People
in the News
1993

People in the News 1993

David Brownstone

Irene Franck

MACMILLAN PUBLISHING COMPANY
NEW YORK

Maxwell Macmillan Canada
TORONTO

Maxwell Macmillan International
NEW YORK   OXFORD   SINGAPORE   SYDNEY

Acknowledgments for illustrative materials are on pp. 429–431, which shall be considered a continuation of the copyright page.

Macmillan Publishing Company   Maxwell Macmillan Canada, Inc.
866 Third Avenue   1200 Eglinton Avenue East, Suite 200
New York, NY 10022   Don Mills, Ontario M3C 3N1

Macmillan Publishing Company is part of the Maxwell Communication Group of Companies

Printed in the United States of America

printing number

1 2 3 4 5 6 7 8 9 10

Library of Congress Cataloging-in-Publication Data
The Library of Congress has catalogued this serial as follows:

Brownstone, David M.
  People in the news / David Brownstone Irene Franck.
    p.   Cm.
  Includes bibliographical references and index.
  Summary: Presents clear, up-to-date biographical information on a wide selection of the most newsworthy people in the world.

Annual
Began with issue for 1991.

ISSN 1062-2713
  1. Celebrities—Biography. 2. Biography—20th century. [1. Celebrities.
2. Biography.] I. Franck, Irene M. II. Title.
CT120.B76 1991
920—dc20
                            91-14962
                            CIP

The paper used in this publication meets the minimum requirements of American National Standard for Information Sciences—Permanence of Paper for Printed Library Materials. ANSI Z39.48–1984 ⊗ ™

Contents

Preface

In this third edition of **People in the News**, we have again developed current profiles of a wide selection of the world's most newsworthy people—the presidents, prime ministers, generals, musicians, film stars, directors, scientists, doctors, sports notables, business leaders, spies, criminals, victims, writers, judges, and the rest who are the main stuff of day-to-day reportage on screen, on radio, and in print throughout the year. The profile for each person first stresses 1992 activities, then presents a concise biography, and finally offers a further reading list, for those who want to dig deeper into the person's current and past history. Each obituary offers a capsule overview of the person's life, also with a further reading list.

As in the second edition, we have included a cumulative alphabetical index and a cumulative occupational index, covering the first three editions of **People in the News**. These make it possible for readers to reach quickly and easily the whole set of people covered in any edition of **People in the News**. Each individual volume is also self-indexed by alphabet.

We should note that approximately 75–80 percent of the material in this edition of **People in the News** is completely new, even though the majority of the entries cover people previously profiled. That will always be so, and stems from the nature of the work, for in each such entry material from the previous year has been merged into the biographies, leaving room for the entirely new material comprising the current and usually largest portion of the entry. Entries on living people are current to the end of 1992, and sometimes later. So are suggestions for further reading; these have also been updated, with newer bibliographic citations added and older ones dropped.

This edition of **People in the News** once again covers approximately 700 people in all, including 200 key obituaries. As is our pattern in this work, we have added many newsworthy people and dropped others, and some from earlier editions are back in this edition or will return in future editions, as their newsmaking activities warrant. This third edition includes a few more political figures, since it covers both the outgoing Bush and then-incoming Clinton administrations. It also includes more literary figures and (by popular request) sports notables, and slightly fewer movie people, a reflection of the recession in Hollywood.

Our thanks to Philip Friedman, president and publisher of Macmillan's Reference Division; his assistant, Alicia Cheng; and managing editor Michael Sander, who have so capably seen this book through the publishing process. We also thank the staff of the Chappaqua Library—Director Mark Hasskarl; the expert reference staff, including Martha Alcott, Teresa Cullen, Carolyn Jones, Paula Peyraud, Mary Platt, and Carolyn Reznick; and the circulation staff, including Marilyn Coleman, Lois Siwicki, and Jane McKean—and their colleagues throughout the northeastern library network, who have once again been so helpful in fulfilling our research needs. Our thanks also to our expert photo researcher, visual resources consultant Susan Hormuth, and to Mary Racette for her invaluable assistance.

David Brownstone
Irene Franck
Chappaqua, New York

Abdul, Paula (1962–) Singer, dancer, and choreographer Abdul toured widely in 1992; on February 24, during her Far Eastern tour, she gave a concert before an unprecedented crowd of 6,000 at Guangzhou (Canton), even though her *Spellbound* album was banned by Chinese censors for its sexual openness. She took her *Under My Spell* tour to large audiences throughout the Far East, including concerts in Japan, Hong Kong, Singapore, Malaysia, and Korea; at Seoul, Korea, teenagers without accompanying adults were banned because a disturbance and panic at an earlier New Kids On the Block concert had killed one fan and injured 50 more.

Abdul then took her show, which had pre-miered in Atlanta in November 1991, on a 31-city North American tour, through the summer of 1992. She took a little time off on May 1 to marry actor Emilio Estevez in a civil ceremony in Santa Monica; it was for both their first marriage. Then it was back on tour, with another small pause for a bout of flu in mid-June.

On the recording side, she released the cassette single "Will You Marry Me?" She was also named favorite female pop artist at the American Music Awards.

Busy or not, Abdul continued to fight AIDS, appearing in Arsenio Hall's AIDS-awareness home video *Time Out: The Truth About HIV, AIDS, and You*, hosted by Magic Johnson, and in September joining many other artists in a Disney benefit concert for the Pediatric AIDS Foundation, which was also to generate a fundraising video and be part of a later Disney Channel AIDS telethon. She was also a face on the video screen in another way: Abdul was seen dancing with Groucho Marx, Cary Grant, and Gene Kelly in a widely shown series of Coca-Cola commercials.

Of Syrian, Brazilian, and French Canadian descent, California-born Abdul studied tap and jazz dancing as a child, performing summers in a traveling group. She began her work as a choreographer during her six-year engagement as one of the Laker Girls, cheerleaders at the Los Angeles Lakers basketball games. In 1984, she also began to choreograph for Michael Jackson and his brothers, then for Janet Jackson and other entertainment figures, including the Pointer Sisters, Eddie Murphy in *Coming to America*,

A

1

and Tracey Ullman, winning an Emmy for her choreography of the "Tracey Ullman Show." In 1988, her career took an entirely new turn, as her first album, *Forever Your Girl*, hit the top of the bestseller charts, with such hits as "Straight Up," "(It's Just) The Way That You Love Me," "Knocked Out," "Forever Your Girl," "Cold-Hearted," and "Opposites Attract." "Straight Up" was named the most performed song of 1989 by ASCAP (American Society of Composers, Authors and Publishers). Abdul also won a 1990 Emmy for her choreography of the American Music Awards. Her second hit album was *Shut Up and Dance (The Dance Mixes)* (1990), and her third was *Spellbound* (1991). She attended California State University.

FURTHER READING

Paula Abdul: Straight Up. M. THOMAS FORD. Dillon/Macmillan, 1992.
"Abdul, Paula." *Current Biography*, Sep. 1991.
Magic of Paula Abdul: Straight up To Spellbound. DEVRA NEWBERGER. Scholastic, 1991.
"Janet Jackson and Paula Abdul. . . ." *Jet*, May 7, 1990.
"The many talents of Paula Abdul. . . ." LYNN NORMENT. *Ebony*, May 1990.
"Paula Abdul." *People*, Spring 1990.
"Straight up . . . and up and up." JEANNIE PARK. *People*, Mar. 12, 1990.
Paula Abdul: Forever Yours. GRACE CATALANO. New American Library-Dutton, 1990.

Accardo, Anthony Joseph (1906–92)
Chicago-born Accardo began his long career in American organized crime in the 1920s, as an "enforcer" or gunman for Al Capone. He was widely accused of being one of the five men who murdered seven members of the competing "Bugs Moran" gang in Chicago in 1929; no prosecution was ever brought against any of the killers. Nor was Accardo ever successfully prosecuted for anything; he spent one day in jail, in 1945, when being questioned, and was convicted of tax evasion in 1960, but that conviction was reversed on appeal, and a second trial resulted in acquittal. He was, however, clearly recognized by criminals and law enforcement officers alike to be a major figure in organized crime in Chicago from the mid-1920s and a national Mafia crime figure from the mid-1930s through the late 1950s, in all probability conti-

nung to be greatly influential at least through the mid-1970s. His last public appearance was before a U.S. Senate subcommittee in 1984; he once again denied having any criminal ties. He was survived by his wife, Clarice, and four children. (d. Chicago; May 27, 1992)

FURTHER READING

Obituary. *The Times* (of London), May 30, 1992.
Obituary. *New York Times*, May 29, 1992.
War of the Godfathers: The Bloody Confrontation Between the Chicago and New York Families for Control of Las Vegas. WILLIAM F. ROEMER, JR. Fine, 1990.

Acuff, Roy Claxton (1903–92)
Tennessee-born singer, fiddler, bandleader, and composer Acuff, one of the foremost figures in the history of American country music, was headed for a career in baseball until a series of sunstrokes prematurely ended his athletic career in the late 1920s. He played in a traveling medicine show in 1932, and then formed his country music band, named successively "The Tennessee Crackerjacks," "The Crazy Tennesseans," and ultimately achieving fame as "The Smokey Mountain Boys." He emerged as a major figure with his early recordings, which included two of the greatest of country music classics: "Great Speckled Bird" and "Wabash Cannon Ball." Acuff joined radio's "Grand Ole Opry" in 1938, and soon starred in the show,

hosting it during the 1940s and 1950s. He also starred in the film *Grand Ole Opry* (1940), and in several other films as well. During World War II, he toured the world entertaining Allied troops, and in the process further popularizing country music.

In 1943, he ran for governor of Tennessee, after the incumbent governor had insulted country music; Acuff lost, and lost again in 1947, after which he returned to music. In 1962, he became the first living member of the Country Music Hall of Fame. Later in his career he led the building of two country music museums in Nashville. He also wrote *Roy Acuff's Nashville: The Life and Good Times of Country Music* (1983) with William Neely. Acuff continued to appear in concert and at the Grand Ole Opry until shortly before his death. He was survived by a son. (d. Nashville, Tennessee; November 3, 1992)

FURTHER READING

" 'I'm able to reach the people.' " DAVID GATES. *Newsweek*, Dec. 7, 1992.
Obituary. *Billboard*, Dec. 5, 1992
Obituary. *Variety*, Nov. 30, 1992
Obituary. *The Times* (of London), Nov. 25, 1992.
Obituary. *New York Times*, Nov. 24, 1992.
Roy Acuff: The Smokey Mountain Boy, 2nd ed. ELIZABETH SCHLAPPI. Pelican, 1992.
"Roy Acuff. . . ." JOHN MORTHLAND. *Country Music*, Nov.–Dec., 1989.
Behind Closed Doors: Talking with the Legends of Country Music. ALANNA NASH. Knopf, 1988.

Adler, Stella (1901–92)

Adler, Stella (1901–92) A leading American interpreter of Constantin Stanislavsky, and a gifted acting teacher, Adler was the child of a theater family, the daughter of Jacob Adler and Sara Levitsky Adler, and the sister of actor Luther Adler. She made her debut as a child actor at the age of four, in 1905, and was a thoroughly experienced professional by the time she became a student of Stanislavsky disciples Maria Ouspenskaya and Richard Boleslavsky at the American Actors Theater School in the mid-1920s. Adler became a leading member of the Stanislavsky-based Group Theater in the 1930s, in such plays as Clifford Odets' *Awake and Sing* and *Paradise Lost*. She met with Stanislavsky in Europe in 1934, and on her return to the United States more fully formed the interpretation of his theories that was to characterize her own teaching, which stressed the use of imagination in applying the actor's own experience to each role, rather than wholly depending on the actor's emotions.

Adler appeared in minor film roles in the 1930s and 1940s, and in several theater roles during the balance of her long career, and directed several plays, but it was as a teacher that she made great impact. She founded the Stella Adler Conservatory of Acting in 1949, and numbered among her thousands of students such actors as Marlon Brando, Robert De Niro, Candice Bergen, Warren Beatty, and Shelley Winters. She also taught at Yale University and New York University. Among her written works were *Stella Adler on Acting* (1988) and *The Technique of Acting* (1990).

Three times married, she was survived by a daughter and a sister. (d. Los Angeles; December 21, 1992)

FURTHER READING

Obituary. *Variety*, Jan. 4, 1993.
Obituary. *The Times* (of London), Dec. 26, 1992.
Obituary. *New York Times*, Dec. 22, 1922.
Real Life Drama: The Group Theatre and America 1931–1940. WENDY SMITH. Random, 1990.
"Stella Adler. . . ." POPE BROCK. *People*, July 17, 1989.

Aiello, Danny

Aiello, Danny (Danny Louis Aiello, Jr.; 1935–) His career as a film star firmly established after almost two decades as a supporting player, Aiello followed his several 1991 starring roles with two more in 1992. One was a very serious and timely drama; he starred as Jack Ruby opposite Sherilynn Fenn in John Mackenzie's *Ruby*, his biofilm about the small-time gangster who murdered Lee Harvey Oswald before an international television audience. In a country resensitized to the continuing debate over the assassination of President John F. Kennedy by Oliver Stone's 1990 *JFK*, the film and Aiello's portrayal of Ruby won great attention—and Aiello's work was very well received. On a lighter note, he starred in Barry Primus' comedy-drama *Mistress*, set on the fringes of the movie business in modern Hollywood. Forthcoming was a starring role in the film *Cemetery Club*, in a cast that included Ellen Burstyn, Olympia Dukakis, and Diane Ladd; and a lead in Dan

Curtis's film *Taking Gary Feldman*, which began filming in October, 1992.

New York City-born Aiello played modest supporting roles on stage and screen from the early 1970s, appearing in such films as *The Godfather Part II* (1974), *The Front* (1976), *Fort Apache, the Bronx* (1981), and *The Purple Rose of Cairo* (1984), and emerging in substantial roles in the late 1980s, with leads opposite Cher in *Moonstruck* (1987) and Eddie Murphy in *Harlem Nights* (1989). Aiello won a Best Supporting Actor Oscar nomination and Chicago and Los Angeles film critics awards for his role as Sal, the Italian pizza parlor owner in a racially troubled Brooklyn neighborhood, in Spike Lee's *Do the Right Thing* (1989). Recent films include the ill-starred *Hudson Hawk, The Closer, Jacob's Ladder*, and *The Pickle*, all in 1991. He married Sandy Cohen in 1955; the couple have four children.

FURTHER READING

"Broadway Danny. . . ." GAVIN SMITH. *Film Comment*, July–Aug. 1991.
"Danny Aiello." LORENZO CARCATERRA. *People*, Feb. 19, 1990.
"His bus came in." MICHAEL NORMAN. *New York Times Magazine*, Jan. 21, 1990.

Albright, Madeleine Korbel (1947–)
President Bill Clinton's incoming United Nations Ambassador brings three decades of training, teaching, and consulting experience to her new job. Prague-born Albright also brings fluency in Czech, Russian, Polish, and French, and special interest in the affairs of newly free Eastern Europe and the countries of the former Soviet Union. Albright's 1959 B.A. was from Wellesley College; she also attended the Johns Hopkins School of Advanced International Studies from 1962–63, and earned her M.A. and Ph.D. at Columbia University's Department of Public Law and Government. In 1976, she began her Washington career, as a staff assistant to Senator Edmund Muskie, and from 1978 worked on the White House National Security Council staff. From 1982 until the present, she has been Research Professor of International Affairs and Director of Women in Foreign Service at Georgetown University's School of Foreign Service. From 1989 to 1992, she was president of the Center of National Policy. She was a foreign policy advisor in the Mondale, Dukakis, and Clinton presidential campaigns. Her books include *The Role of the Press in Political Change: Czechoslovakia 1968* (1976) and *Poland: the Role of the Press in Political Change* (1983).

FURTHER READING

"Albright: right at home." *Washington Post*, Dec. 7, 1992.
"Woman on top of the world. . . ." MOLLY SINCLAIR. *Washington Post*. Jan. 6, 1991.
"Dukakis's foreign policy adviser. . . ." ELAINE SCIOLINO. *New York Times*. July 26, 1988.

Alda, Alan (1936–)
After his 1991 warmup in the London revival of *Our Town*, Alda appeared for the first time in 20 years on the Broadway stage, starring opposite Kate Burton and Tracy Pollan in Neil Simon's new comedy *Jake's Women*, which finally opened on Broadway after closing on the road in 1990—the first of Neil Simon's 24 plays ever to do so. The play, about a warring couple and Jake's recollection of all the women in his life, was well received, and Alda even more so; he won a Tony nomination for his creation of the title role. The play, which ran on Broadway from March to October 1992 was scheduled to open in Los Angeles in April 1993, with Alda again in the title role. On screen, Alda starred as a psychiatrist in Christopher Crowe's psychological sex-and-murder thriller *Whispers in the Dark*, centered around Annabella Sciorra

as a New York psychologist who becomes emotionally involved with her patients.

New York-born Alda, the son of actor Robert Alda, appeared on the New York stage from the late 1950s, in such plays as *Purlie Victorious* (1961), *The Owl and the Pussycat* (1964), and *The Apple Tree* (1966). He became a television star in the 1970s, in *The Glass House* (1972), and then as Korean War surgeon Benjamin Franklin "Hawkeye" Pierce, in the long-running series "M*A*S*H" (1972–83). He has also starred in such films as *The Moonshine War* (1970), *California Suite* (1978), *Same Time Next Year* (1978), and *The Seduction of Joe Tynan* (1979), and appeared in many other films, including *Crimes and Misdemeanors* (1989), for which he won the Directors Guild of America's award for best supporting actor. Alda wrote, directed, and starred in the films *The Four Seasons* (1981), *Sweet Liberty* (1986), and *Betsy's Wedding* (1989). He married Arlene Weiss in 1957; they have three children. He attended Fordham University.

FURTHER READING

"Alan Alda. . . ." CLIFF JAHR. *Ladies Home Journal,* Mar. 1985.
The Last Days of Mash. ARLENE ALDA and ALAN ALDA. Unicorn, 1984.
Alan Alda: A Biography. RAYMOND STRAIT. St. Martin's, 1983.
Alan Alda: An Unauthorized Biography. JASON BONDEROFF. New American Library-Dutton, 1982.

Alexander, Jane (Jane Quigley; 1939–) One of the leading actresses of the American theater, Alexander starred in two major stage roles in 1992. In January, she opened opposite Harris Yulin in a very well-received Roundabout Theater revival of Friedrich Durrenmatt's *The Visit*, as Claire Zachanassian, the rich woman who returns to her Swiss hometown to expose the hypocrisy of its leading citizens and to destroy them. Alexander won a Tony nomination for her portrayal. In October, she starred at New York's Lincoln Center as Sara Goode, opposite Frances McDormand and Madeline Kahn as her sisters, in Wendy Wasserstein's new play *The Sisters Rosensweig*, a study of the greatly differing paths taken by three Jewish-American sisters.

On screen, Alexander starred opposite Barbara Hershey in the telefilm *Stay the Night*, as the mother of a teenage boy who murders his older lover's husband and goes to jail, although the woman, played by Hershey, does not. Alexander unsuccessfully seeks evidence that will implicate the woman and clear her son.

Alexander played in regional theatre in the mid-1960s. She emerged as a major dramatic actress on Broadway in 1968, in her Tony-winning role opposite James Earl Jones in *The Great White Hope*. Some of her most notable stage roles were in *6 Rms Riv Vu* (1972), *Find Your Way Home* (1974), *The Heiress* (1976), *First Monday in October* (1978), *Hedda Gabler* (1981), *Old Times* (1984), *Night of the Iguana* (1988), and *Shadowlands* (1990). On screen, she was nominated for a Best Actress Oscar for the film version of *The Great White Hope* (1970), and she also appeared in such films as *All the President's Men* (1976), *Kramer vs. Kramer* (1979), *Testament* (1983), and *Glory* (1989). She has also made several telefilms, most notably *Eleanor and Franklin* (1976) as a classic Eleanor Roosevelt, *Playing For Time* (1980), *Calamity Jane* (1984), and *A Marriage: Georgia O'Keefe and Alfred Stieglitz* (1991). Alexander attended Sarah Lawrence College and the University of Edinburgh. She has been married twice, last to Edwin Sherin in 1975, and has one child.

FURTHER READING

"Liz and Jane. . . ." BILL DAVIDSON. *TV Guide,* Apr. 20, 1985.
"Jane Alexander launching. . . ." JIM ROBBINS. *Variety,* Jan. 30, 1985.

Alexander, Lamar (Andrew Lamar Alexander, Jr.; 1940–   ) Outgoing U.S. Secretary of Education Alexander spent a mainly fruitless final year in office. During 1992, with a Republican President and Democratic Congress "gridlocked," no significant new education reforms were enacted, while the nation's schools continued to deteriorate, as impoverished state and local authorities made further sharp cuts in school funding and the federal government made very little new help available. In a year that focused on the Presidential election and the worsening economy, education became a much-talked-about and increasingly sick political football. Alexander continued to stress the Bush administration's controversial "choice" approach, featuring federal funding of tuition grants for parents to use in choosing their childrens' schools, with its implication of government aid for religious schools; with no chance of Congressional funding, the program was literally a nonstarter. Alexander spent much of his time deploring the situation and defending the Bush administration's record on education. In April, he reported little progress in American education, but publicly doubted that education would become a campaign issue, because he felt that there were few differences between Clinton and Bush in that area, an assertion Clinton quickly rebutted. By July, Alexander attacked the National Education Association for making an unprecedented endorsement of Clinton, signaling a powerful repudiation of the Bush administration.

Tennessee-born Alexander began his career as an assistant to U.S. Senator Howard S. Baker (1967–69), and briefly during 1969 worked in the White House, as a Congressional liaison. He practiced law in Tennessee during the 1970s, made an unsuccessful gubernatorial run in 1974, and won next time around, serving as state governor from 1979 to 1987, also serving a term as chairman of the National Governors Association (1985–86), and then was president of the University of Tennessee (1988–1990). He was appointed U.S. Secretary of Education in 1990. His 1940 B.A. was from Vanderbilt University, his 1965 LL.D. from New York University. In addition to some works on Tennessee, Alexander has published *Steps Along the Way: A Governor's Scrapbook* (1986) and *Six Months Off: An American Family's Australian Adventure* (1988). He and his wife, Honey Alexander, have four children.

FURTHER READING

"Taking it to the top." JOE AGRON. *American School & University*, Sep. 1992.
"Lamar Alexander and. . . ." GEORGE R. KAPLAN. *Phi Delta Kappan*, June 1992.
"Lamar's choice." WILLIAM MCGURN. *National Review*, May 25, 1992.
"Alexander the Great?" JON STEWART. *Parenting*, May 1992.
"Lamar Alexander's. . . ." SUSAN CHIRA. *New York Times Magazine*, Nov. 24, 1991.
"George Bush's point man." SAM ALLIS. *Time*, Sep. 16, 1991.
"Alexander, Andrew Lamar, Jr." *Current Biography*, July 1991.
"Meet: the Tennessee 'sparkplug.' " ANITA MERINA. *NEA Today*, May–June 1991.

Allen, Peter (1944–92) Songwriter and entertainer Allen began his career as a child, playing in variety in his home town of Tenterfield, New South Wales, Australia, and while still in his teens entertained throughout Australia and the Far East. Judy Garland, then on a world tour, discovered him in Hong Kong in 1964, and took him on tour with her. He joined her in the United States in 1965, and in 1967 married her daughter, Liza Minnelli; they separated in 1970. Allen went on to become a recording, cabaret, and concert star, as well as a Grammy- and Oscar-winning songwriter, his Oscar coming for the theme music of the 1981 film *Arthur*, starring Dudley Moore and Minnelli. In 1979, he starred on Broadway in a one-man show, and in 1988 wrote the score and lyrics, and starred on Broadway in *Legs Diamond*. Allen, who died in connection with AIDS, was survived by his mother and sister. (d. San Diego; June 18, 1992).

FURTHER READING

"A blazing star flickers out." MARK GOODMAN. *People*, July 6, 1992.
Obituary. *The Times* (of London), June 22, 1992.
Obituary. *Variety*, June 22, 1992.
Obituary. *New York Times*, June 19, 1992.

Allen, Woody (Allen Stewart Konigsberg; 1935–   ) The veteran filmmaker and star Woody Allen ran into some highly publicized personal problems in 1992, stemming from the breakup of his long-term relationship with Mia Farrow, which had begun in 1980, but had never included marriage. Allen sued for custody of their three children and Farrow opposed his suit. Shortly afterward, Allen and Farrow's 21-year-old adopted daughter, Soon-Yi Farrow Previn, announced that they were in love. The media, encouraged by lawyers eager to fight their clients' cases very publicly, seized a massive story opportunity, created an implication of incest, and soon were able to also report that the Farrow side had caused a child molestation charge involving one of their children to be filed against Allen in Connecticut. Finally, after enormous damage had been done to Allen, Farrow, Soon-Yi Farrow Previn, and all the children, the judge in the case issued a "gag" order, forbidding the parties to fight the case anywhere but in court.

On the artistic side, Allen had a very successful year, creating two major films that opened during 1992. The first, his 21st film, was *Shadows and Fog*; he wrote, directed, and starred opposite Farrow, heading a multistar cast that included John Malkovich, Madonna, Jodie Foster, and Kathy Bates. The film, shot in black and white, opened in Paris in February, reflecting Allen's huge European popularity, and in the United States in April. The second was *Husbands and Wives*; he wrote, directed, and starred as a college teacher who becomes sexually involved with a 21-year-old student, played by Juliette Lewis, and breaks with his wife, played again by Farrow. Costarring were Blythe Danner, Judy Davis, Sidney Pollack, Liam Neeson, and Lysette Anthony. In a studio attempt to gain audiences from the obvious similarity between the story line and the specifics of the Allen-Farrow breakup, the film opened earlier than scheduled—but did not do as well at the box office as expected. Allen will write, direct, produce, and star in the forthcoming film *Manhattan Murder Mystery*, costarring Diane Keaton (in a role originally intended for Farrow), Anjelica Huston, and Martin Landau. Forthcoming in 1993 is the book *The Woody Allen Illustrated Reader*, to be published by Knopf.

A New Yorker, Allen emerged as a leading television comedy writer in the late 1950s, and during the 1960s also worked in cabaret and theater, beginning a long series of hit films as the writer and star of *What's New Pussycat?* (1965). He then became one of the leading filmmakers of the 1970s and 1980s, with such films as his Oscar-winning *Annie Hall* (1977), *Manhattan* (1979), *Hannah and Her Sisters* (1984), and *Crimes and Misdemeanors* (1989), and *Scenes from a Mall* (1991). Allen attended City College and New York University. He was formerly married to Louise Lasser. He and Farrow have three children; their biological son Satchel, an adopted daughter Dylan, and an adopted son Moses.

FURTHER READING

"Everything you always. . . ." PHOEBE HOBAN. *New York*, Sep. 21, 1992.
"Bananas. . . ." ROGER ROSENBLATT. *New Republic*, Sep. 21, 1992.
"Woody working. . . ." Steven Daly. *Entertainment*, Sep. 18, 1992.
"Love and fog." JESS CAGLE. *Entertainment*, Sep. 18, 1992.
" 'But she's not part of my family.' " JACK KROLL. *Newsweek*, Aug. 31, 1992.
" 'The heart wants what it wants.' " WALTER ISAACSON. *Time*, Aug. 31, 1992.
"A family affair." TOM GLIATTO. *People*, Aug. 31, 1992.
Brooklyn Is Not Expanding: Woody Allen's Comic Universe. ANNETTE WERNBLAD. Fairleigh Dickinson, 1992.
"Woody Allen. . . ." ERIC LAX. *Vogue*, May 1991.
"Woody and Mia. . . ." ERIC LAX. *New York Times Magazine*, Feb. 24, 1991.
Woody Allen: A Biography. ERIC LAX. Knopf, 1991; Random, 1992.
Woody Allen Encyclopedia. MARK A. ALTMAN. Movie Publications, 1991.
Woody Allen: His Films and Career. DOUGLAS BRODE. Carol, 1991.
Loser Take All: The Comic Art of Woody Allen, expanded ed. MAURICE YACOWAR. Continuum, 1991.
Woody Allen. GRAHAM MCCANN. Basil Blackwell, 1990.
Love, Sex, Death, and the Meaning of Life: The Films of Woody Allen, rev. ed. FOSTER HIRSCH. Limelight, 1990.

Alley, Kirstie (1955–) Televison star Alley was once again honored by her peers in 1992, with an Emmy nomination as lead actress in a comedy series for her role as Rebecca Howe, opposite Ted Danson as bartender Sam Malone in the longrunning, top-rated, award-winning comedy series "Cheers." The series continued to do well, too, and NBC announced that it had been renewed for the 1993–94 series. But late in 1992, it became clear that Danson wanted to end the series and move on, although it was equally clear that Alley would have been satisfied to continue; the announced renewal was withdrawn, leaving both stars free to pursue other roles.

Alley in 1992 appeared in the nonprofit AIDS-awareness home video *Time Out: The Truth About HIV, AIDS, and You*, hosted by Magic Johnson, produced by Arsenio Hall, and also featuring such stars as Paula Abdul, Neil Patrick Harris, and Bobby Brown. On the personal side, she and her husband, actor Parker Stevenson, adopted a baby boy.

Kansas-born Alley worked as an interior decorator before taking up an acting career in the early 1980s. Her most notable early work was her role as Lieutenant Saavik in *Star Trek II: The Wrath of Khan* (1982), which was followed by supporting roles in several other theatre and television films. She made her major breakthrough in 1987, when she joined the cast of "Cheers". Her film breakthrough came opposite John Travolta in the film comedy *Look Who's Talking* (1989; and the 1990 sequel). She went on to star in the 1990 film comedies *Madhouse* and *Sibling Rivalry*. Alley attended Kansas State University.

FURTHER READING

"What she did to become a star." JEFF ROVIN. *Ladies Home Journal*, June 1992.
"Kirstie Alley." MARK MORRISON. *US*. Feb. 1992.
"What's hot. . . ." KATHLEEN NEUMEYER et al. *Ladies Home Journal*, Oct. 1991.
"Feisty, funny Kirstie Alley." GREGG KILDAY. *Cosmopolitan*, Dec. 1990.
"The tears behind the Cheers." J.D. REED. *People*, Oct. 29, 1990.
"Kirstie Alley." RICHARD BLAINE. *Good Housekeeping*, Mar. 1990.
"Chez Alley." FRED ROBBINS. *Saturday Evening Post*, Jan.–Feb. 1990.

Almendros, Nestor (1930–92) Barcelona-born Almendros, one of the world's leading cinematographers, left his native Spain in 1948 to join his father in Havana, Cuba, and begin his career. He lived and studied in Rome and New York before returning to Cuba after Fidel Castro's 1959 victory to make government films. But he soon broke with Castro, moving to Paris, where in the mid-1960s he began his long association with several leading New Wave directors, shooting such films as Eric Rohmer's *My Night at Maud's* (1969), *Claire's Knee* (1970), *Chloe in the Afternoon* (1972), and *Pauline at the Beach* (1983), and Francois Truffaut's *The Wild Child* (1970), *Bed and Board* (1970), and *The Last Metro* (1980). He won an Oscar as best cinematographer for Terence Malik's *Days of Heaven* (1978), and received Oscar nominations for several other films: *Kramer vs. Kramer* (1979), *The Blue Lagoon* (1980), *Sophie's Choice* (1982), and *Places in the Heart* (1984). His documentary work also included such anti-Castro films as *Nobody Listened* (1988). His autobiography was *A Man With a Camera* (1984). He was survived by his mother, a sister, and a brother. (d. New York City; March 4, 1992)

FURTHER READING

Obituary. *Variety*, Mar. 9, 1992.
Obituary. *The Times* (of London), Mar. 6, 1992.
Obituary. *New York Times*, Mar. 5, 1992.
"Almendros, Nestor." *Current Biography*, Nov. 1989.
"Nobody listened." CATHERINE MARIN. *Hispanic*, Apr. 1989.

Altman, Robert (1925–) In what he describes as his fourth comeback, celebrated film director Altman in 1992 directed the acclaimed *The Player*, a mercilessly dark comedy exposé of modern Hollywood, with a multistar cast that included Tim Robbins, Greta Scacchi, Fred Ward, Whoopi Goldberg, and more than a score of major stars appearing in cameos as themselves. Altman won a Cannes Film Festival Best Director award for *The Player*, and Robbins won the festival's Best Actor award.

In 1992, Altman filmed another multistar, multiplot, highly textured work, the forthcoming *Short Cuts*, based on eight stories and a poem by Raymond Carver. Some of those who starred in *The Player* also star in his new film, including Tim Robbins and Fred Ward—and a large number of Hollywood stars again appear in small roles, including Anne Archer, Robert Downey, Jr., Jennifer Jason Leigh, Jack Lemmon, Andie MacDowell, Matthew Modine, Lily Tomlin, and Tom Waits. After completing the filming of *Short Cuts* in September 1992, Altman directed *McTeague*, William Bolcom's new opera, at the Lyric Opera of Chicago; the work is based on the Frank Norris novel and the Erich von Stroheim film.

Altman directed in television and films from

the late 1950s, emerging as a major film director in the 1970s, with such films as *M*A*S*H* (1970), *Brewster McCloud* (1971), *McCabe and Mrs. Miller* (1972), *California Split* (1974), *Nashville* (1975), and *Buffalo Bill and the Indians* (1976). He received Best Picture and Best Director Oscar nominations for *M*A*S*H* and *Nashville*. But his film career sagged as the American film industry moved toward the theatre of spectacle, and away from his kind of social commentary. During the 1980s, he directed a variety of films, plays, and telefilms, most notably *Come Back to the Five and Dime, Jimmy Dean, Jimmy Dean* (1982), *Streamers* (1983), *Vincent and Theo* (1990), and (with Garry Trudeau) the innovative pseudo-documentary series, *Tanner* (1988), in which Michael Murphy played a fictitious presidential candidate. Altman has been married three times and has five children. He attended the University of Missouri.

FURTHER READING

"Tarnishing the gilded age. . . ." CARRIE RICKEY. *Opera News*, Nov. 1992.
"Game boy squares the circle." RICHARD COMBS. *Observer*, June 21, 1992.
"Robert Altman on 'The Player.' " RICHARD T. JAMESON. *Film Comment*, May–June 1992.
" 'The movie you saw is. . . .' " GAVIN SMITH and RICHARD T. JAMESON. *Film Comment*, May–June 1992.
"Robert Altman gives something back." JACK KROLL. *Esquire*, May 1992.
"Robert Altman. . . ." DAVID BRESKIN. *Rolling Stone*, Apr. 16, 1992.
"Home movie." JEANIE KASINDORF. *New York*, Mar. 16, 1992.
"Altman '91." BEVERLY WALKER. *Film Comment*, Jan.–Feb. 1991.
Robert Altman's America. HELENE KEYSSAR. Oxford University Press, 1991.
Robert Altman: Jumping Off the Cliff. PATRICK MCGILLIGAN. St. Martin's, 1989.

Altman, Roger C. (1945–) President Bill Clinton's incoming Deputy Treasury Secretary is an investment banker, with strong Wall Street credentials and much prior government service. He began his financial career in 1969, as a Lehman Brothers associate, and was very much a "whiz kid" at the firm, becoming its

youngest post-World War II general partner in 1974. In 1977, he moved to Washington as a Carter administration Assistant Treasury Secretary for domestic finance, playing a substantial role in the bailouts of Chrysler and New York City. With Republican victory in 1980, he returned to Lehman Brothers, and was one of three managing directors of the firm when it was sold in 1984. From 1985–89, he was chairman of New York City's Public Development Corporation, and in the early 1990s was a key economic advisor to mayor David Dinkins. Altman's 1967 B.A. was from Georgetown University, and his M.B.A. from the University of Chicago. He is married to documentary filmmaker Jurata Kazakis; they have three children.

FURTHER READING

"Head to head." S.C. GWYNNE and STEPHEN KOEPP. *Time*, Oct. 12, 1992.

Alzado, Lyle Martin (1949–92) New York City-born Alzado was one of the leading professional football players of the 1970s and 1980s. After receiving his B.A. from Yankton College in 1971, he played with the Denver Broncos for eight years (1971–79), winning several awards; in 1977 he was an All-Pro defensive lineman, American Football Conference defensive player of the year, and National Football League man of the year. He went on to play for the Cleveland

Browns (1979–82) and Los Angeles Raiders (1982–85), helping the Raiders win the Superbowl XVIII national championship in 1983. He unsuccessfully attempted a comeback in 1990. In 1991, stricken with central nervous system lymphoma, a deadly and inoperable form of cancer, he triggered a national debate on the use of steroids and human growth hormone by athletes, blaming his own long-term use of steroids for suppression of his immune system. With Doug Moe, he wrote *Still Hungry: The Autobiography of Lyle Alzado* (1985). He was survived by his second wife, Kathy Davis, and a son. (d. Portland, Oregon; May 14, 1992).

FURTHER READING

Obituary. *Variety*, May 19, 1992.
Obituary. *New York Times*, May 15, 1992.
"Fourth down and long. . . ." WAYNE EDWARDS. *People*, July 29, 1991.
"A doctor's warning ignored." SHELLEY SMITH. *Sports Illustrated*, July 8, 1991.
"Lyle Alzado. . . ." SHELLEY SMITH. *Sports Illustrated*, July 2, 1990.

Anderson, Judith (Frances Margaret Anderson, 1898–1992) Australian-born Anderson was one of the leading actresses of the English-speaking theater. She made her debut in Sydney in 1915, in *A Royal Divorce*, and moved to the United States in 1918. Her first starring role on Broadway was in *Cobra* (1924); she emerged as a leading player in the 1930s, most notably as Olivia Manion in Eugene O'Neill's *Mourning Becomes Electra*, as Gertrude to John Gielgud's *Hamlet*, and opposite Laurence Olivier in *Macbeth* (1937). Her Tony-winning *Medea* (1947) was generally accepted as her greatest role. She also played strong character roles in many films, winning an Oscar nomination as Mrs. Danvers in *Rebecca* (1940). Late in her career, she played a leading role in the television series *Santa Barbara*. She was survived by a niece. (d. Santa Barbara, California; January 3, 1992)

FURTHER READING

Obituary. *Variety*, Jan. 13, 1992.
Obituary. *The Times* (of London), Jan. 6, 1992.
Obituary. *New York Times*, Jan. 4, 1992.

Andreotti, Giulio (1919–   ) In the Italian general elections, held April 5–6, 1992, Premier Andreotti's four-party coalition lost its majority. His Christian Democratic Party, in power since the end of World War II, saw its vote slip to below 30 percent, as dissatisfied voters—faced with multiple unsolved crises—splintered already-diverse Italian politics even further. None of Andreotti's promises had borne fruit: the enormous Italian government debt had grown larger, rather than smaller, as promised; a deep recession gripped the country; the Mafia continued to assassinate its opponents, seemingly at will and in collusion with some in government; and the promised relief that was to come through European Community membership was not yet in sight. On April 24, Andreotti stepped down, staying on as caretaker premier until a new premier was named. President Cossiglia stepped down the next day, amid predictions that Italian politics had been irrevocably changed. A month later, Andreotti's candidacy for the presidency failed, but Luigi Calfaro, a veteran Christian Democratic politician, was selected to replace Cossiglia. On June 28, Socialist Giuliano Amato replaced Andreotti. Amato's governing coalition consisted of the same four parties that had been in Andreotti's coalition, and proceeded to take up the same issues, making no visible progress. There were budget cuts and plans to privatize industries, in support of an attack on the deficit—but there was also a depressive 7 percent currency devaluation, made in response to the virtual collapse of the European money system. After the European currency crisis and the virtual demise of the Maastricht Treaty, the promise of the European Community seemed much further away than it had been any time in the 1990s. Andreotti's work *The U.S.A. Up Close: From the Atlantic Pact to Bush* was published in English in 1992.

Rome-born Andreotti began his long political career just after World War II. He entered the Italian parliament in 1947 and was parliamentary chairman of the Christian Democratic Party from 1954 to 1972. He has held many cabinet posts from the 1950s through the early 1990s, and has been premier seven times in three periods (1972–73, 1976–79, and 1989–92). When out of office, he has been a leading Italian journalist. He attended the University of Rome. Andreotti married Livia Danese in 1945; the couple have four children.

FURTHER READING

"Andreotti, Italian Prime Minister." *Business Week*, Dec. 24, 1990.

Andrew Albert Christian Edward (1960–) and Sarah Margaret Ferguson (1959–), the Duke and Duchess of York

Prince Andrew is the third child and second son of Britain's Queen Elizabeth II. He is a serving Royal Navy helicopter pilot and flight instructor. The former Sarah Ferguson, known as "Fergie" in the media, worked in publishing before her marriage. In 1986, the couple married, and from then on they became worldwide media-created celebrities; 1992 marked their sixth and probably last year together in the spotlight.

On March 19, 1992 it was announced that lawyers for the Duchess of York had moved for a legal separation, climaxing great media speculation on the state of their marriage, stimulated in January by publication of rather innocuous photos taken of her and a friend, Steven Wyatt, on holiday together. In late August, British newspapers published topless photos of Ferguson on holiday with another friend, John Bryan, which gave the media an enormous opportunity, became a major scandal, and brought new calls to take away her title and to reexamine the monarchy. One of the earliest,

but surely far from the last television film exploiting the scandal was *Fergie and Andrew: Behind Closed Doors* (1992). On a different front, the Duchess of York in 1992 published *The Adventures of Budgie*, a sequel to her *Budgie the Little Helicopter* (1989).

The Duke of York attended the Royal Naval College, seeing active service in the Falklands War, and is also a photographer who has published and exhibited his work. The Duchess of York attended secretarial college. With Benita Stoney, she wrote *Victoria and Albert: A Family Life at Osborne House* (1991), about the royal figures and their house on the Isle of Wight; royalties for the book go to the Prince Andrew Charitable Trust. The couple have two daughters, Beatrice and Eugenie.

FURTHER READING

"Duchess in dutch." MICHELLE GREEN. *People*, Sep. 7, 1992.
"Farewell Fergie?" MICHELLE GREEN. *People*, Mar. 30, 1992.
Fergie: A Fascinating, Behind-the-Scenes Look at the Real Duchess of York. INGRID SEWARD. St. Martin's, 1992.
"Royalty most raucous. . . ." ADAM HELLKNER et al. *Ladies Home Journal*, Aug. 1991.
"How this sweet little girl. . . ." INGRID SEWARD. *Good Housekeeping*, May 1991.
"Dallas at the palace? . . ." J.D. REED. *People*, Mar. 11, 1991.

Two Royal Women: the Public and Private Lives of Fergie and Di. NORMAN KING. Knightsbridge, 1991.

The Princess and the Duchess: A Behind the Scenes Biography of the Princess of Wales and the Duchess of York. JANE ARTHUR. State Mutual, 1990.

The Private Lives of Britain's Royal Women: Their Passions and Power. UNITY HALL. Contemporary, 1990.

"Fergie at 30." INGRID SEWARD. *Woman's Day*, Oct. 24, 1989.

The Princess and Duchess. JOSEPHINE FAIRLEY. St. Martin's, 1989.

Duchess: An Intimate Portrait of Sarah, Duchess of York. ANDREW MORTON. Contemporary, 1989.

Sarah Ferguson: The Royal Redhead. DAVID BANKS. Dillon, 1987.

Their Royal Highnesses the Duke and Duchess of York. CHRISTOPHER WARWICK and VALERIE GARNER. Salem House, 1986.

Andrews, Dana (Carver Dana Andrews; 1909–92) A film star of the 1940s, Andrews's classic role was that of returned war hero Fred Derry in William Wyler's *The Best Years of Our Lives* (1946), with Fredric March, Myrna Loy, Teresa Wright, and handless veteran Harold Russell, a work summing up the spirit of the time and the turn from war to peace. Andrews made his film debut in 1940 in *The Westerner*, and played in supporting roles for three years, moving into starring roles with *The Ox-Bow Incident* (1943), and as the detective in *Laura* (1944). He also starred in *A Walk in the Sun* (1946) and *Boomerang* (1947), then moving into supporting roles. He also appeared in the theater, and in television in the series "Bright Promises" (1969–72). Andrews was active in the Screen Actors Guild, becoming Guild president in 1963. He was survived by his wife, actress Mary Todd, two daughters, and a son. (d. Los Alamitos, California; December 17, 1992)

FURTHER READING

Obituary. *Variety*, Dec. 21, 1992.
Obituary. *New York Times*, Dec. 19, 1992.
Obituary. *The Times* (of London), Dec. 19, 1992.

Andronikos, Manolis (1919–92) A leading Greek archeologist, Professor Andronikos began his historic work at Vergina, south of Salonica, while still a student in 1937. He fought with Free Greek forces during World War II, completing his studies and beginning his teaching career after the war. He conducted several excavations in northern Greece during the 1950s and early 1960s, always focusing on Vergina, which he believed to be the early Macedonian capital city of Algae. In 1977, he announced the discovery there of the tomb of Philip II, father of Alexander the Great, and later excavated many other noble tombs in the area, identifying at least ten as royal tombs. Although archeologists differ as to whether or not his finds were indeed royal tombs, they agreed that the tombs and artifacts discovered with them were among the greatest "finds" of the postwar period. He was survived by his wife, Olympia, and a brother. (d. Salonica, Greece; March 30, 1992)

FURTHER READING

Obituary. *The Times* (of London), Apr. 6, 1992.
Obituary. *New York Times*, Mar. 31, 1992.

Antall, Jószef (1932–) Hungarian Premier Antall, president of the ruling Hungarian Democratic Forum, focused on economic matters during 1992, as Hungary struggled to develop a viable economy, along with the other recently free Eastern European nations. But with Soviet markets and support gone, and without a competitive industrial plant, it proved difficult; despite the March 1 beginning of Hungary's tariff-lowering association with the European Community, and despite the voiding of prior Western curbs on high-technology sales to Hungary, Hungarian industrial production dropped sharply during 1992.

Antall also continued to deal with the aftermath of the Communist period. He supported the February 1992 voiding of all political "crimes" committed from 1963 to 1989, and accelerated government handling of compensation claims stemming from property seizures during that period. He also supported a law aimed at prosecuting former Communist officials, but in March Hungary's Constitutional Court declared the law invalid, forestalling multiple political trials.

Far more difficult was the problem of resurgent anti-Semitism and fascism; Hungary, after all, had been a fascist state under the Horthy dictatorship (1920–44), and a Nazi ally during

World War II. Anti-Semitic and antiforeign skinhead riots took place in Budapest in January, and during the year in many locations. On August 20, neo-fascist Istvan Csurka, a vice-president of Antall's Democratic Forum, published an essay in the party's newspaper, which among other things charged a widespread Jewish-led plot against Hungary—a message and tone very reminiscent of the Nazi period. Antall did not publicly respond; later, under pressure from many quarters, he criticized Csurka's position; but Antall's handlng of the matter raised grave questions as to his own antifascist commitment.

Antall was active in the right-of-center Small-holders Party before the 1947 Communist take-over, was mostly out of politics until 1956, and was arrested after joining the failed Hungarian revolution against Soviet domination. He stayed in Hungary after the revolution and was barred from travel abroad until 1973. A historian, he led the Hungarian Democratic Forum to electoral victory in April 1990, and on May 3 became the premier of Hungary, succeeding Socialist Miklos Nemeth. His earned his doctorate at Budapest's Eokvos University.

FURTHER READING

"Antall, József, Jr." *Current Biography*, Sep. 1990.

Antoon, A.J. (Alfred Joseph Antoon, Jr.; 1944–92)

Born in Metheun, Massachusetts, Antoon set out first to be a Jesuit priest, later turning to the theater at the Yale School of Drama. He began his long association with Joseph Papp and the New York Shakespeare Festival in 1971, directing *Subject to Fits*, and went on to win a Tony for his direction of *That Championship Season* for the theater in 1973, a year that also saw his Shakespeare Festival Tony-nominated production of *Much Ado About Nothing*. Both shows went on to Broadway runs. He directed many other classic and modern plays at the Shakespeare Festival, and directed such Broadway shows as the musical *The Rink* and Strindberg's *The Dance of Death*. Antoon, who died of AIDS, was survived by his companion, Peter Perez, his brother, and two sisters. (d. New York City; January 22, 1992)

FURTHER READING

"A.J. Antoon in spirit." JAN WOJCIK. *America*, Mar. 21, 1992.

Obituary. *Variety*, Jan. 27, 1992.
Obituary. *New York Times*, Jan. 23, 1992.

Aoun, Hacib (1956–92)

Dr. Aoun, a cardiologist, became infected with the AIDS virus in 1982, from HIV-carrying blood in a broken test tube that cut a finger. He was diagnosed as having AIDS in 1986, while a chief resident in medicine at the Johns Hopkins University Hospital. Removed from his hospital post because he had AIDS, he sued the hospital, which he felt had abandoned him. His highly publicized case helped to focus national and world attention on the plight of people with AIDS, so often in those early years of the epidemic rejected and denied needed help by frightened health professionals, and by adminstrators afraid to risk public condemnation and loss of funds and jobs. Dr. Aoun's case was settled out of court in 1988; he continued to be a spokesperson for those afflicted with AIDS for the rest of his life. He was survived by his wife, Dr. Patricia Aoun, a daughter, his parents, and two brothers. (d. Glen Arm, Maryland; February 16, 1992)

FURTHER READING

Obituary. *The Times* (of London), Mar. 6, 1992.
Obituary. *New York Times*, Feb. 18, 1992.

Aquino, Corazon (Maria Corazon Cojuangco Aquino; 1933–)

President Aquino achieved one last great triumph during her final months in office—she took her country through a hard-fought but democratic national election, assuring an orderly succession and thereby making a great contribution to the future of Philippine democracy. There certainly was preelection and election day violence, but far less than in previous elections, and there was no eighth attempt to overthrow her from the right and no acceleration of guerrilla warfare from the left. Her accomplishment seemed all the more notable in light of the continuing major problems faced by her country. As had been the case throughout her administration, massive population increases continued, accompanied by 20–25 percent unemployment figures, and deepening poverty throughout the country. In one way the situation was even worse, as the massive American naval base at Subic Bay was closed after she lost her fight to have its lease renewed. On January 4, 1992, President George Bush announced that Seventh Fleet headquarters would be relocated from Subic Bay to Singapore.

Aquino also solved the problem posed by the Imelda Marcos candidacy, not interfering with Marcos in any way until after Marcos had won only 10 percent of the votes in the May election; then Marcos was ordered arrested under long-standing tax evasion and other charges. In the election for her successor to the presidency, Aquino in January backed the candidacy of Fidel Ramos, who won the election and was sworn in on June 30, 1992.

In 1980, Corazon Aquino went into exile with her husband, opposition leader Benigno Aquino. On their return to the Philippines in 1983, he was assassinated by agents of then-dictator Ferdinand Marcos. She took her husband's place as head of the Liberal Party and three years later, in 1986, swept Marcos from power and into exile in the elections and following a series of events that became the Philippine Revolution. She then introduced a new democratic constitution and government and, in the years that followed, survived seven right-wing coup attempts. She also survived a continuing left-wing insurrection, opening negotiations that seemed quite promising during the last year of her administration. Corazon Cojuangco and Benigno Aquino were married in 1954 and had five children. She attended New York's Mount St. Vincent College.

FURTHER READING

Democracy in the Philippines?: The Precarious Aquino Regime. DAVID WURFEL. Westview, 1993.
From Marcos to Aquino: Local Perspectives on Political Transition in the Philippines. BENEDICT J. KERKVLIET and RESIL B. MOJARES, eds. University of Hawaii Press, 1992.
"Aquino may yet. . . ." DENIS MURPHY. *National Catholic Reporter*, Feb. 8, 1991.
"Cory Aquino. . . ." DENIS MURPHY. *America*, Apr. 21, 1990.
Corazon Aquino: Leader of the Phillipines. JAMES HASKINS. Enslow, 1988.
Corazon Aquino. LUCY KOMISAR. Braziller, 1987.
Picture Life of Corazon Aquino. MARGARET M. SCARIANO. Watts, 1987.
Corazon Aquino: The Miracle of a President. CECILIA K. GULLAS. Cultural House, 1987.

Arafat, Yasir (1929–) For Palestine Liberation Organization (PLO) leader Arafat, 1992 was a difficult year. He entered the year in severely impaired political condition; after his support of Saddam Hussein in the Gulf War, many of his Arab allies had turned against him, sending no more arms, supplies, and money (the PLO was running out of all three), while Arafat's personal prestige was at an all-time low. The PLO had also lost its main military base at Sidon, with its heavy weapons, to Syrian-backed Lebanese army forces. In response, Arafat had moved to a moderate position, endorsing the Middle East peace talks and expelling militant Abu Abbas from the PLO executive committee. But the peace talks made little progress early in 1992, and these moves in turn were challenged by PLO and other Palestinian militants, who wanted a return to terrorist tactics.

Arafat survived a plane crash in the Libyan desert on April 7, and his survival was apparently greeted with relief by Palestinian moderates and militants alike; for all the criticism, it suddenly seemed clear that no one else with his kind of prestige and history was available to lead their cause. Then, with the June victory of Labor in the Israeli elections, some progress toward Palestininian goals suddenly seemed possible, and his approach and prestige seemed once again quite attractive to his PLO colleagues. The Israelis still refused to meet directly with him, but it seemed possible that attitudes had changed on both sides, especially after Israeli Arabs who met with him in Tunis in October, including a member of the Israeli Parliament, were not prosecuted under existing Israeli law. However, at year's end the Intifada intensified, after Israeli expulsion of more than 400 fundamentalists following the assassination of an Israeli, and the hope for changed attitudes remained only a possibility.

On the personal side, Arafat and Suha Tawil married in February 1992.

Jerusalem-born Arafat was a founder of Al Fatah in 1956 and of its guerrilla army in 1959. He has headed the PLO and been the top leader of the Palestinian national movement since 1969. He suffered major personal defeats when his forces were expelled from Jordan in 1970–71, and from Lebanon in 1983. In the mid-1980s, he moved toward negotiation and publicly renounced terrorism, and seemed for a time all but overwhelmed by the more extreme terrorist elements within his own movement. In late 1988, he forced Palestine National Council and PLO acceptance of key United Nations resolutions 242 and 338. On November 15, 1988, he issued a Palestinian declaration of independence, and the proclaimed Palestinian state has since been recognized by more than 50 countries. Arafat attended Cairo University, and was an engineer before becoming a full-time political leader.

FURTHER READING

"Better without the boss?" LISA BEYER. *Time*, June 15, 1992.
"Arafat talks. . . ." TOM POST. *Newsweek*, May 4, 1992.
Behind the Myth: Yasser Arafat and the Palestinian Revolution. ANDREW GOWERS and TONY WALKER. Interlink, 1992.
"Yasir Arafat . . . ." *Time*, Oct. 21, 1991.
Behind the Myth: Yasser Arafat and the Palestinian Revolution. ANDREW GOWERS and TONY WALKER. Interlink, 1991.
Arafat and the Palestine Liberation Organization. DIANA REISCHE. Watts, 1991.
Arafat: In the Eyes of the Beholder. JANET WALLACH and JOHN WALLACH. Carol, 1990; Prima, 1991.
Arafat: A Political Biography. ALAN HART. Indiana University Press, 1989.

Arletty (Léonie Bathiat; 1898–1992) French actress Arletty was by far best known to the world's moviegoers as Garance, opposite Jean-Louis Barrault as the mime Deburau, in Marcel Carne's classic *Les Enfants Du Paradis (Children of Paradise)* (1945).

After 20 years as a model and stage and screen actress, Arletty emerged as a film star in Carné's *Hotel Du Nord* (1938), going on to star in his *Daybreak* (1939) and *The Devil's Envoys* (1942). Although she was a world figure after *Les Enfants Du Paradis*, and refused to work in Nazi films during World War II, her career was greatly damaged by her wartime affair with a German officer. Much of her later work was on stage, although there were a few films, including *No Exit* (1954) and a small role in *The Longest Day* (1962). She was partially blinded in 1963, and her vision worsened in her later years. Her autobiography was *I Am What I Am* (1967). There were no survivors. (d. Paris; July 24, 1992)

FURTHER READING

Obituary. *Variety*, Aug. 3, 1992.
Obituary. *New York Times*, July 25, 1992.
Obituary. *The Times* (of London), July 25, 1992.

Arnall, Ellis Gibbs (1907–92) Georgia-born Arnall was a leading Southern liberal politician long before it seemed possible to many that a Southern liberal could possibly survive in what was then the solidly segregated South. A New Deal Democrat, he served two terms in the Georgia House of Representatives, and was Speaker pro tem of that body. He was Georgia attorney general (1939–43), and in 1943, at 35, defeated incumbent Eugene Talmadge to become governor of Georgia. In office, he abolished Georgia's notorious chain gang system, fumigated the state's parole and pardon system, and initiated a series of measures that resulted in the reaccrediting of the state's colleges and universities. He was head of the U.S. Office of Price Stabilization during 1952, and was active in United Nations affairs. A lawyer, Arnall formed his own Atlanta-based firm after his term as governor, and later became president and board member of several companies, industrial associations, and other institutions. His 1928 B.A. was from the University of the South, and his 1931 LL.B. from the University of Georgia. He was survived by his second wife, Ruby Arnall, a son, and a brother. (d. Atlanta, Georgia; December 13, 1992)

FURTHER READING

Obituary. *New York Times*, Dec. 15, 1992.
The Politics of Change in Georgia: A Political Biography of Ellis Arnall. Harold P. Henderson. University of Georgia Press, 1991.
Georgia Governors in an Age of Change: From Ellis Arnall to George Busbee. Hal Henderson and Gary L. Roberts, eds. University of Georgia Press, 1988.

Arnold, Roseanne Barr (1952–) Recognition from her peers was long in coming, but in 1992 the flamboyant Roseanne Barr Arnold received an Emmy nomination as lead actress in her long-running hit comedy series "Roseanne." In its fourth season, the television show was not quite as popular as before, but was still generally found in the top 5 and always in the top 10 in the ratings. In its fifth season, which began in September 1992, the show rebounded, again often going to the top of the television ratings.

On June 20, 1992, Roseanne starred before a live audience in Minneapolis in her third *HBO Comedy Hour*, co-producing it with her husband, Tom Arnold, and providing the kind of standup comic routines that had been her earliest work in entertainment. She and Tom Arnold also co-starred in the forthcoming television movie *Graced Land*, the story of welfare mother Joyce Jackson, who turns her home into a shrine for Elvis Presley after her husband walks out on her. She also acted as executive producer of "The Jackie Thomas Show," starring Tom Arnold, which was added to the lineup in autumn 1992 following "Roseanne." On the personal side, Roseanne Arnold reportedly had surgery to untie her Fallopian tubes, and was attempting to conceive.

Salt Lake City-born Arnold began her career as a stand-up comedian in variety in the late 1970s. A decade later, she emerged as the star of the very popular television series "Roseanne" (1988–), which was at or near the top of the ratings during most of 1989–1992. Propelled by her personal style, she also emerged as a major celebrity. In 1989, she starred in her first feature film, *She-Devil*, and in 1991 in her first television film, *Backfield in Motion*. An animated series "Little Rosey," based on the Roseanne character, aired during the 1990–91 television season. She has published *Roseanne: My Life as a Woman* and *Stand Up!*. In September 1991, speaking to an incest survivors group, Arnold went public with charges that she had been sexually abused as a child, a charge her parents denied. She has been married twice, and has four children, one of whom she bore as a teenager and gave up for adoption.

FURTHER READING

"Everything's coming up Rosie." BOBBIE KATZ. *First for Women*, Nov. 9, 1992.
"The King's biggest fans." MELANIE BERGER. *Ladies Home Journal*, Nov. 1992.
"Lady in waiting." *TV Guide*. Aug. 29, 1992.
"Roseanne!" LESLIE VAN BUSKIRK. *US*, May 1992.
"Tom Arnold and the little woman." MICHAEL ANGELI. *Esquire*, Apr. 1992.
"Roseanne Arnold." ED DWYER. *Los Angeles*, Mar. 1992.
"The Roseanne report." MARY MURPHY and FRANK SWERTLOW. *TV Guide*, Jan. 4, 1992.
"A star cries incest. . . ." VICKIE BANE. *People*, Oct. 1991.
"Roseanne bares all! . . ." RYAN MURPHY. *Advocate*, Mar. 12, 1991.
"Roseanne sings. . . ." JOBETH MCDANIEL. *Ladies Home Journal*, Jan. 1991.
"The wretched. . . ." BARBARA EHRENREICH. *New Republic*, Apr. 2, 1990.
"Roseanne unchained." JIM JEROME. *People*, Oct. 9, 1989.
"The real Roseanne." KATHRYN CASEY. *Ladies Home Journal*, Sep. 1989.
"Barr, Roseanne." *Current Biography*, May 1989.

Ashe, Arthur Robert, Jr. (1943–) One of the major AIDS stories of the year was that of tennis great Arthur Ashe. On April 8, 1992, flanked by his wife and New York mayor David Dinkins, a personal friend, Ashe announced at a press conference that he had the HIV virus, which causes AIDS. His doctors had detected the condition after his 1988 brain surgery. It was probably caused by the blood in transfusions connected with his 1979 or 1983 heart operations, most likely the latter. His was one of many such cases from that period; in the early 1980s, information about the HIV virus and AIDS was scant, and the U.S. blood supply had not been tested for the virus. Although Ashe had chosen not to "go public" with his story, some of his friends and associates—including some journalists—knew that he had the HIV virus; but all respected his right to privacy, and quietly decided to keep his secret. Nor would he have announced it when he did; but on April 7 the decision was effectively made for him, when a reporter for *USA Today* called to confirm information that Ashe "had AIDS." Sure that the story was about to break, Ashe decided to tell it fully and publicly, and in the process made a major contribution to public understanding of the disease, as had Earvin "Magic" Johnson five months earlier.

Afterward, Ashe became active in fundraising for AIDS research and worked to help victims of the disease, organizing the Foundation for the Defeat of AIDS, with the top players in tennis playing benefit exhibitions to help the cause. He also continued his long fight against racism, and was one of 95 people arrested outside the White House in early September in a protest against the forced return home of Haitian refugees. In mid-September, he was hospitalized with a mild heart attack. He also continued his work as an HBO tennis commentator. Though long retired from professional competition, Ashe was named *Sports Illustrated*'s Sportman of the Year.

Richmond-born Ashe, a trailblazing African-American tennis player, was an amateur champion during his college years, and went on to become a leading professional. He was the first African-American to be named to the U.S. Davis Cup team (1963), win the U.S. Amateur title (1968), win the U.S. Open (1968), win the Australian Open (1970), and win at Wimbledon (1975). He retired from play in 1979, after three heart attacks, then becoming a sports consultant and holding several corporate positions. Always active in equal rights struggles, he was an early and highly visible opponent of South African apartheid. He has also been an active author, whose major work was the three-volume *A Hard Road to Glory: The History of the African-American Athlete* (1988). His other works include *Arthur Ashe: An Autobiography* (1970), *Portrait in Motion* (1973), and *Off the Court* (1981). Ashe's 1966 B.S. was in business administration, from the University of California at Los Angeles. He is married to the former Jeanne-Marie Moutoussamy, and has one child.

FURTHER READING

"The eternal example." KENNY MOORE. *Sports Illustrated*, Dec. 21, 1992.

"The righteous rage of. . . ." MIKE LUPICA. *Esquire*, Oct. 1992.

"Aids: my toughest match." RONALD ATKIN. *Observer*, June 21, 1992.

"Arthur Ashe vows to go forward. . . ." *Jet*, Apr. 27, 1992.

Arthur Ashe: Black Americans of Achievement. TED WEISSBERG. Chelsea House, 1992.

"Arthur Ashe remembers. . . ." SUSAN REED. *People*, Mar. 6, 1989.

"Arthur Ashe doing OK. . . ." *Jet*, Sep. 26, 1988.

"Inside the heart and mind of. . . ." BARRY LORGE. *Tennis*, Sep. 1988.

Profiles in Achievement. CHARLES M. HOLLOWAY. College Board, 1987.

Asimov, Isaac (1920–92)

Russian-born Asimov emigrated to the United States with his family at the age of three, graduated from high school at the age of 15, and published his first science fiction story at the age of 18, beginning a long, exceedingly prolific writing career in science fiction, popular science, and a considerable range of other areas. Three of his early works became science fiction classics: the story "Nightfall," published in the 1941 *Astounding Stories* magazine, the story "I, Robot" (1950), and the "Foundation" trilogy of novels, consisting of *Foundation* (1951), *Foundation and Empire* (1952), and *Second Foundation and Empire* (1953). His approximately 500 published works include guides to and chronologies of science and technology, guides to Shakespeare and the Bible, history, poetry, and much more. He was survived by his second wife, Janet Jeppson, two children, a sister, and a brother. (d. New York City; April 6, 1992)

FURTHER READING

"Asimov's vision." ABE DANE. *Popular Mechanics*, Aug. 1992.

Obituary. HARLAN ELLISON and EDWARD L. FERMAN. *Magazine of Fantasy and Science Fiction*, Aug. 1992.

"Giants fall." LEONARD DAVID. *Ad Astra*, July–Aug. 1992.

"Quantum leap." THOMAS M. DISCH. *Entertainment*, Apr. 17, 1992.

Obituary. *Variety*, Apr. 13, 1992.

"Nightfall. " *Economist*, Apr. 11, 1992.

Obituary. *New York Times*, Apr. 7, 1992.

Obituary. *The Times* (of London), Apr. 7, 1992.

"Isaac Asimov." KAREN BOEHLER. *Ad Astra*,
 July–Aug. 1991.
Isaac Asimov. Donald M. Hassler. Borgo Press,
 1991. Reprint.
Reader's Guide to Isaac Asimov. DONALD M. HASSLER.
 Starmont House, 1991.
"Isaac Asimov speaks. . . ." BILL MOYERS. *Humanist*,
 Jan.–Feb. 1989.
"The protean penman." STEFAN KANFER. *Time*, Dec.
 19, 1988.

Aspin, Les (1938–)

President Bill Clinton's incoming Secretary of Defense, Aspin was one of the most powerful Democrats in the House of Representatives even before his December 1992 appointment. As chairman of the House Armed Services Committee, he continued to call for massive cuts in military spending during 1992, against sharp Defense Department opposition, which in February publicly called his plans "merely political." During 1992, he voted with his party to cut Strategic Defense Initiative ("Star Wars") funds, further develop test ban talks, and cut military aid to El Salvador—all part of his drive to cut military spending and use the monies saved to create a "peace dividend," which could be used to create jobs and reduce the deficit. In November 1992, he was reelected by a landslide, winning 58 percent of the vote in his district.

Milwaukee-born Aspin began his long Congressional career in 1970. During the 1980s, he emerged as a leading Wisconsin Democrat, with powerful influence on military appropriations through his House committee memberships. He was cautious at first, and then fully supported the 1991 Persian Gulf War, but after the war strongly attacked Bush administration defense policies and called for far greater military spending cuts than those proposed by the Pentagon.

Aspin's 1960 B.A. was from Yale University, his 1962 M.A. from Oxford University, and his 1965 Ph.D. from the Massachusetts Institute of Technology. He taught economics at Marquette University (1969–70). He has published the *The Aspin Papers: Sanctions, Diplomacy and War in the Persian Gulf* (1991).

FURTHER READING

"The Aspin papers. . . ." MORTON KONDRACKE. *New
 Republic*, Apr. 27, 1992.

Assad, Hafez al (1928–)

Syrian President Assad, in his mid-60s and in his twenty-first year in power, continued to play a major role in the complicated politics of the Middle East. Fully aware of his new post-Cold War, post-Persian Gulf War political situation, he continued to seek ties with the United States, in return for taking a far more moderate position on Arab-Israeli issues. To those ends, he joined the Middle East peace talks in 1991 and continued to fully participate in those talks during 1992, through the wholly unfruitful negotiations with Israel's hard-line Shamir government and into the much more promising negotiations with the Rabin government after the Labor Party victory in the June Israeli elections. In April, Assad ended the long-standing travel bans faced by Syrian Jews. However, he came into sharp conflict with the new Israeli government at year's end, with deportation of more than 400 Arab fundamentalists to Lebanon, which (with Syrian approval) refused to take them.

During 1992, Assad continued to pursue regional goals, recognizing the independence of Lebanon while at the same time actually consolidating his position in the country, supporting and training Kurdish nationalist forces in Turkey and Iraq, and cultivating relations with Egyptian President Mubarak and other Arab leaders.

Assad began his political and military career as a Baath Party activist and air force officer. He became an air force general after the 1963 Baathist coup, and air force commander in chief and minister of defense in 1966. He took power in 1970 and was named President of Syria in 1971. During the Cold War, he was closely allied with and his armed forces were supplied by the Soviet Union. His forces were badly defeated by Israel in the fourth Arab-Israeli (Yom Kippur) war of 1973. Since 1976, his forces have partially occupied Lebanon, although they were defeated again by the Israelis in Lebanon in 1976. During the Iran-Iraq war of the 1980s, he supported Iran against Iraq, a long-term enemy. Assad is married, and has five children. He attended Syria's armed forces colleges.

FURTHER READING

"Hafez Assad: land before peace." *Time*, Nov. 30,
 1992.
"Syria's game. . . ." JUDITH MILLER. *New York Times
 Magazine*, Jan. 26, 1992.

"When Shamir blinked. . . ." ELIAHU SALPETER. *New Leader,* Aug. 12, 1991.

" 'It's now up to the Israelis:. . . ." LALLY WEYMOUTH. *Newsweek,* Aug. 5, 1991.

"Trouble in Damascus." ALAN COWELL. *New York Times Magazine,* Apr. 1, 1990.

Hafez al-Assad. MATTHEW GORDON. Chelsea House, 1989.

Aubuisson Arrieta, Robert d': See D'Aubuisson Arrieta, Robert.

Aung San Suu Kyi, Daw (1945–   ) Now

a legendary world human rights leader, recipient of the 1991 Nobel Peace Prize, Aung San Suu Kyi remained the prisoner of the military dictatorship in Myanmar (traditionally Burma) throughout 1992. In her fourth year of house arrest, she continued to defy the dictatorship's demands that she renounce politics and the cause of Burmese democracy as the price of her freedom. She has been held without charge or trial at her family home at Yangon, near Rangoon.

In late November 1992, her husband Michael Aris told reporters in London that she had cancelled a planned Christmas visit from Aris and their two sons, and that he believed that her life was now in grave danger, as she lived under poverty-stricken conditions, in much worsened health, and had decided to refuse all food and support from the military dictatorship. In mid-December, the government denied that she was on a hunger strike, threatened to try her for alleged crimes, and stated that she had been held for more than three years for "disturbing the peace." As the United Nations pressed the dictatorship to release her, and concern grew for her life and safety, the whole world watched.

Rangoon-born Daw Aung San Suu Kyi is the daughter of the founder of modern Burma (now Myanmar), Aung San (1914–47), who became Burma's first prime minister in 1947, and was assassinated on July 19, 1947. She grew up in Burma, leaving her country in 1960, when her mother became Burmese ambassador to India. She was educated in India and at Oxford University. She married archeologist Michael Aris in 1972; they have two sons. She lived with her husband and children in Oxford until 1988, during those years publishing a biography of her father, *Aung San* (1984); she then returned to Burma to nurse her sick mother, who died later in 1988.

Although her reasons for returning to Burma had nothing to do with politics, she arrived during a revolutionary period, often called the Burmese Spring, with hundreds of thousands involved in massive street demonstrations against the 26-year-old military dictatorship of army leader Ne Win. She soon became a leader of the democratic opposition, heading the nonviolent National League for Democracy, and was in 1988 placed under house arrest and forbidden to run for office.

Ne Win resigned in July 1988, but remained in control of the army, while demonstrations continued. A democratic government briefly ruled in August and September 1988, but was overthrown by the September army coup, in which thousands were killed. The military dictatorship that then took over Burma was led by General Saw Maung.

Aung San Suu Kyi, under house arrest, stayed on in Burma to lead the democratic opposition to the military dictatorship. When the military, facing powerful democratic opposition, promised and held democratic elections in May 1990, her party swept the election. The military then refused to honor the election results, and tightened its control, publicly attacking her for marrying a foreigner and at the same time trying to convince her to leave the country by making the terms of her imprisonment more difficult and keeping her family from visiting her. Various of her writings were published in 1992 under the title *Freedom from Fear,* edited by Aris.

FURTHER READING

"Burma's Gandhi." DAVID S. TOOLAN. *America,* Feb. 8, 1992.

"Aung San Suu Kyi." *Current Biography,* Feb. 1992.

"The wages of courage." *People,* Oct. 28, 1991.

Aykroyd, Dan (Daniel Edward Aykroyd;

1952–   ) Comedy film star Aykroyd starred in 1992 as Mack Sennett in *Chaplin,* Richard Attenborough's biographical film about the legendary Charles Chaplin, starring Robert Downey, Jr. in the title role, and costarring Geraldine Chaplin as her own grandmother Hannah Chaplin; Kevin Dunn as J. Edgar Hoover; Kevin Kline as Douglas Fairbanks, Moira Kelly as Hetty Kelly and Oona O'Neill; Diane Lane as Paulette Goddard; Penelope Anne Miller as

Edna Purviance; Anthony Hopkins as George Hayden; and Paul Rhys as Sydney Chaplin.

Aykroyd also co-starred as a show business agent in Nora Ephron's film directorial debut *This is My Life*, starring Julie Kavner as a stand-up comedian juggling her growing career and her role as mother of two young girls, and co-starring Carrie Fisher. A third major role was in Phil Alden Robinson's well-received fast-paced comedy thriller *Sneakers*, a work that included computer hackers, national security, and assorted murders, in a cast that co-starred Robert Redford, Ben Kingsley, Sidney Poitier, Mary McDonnell, River Phoenix, and James Earl Jones.

Canadian-born Aykroyd became a star in television comedy as one of the original members of the *Saturday Night Live* troupe (1975–79); he also wrote for the program. He and John Belushi created The Blues Brothers for the show, then starred in the film, *The Blues Brothers* (1980), which Aykroyd wrote. He went on to star in many other films, including *Neighbors* (1981), *Trading Places* (1983), *Ghostbusters* (1984), *Spies Like Us* (1985), *Dragnet* (1987), *The Great Outdoors* (1988), *My Stepmother Is an Alien* (1988), *Ghostbusters II* (1989), *Loose Cannons* (1990), *Nothing But Trouble* (1991; he also wrote and directed), and *My Girl* (1991). He won an Oscar nomination for best supporting actor as the son in *Driving Miss Daisy* (1989). Aykroyd attended Ottawa's Carleton College. He has been married twice, and has three children.

FURTHER READING

"Architectural Digest visits. . . ." Susan Cheever. *Architectural Digest*, Aug. 1992.
"Aykroyd, Dan." *Current Biography*, Jan. 1992.
"A haunted humorist. . . ." Brian Johnson. *Maclean's*, June 26, 1989.

Aylwin Azócar, Patricio (1919–) Chilean

President Aylwin continued the long process of restoring Chilean democracy in 1992, while at the same time continuing to co-exist with former dictator General Augusto Pinochet Ugarte, head of the Chilean military. Aylwin continued to pursue a stabilizing course, stressing social welfare legislation within the context of a relatively strong economy, although the question of inflation control was—as always—

very difficult. Chile's anticipated 15 percent inflation rate for 1992, down from more than 25 percent in 1991, was generally regarded as very good for Latin America, but was still very high. Aylwin felt strong enough to pursue improved trading and political relations with the United States, following up the 1991 U.S.-Chile debt reduction agreement with a move toward free trade agreement negotiations in 1992. After the Clinton-Gore Presidential election victory, all such negotiations were effectively put on hold until the new American administration took power in 1993.

Aylwin, a lawyer and Christian Democrat, became a senator in 1965 and leader of his party in 1973. He opposed the socialist Allende government in the early 1970s. In the early years he did not openly oppose the Pinochet dictatorship, but did join other lawyers in defending some of those imprisoned by the government, and later more openly opposed military rule. Aylwin led the democratic coalition that replaced military dictator Pinochet, and was elected to the Chilean presidency in December 1989. In power, he played a major role in restoring Chilean democracy, quickly freeing many of Chile's political prisoners, and setting up a national commission to study and report on the human rights violations of the Pinochet government. In March 1991, the commission reported that over 2,000 cases of murder, disappearance, and torture had occurred during the Pinochet years, including the long-charged murder of folksinger Victor

Jara and 1976 car bombing murders in Washington, D.C., of former cabinet minister Orlando Letelier and Ronni Moffitt. Aylwin Azócar married Leonor Oyarzun in 1948; they have five children.

FURTHER READING

"Seeking a free trade agreement." JEAN A. BRIGGS. *Forbes*, May 11, 1992.
"Chile's uncommon way." JONATHAN KANDELL. *Town & Country*, Oct. 1991.
"Aylwin Azocar, Patricio." *Current Biography*, Aug, 1990.

Aziz, Tariq (Michael Yuhanna; 1936–) Although he had changed jobs after the Persian Gulf War, becoming Iraq's deputy premier after having been Iraq's highly visible foreign minister, Aziz continued during 1992 to be Saddam Hussein's chief international spokesperson. Aziz once again addressed a world audience in March 1992, unsuccessfully leading an Iraqi delegation to the United Nations to demand a relaxation of the UN trade sanctions imposed after the Gulf War. The UN Security Council refused to do so, because of Iraq's failure to comply with its cease-fire agreements, in a range of areas that included failure to allow comprehensive inspection and destruction of Iraq's weapons of mass destruction and weapons production facilities. Aziz figured again in weapons destruction talks during the July weapons inspection standoff, as Iraq tested the resolve of the the UN on the issue.

As Iraq's foreign minister, Aziz became a well known figure during the run-up to the Persian Gulf War, as he attempted with very little success to defend Saddam Hussein's conquest of Kuwait. He and U.S. Secretary of State James Baker were the central figures in the flurry of unsuccessful diplomatic initiatives that preceded the January 17, 1991 opening of the Allied air war against Iraq. Aziz appeared as a main figure again once the war was lost, in a prolonged attempt to use Soviet mediation as a means of securing easier surrender terms and perhaps to save face, but he did not succeed, ultimately agreeing to United Nations demands.

Aziz is one of the few Christians in the largely Muslim Iraqi leadership. He attended Baghdad University and was a journalist before the Baath Party coup of 1968. Long an associate of Saddam Hussein, he became a key media specialist for Hussein after the 1970 coup that brought Hussein to power. He was Minister of Information (1974–77), and has been a member of Hussein's small inner group, the Revolutionary Command Council, since 1977. He became a deputy prime minister in 1979.

FURTHER READING

"Tariq Aziz. . . ." PETER HEBBLETHWAITE. *National Catholic Reporter*, Dec. 14, 1990.

B

Babbitt, Bruce Edward (1938–   ) President Bill Clinton's incoming Secretary of the Interior brings to the job strong pro-environmentalist views and affiliations and a great deal of practical experience. Babbitt practiced law in Phoenix (1965–74), and again in Phoenix and Washington (1988–92), focusing largely in environmental matters, water, and natural resources. He began his political career as Arizona attorney general (1975–78), and was governor of Arizona (1978–87); in 1985, he was chairman of the Democratic Governors Association. In 1988, he made an unsuccessful run for the Democratic Presidential nomination. He is the national president of the League of Conservation Voters, chairman of the National Groundwater Policy Forum, and served on the Presidential commission set up to investigate the nearly catastrophic 1979 Three Mile Island nuclear accident. His books include *Color and Light: The Southwest Canvases of Louis Akin* (1973) and *Grand Canyon: An Anthology* (1978).

Babbitt's 1960 B.A. was from the University of Notre Dame, his 1962 M.S. in geophysics from Britain's University of Newcastle, and his 1965 LL.B. from Harvard Law School. He is married to the former Hattie Coons; they have two children.

FURTHER READING

"Bye-Bye Bruce." *New Republic*, Mar. 7, 1988.
"The men who would be president." *Black Enterprise*, Mar. 1988.
"Campaign diary. . . ." ANDY PLATNER. *U.S. News & World Report*, Feb. 15, 1988.
"The poker player. . . ." DAVID OSBORNE. *Washington Monthly*, Feb. 1988.
"Stand-up guy. . . ." HENDRICK HERTZBERG. *New Republic*, Jan. 4, 1988.
"Standing up for substance. . . ." DAN GOODGAME. *Time*, Jan. 4, 1988.
Laboratories of Democracy. DAVID OSBORNE. Harvard Business, 1988.

Bacon, Francis (1909–92) A leading British artist, Bacon began to paint in the late 1920s and early 1930s, but so disliked his work that he destroyed almost he produced in that period, and stopped painting from 1936 to 1944. But with the 1945 showing of his highly regarded triptych *Three Studies for Figures at the Base of a Crucifixion*, painted in 1944, he emerged as one of the leading painters of the period, his depictions of the most loathesome qualities of humanity and of the human experience quite fitting the postwar disillusion of that time. His main focus continued to be on the torn, bleeding, disintegrating human figures that peopled his work in the decades that followed; as he grew into a major figure, his work was much sought by collectors and museums. Bacon was survived by a sister. (d. Madrid; April 28, 1992)

FURTHER READING

Francis Bacon and the Loss of Self. ERNST VAN ALPHEN. Harvard University Press, 1993.
"Francis Bacon. . . ." WILLIAM FEAVER. *ARTnews*, Summer 1992.

"Of hopelessness and hope." PETER PLAGENS. *Newsweek*, May 11, 1992.

"Raffish old master of the elusive." WILLIAM FEAVER. *Observer*, May 3, 1992.

"The horror of Francis Bacon." *Economist*, May 2, 1992.

Obituary. BRUCE BERNARD. *Independent*, Apr. 29, 1992.

"Francis Bacon. . . ." ANDREW GRAHAM-DIXON. *Independent*, Apr. 29, 1992.

"The artist as a beloved adventurer." DAVID LISTER. *Independent*, Apr. 29, 1992.

Obituary. *New York Times*, Apr. 29, 1992.

Obituary. *The Times* (of London), Apr. 29, 1992.

The Artist Observed: Twenty-Eight Interviews with Contemporary Artist. JOHN GRUEN. Chicago Review, 1991.

"Unnerving art." MICHAEL KIMMELMAN. *New York Times Magazine*, Aug. 20, 1989.

Francis Bacon. LAWRENCE GOWING and SAM HUNTER. Thames Hudson, 1989.

Francis Bacon. JAMES T. DEMETRION et al. Hirshhorn, 1989.

The Brutality of Fact: Interviews with Francis Bacon, rev. ed. DAVID SYLVESTER. Thames Hudson, 1988.

Francis Bacon. MICHAEL LEIRIS. Rizzoli, 1988.

Francis Bacon. HUGH DAVIES and SALLY YARD. Abbeville, 1986.

Francis Bacon. JOHN RUSSELL. Thames Hudson, 1985.

Francis Bacon. DAWN ADES and ANDREW FORGE. Abrams, 1985.

Baker, James (James Addison Baker 3rd; 1930–)

As U.S. Secretary of State, Baker played a major role in world affairs during the first seven months of 1992. A major focus continued to be the Middle East peace talks, begun in Madrid in November 1991, which continued in several Washington, D.C. rounds throughout the year. Another was a continuing attempt to affect the course of events in the countries of the former Soviet Union, coupled with an only moderately successful attempt to funnel aid to Russia, to help shore up the weak Yeltsin government and to stimulate the development of a market economy. As always, the American Secretary of State also continued to function in a worldwide way, in many countries and for a wide variety of purposes.

On August 13, his reelection campaign badly fragmented and ineffective, President George Bush announced that Baker, his old friend and political manager, would once again manage his Presidential campaign. Baker then did so all the way to the November 3 defeat, his old political "magic" failing to work this one last time. In December, Baker was reportedly planning to write an autobiography.

Houston-born Baker, a lawyer, has long been a personal friend and political ally of George Bush; their alliance goes back to the early 1970s, a period in which both men moved from Texas Republican politics onto the national scene. Baker was an undersecretary of commerce (1975–76), was active in the 1976 Ford campaign, and in 1979–80 managed the Bush presidential nomination campaign, from which Bush emerged as Ronald Reagan's vice-president. Baker went into the Reagan administration, too, in the central role of White House Chief of Staff. In 1985, he switched jobs with Treasury Secretary Donald Regan and became Treasury Secretary (1985–88). He went on to manage the successful 1988 Bush presidential campaign, and then became Secretary of State in the new Bush administration. Baker's 1952 B.A. was from Princeton University, and his 1957 LL.B. from the University of Texas. He married Susan Garrett in 1973; they have eight children.

FURTHER READING

"I, Baker. . . ." SIDNEY BLUMENTHAL. *New Republic*, Nov. 2, 1992.

"Baker on Baker." INA GINSBURG. *Town & Country*, Nov. 1992.

"His master's voice." MARJORIE WILLIAMS. *Vanity Fair*, Oct. 1992.

"What foreign policy?. . . ." MORTON KONDRACKE. *New Republic*, Feb. 24, 1992.

"The tactician." JOHN NEWHOUSE. *New Yorker*, May 7, 1990.

"James Baker. . . ." ROWLAND EVANS and ROBERT NOVAK. *Reader's Digest*, Nov. 1989.

Baldwin, Alec (Alexander Rae Baldwin 3rd; 1958–)

Choosing art over commerce, stage and screen star Baldwin rejected the multimillion dollar *Patriot Games* film project in favor of starring on Broadway in the classic Stanley Kowalski role in a 1992 revival of Tennessee Williams's *A Streetcar Named Desire*, opposite Jessica Lange, Amy Madigan, and Timothy Carhart. He and the play were a hit, and Baldwin won critical raves and a Tony nomination as leading actor in a play for the role.

On screen, Baldwin was part of another artis-

Alec Baldwin (right) and Meg Ryan.

tic triumph, starring as a shady real estate sales executive in James Foley's film adaptation of David Mamet's dark drama *Glengarry Glen Ross*. Co-starring were Al Pacino, Jack Lemmon, Ed Harris, Alan Arkin, Kevin Spacey, and Jonathan Pryce. On screen, he also starred opposite Meg Ryan and Kathy Bates in Norman René's fantasy film *Prelude to a Kiss*, adapted by Craig Lucas from René's play. Forthcoming was a starring role opposite Nicole Kidman in Harold Becker's *Damages*.

Long Island-born Baldwin starred in the television series "Knots Landing," and in the New York theater in such plays as *Serious Money* and *Prelude to a Kiss*, for which he won an Obie award. He became a film star in the late 1980s, in such films as *She's Having a Baby* (1988), *Beetlejuice* (1988), *Married to the Mob* (1988), *Talk Radio* (1988), and *Working Girl* (1988), making his major breakthrough in *The Hunt for Red October* (1990). His films also include *Miami Blues* (1990), *Alice* (1990), and *The Marrying Man* (1991). Baldwin attended George Washington University (1976–1979), and studied theater at New York University and the Lee Strasberg Institute (1979–80).

FURTHER READING

"Baldwin, Alec." *Current Biography*, July 1992.
"Kim and Alec. . . ." ELIZABETH SPORKIN. *People*, Apr. 22, 1991.

"Not just another hunk." CATHLEEN McGUIGAN. *Newsweek*, Apr. 23, 1990.
"The hunk from 'Hunt.' " PETER TRAVERS. *Rolling Stone*, Apr. 5, 1990.
"Smart Alec." STEPHANIE MANSFIELD. *GQ—Gentlemen's Quarterly*, Feb. 1990.

Barber, Red (Walter Lanier Barber; 1908–92) Mississippi-born Barber, a pioneer sports broadcaster, began his long radio career with the campus radio station at the University of Florida in the late 1920s. His sportscasting career began in 1934; from then until 1938 he was the voice of the Cincinnati Reds. From 1939 to 1953, known to millions of listening sports fans as "the old redhead," he was the radio voice of the Brooklyn Dodgers, his play-by-play including the first night game in 1935, the first televised game in 1953, and the first unsegregated major league baseball game in 1947, when Jackie Robinson, under Branch Rickey, broke through the color line, making it possible for baseball to honestly call itself America's national pastime. Barber moved to the New York Yankees in 1953; he was fired in 1966 for being too honest on the air about how few people were attending the then-last-place Yankees's games. From 1981 to 1992, his broadcast commentary was carried on National Public Radio's "Morning Edition." Barber also wrote several books on sports themes. He and sportcaster Mel Allen were in 1978 the first broadcasters to be inducted into the Baseball Hall of Fame. He was survived by his wife, the former Lylah Scarborough, and a daughter. (d. Tallahassee, Florida; October 22, 1992)

FURTHER READING

"The catbird seat is empty." JACK KROLL. *Newsweek*, Nov. 2, 1992.
"The ol' Redhead." ROBERT CREAMER. *Sports Illustrated*, Nov. 2, 1992.
Obituary. *Variety*, Oct. 26, 1992.
Obituary. *New York Times*, Oct. 23, 1992.
"His words let listeners see. . . ." LISA TRYMAN BESSONE. *Sports Illustrated*, Aug. 13, 1990.
Voices of the Game: The First Full-Scale Overview of Baseball Broadcasting, 1921 to the Present. CURT SMITH. Diamond Communications, 1987.

Barkley, Charles Wade (1963–)
Charles Barkley was a star among stars in 1992. As part of the U.S. basketball "Dream Team" that went to the Barcelona Summer Olympics,

one might have expected Barkley to be overshadowed by players like Earvin "Magic" Johnson, Larry Bird, and Michael Jordan. But Barkley's competitiveness, enthusiasm, energy, and talent made him a standout even in that stellar crowd and won him new fans among international basketball audiences, even though some were offended by Barkley's usual aggressive play and general combativeness.

Barkley's attitudes strongly contributed to a souring of his relationship with the Philadelphia 76ers—the management, the fans, the media, and his own teammates. Part of it, as Barkley had said many times—and loudly—was that he wanted to be on a winning team, and did not want to stay in Philadelphia if they were not going to be in championship contention. So in June, in an unusual trade for a major player, Barkley was sent to the Phoenix Suns for three other players, Jeff Hornacek, Andrew Lang, and Tim Perry. By year's end, Barkley seemed well-satisfied with his new professional home, and had energized the talented but previously more "laid back" Phoenix team, which went to the top of the league in winning percentage, putting them in a position to challenge the two-time champion Chicago Bulls. Late in the year, Barkley also began a local television show in Phoenix with former head coach, now general manager, Cotton Fitzsimmons, the man who brought him to the Suns. One local Phoenix newspaper even started a column tited "The Barkley Beat," covering "Sir Charles's" always quot-

able quotes. In June, Barkley was acquitted on battery and disorderly conduct charges regarding a December 1991 incident in Milwaukee, in which he broke a heckler's nose.

Also in 1992, Barkley reached two career landmarks—14,000 career points and 7,000 career rebounds—and was named starting forward for the Eastern Conference All-Star game for the fifth consecutive season, his seventh appearance overall.

Born in Leeds, Alabama, Barkley emerged as a nationally recognized player during his years at Alabama's Auburn College (1981–84). Although often overweight and at odds with his coaching staff, he was the leading rebounder in the Southeastern Conference and a strong scorer during all three of his college seasons. He did not make the final cut for the 1984 U.S. Olympic team, but was a first round choice in the National Basketball Association draft after his junior year, going to the Philadelphia 76ers. There he became a fixture, one of the league's leading rebounders and scorers, and a perennial All-Star forward; he was on the second team in 1986 and 1987, on the starting team from 1988 to 1992, and most valuable player in the 1991 All-Star game. But Philadelphia, while often in the playoffs, never made it all the way to an NBA championship during Barkley's time there, although it had done so in 1983. Always highly individual, quotable, and contentious, Barkley has spent much of his career in the center of a self-created media storm, often accompanied by large NBA fines for misconduct and arguments with players, fans, referees, and the staffs of his own and other clubs. He published an autobiography, *Outrageous*, written with Roy Johnson, Jr. Barkley is married and has one child.

FURTHER READING

"Hot head." RICK REILLY. *Sports Illustrated*, Nov. 9, 1992.

"Charles Barkley says goodbye." LARRY PLATT. *Philadelphia*, Nov. 1992.

"Charles Barkley." RICK REILLY. *Sports Illustrated*, Mar. 9, 1992.

"Has mouth, will shoot." MIKE LUPICA. *Esquire*, Mar. 1992.

"Charles Barkley. . . .'" LARRY PLATT. *Sport*, Feb. 1992.

"The round mound unbound." BEN YAGODA. *Philadelphia*, Jan. 1992.

Sports Great Charles Barkley. GLEN MACNOW. Enslow, 1992.

"Headstrong." JEFF COPLON. *New York Times Magazine*, Mar. 17, 1991.
"Barkley, Charles." *Current Biography*, Oct. 1991.
"Sir Charles." RICHARD REGEN. *Interview*, June 1990.

Barnett, Marguerite Ross (1942–92) A

leading university administrator, Dr. Barnett was the first African-American woman to head a major American university, having in 1990 become president of the University of Houston, where she was also the first woman president. Barnett was a political scientist, who taught at several universities before moving into administration, and was an advocate of university activism in pursuit of social goals. She was a vice-chancellor of the City University of New York (1983–86) and a chancellor of the University of Missouri at St. Louis (1986–90). She also served on the boards of several organizations, including the Educational Testing Service, and published works on education policy. She was survived by her husband, Walter E. King, a daughter, and her mother. (d. Wailuku, Hawaii; February 26, 1992)

FURTHER READING

"Marguerite Barnett. . . ." *Jet*, Mar.16, 1992.
Obituary. *New York Times*, Feb. 27, 1992.
"Barnett is first Black prexy. . . ." *Jet*, May 21, 1990.

Barr, Roseanne: See Arnold, Roseanne Barr.

Barry, Marion Shepilov, Jr. (1936–)

Convicted on one misdemeanor count of cocaine possession while mayor of Washington, D.C. in 1990, Barry lost all appeals and in October 1991 began a six-month prison term at a Petersburg, Virginia federal prison. In January 1992, he was accused of having sex with a woman visitor, and transferred to a prison at Loretto, Pennsylvania. Completing his term, he returned to Washington, and immediately reentered politics, with a sharply changed image that included very strong expressions of religious conviction, frequent Bible quotes, clothing that expressed his African-American ethnic heritage, expressions of concern for African-American convicts, and announcement of a turn away from alcohol and drugs.

In September 1992, still very popular in Washington, Barry won a Democratic Party nomination for the Ward 8 City Council seat—which in Washington amounted to election—and emerged once again as a power in city politics. Many observers questioned the sincerity of his new beliefs and image, and further suggested that his reemergence might harm the movement for District of Columbia statehood, by giving Congressional conservative opponents of statehood new excuses for further delay.

Mississippi-born Barry was active in the civil rights movement of the 1960s, and moved into Washington, D.C. politics in the early 1970s, as a member of the School Board and then in 1976 of the City Council. He began his long, highly controversial tenure as mayor of Washington in 1979. His 1958 B.S. was from Lemoyne College and his 1960 M.S. was from Fisk University. He married Effi Barry in 1978; they have one child.

FURTHER READING

"Barry and his city. . . ." JEFFERSON MORLEY. *Nation*, Feb. 19, 1990.
Marion Barry: The Politics of Race. JONATHAN I. AGRONSKY. British American, 1990.
"A bright, broken promise." MICHAEL RILEY. *Time*, June 26, 1989.
"Washington's mayor. . . . " MONTGOMERY BROWER. *People*, Jan. 16, 1989.

Bartholomew, Freddie (Frederick

Llewellen; 1924–92) A leading child actor of the 1930s, Bartholomew made his stage debut at the age of four, and his screen debut in *Fascination* (1930). He emerged as a major star in the title role of *David Copperfield* (1935), in that year also playing Greta Garbo's son in *Anna Karenina*. The following year brought a starring role in *Little Lord Fauntleroy*, for which he is best known, with another in *Captain's Courageous* (1937). In 1938, Bartholomew made *Kidnapped* and several other films, but his career sagged with the onset of adolescence, although in 1940 he made *The Swiss Family Robinson* and *Tom Brown's School Days*. After service during World War II, his career was essentially over, though he continued to make personal appearances and made one more film. He later made a career in advertising. He was survived by his wife, Elizabeth, a daughter, and a son. (d. Sarasota, Florida; January 23, 1992)

FURTHER READING

Obituary. *Variety*, Jan. 27, 1992.
Obituary. *Independent*, Jan. 27, 1992.
Obituary. *The Times* (of London), Jan. 25, 1992.
Obituary. *New York Times*, Jan. 24, 1992.

Baryshnikov, Mikhail (1948–) A great

figure in world dance, Baryshnikov in 1992 continued to develop his White Oak Dance Project, a dance company that he co-founded with ultra-modern dancer-choreographer Mark Morris in the fall of 1990. In March and April, the company toured Europe for the first time, performing in Paris, London, Rome, Milan, Hamburg, Copenhagen, and Stockholm. But Baryshnikov cancelled its projected South African tour after the June massacre of more than 40 people in the Black township of Boipatong.

In June 1992, Baryshnikov danced with the New York City Ballet in George Balanchine's *Duo Concertante*, and as a soloist in the New York premiere of Mark Morris's *Three Preludes*. In October, Baryshnikov and Twyla Tharp appeared together in a segment of PBS's *Great Performance's 20th Anniversary Special*, and in late November began a national tour that would carry them through early February 1993. They premiered Tharp's new ballet "Cutting Up" at Columbus, Ohio on November 30, 1992. With Liza Minelli, Baryshnikov also hosted the opening of the Martha Graham Dance Company season at New York's City Center on October 13. On screen, Baryshnikov's 1991 film *Company Business* opened in New York; he starred as former Soviet mole Pyotr Grushenko who—after the failure of an exchange to return him—goes on the run with CIA agent Sam Boyd (Gene Hackman).

Russian-born Baryshnikov was well on his way to becoming a world figure in ballet when he defected to the West in 1974, after 5 years as a leading dancer with the Kirov Ballet (1969–74). The promise came to pass: in the years that followed, he danced as a leading guest artist with most of the world's great ballet companies and was artistic director of the American Ballet Theater (1980–89). His work included the creation of leads in such new ballets as *Vestris* (1965), *Hamlet* (1970), *Santa Fe Saga* (1978), and *Rhapsody* (1980); the choreography of new versions of *The Nutcracker* (1976), *Don Quixote* (1978), and *Cinderella* (1984); and appearances in several films, including *White Nights* (1985) and *The Dancers* (1987). After abruptly leaving the American Ballet Theatre late in 1989, he and Morris founded the White Oak Dance Project. On Broadway, Baryshnikov appeared as Gregor Samsa in a stage version of Franz Kafka's *Metamorphosis* (1989). With Peter Anastos, he wrote *The Swan Prince* (1987).

FURTHER READING

"Misha's moment. . . ." ELIZABETH KAYE. *Connoisseur*, Nov. 1991.
"And now, superstar? . . ." IRIS M. FANGER. *World Monitor*, June 1991.
Mikhail Baryshnikov. BRUCE GLASSMAN. Silver Burdett, 1991.
"Baryshnikov. . . ." DEBORAH JOWITT. *Dance Magazine*, Jan, 1990.
"Baryshnikov's transformation. . . ." JACK KROLL. *Newsweek*, Mar. 20, 1989.
"The next stage." PATRICIA CORBETT. *Connoisseur*, Jan. 1989.
Misha!: The Mikhail Baryshnikov Story. BARBARA ARIA. St. Martin's, 1989.

Basinger, Kim (1953–) In February

1992, Basinger starred opposite Richard Gere in Phil Joanou's psychological melodrama-murder film *Final Analysis*; unfortunately, the film was very adversely reviewed, did poorly at the box office, and was in film rentals by year's end. But it did do well in rentals, a testimonial to Basinger's continuing drawing power. In July, Basinger starred opposite Gabriel Byrne in the animated film *Cool World*, which also was not well received. Considerable publicity was generated prior to the film, when a 75-foot blowup of Basinger was attached to the famous Hollywood sign, to sharp protests from those living nearby. Forthcoming was a starring role opposite Val Kilmer in Russell Mulcahy's film *The Real McCoy*.

On the legal front, Basinger won a libel award and published apology from Britain's Express Newspapers, over a newspaper article falsely alleging that she was a cocaine addict. Still on the legal front, she was sued by the producers of the film *Boxing Helena*; she had pulled out of the project in 1991.

Georgia-born Basinger worked as a New York model in the mid-1970s, then moved into television, most notably in *Katie—Portrait of a Centerfold* (1978), and in the 1979 remake of *From Here to Eternity*. On screen, she starred in *Hard Country* (1980) and *The Man Who Loved Women* (1983), and became one of Hollywood's leading sex symbols of the 1980s as Domino in Sean Connery's last James Bond film *Never Say Never Again* (1983) and opposite Mickey Rourke in *9½ Weeks* (1986). She also starred in *The Natural* (1984), *Fool for Love* (1985), and *Batman* (1989). Basinger attended New York's Neighborhood Playhouse. She was formerly married.

FURTHER READING

"Kim up close. . . ." JONATHAN VAN METER. *Vogue*, May 1991.
"Kim and Alec. . . ." ELIZABETH SPORKIN. *People*, Apr. 22, 1991.
"Basinger, Kim." *Current Biography*, Feb, 1990.

Bates, Alan (1934–) British stage and screen star Alan Bates was once again honored by his peers in 1992, winning a British Academy of Film & Television Arts best supporting actor nomination for his Claudius in Franco Zeffirelli's film version of *Hamlet* (1990; released in video in 1991). His film *Secret Friends*, which had opened at the November 1991 London Film Festival, opened in New York in 1992 to mixed reviews, although his performance was well received. In the film, directed by Dennis Potter and inspired by Potter's novel *Ticket to Ride*, Bates starred as John, an illustrator who dreams of murdering his wife Helen (Gina Bellman). Bates also starred in Simon Gray's BBC televison film *Unnatural Pursuits*. On stage, Bates created the role of Fenchurch in David Storey's new one act play *Stages*. Directed by Lindsay Anderson, and co-starring Gabrielle Lloyd, Marjorie Yates, Joanna David, and Rosemary Martin, the Royal National Theatre production opened in November.

Forthcoming were starring roles opposite River Phoenix and Dermot Mulroney in Sam Shepherd's Western ghost story film *Silent Tongue*, set in 1893 New Mexico; and opposite Maggie Smith and Bob Hoskins in Lindsay Anderson's film version of Anton Chekhov's *The Cherry Orchard*.

Bates became a star in Harold Pinter's *The Caretaker* (1960; and the 1964 film version). He went on to such plays as *Butley* (1972; he won a Tony), *Otherwise Engaged* (1975), *A Patriot for Me* (1983), and *Ivanov* (1989). He has appeared in such films as *A Kind of Loving* (1962), *King of Hearts* (1966), *Far from the Madding Crowd* (1967), *A Day in the Death of Joe Egg* (1972), *In Celebration* (1974), *An Unmarried Woman* (1977), *Nijinsky* (1979), *The Return of the Soldier* (1982), and *A Prayer for the Dying* (1987), and in such telefilms as *An Englishman Abroad* (1983), *Pack of Lies* (1987), and *101 Boulevard Haussmann* (1991). Bates attended the Royal Academy of Dramatic Arts. He married Victoria Ward in 1970; they have two children.

FURTHER READING

"Alan Bates returns. . . ." CAROL LAWSON. *New York Times*, Dec. 30, 1983.

Kathy Bates (right) and Jessica Tandy.

Bates, Kathy (1948–) Continuing to emerge as an actress of great power and range, Kathy Bates starred in several films during 1992. She was Elsa, the Cape Town schoolteacher, in the notable film adaptation of the Athol Fugard play *The Road to Mecca*, costarring Yvonne Bryceland (who died in 1992) and Fugard. She also starred in Woody Allen's *Shadows and Fog*, in a multistar cast that included Allen, Mia Farrow, John Malkovich, Madonna, and Jodie Foster. Yet another starring role was opposite Alec Baldwin and Meg Ryan in Norman René's fantasy film *Prelude to a Kiss*, adapted by Craig Lucas from René's play. A fourth starring role came as one of Shirley MacLaine's daughters in Beeban Kidron's comedy-melodrama film *Used People*.

In television, she starred as Peggy Say, sister of hostage Terry Anderson, opposite Jay O. Sanders as Anderson and Colin Firth in the highly controversial and very well-received film *Hostages*, which opened in Britain in 1992 and was scheduled for U.S. release as a television film in 1993. Forthcoming was a starring role in Tony Bill's film *A Home of Our Own*.

Memphis-born Bates began her acting career in New York in 1970, often working in children's and regional theater, with occasional small film roles, as in Milos Forman's *Taking Off* (1971) and Dustin Hoffman's *Straight Time* (1978), and guest spots on television series and telefilms. Her first lead was in the Off-Broadway play *Vanities* (1976), and she originated the role of Lenny McGrath in Beth Henley's Pulitzer Prize-winning play *Crimes of the Heart* (1979). Her breakout stage role was as the suicidal Jessie Cates in Marsha Norman's Pulitzer Prize-winning *'Night Mother* (1983), for which she won the Outer Critics Circle Award and a Tony nomination. This was followed by a string of leading stage roles, including *Come Back to the Five and Dime, Jimmy Dean, Jimmy Dean* (1982) and *Frankie and Johnny in the Claire de Lune* (1987) for which she won an Obie Award.

She began to play supporting roles on film after her 1985 move to Los Angeles, as in *Arthur 2 on the Rocks* (1988) and *Dick Tracy* (1990). She won a Best Actress Oscar for *Misery* (1990), and also starred in *At Play in the Fields of the Lord* (1991) and *Fried Green Tomatoes* (1991). Bates graduated from Southern Methodist University in Dallas. She married actor Tony Campisi in 1991.

FURTHER READING

"Kathy Bates. . . ." WAYNE MILLER. *First for Women*, June 8, 1992.
"Kathy Bates talks about. . . ." BROOK HERSEY. *Glamour*, Feb. 1992.
"Bates, Kathy." *Current Biography*, Sep. 1991.
"Kathy Bates. " MICHAEL LASSELL and TIMOTHY GREENFIELD-SANDERS. *Interview*, Aug. 1991.
" 'I never was an ingenue'." DAVID SACKS. *New York Times Magazine*, Jan. 27, 1991.

"Wallowing in Misery. . . ." MARY H. J. FARRELL. *People*, Dec. 24, 1990.

Bean-Bayog, Margaret (1944–) In a

headline-catching case, Dr. Bean-Bayog, a psychiatrist and assistant professor at Harvard Medical School, was accused of having led former Harvard medical student Paul Lozano (then her patient) into a sexual relationship with her and of contributing to his April 1991 suicide. The charges were made in late March, in papers totaling several thousand pages filed as part of a medical malpractice lawsuit brought by Lozano's family against Dr. Bean-Bayog. She denied all charges, stating that some of the sexual fantasy material filed consisted of her own personal papers, having nothing to do with the Lozano case. She did affirm that some of her treatment of Lozano had been unorthodox, but asserted that she had been attempting to build a therapeutic situation between them by developing the fantasy that she was his mother and he a small child, a "regression" approach aimed at making it possible to find what the therapist using it believes to be the early-childhood roots of some problems.

Lozano, then a third year medical student, was her patient from July 1986 to June 1990, a period during which she had him committed to institutions on several occasions; he was institutionalized at the time when she terminated their professional relationship. As a state medical board investigation of the case proceeded, Bean-Bayog was in May 1992 placed on leave by Harvard. On September 18, facing a public hearing before the state medical board, Dr. Bean-Bayog resigned her medical license unconditionally, permanently barring her from practicing medicine anywhere in the United States, although leaving her free to practice as a psychotherapist or therapist. In December 1992, she settled a wrongful death lawsuit brought by Lozan's family for a reported $1 million. Late in 1992, two television films about the case were reportedly in development, one an NBC film starring Jamie Lee Curtis as Bean-Bayog, the other a Republic Pictures-ABC film. Among Bean-Bayog's published works is *Children of Alcoholics* (1987).

FURTHER READING

"Dr. Bean and her little boy." JERRY ADLER. *Newsweek*, Apr. 13, 1992.

Beatty, Warren (Warren Beaty; 1937–)

Celebrated actor and director Beatty was honored by his peers in 1992, winning a Best Actor Oscar nomination for his role as Bugsy Siegel in *Bugsy*, Barry Levinson's 1991 film about the 1940s Las Vegas gangster. The film also won Art Direction and Costume Design Oscars. Beatty became more active in film industry matters in 1992, succeeding Quincy Jones as chairman of the Permanent Charities Committee of the Entertainment Industries. He also joined legislators and film people calling for federal legislation mandating the labeling of films that had been altered, as by colorization or soundtrack changes.

On the personal side, Beatty and costar Annette Bening, who met on the set of *Bugsy*, married in early 1992; Bening had given birth to their daughter Kathlyn in early January.

Virginia-born Beatty, the brother of actress Shirley MacLaine, acted in television and theater from the late 1950s, moving into films in the early 1960s. He starred in *Splendor in the Grass* (1961), but his breakthrough role was that of Clyde Barrow in *Bonnie and Clyde* (1961). He produced that film, and went on to produce and star in such films as *McCabe and Mrs. Miller* (1971) and *Heaven Can Wait* (1978), which he also wrote. His most substantial work, so far, has been the epic film *Reds* (1981); he produced, directed, co-wrote, starred as John Reed, and won a Best Director Oscar for the film. In 1987, he starred in the disastrous *Ishtar*. In 1990, he directed and produced *Dick Tracy*. Beatty attended the Stella Adler theatre school.

FURTHER READING

"The Annette effect." JOAN JULIET BUCK. *Vanity Fair*, June 1992.
"Beatty & Bening & baby Bugsy'." MARY MURPHY. *TV Guide*, Mar. 28, 1992.
"Warren's curse." MASON WILEY and DAMIEN BONA. *Entertainment*, Mar. 27, 1992.
"Just a minute, Mr. Beatty." WALTER THOMAS. *Interview*, Mar. 1992.
"Warren in love." SUSIE LINFIELD. *McCall's*, Feb. 1992.
"A question of control." GAVIN SMITH. *Film Comment*, Jan.–Feb. 1992.
"The Warren report. . . ." NORMAN MAILER. *Vanity Fair*, Nov. 1991.
The Films of Warren Beatty. LAWRENCE J. QUIRK. Carol, 1990.
Actors: A Celebration. RITA GAM. St. Martin's, 1988.
Warren Beatty and Desert Eyes: A Life and a Story. DAVID THOMSON. Doubleday, 1987.

Begin, Menachem Wolfovitch (1913–92)

Born in Poland, Zionist leader and former Israeli prime minister Begin was imprisoned by the Soviets before the 1941 Nazi invasion of the Soviet Union. He joined free Polish forces, emigrated to Palestine in 1942, and in 1943 quickly emerged as a leader of the terrorist Irgun Zvai Leumi organization, developing a series of anti-British terrorist actions, in opposition to the policies of the World Zionist Organization and Haganah, the Jewish army.

A temporary postwar alliance with the Haganah broke down when the Irgun, following Begin's direct orders, bombed British offices in Jerusalem's King David Hotel on July 22, 1946, killing 91 people, 17 of them Jews. The Irgun was thereafter effectively outlawed, and in 1948 its military organization was dissolved by the new Israeli government, after government forces sank an Irgun munitions ship off the Israeli coast.

Begin then moved into conventional politics, founding the right-wing Herut Party in 1948. He gained power for the first time in 1967, as a member of the coalition government, and was Likud Party prime minister of Israel from 1977 to 1983. He and Anwar Sadat signed the 1978 Egyptian-Israeli peace treaty, and shared the 1978 Nobel Peace Prize. His prestige and government were greatly damaged by the 1982 invasion of Lebanon, and the Sabra and Shatilla massacres. Begin retired from public life in 1983. He was survived by two daughters and a son. (d. Jerusalem; March 9, 1992).

FURTHER READING

"The legacy of a 'fighting Jew'. . . ." RUSSELL WATSON. *Newsweek*, Mar. 23, 1992.
"Zion's man of iron." *People*, Mar. 23, 1992.
"Fighter, first and last. . . ." MARGUERITE JOHNSON. *Time*, Mar. 23, 1992.
Obituary. *The Times* (of London), Mar. 10, 1992.
Obituary. *New York Times*, Mar. 10, 1992.
Menachem Begin: His Life and Legacy. HILLEL SEIDMAN and MORDECAI SCHREIBER. Shengold, 1990.
Menachem Begin. RICHARD AMDUR. Chelsea House, 1988.
Begin: An Anatomy of Leadership. SASSON SOFER. Blackwell, 1988.
Life and Times of Menachem Begin. AMOS PERLMUTTER. Doubleday, 1987.
To Win or to Die: A Personal Portrait of Menachem Begin. NED TEMKO. Morrow, 1987.
Begin's Foreign Policy, 1977–1983: Israel's Move to the Right. ILAN PELEG. Greenwood, 1987.

The Rhetoric of Menachem Begin: The Myth of Redemption Through Return. ROBERT C. ROWLAND. University Press of America, 1985.

Benedek, Laszlo (1907–92) Budapest-born Benedek studied medicine before beginning his long film career. He worked as a screenwriter, film editor, and camera operator in Europe during the early 1930s, and continued to work in a considerable variety of film jobs until emerging as a director in 1948 with *The Kissing Bandit*, starring Frank Sinatra. His two major films were *Death of a Salesman* (1951) and *The Wild One* (1953); these were followed by several more feature films and a great deal of work in television. Late in his career, he also taught film, as chairman of New York University's graduate film program from 1976 to 1980, and at several other major institutions. He was survived by his companion, Danielle DeMers, and by two daughters. (d. New York City; March 13, 1992)

FURTHER READING

Obituary. *New York Times*, Mar. 14, 1992.
Obituary. *The Times* (of London), Mar. 14, 1992.

Bentsen, Lloyd (Lloyd Millard Bentsen, Jr.; 1921–) Incoming Treasury Secretary Bentsen began his long political career in 1948. A much-decorated B-24 bomber pilot during World War II, and a practicing lawyer after the war, he was a Hidalgo County, Texas judge (1946–48), winning election to House of Representatives in 1948. He served three terms in the House, and left to go into the financial business in Houston for 16 years, as president of Lincoln Consolidated. He returned to politics in 1970, making a successful Democratic primary run as a conservative against liberal Democratic Senator Ralph Yarborough. Bentsen then defeated Republican George Bush in the Senatorial race, winning the first of his four successive terms in the Senate.

In the Senate, Bentsen ultimately became a very powerful figure. As chairman of the Senate Finance Committee, he exercised great influence on a wide range of matters very important to other legislators and to large numbers of Washington lobbyists, and was able in one period to run a series of $10,000-per-plate "power breakfasts" for lobbyists, for whom the $10,000 campaign funds contribution to Bentsen was just the beginning of a complicated and, for them, often a very rewarding game. As a Senator, Bentsen was responsive to the interests of his constituents, especially on oil, gas, and real estate tax matters. In 1988, he was the Democratic Vice-Presidential candidate on the Dukakis ticket.

Bentsen's 1942 LL.B. was from the University of Texas. He is married to the former Beryl Ann Longino; they have three children.

FURTHER READING

"The eyes of Texas are upon them." *Life*, Feb. 1989.
"Federal elections of 1988." *Congressional Digest*, Oct. 1988.
"Is Bentsen a Democrat? . . ." MORTON KONDRACKE. *New Republic*, Sep. 26, 1988.
"I'm not running against Bentsen." HUGH SIDEY. *Time*, July 25, 1988.
"Patrician power player. . . ." MARGARET B. CARLSON. *Time*, July 25, 1988.

Bergen, Candice (1946–) The star of the hit television show "Murphy Brown" quite unexpectedly became the center of a political storm during the 1992 Presidential campaign. In the May 18th final episode of the 1991–92 season, Murphy Brown had given birth and become a single mother, having decided to keep the baby and not marry its father, her ex-husband. On

May 19th and 20th, then-Vice President Dan Quayle attacked her, the show, and Hollywood in general for encouraging "illegitimacy" and thereby attacking "family values," at the time a major theme in the Republican campaign. Then-President George Bush warmly endorsed Quayles's remarks.

Quayle's attack turned out to be a major miscalculation, for what resulted was a storm of adverse publicity for the Bush-Quayle ticket; massive support for Bergen made a considerable contribution to the Clinton-Gore campaign, which was seen by many analysts as having benefited right up to election day, as working women voted in record numbers for Bill Clinton and Al Gore. Although the White House quickly attempted damage control by soft-pedaling its support for Quayle's attack, and Quayle said that he had been misunderstood, the damage was done. Many entertainment industry people stepped up their attacks on Bush and Quayle, not least during the August 30 Primetime Emmy Awards, which turned into a demonstration of support for Bergen and a mass attack on Quayle. Bergen won an Emmy as best actress in a comedy series, and "Murphy Brown" won a best comedy series Emmy. In her September 21st show, opening the 1992–93 season, Bergen answered Quayle directly, before a record-breaking television audience estimated at 70 million viewers.

Daughter of famed ventriloquist Edger Bergen, the creator of Charlie McCarthy, California-born Bergen is a star in her own right, with a long series of major roles in such films as *Carnal Knowledge* (1971), *Starting Over* (1979), *Rich and Famous* (1981), and *Gandhi* (1982). In 1988, she began a whole new aspect of her career, playing the lead (reportedly modeled on Diane Sawyer, among others) in television's "Murphy Brown." She won two consecutive Emmys as best actress in a comedy (1989 and 1990), and the show won a Best Comedy Series Emmy in 1990. She has also written and photographed articles for several major magazines, and wrote the autobiographical *Knock Wood* (1984). Bergen is married to film director Louis Malle, and has one daughter. She attended the University of Pennysylvania.

FURTHER READING

"Having it all." RICHARD CORLISS. *Time*, Sep. 21, 1992.
"Candy is dandy, ..." JOE RHODES. *TV Guide*, Sep. 19, 1992.

"Women we love: 1992." JIMMY BRESLIN et al. *Esquire*, Aug. 1992.
"The essential 'Murphy Brown' interview." ALAN CARTER. *Entertainment*, May 15, 1992.
"Candice Bergen. ..." MAYNARD GOOD STODDARD. *Saturday Evening Post*, May–June 1992.
"Murphy's laws. ..." JIM JEROME. *People*, Dec. 2, 1991.
"Candice Bergen. ..." MAUREEN DOWD. *McCall's*, Oct. 1991.
"Candid Candice." LINDA ELLERBEE and MICHAEL J. BANDLER. *Ladies Home Journal*, June 1990.
"Playboy interview. ..." DAVID SHEFF. *Playboy*, Dec. 1989.
"Candice Bergen. ..." MICHAEL SEGELL. *Cosmopolitan*, Nov. 1989.

Berger, Samuel R. "Sandy" (1945–)

President Bill Clinton's incoming Deputy National Security Advisor goes back two decades with the new President, to the days when they were young campaigners for Democratic presidential candidate George McGovern. Berger went from writing speeches for McGovern to a New York and Washington political and legal career; in the mid-1970s, he was an aide to New York Mayor John Lindsay, Senator Harold Hughes, and Congressman Joseph Resnick, and during the Carter years was Deputy Director of the State Department's policy planning staff (1977–80), reporting to Anthony Lake, now Clinton's National Security Advisor.

In the 1980s, Berger became a Washington-based international trade lawyer, as partner in Hogan and Hartson. An active Democrat, he was an early key figure in the Clinton campaign, as a senior foreign policy advisor, once again working with Lake. He continued to advise the President-elect as a member of Clinton's transition team, and was expected to play the same role in the White House. Berger's 1967 B.A. was from Cornell University, and his 1971 LL.B. from Harvard Law School.

FURTHER READING

"An instinct for the important." J. F. O. McALLISTER. *Time*, Jan. 11, 1993.

Bergman, Ingmar (1918–)

The great Swedish director, writer, and producer Ingmar Bergman made his main contributions as a writer in 1992. He wrote the screenplay for and selected Bille August to direct *The Best Intentions*, the story of the courtship and early, very difficult marriage of his parents. Pernilla August, Bille August's wife, starred as Anna Bergman and Samuel Froler as Henrik Bergman, with Max von Sydow as Johan Akerblom. The film was shown first as a six-part television series in Scandinavia, and then premiered as a theatrical film at the 1992 Cannes International Film Festival, winning the Golden Palm award. Although Bergman did not direct, it was widely seen as a companion piece to his classic 1982 film *Fanny and Alexander*. Bergman also wrote the screenplay of the autobiographical *Sunday's Children (Söndagsbarn)* in 1992, directed by his son Daniel Bergman.

Forthcoming was a very unusual event, the first Bergman play since 1949, *Sista Skrilet (The Latest Thing)*; it was scheduled to begin its run at Sweden's Royal Dramatic Theater in February 1993, and later to be adapted for television. Also forthcoming was the book *Pictures*, the next installment of his autobiography, a sequel to *The Magic Lantern* (1987).

Bergman is a central figure in world film history and at the same time a major figure in the Swedish theater. From the mid-1950s, he created a series of film masterworks that have been tremendously important to all who followed, including such classics as *Smiles of a Summer Night* (1955), *Wild Strawberries* (1957), *The Magician* (1958), *The Virgin Spring* (1960), *Through a Glass Darkly* (1961), *Scenes From a Marriage* (1974), *After the Rehearsal* (1984), and *Good Intentions* (1989). In March 1990, he received the D.W. Griffith award from The Directors Guild of America, for lifetime contribution to film. In 1991, he brought three Swedish language productions to the Brooklyn Academy of Music (BAM), as part of the New York International Festival of the Arts: August Strindberg's *Miss Julie*, Eugene O'Neill's *Long Day's Journey into Night*, and Henrik Ibsen's *A Doll's House*. Bergman attended Stockholm University. He has been married six times, and has eight children. His son, Daniel Bergman, is also a film director, while his sister, Margareta Bergman, is a novelist.

FURTHER READING

"Ingmar Bergman." JOHN CLARK. *Premiere*, Sep. 1992.
Ingmar Bergman: A Critical Biography, rev. ed. PETER COWIE. Limelight, 1992.
The Poet at the Piano: Portraits of Writers, Filmmakers, and Performers at Work. MICHIKO KAKUTANI. Random, 1988.
Ingmar Bergman: A Guide to References and Resources. BIRGITTA STEEN. G.K. Hall, 1987.

Bhutto, Benazir (1943–) The former Prime Minister of Pakistan, forced out of office by the military-dominated government in 1990, and subsequently defeated at the polls in a controversial election, Benazir Bhutto showed greatly increased strength in 1992. At the head of a coalition led by her Pakistan People's Party (PPP), she demanded that national elections be moved up from their scheduled 1995 date, charging the government with corruption and electoral fraud. In late November 1992, she a began series of marches on Parliament to dramatize her demands, and quickly drew audiences of tens of thousands of supporters, much to the discomfort of the government, which responded with mass arrests of opposition leaders and flatly rejected her demands.

In the aftermath of the November Hindu-Muslim riots in India and Pakistan, some voiced renewed concern for Bhutto's safety, fearing that if relations with India again deteriorated, Pakistan's military, fundamentalist religious leadership and government might make good their often-repeated threats to move against her personally, to remove an internal threat.

Bhutto and her mother, Nusrat Bhutto, were under house arrest in Pakistan from 1977 to 1984, after the coup that deposed her father. She left Pakistan in 1984, returned for the funeral of her brother in 1985, and was rearrested and expelled from her country. She returned again in 1986, as head of the Pakistan People's Party, and led the opposition to the government.

After the death of military dictator Zia Ul-Haq in an August 1988 plane crash, Bhutto was elected prime minister of Pakistan in the free election of December 2, 1988. She was the second Bhutto to become prime minister. Her father, Zulfikar Ali Bhutto, had been Pakistani prime minister (1972–77); he was executed in 1979 by Zia's military government.

In office, Benazir Bhutto was hailed as one of the world's leading women; but at home, she faced increasing opposition from the Pakistani army and fundamentalist religious leaders. On August 6, 1990, she was removed from office by president Ishak Khan, acting with the support of the military; she was charged with corruption, her husband and many supporters were arrested, and she was forbidden to leave the country. She and her party were defeated in the October 24, 1990 elections, which she called fraud-ridden.

Bhutto attended Harvard University and Lady Margaret Hall, Oxford University. In 1989 she published *Daughter of Destiny: An Autobiography*. She married Asif Ali Zardari in 1987; they have two children.

FURTHER READING

Benazir Bhutto. DIANE SANSEVERE-DREHER. Bantam, 1991.
Benazir Bhutto. KATHERINE M. DOHERTY and CRAIG A. DOHERTY. Watts, 1990.
From Prison to Prime Minister: A Biography of Benazir Bhutto. LIBBY HUGHES. Dillon, 1990.
Women and Politics in Islam: the Trial of Benazir Bhutto. RAFIG ZAKARIA. New Horizons, 1990.
"Dynasty's daughter." TARIQ ALI. *Interview*, Feb. 1989.

Biden, Joseph Robinette, Jr. (1942–   )

After being at the center of the 1991 firestorm that was the Anita Faye Hill–Clarence Thomas confrontation before his Senate Judiciary Committee and a worldwide audience, Biden's legislative year was relatively uneventful. Nor was he up for reelection until 1996, so that his participation in the 1992 Presidential election was limited to supporting the winning Clinton–Gore ticket and other Democratic candidates. He did, however, in late June make a little-noticed move of great significance for the conduct of further Judiciary Committee confirmation proceedings. In the future, all sources of information will be informed that any information received will be filed with the FBI and available to all senators; all senators will be invited to "closed, confidential briefing sessions" on the nominees; and each nominee will queried under oath in closed committee sessions about any charges developed during the course of investigation. Biden also stated in June that he would oppose any further Supreme Court nominations until after the November election, though as it turned out there were no Supreme Court vacancies in that period. Biden also continued to be a leading Senate liberal, on such issues as abortion choice, civil rights, and military spending cuts.

After briefly practicing law in Delaware, Biden became a Democratic senator from that state in 1972, later moving into a key position as head of the Senate Judiciary Committee. In 1986, he played a major role in the rejection of President Reagan's nomination of Robert Bork to the Supreme Court. He was a leading candidate for the 1988 Democratic presidential nomination, but withdrew after allegations that he had plagiarized some of the material in his campaign speeches from the speeches of British Labor leader Neil Kinnock. In early 1990, he survived two brain operations, both for aneurysms, then resumed his Senate career. He received his A.B. from the University of Delaware and his J.D. from Syracuse University. Pennsylvania-born Biden, a four-term Senator, was previously married to Neilia Hunter, and married Jill Tracy Jacobs in 1977; he has had four children, including two sons from his first marriage, who survived the 1972 automobile accident that killed their mother and infant sister.

FURTHER READING

"Biden is also reborn." MARGARET CARLSON. *Time*, Sep. 12, 1988.

Bird, Larry Joe (1956–   )

On August 18, 1992, basketball great Larry Bird announced his retirement, due to a chronic back condition that had caused great pain and severely impeded his play for the previous two years. Indiana-born

Bird was, with Magic Johnson, one of the two leading players in the game from the late 1970s through the "Dream Team" of the 1992 Barcelona Olympics. The pair and their friendly rivalry were widely credited for the great spread in basketball's popularity in the 1980s. Bird maintained a connection with the Celtics, acting as special assistant to the executive vice president, and in December was named to the board of directors of USA Basketball, where he will help select players for future international competitions, including the 1994 world championships in Toronto and the 1996 Olympics in Atlanta.

From 1976 to 1979, Bird was the high-scoring star forward of the Indiana University team, named Collegiate Player of the Year by AP, UPI, and the National Association of Coaches (1978–79), who led the team to the 1979 National Collegiate Athletic Association (NCAA) championship, ultimately losing to Earvin "Magic" Johnson's Michigan State team. Bird and Johnson became basketball's two major stars from then on, their friendly rivalry being considered largely responsible for the widened popularity of the sport. Joining the Boston Celtics in 1979, Bird was named National Basketball Association Rookie of the Year in 1980, the league's most valuable player (MVP) three times (1984, 1985, and 1986), and an All-Star 12 times, as a starter for nine straight years (1980–88), he was named most valuable player of the All-Star game 1982. He led the team to three championships (1981, 1984, 1986), and was himself named playoff MVP in 1984 and 1986, as well as being NBA scoring leader in 1984 and winning the first three of the popular three-point shot contests held on All-Star weekend. Bird ran into a series of injuries in the late 1980s, and was sidelined for long periods during the 1990–91 and 1991–92 seasons, returning only for limited periods. He wound up his career with the U.S. "Dream Team" that won the 1992 Olympic basketball gold medal. His autobiography, *Drive: The Story of My Life*, written with Bob Ryan, was published in 1989. Bird married the former Dinah Mattingly in 1989; they adopted a baby in 1991.

FURTHER READING

"The two and only." BOB RYAN. *Sports Illustrated*, Dec. 14, 1992.
"The brother from another planet." CHARLES P. PIERCE. *Esquire*, Feb. 1992.

Larry Bird. BOB ITALIA. Abdo & Daughters, 1992.
Sports Great Larry Bird. JACK KAVANAGH. Enslow, 1992.
"Guts and glory. . . ." J. DAVID MILLER et al. *Sport*, July 1991.
"A player for the ages. . . ." FRANK DEFORD. *Sports Illustrated*, Mar. 21, 1988.
Magic Johnson Larry Bird. BRUCE WEBER. Avon, 1986.
Larry Bird. MATTHEW NEWMAN. Crestwood, 1985.

Black, Eugene Robert (1898–1992)

A leading international banker, Atlanta-born Black began his long career after World War I naval service, in the Atlanta office of Harris Forbes and Company. He became a bond dealer, moving to the Chase National Bank in 1937. In 1947, John J. McCloy, president of Chase, became president of the World Bank, where Black joined him. He succeeded McCloy to the presidency of the World Bank in 1949, and until his retirement in 1962 was one of world's leading bankers. During his presidency, the World Bank became a massive international lending presence, focusing lending efforts on such major development projects as electricity-generating dams and chemically-aided agriculture, approaches that were later considerably modified. In retirement, he served on many corporate boards and as a United Nations financial consultant. He was survived by his second wife, the former Suzette Heath, a daughter, two sons, and a sister. (d. February 20, 1992)

FURTHER READING

Obituary *The Times* (of London), Feb. 22, 1992.
Obituary. *New York Times*, Feb. 21, 1992.

Blackmun, Harry Andrew (1908–)

"I am 83 years old. I cannot remain on this court forever, and when I do step down, the confirmation process for my successor well may focus on the issue before us today." So wrote Justice Blackmun in his concurring opinion in *Planned Parenthood of Southeastern Pennsylvania v. Casey*, the landmark abortion rights case decided on June 29, 1992, on the eve of the Democratic and Republican nominating conventions, during the Clinton and Bush presidential campaigns. A 5–4 majority, led by a newly emerging court center, upheld the essence of *Roe v. Wade* (which in 1972 had established the right of a woman to choose to have an abortion) while at the same time upholding most of the restrictive 1989 Pennsylvania abortion law and so giving the states broader powers to restrict abortion.

Although Justices O'Connor, Souter, and Kennedy were emerging as a new Court center, they were all conservatives in a very conservative Court; yet liberal Justice Blackmun found himself voting with a somewhat centrist majority on several occasions during the 1991–92 Court term. He joined all of his colleagues in a rare, unanimous landmark sexual harassment decision; in *Franklin v. Gwinnett County Public Schools*, the Court unanimously ruled that Title IX of the 1972 education act allowed a sexually harassed student to collect damages from a school district where a teacher-coach had sexually harassed Christine Franklin and pressed her to have sexual intercourse with him, ultimately succeeding.

Blackmun also wrote the landmark 7–2 majority opinion in *Georgia v. McCollum*, ruling that criminal case defendants could not bar prospective jurors solely because of their race. Two of his other substantial majority opinions were *Nordlinger v. Hahn*, upholding the right of California to enact Proposition 13, with its unequal property taxes on newcomers; and *Forsyth County v. Nationalist Movement*, ruling that an advance fee for a public meeting or march was in violation of free speech. He also joined the majority in *Lee v. Weisman*, barring nonsectarian or any other prayers at public high school graduations; *Hudson v. McMillian*, ruling that the excessive use of force by prison guards was an Eighth Amendment violation even if the prisoner was not seriously hurt; *Riggins v. Nevada*, ruling that the state could not force an insane criminal defendant to take medication during a trial; *U.S. v. Fordice*, ruling that Mississippi had not fulfilled its obligation to desegregate its public colleges and universities; and *Jacobson v. U.S.*, ruling that the federal government had illegally entrapped a defendant into buying child pornography through the mail. Blackmun wrote a concurring opinion in the landmark *R.A.V. v. St. Paul*, overturning a St. Paul, Minnesota ordinance making sexist, racist, or otherwise bigoted speech or behavior a crime.

Justice Blackmun wrote strongly dissenting opinions in *Lujan v. Defenders of Wildlife*, ruling that the plaintiff, an environmental organiza-

tion, had no standing to bring suit because no determinable specific interest was at issue. He also dissented in such key cases as *U.S. v. Alvarez Machain*, upholding the 1990 U.S. kidnapping of a Mexican doctor suspected of a role in the torture of a U.S. Drug Enforcement agent; *Lechmere Inc. v. National Labor Relations Board*, ruling that companies did not have to allow union organizers access to such company-owned lands as parking lots and shopping malls; *Keeney v. Tamayo-Reyes*, which sharply limited the federal habeas corpus appeals of state prisoners; *New York v. U.S.*, which invalidated a federal law forcing states to handle their own radioactive waste; and *International Society for Krishna Consciousness v. Lee*, ruling that airports could ban groups from soliciting money. He also disagreed with the majority ruling that the Coast Guard could continue to intercept at sea and return Haitian refugees to Haiti; and in the decision barring return of RU-486 pills to Leona Benten, a pregnant woman who tried to import them into the U.S. for her personal use, in a challenge to their ban.

Nashville-born Blackmun practiced and taught law in Minneapolis during the 1930s and 1940s, and was then counsel to the Mayo Clinic (1950–59). He was named to the 8th Circuit of the U.S. Court of Appeals in 1959 and was appointed by president Richard Nixon to the Supreme Court in 1970. His course in the liberal Warren Court of the time was thought to be moderately conservative; but in later years Blackmun's unwavering commitment to what were seen by most as a set of liberal positions on civil and personal rights placed him with the liberal minority in a more conservative Court. His 1929 B.A. and 1932 LL.B. were from Harvard University. He married Dorothy Clark in 1941; they have three children.

FURTHER READING

Harry Blackmun. BOB ITALIA. Abdo & Daughters, 1992.
"A new day in court." LAUREN TARSHIS and JAMES EARL HARDY. *Scholastic Update*, Nov. 1, 1991.

Bloom, Allan (1930–92) Indianapolis-born Bloom, a teacher, writer, and social critic, taught at the University of Chicago (1955–60), Yale University (1960–63), and Cornell University

(1963–70), and then at several other universities before returning to the University of Chicago in 1979, where he spent the rest of his career. He is best known for his book *The Closing of the American Mind; How Higher Education Has Failed Democracy* (1987), a sharp, ultraconservative critique of what he felt had been very wrong trends in American higher education since the 1960s, in curriculum, student-teacher-administration relationships, and a wide range of other areas. In that book, and in the years that followed, Bloom extended his criticisms to nearly every aspect of American society, becoming an extremely controversial figure in and out of academe. His works include a 1968 translation of Plato's *Republic* and Rousseau's *Emile*, the essays collected in *Giants and Dwarfs* (1990), and *Love and Friendship* (1991). He was survived by his mother, a sister, and his stepfather. (d. Chicago, October 7, 1992)

FURTHER READING

"A most uncommon scold." WILLIAM McWHIRTER. *Time*, Oct. 17, 1988.
Obituary. *The Times* (of London), Oct. 13, 1992.
"Professor Allan Bloom." KEITH BOTSFORD. *Independent*, Oct. 12, 1992.
Obituary. *New York Times*, Oct. 8, 1992.
"Our finest moment." "Too much tolerance." *New Perspectives*, Winter, 1988.
"Democracy and the great books." HARVEY C. MANSFIELD, JR. *New Republic,* Apr. 4, 1988.
"Bloomsyear. . . ." JOHN W. DONOHUE. *America*, Mar. 26, 1988.
"Bloom, Allan David." *Current Biography*, Mar. 1988.
"Chicago's grumpy guru . . ." JAMES ATLAS. *New York Times Magazine*, Jan. 3, 1988.

Booth, Shirley (Thelma Booth Ford; 1907–
92) New York City-born Booth made her stage debut in 1919, and her Broadway debut in 1925, in *Hell's Bells*, also featuring Humphrey Bogart. Her breakthrough stage role was in *Three Men on a Horse* (1935). She was a star on radio in "Duffy's Tavern" (1940–43), with her first husband Ed Gardner (married 1939–43). She became a Broadway star as Lola Delaney in *Come Back Little Sheba* (1950), winning a Best Actress Tony, and a Best Actress Oscar in the 1952 film version. She later starred on screen in *The Matchmaker* (1958). She also appeared in such plays as *The Philadelphia Story* (1939), *My Sister Eileen* (1940), *Tomorrow the World* (1943), and *A Tree Grows in Brooklyn* (1951). She was best known to worldwide audiences as maid Hazel Burke in the hit situation comedy series "Hazel" (1961–66), winning two Emmys in the role. She was survived by sister. (d. North Chatham, Massachusetts; October 16, 1992)

FURTHER READING

Obituary. *Variety*, Oct. 26, 1992.
Obituary. *The Times* (of London), Oct. 23, 1992.
Obituary. *Independent*, Oct. 22, 1992.
Obituary. *New York Times*, Oct. 21, 1992.

Borsellino, Paolo (1940–92) Palermo-born Borsellino, a leading Sicilian lawyer, magistrate, and state prosecutor, was a lifelong opponent of the Sicilian Mafia and, in this work, a key associate of anti-Mafia judge Giovanni Falcone. He became a magistrate in 1964, and in 1975 joined Falcone and judge Rocco Chinnici in Palermo, helping to prosecute the anti-Mafia campaign that resulted in the successful mass Mafioso convictions of 1985. Borsellino became chief prosecutor in Marsala in 1987, and in Palermo in 1990, there replacing Falcone, who had been reassigned to Rome to head a nationwide anticrime magistrate's group. Chinnici had been assassinated by a Mafia bomb in Palermo in 1983. Falcone was assassinated by a Mafia bomb in Palermo in early 1992. Borsellino and five bodyguards were assassinated in Palermo by a Mafia bomb on July 19, 1992, others then taking up the anti-Mafia fight. Borsellino was survived by his wife, two daughters, and a son. (d. Palermo, Sicily; July 19, 1992)

FURTHER READING

Obituary. *The Times* (of London), July 21, 1992.
Obituary. *Independent*, July 21, 1992.

Boskin, Michael Jay (1945–) The outgoing chairman of President George Bush's Council of Economic Advisors spent 1992 much as he had spent 1991, attempting to put a more acceptable face on a series of enormous economic problems. He no longer denied the existence of the patently obvious recession, as he had in

1990, or called the recession a temporary lag in the growth of a healthy economy, as he had in 1991. Instead, his February 5, 1992 annual Economic Report predicted a modest recovery, beginning in the first quarter of 1992 and becoming stronger as the year progressed; that did not happen, and it is generally accepted that the state of the economy was the chief reason for President Bush's huge decline in popularity and November defeat by Bill Clinton. Boskin's report also placed some of the blame for the recession on the Federal Reserve's failure to lower interest rates sooner. In the report, and during the balance of the year, Boskin also acknowledged the scope and persistence of the enormous federal deficit, no longer predicting that it would be paid off by the mid-1990s, as he had in 1990. Boskin continued attempting to generate optimism throughout the year, although many published reports indicated that he was probably considerably less optimistic than he seemed, and in contention with other Bush administration officials about their even greater publicly expressed optimism. Very late in the presidential campaign, President Bush promised great changes in the White House economic advisory team in his second administration; reports indicated that he intended to replace all his economic advisors, including Boskin, and place James Bakers in control of all administration economic functions.

New York-born Boskin taught economics at California's Stanford University for almost two decades, and was director of Stanford's Center for Economic Policy Research (1986–1989), before going to Washington as Bush's chairman of the Council of Economic Advisors. His 1967 B.A., 1968 M.A., and 1971 Ph.D. were from the University of California at Berkeley. He married Chris Dornin in 1981.

FURTHER READING

"Mr. Bush's forecaster. . . ." THOMAS G. DONLAN. *Barron's*, Nov. 12, 1990.
"Free markets. . . ." *Challenge*, May–June, 1990.
"Boskin, Michael Jay." *Current Biography*, Sept. 1989.

Botha, Roelof Frederik "Pik" (1932–)

South African foreign minister Botha, by virtue of his position, played a major role in bringing South Africa back into the world community during 1992, although some coolness developed from June through September 1992, when the African National Congress (ANC) withdrew from negotiations with the government, went over to mass demonstrations, and Nelson Mandela went to the United Nations to appeal for help in stopping the mass murders in the Black townships, blaming much of what was happening on the government. Botha responded in a speech to the UN Security Council, in which he welcomed the dispatch to South Africa of special envoy Cyrus Vance. Botha also continued to be a key government representative in the Codesa (Convention For a Democratic South Africa) talks.

In late October, Botha attempted to help mediate the redeveloping civil war in Angola, South Africa having played a major role in supporting Jonas Savimbi's UNITA forces during the long war; but his offices were quickly rejected by the Dos Santos government, which asked him to leave the country. South Africa had also supported Renamo insurgent forces during the Mozambique civil war, and Botha attended the October peace treaty signing ending that war—continuing the settlement of outstanding disputes in southern Africa made possible by the end of the Cold War.

Botha, a lawyer, has spent his whole career in South African government service. He joined the foreign service in 1953, and held a long series of diplomatic and legal posts at home and in Europe during the 1950s and 1960s. He was elected to parliament in 1970, serving until 1974. He was South African ambassador to the United Nations (1974–77), and to the United States, as well (1975–77). He went home to become South African Foreign Minister in 1977, and was his government's chief international spokesperson during its long fight to maintain and deepen the apartheid system. He failed in his February 1989 bid to succeed president Pieter William Botha as National Party leader, and stayed on as foreign secretary in the new De Klerk government, becoming a key negotiator in the long African National Congress–government talks that resulted in the August 7, 1990 ceasefire. Botha attended the University of Pretoria. He married Helen Bosman in 1953; they have four children.

FURTHER READING

"Giving as good as he got." *Time*, Nov. 21, 1988.

Boudiaf, Muhammad (1919–92) Recently installed Algerian president Boudiaf was assassinated on June 29, 1992, his death a major incident in the continuing near-war between Algerian Muslim fundamentalists and the army-backed National Liberation Front (FLN) government. Boudiaf was a French Army noncommissioned officer in the late 1940s, deserting to join the FLN guerrilla movement. He became a rebel leader, and was one of those captured in 1956, with Ahmed Ben Bella; released with Ben Bella in 1962, he became a member of the new Algerian government. But Boudiaf, a dedicated democrat, soon split with Ben Bella, and after two years in and out of prison went into exile in 1964. He remained in exile until January 1992, when he was invited home to become president of the republic, to lend his reputation for honesty and democracy to a government and party perceived by most Algerians as corrupt and incapable of solving Algeria's problems. (d. Annaba, Algeria; June 29, 1992)

FURTHER READING

"Murder in Annaba." *Economist,* July 4, 1992.
Obituary. *The Times* (of London), June 30, 1992.

Boutros Ghali, Boutros (1922–) On January 1, 1992, Egyptian diplomat and lawyer Boutros Ghali began his five-year term as the sixth United Nations secretary general, following Javier Pérez de Cuéllar, whose second five-year term expired on December 31, 1991. Boutros Ghali had campaigned long and hard for the job; an experienced mediator who played a significant role in negotiating the 1978 Camp David Accords and the 1979 Egypt-Israel peace treaty, he was thought by many to be a logical choice to continue the expanded worldwide UN mediating role developed so successfully by Pérez de Cuéllar.

Boutros Ghali's 1992 agenda certainly confirmed those early expectations. He turned out to be a thoroughly activist secretary-general, who quickly moved to streamline cumbersome UN staff operations in New York and elsewhere, and simultaneously moved to expand UN peacekeeping operations throughout the world, although greatly hampered by lack of funds. At the start of the year, the UN had major peacekeeping commitments in several areas, including Cambodia, Iraq, the western Sahara, and long-standing commitments elsewhere, as well; 1992 saw major new commitments in Bosnia-Herzogivina and Somalia, as well as a great expansion of the UN role in Cambodia and smaller commitments in Angola, Mozambique, and several other countries. Boutros Ghali also called for a refocus on matters other than war; opening the June 1992 Rio de Janiero Earth Summit, he called for the nations of the world to move money from their defense budgets into matters of environmental concern.

Cairo-born Boutros Ghali attended Cairo University and the University of Paris. He was a professor of international law and head of the political science department at Cairo University, and has long been active in international law, political studies, and human rights organizations. He was Egypt's Minister of State for Foreign Affairs (1997–91) and became deputy prime minister in 1991.

FURTHER READING

"A secretary-general. . . ." AHMED MURSI. *World Press Review,* Oct. 1992.
"North/south squaring off. . . ." CAROLE COLLINS. *National Catholic Reporter,* Sep. 25, 1992.
" 'Give me the battalions. . . .' " HARVEY MORRIS. *Independent,* Aug. 3, 1992.
"Challenge for the new boss." BONNIE ANGELO. *Time,* Feb. 3, 1992.
"The new boss will work. . . ." DIETER BUHL and FREDY GTSEIGER. *World Press Review,* Feb. 1992.

"New U.N. chief confronts. . . ." CAROLE COLLINS. *National Catholic Reporter*, Jan. 10, 1992.
"Hello, Ghali." *Nation*, Dec. 16, 1991.
"A man for all nations." BONNIE ANGELO. *Time*, Dec. 2, 1991.

Bovet, Daniel (1907–92)

Swiss-born biochemist Bovet was one of the world's leading research scientists. After earning his doctorate at the University of Geneva in 1929, he worked at the Pasteur Institute in Paris, there with Ernest Fourneau discovering sulfanilamide, the first of the wonder drugs; his laboratory synthesized sulfanilamide in 1936. From 1937 to 1941, he experimented in search of anti-allergic drugs, in the process discovering antihistamines. He moved from the Pasteur Institute to Rome's Instituto Superiore di Sanita in 1947, and there worked with his wife, Filomena Nitti, ultimately discovering the mechanism of the South American drug curare, and laying the basis for muscle relaxants used in major surgery. For his work with antihistamines and curare, he was awarded the 1957 Nobel Prize for Physiology and Medicine. His later work focused on synthetic foods and the effect of mental illness on brain chemistry. He was survived by his wife and a son. (d. Rome; April 8, 1992)

FURTHER READING

Obituary. *The Times* (of London), Apr. 14, 1992.
Obituary. *New York Times*, Apr. 11, 1992.

Bowe, Riddick (1967–)

On November 13, 1992, heavyweight boxing got a new champion by a unanimous decision, at the Thomas & Mack Center in Las Vegas, Nevada, in what was hailed as the best fight since Muhammad Ali and Joe Frazier's first battle 21 years earlier. With impeccable execution and patience, the much bigger, stronger Riddick Bowe took Evander Holyfield apart in 12 rounds, including one knockdown in the 11th round, with Holyfield showing a widely praised magnificence in defeat that had not been seen during his reign. Even Bowe was surprised that Holyfield—30 pounds lighter and five years older—kept coming back, despite the 132 blows Bowe landed, and finished on his feet. Immediately after the fight, Bowe got into an on-air verbal battle with British boxer Lennox Lewis, who was doing commentary; it was Lewis who had won the gold medal over Bowe in the 1988 Seoul Olympics, after a controversial fight stoppage.

Bowe has empathy for Mike Tyson, to whom he dedicated the Holyfield fight and who came from the same mean streets of Brooklyn, which Bowe visited on a whirlwind homecoming tour. But Bowe also wants to be a different kind of champion, using his celebrity for social good. For his appearance on the "Arsenio Hall Show," he wore a red lapel ribbon to indicate support for the fight against AIDS. He urged young people to stay in school, and said that he and his wife Judy plan to enroll at Howard University in 1993, and to hire a tutor to travel with him while training, to prepare him to "get on with my real life" after boxing.

After his win, Bowe negotiated to defend his title against Lennox Lewis, as he had previously agreed to do and as the World Boxing Council (WBC) demanded. But he then decided to fight in New York instead, and literally threw his WBC belt into the trash; WBC then made Lewis champion by default, the first time the titles had been divided since Tyson united them in 1987. At year's end, Bowe signed a two-fight deal, under which he was scheduled to make the first defense of his two remaining titles against Michael Dokes in February 1993 at Madison Square Garden.

Born in the Brownsville section of Brooklyn, Bowe was the youngest boy of 13 children raised by an abandoned mother, and was the family's only high school graduate, from Thomas Jefferson High, in 1986. Inspired by Muhammad Ali, he started training at the Bedford Stuyvesant Boxing Association in 1981, and won four New York Golden Gloves titles, going on to win a silver medal at the 1988 Seoul Olympics. He had a record of 31 wins and no losses before the championship bout. Bowe and his wife Judy grew up in the same neighborhood and married in 1986; they have three children.

FURTHER READING

"The family man." STEVE HYMON. *Sports Illustrated*, Nov. 30, 1992.
"Riddick Bowe." JEFF RYAN. *Sport*, July 1992.
"But seriously folks, . . ." RICHARD HOFFER. *Sports Illustrated*, Dec. 10, 1990.

Bowie, David (David Robert Jones, 1947–)

Rock star and songwriter Bowie continued to pursue his parallel career as an actor in 1992, starring opposite Rosanna Arquette in Richard Shepard's New York comedy *The Linguini Incident*. The story involved a romance between the two stars while each was trying to rob the restaurant in which they work, he as a bartender, she as a waitress; the cast included Viveca Lindfors, Eszter Balint, André Gregory, Buck Henry, and Marlee Matlin. Unfortunately, the film was poorly received, critically and commercially. Bowie also appeared in David Lynch's film *Twin Peaks Fire Walk With Me*, a retelling of the Laura Palmer story featured in Lynch's television series.

Reportedly working on a new album, Bowie in 1992 cut the single "Real Cool World" taken from the soundtrack of *Cool World*. In April, he also joined many other artists in the Wembley Stadium "Freddie Mercury Tribute: Concert for AIDS Awareness."

On the personal side, Bowie and famed model Iman married at Lausanne, Switzerland in April; both have been previously married. A Somali, whose family had fled the country 20 years earlier, Iman returned for the first time to Somalia in 1992, came away horrified by what she saw there, and began working on Somali relief and educational efforts.

Bowie became a leading rock singer and songwriter in 1969, with publication of his first song, "Space Oddity," followed by such albums as *The Man Who Sold the World* (1970), *Hunky Dory* (1971), *The Rise and Fall of Ziggy Stardust and the Spiders from Mars* (1972), *Pin Ups* (1973), *Young Americans* (1975), *Lodger* (1979), *Let's Dance* (1983), *Tin Machine* (1989), *Sound + Vision* (1989), and the retrospective *Changesbowie* (1990), which added seven songs and 27 minutes to the original 1976 *Changesonebowie* album. As an actor, Bowie also starred as the alien in the film *The Man Who Fell to Earth* (1976), and appeared in such films as *Merry Christmas Mr. Lawrence* (1983) and *The Last Temptation of Christ* (1988), and on Broadway in *The Elephant Man* (1980). Among his written works are *David Bowie in His Own Words* (1981), *David Bowie: Tonight* (1984), and *David Bowie Anthology* (1985). Bowie was formerly married and has one child.

FURTHER READING

Backstage Passes: Life on the Wild Side with David Bowie. ANGELA BOWIE and PATRICK CARR. Putnam, 1993.

"A session with David Bowie." JIM JEROME. *Life,* Dec.1, 1992.

"Architectural Digest visits. . . ." CHRISTOPHER BUCKLEY. *Architectural Digest,* Sep. 1992.

Alias David Bowie. PETER GILLMAN and LENI GILLMAN. Holt, 1987.

Stardust: The David Bowie Story. TONY ZANETTA and HENRY EDWARDS. McGraw-Hill, 1986.

Bowie. JERRY HOPKINS. Macmillan, 1986.

Boxer, Barbara Levy (1940–)

Newly-elected California Democratic Senator Boxer became a major figure in 1992, the "Year of the Woman," when she won a hotly contested primary to select a candidate for the vacancy created by Senator Alan Cranston's retirement, in spite of the fact that she had a total of 143 overdrafts in the highly publicized House of Representatives bank scandal. She ran for the Senate as a straightforward liberal, stressing such issues as abortion rights, military spending cuts, and environmental protection, against conservative Republican and former television personality Bruce Herschensohn, who ran on a diametrically opposed set of programs. Faced with a clear choice, California voters selected her by a 5-point margin, down considerably from her 18-point margin earlier in the race, but enough to elect her for a 6-year term. In the same election, California also sent Dianne Feinstein to the Senate, becoming the only state with two women Senators.

Brooklyn-born Boxer was a New York City stockbroker before moving west to California's Marin County. She was a journalist and then a Congressional aide in the early 1970s, in 1976 winning her first elective office, as a county supervisor. She served for six years, and was president of the Marin County Board of Supervisors (1980–81). In 1982, she won the first of her five Congressional terms, in that as in all successive elections stressing her commitment to women's rights and environmental issues. In the early 1990s, as the women's rights movement regathered its strength, especially around the issues of abortion rights and sexual harassment, she became one of the Congressional spokeswomen of the revitalized movement, as when in 1991 she and other Congresswomen demanded that the Senate Judiciary Committee take up Anita Faye Hill's sexual harassment charges against Clarence Thomas. Boxer is a 1962 graduate of Brooklyn College. She is married to Stuart Boxer and has two children.

FURTHER READING

"Scramble for the Senate." *California*, Aug. 1991.
"U.S. congresswoman. . . ." KEN KELLEY. *California*, Mar. 1991.
Answers to the Mommy Track: How Wives-Mothers in Business Reach the Top and Balance Their Lives. TRUDI FERGUSON and JOAN DUNPHY. New Horizon (NJ), 1991.

Bradley, Bill (1943–) Widely seen as a possible Presidential candidate in 1992, New Jersey Senator Bradley decided early not to run, and entered no primaries. He also made it clear that did he not want to be considered for the Vice Presidential slot on the Clinton ticket. What he did do was to become a key campaigner for Bill Clinton during the Presidential primary races, and for the Clinton-Gore ticket during the Presidential campaign. Time after time, he answered then-President George Bush, on such issues as the cause of the Los Angeles riots, and on the issue of Bill Clinton's character, which Bradley

identified as a mudslinging Bush campaign tactic. Bradley delivered one of the three speeches nominating Clinton for the Presidency at the July Democratic convention.

In the Senate, Bradley continued to press for massive cuts in military spending, thereby hoping to create a "peace dividend" that could be used to create jobs and cut the deficit. He voted for cuts in military forces based abroad, cuts in massive weapons systems, and cuts in aid to military regimes abroad. At the same time, the liberal Democrat voted for a wide range of domestic issues, such as abortion rights, civil rights, and environmental measures aimed at preserving the natural world. He was expected to become a major figure in the new Congress.

Missouri-born Bradley received his 1965 B.A. from Princeton University and his 1968 M.A. from Oxford University, which he attended as a Rhodes scholar. He was a highly successful professional basketball player with the New York Knicks (1967–77), a mobile forward with an outstanding long shot, who helped his team to two National Basketball Association (NBA) championships (1970 and 1973). He served with the U.S. Air Force Reserves (1967–78). On his retirement from sports, Bradley moved into politics, as a senator from New Jersey in 1979, active on the finance and energy committees, as well as on the select committee on aging. Often talked of as a potential presidential or vice-presidential candidate, he is also a member of the National Advisory Council on Rights of the Child and the National Commission to Prevent Infant Mortality. Among his written works are the autobiographical *Life on the Run* (1976), *The Fair Tax* (1984), and (with several co-authors) *Implications of Soviet New Thinking* (1988). Bradley married Ernestine Schlant in 1974; they have one daughter.

FURTHER READING

"Major crisis brings out. . . ." *Independent*, May 9, 1992.

"Senator Lazarus. . . ." MORTON KONDRACKE. *New Republic*, Sep. 2, 1991.

"Bill folds. . . ." JOHN B. JUDIS. *New Republic*, Jan. 28, 1991.

"Bradley's time." GERRI HIRSHEY. *Rolling Stone*, June 14, 1990.

"Sharing a dream with. . . ." DAWN GRAFF-HAIGHT. *Current Health*, Feb. 1990.

Brady, James (1944–) and Sarah Kemp Brady (1942–) Sarah and James Brady continued to fight for gun control during 1992. James Brady, President Ronald Reagan's press secretary, was seriously wounded during John Hinckley's March 31, 1981 presidential assassination attempt, shot with a cheap $29 handgun, and remains partially paralyzed. After the incident, Sarah Kemp Brady, his wife, became an extraordinarily effective crusader for gun control, her work continuing and expanding throughout the 1980s and into the 1990s. She is chairman of Handgun Control Inc. James Brady joined her in the fight for gun control after leaving his job as Reagan's press secretary in 1988.

The Bradys had seemed to score a major victory in 1991, with Congressional passage of the Brady Handgun Violence Prevention Act, the "Brady Bill," as part of the 1991 Crime Bill, with the help of former President Reagan and the seeming agreement of then-President George Bush. But ultimately Bush threatened to veto the entire Crime Bill, and without enough votes to overturn a veto, no gun control law was enacted.

The Bradys came back in 1992, in January joining Maryland Governor William Schaefer in his attempt to ban military-style assault weapons, and campaigned again very effectively during the Presidential campaign. Still pressing for passage of the Brady Bill, Handgun Control Inc. ran ads featuring President Reagan endorsing handgun control, and campaigned for Congressional passage throughout the year. And on October 18, three weeks before the Presidential election, Sarah Brady, a lifelong Republican, strongly endorsed Bill Clinton, calling Bush a president "fearful of crossing special interest gun lobbies." Clearly, gun control was to be part of the agenda of the new Clinton administration.

On the personal side, a federal judge on August 14 ruled that James Brady and two other men wounded in the assassination attempt on President Reagan could sue Hinckley.

Grand Rapids-born James Brady practiced law in Michigan (1969–77), and was a U.S. attorney in western Michigan (1977–81), then becoming presidential press secretary. He attended the University of Western Michigan and Notre Dame. Sarah Kemp Brady is an experienced political professional, who worked for the Republican Congressional Committee in the late 1960s and then was an administrative assistant to two Republican congressmen (1970–74) and an administrator with the Republican National Committee (1974–78). James and Sarah Brady have one son; he also has a daughter from a previous marriage.

FURTHER READING

"Brady, James S." *Current Biography*, Oct. 1991.

Thumbs Up: The Jim Brady Story. MOLLIE DICKENSON. Morrow, 1987.

Brady, Nicholas Frederick (1930–) Outgoing Treasury Secretary Brady spent much of 1992 enveloped in Bush Administration infighting and in the election year "gridlock" generated by a Republican President and Democratic Congress, both determined to make political capital out of every possible issue. Internationally, he participated in the administration's largely unsuccessful attempt to wring some meaningful trade concessions from the Japanese government, starting with the January Tokyo meeting that was overshadowed by President Bush's collapse at a state dinner.

Later in the year, deep into the Presidential campaign, Brady provided a moment of embarassment for the administration, when he used the term "Japs" at an August press conference, triggering Democratic calls for his resignation. Earlier, in February, a group of Congressional conservatives in his own party had called for his resignation, as he was too moderate for them. Adding to his frustrations was a continuing power struggle within the administration, involving Brady, White House Chief of Staff Samuel Skinner, Richard Darman, and Michael Boskin, all played out within the context of a disastrously worsening domestic economy, deepening deficit, the increasingly expensive savings and loan bailout, and a losing presidential campaign. On August 18, when President Bush said that there would be "plenty of new faces" in his second-term cabinet, all of the above were thought to be candidates for early departure.

Brady went to Washington after a long career in investment banking. He spent 28 years with Dillon, Read, ultimately becoming its chief executive officer and chairman, and leaving to become a U.S. senatorial appointee from his home state of New Jersey in 1982. He was chairman of the Purolator Company (1983–88), leaving the business world again in 1989, to become Treasury Secretary in the Bush administration.

Brady's 1952 B.A. was from Yale and his 1954 M.B.A. from Harvard. He and Katherine Douglas married in 1952; they have three children.

FURTHER READING

"George Bush's white men." RICHARD BEN CRAMER. *Esquire*, Feb. 1992.
"Who is Nick Brady? . . ." LOUIS S. RICHMAN. *Fortune*, May 22, 1989.

Branagh, Kenneth (1960–) British actor and director Branagh continued to develop his multifaceted career in 1992. On stage, he starred in Adrian Noble's Royal Shakespeare Company production of *Hamlet*, heading a cast that included Jane Lapotaire, Joanne Pearce, David Bradley, and John Shrapnel. He did the play on radio, as well—in a full-length, 3 hour and 25 minute multistar *Hamlet*, joined by John Gielgud, Judi Dench, Derek Jacobi, and Emma Thompson. With his Renaissance Theatre Company, Branagh also appeared as Shakespeare's *Coriolanus*, in a May production of the play at Britain's Chichester Festival.

On screen, he directed, produced, and starred in *Peter's Friends*, a comedy-drama about the reunion of a group of friends that reminded many of the American film *The Big Chill*. The cast included Emma Thompson, Hugh Laurie, Imelda Stanton, Stephen Fry, and Rita Rudner. Scheduled for 1993 release was Branagh's film version of *Much Ado About Nothing*, which he shot in 1992, with Branagh as Benedick, opposite Emma Thompson as Beatrice, Denzel Washington as Don Pedro, and Michael Keaton as Dogberry. He was also set to direct and star as Victor Frankenstein in a new film version of *Frankenstein*.

Belfast-born Branagh was one of the most promising theater people to come out of the 1980s. After attending the Royal Academy of Dramatic Art (RADA), Branagh debuted in London in *Another Country*, then quickly became a notable Shakespearean actor, starring on stage as *Hamlet* and *Henry V* (at age 23) and directing and producing *Romeo and Juliet*, all in Britain. In 1987, he starred in the highly regarded television series "The Fortunes of War," co-starring Emma Thompson, and in the film *A Month in the Country*. After a notable split with the Royal Shakespeare Company, he founded the Renaissance Theatre Company in 1987, and two years later brought to the United States stage productions of Shakespeare's *Midsummer Night's Dream* and *King Lear*, and Ibsen's *Ghosts*, starring in the latter two; *Ghosts* also appeared on television. In 1989, he also made his directorial debut and starred in a new film version of Shakespeare's *Henry V*; he won the Directors Guild of America's D. W. Griffith Award for best director, the movie was named the British Film Institute's best film, and both he and the film gained Oscar nominations. His first American film was *Dead Again* (1991). Branagh published an autobiography, *Beginning*, in 1990, at age 28; he had earlier written and produced a play, *Public Enemy*. He married Emma Thompson in 1989.

FURTHER READING

"Baby grand old man." PAUL DONOVAN. *Sunday Times*, Apr. 19, 1992.
"Branagh. . . ." *Cosmopolitan*, Oct. 1991.
"Vaulting ambition. . . ." F.X. FEENEY. *American Film*, Sep.–Oct. 1991.
"Stratford on Sunset. . . ." JOHANNA SCHNELLER. *GQ—Gentlemen's Quarterly*, Sep. 1991.
"Renaissance man." GEORGINA HOWELL. *Vogue*, Sep. 1991.

"L.A. bard." *Esquire*, Sep. 1991.
"The man who would be king. . . ." KIM HUBBARD.
  People, Feb. 12, 1990.
"A rising star enlivens Shakespeare." GARY ARNOLD.
  Insight, Jan. 15, 1990.

Brand, Neville (1921–92)

Illinois-born Brand joined the U.S. Army in 1936, while still in his mid-teens. Nine years later, he came out of World War II as his country's fourth-most-decorated soldier. He studied acting and worked in the New York theatre after the war, breaking into films with the first of his scores of gangster roles, in *D.O.A.* (1948). He went on to such films as *Stalag 17* (1952), *Riot in Cell Block 11* (1954), and *Birdman of Alcatraz* (1962). His many television roles included that of Willie Stark in *All the King's Men* (1958), Al Capone in "The Untouchables" (1959–62), and Texas Ranger Reese Bennett in the series "Laredo" (1966–67). He was survived by his wife, Mae, three daughters, two sisters, and a brother. (d. Sacramento, California; April 16, 1992)

FURTHER READING

Obituary. *The Times* (of London), May 9, 1992.
Obituary. *Variety*, Apr. 27, 1992.
Obituary. *New York Times*, Apr. 19, 1992.

Brando, Marlon (Marlon Brando, Jr.; 1924–)

Now late in his career, Brando made a relatively brief appearance, but as always had star billing, as notorious Spanish Inquisition figure Torquemada, opposite Tom Selleck as Ferdinand, George Corraface as Columbus, and Rachel Ward as Isabella in John Glen's *Christopher Columbus: the Discovery*. The expensive film had substantial financial and artistic difficulties during production, and Brando was reported to have unsuccessfully asked that his name be removed from the film before release. The film was almost universally panned by the critics, and was also a commercial failure. Still forthcoming was Brando's autobiography, signed in 1991 with Random House for a reported $3.5 million advance.

On the personal side, Brando's daughter, Cheyenne, was still awaiting a court decision on whether she would be prosecuted in relation to the murder of Dag Drollet, father of her child. Her half-brother, Christian, was serving a 10-year prison sentence for voluntary manslaughter for the 1990 Los Angeles shooting of Drollet.

Omaha-born Brando is one of the leading stage and screen actors of his time. In 1947, he created the role of Stanley Kowalski in Tennessee Williams's *A Streetcar Named Desire* (recreated in the 1951 film). This major role also signaled the breakthrough of "method" acting, the enormously influential American version of the Stanislavski school, as taught at New York's Actors Studio. Brando's first Best Actor Oscar was for his film role in *On the Waterfront* (1951), his second for creation of another landmark role, that of Vito Corleone, in *The Godfather* (1972). He also starred in such films as *Julius Caesar* (1953), *One-Eyed Jacks* (1961), *Last Tango in Paris* (1972), and after some years of seclusion in *The Dry White Season* (1989) and in his sendup of his own Godfather role in *The Freshman* (1990). He has been married to Anna Kashfi and Movita. He has seven children.

FURTHER READING

"Marlon Brando." BENJAMIN SVETKEY et al.
  Entertainment, Oct. 2, 1992.
The Films of Marlon Brando, rev. ed., TONY THOMAS.
  Carol, 1992.
"Runnin' into Marlon." WILLIAM A. WELLMAN, JR.
  Film Comment, July–Aug. 1991.
Brando: A Life in Our Times. RICHARD SCHICKEL.
  Macmillan, 1991.
"Marlon Brando. . . ." *Life*, Fall 1990.

"Brando." MARK KRAM. *Esquire*, Nov. 1989.
Brando: The Unauthorized Biography. CHARLES HIGHAM. NAL-Dutton, 1987.
Brando: A Biography in Photographs. CHRISTOPHER NICKENS. Doubleday, 1987.
Marlon Brando: The Only Contender. GARY CAREY. St. Martin's, 1985.

Brandt, Willy (Carl Herbert Frahm; 1913–92)

One of postwar West Germany's leading politicians, Brandt was a staunch anti-Nazi from the beginning of the Hitler era, who fled Germany in 1933, worked with the anti-fascist German underground during the 1930s and World War II, and returned to Germany in 1945. A socialist, he was a member of the West German assembly (1949–57) and was mayor of West Berlin during the crucial Cold War years of 1957 to 1966, becoming a world figure in 1961, when the Berlin Wall was built. He became chairman of the Social Democratic Party in 1964, was foreign minister from 1966 to 1969, and West German chancellor from 1969 to 1974, in both periods making substantial contributions to the easing of Cold War tensions. His resignation came when a key aide was exposed as an East German spy, although Brandt was in no way implicated in the matter. He stayed on in politics as chairman of the Social Democratic Party until 1987, and was chairman of the Socialist International, as well as chairman of the Brandt Commission, which published reports on world economic prospects and policies in 1980 and 1983. Brandt was awarded the 1971 Nobel Peace Prize. He was survived by his third wife, Brigitte. (d. Unkel, Germany; October 8, 1992)

FURTHER READING

"A bold peacemaker. . . ." JAMES O. JACKSON. *Time*, Oct. 19, 1992.
"A moral beacon. . . ." RUSSELL WATSON. *Newsweek*, Oct. 19, 1992.
"The end of an era." DENIS MACSHANE. *New Statesman & Society*, Oct. 16, 1992.
Obituary. *The Times* (of London), Oct. 10, 1992.
Obituary. *Independent*, Oct. 10, 1992.
Obituary. *New York Times*, Oct. 9, 1992.
"The difference Willy Brandt. . . ." ARTHUR M. SCHLESINGER, JR. *New Leader*, Oct. 29, 1990.

Bratby, John (1928–92)

British painter and writer Bratby was, on the occasion of his first show in 1954, hailed as a new Van Gogh and the creator of what some critics called the Kitchen Sink School, a description that stuck to his thickly textured figures, many of which incorporated such household objects as bottles and cereal boxes. He simply described himself as a modern realist. His work appeared before wide popular audiences rather unexpectedly as the paintings done by the failed artist played by Alec Guinness in the 1958 film *The Horse's Mouth*. As more abstracted styles of painting became popular, however, Bratby's work lost much of its appeal to critics and collectors, although he continued to produce large numbers of works, many of them portraits. He began a writing career with the novel *Breakdown* (1961), which was followed by several other books and many articles. He was survived by his second wife, the actress Patti Prime, a daughter, and three sons. His first wife was the painter Jean Cooke. (d. Hastings, England; July 10, 1992)

FURTHER READING

Obituary. *New York Times*, July 23, 1992.
Obituary. *Independent*, July 23, 1992.
Obituary. *The Times* (of London), July 22, 1992.
John Bratby Portraits. ROBIN GIBSON. Antique Collect, 1991.

Braun, Carol Elizabeth Moseley (1947–)

In the "Year of the Woman," Illinois Democratic Senator Braun was the first African-American woman to become a U.S. Senator; she was elected November 3 by a landslide 55 per-

FURTHER READING

"Carol Moseley Braun. . . ." *Jet*, Nov. 23, 1992.
"Behind the Braun phenomenon." GRETCHEN
  REYNOLDS. *Chicago*, Oct. 1992.
"A woman's place is in the house. . . ." LYNN SWEET.
  Self, Oct. 1992.
"Carol Moseley Braun. . . ." JILL NELSON. *Essence*,
  Oct. 1992.
"Woman of the year?" JOHN R. COYNE, JR. *National
  Review*, Sep. 14, 1992.

cent of the vote, over her opponent, Republican Richard S. Williamson. Braun, who had been Cook County Recorder of Deeds since 1990, had not originally planned to run for the Senate, but had been appalled by the treatment of Anita Faye Hill by the then-all-male Senate Judiciary Committee, as had many other women who then decided to run for office in 1992. On March 17, in a close three-way Democratic primary, she defeated incumbent Senator Alan J. Dixon, who had voted for the Supreme Court nomination of Clarence Thomas, and lawyer Alfred Hofeld. With that primary victory, she became a national celebrity, gaining massive media recognition and raising substantial funds from many national women's organizations. She ran far ahead of Williamson until early October, when Williamson gained some ground by publicizing a Braun family Medicare payment dispute, casting doubt on her ethics. But her voter acceptance and lead were far too great by then to deny her victory.

Chicago-born Braun's 1967 B.A. was from the University of Illinois, and her 1972 J.D. from the University of Chicago. She was an assistant district attorney (1973–77), a member of the Illinois Assembly (1979–89), and Cook County Recorder of Deeds (1990–92). She was formerly married to lawyer Michael Braun and has one child.

Bridenbaugh, Carl (1903–92) A leading American historian, Philadelphia-born Bridenbaugh was a major figure in the study of colonial American history. His many books included *Cities in the Wilderness* (1938), *Rebels and Gentlemen* (1942; with Jessica Bridenbaugh), *Peter Harrison* (1949), *Seat of Empire* (1950), *Colonial Craftsmen* (1950), *Myths and Realities* (1952), *Cities in Revolt* (1955), *Mitre and Sceptre* (1962), *Vexed and Troubled Englishmen* (1968; with Roberta Herriott Bridenbaugh), *No Peace Beyond the Line* (1971), *Silas Downer, Forgotten Patriot* (1974), *Fat, Mutton, and Liberty of Conscience* (1974), *The Spirit of '76* (1975), and *Jamestown in Virginia 1544–1689* (1980). Bridenbaugh was director of the Institute of Early Amercan History and Culture at Williamstown, Virginia from 1945 to 1950. He taught at several colleges and universities, including the Massachusetts Institute of Technology, the University of California at Berkeley, and Brown University, from which he retired in 1969. In 1962, he was president of the American Historical Association. He was survived by his second wife, the former Roberta Haines Herriott. (d. Providence, Rhode Island; January 6, 1992)

FURTHER READING

Obituary. *New York Times*, Jan. 12, 1992.

Bridges, Jeff (1949–) Once again playing a compelling character lead, Bridges in 1992 coproduced and starred in *American Heart*, a powerful father-and-son story set in Seattle and on the underside of American life. The film, directed by Martin Bell, premiered at the 1992 Cannes Film Festival in May. Bridges played

Jack Keely, an ex-convict who ultimately comes to terms with himself and with his 14-year-old son, played by Edward Furlong, in the process saving his son from going down the criminal road Bridges had taken long before. Forthcoming were a starring role opposite Isabella Rossellini, Rosie Perez, John Turturro, and Tom Hulce in Peter Weir's film *Joy Ride*, which began shooting in August 1992; and another in George Sluizer's *The Vanishing*.

Los Angeles-born Bridges is one of the leading American film actors of the last two decades, in such films as *The Last Picture Show* (1971; and its 1990 sequel *Texasville*); *Hearts of the West* (1975); *Starman* (1984); *Tucker* (1989); *The Fabulous Baker Boys* (1989) opposite his brother, Beau Bridges; and *The Fisher King* (1990). Jeff and Beau Bridges are the sons of actor Lloyd Bridges; Jeff played his first screen role at the age of eight, in his father's television series, "Sea Hunt". He is married to photographer Susan Geston; they have three children.

FURTHER READING

"Jeff Bridges." TIM CAHILL. *Esquire*, Oct. 1991.
"Jeff Bridges." JOHN CLARK. *Premiere*, May 1991.
"Bridges, Jeff." *Current Biography*, Mar. 1991.
"Lone star Bridges." MARTHA FRANKEL. *American Film*, Oct. 1990.

Brody, Samuel (1926–92) A leading American architect, Brody and his longtime partner Lewis Davis were by far best known for their highly successful urban apartment projects, and especially for their large New York City low- and moderate-income housing complexes, which consciously built links between apartments and urban settings and services, and joined beauty to economy, rather than settling for the creation of forbidding apartment blocks in a wasted urban landscape, as was so typical of many post-World War II modernist mass housing projects. One of their most notable efforts was Harlem's Riverbend complex, its first section completed in 1967; Brody and Davis also won extension of city bus service to the complex as part of their concept. Two other major projects were Manhattan's Waterside (1974) and the Bronx's River Park Towers (1975). Their work also included several luxury apartment complexes, the U.S. pavilion at the 1970 Osaka exposition, and the Steinhardt Conservatory at the Brooklyn Botanic Gardens. Brody was survived by his wife, the former Sally Rosenthal, a daughter, and two sons. (d. New York City; July 29, 1992)

FURTHER READING

Obituary. *The Times* (of London), Aug. 20, 1992.
Obituary. *New York Times*, July 30, 1992.

Brokaw, Tom (Thomas John Brokaw; 1940–) To his evident surprise, "NBC Nightly News" anchor Brokaw was during 1992 rumored to be considering a run for the U.S. Senate from his native South Dakota or from Montana, where he spends one month a year. He denied the rumors. In fact, Brokaw continued his solid work at NBC, with stronger emphasis on hard news over features, though his news show was generally in third place, behind his counterparts at ABC and CBS, Peter Jennings and Dan Rather. Brokaw also began anchoring a series of prime-time hour-long documentaries called "The Brokaw Report," focusing on key problems facing America, such as the multiple crises involving families, schools, health care, and violence; in a special edition, he hosted an hour-long talk with then-candidate Bill Clinton. Brokaw also went on the road, as when reporting live in February from Moscow, there interviewing former Soviet President Mikhail Gorbachev, and in December from Somalia. In one unusual break with tradition, Brokaw reported on 1992's Democratic and Republican presidential nominating conventions partly from PBS, in tandem with public television's Robert MacNeil and Jim Lehrer, reporting on NBC itself only in late-evening coverage of prime convention events. In January, he helped toast the 40th anniversary of the "Today" show, of which he was once co-host.

South Dakota-born Brokaw began his long career in broadcasting in 1962, and anchored news shows in Atlanta and Los Angeles during the mid-1960s, before becoming NBC White House correspondent in 1973. He became a nationally known figure as the host of the "Today" show (1976–82), and has anchored the "NBC Nightly News" since 1982, as one of the three chief American reporters and interpreters of the news. His

B.A. was from the University of South Dakota. He married Meredith Lynn Auld in 1962; they have three children.

FURTHER READING

"50/50: happy birthday. . . ." JOANNA ELM. *TV Guide*, Feb. 3, 1990.
Anchors: Brokaw, Jennings, Rather and the Evening News. ROBERT GOLDBERG and GERALD J. GOLDBERG. Carol, 1990.
"NBC's power-Brokaw. . . ." JOHN LIPPMAN. *Variety*, Aug. 3, 1988.
"Tom Brokaw. . . ." JAMES KAPLAN. *Vogue*, Apr. 1988.

Brooks, Garth (1962–) Country music star Brooks was very much at the top of his world throughout 1992. He was honored by his peers on many occasions, most notably as entertainer of the year and top male vocalist at the annual Country Music Awards on April 27th, and with a best male country vocal Grammy for "Ropin' the Wind." His 1990 album *No Fences* topped nine million sales in September 1992; only Hammer's *Please Hammer Don't Hurt 'Em*, had sold more in the 1990s, at more than 10 million sales. And his *Ropin' the Wind* album, issued in September 1991, went right to the top of the charts and stayed there in early 1992, with seven of its ten songs written by Brooks, including such singles as "Rodeo," "Against the Grain," "Papa Loved Mama," "What's She Doing Now," and "The River."

There was more: his fourth album, *The Chase*, issued in the fall of 1992, also went to the top of charts, as did his Christmas album *Beyond the Season*. Brooks was named Billboard's top artist of the year. As 1992 closed, there was no end in sight; so far, 1993 was scheduled to bring a television special, a European tour, and more hit albums.

On the personal side, Brooks's wife, Sandy Mahr Brooks, gave birth in July to their first child, Taylor Mayne Pearl.

Oklahoma-born Brooks began his career singing country music in cabaret. He and his wife made an unsuccessful bid to enter the Nashville country music world in 1985, but soon went home to Oklahoma. A second bid, in 1987, worked spectacularly well, resulting in his first country album *Garth Brooks* (1989), with the hit singles "If Tomorrow Never Comes" (his signature song), "Much Too Young," "The Dance," and "Not Counting You." The album sold more than 2 million copies, and Brooks became a star. His second album *No Fences* was equally successful, and contained such hit singles as "The Thunder Rolls" and "Friends in Low Places." That year saw his induction into Grand Ole Opry, and a long string of country music awards, including the Academy of Country Music and Country Music Association entertainer of the year awards, as well as Best Album awards for *No Fences* and "Friends in Low Places." Brooks's B.A. was from Oklahoma State University. He is married to the former Sandy Mahr, and has one child.

FURTHER READING

Garth Brooks: One of a Kind, Workin' on a Full House. Rick Mitchell. Simon & Schuster, 1993.
"He's Garth Brooks. . . ." CHARLES HIRSHBERG and NUBAR ALEXANIAN. *Life*, July 1992.
"Garth Brooks. . . ." MARJIE MCGRAW. *Saturday Evening Post*, July-Aug. 1992.
"Garth Brooks. . . ." MARJIE MCCRAW. *Ladies Home Journal*, June 1992.
"Garth Brooks." ALANNA NASH. *Stereo Review*, Apr. 1992.
"Brooks, Garth." *Current Biography*, Mar. 1992.
"Garth power. . . ." MICHAEL MCCALL. *Country Music*, Jan.–Feb. 1992.
The Garth Brooks Scrapbook. Lee Randall. Carol, 1992.
"Garth Brooks. . . ." *People*, Dec. 30, 1991.
"The new king of country." JIM JEROME. *People*, Oct. 7, 1991.
"Country classicists. . . ." JAY COCKS. *Time*, Sep. 24, 1990.

"For Garth Brooks. . . ." JANE SANDERSON. *People*, Sep. 3, 1990.

"New kids on the country block." BOB MILLARD. *Country Music*, May–June 1990.

Brooks, Richard (1912–92) Philadelphia-born Brooks worked in journalism and broadcasting during the 1930s, and began his long career as a screenwriter, director, and producer after his 1940 move to Los Angeles. He co-wrote the screenplay for *Key Largo* in 1948, directed his first film, *The Crisis* in 1950, and emerged as a major film figure with his co-written screenplay and direction of *The Blackboard Jungle* (1955); the screenplay brought the first of eight Oscar nominations, five for screenplays and three for directing. His 1960 *Elmer Gantry* screenplay won an Oscar. His other major films included *Cat on a Hot Tin Roof* (1958), *Sweet Bird of Youth* (1962), *Lord Jim* (1965), *The Professionals* (1966), *In Cold Blood* (1967), and *Looking for Mr. Goodbar* (1975). Brooks also published several novels. His second wife was actress Jean Simmons. He was survived by a daughter and a stepdaughter. (d. Beverley Hills; March 11, 1992)

FURTHER READING

Obituary. *Variety*, Mar. 16, 1992.
Obituary. *New York Times*, Mar. 14, 1992.
Obituary. *The Times* (of London), Mar. 13. 1992.
"Richard Brooks. . . ." FRANK SPOTNITZ. *American Film*, June 1991.
"The script men." PATRICK MCGILLIGAN. *American Film*, Aug. 1990.

Brown, Georgia (Lillie Klot; 1933–92) British singer and actress Brown began her career as a jazz singer in London cabaret. In the mid-1950s, she also emerged as an actress, in musicals, on television, and in Sam Wanamaker's 1955 London production of Brecht and Weill's *Threepenny Opera*, a play she later did in New York. She also played in the 1989 Broadway revival of the play. Brown was best known by far for her role as Nancy in Lionel Bart's musical *Oliver*, which brought her a 1963 Tony nomination. She also appeared in several films and in television, and starred on stage in her one-woman show *Georgia Brown and Her Friends*, in a London producton of *42nd Street*, and in several other musicals, including the failed *Carmelina* (1979). She was a women's rights movement activist, and, as a BBC producer in 1970s, produced and appeared in the television series "Shoulder to Shoulder." She was survived by a son. (d. London; July 5, 1992)

FURTHER READING

Obituary. *Variety*, July 13, 1992.
Obituary. *Independent*, July 7, 1992.
Obituary. *The Times* (of London), July 6, 1992.
Obituary. *New York Times*, July 6, 1992.

Brown, Jerry (Edmund Gerald Brown, Jr.; 1938–) In an anti-incumbent election year, the former California governor ran a strong, innovative populist campaign for the Democratic presidential nomination. Like Ross Perot—but without Perot's money—Brown launched a slashing attack on the Washington "establishment," including by implication the leadership of his own party, and vowed not to accept contributions of more than $100, instead relying for funds on a mass of small contributions phoned in to the 800 telephone number he mentioned at every opportunity. On the issues, he embraced the most traditionally liberal elements of the Democratic Party, at one point suggested that Jesse Jackson might be a very good vice-presidential running mate, and attacked Governor Clinton as the candidate of his party's conservative elements, in particular attacking

Clinton's environmental record while governor of Arkansas.

The high point of Brown's campaign came with his victory in the March Connecticut primary, shortly after Paul Tsongas dropped out of the race. But he was unable to sustain that momentum and, although winning more than 4 million Democratic primary votes, went to the party convention without enough strength to seriously challenge Clinton. At the convention, Brown refused to endorse Clinton, and was at first denied the right to speak, but ultimately spoke without attacking, endorsing, or even mentioning Clinton.

The son of former California governor Edmund G. "Pat" Brown, Jerry Brown practiced law (1964–69), and then began his long political career, becoming California secretary of state (1970–74). He was a highly innnovative, always controversial two-term California governor (1975–83). A liberal Democrat, he emerged as a national leader on such issues as antilobbyist campaign reforms, environmental and farm labor protective legislation, and the appointment of women, African-Americans, Hispanics, and other minority group members to state positions. As federal funding dried up, property taxes rose, and a conservative national mood grew in the early Reagan years, he encountered very substantial conservative opposition, which succeeded in recalling Rose Bird, his liberal State Supreme Court Chief Justice appointee, and in passing the property tax-cutting Proposition 13. Brown was defeated by Republican Pete Wilson in the 1982 U.S. Senate race. With Dick Adler, Brown wrote *Public Justice, Private Mercy: A Governor's Education on Death Row* (1989). Brown's 1961 B.A. was from the University of California at Berkeley, and his 1964 J.D. from Yale University.

FURTHER READING

"Showtime for Jerry." ROBERT SCHEER. *Playboy*, Aug. 1992.
"Who's on main street?" BARBARA EHRENREICH and HOWARD KOHN. *Mother Jones*, July–Aug. 1992.
"Governor Brown." HENRY SCHIPPER. *Rolling Stone*, May 14, 1992.
"Late night with. . . ." ALEXANDER COCKBURN and ANDREW KOPKIND. *Nation*, Apr. 20, 1992.
"Jerry Brown's grassroots. . . ." *Rolling Stone*, Mar. 5, 1992.
"Brownian motion." SIDNEY BLUMENTHAL. *New Republic*, Mar. 2, 1992.
"Strong message, wrong messenger." JORDAN BONFANTE. *Time*, Jan. 13, 1992.
"Student of Mother Teresa. . . ." ARTHUR JONES. *National Catholic Reporter*, Oct. 18, 1991.
"A flash in the pan?" BILL WHALEN. *Insight*, Sep. 30, 1991.
"That was zen. . . ." RICHARD LACAYO. *Time*, Feb. 27, 1989.
"Jerry Brown. . . ." LYNDA WRIGHT. *Newsweek*, Feb. 27, 1989.
"Tanned, rested, and ready. . . ." RONALD BROWNSTEIN. *New Republic*, Jan. 30, 1989.

Jesse Brown.

Brown, Jesse (1944–) and Hershel Gober (1936–)

With the selection of veteran's advocate Jesse Brown to be his Secretary of Veterans Affairs, incoming President Bill Clinton set in motion a train of events that was expected to have major impact on the nation's huge veterans' hospital and benefits systems. When announcing the appointment, Clinton made it clear that he was not satisfied with the Veterans Administration (VA), for its treatment of many veterans and for its administration of the VA hospitals and related functions. Brown is the first veterans' organization staff member ever to head the VA.

Brown was a marine in Vietnam; wounded in action near Danang in 1965, his right arm is partly paralyzed. He joined the Disabled American Veterans (DAV) staff in Chicago in 1967, and during the following 25 years moved up in the organization, ultimately becoming the

Hershel Gober.

Washington-based Executive Director of the DAV national service and legislative headquarters. Brown attended Chicago City College

Clinton underscored his desire to effect major change in the veterans' affairs area by appointing another veterans' advocate, Arkansas Director of Veterans' Affairs Hershel W. Gober, to the position of Deputy Secretary of Veterans Affairs.

Gober was a career military officer, who served 17 years in the Army and three years in the marines; he served two tours of duty in Vietnam and retired a major. He was appointed to his Arkansas post by Bill Clinton in 1988.

FURTHER READING

"Four Cabinet Nominees. . . ." *The Washington Post*, Jan. 8, 1993.
"Veterans Leader. . . ." *The Washington Post*, Dec. 17, 1992.

Brown, Ron (Ronald Harmon Brown, 1941–) As chairman of the Democratic National Committee, Brown played a major role in 1992 presidential politics, for with the election of President Bill Clinton and Vice President Al Gore, he saw the climax of a political miracle he had helped create. Clinton led a revived Democratic Party into the nominating convention, a party that Brown had largely rebuilt since tak-

ing office as chairman in 1989, after the near-disastrous 1988 Dukakis defeat. The convention was a unified one, a rarity for modern Democrats: Jesse Jackson, whom Ron Brown had helped convince not to run again, publicly supported Clinton, and even maverick candidate Jerry Brown, who had threatened to split the convention, did not do so, speaking to the convention without endorsing Clinton, but attacking Bush on the issues. On December 12, 1992 Clinton named Ron Brown to be his Secretary of Commerce.

Born in Washington, D.C., Brown began his career as a Washington "insider" soon after his graduation from the St. John's University School of Law in 1970. He worked in a series of increasingly responsible posts at the National Urban League (1971–79); was counsel for the Senate Judiciary Committee in 1980; worked in the 1979–80 presidential campaign of Senator Edward Kennedy, remaining with him in 1981; and was a partner in Patton, Boggs & Blow (1981–89). He worked with the Democratic National Committee from 1981. He was Jesse Jackson's 1988 Democratic Convention manager, a Dukakis political adviser during the 1988 presidential campaign, and in February 1989 became the trailblazing first African-American Democratic National Committee chairman. Brown's 1962 B.A. was from Middlebury College, and his 1970 J.D. was from St. John's. He married Alma Arrington in 1962; they have two children.

Ron Brown.

FURTHER READING

"Talking to the chairmen." MARY ANN FRENCH. *Essence*, July 1992.
"Face-off. . . . " FRANK McCOY. *Black Enterprise*, Mar. 1992.
"From two new party chairmen. . . . " *American Visions*, June 1989.
"Brown, Ronald Harmon." *Current Biography*, July 1989.
"Ron Brown. . . . " *Ebony*, May 1989.
"Running as his own man." WALTER ISSACSON. *Time*, Jan. 30, 1989.

Brown, Tina (1953–) British editor and writer Brown moved from London to New York in 1984, as the editor-in-chief of the highly regarded, then-failing *Vanity Fair* magazine, and during the balance of the 1980s and the early 1990s dramatically changed its by-then somewhat "dated" image, injecting far more more sex, scandal, and wide-ranging controversy, and in the process finding much wider audiences and great commercial success.

On June 30, 1992, in a move that surprised many in the magazine world, she replaced Robert Gottlieb as editor-in-chief of *The New Yorker*, becoming only the magazine's fourth editor, after Harold W. Ross, William Shawn, and Gottlieb, a trade book editor and publisher who had taken the post five years earlier, and who had made very few changes in the magazine during his tenure. *The New Yorker*, owned by the Newhouse media empire, had been widely reported to be unprofitable, and Brown was expected to try to do with it some of what she had done with *Vanity Fair*, in an attempt to attract new readers and increase advertising revenue.

Her first major dispute came in October, when British author John Le Carré publicly attacked her journalistic standards for printing an article he felt had unfairly attacked an author who had written unfavorably about her husband, Harold Evans. Brown denied Le Carré's charges.

Born in Maidenhead, England, Brown was a columnist at London's *Punch* magazine in 1978, and then was editor-in-chief of London's *Tatler* magazine (1979–83). Her own published works include the plays *Under the Bamboo Tree* (1973) and *Happy Fellow* (1977), and the books *Loose Talk* (1979) and *Life As a Party* (1983). Oxford-educated Brown is married to editor Harold Evans, whose position at Random House makes him another major player in the Newhouse companies, and has two children.

FURTHER READING

"Tina's turn: the New Yorker's head transplant." MICHEAL GROSS. *New York*, July 20, 1992.
"Brown, Tina." *Current Biography*, Feb. 1990.
"The dynamic duo. . . . " LAURANCE ZUCKERMAN. *Time*, June 13, 1988.

Browner, Carol (1955–) President Bill Clinton's incoming Environmental Protection Agency (EPA) administrator began her career as a strongly environmentalist Florida House of Representatives lawyer in 1980, soon after receiving her 1979 J.D. from the University of Florida, where she had also done her undergraduate work. Moving to Washington, she worked for Common Cause on environmental matters, and in the late 1980s as legislative director for then-Senator Al Gore, a Congressional leader on environmental issues.

In January 1991 she moved back to her home state, as head of the Florida Department of Environmental Protection; in that post, she negotiated a federal-state settlement aimed at restoring ecological damage in Everglades National Park. She also developed a reputation for working with industry and ecologists to simultaneously foster development and preservation, and for speeding the pace of agency decisions, approaches criticized by some ecologists and welcomed by others. Her stated early intentions as EPA administrator ran along similar lines; she also very strongly stressed the need to restore public faith in the EPA, which she felt had sagged very greatly during the Reagan and Bush years.

Browner is married to Michael Podhorzer; they have one son.

FURTHER READING

"No longer home alone." *Time*, Dec. 21, 1992.

Bryceland, Yvonne (Yvonne Heilbuth; 1924–92) South African actress Bryceland made her stage debut at Capetown in 1947, in *Stage Door*, and played a wide range of conventional roles until her long association with playwright Athol Fugard began in the early 1960s. She created the roles of Hester in Fugard's *Hello and Goodbye* (1965) and Lena in his *Boesman and Lena* (1969), and won a 1985 Laurence Olivier Best Actress Award for her creation of the Africaaner sculptress in Fugard's *The Road to Mecca*, also starring in the 1992 film version of the play. She and her second husband, Brian Astbury, founded The Space, a Capetown theater presenting new plays to mixed audiences. There she created Frieda in Fugard's *Statements after an Arrest under the Immorality Act* (1972), and played in many classic leading roles. Bryceland and Astbury moved to London in 1978, and she continued to play leading stage roles, joining the National Theatre for eight years. She also worked in several other films and in television. She was survived by her husband and three daughters. (d. London; January 13, 1992)

FURTHER READING

Obituary. *Variety*, Apr. 27, 1992
Obituary. *The Times* (of London), Jan. 15, 1992.
"South African. . . ." KIM HUBBARD. *People*, July 18, 1988.

Buchanan, Pat (Patrick Joseph Buchanan; 1938–) A celebrity talk-show host and columnist, Buchanan emerged as quite a different kind of celebrity during the 1992 Republican presidential primary campaign. Buchanan chal-

lenged President George Bush from the extreme right of the Republican Party and ran on an "America First" platform that to many Americans seemed reminiscent of the pre-World War II isolationist "America First" movement. In the months that followed, Buchanan attacked George Bush, women's rights advocates, homosexuals, AIDS victims, abortion, vagrants, immigrants, advocates for African-American, Hispanic-American, and Native American rights, and a host of individual Americans and foreign leaders. In the process, he was himself attacked by a wide range of people; perhaps most notably and damagingly attacked as anti-Semitic by William Buckley, editor of the *National Review*, long the chief far-right U.S. conservative magazine.

Buchanan found a considerable constituency within the Republican Party, receiving more than 2.8 million primary votes and more than 22 percent of the entire vote. Although it soon became clear that he had no prospect of defeating George Bush for the nomination, Buchanan stayed in the race until the Republican National Convention. There, on August 17, he delivered a notably intemperate speech, in which he supported the Bush-Quayle ticket and attacked Hillary Clinton, gays, lesbians, pornography, abortion, and many other favorite targets, and declared that there "is a religious war going on in our country for the soul of America." His speech was well received by the convention, but its identification of the Republican Party with the far right was widely thought to have contributed greatly to the Bush-Quayle defeat in the November election.

Washington, D.C.-born Buchanan began his career in journalism as an editorial writer for the *St. Louis Globe Democrat* from 1962–66. He moved into politics as an executive assistant to Richard M. Nixon in 1966, and moved into the White House as a special assistant to Nixon in 1969, during the years that followed becoming a leading speechwriter for Nixon and for then-Vice President Spiro Agnew. Although Buchanan left the White House in 1973, he remained loyal to Nixon throughout the Watergate scandals that cost Nixon his Presidency. Buchanan became a widely followed syndicated columnist and broadcasting personality from the mid-1970s, most notably as the ultraconservative half of the Cable News Network's "Buchanan-Braden Show" (1978–83) and "Crossfire" (1982–85; 1987–92). He went back into the White House as President Ronald Reagan's communications director (1985–87), then resuming his media career. His books include *The New Majority* (1973), *Conservative Votes, Liberal Victories* (1975), and his autobiography *Right from the Beginning* (1988). Buchanan's 1961 A.B. was from Georgetown University, and his 1962 M.S. in journalism from Columbia University. He is married to the former Shelley Scarney.

FURTHER READING

"By heaven inspired. . . ." NORMAN MAILER. *New Republic*, Oct.12, 1992.
"Rot on the right." LAURENCE I. BARRETT. *Time*, Aug. 24, 1992.
"Outsiders get on the inside track." PIERRE BRIANCON. *World Press Review*, May 1992.
"Ex cathedra. . . ." PAUL ELIE. *New Republic*, Apr. 6, 1992.
"Heir apparent. . . ." FRED BARNES. *New Republic*, Mar. 30, 1992.
"Springtime for Buchanan." SIDNEY BLUMENTHAL. *New Republic*, Mar. 9, 1992.
"The case for Buchanan." TOM BETHELL. *National Review*, Mar. 2, 1992.
"Waning cry from the right." MATTHEW COOPER. *U.S. News & World Report*, Feb. 17, 1992.
"Pat Buchanan. . . ." WILLIAM McGURN. *National Review*, Feb. 17, 1992.
"The thorn in Bush's right side." MARGARET CARLSON. *Time*, Feb. 17, 1992.
"President Buchanan?" ANN REILLY DOWD. *Fortune*, Feb. 10, 1992.
"The Pat Buchanan show." PETER ROSS RANGE. *TV Guide*, Feb. 8, 1992.
"Why is Buchanan so angry?" TOM MATHEWS. *Newsweek*, Jan. 27, 1992.
"Bush's bad dream." HOWARD FINEMAN. *Newsweek*, Jan. 27, 1992.
"Live tough or die." BILL HEWITT and LINDA KRAMER. *People*, Jan. 27, 1992.
"Can we stand Pat?" MICHAEL KINSLEY. *New Republic*, Jan. 27, 1992.
"Waiting for righty." RICHARD BROOKHISER. *National Review*, Jan. 20, 1992.
"Tomorrow belongs to me. . . ." SIDNEY BLUMENTHAL. *New Republic*, Jan. 6, 1992.
"Buchanan—we'd rather be right." ANDREW KOPKIND. *Nation*, Jan. 6, 1992.
"The conservative bully boy." DAVID FRUM. *American Spectator*, July 1991.
"The heresies of. . . ." JACOB WEISBERG. *New Republic*, Oct. 22, 1990.
"Pat Buchanan keeps. . . ." DANIEL LAZARE. *Present Tense*, Jan.–Feb. 1990.

Buckmaster, Maurice (1902–90) A leading British spymaster during World War II, Buckmaster was from 1941 to 1945 head of the French section of the British Special Operations Executive (SOE), which was responsible for British secret operations in occupied France, working with but not attached to French Resistance organizations. His highly effective work also cost the lives of many British agents, though postwar criticism of his work and highly individual style in no way diminished his wartime accomplishments. Fluent in French and German, Buckmaster worked as a journalist, banker, and Ford motor company executive in France during the interwar period. After the war, he returned to Ford, in Britain; worked in public relations; and represented the French champagne industry. He appeared as himself in the film *Odette* (1951). He was survived by two daughters and a son. (d. April 17, 1992)

FURTHER READING

Obituary. *The Times* (of London), Apr. 20, 1992.

Buettner-Janusch, John (1924–92) Once a leading American anthropologist and geneticist, Dr. Buettner-Janusch ended his life in a federal prison medical center. After earning his doctorate at the University of Michigan in 1957, he taught at Yale and Duke universities, and from 1973 at New York University. He was a vice-president of the American Association of Physical Anthropologists (1974–76). He was also a leading author in his field, most notably of the textbook *The Origins of Man* (1966), and was a prolific contributor to professional journals. But in 1979 he was indicted for creating a drug factory in his laboratory, and of selling the drugs manufactured. He was convicted, spent several years in jail, and in 1983 was released on parole. In 1987, he was convicted of sending poisoned candy to Charles L. Brieant, the judge in his drug conviction, and to several others, as well. Judge Brieant's wife was poisoned by the candies, but survived. Buettner-Janusch was sentenced to a 20-year prison term, and died in prison. He was survived by a sister. (d. Springfield, Missouri; July 2, 1992)

FURTHER READING

Obituary. *New York Times*, July 4, 1992.

Burdick, Quentin (1908–92)

North Dakota-born Burdick was a lawyer and long-term liberal politician, the son of a lawyer and ten-time Congressman. He practiced law in his father's firm from 1932, and ran for office unsuccessfully several times before his first election to the U.S. House of Representatives in 1958, succeeding his father. He was elected to the U.S. Senate in 1960, serving the the remainder of deceased Senator William Langer's term, and was then elected to full terms five times, dying in office after serving four years of his final term. At his death, he was the second oldest and third-longest-serving member of the Senate. During his 34 years in the Senate, he achieved the well-deserved nickname "the king of pork," for his dedication and skill in securing "pork barrel" federal appropriations benefitting his home state, although he did overreach in 1990, securing an appropriation that funded a Russian-American museum at bandleader Lawrence Welk's birthplace, later canceled by the Senate. Burdick was survived by his second wife, Jocelyn, six children, a sister, and a brother. (d. Fargo, North Dakota; September 8, 1992)

FURTHER READING

Obituary. *The Times* (of London), Sep. 15, 1992.
Obituary. *New York Times*, Sep. 9, 1992.

Burnett, Carol (1936–)

After her successful 1990–91 television season comeback in "Carol & Company," Burnett moved from NBC to CBS, expanding her show in the 1991–92 season into an hour-long comedy-variety series, "The Carol Burnett Show." Unfortunately, the show did not do well in the ratings and was quickly dropped by CBS, though Burnett and the network announced that she would continue to develop films and series for the network. Also announced was a forthcoming "Carol Burnett Show" 25th anniversary special.

Beyond television, Burnett starred opposite Michael Caine in Peter Bogdanovich's film farce *Noises Off*, based on the Michael Frayn play, in a cast that included Denholm Elliott, Julie Hagerty, Marilu Henner, Mark Linn-Baker, Christopher Reeve, and Nicollette Sheridan. Forthcoming was a set of three stage mini-musicals, based on the songs of Cole Porter, George and Ira Gershwin, and Irving Berlin, to be presented in Los Angeles in the spring of 1993.

San Antonio-born Burnett became a highly regarded television comedian in the early 1960s, and was the enormously popular star of her own "The Carol Burnett Show" (1967–79). Through the early 1980s, she also appeared in several plays, including *Plaza Suite* (1970) and *I Do, I Do* (1973) on Broadway, and in such films as *Pete 'n' Tillie* (1972), *A Wedding* (1977), and *Annie* (1982), then falling into a difficult period through the 1980s. She began what became a major comeback with the Christmas 1989 television special *Julie and Carol*, shared with Julie Andrews; her "Carol & Company" (1990–91) followed. In 1986, she published the autobiographical *One More Time*. Burnett attended the University of California at Los Angeles. She was formerly married to Joseph Hamilton and has three children.

FURTHER READING

"Carol Burnett. . . . " ALAN W. PETRUCELLI. *First for Women*. Mar. 30, 1992.
"Burnett, Carol." *Current Biography*, Nov. 1990.
"Carol Burnett. . . . " ERIC SHERMAN. *Ladies Home Journal*, Sep. 1990.
"Carol Burnett. . . ." MARK MORRISON. *Woman's Day*, Aug. 7, 1990.
"Carol Burnett. . . . " CHARLES BUSCH. *Interview*, Mar. 1990
Laughing Till It Hurts. J. RANDY TARABORELLI. Morrow, 1988.

Carol Burnett: The Sound of Laughter. JAMES HOWE. Viking Penguin, 1987.

Carol Burnett. CAROLINE LATHAM. New American Library-Dutton, 1986.

Bush, Barbara Pierce (1925–)

Although Barbara Bush continued on with work for literacy and against cancer during 1992, her year was dominated by her husband's re-election campaign. She accompanied him throughout the primary season, at the August Republican National Convention, and throughout the presidential campaign. Her popularity remained very high during the entire year, far higher than that of George Bush, and she made the most of that popularity in her campaigning. Generally, she continued to be a warm presence, whose role was limited to defending her husband's motives and character, a symbol of the kind of "family values" that were a main Bush-Quayle campaign theme. She spoke out only once sharply on the issues, in August maintaining that abortion was a private matter that did not belong on a party platform. The Republican platform committee did not agree, and the convention passed an anti-abortion plank so severe as to alienate many voters and harm Bush's re-election chances, even though he, with Barbara Bush's help, attempted to distance himself from that aspect of his platform after the convention. In November, despite her husband's loss in the presidential campaign, she began the third season of her radio program "Mrs. Bush's Story Time," in which she and various celebrities read stories for children.

Barbara Pierce married George Bush in 1945. They have five living children: George, John, Neil, Marvin, and Dorothy; their second child, Robyn, died of leukemia in 1953, at the age of three. She attended Smith College. She continues to be active in a wide range of voluntary organizations. Since 1983, she has been a trustee of the Morehouse School of Medicine. Her books include *C. Fred's Story* (1984) and the best-selling *Millie's Book: As Dictated to Barbara Bush* (1990), a dog's-eye look at Washington life, as seen through the eyes of Millie, the Bush's springer spaniel.

FURTHER READING

"Lunch with Bar. . . ." BARBARA GRIZZUTI HARRISON. *New Republic*, Nov. 9, 1992.

"Mommy dearest. . . ." MARJORIE PERLOFF. *New Republic*, Oct. 5, 1992.

"Who should be first lady?" CATHERINE BRESLIN and DIANA McLELLAN. *Ladies Home Journal*, Oct. 1992.

" 'Abortion is a personal choice.' " *Newsweek*, Aug. 24, 1992.

"The best days of their wives." MICHAEL DUFFY. *Time*, Aug. 24, 1992.

"Biographies of the Republican candidates." *Facts on File*, Aug. 20, 1992.

"Barbara's backlash." MARJORIE WILLIAMS. *Vanity Fair*, Aug. 1992.

"White House adventures." JACQUELINE LEO. *Family Circle*, June 23, 1992.

"First lady culture clash." ELEANOR CLIFT. *Newsweek*, June 8, 1992.

Barbara Bush: A Biography. PAMELA KILIAN. Thomas Dunne/St. Martin's, 1992; Thorndike, 1992.

Barbara Bush. ARLEEN McGRATH-HEISS. Chelsea House, 1992.

Barbara Bush. DIANE SANSEVERE-DREHER. Bantam, 1991.

Barbara Bush. KAREN B. SPIES. Macmillan, 1991.

Barbara Bush: First Lady. ROSE BLUE and CORINNE J. NADEN. Enslow, 1991.

First Ladies: The Saga of the Presidents' Wives and Their Power. CARL S. ANTHONY. Morrow, 1991.

Barbara Bush. ARLEEN HEISS. Chelsea House, 1991

"Barbara Bush. . . ." CINDY ADAMS. *Ladies Home Journal*, Nov. 1990.

"In the eye of the storm." PAULA CHIN. *People*, Oct. 1, 1990.

"The hidden life. . . ." KENNETH T. WALSH. *U.S. News & World Report*, May 28, 1990.

Barbara Bush: First Lady of Literacy. JUNE BEHRENS. Childrens, 1990.

Simply Barbara Bush: A Portrait of America's Candid First Lady. DONNIE RADCLIFFE. Warner, 1990.

"Bush, Barbara Pierce." *Current Biography*, Oct. 1989.

Bush, George (George Herbert Walker Bush; 1924–)

On November 3, 1992, George Bush, the 41st President of the United States, became a one-term President, losing his bid for re-election to Arkansas Governor Bill Clinton, in a three-way race that included independent candidate Ross Perot. With only 38 percent of the popular vote, and a Clinton electoral vote landslide, Bush's defeat was decisive. His defeat with so low a vote would have seemed almost inconceivable less than two years earlier, for he had emerged from the Gulf War with 90 percent popularity ratings. But as the American econ-

omy faltered, and he was seen as unable to do anything about it, his popularity plummeted. To the end, he insisted that the economy was in far better condition than his opponents claimed, and that everything would be all right in the end, if only the free market were left alone to correct itself; but in the end, very few voters believed him—so few that even enduring doubts about Bill Clinton could not save George Bush.

President Bush's last year in office was dominated by the presidential campaign and the state of the economy. His deep political problems became apparent even in the Republican primaries, where Pat Buchanan, a right-wing conservative, challenged him and in state after state won 20–25 percent of the Republican primary vote. His deep economic problems became more and more apparent as repeated Federal Reserve interest rate cuts failed to stimulate recovery; mass unemployment and fear of unemployment grew; the national debt continued to soar; savings and loan bailout costs escalated; and consumer confidence dropped and kept on dropping throughout the year. Bush's relations with the Democratic-controlled Congress worsened, as "gridlock" became a fact of American life and Bush vetoed a wide range of legislation, including highly publicized family leave plans, middle-class tax cuts, campaign financing reforms, and fetal tissue research, while continuing to call for a ban on abortions and the overturn of *Roe v. Wade*. He was also pursued by the Iran-Contra scandal, although continuing to deny any complicity. In the end, though, it was the economy that triggered his downfall, and ultimately even a highly negative campaign, complete with a great deal of name-calling and investigations of the private lives of his opponents and their families.

On December 24, President Bush announced full pardons for six Reagan administration figures allegedly implicated in the Iran-Contra affair, including former Defense Secretary Caspar W. Weinberger, who was about to go to trial; Clair George, Elliott Abrams, Alan G. Fiers, and Robert C. McFarlane, all of whom had been previously found guilty or pleaded guilty; and Duane Clarridge, awaiting trial. His act generated a storm of controversy, sure to follow him long beyond his presidency; on December 30, the White House announced that he had hired former Attorney General Griffin T. Bell to represent him in the continuing investigation of his own connections with the Iran-Contra affair. During the transition period, President Bush also initiated the Somali intervention. Presidents Yeltsin and Bush signed a major arms reduction treaty in Moscow on January 3, 1993.

On the personal side, President Bush collapsed and blacked out briefly at a January 8, 1992 state dinner in Tokyo; his collapse was attributed to a stomach virus. However, it occurred while television cameras were recording the event, and his collapse was shown worldwide, generating great concern for his health.

George Bush defeated Michael Dukakis in the bitterly contested 1988 presidential race, becoming the 41st President of the United States in 1989, the climax of a political career that began in Texas in the early 1960s. He had grown up in a Republican Party family, the son of Connecticut senator Prescott Bush, and then left New England to enter the oil business in Texas in the early 1950s, co-founding the Zapata Petroleum Company in 1953 and becoming president and then board chairman of the Zapata Off Shore Company in 1956. He was an unsuccessful Republican senatorial candidate from Texas in 1964, but won a House seat in 1966, moving to Washington as a Houston congressman for two terms (1967–71). In 1970, he made another unsuccessful run for the Senate on the Republican ticket.

Bush was United States Ambassador to the United Nations during the waning days of the Vietnam War (1971–72), and then Republican National Committee chairman (1973–74). He was the chief American liaison officer in Peking (1974–76), then returning to Washington as head of the CIA (1976–77). He made an unsuccessful Republican presidential nomination run in 1980, but withdrew in favor of Ronald Reagan, and subsequently became Reagan's two-term vice president, operating in those eight years in a largely ceremonial and standby fashion, as have most vice presidents. He then succeeded Reagan as President.

The early Bush years saw a series of major international triumphs as the Cold War ended and the Soviet empire collapsed. First came the quick and easy invasion of Panama that toppled the Noriega dictatorship. Then came a series of major Soviet-American peace moves, with planned troop pullbacks and real progress on arms control and on the ending of a whole series of regional conflicts that had for decades been spurred by Soviet and American sponsorship of the combatants. With both countries acting in concert as peacemakers, and with the direct intervention of George Bush and Mikhail Gorbachev, the continuing conflicts in Nicaragua, Cambodia, Angola, Mozambique, Namibia, Ethiopia, and several other countries moved swiftly toward resolution. His last triumph was the successful prosecution of the 1991 Persian Gulf War.

George Bush's 1948 B.A. was from Yale. A navy pilot in World War II, he married Barbara Pierce in 1945. Their five surviving children are George, John, Neil, Marvin, and Dorothy; their second child, Robyn, died of leukemia at age three. During the 1988 Presidential campaign, Bush published two books, *Man of Integrity* (with Doug Wead) and *Looking Forward: The George Bush Story* (with Victor Gold). (For additional Photo, see Powell, Colin.)

FURTHER READING

"Life in Bush hell." JAMES PINKERTON. *New Republic*, Dec. 14, 1992.

"Rubbers. . . ." SIDNEY BLUMENTHAL. *New Republic*, Nov. 30, 1992.

"George Bush just didn't get it." LEE WALCZAK. *Business Week*, Nov.16, 1992.

"Bush's desperate game. " JOE KLEIN. "Face to face." ANN MCDANIEL. *Newsweek*, Oct. 19, 1992.

"Bush's gamble." WILLIAM SAFIRE. *New York Times Magazine*, Oct. 18, 1992.

"War story. . . ." SIDNEY BLUMENTHAL. *New Republic*, Oct. 12, 1992.

"The final battle. " GUS TYLER. *New Leader*, Oct. 5, 1992.

"Bushism, found. . . ." WALTER RUSSELL MEAD. *Harper's*, Sep. 1992.

"The case for Bush. . . ." RICHARD VIGILANTE. "The wilderness year." *New Republic*, Aug. 31, 1992.

"A conversation with. . . . " ANN MCDANIEL and TOM DEFRANK. *Newsweek*, Aug. 24, 1992.

"Finding a road. . . ." HILARY MACKENZIE. *Maclean's*, Aug. 24, 1992.

"Warrior for the status quo." MICHAEL DUFFY and DAN GOODGAME. *Time*, Aug. 24, 1992.

"Bush on the record." MICHAEL KRAMER and HENRY MULLER. *Time*, Aug. 24, 1992.

"The fight of his life." DAN GOODGAME. *Time*, Aug. 24, 1992.

"What's wrong with Bush?" *Time*, Aug. 10, 1992.

"A visit with. . . ." RICHARD BROOKHISER. *Atlantic*, Aug. 1992.

"The goofy politics of. . . ." JOHN O'SULLIVAN and WILLIAM MCGURN. *National Review*, Feb. 3, 1992.

Chameleon: The Unauthorized Biography of George Bush. JONATHAN SLEVIN and STEVEN WILMSEN. Krantz, 1992.

George Bush: His World War II Years. ROBERT B. STINNETT. Macmillan, 1992.

The Renegade CIA: Inside the Cover Intelligence Operations of George Bush. JOSEPH J. TRENTO. Putnam, 1992.

George Bush's War. JEAN E. SMITH. Holt, 1992.

George Bush: His World War Two Years. ROBERT B. STINNETT. Pictorial History, 1991.

George Bush. KAREN B. SPIES. Macmillan, 1991.

The Postmodern President: George Bush Meets the World, 2nd ed. RICHARD ROSE. Chatham House, 1991.

Flight of the Avenger: George Bush at War and in Love. JOSEPH HYAMS. Harcourt Brace, 1991; Berkeley, 1992.

Buthelezi, Mangosuthu Gatsha

(1928–   ) Zulu leader Buthelezi seemed to lose some ground in 1992. Although still playing a key role in the complicated negotiations leading to a South African interim government, constitutional convention, and majority rule, his prestige was hurt greatly by worldwide condemnation of Inkatha-organized massacres in the Black townships, and at home in South Africa especially by rather convincing proof that, at least in some and possibly in many instances, there had been police and military help for the Zulus. In 1992, Buthelezi no longer freely met with world leaders, and when Nelson Mandela went to seek help at a special session of the United Nations Security Council in July, Buthelezi also spoke, but had no effective way to answer, failing to block the dispatch of special envoy Cyrus Vance.

Ultimately, adverse publicity and government investigations limited the police and military help available to Inkatha, while the African National Congress (ANC) mounted a considerable force against Inkatha in the civil war in the townships. In September, when Codesa (Convention for a Democratic South Africa) talks restarted after a four-month suspension by the ANC, the government pledged to effectively disarm the main body of Inkatha militants, by prohibiting the carrying of weapons in public. Buthelezi then boycotted the talks, but the move proved self-isolating, as the talks went forward without him.

Buthelezi became chief of the Buthelezi tribe in 1963, succeeding his father, Mathole Buthelezi. He was a Zulu administrator for two decades, becoming chief minister of the Kwa-Zulu in 1976. As the long fight for South African democracy developed during the 1970s and 1980s, he emerged as the main spokesperson and leader of the Zulus, and a third force in South African politics, for he negotiated with the White South African government on behalf of the Zulus, and often opposed the African National Congress. His followers, organized into the Inkatha movement, carried those disagreements into anti-ANC street fighting throughout the 1980s. Buthelezi emerged as a powerful independent force in South African politics during 1990, as negotiations over the future of the country began between the De Klerk government and the ANC, led by newly-freed Nelson Mandela, which had tried to bypass Buthelezi, but found itself engaged in a hot and growing civil war. In 1990, he published *South Africa: My Vision of the Future*. Buthelezi married Irene Audrey Thandekile Mzila in 1952; they have seven children. He attended Adams College and Fort-Hare University.

FURTHER READING

"Buthelezi. . . ." SCOTT MACLEOD. *Time*, July 6, 1992.

"The chief steps forward. . . ." CHRISTOPHER S. WREN. *New York Times Magazine*, Feb. 17, 1991.

Gatsha Buthelezi: Chief with a Double Agenda. MZALA. Humanities, 1988.

An Appetite for Power: Buthelezi's Inkatha and South Africa. GERHARD MARE and GEORGINA HAMILTON. Indiana University Press, 1988.

C

Caan, James (1939–) His strong comeback career somewhat damaged by the box office failure of *For the Boys*, Caan made a powerful comeback-within-a-comeback in 1992, with his starring role in Andrew Bergman's *Honeymoon in Vegas*, a romantic satire-drama about gambling, love, and the Las Vegas lifestyle, and a great surprise as one of the year's strongest box office draws. Caan played a professional gambler in the film, opposite Nicolas Cage as a young amateur gambler drawn to Las Vegas and Sarah Jessica Parker as Cage's fiancée. Ultimately,

Cage wants to use her as a gambling stake with Caan, who is drawn to her. She does not object, being greatly attracted to the older man, and the story develops from there. Forthcoming for Caan was a starring role opposite Dennis Quaid and Meg Ryan in Steve Klove's film *Flesh and Bone*; a starring role in David S. Ward's film *The Program*; and another starring role in *The Dark Backward*, written and directed by Adam Rifkin.

New York City-born Caan played in New York theater and television in the early 1960s, and emerged as a major player in the early 1970s, with his notable television lead in *Brian's Song* (1971), which was followed by his star-making role in *The Godfather* (1972), creating the classic "tough guy" role of Sonny Corleone. He went on to such films as *Cinderella Liberty* (1974), *Funny Lady* (1975), *Rollerball* (1975), *A Bridge Too Far* (1977), *Chapter Two* (1979), *Hide in Plain Sight* (1980; he also directed), and *Kiss Me Goodbye* (1982). He retired from filmmaking during the mid-1980s, returning in *Gardens of Stone* (1987) and *Alien Nation* (1988). In 1990, he starred in *Misery*, and in 1991 opposite Bette Midler in *For the Boys*. Caan attended Michigan State University, Hofstra College, and New York's Neighborhood Playhouse. He has been married three times, since 1990 to Ingrid Hajek, and has four children, one of them adopted.

FURTHER READING

"Raising Caan." AL REINERT. *Premiere*, Dec. 1991.

Cage, John (1912–92)

A leading 20th-century modernist composer, Cage was until the late 1930s one of many who worked in atonal and serial musical forms. In the early 1940s, he began his long professional association with the dancer Merce Cunningham. But by the late 1930s he was also experimenting in the ways that would make him famous—to some, notorious. Perhaps most notable was his creation of the "prepared piano," a piano intended to function as a whole percussion orchestra, with weighted objects inserted between the strings and under the dampers; nuts and bolts were among the objects used. From the early 1940s, he also experimented with electronic music. He became greatly interested in some aspects of Buddhism in the mid-1940s, and in music moved toward random, unscored work, and to indeterminacy, finally even moving into silence in his best known work *4' 33"* (1952), which consisted merely of several minutes of silence, the players sitting soundless on stage. He also wrote several books on musical and philosophical matters. There were no immediate survivors. (d. New York City; August 12, 1992)

FURTHER READING

Writings about John Cage. RICHARD KOSTELANETZ, ed. University of Michigan Press, 1993.
Obituary. *Down Beat,* Nov. 1992.
Obituary. *Dance,* Nov. 1992.
"John Cage: 1912–1992." SUSAN RICHARDSON. *Rolling Stone.* Oct. 1, 1992.
"UnCaged." *Economist,* Aug. 22, 1992.
Obituary. *Variety,* Aug. 17, 1992.
Obituary. *The Times* (of London), Aug. 14, 1992.
Obituary. *New York Times,* Aug. 13, 1992.
Cage Cunningham Johns: Dancers on a Plane. SUSAN SONTAG et al. Knopf, 1990.
John Cage at Seventy-Five. RICHARD FLEMING and WILLIAM DUCKWORTH, eds. Bucknell University Press, 1989.

Cage, Nicolas (Nicholas Coppola; 1965–)

Young film star Nicolas Cage had a major success in 1992 with his starring role in Andrew Bergman's *Honeymoon in Vegas,* as an amateur gambler who "loses" his fiancée, played by Sarah Jessica Parker, to a professional gambler, played by James Caan. The film was well reviewed, and also a commercial success. Forthcoming were starring roles in Christopher Coppola's film *Deadfall,* which started shooting in October 1992; Max Frye's *Amos and Andrew;*

and John Dahl's *Red Rock West.* On a celebrity note, Cage hosted the September television season premiere of "Saturday Night Live."

California-born Cage, Francis Ford Coppola's nephew, began his career with strong supporting roles in such 1980s films as *Valley Girl* (1983), *Rumble Fish* (1983), *Racing with the Moon* (1984), *Birdy* (1984), and *The Cotton Club* (1984), and moved into leads with his role opposite Kathleen Turner in *Peggy Sue Got Married* (1986). He went on to star in *Raising Arizona* (1987); in *Moonstruck* (1988) as the one-armed baker who becomes Cher's lover; *Vampire's Kiss* (1989); *Firebirds* (1990); in the David Lynch film *Wild at Heart* (1990) as Sailor Ripley opposite Laura Dern as Lula Pace Fortune; and in *Zandalee* (1991).

FURTHER READING

"Nicolas Cage. . . ." RICHARD NATALE. *Cosmopolitan,* Dec. 1992.
"Nicolas Cage." STEVE POND. *US,* Sep. 1992.
"Nicolas Cage. . . ." MARK ROWLAND. *Cosmopolitan,* Sep. 1990.
"Rebel without. . . ." STEPHANIE MANSFIELD. *GQ—Gentlemen's Quarterly,* Aug. 1990.
"Nicolas Cage." JOHN CLARK. *Premiere,* Sep. 1990.
"The beasts within. . . ." MARK ROWLAND. *American Film,* June 1990.
"20 questions. . . ." ROBERT CRANE. *Playboy,* June 1989.
"Nicolas Cage. . . ." T. KLEIN. *Cosmopolitan,* Oct. 1988.

Caine, Michael

Caine, Michael (Maurice Joseph Micklewhite; 1933–) Three 1992 film roles demonstrated veteran British actor Michael Caine's range and versatility. The first, opening in March, was his starring role opposite Carol Burnett in Peter Bogdanovich's film farce *Noises Off*, based on the Michael Frayn play, in a cast that also included Denholm Elliott, Julie Hagerty, Marilu Henner, Mark Linn-Baker, Christopher Reeve, and Nicollette Sheridan. The second was his starring role in Russell Mulcahy's *Blue Ice*, a spy thriller that echoed hundreds of similar films all made during the almost half century of the Cold War. And the third was his role as Scrooge in *The Muppet Christmas Carol*, opposite Kermit the Frog, Miss Piggy, and many other familiar faces and bodies. Forthcoming was another action film, *Bullseye*, a British movie co-starring Roger Moore and directed by Michael Winner. During 1992, Caine also published the autobiography *What's It All About*.

London-born Caine has been a durable, versatile film star since the mid-1960s, beginning with such films as *Zulu* (1964), *The Ipcress File* (1965), *Alfie* (1966), *The Wrong Box* (1966), *Gambit* (1966), and *Funeral in Berlin* (1966). His work also includes such films as *Sleuth* (1973), *The Wilby Conspiracy* (1975), *California Suite* (1978), *Educating Rita* (1982), *The Holcraft Covenant* (1985), *Hannah and Her Sisters* (1986; he won a Best Supporting Actor Oscar), *Dirty Rotten Scoundrels* (1988), *To Kill a Priest* (1989), *Mr. Destiny* (1990), and *A Shock to the System* (1990). In 1989, he also published a book, *Acting in Film: An Actor's Take on Movie Making*, based on his one-hour BBC special on movie acting. Also for television, he did *Jekyll & Hyde* (1990). He has also written *Michael Caine's Moving Picture Show* (1989). Formerly married to Patricia Haines, Caine married Shakira Khatoon Baksh in 1973. He has two children.

FURTHER READING

"The mark of Caine. . . ." MICHAEL A. LIPTON. *People*, Dec. 7, 1992.
"Still reaching. . . ." CHRISTA D'SOUZA. *Sunday Times* (of London), Oct. 11, 1992.
Candidly Caine: Everything Not Many People Know about Michael Caine . . . from Those in the Know! ELAINE GALLAGHER and IAN MACDONALD. Robson-Parkwest, 1992.
"The extraordinary. . . ." JOHN CULHANE. *Reader's Digest*, Nov. 1991.
"Michael Caine. . . ." JOHN ENNIS. *Reader's Digest* (Canadian), Dec. 1988.
"Caine, Michael." *Current Biography*, Jan. 1988.

Caminos, Ricardo

Caminos, Ricardo (1915–92) A leading Egyptologist, Buenos Aires-born Caminos graduated from the University of Buenos Aires in 1938 and did his postgraduate work at Oxford during and after World War II. A field archeologist for almost four decades, his first major fieldwork was at Luxor (Thebes) from 1947 to 1950. He later did much work at Gebel es-Silsila, Karnak, Qasr Ibrim, Buhen, and Semna-Kumma, the latter three in the late 1960s, in advance of the flooding of part of the Nile valley by the Aswan High Dam. His many publications included substantial works on Qasr Ibrim and Buhen. From the early 1950s, his fieldwork was sponsored by the Egypt Exploration Society. Caminos taught at Brown University (1952–79), and was department chairman from 1971 to 1979. He retired to London, continuing his research from a home close to the offices and library of the Egypt Exploration Society. He was survived by a sister and a brother. (d. London; May 26, 1992)

FURTHER READING

Obituary. *New York Times*, June 6, 1992.
Obituary. *The Times* (of London), June 1, 1992.
"Professor Ricardo Caminos." A.F. SHORE. *Independent*, May 30, 1992.

Campbell, Ben Nighthorse (1933–)

A Northern Cheyenne, Campbell is the second Native American ever to be elected to the U.S. Senate. On November 3, moderate Democrat Campbell defeated conservative Republican Terry Considine for the Colorado Senate seat vacated by Democrat Tim Wirth, who had not run for a second term. A rancher in Ignacio and a three-term Representative from the Third District, in western Colorado, Campbell won by a landslide 55 percent to 45 percent vote, although Considine had come from even further behind during the course of the race, with a barrage of negative ads. Campbell's campaign also did some negative advertising, but far less, rather stressing such issues as abortion rights and his Native American heritage. Campbell had won the Democratic nomination in a three-way contest with Josie Heath, who had lost the 1990 Senate race to Republican Hank Brown, and three-term former governor Richard Lamm.

California-born Campbell's 1957 B.A. was from San Jose State University. After Air Force service (1951–54), he attended Japan's Meiji University (1960–64). He served in the Colorado House of Representatives (1982–86), then serving in the U.S. House of Representatives, the only Native American member of Congress (1986–92). Campbell was a gold medalist in judo at the 1964 Olympic Games. He is also a well-known designer of Native American-inspired jewelry. He is married.

FURTHER READING

"An artist first. . . ." Judith Colp. *Insight*, Oct. 28, 1991.

Capriati, Jennifer (1976–)

Young Jennifer Capriati took the Olympic gold medal at the Summer Olympics in Barcelona, Spain, in July 1992, on the way defeating the Spanish favorite Arantxa Sanchez-Vicario and, in the finals, Germany's second-ranked Steffi Graf. In so doing, she defeated the last of the current women's tennis powers against whom she had not previously won a match. In March, in the Lipton International Players Championship at Key Biscayne, Florida, she had defeated top-ranked player Monica Seles. Though Capriati was still not ranked among the top five, she had clearly demonstrated that she was a contender. Elsewhere she did not fare well, exiting early from the year's Grand Slam tournaments; her only other tour win was at the San Diego Kraft Tour event in August. Capriati herself said about her 1992, "Wow, what a waste." At the end of 1991, Capriati had adopted as her new coach Pavel Slozil, formerly Graf's mentor; but in April 1992, she decided to stay under the supervision of her father and the staff of instructor Harry Hopman.

Capriati was trained for tennis from the age of four, first by her father Stefano Capriati, and then by Florida tennis professional Jimmy Evert, father of tennis star Chris Evert, also a mentor. She began winning junior tennis cham-

pionships at the age of 12. At 13, she won junior titles at the U.S. and French Open tournaments. In 1990, then barely 14 and still an eighth-grade student at the Saddlebrook Tennis Academy, she turned professional. She won one singles tournament that year, and two singles events in 1991, plus a doubles title with Seles.

FURTHER READING

Jennifer Capriati, Teenage Tennis Star. BILL GUTMAN. Millbrook, 1993.
"Net success." *Sporting News*, Sep. 7, 1992.
"Tennis menace." CINDY SHMERLER. *Women's Sports and Fitness*, Mar. 1992.
"Learn from the game's. . . ." TIM GULLIKSON et al. *Tennis*, Dec. 1991.
"But seriously folks. . . ." CINDY SCHMERLER. *World Tennis*, June 1991.
Jennifer Capriati. MIKKI MORRISSETTE. Little, Brown, 1991.
Jennifer Capriati. JAMES R. ROTHAUS. Child's World, 1991.
Jennifer Capriati. ELLEN E. WHITE. Scholastic, 1991.
"Tennis' new legend. . . ." DAVE SCHEIBER. *Saturday Evening Post*, July–Aug. 1990.

Carey, Mariah (1970–) New recording star Carey was again honored by her peers in 1992, most notably with a Best Female Pop Vocal Grammy nomination, as American Music Awards Favorite Female Soul-Rhythm Artist, and with a Soul Train Best Rhythm-and-Blues Female Soul Album award for her second album, *Emotions*, released in September 1991. During 1992, sales of that album went well over 3 million.

Carey, who had not yet toured, spent much of 1992 working on her third album, scheduled for release in spring 1993. She appeared in concert on the MTV series "Unplugged," and issued a seven-song selection from that concert that scored very well in the charts, as did her remake of The Jackson 5's "I'll Be There," which became a number one pop single. Carey was named Billboard's top female pop artist of the year. There was considerable talk of a concert tour after release of her forthcoming album.

Long Island-born Carey left high school to live and work in New York City in 1987. She worked as a waitress and backup singer before signing her first recording contract, with Columbia Records. She became a star overnight in 1990,

with her first album *Mariah Carey*, which sold well over 4 million copies; its ten songs included "Vision of Love," which stayed at the top of the charts as the number one single for four weeks. She won a 1991 Grammy award as the best new artist of 1990 and a second 1991 Grammy for top female pop vocal for her hit single "Vision of Love." She had also been nominated for top album, top record, and top song. Carey won several other awards during 1991 as well, including *Billboard*'s Top Artist of the Year award and three Soul Train awards. Her songs "Someday" and "I Don't Wanna Cry" were also 1991 number one singles.

FURTHER READING

"Carey, Mariah." *Current Biography*, July, 1992.
"Pop meteor. . . ." CHRIS SMITH. *New York*, Sep. 23, 1991.
"Mariah Carey tells why. . . ." *Jet*, Mar. 4, 1991.
"Careerwise or couchwise. . . ." *People Weekly*, Jan. 28, 1991.
"Building the perfect diva." ROB TANNENBAUM. *Rolling Stone*, Aug. 23, 1990.
"Pop's new vision." CHRIS SMITH. *New York*, May 28, 1990.
"In person. . . ." *Seventeen*, Oct. 1990.

Carnovsky, Morris (1897–1992) St. Louis-born Carnofsky made his professional debut in Boston in 1920, and his New York debut in 1922. From 1924 to 1933, he played in a wide range of roles with the Theater Guild, very notably including his title role in the 1929 production of *Uncle Vanya*. He was a founding member of the Group Theater in 1933, playing a succession of strong characters, as in his Mr. Bonaparte in *Golden Boy*. He also appeared in several films, including *The Life of Anatole France* (1937), *Rhapsody in Blue* (1945), and *Cyrano de Bergerac* (1950). In the early 1950s, he became a McCarthy-period witchhunt victim, blacklisted after refusing to name names before the House Un-American Activities Committee. Returning to the New York stage, he enjoyed a two-year run in *The World of Sholom Aleichem*, followed in 1956 by the beginning of his long association with John Houseman and the American Shakespeare Festival at Stratford, Connecticut. In 1957, he played his first Shylock, opposite Katharine Hepburn as Portia in *The Taming of the Shrew*, and in 1965 played the

title role in *King Lear*. With Peter Sander, he wrote *The Actor's Eye* (1983). He was survived by his wife, Phoebe Brand Carnovsky, a son, and two sisters. (d. Easton, Connecticut; September 1, 1992)

FURTHER READING

Obituary. *Variety*, Sep. 7, 1992.
Obituary. *New York Times*, Sep. 1, 1992.

Carradine, Keith Ian (1949–) During the final months of 1992, Carradine went on the road, taking on national tour his Tony-nominated performance as the rope-twirling, wise-cracking title character in Tommy Tune's Tony-winning musical *The Will Rogers Follies*. He and the show were very well received, by critics and audiences, and the national tour was scheduled to continue through the summer of 1993. On screen, Carradine starred as Goldie Hawn's ex-husband in Chris Menges's film drama *Criss Cross*, set in 1969 Florida; he plays a former Vietnam War pilot, who has been all but destroyed by his wartime experiences, and is in no condition to help his 12-year-old son come to terms with his mother's occupation as a stripper.

Carradine made his film debut in *A Gunfight* (1970), and went on to such films as *McCabe and Mrs. Miller* (1971), *Emperor of the North* (1972), *Thieves Like Us* (1973), *Nashville* (1975), *The Duellists* (1976), *Pretty Baby* (1977), *Lumiere* (1976), *Welcome To L.A.* (1977), *Old Boyfriends* (1979), *An Almost Perfect Affair* (1979), *The Long Riders* (1980), *Southern Comfort* (1981), *Choose Me* (1983), *Maria's Lovers* (1983), *Blackout* (1985), *Half a Lifetime* (1986), *Backfire* (1987), *The Moderns* (1988), *Backfire* (1987), *Cold Feet* (1989), *Judgment* (1990), *The Ballad of the Sad Cafe* (1991), and *The Bachelor* (1991). His theater appearances include *Hair* (1969–70) and *Foxfire* (1982–83). He has also appeared often in television, in such works as *A Rumour of War* (1981), *Chiefs* (1983), *Half a Lifetime* (1986), *Eye on the Sparrow* (1987), *Murder Ordained* (1987), and *The Forgotten* (1989). He won an Oscar as composer of the song "I'm Easy," which he introduced in *Nashville*. The son of actor John Carradine and the brother of actors David and Robert Carradine, he attended Colorado State University. He is married to Sandra

Will, they have two children. He is also the father of actress Martha Plimpton.

FURTHER READING

"Roping in the raves." MARK GOODMAN and TOBY KAHN. *People*, Sep. 30, 1991.
"Carradine, Keith." *Current Biography*, Aug. 1991.
"Ballad of a quiet man. . . ." WOLF SCHNEIDER. *American Film*, Apr. 1991.

Carson, Johnny (1925–) After a 30-year run that began on October 1, 1962, comedian and late-night host par excellence Johnny Carson ended his NBC "Tonight Show." As his tenure drew to a close, amid a blitz of media coverage, fans lined up for hours to get tickets for his shows, and a stream of celebrities came to pay tribute to an institution, including many (such as Elizabeth Taylor) rarely, if ever, seen on a live talk show. In addition to regulars Ed McMahon and Doc Severinsen, Carson's final guests, on May 21st, were Robin Williams and Bette Midler, with whom he sang an impromptu duet of "Here's That Rainy Day," and who made her final salute with "One for My Baby." For his farewell show, on May 22, 1992, Carson was alone, reminiscing with clips from past shows. NBC later announced that the show was watched by an estimated 55 million viewers, its largest audience ever. The all-comedy service Comedy Central even pre-empted its own programming during that final hour, with on-screen recommendations that viewers turn to the "Tonight Show."

But the "Tonight Show" did not end with Carson's retirement; he was succeeded by Jay Leno, his musical backup headed by jazzman Branford Marsalis. Nor did Carson go into "retirement;" instead, just seven weeks later, he and NBC signed a new seven-year contract, for Carson to develop several network projects, though the specifics of the contract and possible projects were not announced.

Iowa-born Carson began his four-decades-long career in radio in 1948, as an announcer with station KFAB, in Lincoln, Nebraska, and worked in radio until emerging as a television variety show host and quiz show master of ceremonies in the early 1950s. His early shows included "Carson's Cellar" (1951), and the quiz shows "Earn Your Vacation" (1954), "The Johnny Carson Show" (1955), and "Who Do You Trust" (1958–63). He also wrote for Red Skelton's television show and, from the mid-1950s, appeared in cabaret. He wrote the book *Happiness Is a Dry Martini* (1965). Carson's 1949 B.A. was from the University of Nebraska. Three times married, his wife is the former Alexis Maas. He has two surviving children; a third, his son Rick, was killed in an auto crash in 1991. (For additional photo, see Taylor, Elizabeth.)

FURTHER READING

"The pro holes out." MARK GOODMAN and MICHAEL A. LIPTON. *People*, May 25, 1992.
"Good night, Johnny." CALVIN TRILLIN. *Life*, May 1992.
"Johnny, we hardly knew ye. . . ." JAMES WOLCOTT. *Vanity Fair*, May 1992.
"End of an era." STEPHEN COX. *TV Guide*, May 9, 1992.
"A: laughs uncanned. . . ." *Entertainment*, May 8, 1992.
"And what a reign. . . ." RICHARD ZOGLIN. *Time*, Mar. 16, 1992.
"Behind the laughter. . . ." MARJORIE ROSEN. *People*, Aug. 19, 1991.
"Johnny mourns a son. . . ." *People*, July 8, 1991.
"Johnny Carson." LAURENCE LEAMER. *Good Housekeeping*, July 1989.
King of the Night: The Life of Johnny Carson. Laurence Leamer. Morrow, 1989; St. Martin's, 1990.
Carson: The Unauthorized Biography. PAUL CORKERY. Randt, 1987.
Johnny Carson. RONALD L. SMITH. St. Martin's, 1987.

Carstens, Karl (1914–92)

Bremen-born Carstens received his law degree from the University of Hamburg in 1936. He joined the Nazi Party in 1937, and served as an officer in the German Army from 1939 to 1945, but was not indicted for any war crimes. After the war, Carstens practiced law and went into West German politics and was elected to the federal parliament, the Bundesrat, in 1949. At first a Social Democrat, he became a Christian Democrat in 1955, joining the Foreign Office and then holding a series of other posts until the 1969 victory of the Social Democrats. He re-entered parliament in 1972, was Christian Democratic leader in the Bundesrat, and from 1976 to 1979 was Bundesrat president. He was President of West Germany (1979–84), despite massive opposition from those who felt that his Nazi Party membership should have disqualified him from holding that post. He was survived by his wife, Veronica. (d. Meckenheim, Germany; May 30, 1992)

FURTHER READING

Obituary. *The Times* (of London), June 1, 1992.
Obituary. *Independent*, June 1, 1992.
Obituary. *New York Times*, May 31, 1992.

Carswell, George Harrold (1920–92)

Georgia-born Carswell practiced law in his home state after his 1948 graduation from Mercer Law School. A Democrat who supported Dwight D. Eisenhower in the 1952 elections, he was appointed U.S. Attorney for northern Florida by Eisenhower in 1953, and to the federal bench in 1958; he was then the youngest federal judge. In 1969, after the Supreme Court resignation of Justice Abe Fortas, President Richard M. Nixon nominated Clement Haynesworth to fill the vacancy, but Haynesworth was rejected by the Senate. Nixon then nominated Carswell, at the time a federal Court of Appeals judge. But opponents quickly found a 1948 white supremacist speech, an anti-integration private golf course involvement, and anti-civil rights legal positions; the Senate rejected Carswell, then unanimously accepting Nixon's third choice, Harry Blackmun. Carswell resigned his court post, unsuccessfully ran for a Florida U.S. Senate nomination, and then practiced law in Tallahassee. He was survived by his wife, the former Virginia Simmons, two daughters, and two sons. (d. Tallahassee, Florida; July 31, 1992)

FURTHER READING

Obituary. *The Times* (of London), Aug. 7, 1992.
Obituary. *New York Times*, Aug. 1, 1992.

Carter, Jimmy (James Earl Carter, Jr.; 1924–) Former President Jimmy Carter played a new role in 1992, as a key foreign policy advisor to presidential candidate and then President-elect Bill Clinton. Carter's advice was especially sought on Middle Eastern affairs, although he and Clinton developed a wide-ranging relationship. On July 14, he addressed the Democratic National Convention in support of Clinton, his presence as the only living Democratic former President and his enthusiastic endorsement greatly helping the convention's unity theme. Immediately after the election, Clinton and Carter appeared together, both affirming that Carter would continue to play a major senior advisory role, although Carter did not want any formal post.

During 1992, Carter also continued to develop major programs to help America's depressed inner cities. In October 1991, he announced that he would be developing the massive "Atlanta project," a program to help solve the problems faced by poor people in his home state's capitol city, Atlanta, Georgia, such as "teen pregnancy, crack babies, drug addiction, juvenile delinquency, school dropouts, homelessness, unemployment, and divided families." Throughout the year that followed, he moved the project forward, gaining citizen "bottom up" participation, corporate and public support and funding, and late in the year moving to convince leaders throughout the country to expand the concept for use in many other cities, as the "America Project." During 1992, Carter also published *One Man, One Vote: A Candidate and a State Come of Age* and, for children, *Talking Peace.*

Georgia-born Carter became the 39th President of the United States in 1977, the climax of a political career that began with his four years in the Georgia Senate (1963–67). He went on to become governor of Georgia (1971–75), emerged as the surprise "outsider" winner of the Democratic presidential nomination after a long series of primary campaigns, and defeated incumbent Gerald Ford in the 1976 presidential race. His earlier career included seven years as a naval officer (1946–53), and ten years as a successful Georgia farmer and businessman at Plains, Georgia.

Jimmy Carter's very difficult presidential term was dominated by largely adverse foreign affairs matters, including the Arab oil embargo of the mid-1970s, the Iran hostage crisis that began in late 1979 and colored the rest of his presidency, and the worsening Soviet-American relations that began with the Soviet invasion of Afghanistan and resulted in the American boycott of the 1980 Moscow Olympics. His major accomplishment was the 1978 Camp David Accords, which paved the way for the 1979 Egyptian-Israeli peace treaty. After leaving the presidency, he initiated several pilot projects aimed at bringing sound low-income housing to decaying American inner cities. Carter has also been active in international mediation and human rights efforts, as in 1989 in Nicaragua, in 1990 in Ethiopia, the Sudan, and Haiti, and in 1991 in Zambia and Nicaragua. He has also been a distinguished professor at Emory University.

Carter's 1947 B.S. was from the U.S. Naval Academy. He married Rosalynn Smith in 1946; they have four children. After he left office, they collaborated in writing *Everything to Gain: Making the Most of the Rest of Your Life* (1988). He has also written several other works, including *An Outdoor Journal* (1988) and *America on My Mind* (1991).

FURTHER READING

Jimmy Carter and the Politics of Frustration.
    GARLAND A. HAAS. McFarland, 1992.
*The Native Son Presidential Candidate: The Carter
    Vote in Georgia.* HANES WALTON, JR.
    Praeger/Greenwood, 1992.
"Jimmy Carter." ROBERT N. HOFFMAN. *Workbench,*
    Nov. 1991.
"The Carter connection. . . ." DEBBIE S. MILLER.
    Wilderness, Winter 1990.
"Hail to the ex-chief. . . ." STANLEY CLOUD. *Time,* Sep.
    11, 1989.
Jimmy Carter. ED SLAVIN. Chelsea House, 1989.
*The President Builds a House: The Work of Habitat
    for Humanity.* TOM SHACHTMAN. Simon and
    Schuster, 1989.

Castro Ruz, Fidel (1926–) His old So-

viet ties and subsidies now very uneasy trading
relationships, his Eastern European Communist
trading partners now democracies and highly
critical of him, Castro still remained a hardline
Communist in 1992. During 1991, he had
seemed to soften just a bit internally, as small
dissident groups began to appear in Cuba, and
as Carlos Aldana Escalante emerged as a somewhat more moderate leader in Castro's own
Communist Party. But he soon made it clear
that he was having none of that. In late 1991,
several Cuban human rights activists were
arrested and jailed. In January, he ignored
worldwide protests and executed a "terrorist,"
Eduardo Diaz Betancourt, who had not yet committed any terrorist acts. Nor did dissent flour-
ish in his own party; in September, Aldana
Escalante was dismissed from Castro's Politburo
and all party positions, as were many other
Havana-based relative moderates.

Not surprisingly, Castro and Cuba further iso-
lated themselves in the process. For hardline
Communist Cuba, little hoped-for foreign investment materialized. It even became impossible to
go forward to completion of the expensive and
much-awaited Juragua nuclear plant, a joint
Russian-Cuban project, for the Russians demanded economic terms that Castro could not or
would not meet. Castro even dismissed his son
as head of the country's nuclear energy program.
Russia also announced plans to remove its final
major military unit, a brigade. As Cuba's economic situation worsened, Castro attempted to
tighten his party's hold and eliminate all possible opposition—but there were real questions as

to his ability to hold power for very much longer.

After leading the successful 1959 revolution
against the government of Fulgencio Batista,
Castro was a leading figure in world politics until the late 1980s. He survived the U.S.-backed
Bay of Pigs invasion of 1961 and also the Soviet
missile withdrawal after the 1962 Cuban Missile Crisis came very close to igniting World War
III, remaining in power as a Soviet ally and economic dependent through the late 1980s. Castro
has played a major role in supplying and training left revolutionaries throughout Latin America, and sent tens of thousands of troops to
Angola and Ethiopia in the late 1970s; withdrawal of those forces was agreed upon only in
the late 1980s, under pressure from the Soviet
Union. Castro attended the University of Havana, and practiced law in Havana before beginning his political career. He is married to Mirta
Diaz-Bilart and has one son.

FURTHER READING

"Is Fidel washed up?" SAUL LANDAU. *Progressive,*
    Aug. 1992.
"Fidel's world." PATRICK SYMMES. *American Spectator,*
    July 1992.
"Fidel's last resort." ANNE-MARIE O'CONNOR. *Esquire,*
    Mar. 1992.
*Fidel by Fidel: A New Interview with Dr. Fidel
    Castro Ruz, President of the Republic of Cuba.*
    FIDEL CASTRO et al. Borgo Press, 1992.
*The Tiger and the Children: Fidel Castro & the
    Judgment of History.* ROBERTO L. ESCALONA.
    Transaction, 1992.
"Maximum leader." GEORGIE ANNE GEYER. *American
    Heritage,* Nov. 1991.
"The last Communist." GEORGIE ANNE GEYER.
    Reader's Digest (Canadian), July 1991.
"The last communist." MARK FALCOFF. *Commentary,*
    June 1991.
"Guerrilla Prince. . . ." ARTURO CRUZ, JR. et al. *New
    Republic,* Apr. 22, 1991.
"Low fidelity. . . ." CHARLES LANE. *New Republic,* Jan.
    7, 1991.
*Guerrilla Prince: The Real Story of the Rise and
    Fall of Fidel Castro.* GEORGIE A. GEYER. Little,
    Brown, 1991.
Fidel Castro. JUDITH BENTLEY. Messner, 1991
Castro's Cuba, Cuba's Fidel. LEE LOCKWOOD.
    Westview, 1990.

Chamorro, Violeta (Violeta Barrios de

Chamorro; 1939–) Although Nicaraguan President Chamorro made considerable progress on
economic matters during 1992, many still-

unresolved problems stemming from Nicaragua's long civil war continued to plague her presidency. On the economic side, a substantial move toward recovery began, with stablilization of the cordoba, the basic unit of currency, and economic aid from abroad. But $104 million in much-needed economic aid from the United States was stopped for political reasons in June, as the Bush Administration and its Congressional supporters attacked her retention of Sandinistas in high military and police positions, along with her refusal to act on a mass of property claims against Sandinistas. But giving in to U.S. demands also posed problems; in September, after Chamorro did go a small part of the way, replacing the highly controversial Sandinista police chief with a somewhat less controversial Sandinista police chief, former President Daniel Ortega Saavadra made a thinly veiled threat of renewed civil war if she were to go much further to satisfy the United States. At year's end, Chamorro, Ortega, and Nicaragua continued on in an uneasy peace, as they waited for newly elected American President Bill Clinton to take office.

Chamorro became the elected President of Nicaragua on February 25, 1990, after Sandinista leader Ortega had quite surprisingly agreed to a free election, and to honor the election results. Her election was the start of a new chapter in a story that began on January 10, 1978, when her husband, crusading newspaper editor Pedro Joaquin Chamorro Cardenal, a leading opponent of the dictator Anastasio Somoza Debayle, was murdered on a street in Managua. That murder made him a martyr, and helped trigger the series of events that led to the Sandinista revolution and the overthrow of Somoza.

Violeta Chamorro was a member of the first Sandinista government, but withdrew within a year, when she saw the Sandinistas moving toward a dictatorship of their own, and took her husband's place as the crusading editor of *La Prensa*, in opposition to Sandinista attacks on freedom. Then came ten years of civil war between Contra and Sandinista forces, with the United States helping the Contras, and Cuba and the Soviet Union helping the Sandinistas. In her first year as president of a free Nicaragua, Chamorro successfully reached agreements to disarm the former combatants, guaranteeing the freedoms that she and her husband had fought for, and trying to set her very poor and damaged country on the road to economic recovery.

Violeta Barrios and Pedro Chamorro had four children.; Carlos Fernando and Claudia became highly placed Sandinistas, while Pedro Joaquin became a Contra leader and Cristiana an editor of *La Prensa*.

FURTHER READING

"The woman who. . . ." TREVOR ARMBRISTER. *Reader's Digest* (Canadian), Feb. 1991.
"Flowers for Violeta." DENNIS COVINGTON. *Vogue*, Aug. 1990.
"Chamorro, Violeta Barrios de." *Current Biography*, June 1990.
"A defiant widow. . . ." RON ARIAS. *People*, Mar. 19, 1990.
"A family affair. . . ." D'ARCY JENISH. *Maclean's*, Mar. 12, 1990.
"Chamorro. . . ." JOHN MOODY. *Time*, Mar. 12, 1990.
Life Stories of the Nicaraguan Revolution. DENIS L. HEYCK. Routledge Chapman and Hall, 1990.
Nicaragua Divided: La Prensa and the Chamorro Legacy. PATRICIA T. EDMISTEN. University Presses of Florida, 1990.

Chapman, Tracy (1963–) Singer, songwriter, and guitarist Chapman issued her third album in 1992, *Matters of the Heart*. Once again, she focused on questions of social justice, or lack of it, and once again wrestled with the uncertainties brought by her own still-new celebrity and concern about selling out or keeping the faith with social justice, as reflected in such songs as "I Used to be a Sailor," and "Bang Bang Bang." But she also now focused on such very personal matters as love and loss, as in the long title song "Matters of the Heart." Like her *Crossroads* album, *Matters of the Heart*, while finding substantial audiences, was not a commercial smash hit, but still an important part of her developing body of work.

Cleveland-born Chapman emerged very suddenly in 1988 as a leading writer and singer of social protest. She won three Grammys and several other awards for her first album, *Tracy Chapman*, which eventually sold an estimated 10 million copies worldwide. In 1989, she joined the worldwide Amnesty International tour; and also enjoyed the distinction of having her song "Freedom Now," about then-jailed African National Congress leader Nelson Mandela, banned from South African state radio and television. Her second album was *Crossroads* (1989), which expressed similar sentiments, but was less of a popular hit. She attended Connecticut's Wooster School and Tufts University.

FURTHER READING

"Singing for herself. . . ." RICHARD STENGEL. *Time*, Mar. 12, 1990.
"Women popsters. . . ." KEVIN ZIMMERMAN. *Variety*, Sep. 20, 1989.
"Chapman, Tracy." *Current Biography*, Aug. 1989.
"Tracy Chapman." *People*, Dec. 26, 1988.
"Good 'n' gritty. . . ." JENNIFER ASH and MARY FRAKES. *Life*, Aug. 1988.
"On her own terms." STEVE POND. *Rolling Stone*, Sep. 22, 1988.
"Tracy Chapman's. . . ." ANTHONY DeCURTIS. *Rolling Stone*, June 30, 1988.

Charles Philip Arthur George, the Prince of Wales

(1948–) The Prince of Wales is the oldest son of Elizabeth II and Prince Philip, and heir to the British throne. As such, he is, like the other British "royals," the object of enormous worldwide media attention, directed at every aspect of his personal life. So it was that in 1992 massive media attention was focused on his marital difficulties, especially after the June serialization of Andrew Morton's book *Diana: Her True Story* in London's *The Sunday Times*. The book, which made much of the couple's problems, also alleged that Diana had attempted suicide several times. On December 9, 1992, the Prince and Princess of Wales announced their separation.

However well publicized his marital problems, the Prince of Wales is scarcely an international playboy. He is a respected and effective environmentalist, who made a considerable contribution to the development of the 1992 Rio de Janiero Earth Summit, on a wide range of ecological issues and particularly on the future of the Amazon Basin.

Prince Charles has also for some years been a highly visible critic of modern architecture. Major objects of his attack have included such massive buildings as Britain's National Theatre, National Gallery, and National Library. In 1991, he resigned as president of the patrons of the Museums of Scotland, opposing the prize-winning modernist design of the new Edinburgh Museum. Early in 1992, he announced the formation of a new institute of architecture, named after him, aimed at creating a new modern architecture that incorporated classical forms, an "architecture of the heart," and an Institute that "will become a kind of crucible in which the architecture of the 21st century can be forged."

Prince Charles attended Trinity College, Cambridge, and the University College of Wales. He married Lady Diana Spencer in 1981; they have two children: William Arthur Philip, born June 21, 1982; and Henry Charles Albert David, born September 15, 1984. His books include *The Old Man of Lochnagar* (1980), *A Vision of Britain* (1989), and *The Prince of Wales' Watercolours* (1991). Forthcoming in 1993 is *Highgrove: Portrait of an Estate.*

FURTHER READING

"Royal marriage. . . ." DAME BARBARA CARTLAND. *Newsweek*, Dec. 21, 1992.
"Throne out." JERRY ADLER. *Newsweek*, Dec. 21, 1992.
"Separate lives." MICHELLE GREEN. *People*, Dec. 21, 1992.
"Royal fire storm." ANDREW PHILLIPS. *Maclean's*, Nov. 30, 1992.
"The warring Windsors." DERMOT PURGAVIE and GARTH PEARCE. *TV Guide*, Aug. 8, 1992.
"Alone together." ROBERT LACY. *Life*, Aug. 1992.
"Heartache in the palace. . . ." ANNE EDWARDS. *McCall's*, Aug. 1992.
"Royal rumpus. . . ." GEORGE RUSSELL. *Variety*, July 13, 1992.
"Love on the rocks." MICHELLE GREEN. *People*, June 29, 1992.
"Portrait of a marriage." *Newsweek*, June 22, 1992.
"What's it all about, Charlie?" ADAM PLATT. *Esquire*, June 1992.
Diana: A Princess and Her Troubled Marriage. NICHOLAS DAVIES. Birch Lane/Carol, 1992.
"Windsor knot. . . ." CHRISTOPHER HITCHENS. *New York Times Magazine*, May 12, 1991.
"Diana and Charles. . . ." ANTHONY HOLDEN. *McCall's*, June 1991.
Charles and Diana: The Tenth Anniversary. BRIAN HOEY. Studio Books, 1991.

Chase, Chevy

(Cornelius Crane Chase, 1943–) Film star Chase in 1992 starred in James Carpenter's film comedy *Memoirs of an Invisible Man*, playing Nick Holloway, who (along with considerable parts of the building he is in) becomes invisible after an accident. The film features a considerable number of creative special effects. Co-starring were Daryl Hannah as Nick's love interest and Sam Neill as a spy who wants to use Nick as a superspy. The film was not very well received by the critics.

In April 1992, Chase and the Fox Broadcasting Company announced a multiyear agreement covering Chase's development of television series and feature films for Fox's 20th Television and 20th Century Fox. Chase was also to host "The Chevy Chase Show," a six-nights-a-week late-night talk show, scheduled to begin in September 1993.

New York City-born Chase was a comedy writer and off-Broadway comedian in cabaret in the late 1960s and early 1970s, emerging in the mid-1970s as a nationally recognized television comedian as a member of "Saturday Night Live" troupe. In the late 1970s, he also became a leading film comedian, in such movies as *Foul Play* (1978), *Oh Heavenly Dog* (1980), *Caddyshack* (1980; and the 1988 sequel), *Modern Problems* (1981), *Deal of the Century* (1983), *Fletch* (1985; and the 1988 and 1989 sequels), *Spies Like Us* (1985), *Three Amigos* (1986), *Funny Farm* (1988), *National Lampoon's Christmas Vacation* (1989), and *Nothing But Trouble* (1991). His 1967 B.S. was from Bard College and his 1970 C.C.S. from the Institute for Audio Research. Chase has been married three times and has three children.

FURTHER READING

"I'm finally growing up." DOTSON RADER. *Parade.* April 19, 1992.
"Chevy Chase." MARK MORRISON. *US*, March, 1992.
"Playboy interview. . . ." JOHN BLUMENTHAL. *Playboy*, June 1988.

Chase, Gilbert (1906–92) A leading American musicologist, teacher, and writer, especially in the areas of U.S. and Latin American music, Chase began his career as a music critic for the *Daily Mail* in Paris (1929–35). Back in the United States from the mid-30s, he worked in a wide range of music-related jobs, and as a music advisor and reviewer for the Book-of-the-Month Club, while also producing his first major work, *The Music of Spain* (1941). From 1951 to 1955, he was a U.S. cultural attache in Lima and then Buenos Aires, returning to the U.S. to head the University of Oklahoma School of Music. He

later taught at several other colleges and universities. His best-known books include *A Guide to Latin American Music* (1945), *American's Music: From the Pilgrims to the Present* (1955), and *A Concise Handbook of Latin American Culture* (1966). He was survived by his wife, Kathleen, and three sons. (d. Chapel Hill, North Carolina; Feb. 22, 1992)

FURTHER READING

Obituary. *New York Times*, Feb. 27, 1992.
Obituary. *Variety*, Mar. 2, 1992.

Cheney, Dick (Richard Bruce Cheney, 1941–) In the aftermath of the Cold War, and with the Persian Gulf War receding into history, the outgoing U.S. Secretary of Defense spent much of 1992 walking a tightrope between those who wanted very sharp military cuts and a massive conversion to peacetime pursuits, and those who wanted to maintain as much as possible of the enormously expensive Cold War military establishment. That most of those calling for massive cuts were Democrats, and most of those on the other side Republicans, and that 1991 was a presidential election year made his situation all the more delicate. That Cheney was widely considered to be a potential Republican 1996 presidential candidate filled out his situation. Still, he did propose major National Guard and Reserve cuts in March, and continued the base closings and personnel cuts started in 1990 and 1991, while at the same time strongly resisting the much larger cuts proposed by some Congressional Democrats—although other Democrats, concerned about job losses, especially in their states and districts, called for go-slow policies on many cuts. On the international scene, Cheney defended the administration's early conclusion of the Persian Gulf War, supported administration arms sales in the Middle East and elsewhere, supported administration hesitation to intervene in the civil war among peoples in the former Yugoslavia, and supported the Somalia intervention.

Nebraska-born Cheney is a long-term Washington "insider," who worked in several Washington administrative positions during the 1970s, ultimately becoming a White House assistant of President Gerald Ford (1975–77). He became a Republican congressman from Wyoming in 1979, and during the 1980s became a leading House Republican. He became defense secretary in early 1989, after the John Tower nomination had been rejected in a long, bitter Senate fight. Cheney's 1965 B.A. and 1966 M.A. were from the University of Wyoming. He married Lynne Anne Vincent in 1964; they have two children.

FURTHER READING

"Cheney for the defense." ROWLAND EVANS et al. *Reader's Digest*, Dec. 1991.
"Five who fit the bill. . . ." *Time*, May 20, 1991.
"Cracking the whip. . . ." MICHAEL R. GORDON. *New York Times Magazine*, Jan. 27, 1991.
"Cheney, Richard Bruce." *Current Biography*, Aug. 1989.

Cher (Cherilyn LaPiere Sarkisian; 1946–) Popular singer, actress, and enduring celebrity Cher continued to follow up on the success of her 1991 album *Love Hurts*, with her long *Love Hurts* tour in 1992, although she was forced to postpone several scheduled New York concerts in June due to illness. On screen, she appeared as herself in Robert Altman's *The Player*, his slashing hit lampoon of Hollywood. But she was by far most often seen on screen in a wide range of commercials, many of them long "infomercials," and many of those for her own exercise and other products. In 1992, she issued another tremendously successful exercise video, adding *Cherfitness: Body Confidence* to her earlier *Cherfitness: A New Attitude*. And her celebrity continued to be such that the tattoo craze she did so much to start continued to grow and grow. On the political side, she strongly supported Ross Perot's Presidential candidacy; on his withdrawal from the race, she announced that she would drop everything to campaign for him if he would reconsider. Forthcoming is an autobiography.

California-born Cher became a popular singer in the mid-1960s, teamed with her first husband, Sonny Bono, as Sonny and Cher. On her own from the late 1970s, she emerged as a star entertainer and recording artist, and continued as one of the leading celebrities of the 1980s. She turned to acting in Robert Altman's New York stage production of *Come Back to the Five and Dime, Jimmy Dean, Jimmy Dean* in 1981, and then emerged as a leading dramatic actress, whose no-table body of work includes *Silkwood* (1983), *The Witches of Eastwick* (1987), her Oscar-winning lead in *Moonstruck* (1987), and *Mermaids* (1990). In addition to Bono, she was formerly married to Gregg Allman, and has two children.

FURTHER READING

"Dress minimal. . . ." ALAN JACKSON. *Times*, Apr. 27, 1992.
"Cher." LAWRENCE GROBEL. *Architectural Digest*, Apr. 1992.
"Mirror, mirror. . . ." LAVINIA EDMUNDS. *Family Circle*, June 2, 1992.
Totally Uninhibited: The Life & Wild Times of Cher. LAWRENCE J. QUIRK. Morrow, 1991.
"Cher." *Current Biography*, June 1991.
"Cher today. . . ." JIM JEROME. *People*, Jan. 21, 1991.
"Cher the unstoppable." CLIFF JAHR. *Ladies Home Journal*, Nov. 1990.
Cher. J. RANDY TARRABORRELLI. St. Martin's, 1986.

Cheshire, Geoffrey Leonard (1917–92) One of the leading British bomber pilots of World War II, Cheshire joined the Bomber Command in 1940. He quickly moved up in rank and responsibility; at the age of 25, he was Britain's youngest bomber group captain, at Marston Moor. But he wanted to fly, and went one step back, to wing commander of the highly regarded precision-bombing 617 Squadron, the Dambusters, ending his active bombing career after his 100th mission. Winner of many decorations, he was awarded the Victoria Cross in 1944. In 1945, he was Britain's observer at the American atom-bombing of Nagasaki; the horror observed was to change his life.

Cheshire had some difficulty getting started after the war, but in 1948 began the movement that was to become the Cheshire Foundation, with missions in many countries. He wrote several books, including *Bomber Pilot* (1943), *The Face of Victory* (1961), and *The Light of Many Suns* (1985), the latter on the 40th anniversary of the atom-bombings of Japan. He was survived by his second wife, Sue Ryder, who joined him in his work in 1956 (they married in 1959), a daughter, and a son. (d. London; July 31, 1992)

FURTHER READING

Obituary. *The Times* (of London), Aug. 3, 1992.
Obituary. *New York Times*, Aug. 2, 1992.
Obituary. *Independent*, Aug. 1, 1992.

Chikatilo, Andrei (1936–)

A serial killer, Chikatilo murdered at least 53 people throughout the Soviet Union from 1978 to 1990, most of them in and around Rostov-on-Don, where he lived and worked as a teacher and then a clerk, and in smaller numbers throughout the country. The number of the murders, that most of his victims were children and teenagers, and that the murders were accompanied by sexual abuse, dismemberment, and cannibalism, made him one of the most wanted mass murderers of the century, who was known throughout the world as the "Rostov Ripper."

Chikatilo was captured near the scene of a killing in November 1990, and quickly admitted many of the murders, showing no remorse. His several-month trial ended on October 14, 1992, with a verdict of guilty on 52 counts of murder. On October 15, the presiding judge, Leonid Akubzhanov, sentenced him to death. The judge also attacked the former Soviet government for hiding the fact of the mass murders for many years from its own citizens and for fostering the authoritarian conditions in which Chikatilo, a Communist Party member, was able to more easily lure his victims to their deaths. Akubzhanov also charged that an innocent man had been charged and executed in error for one of Chikatilo's murders in 1978. A further charge was that Chikatilo had been arrested in 1986, but had been released after blood tests (later shown to have been mishandled) had pointed to his probable innocence. Late in 1992, several books on the case were reportedly in preparation.

FURTHER READING

"Good riddance. . . ." *Time*, Oct. 26, 1992.
"A monster caged at last. . . ." JOE TREEN. *People*, Oct. 19, 1992.
"Russia's ripper." MALCOLM GRAY. *Maclean's*, June 29, 1992.
"A Slavic Hannibal? . . ." *Time*, Apr. 27, 1992.
"Smiling Rostov Ripper. . . ." JONATHON BASTABLE. *Sunday Times* (of London), Apr. 19, 1992.

Chissanó, Joaquim Alberto (1939–)

On August 7, 1992, after two years of on-and-off negotiations, Mozambique President Chissanó was able to negotiate a lasting ceasefire in his country's long civil war. He and Afonso Dhlakama, leader of Renamo (Mozambique National Resistance), signed a peace agreement in Rome; in addition to a ceasefire leading to a formal peace treaty, it provided for United Nations monitoring and establishment of democracy in Mozambique.

Sixteen years of civil war, on top of ten years of war with the Portuguese, had left an estimated one million dead; three to four million more were refugees in other countries. The country was devastated, the long drought in southern Africa had worsened, and mass starvation and accompanying disease threatened the lives of millions. What ended the war, however, was the withdrawal of Renamo support by South Africa, as part of the general settlement of hostilities in the region.

The formal peace treaty was signed by Chissanó and Dhlakama on October 4. It provided for demobilization of both armies and formation of a new national army drawn equally from both sides. With the way now open, international humanitarian organizations could begin to bring in the kinds of massive foodstocks needed, without interference by the warring parties, and the long work of reconstruction could begin—if, in the long run, the ceasefire and peace treaty held.

Chissanó has spent his whole career as a Mozambiquan revolutionary and then government official. After holding several responsible posts in Frelimo (Mozambique National Liberation Front) during the long war against the Portuguese colonizers of his country, he was foreign minister of newly independent, one-party, Marxist Mozambique (1975–86), and succeeded Samora Machel as president in 1986. In 1989, he began to move his party away from Marxism and one-party rule, toward multi-party democracy, a market-driven economy, and a peaceful reconciliation with the Renamo insurgents. The process was helped greatly by withdrawal of South African support for Renamo, as part of the general settlement of hostilities in southern Africa, and was part of a worldwide American-Soviet post-Cold War attempt to settle regional conflicts. In July 1990, Chissanó declared that his government would give up its one-party rule and participate in free elections, and on November 3, 1990, a new democratic constitution was adopted. Chissanó is married to Marcelina Rafael Chissanó; they have four children.

FURTHER READING

"Chissano, Joachim Alberto." *Current Biography*, Nov. 1990.

Christopher, Warren (1925–) President Bill Clinton's incoming Secretary of State

played a substantial role in the 1992 presidential elections. During the campaign, he was a key Clinton advisor, and was part of the selection committee that recommended choosing Al Gore as the vice-presidential candidate. Immediately after the campaign, he was chosen manager of the Clinton transition team, to take day-to-day responsibility for developing recommendations for the key posts in the new administration. A top corporate lawyer, with extensive government and foreign policy experience, he was expected to bring strong negotiating and other practical skills to his new assignment.

Pennsylvania-born Christopher began his career as a law clerk to U.S. Supreme Court Justice William O. Douglas (1949–50). Returning to California, he began his long career with the Los Angeles law firm O'Melveny and Myers, becoming a partner in 1958, and going back to the firm after periods of government service. He was a deputy U.S. Attorney General during the Johnson Administration (1967–69), and a deputy Secretary of State during the Carter years (1977–81), in 1980 becoming heavily involved in negotiations for the release of the Iran hostages, about which he wrote (with others) *American Hostages in Iran: The Conduct of a Crisis* (1985). In 1991, he chaired the Independent Commission on the Los Angeles Police Department, formed after the Rodney King beating, which established a pervasive pattern of racism in the department and called for the resignation of police chief Daryl F. Gates. Christopher's 1945 B.S. was from the University of Southern California and his 1949 LL.B. from Stanford University. He is married and has four children.

FURTHER READING

"The transition. . . ." BILL TURQUE. *Newsweek*, Nov. 16, 1992.

Cisneros, Henry Gabriel (1947–)

President Bill Clinton's incoming Secretary of Housing and Urban Development is widely regarded as one of the most highly qualified urban affairs and public administration experts ever to hold the post. San Antonio-born Cisneros holds a B.A. and M.A. in urban and regional planning from Texas A&M University, an M.A. in public

administration from Harvard University's John F. Kennedy School, and a Ph.D. in public administration from George Washington University, then serving a year as a White House Fellow under Secretary of Health, Education, and Welfare Elliot Richardson. His qualifications are practical, as well; he was elected to the San Antonio City Council in 1975, the year before he received his Ph.D., and in 1981 at age 33 became mayor of his home city—the first Mexican-American to hold the job in 140 years—serving until 1989. He has also served a stint as president of the National League of Cities. When then-Texas senator Lloyd Bentsen was appointed Treasury Secretary, Cisneros was atop the short list of candidates to replace him, but he chose instead to take an appointment in the Clinton cabinet.

One of the country's leading urban figures, and a leading Hispanic-American politician, as well, Cisneros seemed headed for either much higher office or for a lifetime job at San Antonio; he won more than two thirds of the vote in his 1987 re-election. But in late 1988, he withdrew from politics, citing financial reasons, though probably because of media outcry over an extramarital affair with a political coworker. In private life, he founded a successful financial firm; hosted *Texans*, a quarterly television show; hosted "Adelante," a national daily Spanish-language radio show; and became deputy chairman of the Dallas Federal Reserve Bank, before leaving to join the Clinton campaign in mid-

1992. Earlier, he had contributed to the book *Texas in Transition* (1986). Cisneros is married to Mary Alice Perez; they have three children.

FURTHER READING

Henry Cisneros: A Leader for the Future, rev. ed. MAURICE ROBERTS. Childrens, 1991.
"Henry Cisneros on sabbatical." *Hispanic*, July 1989.
"Remembering Henry." *Texas Monthly*, Dec. 1988.
"Whither Henry?" ALISON COOK. *Texas*, May 1988.
Henry Cisneros: Señor Alcade: A Biography of Henry Cisneros. JOHN GILLIES. Dillon/Macmillan, 1988.
Profiles in Achievement. CHARLES M. HOLLOWAY. College Board, 1987.

Clarke, Mae (1907–92) A movie star in the early 1930s, Clarke was best known by far for the 1931 *The Public Enemy* film sequence in which James Cagney pushed a grapefruit into her face. Clarke started her career as a dancer in New York cabaret, made her film debut in 1929, and starred in several major films, including *The Front Page*, *Waterloo Bridge*, and *Frankenstein*, all in 1931. But her career quickly sagged, and although there were strong supporting roles in the following years, she never had another year like that one, although her film career lasted almost four decades and she appeared in more than 80 films, as in *Parole Girl* (1933), *Nana* (1934), *Flying Tigers* (1942), *Annie Get Your Gun* (1950), *Singin' In the Rain* (1952), and *Magnificent Obsession* (1954). She was survived by a nephew. (d. Woodland Hills, California; April 29, 1992)

FURTHER READING

Obituary. *Variety*, May 4, 1992.
Obituary. *The Times* (of London), May 2, 1992.
Obituary. *New York Times*, May 1, 1992.

Clifford, Clark McAdams (1906–) Long-term Washington insider Clark Clifford, a key advisor to three presidents and a former Secretary of Defense, in 1991 became a central figure in the Bank of Credit and Commerce International (BCCI) affair, one of the most highly publicized bank scandals of the century. The scandal began with Senator John Kerry's discovery of the secret $20 million BCCI account of Panama's General Manuel Noriega, and included BCCI involvement in bribery, larceny, conspiracy to illegally acquire interests in other financial institutions, money-laundering, the funding of illegal arms dealing, and a host of other illegal activities, as well as possible ties with the CIA. It also included the secret ownership and use of First American Bankshares, a large Washington-area bank; Clifford had been chairman of First American since 1982, and his law partner, Robert Altman, had been president of the bank. Both men resigned their positions under pressure on August 13, 1991, and denied any wrongdoing in a highly publicized September 11 appearance before the House Banking Committee.

Seven countries closed down BCCI activities in July 1991. On December 15, 1991, BCCI settled outstanding United States charges against it for $550 million, although massive criminal and civil suits against the bank and those connected with it continued in many countries. On July 29, 1992, Federal and New York State prosecutors filed a wide range of criminal charges against BCCI; among them were charges against Clifford that included conspiracy, concealing material facts, fraud, and bribery. A long series of legal maneuvers followed during the balance of 1992, while federal and state prosecutors argued over who would prosecute first, and Clifford's lawyers attempted to block his trial, contending that it would be likely to result in a fatal heart attack.

Kansas-born Clifford began his long career as a practicing lawyer in St. Louis (1928–43). He became a White House naval aide in 1945, and quickly became a key political advisor to fellow Missourian Harry S. Truman, who was the first of the several Democratic presidents who came to rely on his advice, as he described in *Counsel to the President* (1991). Clifford was a special counsel to Truman (1946–50), and to presidents John F. Kennedy and Lyndon Johnson until becoming Secretary of Defense in 1968–69. After his years in government, he stayed in Washington, becoming one of the country's most powerful, politically connected Washington "insiders." Clifford's LL.B. was from Washington University, in St. Louis.

He is married to the former Margery Pepperell Kimball; they have three daughters.

FURTHER READING

"The fall of. . . ." WARREN I. COHEN. *Nation*, Oct. 5, 1992.

"How they broke the bank. . . ." MARIE BRENNER. *Vanity Fair*, Apr. 1992.

Dirty Money: BCCI—The Inside Story of the World's Sleaziest Bank. MARK POTTS et al. National Press, 1992.

"A matter of influence. . . ." EVAN THOMAS. *Newsweek*, May 20, 1991.

"All the presidents' man." *M Inc.*, Mar. 1991.

Clinton, Bill (William Jefferson Blythe IV; 1946–) On November 3, 1992, Arkansas Democratic Governor Bill Clinton was elected 42nd President of the United States, defeating incumbent Republican President George Bush and independent candidate H. Ross Perot. Clinton won in an electoral vote landslide, 370 electoral votes to Bush's 168 electoral votes; Perot won none. However, Clinton won these with only 43 percent of the popular vote (43.7 million votes), to Bush's 38 percent (38.2 million votes) and Perot's 19 percent (19.2 million votes).

The road to the Presidency had been far from smooth for Clinton. He entered the Democratic presidential nomination race on October 3, 1991, sounding the same themes he had been developing as chairman of the middle-of-the-road Democratic Leadership Council since 1990. He ran as a centrist trying to gain the votes of the "forgotten middle class," and simultaneously as a liberal Democrat stressing some traditional Democratic issues. Clinton advocated taking major steps to turn around the ailing American economy, widening health insurance coverage to include all Americans, freedom of choice for women on the question of abortion, education reform, child support and welfare system reforms, deficit reduction, and middle class tax relief coupled with increases in taxes for higher-income people and foreign corporations. Such themes were outlined in the book *Putting People First* (1992) by Clinton and Al Gore.

Early in 1992, Clinton became a primary campaign frontrunner, while at the same time suffering a series of attacks from other candidates and in the media on such questions as his alleged extramarital affairs with Gennifer Flowers and others; his alleged "draft-dodging" during the Vietnam War; and his alleged general untrustworthiness. During the election campaign, Clinton was also attacked indirectly through attacks on his wife, Hillary Clinton, who was depicted by his opponents as a radical feminist. Late in the campaign, some Republicans even illegally caused his passport files to be searched for possibly derogatory information—and went so far as to seek derogatory information on his mother. But in the long run, Clinton surmounted all such negative attacks, from within his own party and during the election campaign from the Republican Party and directly from George Bush, by focusing on the economy in a period of great economic distress, with a major second focus on the issue of health insurance reform, and a third focus on women's choice.

Clinton's election was widely described as an extraordinary repudiation of George Bush, who had been enormously popular after the Persian Gulf War, in some polls in the 90+ percent range. After his election, and during the transition period before his January 20, 1993 inauguration, Clinton and Vice President-elect Al Gore adopted as low a profile as possible on the specific matters being handled by the outgoing Bush Adminstration, instead focusing on the key appointments to be made and on turning the main themes of the campaign into programs to be put into effect during the Clinton Presidency.

Arkansas-born Clinton taught law at the University of Arkansas Law School and was in private practice (1973–76) before entering politics in 1977 as state attorney-general, a position he held until becoming governor. He was governor from 1979 to 1981, and again from 1983–92. His

1968 B.S. was from Georgetown, his 1973 J.D. from Yale; in between, he was a Rhodes Scholar at Oxford (1968–70). Born three months after his father's death, he later took his stepfather's surname, Clinton. He and Hillary Rodham met when both were at Yale Law School; they married in 1975 and have one daughter, Chelsea.

FURTHER READING

"Bill Clinton and. . . ." LANDON Y. JONES, JR. and GARRY CLIFFORD. *People*, Dec. 28, 1992.

"A generation takes power." WALTER SHAPIRO. "A new coalition for the 1990s." LAURENCE I. BARRETT. "The final 48 hours." WALTER SHAPIRO. "What he will do." MICHAEL KRAMER. "A time for courage." WALTER ISAACSON. *Time*, Nov. 16, 1992.

"Cool hand Bill. . . ." FRED BARNES. *New Republic*, Nov. 16, 1992.

"A man of Hope (Ark.)." SCOTT STEELE. *Maclean's*, Nov. 16, 1992.

"Man who just wants to be loved." ANDREW STEPHEN. *Observer*, Nov. 8, 1992.

"Clinton emerges. . . ." MARTIN FLETCHER. *Times* (of London), Oct. 21, 1992.

"Face to face." ANN MCDANIEL. *Newsweek*, Oct. 19, 1992.

"About-face." MICHAEL NORMAN. *New York Times Magazine*, Oct. 11, 1992.

"A visit with. . . ." *Atlantic*, Oct. 1992.

"Bill Clinton. . . ." WILLIAM GREIDER et al. *Rolling Stone*, Sep. 17, 1992.

"Bill Clinton." P.J. O'ROURKE. *Independent*, Sep. 15, 1992.

"The reanointed." *New Republic*, July 27, 1992.

"Mr. Clinton. . . ." WILLIAM MCGURN. *National Review*, July 20, 1992.

" 'Change is very painful.' " ELEANOR CLIFT. "Running mates." *Newsweek*, July 20, 1992.

"An interview with Clinton." HENRY MULLER and JOHN F. STACKS. "Clinton's second chance." MICHAEL KRAMER. "Beginning of the road." GARRY WILLS. *Time*, July 20, 1992.

"Bill Clinton's hidden life. . . ." DONALD BAER et al. "How the lessons. . . ." MATTHEW COOPER. *U.S. News & World Report*, July 20, 1992.

"William Jefferson Clinton." *Facts on File*, July 16, 1992.

"The blur. . . ." JOHN TAYLOR. *New York*, July 13, 1992.

" 'They'll vote for me because. . . .' " LEE WALCZAK and HOWARD GLECKMAN. *Business Week*, July 6, 1992.

"Clinton's forgotten childhood." GARRY WILLS. *Time*, June 8, 1992.

"Clinton on the brink." JULIA REED. *Vogue*, June 1992.

"Governor Clinton." HENRY SCHIPPER. *Rolling Stone*, May 14, 1992.

"Loser. . . ." FRED BARNES. *New Republic*, May 4, 1992.

"Questions questions questions." GEORGE J. CHURCH. *Time*, Apr. 20, 1992.

"Greaseman. . . ." MORTON KONDRACKE. "The pol. . . ." SIDNEY BLUMENTHAL. *New Republic*, Apr. 6, 1992.

"Testing ground. . . ." ELEANOR CLIFT. " 'You didn't reveal. . . .' " JONATHAN ALTER and ELEANOR CLIFT. "The real character issues." JONATHAN ALTER. "Can he beat Bush?" HOWARD FINEMAN and ANN MCDANIEL. *Newsweek*, Mar. 30, 1992.

"The making of Bill Clinton." DONALD BAER and STEVEN V. ROBERTS. *U.S. News & World Report*, Mar. 30, 1992.

"Clinton. . . ." RICHARD BROOKHISER. *National Review*, Mar. 30, 1992.

"A talk with. . . ." LEE WALCZAK. *Business Week*, Mar. 23, 1992.

"An uncertain embrace." MATTHEW COOPER. *U.S. News & World Report*, Mar. 23, 1992.

"Political ambitions. . . ." ELEANOR CLIFT. *Newsweek*, Mar. 9, 1992.

"Bill Clinton's. . . ." PETER APPLEBOME. *New York Times Magazine*, Mar. 8, 1992.

"Clinton on trial." BILL HEWITT et al. *People*, Feb. 10, 1992.

"The anointed. . . ." SIDNEY BLUMENTHAL. *New Republic*, Feb. 3, 1992.

"The manufactured candidate." Andrew Kopkind. *Nation*, Feb. 3, 1992.

"The self-making. . . ." MICHAEL KRAMER. "Is Bill Clinton for real?" GEORGE J. CHURCH. *Time*, Jan. 27, 1992.

"Tough love child of Kennedy." MARTIN WALKER and PETER CLARKE. *Guardian*, Jan. 6, 1992.

The Comeback Kid: The Life and Career of Bill Clinton. CHARLES F. ALLEN and JONATHAN PORTIS. Birch Lane/Carol, 1992.

Bill Clinton: The Inside Story. ROBERT E. LEVIN. Shapolsky, 1992.

Slick Willie: Why America Cannot Trust Bill Clinton. FLOYD G. BROWN. Annapolis, 1992.

Clinton, Hillary Rodham (1947–) Incoming U.S. First Lady Hillary Clinton is also a distinguished lawyer and law professor, children's advocate, educational reformer, and women's rights leader; indeed, she kept her own name, Hillary Rodham, until 1982, adopting Bill Clinton's name only for Arkansas political purposes, because of mounting local objections to her views on the question of keeping her own name. As the Clinton Presidency began, all indications were that she was going to be a very unusual First Lady.

Hillary Rodham Clinton's 1969 B.A. was from Wellesley College, where she was President of College Government, and her 1973 J.D. from Yale Law School, where she served on the *Yale Review of Law and Social Action*. During and after law school, she worked at Cambridge and then in Washington with Marian Wright Edelman at the Children's Defense Fund; in later years, she was the chairman of the Fund's Board of Directors. In 1974, she was a staff member of the Impeachment Inquiry Staff of the House of Representatives Judiciary Committee, investigating the Watergate affair and the possible impeachment of President Richard M. Nixon.

She and Bill Clinton met when both were at Yale Law School. They married in 1975; she then joined him in Arkansas, where she taught law and joined the Rose Law Firm in Little Rock, there becoming a very successful litigator. She also became a nationally known figure, for her work in several areas. Active in her profession, she was chairman of the American Bar Associaton (ABA) Commission on Women in the Professions (1987–91); in August 1992, she paid tribute to Professor Anita Hill at an awards meeting, during the annual ABA convention, held in San Francisco. She also continued her nationwide work with the Children's Defense Fund and several other organizations, and in Arkansas in 1977 founded Arkansas Advocates for Children and Families, and in 1983–84 chaired the Arkansas Education Standards Committee.

Hillary Rodham Clinton grew up in Park Ridge, Illinois. She and Bill Clinton have one daughter, Chelsea.

FURTHER READING

"Bill Clinton and. . . ." LANDON Y. JONES, JR. and GARRY CLIFFORD. *People*, Dec. 28, 1992.

"Interview. . . ." ELEANOR CLIFT. *Newsweek*, Dec. 28, 1992.

"Hillary's kids. . . ." ROGER ROSENBLATT. *New Republic*, Dec. 14, 1992.

"First friends. . . ." HOWARD G. CHUA-EOAN. *People*, Nov. 16, 1992.

"A different kind. . . ." MARGARET CARLSON. *Time*, Nov. 16, 1992.

"Lessons of a lightning rod." MARK MILLER. *Newsweek*, Nov.–Dec. 1992.

"At home with. . . ." JILL BROOKE and BARBARA GRAUSTARK. *Metropolitan Home*, Nov. 1992.

"Who should be first lady?" CATHERINE BRESLIN and DIANA MCLELLAN. *Ladies Home Journal*, Oct. 1992.

"Hillary Clinton's. . . ." ELEANOR CLIFT. *Newsweek*, Sep. 21, 1992.

"All eyes on Hillary. " MARGARET CARLSON. *Time*, Sep. 14, 1992.

"The first lady with a career?" PATRICIA O'BRIEN. *Working Woman*, Aug. 1992.

"Hillary speaks. . . ." SHIRLEY ABBOTT. *Glamour*, Aug. 1992.

"Hillary Clinton. . . ." MARIAN BURROS. *Family Circle*, July 21, 1992.

"Hillary then and now." ELEANOR CLIFT. *Newsweek*, July 20, 1992.

"The political wife. . . ." DEIRDRE MCMURDY. *Maclean's*, July 20, 1992.

"First lady culture clash." ELEANOR CLIFT. *Newsweek*, June 8, 1992.

"What Hillary wants." GAIL SHEEHY. *Vanity Fair*, May 1992.

"The Hillary factor." MATTHEW COOPER. *U.S. News & World Report*, Apr. 27, 1992.

"Will Hillary hurt or help." GINNY CARROLL. *Newsweek*, Mar. 30, 1992.

"Entering the combat zone." MICHAEL BARONE. *U.S. News & World Report*, Mar. 30, 1992.

"H.R. Clinton's case." GARRY WILLS. *New York Review of Books*, Mar. 5, 1992.

"Running mate." KAREN S. SCHNEIDER. *People*, Feb. 17, 1992.

" 'I think we're ready.' " ELEANOR CLIFT. *Newsweek*, Feb. 3, 1992.

"Hillary Clinton. . . ." MARGARET CARLSON. *Time*, Jan. 27, 1992.

The Comeback Kid: The Life and Career of Bill Clinton. CHARLES F. ALLEN and JONATHAN PORTIS. Birch Lane/Carol, 1992.

Close, Glenn (1947–) Stage and screen star Close starred on Broadway in early 1992, opening in March in Ariel Dorfman's play *Death and the Maiden*, as Paulina Salas, a woman who takes revenge on the Latin American police officer who raped and tortured her 15 years earlier. Co-starring were Gene Hackman as torturer Dr. Miranda, and Richard Dreyfuss as her husband; Mike Nichols directed. The play received mixed reviews, but Close won a Tony for her performance in the role. She also hosted the televised Tony awards presentation in May. On television, she was among the narrators in the four-hour ABC documentary *Lincoln*, as the voice of Mary Todd Lincoln, joining Jason Robards, Richard Dreyfuss, and Ossie Davis. She also used her voice in other areas, as in an audio version of *The Legend of Sleepy Hollow*.

Forthcoming is a starring role opposite Meryl Streep, Jeremy Irons, and Winona Ryder in the film *House of the Spirits*, based on the Isabel Allende novel, set in Chile. Also forthcoming is a reprise of her role opposite Christopher Walken in *Skylark*, a sequel to the highly successful 1991 telefilm *Sarah, Plain and Tall*, in which she played a New England spinster who answers an advertisement for a mail-order bride placed by a Kansas man (Walken) with two children. Close was also to be a voice in Dave Michener's forthcoming animated film *Once Upon a Forest*.

Connecticut-born Close, on stage from the early 1970s, emerged as a stage and screen star in the 1980s, winning a Tony for her Broadway role in *The Real Thing* (1984) and playing leads in such films as *The World According to Garp* (1982), *The Big Chill* (1983), *The Natural* (1984), *Fatal Attraction* (1987), *Dangerous Liaisons* (1988), *Reversal of Fortune* (1990), *Hamlet* (1990), and *Meeting Venus* (1991). Her 1974 B.A. was from the College of William and Mary. She was previously married, to Cabot Wade and then to James Marlas, and has one child.

FURTHER READING

"Glenn Close." FRANK SPOTNITZ. *American Film*, Nov.–Dec. 1991.

"Getting Close. . . ." STEPHEN FARBER. *Connoisseur*, Aug. 1991.

"Glenn gets close." CLIFF JAHR. *Ladies Home Journal*, Jan. 1991.

Cole, Natalie (1950–) Jazz musician Nat "King" Cole was a great popular singing star in the 1940s and 1950s, who died in 1965; in the early 1990s, his daughter Natalie, herself a very popular singer, in homage to him sang many of his old songs—adding her voice to his in one song—in the album *Unforgettable*. The album was a hit, but not enormously so at first. Then, at the February 25th, 1992, 34th annual Grammy Awards ceremonies, she and the album won an unexpected six Grammy Awards, and she quite suddenly emerged as a new superstar. *Unforgettable* was Record of the Year, Album of the Year, Best-Engineered Album, Best Non-Classical, and Best Instrumental Arrangement Accompanying Vocals. "Unforgettable" was Song of the Year. Natalie Cole with Nat "King" Cole won best Traditional Pop Single. Many more awards followed, including a television Emmy nomination for best individual performance in a variety or music program for *Unforgettable, With Love: Natalie Cole Sings the Songs of Nat King Cole*, a "Great Performances" presentation occurring shortly after the Grammy awards. Forthcoming in 1993 is another album of standards.

Los Angeles-born Cole emerged as a star with her first recording, the album *Inseparable*, which included "This Will Be." She won a 1975 Grammy award as best new artist, and a 1976 Grammy as best rhythm and blues female vocalist. Always popular, but not until the early 1990s a superstar, her albums included *Natalie* (1976), *Unpredictable* (1977), *I Love You So*

(1979), *Don't Look Back* (1980), and *I'm Ready* (1983). Cole has also won a wide range of other awards, including two National Association for the Advancement of Colored People (NAACP) Image awards and an American Music Award. Her 1972 B.A. was from the University of Massachusetts. She is married to Marvin J. Yancy.

FURTHER READING

"Natalie Cole. . . ." *Jet*, Feb. 24, 1992.
"Cole, Natalie." *Current Biography*, Nov. 1991.
"The untold story. . . ." LAURA B. RANDOLPH. *Ebony*, Oct. 1991.
"Natalie Cole's. . . ." DAVID WILD. *Rolling Stone*, Sep. 19, 1991.
"Natalie Cole sings. . . ." *Jet*, June 17, 1991.

Coleman, Roger Keith (1969–92)

On May 20, 1992, Coleman was executed by the state of Virginia for the March 10, 1981 murder of his sister-in-law, Wanda Fay McCoy, at Grundy, Virginia. The execution generated yet another national controversy over the death penalty, this one over the denial of the final appeal.

Then a coal miner, with a record of having been imprisoned from 1977 to 1979 for attempted rape, Coleman was arrested a month after the murder. In early 1982, after a four-day trial, a jury took three hours to convict him of rape and murder. Ten years of appeals followed, accompanied by the entrance on his behalf of new pro bono (unpaid) public service lawyers from the large Washington law firm of Arnold and Porter. Coleman maintained his innocence to the end, and his lawyers filed appeal after appeal, making several new charges as to his allegedly inadequate representation and conviction by use of allegedly tainted evidence. Shortly before his execution, several national magazines and newspapers, including *New York Times* and *Time*, raised very serious questions on the merits of the case, questioned denial of a recent appeal on procedural grounds, and charged the Supreme Court and judiciary system with undue haste in executing Coleman. But all appeals failed, including an appeal for executive clemency denied by Virginia governor L. Douglas Wilder.

FURTHER READING

"Must this man die?" JILL SMOLOWE. *Time*, May 18, 1992.
"Dead end. . . ." JOHN TUCKER. *New Republic*, May 4, 1992.

Coles, Charles "Honi" (1911–92)

Philadelphia-born Coles was a leading tap dancer for six decades, a figure out of jazz history who was at the same time an acclaimed contemporary dancer throughout his long career. He began dancing professionally in the early 1930s, and in the two decades that followed, danced with many of the big bands of the era, including those of Cab Calloway, Duke Ellington, and Count Basie. Coles and his long-time dance partner, Choly Atkins, met while dancing with Calloway. Cole and Atkins appeared on Broadway in *Gentlemen Prefer Blondes* (1949), and Coles went on to appear in *Bubbling Brown Sugar* (1976) and *My One and Only* (1982), for the latter winning a Best Featured Actor in a Musical Tony Award and a Best Featured Actor Drama Desk Award. When tap dancing went out of style in the mid-1960s, Coles worked as a production manager at Harlem's Apollo Theater; and when tap revived, his career revived with it—now late in his career —in a few featured performances, as a guest professor at several colleges and universities, and as a tap teacher throughout the United States.

He was survived by his wife Marian Coles, a daughter, a son, a sister, and a brother. (d. New York City; November 12, 1992)

FURTHER READING

Obituary. *The Times* (of London), Dec. 28, 1992.
"Taps." MINDY ALOFF. *New Republic*, Dec. 21, 1992.
Obituary. *Variety*, Nov. 16, 1992
Obituary. *New York Times*, Nov. 13, 1992.

Collins, Phil (1951–)

Singer, drummer, and actor Collins toured widely with his rock band Genesis in 1992, deriving two related albums from the tour, jointly titled "Genesis Live: The Way We Walk." The first album, released in November 1992 was "The Shorts," a collection of material performed on previous albums, but here done from live concert versions, including such songs as "I Can't Dance." The second, forthcoming in early 1993, was to be "The Longs," a collection of such longer pieces as "Domino" and "Home By the Sea." Collins in 1992 also released the concert documentary *Phil Collins—No Ticket Required*. Collins won a nomination as Best British Male Artist in the 1992 Brits Awards. Forthcoming is a starring role opposite Hugo Weaving and Josephine Byrnes in Stephan Elliott's forthcoming film *Frauds*.

London-born Collins joined the rock band Genesis in 1971, as the group's drummer, and became lead singer in 1975, recording such albums as *And Then There Were Three* (1978), *Abacab* (1981), and *Genesis* (1983). He emerged as a major rock soloist in the 1980s, starting with the album *Face Value* (1981), followed by his Grammy-winning, Oscar-nominated song "Against All Odds (Take a Look at Me Now)," title song of the 1984 film, and the Grammy-winning album *No Jacket Required* (1985), with its number one singles "One More Night" and "Sussudio." In 1991, his "Another Day in Paradise," a song about homelessness, won the Grammy for Best Record of the Year. He starred in the film *Buster* (1988), co-writing the Grammy-winning "Two Hearts." He has been married twice, last to Jill Collins in 1984, and has three children.

FURTHER READING

Genesis of Phil Collins. SCOTT NANCE. Movie
   Publications Services, 1991.
Phil Collins. TOBY GOLDSTEIN. Ballantine, 1987.
The Phil Collins Story. JOHNNY WALLER. H. Leonard,
   1986.
Phil Collins. PHILIP KAMIN. H. Leonard, 1985.

Collor de Mello, Fernando Affonso

(1949–) In 1992, it all came apart for Brazilian President Collor de Mello. Elected as a free-enterprise fiscal reformer in 1989, he had seemed to be spending his first two years in office trying hard, though not very successfully, to solve Brazil's huge and growing economic problems, while at the same time having some success in saving the threatened Amazon Basin. In June 1992, he hosted the Rio de Janeiro Earth Summit. There had been some hints of financial irregularities in those first two years, largely because of his lavish lifestyle, which he could not possibly have maintained on his salary, savings, and government allowances, but no substantial proof had emerged.

Then, in June 1992, his younger brother accused him of being the mastermind of a web of corruption, involving payments of millions of dollars in kickbacks from companies doing business with the government, using his former campaign treasurer as his collector. Although Collor's brother quickly withdrew the charges, the Brazilian press and many legislators pur-

sued the matter—and Collor was soon accused of having received millions of dollars from an influence-selling ring that netted more than $55 million. He denied all charges, but by late August his impeachment was being demanded at large public demonstrations in many cities; on September 18, an estimated 750,000 at Sao Paulo attended the largest demonstration in Brazilian history. On September 29, Congress forced him to step aside for six months, so that an impeachment trial could proceed. On November 12, Brazil's attorney general filed formal criminal charges against him; the impeachment and criminal trial were to proceed side by side and, regardless of how they came out, Collor's career had ended. On December 29, a few minutes after his impeachment trial opened, Collor de Mello resigned his presidency, and was replaced by Vice President Itamar Franco.

Collor de Mello spent the early part of his career in his family's communications companies, becoming their president in 1978. He moved into politics in 1979, as the military government-appointed mayor of Maceió, in the state of Alagoas. He was elected to the federal legislature from Alagoas in 1982, and became governor of the state in 1986. He founded Brazil's Reconstruction Party in 1989, and was elected to the presidency in December 1989, with a program that stessed the importance of encouraging private enterprise, paying Brazil's huge international debts, and cutting social welfare programs. He took office in March 1990, succeeding José Sarney Costa. Collor de Mello attended the University of Brasilia. He was formerly married to Lilibeth Monteiro de Carvalho, is married to Rosane Malta, and has two children.

FURTHER READING

"Looting Brazil." JAMES BROOKE. *New York Times
   Magazine*, Nov. 8, 1992.
" 'I keep saying. . . .' " GERI SMITH and ELIZABETH
   WEINER. *Business Week*, May 11, 1992.
"The man and the moment. . . ." *Economist*, Dec. 7,
   1991.
"Collor de Mello, Fernando Affonso." *Current
   Biography*, Mar. 1990.
"Putting his best foot. . . ." MICHAEL S. SERRILL. *Time*,
   Jan. 1, 1990.

Connery, Sean (Thomas Connery, 1930–)

Taking up very contemporary issues indeed, Connery in 1992 starred as research scientist and jungle doctor Dr. Robert Campbell opposite Lorraine Braco as Dr. Rae Crane in John McTiernan's romance-adventure film *Medicine Man*. Set in the Amazon rainforest and shot in Mexico and Brazil, the film centers around a hard-to-reproduce cancer cure found by Connery, and simultaneously on the fate of the greatly endangered Amazon Basin rainforest, one of world's greatest environmental issues. Connery's role as an eccentric, difficult scientist was yet another demonstration of the great range and variety he has demonstrated in the later portion of his career, far beyond the stock qualities of the James Bond character that made him famous. In July, Connery received the seventh American Cinematheque Award. Forthcoming was a starring role opposite Wesley Snipes in Philip Kaufman's film *The Rising Sun*, screenplay by Kaufman and David Mamet, based on the Michael Crichton novel.

Edinburgh-born Connery was on stage and screen in small roles during the 1950s and early 1960s; he became an instant star as sex-symbol James Bond in *Dr. No* (1962), and went on to become a worldwide celebrity in six more James Bond films: *From Russia With Love* (1963), *Goldfinger* (1964), *Thunderball* (1965), *You Only Live Twice* (1967), *Diamonds are Forever* (1971), and *Never Say Never Again* (1982). But he soon became far more than a sex symbol, showing himself to be a strong and flexible actor, in such films as *A Fine Madness* (1966), *The Molly Maguires* (1970), *The Wind and the Lion* (1975), *The Man Who Would Be King* (1975), *Robin and Marian* (1976), *Cuba* (1979), *The Untouchables* (1986; winning a Best Supporting Actor Oscar), *The Name of the Rose* (1987), *Indiana Jones and the Last Crusade* (1989), *Family Business* (1989), and *The Hunt for Red October* (1990). Connery has been married twice and has one child, the actor Jason Connery.

FURTHER READING

" 'It's the books. . . .' " PETER SWET. *Parade*, May 10, 1992.
"Finely aged Scot." STEVEN GOLDMAN. *US*, Mar. 1992.
"Straight talk." JOHN H. RICHARDSON. *Premiere*, Feb. 1992.
Sean Connery: From 007 to Hollywood Icon. ANDREW YULE. Fine, 1992.
The Films of Sean Connery. ROBERT SELLERS. St. Martin's, 1991.
"A man called Connery." SUSAN SCHINDEHETTE. *People*, Dec 18, 1989.
"Sean Connery. . . ." JOHN CULHANE. *Reader's Digest*, Aug. 1989.

"Connery. . . ." BEN FONG-TORRES. *American Film*, May 1989.
Sean Connery. MICHAEL F. CALLAN. Scarborough House/Madison Books, 1985.

Connick, Harry, Jr.

Connick, Harry, Jr. (1967–) Although the quality of his work was still sharply questioned by many music critics, especially for his Frank Sinatra look-alike and sound-alike numbers, young singer, songwriter, and pianist Connick continued to pack houses on tour and produce very popular recordings in 1992. He even sang the national anthem at Super Bowl XXVI in January 1992. He was honored by his peers as well, with a Best Traditional Pop Grammy nomination.

In late November 1992, Connick issued two albums at once. One was on the occasion of his 25th birthday, and titled *25*. It contained a collection of standards, some piano and vocal, others instrumental; one notable standard was "Stardust," with Ellis Marsalis. Connick's second album was *Eleven*, recorded when he was eleven years old, in which he sings, plays the piano, and is accompanied by a Dixieland band in such songs as "Sweet Georgia Brown."

New Orleans-born jazz and pop singer, songwriter, and pianist Connick studied with James Booker, 3rd, and Ellis Marsalis (head of the Marsalis jazz clan) in his hometown while still in high school, and at the same time received much of his practical training playing the piano in French Quarter jazz clubs. Arriving in New York City at age 18, he attended the Manhattan School of Music, and, with door-opening help from Wynton Marsalis, cut his first jazz record, *Harry Connick, Jr.* (1987). A year later, at age 20, he cut his second record, *20* (1988). Then came his breakthrough soundtrack contributions to the film *When Harry Met Sally . . .* (1989), followed by the albums *Lofty's Roach Souffle* (1990), *We Are in Love* (1990), and *Blue Light, Red Light* (1991). He made his film debut in *Memphis Belle* (1990) and also appeared in *Little Man Tate* (1991).

FURTHER READING

"Connick, Harry, Jr." *Current Biography*, Nov. 1990.
"Harry's double take." BECCA PULLIAM. *Down Beat*, Oct. 1990.
"The entertainer. . . ." ROB TANNENBAUM. *Rolling Stone*, Mar. 23, 1989.

Connors, Chuck

Connors, Chuck (Kevin Connors; 1921–92) New York City-born Connors was a Boston Celtics forward and a professional baseball player before turning to films. He began his acting career in the early 1950s, in small movie roles while still playing baseball with the Los Angeles Angels. Although he appeared in more than 40 films, he is best known by far for his role as homesteader and devoted father Lucas McCain in the long-running television western series "The Rifleman," (1958–63) set in late-19th-century New Mexico. The very popular series is still seen in reruns. He also starred in the television series "Arrest and Trial" (1963–64) and "Branded" (1965–66). He won an Emmy nomination for his role as a vicious slaveowner in "Roots." Connors, a political conservative, was active in Republican politics, campaigning for his long-time friend Ronald Reagan. Three times married, he is survived by four sons. (d. Los Angeles; November 10, 1992)

FURTHER READING

"Tall in the saddle." MARK GOODMAN. *People*, Nov. 23, 1992.
Obituary. *Variety*, Nov. 16, 1992
Obituary. *The Times* (of London), Nov. 13, 1992
Obituary. *New York Times*, Nov. 11, 1992.

Connors, Jimmy

Connors, Jimmy (James Scott Connors; 1952–) Now 40-something, Jimmy Connors is no longer a serious contender in championship tennis, and his world ranking is more like 30-something. But his fans set up what the media calls the Jimbo Watch—flocking to see him wherever he plays, whoever his opponents—drawn by his sheer joy, enthusiasm, and grit, especially now that his every appearance may be his last. Nowhere is this more true than at the U.S. Open, where he has shone so often. In September, the opening round fell on his 40th birthday, and the crowded greeted him with a spontaneous chorus of "Happy Birthday." Long-timers noted that, at his first Open, Nixon was in his first term as president and Shaquille O'Neal wasn't even born. However, Connors lost to Ivan Lendl in the second round in 1992. Later in September, Connors had a $500,000 pay-per-view televised "battle-of-the-sexes"-type match against Martina Navratilova in Las Vegas, in which he had the handicap of covering part of the doubles alley and getting only one serve; he won the match, 7–5, 6–2, but some observers felt he resembled nothing so much as a past-it heavyweight fighter.

Connors already is playing a selective schedule. In May, he lost a 4-hour marathon against 23-year-old former Wimbledon champion Michael Stich in the first round. In June, he lost on opening day at Wimbledon, in what he said was probably his last appearance there. In August, he announced that he and others would be starting a new tennis circuit for over-35 players, tentatively called the Champions Tour. Connors turned his fitness regimen to new ends in 1992, with publication of a new book *Don't Count Yourself Out: Staying Fit After 35 with Jimmy Connors*, written with physician and exercise physiologist Neil Gordon.

An All-American in 1971, the year he was National Collegiate Athletic Association (NCAA) men's singles champion, Connors turned professional in 1972 and was named player of the year in 1974. He was number one in the men's world rankings for a record 159 weeks, from July 29, 1974 to August 16, 1977, and also holds the all-time record for number of tournaments won, at 109. He has had eight Grand Slam singles wins: the Australian Open (1974), Wimbledon twice (1974, 1982), and the U.S. Open five times (1974, 1976, 1978, 1982, 1983). Among his 19 doubles titles are two Grand Slams: Wimbledon (1974) and the U.S. Open (1975), both with Ilie Nastase. With Robert J. LaMarch, he wrote *Jimmy Connors: How to Play Tougher Tennis* and *Winning Tennis My Way* (both 1986). Connors attended the University of California at Los Angeles. He is married to Patti McGuire and has a son and a daughter.

FURTHER READING

"The unforgettable run." MARK PRESTON. "Learn from . . . ." NORMAN ZEITCHICK. *Tennis*, Feb. 1992.
"Ten living legends. . . ." STEVE WULF. *Sports Illustrated*, Dec. 23, 1991.
"Jimbo, part X. . . ." MIKE LUPICA. *Esquire*, Sep. 1991.
"He's baaack! . . ." CINDY SCHMERLER. *World Tennis*, June 1991.
"Jimmy Connors. . . ." MARK PRESTON. *Tennis*, May 1991.

Coppola, Francis Ford

Coppola, Francis Ford (1939–) Coppola's major 1992 film was *Bram Stoker's Dracula*, his big-budget, visually striking film adaptation of Stoker's 1897 novel *Dracula*, which Coppola directed and produced, with a cast that included Gary Oldham as the fictional Transylvanian vampire Dracula, Winona Ryder, Anthony Hopkins, and Keanu Reeves. This Dracula film stressed highly sexual and literally bloody aspects of the Dracula story; such classic earlier versions as *Nosfertatu* (1921) and *Dracula* (1931; with Bela Lugosi in the lead) were more conventional horror films. Coppola and James V. Hart co-authored the book *Francis Ford Coppola's Dracula: The Illustrated Story of the Film.*

During 1992, Coppola's American Zeotrope and Warner Bros. shot a film version of Frances Hodgson Burnett's children's story *The Secret Garden*, starring Kate Maberly as Mary Lennox and Maggie Smith as the housekeeper, scheduled for 1993 release. Coppola also added to his many awards, in March winning an American Cinema Editors' Golden Eddie award, and in September winning a special career award at the Venice Film Festival. On the financial side, Coppola went bankrupt again, for the third time in a decade, as American Zeotrope and personally.

Detroit-born Coppola is best known by far for two films: the Oscar-winning *The Godfather* (1972; he directed and co-wrote the screenplay) and the Oscar-winning *The Godfather Part II* (1974; he directed, produced and wrote the screenplay), for which he won Best Director and Best Screenplay Oscars. Together, these Sicilian-American Mafia stories are one of the greatest achievements of the American cinema; Coppola also combined them, with additional material, into a "novel for television" that some observers thought superior to the individual films. Although he created many other films, including the notable *Apocalypse Now* (1979), *Peggy Sue Got Married* (1986), and *Tucker: The Man and His Dream* (1988), nothing else even came close to duplicating the achievement of his massive Godfather films. His 1991 *The Godfather Part III* was generally received as a pale imitation of his two great films. Coppola's 1958 B.A. was from Hofstra University, and his 1968 M.A. in cinema from UCLA. He married Eleanor Neil, and has had three children, one of whom died in a boating accident in 1986. Eleanor Coppola directed *Hearts of Darkness: A Filmmaker's Apocalpyse* (1991), about the filming of *Apocalpyse Now*, with contemporary footage. Actress Talia Shire is Coppola's sister; actor Nicolas Cage is his nephew; the late Carmine Coppola, who scored *The Godfather Part II*, was his father.

FURTHER READING

"Coppola, Francis Ford." *Current Biography*, July 1991.
"Francis Ford Coppola." DAVID BRESKIN. *Rolling Stone*, Feb. 7, 1991.
Coppola. PETER COWIE. Macmillan, 1990.
On the Edge: The Life and Times of Francis Coppola. MICHAEL GOODWIN and NAOMI WISE. Morrow, 1989.
Hollywood Auteur: Francis Coppola. JEFFERY CHOWN. Praeger/Greenwood, 1988.
Francis Ford Coppola. JEAN-PAUL CHAILLET and ELIZABETH VINCENT. St. Martin's, 1985.

Cosby, Bill (1937–) The final episode of "The Cosby Show" aired on April 30, 1992; the NBC primetime series, about a middle-class African-American family, had run for eight years and had been the most popular television series of the 1980s—and Bill Cosby had become one of the most familiar faces on the world's television screens, standing in a quiet way for education, plain decency, and a good many other quite traditional American values, applied across the whole range of cultural, racial, and ethnic heritages that form the American people. The show, of course, was not over; it would go on in syndication all around the world for decades, well into the 21st century.

Neither was Bill Cosby's career over; during the autumn of 1992 he starred briefly in a syndicated new version of the old Groucho Marx quiz show "You Bet Your Life." Forthcoming was the film *The Meteor Man*, written and directed by Cosby, and co-starring Cosby and Robert Townsend. Forthcoming was much more, as well; in June, Paramount Pictures announced a multiyear contract with Cosby, to produce and star in major theatrical films and to develop other unspecified large projects. One very large project did not happen: In the autumn of 1992, Cosby began discussions as to a possible purchase of NBC from the General Electric Company, but the talks reportedly fell through.

Philadelphia-born Cosby became a television star and pioneering African-American performing artist in the thriller "I Spy" (1965–68), and went on to star in his own "The Bill Cosby Show" (1969–71), which later had a second life (1972–

73). He also became a leading solo comedy performer and recording artist, as well as starring in several films, including *Uptown Saturday Night* (1974), *Let's Do It Again* (1975), *Mother, Jugs and Speed* (1976), and *Ghost Dad* (1989). In 1984, with "The Cosby Show," he became one of the leading performers in American television, and with that also a leading celebrity. His books include *The Wit and Wisdom of Fat Albert* (1973), *Fatherhood* (1986), *Time Flies* (1987), *Love and Marriage* (1989), and *Childhood* (1991). Cosby attended Temple University; his 1972 M.A. and 1977 Ed.D. were from the University of Massachusetts. He married Camille Hanks in 1964; they have five children.

FURTHER READING

Bill Cosby. BRUCE W. CONORD. Chelsea House, 1993.
"Bill Cosby stars. . . ." *Jet*, Oct. 26, 1992.
"The Cosby Show ends. . . ." *Jet*, May 4, 1992.
"The Cosby Show's. . . ." LISA SCHWARZBAUM.
   Entertainment, May 1, 1992.
"Should celebrities be. . . ." *Jet*, Apr. 27, 1992.
Bill Cosby. SOLOMON HERBERT and GEORGE HILL.
   Chelsea House, 1992.
"Bill Cosby. . . ." MICHAEL BOURNE. *Down Beat*, Sep.
   1991.
"Cosby talks." BOB THOMAS. *Good Housekeeping*, Feb.
   1991.
Bill Cosby: The Changing Black Image. ROBERT
   ROSENBERG. Millbrook, 1991.
Cosby. RONALD L. SMITH. St. Martin's, 1987.
Bill Cosby: Family Funny Man. LARRY KETTELKAMP.
   Messner, 1987.
Bill Cosby: Superstar. PATRICIA S. MARTIN. Rourke,
   1987.
Cosby. RONALD L. SMITH. St. Martin's, 1986.
The Picture Life of Bill Cosby. BARBARA JOHNSTON
   ADAMS. Watts, 1986.

Costa Mendez, Nicanor (1922–92) Argentine lawyer and diplomat Nicanor Costa Mendez practiced law in Buenos Aires after his 1943 graduation from the University of Buenos Aires. He joined the government in 1962 as a trade advisor, and was in the early 1960s an ambassador to Chile. He was Argentina's Foreign Minister (1966–69) and delegate to the Organization of American States. He joined the Galtieri government as Foreign Minister in 1981, and as such was Argentina's chief international spokesperson during the April–July 1982 Falklands (Malvinas) War. He was removed from office with Galtieri by the Argentine military after

the war was lost. No information was available on survivors. (d. Buenos Aires; August 2, 1992)

FURTHER READING

Obituary. *The Times* (of London), Aug. 5, 1992.
Obituary. *New York Times*, Aug. 3, 1992.

Costner, Kevin (1955–) For film superstar Costner, 1992 was the year of *JFK*. He had emerged in 1990 as a superstar, in *Dances With Wolves*, and in mid-1991 had starred in *Robin Hood: Prince of Thieves*, another worldwide hit. In the 1991 Christmas season, he opened as New Orleans District Attorney Jim Garrison in Oliver Stone's highly controversial film *JFK*, and during 1992 the film ran its extraordinarily visible course throughout the world, with Costner and Jay O. Sanders providing world film history with one of its classic, enduring shots—the two men with a rifle in the Dallas Book Depository window, reenacting the event to see if Lee Harvey Oswald alone could have conceivably fired the shots that killed President John F. Kennedy.

Later in 1992, Costner starred opposite Whitney Houston in the Mick Jackson film *The Bodyguard*, as Frank Farmer, a former Secret Service agent now doing private security work, who is hired to protect popular singer Rachel Marron, played by popular singer Whitney Houston, the situation generating a love affair between the two. The film's soundtrack included the number one song, "I Will Always Love You," which Costner suggested Houston sing for the film. Scheduled was an eight-part CBS television documentary "500 Nations," a review of North American Indian history, to be narrated by Costner, who was also reportedly investing $8 million in the production. Also in 1992, Costner won British Academy of Film & Television Arts nominations as best actor and best director for *Dances With Wolves*, which had opened in Britain in 1991.

California-born Costner emerged as a film star from the mid-1980s, in *Silverado* (1985), *The Untouchables* (1987), *No Way Out* (1987), *Bull Durham* (1988), and the very popular *Field of Dreams* (1989). Costner has also published *Dances with Wolves: The Illustrated Story of the Epic Film* (1990). He attended California State University. He is married to Cindy Silva; they have three children. (For additional photo, see Spacek, Sissy.)

FURTHER READING

"Whitney Houston and Kevin Costner. . . ." *Jet*, Dec. 14, 1992.
"You asked for him!" *Teen*, Jan. 1992.
"Costner in control." EDWARD KLEIN. *Vanity Fair*, Jan. 1992.
"Into the woods. . . ." STEPHANIE MANSFIELD. *GQ—Gentlemen's Quarterly*, July 1991.
"Safe sex symbol. . . ." BARBARA LIPPERT. *M Inc.*, June 1991.
"Kevin Costner. . . ." SALLY OGLE DAVIS. *Ladies Home Journal*, Apr. 1991.
"Kevin Costner." FRED SCHRUERS. *Rolling Stone*, Nov. 29, 1990.
"Pack leader. . . ." MARJORIE ROSEN. *People*, Nov. 19, 1990.
"Dancing with the wolves." FRED SCHRUERS. *Premiere*, Oct. 1990.
"Costner, Kevin." *Current Biography*, June 1990.

Couples, Fred (1960–) American golfer Fred Couples has been coming on strong. After the 1991 season, when he won the St. Jude Classic, the B.C. Open, and the Johnnie Walker World Championship, Couples was named Professional Golfers Association (PGA) Tour Player of the Year. Then he hit 1992 like a cannon. In March he won the Los Angeles Open; tied for second at the Doral Open; lost a playoff Honda Classic; and won the Nestlé Invitational, after which he jumped from fifth to first in the world

in the Sony rankings—the first American to be ranked number one since the ratings came into use in 1985. Then in April he won his first major championship, the Masters, by two strokes over his friend and mentor Ray Floyd, to whom he had lost at the Doral and with whom he had played on the 1989 and 1991 Ryder Cup teams. Couples lost his top Sony ranking in July to Nick Faldo, who regained the lead with his win at the British Open, where Couples failed to make the cut. Though the second half of 1992 did not equal the first, Couples had numerous top-five rankings, won the Vardon Trophy with a stroke average of 69.38, and led the PGA Tour money list. Not surprisingly, he was widely tipped to repeat as PGA Player of the Year for 1992.

Before 1992, in his eleven years as a professional, Seattle-born Couples had won six tournaments, including the Tournament Players Championship in 1984, but he had been a real contender in only one major tournament, the 1990 PGA Championship, and had been considered by some to be in a "career coma," until his 1991 revival. Couples attended the University of Houston, where he played on the golf team. Late in 1992, Couples's wife, Deborah, sued for divorce, after an 11-year marriage.

FURTHER READING

"Laid back." JAMES DODSON. *Golf*, Sep. 1990.

Couric, Katie (Katherine Couric; 1957–) Sprightly Katie Couric is credited with reviving NBC's venerable "Today" show in 1992. Her presence seems to have calmed the waters, troubled since the badly handled replacement of popular Jane Pauley by Deborah Norville, who was herself replaced by Couric, at first during Norville's maternity leave from February 1991, then permanently in April 1991. "Today" may no longer be dominant, as it once was, but it has been at or near the top of the ratings since mid-1992. NBC has paid notice; Couric was signed to a new five-year contract for reportedly over $1 million a year. She has grown so popular that in a pre-election interview with Barbara Bush at the White House, President Bush appeared unexpectedly and submitted to an impromptu interview. Nor is she all fluff; she even irritated presidential candidate Ross Perot with her persistent questioning. In January 1992, Couric and Gumbel anchored a prime-time special celebrating "Today's" 40th anniversary, and featuring previous hosts, including Tom Brokaw, Hugh Downs, Barbara Walters, John Chancellor, and Pauley. Couric was also widely seen as morning host, with Dick Enberg, of NBC's coverage of the Summer Olympics at Barcelona. In May, Couric and several of her real-life colleagues attended the baby shower of their fictional counterpart on CBS's "Murphy Brown," played by Candice Bergen.

Virginia-born Couric began her career in broadcast journalism after her 1979 graduation from the University of Virginia. That year, she worked as an assistant in ABC's Washington, D.C. television news department. She joined the Cable News Network (CNN) as a Washington-based editor in 1980, and moved to Atlanta for CNN, working as an assignment editor and newscaster with the "Take Two" program. She moved to Miami's WTJI as a reporter in 1984, and back to Washington in 1986 as a reporter for WRC, an NBC affiliate. In 1989, she moved to an NBC network job, as a Pentagon correspondent, soon working as a weekend anchor and in 1990 joining the "Today" show as a national correspondent. She is married to Washington, D.C.-based attorney Jay Monahan, and has one daughter, Elinor, born in 1991.

FURTHER READING

"Katie Couric." *People*, Dec. 28, 1992.
"Catching up with. . . ." JUDY FLANDER. *Saturday Evening Post*, Sep.–Oct. 1992.
"Katie and Chris. . . ." JOANNE KAUFMAN. *Ladies Home Journal*, Aug. 1992.
" 'Don't call me perky.' " JENNET CONANT. *Redbook*, June 1992.
"Katie Couric. . . ." CHRIS CHASE. *Cosmopolitan*, May 1992.
"The Today Show's. . . ." CHARLA KRUPP. *Glamour*, July 1991.
"With Deborah Norville. . . ." TOM GLIATTO. *People*, Apr. 22, 1991.
"Heeeere's Katie! . . ." BARBARA MATUSOW. *Washingtonian*, Aug. 1990.

Courier, Jim (James Spencer Courier; 1970–) Jim Courier rose to the top of the world's tennis rankings in 1992, but his stay there was far from secure. A win at the Australian Open put him in position to take the number one spot from Stefan Edberg early in the

year, which he did in February, becoming the first American in the top spot since John McEnroe in 1985. Then he promptly lost five tournaments, losing his number one ranking after 40 days. But he regained the top spot in April after Edberg lost in the semifinals of the Suntory Japan Open in Tokyo, which Courier won. Then Courier went on a roll, winning the Hong Kong Open, the Italian Open, and the French Open, for his second Grand Slam championship of the year. He was positioned for a possible Grand Slam sweep, but it was not to be. Instead of Courier, it was Andre Agassi at Wimbledon and Edberg at the U.S. Open; in fact, Courier had no further tournament wins in the year, though he placed high several times. Still ranked number one, Courier revived in December to help the United States team capture the Davis Cup for the second time in two years. His winning play generated such excitement that Courier was carried off the field by his teammates, Agassi, Pete Sampras, and John McEnroe.

Born in Dade City, Florida, Courier began his tennis training at the Harry Hopman tennis academy at Bardmoor, Florida, then moving to the Nick Bollettieri academy. He won his first tournament, at Florida's Orange Bowl, when only 16 in 1986, and won there again a year later. He joined the professional tennis tour in 1988, but was far from being a shooting star, winning his first singles tournament at Basel, Switzerland in 1989. Courier began working with coach José Higueras in 1990, and in 1991 emerged as a world-class tennis star, as men's singles winner at the French Open, as well as at four other tournaments, and as a finalist at the U.S. Open. In that year, he jumped in the men's singles world rankings from 25th to second.

FURTHER READING

"An American in Paris." RICHARD FINN. *Sporting News*, June 8, 1992.
"Top hat." FRANZ LIDZ. *Sports Illustrated*, Feb. 24, 1992.
"Pardon his dust. . . ." WILLIAM PLUMMER. *People*, July 1, 1991.
"Jim Courier. . . ." MARK WINTERS. *World Tennis*, Feb. 1989.

Crile, George Washington, Jr. (1907–92)

The son of surgeon George Washington Crile, a founder of the Cleveland Clinic, the younger Crile began his own medical career with a residency at the Clinic after his 1929 graduation from Harvard Medical School. He began working as a surgeon at the Clinic in 1937, leaving to become a Navy doctor during World War II. He came home to the Clinic from the war with what was to become a lifelong conviction and crusade—that far too many unnecessary major surgeries were being performed, when less invasive and damaging alternatives were possible. That belief was first expressed in his work with alternative therapies for thryroid cancer. In the late 1950s, he became a powerful opponent of the then almost universal—and for many surgeons very lucrative—treatment of breast cancer by radical mastectomy: the removal of the entire breast, major associated breast muscles, and lymph nodes. He instead advocated such alternatives as partial removal, lumpectomy, and radiation therapy, proving quite conclusively that these were entirely effective procedures. For this, he was attacked and ridiculed by the medical establishment of the day. Standing firm, he published two landmark popular books that informed millions of women of their alternatives: *What Women Should Know About the Breast Cancer Controversy* (1973) and *Surgery, Your Choices, Your Alternatives* (1978). Both became important parts of a major assault on the outmoded radical mastectomy approach, which by the 1990s was being used very sparingly indeed by most highly qualified doctors, although it was still in wide use in some sections of the United

States. An autobiographical work, *The Way It Was: Sex, Surgery, Treasure, & Travel, 1907–1987*, was published shortly after his death. Crile was survived by his second wife, the former Helga Sandburg, daughter of Carl Sandburg, three daughters, a son, and a sister. (d. Cleveland; September 11, 1992)

FURTHER READING

Obituary. *The Times* (of London), Sep. 19, 1992.
Obituary. *New York Times*, Sep. 12, 1992.

Cristaldi, Franco (1924–92)

From the late 1950s a leading Italian film producer, Cristaldi produced three Oscar-winners: *Divorce, Italian Style* (1961), directed by Pietro Germi; *Amarcord* (1973), directed by Federico Fellini; and *Cinema Paradiso*, directed by Giuseppe Tornatore (1988). The first of his films to win international attention was Luchino Visconti's *White Nights* (1957). Other major films were Franco Rosi's *Salvatore Giuliano* (1962) and Mario Monicelli's *The Organizer* (1963), both starring Marcello Mastroianni; *Big Deal on Madonna Street* (1958), *Seduced and Abandoned* (1964), *The Red Tent* (1970), *Christ Stopped at Eboli* (1978), *And the Ship Sails On* (1983), and *The Name of the Rose* (1986). He was survived by his wife, actress Zeudi Araya, and two sons. He was previously long married to actress Claudia Cardinale. (d. Monte Carlo; July 1, 1992)

FURTHER READING

Obituary. *Variety*, July 13, 1992
Obituary. *The Times* (of London), July 7, 1992.
Obituary. *New York Times*, July 3, 1992.

Cristiani Burchard, Alfredo (1948–)

For El Salvador, 1992 meant the end of the 12-year-long civil war, which had cost an estimated 75,000 lives, generated mass killing by right-wing death squads, and involved aid from the United States to the government and from the Soviet Union, Cuba, and Nicaragua to the insurgents of the Farabundi Marti National Liberation Front (FMLN).

For President Cristiani, the peace treaty signed on January 16, 1992 was a personal triumph; after two years of on-and-off talks, he had succeeded in bringing a peace that even once signed was regarded very skeptically by many militants of the right and left, with both camps doubtful that it could be held together. But it did hold. The United Nations-monitored ceasefire, which took effect February 1, was preceded by a general amnesty for both sides, except for several specified especially atrocious crimes committed during the war. The FMLN agreed to disarm by October 1, in return for places in a new national police force and large cuts in army forces, including the disbanding of several elite, intelligence, and paramilitary forces, among them the sources of the worse civil war atrocities. Investigation and prosecution of some atrocities was promised. The FMLN was to become a peaceful political party. What remained to be seen at the end of the El Salvador peace process was how well the peace would hold once UN monitors were withdrawn and the FMLN had given up its arms. Much still depended on President Cristiani.

Cristiani was an executive in his family's companies before going into politics in the early 1980s. In 1985, he became leader of the right-wing Nationalist Republican Alliance Party (ARENA), succeeding Robert D'Aubuisson, under whose leadership ARENA had been widely accused of being implicated in the mass killings perpetrated by Salvadoran death squads. Cristiani was seen as a more moderate business-interests leader, and won a clear majority of those voting in the 1989 presidential elections, athough the elections were boycotted by FMLN and other armed revolutionary organizations. He attended Georgetown University, and is married to Margarita Cristiani.

FURTHER READING

"Delicate peace. . . ." *American Legion Magazine*, July 1991.
"At home with. . . ." *America*, Dec. 8, 1990.
"Cristiani, Alfredo." *Current Biography*, Jan. 1990.

Crowe, William J., Jr. (1925–) Admiral Crowe, the former Chairman of the Joint Chiefs of Staff, is the incoming chairman of President Bill Clinton's Foreign Intelligence Advisory Board, carrying forward into government the advisory role he performed during the 1992 presidential campaign. Forthcoming in 1993 was a book, *The Line of Fire: From Submarine Ensign to Chairman of the Joint Chiefs—the Politics of the Modern Military.*

Kansas-born Crowe, a career officer, was a 1947 graduate of the U.S. Naval Academy, and holds master's degree in education from Stanford University and a 1965 Ph.D. in politics from Princeton University, with a dissertation on the post-World War II British navy. He was a submarine division commander in the mid-1960s, a senior advisor to the Vietnamese navy in the Mekong delta (1970–71), in several Washington-based positions during the early 1970s, becoming rear admiral in 1973, and commander of the Bahrain-based Middle East Task Force (1976–77). He was Deputy Chief of Naval Operations (1977–80), commander of allied forces in southern Europe (1980–83), Commander-in-Chief of the Pacific fleet (1983–85), and Chairman of the Joint Chiefs of Staff (1985–89). In retirement, he became Professor of Geopolitics at the University of Oklahoma, and a much-in-demand lecturer and television commentator on military matters. He is married to Shirley Crowe; they have three children.

FURTHER READING

"Are we safe?" KEN ADELMAN. *Washingtonian*, Nov. 1989.
"There is little question. . . ." *U.S. News & World Report*, Aug. 28, 1989.
"Of war and politics." BRUCE VAN VOORST. *Time*, Dec. 26, 1988.
"Crowe, William James, Jr." *Current Biography*, July 1988.
"The military's new stars." MICHAEL SATCHELL. *U.S. News & World Report*, Apr. 18, 1988.

Cruise, Tom (Thomas Cruise Mapother IV; 1962–) In 1992, film star Cruise starred in the Rob Reiner military courtroom film *A Few Good Men*, adapted for film by Aaron Sorkin from his own long-running play. Co-starring were Jack Nicholson and Demi Moore, in a cast that included Kevin Bacon, Kiefer Sutherland, and Kevin Pollak. In the film, Cruise is a young lieutenant, defending two soldiers charged with murder; Moore is his superior, a lieutenant commander who presses him to fully defend the case; Nicholson is the Guantanamo Bay base com-

"Too live Cruise." DAVID RENSIN. *Movies USA*, June, 1992.

"Tom Cruise." PATRICK GOLDSTEIN. *Rolling Stone*, May 28, 1992.

"Irish risky." MELINA GEROSA. *Entertainment*, May 22, 1992.

Tom Cruise. MARIE CAHILL. Smithmark, 1992.

"From here to maturity. . . ." *Seventeen*, July 1991.

"A Cruise in outer space. . . ." JAN GOLAB. *California*, June 1991.

"Burn a little rubber. . . ." JEANNIE PARK. *People*, July 23, 1990.

"What's driving. . . ." JEANNE MARIE LASKAS. *Life*, June 1990.

"Cruise at the crossroads." TRIP GABRIEL. *Rolling Stone*, Jan. 11, 1990.

"Playboy interview. . . ." ROBERT SCHEER. *Playboy*, Jan. 1990.

Top Gun: The Films of Tom Cruise. ED GROSS. Pioneer, 1990.

Tom Cruise. JOLENE ANTHONY. St. Martin's, 1988.

mander who is his chief courtroom antagonist.

Cruise also starred in Ron Howard's immigration epic *Far and Away*, a story about late-19th century emigrants from Ireland to the United States, with Cruise as a young Irish tenant farmer who emigrates to America with his landlord's daughter, played by Cruise's real-life wife, Australian actress Nicole Kidman. Reviews were mixed, although the film did well at the box office.

Forthcoming was Sidney Pollack's film *The Firm*, with screenplay by Robert Towne, based on the John Grisham novel of that name. On the business side, Cruise and his business partner Paula Wagner signed a multifilm three-year agreement with Paramount Pictures.

Born in Syracuse, New York, Cruise became very popular in the early 1980s, in such films as *Risky Business* (1983), *All the Right Moves* (1983), *Legend* (1984), *Top Gun* (1986), *The Color of Money* (1986), *Rain Man* (1988), and *Days of Thunder* (1990). He won an Oscar nomination for his portrayal of disabled Vietnam War veteran Ron Kovic in Oliver Stone's *Born on the Fourth of July* (1989). He was previously married to Mimi Rogers (1987–90); he married Nicole Kidman in 1990.

FURTHER READING

"Tom Cruise." TRISH DEITCH ROHRER and TY BURR. *Entertainment*, Dec. 11, 1992.

"Crazy for each other." ELIZABETH SPORKIN. *People*, June 8, 1992.

Crystal, Billy (1947–) It was another "awards" year for star comedian Crystal. On March 30, he appeared once again before an audience of more than one billion people, as host of "The 64th Annual Academy Awards," and once again scored a hit, later winning an Emmy nomination for individual performance in a variety or music program. He also won two 1992 American Comedy Awards, as funniest actor in a movie for his role in *City Slickers*, and as best male performer in a special for his 1991 Academy Awards show.

In 1992, Crystal tried something very new for him, directing, cowriting, coproducing, and starring in the film *Mr. Saturday Night*, a fictional biofilm about forty years in the life of obnoxious comedian Buddy Young, Jr. The film received mixed reviews, and had only moderate box office success. For a fifth year, Crystal, Robin Williams, and Whoopi Goldberg joined their talents in a benefit for the homeless; their *Comic Relief V* raised more than $5 million in pledges.

New York-born Crystal worked as a comedian in cabaret in the mid-1970s, and moved into television in the long-running "Soap" (1977–81), which was followed by the short-lived "The Billy Crystal Hour" (1982). He was well received as a continuing character in the 1984–85 season of "Saturday Night Live", and has also appeared in several telefilms. He began playing film leads in the late 1980s, in *Running Scared* (1986), *Throw Momma From the Train* (1987), *Memories of Me* (1988), and *When Harry Met Sally . . .* (1989), for which he and co-star Meg Ryan won American Comedy Awards. He also shared a 1990 Emmy for Best Variety or Musical Show. With Dick Schaap, he wrote *Absolutely Mahvelous* (1986). Crystal attended Nassau Community College and New York University. He is married to Janice Crystal; they have two children.

FURTHER READING

"Billy the kid rides high." MARGARET CARLSON. *Time*, Oct. 19, 1992.

"Mahvelous Billy Crystal." DAVE STONE. *Cosmopolitan*, Oct. 1992.

" 'Scary is good'." DICK SCHAAP. *Parade*, Sep. 13, 1992.

"Billy Crystal." KENT BLACK. *Los Angeles*, Sep. 1992.

"Cover Q&A." FRANK SANELLO. *Los Angeles*, Sep. 1991.

"Billy Crystal. . . ." BARBARA GERBASI. *McCall's*, July 1991.

"Crystal, Billy." *Current Biography*, Feb. 1987.

Culkin, Macaulay (1980–) Child actor

Culkin, a great box-office draw after his worldwide high-grossing 1990 hit *Home Alone*, starred in 1992 in the sequel *Home Alone 2*. In many respects a carbon copy of the original, the sequel is set in New York City; Culkin again wins out over his very stupid bad-guy adversaries, this time with a series of more dangerous and violent tricks than in the earlier film. Chris Columbus

again directed; Joe Pesci and Daniel Stern were the villains, and Catherine O'Hara and John Heard were again the parents, in a cast that included Brenda Fricker.

Several Culkin films were forthcoming. He was set to star in Emile Ardolino's forthcoming *The Nutcracker*, an adaptation of George Balanchine's version of the Tchaikovsky ballet; in *The Pagemaster* directed by Maurice Hunt and Joe Johnston, and co-starring Christopher Lloyd, Mel Harris, and Ed Begley; and in Joel Ruben's forthcoming psychological thriller, *The Good Son*.

Culkin began his career at age four, acting in Off-Broadway plays and later appearing as a featured dancer in the New York City Ballet's annual *The Nutcracker* at Lincoln Center. His films include *Rocket Gibraltar* (1988) as Burt Lancaster's grandson, *See You in the Morning* (1989), *Uncle Buck* (1989) as John Candy's nephew, *Jacob's Ladder* (1990), *Only the Lonely* (1991), and *My Girl* (1991). Culkin comes from a theatrical family, brought onto the stage (along with his four brothers and two sisters) by his father, actor Christopher (Kit) Culkin, now his children's theatrical manager; actress Bonnie Bedelia is his aunt.

FURTHER READING

"The American man at age ten." SUSAN ORLEAN. *Esquire*, Dec. 1992.

"Baby, it's you." ZOE F. CARTER. *Premiere*, Nov. 1991.

"Macaulay Culkin." KAREN JAEHNE and KAREN KUEHN. *Interview*, July 1991.

"Macaulay Culkin. . . ." ERIC SHERMAN. *Ladies Home Journal*, May 1991.

"The kid who. . . ." MAYNARD GOOD STODDARD. *Saturday Evening Post*, Apr. 1991.

"Running away. . . ." TOM GLIATTO. *People*, Dec. 17, 1990.

Cuomo, Mario Matthew (1932–) New

York governor Mario Cuomo, who had run hot and cold about becoming a presidential candidate through much of 1991, began 1992 still very much a possible candidate, seeming to once again re-examine the question, although he had previously ruled himself out. He did little to discourage a "favorite son" movement early in the year; nor did he until quite late do anything to discourage a write-in campaign for him in the New Hampshire primary. A leading liberal, who was reported to have serious disagreements with Bill Clinton's more centrist positions on many matters, he did not endorse Clinton until the nomination fight was over, and Clinton was clearly going to the winner. Ultimately, though, he endorsed Clinton, on July 15 delivering a powerful nominating speech at the Democratic National Convention, and then backing Clinton without reservation during the campaign that followed. During the campaign, he was often mentioned as a possible Supreme Court nominee, and Clinton in a June 16th cable television appearance on MTV said that he would favor appointing Cuomo to the Court if elected.

New York-born Cuomo moved into politics after two decades as a practicing lawyer and law teacher. He was New York Secretary of State (1975–79), lieutenant governor (1979–82), and became his party's candidate and then governor in 1983, after defeating then-New York City mayor Ed Koch in a hotly contested primary campaign. He wrote of the gubernatorial contest in his *Diaries of Mario M. Cuomo: The Campaign for Governor* (1984). As governor, he became a powerful Democratic Party leader. Since his keynote address to the 1984 Democratic national convention, he has been thought to be a leading contender for the American Presidency, even though he is a much-attacked Catholic liberal who has refused to modify his pro-choice views, in spite of one Catholic cleric statement that he was "in serious risk of going to hell"

because of his pro-choice stand, and in spite of Cardinal O'Connor's later-denied threat of excommunication. Cuomo has also declined to reverse his long-standing opposition to the death penalty. Cuomo's B.A. was from St. John's College, in 1953, his LL.B. from St. John's University. He is married to the former Matilda Raffa; they have five children.

FURTHER READING

"Court test. . . ." Jeff Rosen. *New Republic*, Sep. 28, 1992.

"Message from a kibitzer." GLORIA BORGER; DAVID GERGEN. *U.S. News & World Report*, July 20, 1992.

"The man who would not run." BARBARA GRIZZUTI HARRISON. *Playboy*, July 1992.

"The coward." SIDNEY BLUMENTHAL. *New Republic*, Mar. 16, 1992.

"Why Cuomo said no." GARRY WILLS. *New York Review of Books*, Jan. 30, 1992.

"Mario's calling." JACOB WEISBERG. *New Republic*, Dec. 2, 1991.

"Cuomo's hologram. . . ." JOE KLEIN. *New York*, Oct. 7, 1991.

"The state of the governor. . . ." ELIZABETH KOLBERT. *New York Times Magazine*, Feb. 10, 1991.

"Mario the fire god." RICHARD BROOKHISER. *National Review*, May 28, 1990.

"Message for Mario. . . ." MAGIE MAHAR. *Barron's*, Mar. 12, 1990.

"Mario the magician. . . ." JOE KLEIN. *New York*, Feb. 5, 1990.

"Can Mario run?" MARTIN SCHRAM. *Washingtonian*, Jan. 1990.

Mario Cuomo: A Biography. ROBERT S. MCELVAINE. Macmillan, 1988.

Cyrus, Billy Ray (1962–) Pop country

singer Cyrus became a huge hit overnight in the spring of 1992, with his enormously popular single and video "Achy Breaky Heart," followed quickly by the album of which it was part, *Some Gave All*, which headed right for the top of the charts, and stayed at the top of the Billboard 200 chart for 17 weeks in the spring and summer of 1992, until replaced by Garth Brooks's *The Chase*. During 1992, Cyrus played everywhere to soldout audiences, getting a latter-day Elvis Presley kind of sex-symbol response from worshipful fans. His early awards included Billboard Music Video Awards as best male country artist and best new male country artist for "Achy

Breaky Heart." Forthcoming were two music specials and a primetime television film, all with ABC.

Cyrus's hometown is Flatlands, Kentucky. He attended Kentucky's Georgetown College, dropping out when he was 20 to pursue a singing career. He began singing in local bands, and spent five years trying to break into the Nashville country music industry, making his first breakthrough in 1991. He was formerly married, to Cindy Smith.

FURTHER READING

"Billy Ray Cyrus." Marjie McGraw. *Country Music*, Nov.–Dec. 1992.
"Country hunks." Marjie McGraw. *Ladies Home Journal*, Oct. 1992.
"One from the heart." Bob Cannon . *Entertainment*, July 17, 1992.

D

Dalton, Timothy (1946–) British actor Timothy Dalton appeared in another comic-strip hero role in 1992, this time as handsome, dashing Basil St. John opposite Brooke Shields as comic strip reporter Brenda Starr, in the film of that name, directed by Robert Ellis Miller. The film, made in 1986 and released six years later, was not well received, and for the careers of all concerned might well have stayed in the can. Dalton's equally ill-fated 1991 film *The Rocketeer* found its way into home video in 1992; he played Nazi villain Neville Sinclair in a comic-book-style action film set in 1938 Hollywood. Forthcoming was a starring role in the Daniel Algrant film *Naked in New York*, produced by Martin Scorsese and co-starring Whoopi Goldberg, Kathleen Turner, Eric Stolz, and Mary Louise Parker.

Wales-born Dalton made his stage debut in 1966, in British regional theater. His screen debut came in 1968, as Philip II in *The Lion in Winter*. He went on to star as Heathcliff in a 1970 remake of *Wuthering Heights*, and appeared in such films as *Mary, Queen of Scots* (1971), *Permission to Kill* (1975), *Agatha* (1979), *Sextette* (1978), *Flash Gordon* (1980), *Chanel Solitaire* (1981), and *The Doctor and the Devils* (1985), and starred in the 15th and 16th James Bond films, *The Living Daylights* (1987) and *Licence to Kill* (1989). He has also continued to appear on stage, and has played in several other television films. Dalton attended the Royal Academy of Dramatic Art.

FURTHER READING

"Dalton, Timothy." *Current Biography*, May 1988.

Daly, John (1966–) It was a year of extremes for professional golfer John Daly. After a 1991 that included his win of the Professional Golfers Association (PGA) Championship, Daly was named rookie of the year, and was acknowledged as the tour leader in driving power. With his new celebrity, he was quickly signed to write a book about his power style, *Grip It and Rip It! John Daly's Guide to Hitting the Ball Farther Than You Ever Have Before*, written with John Andrisani and published in November 1992. During 1992, Daly also had a six-stroke win at the B.C. Open, and was tied for the lead in the Kemper Open, before bogeying the last hole to come in second. Though "Long John"'s play was still powerful, and he made the cut more often than not, he experienced various disqualifications, reprimands, or withdrawals because of erratic behavior. He also took some criticism for his having played professionally in South Africa, despite the ban because of that country's discriminatory apartheid system.

Personally, Daly's life was in turmoil. In January, after a broken engagement, then-pregnant Bettye Fulford filed palimony and paternity suits against Daly. In May the couple reconciled and were married privately; their daughter,

97

Shynah Hale Daly, was born in June. Daly hit bottom in December, when he was arrested and charged with third-degree assault against his wife, after drinking at a party. He then checked into an alcohol rehabilitation facility, withdrawing from the Tournament of Champions, where he was to have started his 1993 season.

Arkansas-born Daly is a self-taught golfer, who modeled himself after golf great Jack Nicklaus. Before joining the PGA tour, he had played on the Ben Hogan circuit, a "minor league" developmental tour, where his biggest victory was the Utah Open. Daly attended the University of Arkansas. He was previously married.

FURTHER READING

"Full blast." DAVE KINDRED. *Golf*, Nov. 1991.
"A real long shot." MIKE PURKEY. *Golf*, Oct. 1991.

Daly, Tyne (1947–) Still best known to worldwide television viewers for her role as Mary Beth Lacey in the "Cagney and Lacey" series, Daly in 1992 continued to pursue her career in theater and in television guest spots. In November, Daly starred on Broadway as Madame Arkadina, opposite Jon Voight in the National Actors Theater production of Anton Chekhov's *The Seagull*, directed by Marshall Mason. She received mixed reviews in the role, with some reviewers suggesting that she might have been miscast. On stage, she also starred opposite Charles Durning in a Long Beach Civic Light Opera production of a musical version of *Queen of the Stardust Ballroom*, in the role originated by Maureen Stapleton in the 1975 television drama. Daly's television colleagues honored her once again in 1992, this time with a nomination as best guest lead actor in a comedy series for her appearance in an episode of the series "Wings." A notable 1992 guest appearance was as the alcoholic widow of the murder victim in a new episode of "Colombo."

Daly appeared in supporting stage and screen roles throughout the 1970s; she emerged as a television star as Mary Beth Lacey opposite Sharon Gless in the long-running "Cagney and Lacey" (1982–88; she won Best Actress Emmys in 1983, 1984, and 1988). In 1987, she starred in the film *Kids Like These*, directed by her husband, Georg Stanford Brown. In 1989, she starred on Broadway as Rose in the hit revival of

the musical, *Gypsy*, and in 1990 won a Tony as best actress in a musical for the role. Daughter of actor James Daly and sister of actor Timothy Daly, she attended Brandeis University and the American Music and Drama Academy. Daly and Brown have three children; they filed for divorce in 1991.

FURTHER READING

"Lacey lady. . . ." RICHARD MORRISON. *Times* (of London), June 27, 1992.
"Daly, Tyne." *Current Biography*, Mar. 1992.
"Tyne Daly. . . ." LESLIE BENNETTS. *McCall's*, Apr. 1990.

Danson, Ted (1947–) Ted Danson continued to enjoy worldwide popularity as the long-running television series "Cheers" continued through its tenth season; and his show continued to attract massive audiences, in some weeks enjoying television's top ratings. At a reported $250,000 per episode, and perhaps more, Danson also continued to be one of television's top earners. Recognition from his peers continued, as well; Danson won a 1992 Emmy nomination as best lead actor in comedy series for "Cheers." NBC seemed satisfied, as well; the network announced that the show had been renewed for the 1993–94 season. But it was not to be; Danson felt that it was "time to leave," and to end his long run as bartender Sam Malone. Late in 1992 the announcement came that the show would end after the 1992–93 season, although world audiences would continue to see it in reruns well into the next century.

Also in 1992 Danson was narrator on the audiocassette version of Dr. Seuss's *The Lorax*. Forthcoming for Danson was a starring role opposite Whoopi Goldberg in Richard Benjamin's *Made in America*. Danson also continued to work in environmental causes, especially focusing on his American Oceans campaign.

Danson worked in the New York theater and in television in the early 1970s, beginning his film career with *The Onion Field* (1979), followed by such films as *Body Heat* (1981), *Creepshow* (1983), *Just Between Friends* (1986), *Three Men and a Baby* (1987), *Cousins* (1989), *Dad* (1990), and *Three Men and a Little Lady* (1990). In 1982, he became a star of "Cheers," and won a 1990 Emmy as best actor in a comedy series. His large body of television work also includes the Emmy-winning *Something About Amelia* (1984) and the telefilm *When the Bough Breaks* (1986). Danson attended Stanford University and Carnegie-Mellon University. Previously married, he has two children.

FURTHER READING

"Three men and. . . ." JEFF ROVIN. *Ladies Home Journal*, Dec. 1990.
"Danson, Ted." *Current Biography*, Oct. 1990.

Danton, Ray (1931–92) An actor and director, Danton began his career in radio as a child, in the radio show "Let's Pretend." He worked in New York television in the early 1950s, then going to Hollywood, becoming a star opposite Susan Hayward in *I'll Cry Tomorrow* (1955). He went on to star in several films, most notably as Legs Diamond in *The Rise and Fall of Legs Diamond* (1960), as Diamond in *Portrait of a Mobster* (1961), and as George Raft in *The George Raft Story* (1961); also appearing in several other films, and in several stage roles. He also appeared in a continuing role in the television series "The Alaskans" (1959–60). Danton then began a directing career, directing and acting in Italy and France. After his return home in 1975, his work was largely as a director and producer in television. He was survived by his companion, Jeannie Austin, and by two sons. (d. Los Angeles; Feb. 11, 1992)

FURTHER READING

Obituary. *The Times* (of London), June 22, 1992.
Obituary. *Variety*, June 22, 1992
Obituary. *New York Times*, June 19, 1992.

Darby, Henry Clifford (1909–92) A leading British historical geographer, Darby began his long teaching career at Cambridge in 1931, in the 1930s also editing such works as *The University Atlas* and *The Library Atlas*, both in 1937, with H. Fullard. He worked as a naval intelligence geographer during World War II, in 1945 resuming his teaching career, at Liverpool. He later was a geography professor at University College, London (1949–66), and at King's College, Cambridge (1966–76), then retiring to become a professor emeritus. He was also a visiting professor at several American universities. His central work was *The Domesday Geography of England* (1952–77, in seven volumes). He and Fullard also published *The New Cambridge Modern History Atlas* (1975). Darby also published and edited a wide range of other works. He was survived by his wife and two children. (d. April. 14, 1992)

FURTHER READING

Obituary. *Independent*, Apr. 28, 1992.
Obituary. *The Times* (of London), Apr. 17, 1992.

Darman, Richard Gordon (1943–) Outgoing White House Director of Management and Budget Darman again fulfilled his main function early in 1992, providing the basis for President George Bush's budget proposals, submitted to Congress on January 29. This time, his deficit estimates were enormous, rather than overly optimistic, as they had been in 1991, when he had been forced to up them by 24 percent in July 1992. Indeed, they were so large that later in the year he revised them sharply downward, though at the same time he projected a steady, though slow economic recovery, a view that was clearly not shared by most voters, whose rejection of President Bush at the polls in November was based largely on the state of the economy. After the presidential election, the administration's deficit estimates were once again revised upward.

Darman's final year in office included a great deal of political comment on behalf of his President, including strong support for the failed balanced budget amendment, and election campaign attacks on Clinton and Perot economic proposals. He also spent much of his year deeply engaged in intra-administration infighting, also involving Treasury Secretary Nicholas Brady, White House Chief of Staff Samuel Skinner, and Michael Boskin, chairman of President Bush's Council of Economic Advisors. On August 18, when President Bush said that there would be "plenty of new faces" in his second term cabinet, Darman was widely guessed to be one of those who might depart.

North Carolina-born Darman is a long-term Washington "insider," who emerged as a key figure in the 1980s, as a Reagan White House assistant (1981–85) and Deputy Treasury Secretary (1985–87). He left Washington to become managing director of the Shearson Lehman Hutton investment banking firm (1987–88), and returned as Bush Adminstration Director of Office Management and Budget in 1989. Darman's B.A. and M.B.A. were from Harvard. He married Kathleen Emmet in 1967; the couple have two children.

FURTHER READING

"Life in Bush hell." JAMES PINKERTON. *New Republic*, Dec. 14, 1992.
"Head to head." S.C. GWYNNE and STEPHEN KOEPP. *Time*, Oct. 12, 1992.
"Dead wrong again. . . ." WARREN T. BROOKES et al. *National Review*, Oct. 7, 1991.
"Beasts of the beltway. . . ." FRED BARNES. *New Republic*, Dec. 24, 1990.
"Darman, Richard Gordon." *Current Biography*, May 1989.

D'Aubuisson Arrieta, Robert (1943–92)

A professional soldier, D'Aubuisson was a young officer in El Salvador's national guard during the early 1970s, and studied anti-insurgency and police tactics in several countries in that period. He was attached to the El Salvador general staff in 1975. In the late 1970s, he was chief organizer of right-wing death squads in El Salvador, then sliding into civil war. He was expelled from the army and arrested after his implication in the unsuccessful 1980 army coup, but was quickly freed, continu-ing his death squad activities. He founded the Arena political party in 1981, and was elected head of the El Salvador constituent assembly in 1982, but lost his 1984 presidential bid, and did not run again in 1989, although remaining a major force on the right. He was survived by his second wife, Luz Maria, and four children from his first marriage. (d. San Salvador; February 20, 1992)

FURTHER READING

Obituary. *Times*, Feb. 22, 1992.
Obituary. *New York Times*, Feb. 21, 1992.
" 'Absolute, diabolical terror.' " SARAH MILES and BOB OSTERTAG. *Mother Jones*, Apr. 1989.
"Letter from El Salvador. . . ." SCOTT WALLACE. *Interview*, Apr. 1989.

David, Elizabeth (1913–92)

A leading British cookbook writer, especially expert on eastern Mediterranean food and cooking, David became interested in cuisine while a student at the Sorbonne, and in Mediterranean food during World War II, after having been evacuated from Greece to Egypt. Her first work was the very well received *A Book of Mediterranean Food*; it was followed by *French Country Cooking, Italian Food, Summer Cooking,* and *French Provincial Cooking*. In the mid-1950s, she also began to write for such periodicals as *The Sunday Times* (of London) and *Vogue*. In 1965, she opened her London kitchenware shop. Later books included *Spices, Salts, and Aromatics in the English Kitchen* (1970), *English Yeast and Bread Cookery* (1977), and *An Omelette and a Glass of Wine* (1984). There were no survivors. (d. London; May 22, 1992)

FURTHER READING

Obituary. *New York Times*, May 28, 1992.
Obituary. *Independent*, May 25, 1992.
Obituary. *The Times* (of London), May 23, 1992.

Davis, Geena (Virginia Elizabeth Davis; 1957–)

Film star Davis was honored by her peers in 1992, winning best actress nominations from the Academy Awards and also the British Academy of Film & Television Arts for her role as a gun-toting feminist vigilante in the female-buddy action hit *Thelma and Louise* (1991). Dur-

"Geena. . . ." MAX VADUKUL and JAMIE DIAMOND. *Vogue*, Sep. 1992.

"Geena's sheen." KEVIN SESSUMS. *Vanity Fair*, Sep. 1992.

"Whether she's shooting. . . ." JAMES KAPLAN and TY BURR. *Entertainment*, July 24, 1992.

"Catcher in the wry." NANCY MILLS and MERLE GINSBERG. *Movies USA*, July 1992.

"Geena Davis." DAVID RENSIN. *Harper's Bazaar*, June 1992.

"An interview with. . . ." TOM HANKS. *Interview*, Mar. 1992.

"Davis, Geena." *Current Biography*, Oct. 1991.

"Ridin' shotgun. . . ." JIM JEROME. *People*, June 24, 1991.

"Straight shooter." JOE RHODES. *Harper's Bazaar*, May 1991.

"20 Questions. . . ." DAVID RENSIN. *Playboy*, Oct. 1989.

"Geena Davis. " TINA JOHNSON. *Harper's Bazaar*, Sep. 1989.

ing 1992, the film enjoyed a second hit season, this one at the top of the home video rental charts.

During 1992, Davis starred in Penny Marshall's *A League of Their Own*, a big-budget summer blockbuster that was very favorably reviewed and became a worldwide hit. It was the story of the first season of the Rockford, Illinois Peaches, a fictional Midwestern World War II-era women's baseball team, in a newly formed women's league. Davis was the team's catcher and star hitter, Lori Petty her younger sister and the team's pitcher, Madonna the team's lively centerfielder, and Tom Hanks their ex-major-league coach. Davis also starred opposite Dustin Hoffman and Andy Garcia in Stephen Frears's film *Hero*.

Massachusetts-born Davis made her film debut in *Tootsie* (1982), and went on to appear in such films as *Fletch* (1985), *Transylvania 6-5000* (1985), *The Fly* (1986), *Beetlejuice* (1988), *The Accidental Tourist* (1988; she won a Best Supporting Actress Oscar), *Earth Girls Are Easy* (1989), and *Quick Change* (1990). Her television appearances include the series "Buffalo Bill" (1983–84) and "Sara" (1985), and the telefilm *Secret Weapons* (1985). She graduated from Boston University. She was previously married to actor Jeff Goldblum (1987–91).

FURTHER READING

"Geena Davis." FRANK SANELLO. *First for Women*, Nov. 30, 1992.

Davis, Leon Julius (1906–92) Born in Russia, union leader Davis emigrated to the United States in 1921. He became a drug store clerk during the Great Depression, and in 1932 was a founder and became first organizer of Local 1199 of the Drug, Hospital and Health Care Employees Union, becoming the union's first president in 1940. In 1959, the small union, then composed only of four to five thousand drug clerks, began a very successful organizing drive among hospital workers, leading to major organizing strikes in 1959 and 1962, from which the union emerged far larger and stronger. The union went national during the late 1960s and 1970s, beginning with the long Charleston, South Carolina hospital workers strike of 1969, and ultimately reached a national membership of 150,000. In the process, state and federal restrictions on the organization of health care workers were rescinded. Davis retired from his union presidency in 1982. He was survived by his wife, the former Julia Gaberman, and two daughters. (d. New York City; September 14, 1992)

FURTHER READING

Obituary. *New York Times*, Sep. 15, 1992.

Davis, Ossie (1917–) As Ponder Blue, Davis was seen again on television throughout 1992 in the prime-time series "Evening Shade," co-starring in ensemble with Burt Reynolds,

Elizabeth Ashley, Charles Durning, Marilu Henner, Hal Holbrook, and Michael Jeter, and a considerable range of guest stars. In a far more serious vein, he was the voice of Frederick Douglass in the four-hour ABC documentary *Lincoln*, joining Jason Robards as Lincoln, Glenn Close, Richard Dreyfuss, Rod Steiger, and Frank Langella. As always, his year was varied and productive; he was also seen on screen in 1992 as a boxing trainer in Rowdy Herrington's action film *Gladiator*, about corruption in the world of underground amateur boxing. In September, Davis narrated the one-hour PBS documentary *Haiti: Killing the Dream*. October saw publication of his first novel, *Just Like Martin*.

Georgia-born Davis has been on stage for over 50 years, as actor, writer, director, and producer, and is one of the leading African-American theater figures of his time. He is best known for his creation of the Walter Lee Younger role in *A Raisin in the Sun* (1959; and the 1961 film version), opposite his wife, Ruby Dee, as Ruth Younger; and for his play *Purlie Victorious* (1961; and the 1963 film version, titled *Gone Are the Days*), in which he created the title role. He has also directed such films as *Cotton Comes to Harlem* (1970) and *Black Girl* (1972), and has acted in scores of films and telefilms, including his notable *The Emperor Jones* (1955), *Harry and Son* (1983), *Do the Right Thing* (1989), and *Jungle Fever* (1991). He appeared in continuing roles in the television series "B.L. Stryker" (1989–90). He and Dee also had a radio series,

the "Ossie Davis and Ruby Dee Story Hour" (1974–78). His other written works include *Langston: A Play* (1982) and *Escape to Freedom: A Play about Young Frederick Douglass* (1989).

Davis attended Howard University (1935–38). He and Dee married in 1948 and have worked together in the theater and as social activists ever since; they have three children, one of whom is actor-playwright Guy Davis.

FURTHER READING

"One miracle at a time." W. CALVIN ANDERSON. *American Visions*, Apr.–May 1992.

Day-Lewis, Daniel (1957–) In yet another demonstration of his extraordinary range and versatility, stage and screen star Day-Lewis in 1992 created the role of Hawkeye in Michael Mann's film version of James Fenimore Cooper's classic novel *The Last of the Mohicans*. Madeleine Stowe co-starred as Cora, and Native American activist Russell Means as the Mohican Chingachgook. The costume drama was received well by most critics, and Day-Lewis was acclaimed in the role, while the film, which opened in New York in September, went on to become a worldwide hit.

Forthcoming was a starring role as Newland Archer in Martin Scorsese's *The Age of Innocence*, based on the Edith Wharton novel, and co-starring Michele Pfeiffer and Wynona Ryder. Filmed in the spring of 1992, the movie was orig-

inally scheduled for Christmas 1992 release but was rescheduled for the autumn of 1993.

Day-Lewis emerged as a leading dramatic actor in several late 1980s films, including *My Beautiful Laundrette* (1985), *A Room With a View* (1985) and *The Unbearable Lightness of Being* (1988). In 1990, he won a Best Actor Oscar and best actor awards from the British Academy, the National Society of Film Critics, and the New York and Los Angeles critics' circles for his performance in *My Left Foot*, as the late Christy Brown, a gifted Irish writer and painter so severely afflicted by cerebral palsy that he had sure control over only his left foot. In 1989, Day-Lewis starred in Richard Eyre's production of *Hamlet* at Britain's National Theatre. He attended the Old Vic Theatre School. He is the son of writer Cecil Day-Lewis and actress Jill Bolcom.

FURTHER READING

"Actor from the shadows. . . ." JOAN JULIET BUCK. *New Yorker*, Oct.12, 1992.
"The intensely imagined life. . . ." RICHARD B. WOODWARD. *New York Times Magazine*, July 5, 1992.
"Day-Lewis, Daniel." *Current Biography*, July 1990.
"Risk taker supreme. . . ." MATTHEW GUREWITSCH. *Connoisseur*, Dec. 1989.
"Getting the skinny. . . ." CHRISTINA DE LIAGRE. *Interview*, Apr. 1988.
"Daniel Day-Lewis. . . ." DAVID HUTCHINGS. *People*, Feb. 22, 1988.
" 'I bring you. . . .' " HARLAN KENNEDY. *Film Comment*, Jan.–Feb. 1988.
"Day-Lewis' brood. . . ." STEPHEN SCHAEFER. *Harper's Bazaar*, Jan. 1988.

Dee, Ruby (Ruby Ann Wallace, 1924–)

Now into her sixth decade in the theater, and if possible getting better as she grows older, Dee created the central role in Adrienne Kennedy's new play, *Ohio State Murders*, directed by Gerald Freedman, which opened on March 7 at Cleveland's Ohio Theater. Her own play, an adaptation of Rosa Guy's novel *The Disappearance*, was scheduled to open in regional theater in 1993. On television, she narrated Marlon T. Riggs's documentary, *Color Adjustment*, an angry and revealing examination of African-American television images, from the early days of the medium until now. She also continued in guest roles, as in the September miniseries "Middle Ages."

Cleveland-born Dee began her career in 1941, with the American Negro Theater. Some of her most notable stage roles were in *Anna Lucasta* (1946); opposite Ossie Davis in *Jeb* (1946); as Ruth Younger, again opposite Davis, in *Raisin in the Sun* (1959; both also appeared in the 1961 screen version); and again opposite Davis in *Purlie Victorious* (1961; both appeared in the 1963 film, titled *Gone Are the Days*); and in *Boesman and Lena* (1970), *Wedding Band* (1972), and in several classic roles at the Stratford American Shakespeare Festival. Among her other films are *The Balcony* (1963), *Buck and the Preacher* (1972), *Do the Right Thing* (1989), and *Jungle Fever* (1991). Dee has also often appeared on radio and television, perhaps most notably in the radio series, the "Ossie Davis and Ruby Dee Story Hour" (1974–78), which she also coproduced, and in an American Playhouse production on Zora Neale Hurston (1990), writing, narrating, and starring in the title role. She has written a volume of poetry, *Glowchild* (1972), children's books such as *Two Ways to Count to Ten* (1988) and *The Tower to Heaven* (1991), and a wide range of short stories and essays. Dee's 1945 B.A. was from New York's Hunter College. She married Davis in 1948; they have three children, one of whom is actor-playwright Guy Davis.

FURTHER READING

"One miracle at a time." W. CALVIN ANDERSON.
American Visions, Apr.–May 1992.

De Klerk, Frederik Willem (1936–)

Buffeted by a series of government scandals, reviled by a diehard right-wing minority, caught in the crossfire created by the African National Congress (ANC)-Inkatha civil war, South African Prime Minister De Klerk in 1992 still pursued his attempt to peacefully dismantle the apartheid system, bring South Africa back into the world community, and transform South Africa into a multiracial constitutional democracy. It remained an extraordinarily difficult process, even though he had made giant strides since his release of the ANC leaders, legalization of the ANC, and negotiation of a lasting ceasefire only two years before. Yet he was still able to move the process, although it slowed to a crawl after the ANC suspended talks and went over to mass demonstrations following the June 1992 Boipatong massacre. In the months that followed, De Klerk made concession after concession, ultimately agreeing to effectively disarm the Inkatha militants by prohibiting the carrying of arms in public. In return, the ANC agreed to return to the bargaining table, and in November even made a historic offer to share power with the White minority even after the coming of majority rule in South Africa, a major concession never before offered. On December 19, De Klerk dismissed six generals and seventeen other officers for covert activities aimed at opposition movements, including assassinations. Yet De Klerk's position was far from secure, as threats from the right continued and grew when terrorists of the splinter Azanian Peoples Liberation Army began murderous attacks on Whites late in the year.

De Klerk continued to bring South Africa back into the human family, making state visits to Russia, Japan, and several other European and African countries during 1992. South African participation in the 1992 Barcelona Olympics, after years of international boycotts, was very meaningful at home, bolstering his position.

De Klerk practiced law in the 1960s and early 1970s, and was elected to the national assembly in 1972. He became Transvaal leader of the ruling National Party in 1982. He held several cabinet posts from the mid-1970s, was education minister in the government of Pieter Willem Botha, and succeeded Botha as head of the National Party in February 1989. Botha resigned as president in August 1989; De Klerk became acting president, and was named to a full five-year presidential term in September, bringing with him a new spirit of reconciliation between the races. In October 1989, De Klerk released eight long-term political prisoners, including Walter Sisulu and six other ANC leaders, and Jafta Masemola of the Pan Africanist Congress. On February 2, 1990, he legalized the ANC and several other outlawed organizations, and on February 11 freed ANC leader Nelson Mandela, opening a new chapter in South African history. On August 7, 1990 the ANC agreed to a full ceasefire, bringing 30 years of guerrilla war to an end. The government in turn agreed to free many more political prisoners, allow many exiles to freely return home, and relax several repressive laws, and lived up to its promises. Frederik De Klerk attended Potchefstroom University. He married Marike Willemse in 1959; they have three children.

FURTHER READING

" 'The road of conflict. . . .' " LALLY WEYMOUTH.
Newsweek, Sep. 28, 1992.
" 'Our struggle is. . . .' " BARRY SHELBY. *World Press Review*, May 1992.
" 'No racism in the New South Africa.' " *Newsweek*, Mar. 2, 1992.
"Great black hope." *Economist*, Feb. 29, 1992.
Politics in South Africa: From Vorster to de Klerk.
IAN DERBYSHIRE. CKG Publications, 1992.
"The mandate for. . . ." ARNAUD DE BORCHGRAVE.
Insight, July 2, 1990.
"After apartheid. . . ." COLIN VALE and R.W. JOHNSON.
National Review, Oct. 15, 1990.
"The authoritarian center. . . ." SANFORD J. UNGAR.
New Republic, Oct. 1, 1990.
"de Klerk, Frederik Willem." *Current Biography*, Feb. 1990.

Delerue, Georges (1925–92)

A prolific composer in many musical forms, Delerue was best known by far for his film music. He scored more than 160 films, winning a 1979 Oscar for *A Little Romance*, and won Oscar nominations for *Anne of the Thousand Days* (1969), *The Day of the Dolphin* (1973), and *Julia* (1977). Much of his early work was with the French New Wave film directors, for such films as Francois Truffaut's *Shoot the Piano Player* (1960), *Jules and Jim* (1961), *The Soft Skin* (1964), *Day For Night* (1973), and *The Last Metro* (1980), and with such directors as Philippe de Broca, Agnes Varda, Julien Duvivier, Claude Berri, and Louis Malle. Abroad, his work included such major films as *A Man For All Seasons* (1966), *The Day of the Jackal* (1973), *The Conformist* (1970), *Platoon* (1986), *Crimes of the Heart* (1986), and the forthcoming Pierre Schoendorfer film *Dien Bien Phu*. Delerue was a Commander of Arts and Letters, a French cultural award. He was survived by his wife, Micheline Gautron, and two daughters. (d. Los Angeles; March 20, 1992)

FURTHER READING

Obituary. *Variety*, Mar. 31, 1992
Obituary. *The Times* (of London), Mar. 24, 1992.
Obituary. *New York Times*, Mar. 23, 1992.

Demme, Jonathan (1944–)

The extraordinary success of Demme's *The Silence of the Lambs* became apparent in 1992, as it won a string of major awards. The film starred Jodie Foster as FBI agent Clarice Starling, opposite Anthony Hopkins as imprisoned psychopathic killer Dr. Hannibal "the Cannibal" Lecter, whom Starling consults in prison for help in finding a psychopathic killer still at large. Demme directed from Ted Tally's screenplay, based on the Thomas Harris novel. In an extraordinary sweep of the top Academy Awards, the film was named best picture, Demme was named best director, Foster and Hopkins won best actress and actor, and Ted Tally won for best adapted screenplay. Demme also won a Directors Guild of America best feature film award, and several other major awards and nominations. A sequel is being planned.

In an entirely different vein, Demme directed *Cousin Bobby*, a documentary about his cousin the Rev. Robert Castle, a White Episcopal priest whose main work is in Harlem's African-American and Hispanic-American communities. Demme was also directing the forthcoming film *People Like Us*, starring Tom Hanks, Denzel Washington, and Mary Steenburgen. He was also producing the forthcoming film *Amos and Andrew*, directed by E. Max Frye and starring Nicolas Cage.

Long Island-born Demme began his film career in the late 1960s, as a writer in the publicity departments of several film companies and *Film Daily*, and as a producer of television commercials. He cowrote and coproduced several Roger Corman films in the early 1970s, and made his feature film directorial debut with *Caged Heat* (1974). He went on to direct such films as *Crazy Mama* (1975), *Melvin and Howard* (1980), *Swing Shift* (1984), *Something Wild* (1986), *Swimming to Cambodia* (1987), *Married to the Mob* (1988), and *Miami Blues* (1990). He attended the University of Florida. He is married to Joanne Howard; they have one child.

FURTHER READING

"Only lambs are silent." ELIZABETH GLEICK. *People*, June 22, 1992.
"Heavy estrogen." GARY INDIANA. *Interview*, Feb. 1991.
"Identity check." GAVIN SMITH. *Film Comment*, Jan.–Feb. 1991.

Deneuve, Catherine (Catherine Dorléac; 1943–)

In the spring of 1992, Deneuve opened in Régis Wargnier's film *Indochine*, an adventure-romance set in 1930s Indochina, then a French colony. Deneuve starred as Eliane, a French plantation owner, opposite Linh Dan Pham as her adopted Indochinese daughter and Vincent Perez as the French naval officer who has a love affair with the mother and then with the daughter, who has a son with him. Later, Eliane raises their son, and is about to introduce him to his mother at the end of the film, in a flashforward to three decades later, when the daugher has become a Communist Vietnamese leader. Deneuve was also starring in a forthcoming sequel, *Dien Bien Phu*, the story of the siege that effectively ended French involvement in Vietnam, Laos, and Cambodia.

Deneuve, for many years active in Amnesty International on behalf of the world's political prisoners, dedicated the November Los Angeles premiere of *Indochine* to that organization. In 1992, she also starred opposite Philippe Noiret in the Amnesty International film *Against Oblivion*, a plea for the freedom and humane treatment of the world's political prisoners; it opened at the August Montreal film festival.

One of the leading actresses of the French cinema and a major international star, Deneuve is the child of a theater family, her father Maurice Dorléac and her older sister Francois Dorléac. She made her film debut at the age of 13, in 1956, and emerged as a star in Jacques Demy's *The Umbrellas of Cherbourg* (1963). Some of her best known starring roles were in Roman Polanski's *Repulsion* (1965), Luis Bunuel's *Belle de Jour* (1967) and *Tristana* (1970), *Donkey Skin* (1971), and *The Last Metro* (1980). She was formerly married to photographer David Bailey, and has two children, their fathers Roger Vadim and Marcello Mastroianni.

FURTHER READING

"Catherine Deneuve. . . ." SALLY KOSLOW. *Woman's Day*, June 20, 1989.
"Conversation with. . . ." CHARLOTTE AILLAUD. *Architectural Digest*, Jan. 1989.
Bardot, Deneuve, Fonda: An Autiobiography. Roger Vadim. Simon & Schuster, 1986.

Deng Xiaoping

Deng Xiaoping (T'eng Hsiao-ping; 1904–) At 88 still China's undisputed leader, Deng seemed in 1992 to be once again trying the volatile combination of economic liberalization and political repression that had resulted in the the 1989 Tienanmen Square massacre. In January, he made a highly publicized trip to the southern province of Guangdong, publicly approving the pace and nature of the market reforms being introduced. Then, in a series of major defeats for hardline economic conservatives, in early March he pushed through China's Politiburo his program of sharply increased economic development. Premier Li Peng followed up with strong endorsement of his policies at the late March National People's Congress. Part of the plan was a go-ahead for the controversial Three Gorges Dam on the Yangtze River, a focus of worldwide environmental concern. At the same time, speaking through Li Peng and others, Deng continued to call for repression of all political dissent. Time will tell whether the Chinese leadership will be more successful on that score this time than they were during the last wave of economic liberalization.

Deng continued to develop the same twin themes throughout the year, as reflected most notably at the 14th National Communist Party Congress (October 12–18). Like Premier Li Peng, Party General Secretary Jiang Zemin called for major increases in the rate of economic growth, to be achieved largely through liberalization, while at the same time stressing the unquestioned authority of the Communist Party; the new Politburo reflected those views. Deng, reportedly in very poor health, did not attend the congress, making a brief ceremonial appearance afterward. The question of Deng's health and his ability to rule much longer continued to stimulate great speculation in China and abroad, for after Deng, China once again will face the question of succession, in a world that has just seen the Soviet empire dissolve.

Deng joined the Communist Party of China in the 1920s, while a student in France. He fought through the whole length of the Chinese Civil War (1927–49) and is a survivor of the 1934 Long March. During Communist ascendency, he became a major moderate leader, was purged twice (1973 and 1976), and survived to become the primary leader of Chinese communism. Deng attended the French School in Chongqing, studied in France during the 1920s, and attended Moscow's Far Eastern University. He married Cho Lin; the couple had five children.

FURTHER READING

"Deng's new hope: China." *Economist*, Oct. 24, 1992.
"Can Deng square the circle?" BRIAN CROZIER. *National Review*, July 6, 1992.
The New Emperors: China in the Era of Mao and Deng. HARRISON E. SALISBURY. Little, Brown, 1992.
China Under Deng Xiaoping: Political and Economic Reform. DAVID WEN-WEI CHANG. St. Martin's, 1991.
Politics of Disillusionment: The Chinese Communist Party under Deng Xiaoping, 1978–1989. HSI-SHENG CH'I. M.E. Sharpe, 1991.
"Rise of a perfect apparatchik. . . ." WILLIAM R. DOERNER. *Time*, July 10, 1989.
"An unlikely 'emperor.'" MARY NEMETH and LOUISE DODER. *Maclean's*, May 29, 1989.
Deng Xiaoping. ULI FRANZ. Harcourt Brace, 1988.

Deng Yingchao

Deng Yingchao (1904–92) A leading Chinese communist, Deng became a left revolutionary while still a teenager, in 1919 joining in the May Fourth Movement and that year meeting Zhou Enlai (1898–1976), a key figure in Chinese communism for more than five decades. She joined the Communist Party in 1924, and in 1925 married Zhou. With him, she was at the center of the Chinese civil war and anti-

Japanese war, and remained a Communist leader uninterruptedly throughout her lifetime. During Zhou's lifetime, she was active in Communist Party women's groups, but was not otherwise a public figure, although she was a Central Committee member from 1969. In 1978, she joined the Communist Politburo. She resigned her active positions in 1985. A conservative, she supported the violent repression of the 1989 Tienanmen Square student demonstrations. There were no direct survivors, though she and Zhou Enlai adopted several children. (d. Beijing; July 11, 1992)

FURTHER READING

Obituary. *The Times* (of London), July 13, 1992.
Obituary. *New York Times*, July 12, 1992.

Robert De Niro (right) and Jessica Lange.

De Niro, Robert (1945–) De Niro won a

1992 Best Actor Oscar nomination for his role as Max Cady in *Cape Fear* (1991), and in 1992 appeared in another highly regarded starring role, as Harry Fabian, a small-time New York ambulance-chasing lawyer, opposite Jessica Lange in Irwin Winkler's *Night and the City*. The film was the closing feature at the October New York Film Festival. He also played a cameo role in, and was executive producer of, Barry Primus's comedy-drama *Mistress*, set on the

fringes of the movie business in modern Hollywood. On August 31, he began shooting *A Bronx Tale*, in which he makes his directorial debut and stars opposite Chazz Palminteri, who wrote the film's screenplay, based on his own play.

De Niro also produced Michael Apted's *Thunderheart*, the story of a Native American FBI agent torn between conflicting loyalties during a murder investigation on a Sioux reservation, starring Val Kilmer. Forthcoming were *This Boy's Life*, a film based on Tobias Wolff's 1950s autobiographical novel; and John MacNaughton's *Mad Dog and Glory*, produced by Martin Scorsese.

On the personal side, De Niro won a child support suit brought against him by Nina Lisandrello, after blood tests found that he was not the father of her child.

New York-born De Niro became one of the leading actors of the American cinema in the mid-1970s, beginning with his strong supporting roles in *Bang the Drum Slowly* (1973), *Mean Streets* (1973), and as the young Vito Corleone in *The Godfather Part II* (1974), for which he won a Best Supporting Actor Oscar. He went on to star in *Taxi Driver* (1976), *The Deer Hunter* (1978), and *Raging Bull* (1980), for which he won a Best Actor Oscar. In the 1980s, he starred in such films as *Once Upon a Time in America* (1984), *Brazil* (1985), *Midnight Run* (1988), *We're No Angels* (1989), and *Stanley and Iris* (1989). He began the 1990s on two very high notes, in *Goodfellas* (1990) and *Awakenings* (1990), following them with *Guilty by Suspicion* and *Backdraft* (both 1991). He was previously married and has two children.

FURTHER READING

"Awake and sing." FRED SCHRUERS. *Premiere*, Jan. 1991.
"De Niro. . . ." *Video Review*, Mar. 1989.
Robert De Niro: The Hero Behind the Mask. KEITH McKAY. St. Martin's, 1986.

Dennehy, Brian (1939–) In October

1992, the American film, television, and stage star Brian Dennehy opened as Hickey in Eugene O'Neill's *The Iceman Cometh*, at Dublin's Abbey Theatre, in a highlight of the Irish theater season and of his own still-developing career. During the year, he also appeared in several television and theatrical films. In February, he played in a strong supporting role in the television film *Burden of Proof*, a film adaptation of Scott Turow's second novel, winning a Best Supporting Actor Emmy nomination in the role. He also won a nomination as best actor in a miniseries or special, for *To Catch a Killer*. In June, he starred as a police officer opposite Kate Nelligan and Ben Cross in the television thriller *The Diamond Fleece*, revolving around the fate of a large and very valuable diamond. In September, he starred opposite Eli Wallach and Robert Prosky in the title role of the HBO television film *Teamster Boss: The Jackie Presser Story*, and in November he was an honest Chicago cop in *Deadly Matrimony*. In theatrical release was the Rowdy Herrington film *Gladiator*, about the often-crooked world of professional boxing, starring Dennehy as a boxing promoter and Ossie Davis as a trainer.

Connecticut-born Dennehy saw service with the Marine Corps in Vietnam. In the mid-1970s, he emerged as a strong supporting player in a wide range of character roles on stage and screen, with a notable role off-Broadway in *Streamers* (1976) and his film debut in *Semi-Tough* (1977). He became best known for such films as *F.I.S.T.* (1978), *First Blood* (1982), *Gorky Park* (1983), *Never Cry Wolf* (1983), *Finders Keepers* (1984), *Cocoon* (1985), *Silverado* (1985), *F/X* (1986), *Legal Eagles* (1986), *Return to Snowy River* (1988), *Miles from Home* (1988), *Cocoon: The Return* (1988), *The Last of the Finest* (1989), and *Presumed Innocent* (1990). He has also appeared in the television series "Big Shamus, Little Shamus" (1979), and "Star of the Family" (1982–83), as well as several television films. Notable stage appearances were in *The Cherry Orchard* (1988) and *The Iceman Cometh* (1990). Dennehy is a graduate of Columbia University and did postgraduate work at Yale University. He is married and has three children.

FURTHER READING

"Brian Dennehy. . . ." BOB DALY. *Chicago*, Sep. 1990.
"Heavy duty." JEAN NATHAN. *Interview*, Mar. 1990.
"They call him. . . ." MARION LONG. *GQ—Gentlemen's Quarterly*, May, 1989.

Dennis, Sandy (Sandra Dale Dennis; 1937–92) Nebraska-born Dennis studied at the Actors Studio and worked on the New York stage in the late 1950s. On Broadway, she won a 1963 Best

Supporting Actress Tony opposite Jason Robards in *A Thousand Clowns*, and a 1964 Best Actress Tony for *Any Wednesday*. She made her film debut in *Splendor in the Grass* (1961) and won a Best Supporting Actress Oscar in *Who's Afraid of Virginia Woolf* (1967). Other starring film roles were as the New York City schoolteacher in *Up the Down Staircase* (1967) and opposite Jack Lemmon in *The Out-of-Towners* (1970), as well as *The Fox* (1967), *Come Back to the Five and Dime, Jimmy Dean, Jimmy Dean* (1982), *The Four Seasons* (1981), *Parents* (1989), and *The Indian Runner* (1990). Dennis also appeared in several television films and series. She was survived by her mother and brother. (d. Westport, Connecticut; March 2, 1992)

FURTHER READING

Obituary. *People*, Mar. 16, 1992.
Obituary. *Variety*, Mar. 9, 1992.
Obituary. *The Times* (of London), Mar. 6, 1992.
Obituary. *New York Times*, Mar. 5, 1992.
"Sandy Dennis." DAVID HUTCHINGS. *People*, Mar. 13, 1989.

Depardieu, Gérard (1948–   ) In the year of the 500th anniversary of the Columbus voyage, French film star Depardieu starred as Christopher Columbus in the long-awaited Ridley Scott epic film *1492: Conquest of Paradise*, opposite Sigourney Weaver as Queen Isabel and Armand Assante as Sanchez. The film received mixed reviews, ranging from mild praise of its photography and Spanish and Costa Rican sites and the work of its stars to generally negative feelings as to its depth and perceived lack of liveliness. But its box-office response was not equivocal: the very expensive blockbuster film was a resounding box-office failure for whatever the reasons, whether because of overwork of the Columbus theme, generally disapproving reevaluation of the European conquest of the Americas, or the quality of the film itself.

On a considerably happier note, Depardieu won a British Academy of Film and Television Arts Best Actor nomination for his highly acclaimed title role in *Cyrano de Bergerac*. In November 1992, his 1991 film *Tous les Matins du Monde* opened in New York. Forthcoming was an environmentally oriented film, *Welcome to Veraz*, directed by Xavier Castano and shot in southern France in late 1990, also starring Kirk Douglas.

The seeming antithesis of a romantic star, with his chunky physique, skewed nose, and lantern jaw, French-born Depardieu burst on the French film scene as an amoral *Easy Rider*-style juvenile delinquent in *Going Places* (1974) and then emerged as a leading French actor of the 1970s and 1980s, making over 60 films, including *Stavisky* (1974), *1900* (1976), *Get Out Your Handkerchiefs* (1978), *The Last Metro* (1980; he won the French César award as best French actor), *My American Uncle* (1980), *Danton* (1982), *The Return of Martin Guerre* (1982), *Tartuffe* (1984), *Jean de Florette* (1986), *Green Card* (1990), *Cyrano de Bergerac* (1990), *Too Beautiful for You* (1990), *Camille Claudel* (1990), and *Uranus* (1991). He also became a substantial theater actor in France, and has appeared on television. He is married to the actress, singer, and songwriter Elisabeth Guignot; they have one daughter and one son.

FURTHER READING

"Gerard Depardieu. . . ." Tom Conroy. *Rolling Stone*, Mar. 7, 1991.

"Gerard Depardieu. . . ." Jeannie Park. *People*. Feb. 4, 1991.

"Life in a big glass. . . ." Richard Corliss. *Time*, Feb. 4, 1991.

"Deciphering Depardieu." Paul Chutkow. *Vogue*, Dec. 1990.

"Gerard Depardieu." Stephen O'Shea and Brigitte Lacombe. *Interview*, Dec. 1990.

"Depardieu, Gerard." *Current Biography*, Oct. 1987.

Dern, Laura Elizabeth (1967–) The up-and-coming American actress was part of a very notable "first" in 1992; she and her mother, Diane Ladd, won Oscar nominations as best actress and best supporting actress respectively for their roles in Martha Coolidge's *Rambling Rose*, co-starring Robert Duvall. Dern played a wild, straightforward, highly sexually-charged poor girl, working as a live-in maid. Dern also won an Emmy nomination as best leading actress in a miniseries or special for her starring role in the television film *Afterburn*, as the widow of a pilot who died in a jet fighter crash; she ultimately redeems his reputation and exposes Air Force coverup of the plane's faulty design.

Forthcoming was a leading role in Stephen Spielberg's sci-tech special-effects blockbuster *Jurassic Park*, co-starring Sam Neill, Jeff Goldblum, and Richard Attenborough, scheduled for release in the summer of 1993. The film, based on Michael Crichton's novel, about modern, genetically engineered theme park dinosaurs that become a menace, began shooting on Hawaii's Kauai on August 24; cast and crew were trapped on the island briefly after a disastrous early-September hurricane.

Santa Monica-born Dern, the daughter of actors Bruce Dern and Diane Ladd, began her professional career as a teenager, in such films as *Foxes* (1980) and *Ladies and Gentlemen, the Fabulous Stains* (1982). She became a juvenile lead in *Mask* (1985), *Smooth Talk* (1985), and in David Lynch's exploration of the seamy side of American smalltown life, *Blue Velvet* (1986). She emerged a star as Lula Pace Fortune opposite Nicolas Cage as Sailor Ripley in Lynch's *Wild at Heart* (1990). She attended the Lee Strasberg Institute in Los Angeles and London's Royal Academy of Dramatic Art.

FURTHER READING

"Laura Dern." BART BULL. *Harper's Bazaar*, June 1992.

"Wild innocent." MARK ROWLAND. *American Film*, July 1991.

"Screen veteran Bruce Dern and. . . ." MARJORIE ROSEN. *People*, Oct. 8, 1990.

"Childhood's end." PHOEBE HOBAN. *Premiere*, Sep. 1990.

"Laura Dern." GARY INDIANA; KURT MARKUS. *Interview*, Sep. 1990.

"Behind her blue eyes." LAURIE OCHOA. *American Film*, Oct. 1989.

Deutsch, Helen (1907–92) Best known as a screenwriter, Deutsch began her career in 1927, as manager of the Provincetown Players, and co-authored the book *The Provincetown* in 1931. She then worked as a New York theater critic and writer in the 1930s and early 1940s, and was an organizer of the New York Drama Critics Circle. Her first screenplay was the co-written *National Velvet* (1944), starring Elizabeth Taylor, followed by *The Seventh Cross* (1944), a Spencer Tracy vehicle. She won an Oscar nomination for the screenplay of *Lili* (1953), which won Cannes Festival, Writers Guild of America, and Golden Globes awards for the screenplay. Other major films included *King Solomon's Mines* (1950), *I'll Cry Tomorrow* (1956), and *The Unsinkable Molly Brown* (1964). She wrote the screenplay for *Valley of the Dolls* (1967), but disclaimed credit after script alterations, breaking with MGM and leaving Hollywood. She also wrote for television. There were no survivors. (d. New York City; March 15, 1992)

FURTHER READING

Obituary. *The Times* (of London), Apr. 9, 1992.
Obituary. *Variety*, Mar. 30, 1992
Obituary. *New York Times*, Mar. 17, 1992.

DeVito, Danny (Daniel Michael DeVito; 1944–   ) Actor, director, and producer DeVito starred as the Penguin, opposite Michael Keaton as Batman and Michelle Pfeiffer as the Catwoman, in Tim Burton's 1992 blockbuster *Batman* sequel, *Batman Returns*, which went on to become a worldwide commercial hit. Also co-starring were Christopher Walken, Michael Gough, Pat Hingle, and Michael Murphy.

Devito also directed, coproduced, and co-starred in *Hoffa*, a biographical film about the rise of corrupt Teamsters Union president Jimmy Hoffa, who disappeared in 1975, and was thought to have been kidnapped and murdered, probably by criminals who were former associates. In the film, which opened late in the year, Jack Nicholson starred as Hoffa opposite DeVito as his associate Bobby Ciaro, in a cast that included Armand Assante, J. T. Walsh, John C. Reilly, and Robert Prosky. Reviews were mixed, though some were strongly favorable, and the film did not find immediate commercial success.

Still forthcoming was a starring role in Marshall Herskovitz's *Jack the Bear*, playing the newly widowed father of two young boys, who moves to California and becomes a late-night television horror film host.

New Jersey-born DeVito was a New York stage actor before making his main career in Hollywood. He appeared in such off-Broadway productions as *The Man With a Flower in His Mouth* (1969) and *One Flew Over the Cuckoo's Nest* (1971), recreating his role in the 1975 film version, and went on to such films as *Car Wash* (1976), and *Goin' South* (1978). Then came his role as Louie DePalma in the long-running television series "Taxi" (1978–83), for which he won a 1981 Emmy, and roles in such films as *Terms of Endearment* (1983), *Romancing the Stone*

(1984), *Jewel of the Nile* (1985), *Ruthless People* 1986, and starring roles in *Tin Men* (1987), *Throw Momma from the Train* (1987; he also directed), *Twins* (1988), and *Other People's Money* (1991). In 1989, he directed and co-starred in *The War of the Roses*. DeVito is married to actress Rhea Perlman, and has three children.

FURTHER READING

"Danny DeVito. . . ." MICHAEL J. BANDLER. *Ladies Home Journal*, Jan. 1990.
"Funny as hell." ROBERT SEIDENBERG. *American Film*, Sep. 1989.
"DeVito, Danny." *Current Biography*, Feb. 1988.
The Taxi Book: The Complete Guide to TV's Most Lovable Hacks. JEFF SORENSEN. St. Martin's, 1987.

Devlin, Patrick Arthur (1905–92) A leading British lawyer and judge, Devlin began his practice of law in 1929, developing a largely commercial practice throughout the 1930s. After World War II service, he resumed his practice, and became a High Court judge in 1948, the youngest to be appointed in the 20th century. Moving up very quickly, by 1963 he was clearly in line for his country's highest legal position, that of Lord Chancellor. Instead, he suddenly resigned, thereafter writing, lecturing, and serving on many public bodies. From 1965 to 1979, he headed Britain's Press Council. A critic of Britain's criminal justice system, he took a leading public role in the long and ultimately successful fight to force review of the conviction of the Guildford Four, unjustly convicted of murder in 1975, in connection with terrorist bombings. He was survived by his wife, the former Madeleine Oppenheimer, two daughters, and four sons. (d. Pewsey, England; August 9, 1992)

FURTHER READING

Obituary. *The Times* (of London), Aug. 11, 1992.
Obituary. *New York Times*, Aug. 11, 1992.
Obituary. *Independent*, Aug. 11, 1992.

Diana, Princess of Wales (Diana Frances Spencer; 1961–) Diana Spencer married Charles, Prince of Wales, heir to the British throne, in July 1981, in a ceremony watched worldwide by hundreds of millions of viewers

(and replayed on their 10th anniversary). During the eleven years that followed, they remained great celebrities, every step and misstep chronicled and photographed in great detail by the media. In the later years of their marriage, media attention has focused on reported marital strains, and in 1992 it became apparent that some strains did indeed exist. In early June, the book *Diana: Her True Story*, by Andrew Morton, was serialized in London's *The Sunday Times*, became a bestseller, and was later the basis of a television miniseries; it alleged, among other things, that Diana had attempted suicide several times. On December 9, 1992, the Prince and Princess of Wales announced their separation. Under the terms of the agreement, she maintains a London palace for her residence. Controversy and speculation surrounded the question of whether or not she would be named queen, if and when Prince Charles succeeds to the throne.

Diana Spencer, Princess of Wales, worked as a kindergarten teacher in London before her marriage. She has two children: William Arthur Philip, born June 21, 1982; and Henry Charles Albert David, born September 15, 1984.

FURTHER READING

"Princess Diana." *People*, Dec. 28, 1992.
"Royal marriage. . . ." DAME BARBARA CARTLAND. *Newsweek*, Dec. 21, 1992.

"Throne out." JERRY ADLER. *Newsweek*, Dec. 21, 1992.

"Separate lives." MICHELLE GREEN. *People*, Dec. 21, 1992.

"Don't cry for Di." BARBARA GRIZUTTI HARRISON. *Mademoiselle*, Oct. 1992.

"Diana under fire." MICHELLE GREEN. *People*, Sep. 14, 1992.

"Di's private battle." *People*, Aug. 3, 1992.

"The Diana cult. . . ." CAMILLE PAGLIA. *New Republic*, Aug. 3, 1992.

"Heartache in the palace. . . ." ANNE EDWARDS. *McCall's*, Aug. 1992.

"Alone together." ROBERT LACY. *Life*, Aug. 1992.

"Diana, myth and media." CAMILLE PAGLIA. *Guardian*, July 30, 1992.

"Diana in private." COLIN CAMPBELL. *Cosmopolitan*, July 1992.

"To Di for." LISA SCHWARZBAUM. *Entertainment*, July 10, 1992.

"Love on the rocks." MICHELLE GREEN. *People*, June 29, 1992.

"Portrait of a marriage." CHARLES LEERHSEN. *Newsweek*, June 22, 1992.

"A grim fairy tale." ANDREW MORTON. *People*, June 22, 1992.

"Diana's photo album." *People*, June 22, 1992.

"The little princess." ANDREW MORTON. *People*, June 22, 1992.

"Diana's story." ANDREW PHILLIPS. *Maclean's*, June 15, 1992.

"Is nothing sacred?" MICHELLE GREEN. *People*, May 25, 1992.

Diana: Her True Story. ANDREW MORTON. Simon & Schuster, 1992.

Princess Diana: Future Queen. RENORA LICATA. Blackbirch, 1992.

Diana in Private: The Princess Nobody Knows. COLIN CAMPBELL. St. Martin's, 1992.

Diana: A Princess and Her Troubled Marriage. NICHOLAS DAVIES. Birch Lane/Carol, 1992.

Crown Princess: A Biography of Diana. JOSEPHINE FAIRLEY. Thomas Dunne/St. Martin's, 1992.

Dietrich, Marlene (Maria Magdalene Dietrich; 1901–92)

One of the greatest of international film stars, Dietrich began her stage and screen career in her native Germany, making her film debut in *The Little Napoleon* (1923). Her breakthrough came as Lola-Lola opposite Emil Jannings in Josef von Sternberg's film classic *The Blue Angel* (1930). She made six more films with von Sternberg, all in Hollywood: *Morocco* (1930), *Dishonored* (1931), the classic *Shanghai Express* (1932), *Blonde Venus* (1932), *The Scarlet Empress* (1934), and *The Devil Is a Woman* (1935). Several of her most notable later films were the western comedy *Destry Rides Again* (1939), the postwar comedy *A Foreign Affair* (1948), her classic dramatic role in *Witness for the Prosecution* (1957), *A Touch of Evil* (1958), and *Judgment at Nuremberg* (1959). A steadfast foe of Nazism, Dietrich rejected Hitler's invitation to return to Germany, instead becoming an American citizen in 1939. During World War II, she tirelessly entertained Allied troops, her version of the German song "Lili Marlene" ultimately becoming popular with troops on both sides of the conflict. She did not appear live in Germany until 1960. In the early 1950s, Dietrich moved into cabaret and concert, touring in her extraordinarily popular one-woman show until the mid-1970s. *Some Facts about Myself by Marlene Dietrich—Photographs of Berlin* (1992) was published shortly before her death; she had earlier published *Marlene: My Life* (1989) and *Marlene Dietrich's ABC* (1984). She was survived by her daughter. (d. Schöneberg, Germany; May 6, 1992)

FURTHER READING

"Earth angel." STEVEN BACH. *Vanity Fair*, July 1992.

"A bisexual Marlene." DAVID EHRENSTEIN. *Advocate*, June 16, 1992.

"A legend's last years. . . ." MARJORIE ROSEN. *People*, June 1, 1992.

"Der blaue Engel." *Economist*, May 23, 1992.

"The secret in her soul." RICHARD SCHICKEL. *Time*, May 18, 1992.

"The death of a goddess." JACK KROLL. *Newsweek*, May 18, 1992.

Obituary. *Variety*, May 11, 1992

Obituary. *New York Times*, May 11, 1992.

Obituary. *The Times* (of London), May 11, 1992.

"The final curtain. . . ." ALAN HAMILTON and PHILIP JACOBSON. *The Times* (of London), May 7, 1992.

Obituary. *Independent*, May 7, 1992.

Marlene Dietrich: Life and Legend. STEVEN BACH. Morrow, 1992.

The Complete Films of Marlene Dietrich, rev. ed. HOMER DICKENS. Citadel/Carol, 1992.

"Alexander Fleming and. . . ." NANCY CALDWELL SOREL. *Atlantic*, Mar. 1991.

"Marlene Dietrich. . . ." MICHAEL FRANK. *Architectural Digest*, Apr. 1990.

"Marlene." MARCELLE CLEMENTS. *Premiere*, Aug. 1989.

The Idea of the Image: Josef Von Sternberg's Dietrich Films. CAROLE ZUCKER. Fairleigh Dickinson, 1988.

In the Realm of Pleasure: Von Sternberg, Dietrich, and the Masochistic Aesthetic. GAYLYN STUDLAR. University of Illinois Press, 1988.

Marlene Dietrich: Portraits 1926–1960.
KLAUS-JURGEN SEMBACH. Grove, 1985.

Dillon, Matt (1964–) In 1992, Dillon
starred as Cliff, a rock guitarist, in Cameron
Crowe's film comedy *Singles*, about a group of
young people and their various loves, set in Seattle. Co-starring were Campbell Scott, Bridget
Fonda, and Sheila Kelley. The film was moderately well received by the critics. Dillon also
played a starring role opposite Danny Glover in
Tim Hunter's forthcoming *The Saint of Fort
Washington*, shot in the spring of 1992. He also
starred in the forthcoming Anthony Minghella
film comedy *Mr. Wonderful*, co-starring Annabella Sciorra and Mary Louise Parker, as a divorced man looking for the perfect husband for
his ex-wife, to put an end to his alimony payments to her. Also forthcoming were starring
film roles in Andy Wolk's *The Boxer and the
Blonde* and *Golden Gate*, written by David
Henry Hwang.

Born in New Rochelle, New York, Dillon began his movie career as a teenager, in *Over the
Edge* (1979), quickly followed by *Little Darlings*
(1980), which established him as a leading teenage Hollywood star. During the 1980s, he
starred in such films as *My Bodyguard* (1980),
Liar's Moon (1982), *Tex* (1982), *The Outsiders*
(1983), *Rumblefish* (1983), *The Flamingo Kid*
(1984), *Native Son* (1986), *Kansas* (1988), *Drug-
store Cowboy* (1989), *Bloodhounds of Broadway*
(1989), and *A Kiss Before Dying* (1991). His
younger brother is the actor Kevin Dillon.

FURTHER READING

"From here to maturity...." *Seventeen*, July 1991.
"Matt Dillon." BRENDON LEMON. *Interview*, Apr. 1991.
"The Dillon papers...." BRET EASTON ELLIS. *Ameri-
can Film*, Feb. 1991.

Dinkins, David Norman (1927–) For
New York City's first African-American mayor,
1992 was in some respects a little better than
1991, for although the city's massive physical,
human, and economic problems continued and
the deep national recession became worse, he
did not face the same kinds of immediate budget
problems that in 1991 had forced cuts in opera-

tional city jobs and vitally needed school, library, and other social services, accompanied by
massive tax increases. What he did face was continuing and in some respects worsening social
tensions in 1992, most visibly expressed as confrontation and violence between police and people of color and between Jews and African-
Americans.

Dinkins personally appeared in some of the
most troubled situations. In July, on the eve of
the Democratic National Convention held in
Manhattan, he headed off major street riots
in largely Dominican-American Washington
Heights, after police shot and killed Dominican
immigrant Jose Garcia. The many interest-
group street demonstrations that accompanied
the convention were handled without major incident. In late autumn, rioting by outraged Hassidic Jews was averted in Crown Heights, where
an African-American was acquitted of murder
charges in the death of a Jewish student killed
during the 1991 anti-Jewish riots. The mayor
also faced such situations as the refusal of St.
Patrick's Day Parade organizers to allow gay
and lesbian units to march, refusing to march
himself. Late in the year, he also found his office
indirectly involved in a major sexual harassment case, when deputy mayor Randy Daniels
resigned after having been accused of sexual harassment by a former co-worker. And Dinkins
stood by the side of his friend, Arthur Ashe,
when Ashe announced that he was infected with
HIV, the virus that causes AIDS. The mayor
himself was the target of direct racial slurs when
police demonstrators taunted him during a series of confrontations, in a set of disputes that
included charges of widespread police corruption
and bigotry.

Dinkins addressed the Democratic National
Convention on July 13, speaking for candidates
Bill Clinton and Al Gore, and then campaigned
for their election. That accomplished, he looked
forward to renewed federal commitment and direct practical help in addressing New York
City's problems, as did many other big city
mayors.

New Jersey-born Dinkins practiced law and
politics in New York City from the mid-1950s.
He was elected to the State Assembly in 1965
and served in several appointive posts, withdrawing from a deputy's mayor's position in
1973, at least partly because he had failed to file
tax returns for several years. He was City Clerk
(1975–85), and then was the elected borough

president of Manhattan (1985–88). He became the historic first African-American Mayor of New York City in 1989, after defeating incumbent mayor Edward Koch in the 1989 Democratic mayoral primary, and defeating Republican Rudolph Giuliani in the general election. Dinkins attended Howard University and Brooklyn Law School. He married Joyce Burrows in 1953; they have two children.

FURTHER READING

"Mayor Dinkins. . . ." SAM ROBERTS. *New York Times Magazine*, Apr. 7, 1991.
"Being there." MARIE BRENNER . *Vanity Fair*, Jan. 1991.
Changing New York City Politics. ASHER ARIAN et al. Routledge, 1991.
"Dinkins, David Norman." *Current Biography*, Mar. 1990.

Dixon, Sharon Pratt: See Kelly, Sharon Pratt Dixon.

Dixon, Willie (1915–92) Mississippi-born Dixon began his long career as a Chicago-based blues singer, composer, arranger, producer, and bassist in the early 1930s, beginning his recording career with The Five Breezes in 1940. He was jailed as a conscientious objector to military service during World War II. After the war, he formed the Big Three Trio (1946–52), and in 1948 also began his long association with Chess records, becoming a full-time studio musician, songwriter, and producer with Chess in 1952. There he worked with such musicians as Muddy Waters, Howlin' Wolf, Bo Diddley, and Chuck Berry; his first hit song was the 1954 Waters version of his "Hoochie Koochie Man." Some of Dixon's best-known compositions were "Spoonful," "Little Red Rooster," "Back Door Man," "I Can't Quit You Baby," and "My Babe." In the 1960s, Dixon formed The Chicago All Stars group, and toured widely. In his later years, he established the nonprofit Blues Heaven Foundation. In 1990, he published *I Am the Blues: The Willie Dixon Story*. He was survived by his wife, Marie, and eleven children. (d. Burbank, California; January 29, 1992)

FURTHER READING

"Blues for the blues." HANK BORDOWITZ. *American Visions*, Aug.-Sep. 1992.

"Willie Dixon, 1915–1992." JAS OBRECHT. *Guitar Player*, Apr. 1992.
Obituary. DAVID WHITEIS. *Down Beat*, Apr. 1992.
"Bluesman Willie Dixon. . . ." *Rolling Stone*, Mar. 5, 1992.
"The man who remade the blues." RON GIVENS. *Entertainment*, Feb. 14, 1992.
Obituary. *Variety*, Feb. 3, 1992.
Obituary. *The Times* (of London), Feb. 1, 1992.
Obituary. *Independent*, Jan. 31, 1992.
Obituary. *New York Times*, Jan. 30, 1992.
"Willie Dixon." ROGER WOLMUTH. *People*, Sep. 11, 1989.
"Dixon, Willie." *Current Biography*, May 1989.
"Willie Dixon. . . ." ANTHONY DECURTIS. *Rolling Stone*, Mar. 23, 1989.
"Blues in the news." JIM DEJONG. *Down Beat*, June 1988.

Dole, Bob (Robert Joseph Dole; 1923–   ) Republican Senate minority leader Bob Dole was elected to a fifth Senate term in 1992, and by a huge majority, with 64 percent of the vote, although earlier media stories had indicated that he was encountering a stiff fight for his seat. As the Republican Party lost power, and Bill Clinton prepared to take office, Dole publicly announced that he and his party would take on a watchdog role aimed at impeding the anticipated liberal trend of the new Clinton Administration, rather surprisingly going over to the attack even before Clinton took office, rather than making a show of unity during the traditional brief "honeymoon" period that is allowed most new administrations. Dole, a leading conservative, continued during 1992 to press for most of the Republican agenda, resisting massive cuts in military spending, voting against abortion rights and civil rights, and supporting administration economic initiatives. A staunch Republican Party supporter, he campaigned hard for the Bush-Quayle ticket, as he had in 1988, even after his primary defeat by Bush. He was widely regarded as a major possible contender for the Republican Presidential nomination in 1996.

On the personal side, Dole "went public" when he found that he had prostate cancer, in an attempt to help others understand and deal with the problem. His treatment was reportedly entirely successful.

Kansas-born Dole has spent three decades in Washington, starting with his four Congressional terms (1961–69). A leading Republican, he has served in the Senate since 1969, and as Senate Republican leader since 1985. He was chairman of the Republican National Committee (1971–73), and his party's unsuccessful Vice-Presidential candidate in 1976. He made unsuccessful runs for the Republican presidential nomination in 1980 and 1988. His B.A. and LL.B were from Topeka's Washburn Municipal University. In 1975, Robert Dole married Elizabeth Hanford Dole, American Red Cross president and former Secretary of Labor; together they published *Doles: Unlimited Partners* (1988).

FURTHER READING

"Kemp vs. Dole." FRED BARNES. *New Republic*, Dec. 14, 1992.
"Bob Dole speaks. . . ." CORY SERVAAS. *Saturday Evening Post*, July–Aug., 1992.
"The two Bobs." WILLIAM MCGURN. *National Review*, Dec. 2, 1991.
Bob Dole: American Political Phoenix. STANLEY G. HILTON. Contemporary, 1988.

Donato, Pietro di (1911–92) Italian-American Donato was the son of an immigrant who became a bricklayer and was crushed to death in 1923 when a building collapsed and buried him in concrete. The boy also soon lost his mother and, at 12, managed to support his seven younger brothers and sisters, also becoming a bricklayer. Fifteen years later, he published his masterpiece, *Christ in Concrete*, the story of his father's life and death. The book became a bestseller, and was the basis of the 1949 film *Give Us This Day*. Di Donato continued to write and to work as a bricklayer, publishing several stories in magazines. His later work includes a life of Mother Cabrini, *Innocent Saint* (1960), and the novel *The Penitent* (1962). He was survived by two sons and a stepdaughter. (d. Stony Brook, New York; January 19, 1992)

FURTHER READING

Obituary. *The Times* (of London), Jan. 27, 1992.
Obituary. *New York Times*, Jan. 21, 1992.

Dos Santos, José Eduardo (1942–) It was to have been the first full year of peace for Angola and for the Angolan President. In May 1991, thirty years of Angolan war and civil war had ended, with a ceasefire, the withdrawal of Cuban forces, and on May 31 the formal signing of a peace treaty between Dos Santos as leader of the Popular Movement for the Liberation of Angola (MPLA) and Jonas Savimbi as leader of the National Union for the Total Independence of Angola (UNITA).

The agreement had provided for multiparty free elections to take place in the autumn of 1992, preceded by partial demobilization of both armies and merger of the remaining forces into a new national army. But only modest progress was reported; a new national army was formed, but by the summer of 1992 it was clear that both sides remained largely armed and ready for renewed hostilities; there were skirmishes in August and September, as the election approached. Meanwhile, war-scarred Angola remained one of the world's poorest nations, the Dos Santos government unable to seriously begin the work of reconstruction.

Dos Santos won the October 2–3 elections, with 51 percent of the vote to 39 percent for Savimbi, and the MPLA won an absolute majority in the new parliament. Savimbi charged massive fraud, refused to accept the results, and withdrew UNITA forces from the national army. On October 30, the civil war resumed, with heavy fighting between MPLA and UNITA forces in Luanda, the capital; UNITA forces soon resumed control of areas won before the 1991 ceasefire. More than 1,000 deaths were reported. Although the United Nations arranged a truce on November 2, Angola's long wars seemed far from over.

For Dos Santos, the signing of the May 1991 peace treaty seemed the end of two consecutive wars that had occupied his entire adult life. He has been an activist in the MPLA since he joined it in 1961. He went into exile that year and became president of the MPLA youth organization. From 1963 to 1970, he was educated in the Soviet Union, as a petroleum engineer and telecommunications specialist, the latter skills being used when he returned to the Angolan war of independence in 1970. He became a member of the MPLA central committee in 1974, was foreign minister of the new Soviet-backed MPLA Angolan government in 1975, and held several cabinet-level posts during the next four years, as the civil war continued. After the death of president Augustinho Neto, Dos Santos became Angolan president, commander in chief, and head of the MPLA.

FURTHER READING

"Fact sheet. . . ." *U.S. Department of State Dispatch,* Sep. 23, 1991.
" 'We have taken. . . .' " Bruce W. Nelan. *Time,* July 3, 1989.

Kirk Douglas and Sport.

Douglas, Kirk (Issur Danielovich Demsky; 1916–) Veteran film star Kirk Douglas was honored by his peers once again in 1992, winning an Emmy nomination for his role as father to his real-life son Eric, in the final 1991 episode of the television series "Tales From the Crypt." He played a highly acclaimed television role in 1992, as well, as a dyslexic grandfather who overcomes his own lifelong self-imposed guilt to work with his dyslexic grandson in "The Secret," a fictional telefilm, which was followed by a televised talk on dyslexia by then-First Lady Barbara Bush. Forthcoming was an environmentally oriented film, *Welcome to Veraz,* directed by Xavier Castano and shot in southern France in late 1990. In quite another medium, author Douglas published his second novel, *The Gift,* a romantic melodrama that had a less-than-favorable response from most critics, but that sold rather well, for Kirk Douglas continues to have a worldwide audience for whatever he does.

Born "a ragman's son" in Amsterdam, New York, Douglas, the father of actor-producer Michael Douglas, has been a Hollywood star for over four decades, ever since his role in *Champion* (1949). In the peak years of his film career, he starred in *The Glass Menagerie* (1950), as Vincent Van Gogh in *Lust For Life* (1956), and in such diverse films as *Gunfight at the O.K. Corral* (1957), *Paths of Glory* (1959), *Lonely Are the Brave* (1962), and *Seven Days in May* (1964), the latter three produced by his own production company, Bryna. He also produced and starred in *Spartacus* (1960), restored (including originally censored material) and released in 1991. He also wrote the best-selling autobiography *The Ragman's Son* (1988) and the novel *Dance With the Devil* (1990).

Douglas's 1938 B.A. was from St. Lawrence University and he studied at the American Academy of Dramatic Arts (1939–41). After an earlier marriage to Diana Dill, he married Anne Buydens in 1954. He has four children.

FURTHER READING

"A man cut for the screen. . . ." Frank Thompson. *American Film,* Mar. 1991.
Films of Kirk Douglas. Tony Thomas. Carol, 1991.

Douglas, Michael (Michael Kirk Douglas; 1944–) Versatile actor-producer Michael Douglas starred in two very different major commercial films in 1992. In January, he opened opposite Melanie Griffith in David Seltzer's *Shining Through,* a romantic spy thriller set in Berlin and London during World War II, with Liam Neeson, John Gielgud, and Joely Richardson. In March, he opened opposite Sharon Stone in Paul Verhoeven's *Basic Instinct,* which became one of the year's blockbuster sex-and-violence worldwide hits. The unrated version shown in some countries was as successful as the cut version (with some of the sex and violence excised) shown in the United States for purposes of securing an R rating. Stone played Catherine Trammell, a bisexual female novelist and possibly a murderer who seduces and murders her male victims; Douglas played Nick Curran, an investigating detective, who is drawn into an affair with her. The film was the center of a major controversy and unsuccessful campaign to suppress it while it was being made and then while it was being shown, becoming the target of numerous demonstrations, protests, and vandalism from gay and lesbian activists, who criticized the psychological thriller for negative depiction of lesbians. Forthcoming for Douglas was a starring role opposite Robert Duvall in Joel Schmacher's film *The Fall*, which was filmed in the spring of 1992.

Son of actor Kirk Douglas, Michael Douglas first became a star in the television series "The Streets of San Francisco" (1972–75), paired with Karl Malden. Moving into films, he produced the Oscar-winning *One Flew Over the Cuckoo's Nest* (1975) and the notable nuclear-accident film *The China Syndrome* (1979), and produced and starred in such films as *Romancing the Stone* (1984), *Jewel of the Nile* (1985), and *The War of the Roses* (1989), all three with Kathleen Turner, also starring in such films as *A Chorus Line* (1985), *Fatal Attraction*, (1987) and *Wall Street* (1987; he won a Best Actor Oscar and a Golden Globe Award), and *Black Rain* (1989). Douglas's 1967 B.A. was from the University of California. He married Diandra Mornell Luker in 1977; they have one son.

FURTHER READING

"Michael and Diandra Douglas. . . ." DEBORAH NORVILLE. *McCall's*, Nov. 1992.
"Just your basic. . . ." T. KLEIN. *Cosmopolitan*, May 1992.
"Adventures in the skin trade. . . ." TRISH DEITCH ROHRER et al. *Entertainment*, Apr. 3, 1992.
"Michael Douglas." JUDITH THURMAN. *Architectural Digest*, Apr. 1992.
"Steaming up the screen." BRIAN D. JOHNSON. *Maclean's*, Mar. 30, 1992.
"Business as usual." DAVID THOMSON. *Film Comment*, Jan.–Feb., 1990.
Michael Douglas and the Douglas Clan. ANNENE KAYE and JIM SCLAVUNOS. Knightsbridge, 1990.
"A prince. . . ." LINDA BLANDFORD. *New York Times Magazine*, Dec. 3, 1989.

Douglas-Home, William (1912–92)

Edinburgh-born Douglas-Home, a leading British playwright, was educated and began to write plays at Oxford in the mid-1930s, and made his stage debut in 1937. During World War II, then a serving officer, he refused to participate in an attack on Le Havre unless the city's civilians were first evacuated, which was not done; afterward, he was courtmartialed, cashiered, and served a year in prison. His breakthrough play, *Now Barabbas* (1946), drew upon his prison ex-

perience. He went on to write more than 40 plays, his light comedies providing most of his major successes. These included such works as *The Chiltern Hundreds* (1947), *The Reluctant Debutante* (1955), *The Secretary Bird* (1968), *The Jockey Club Stakes* (1970), *Lloyd George Knew My Father* (1972), *The Dame of Sark* (1974), and *The Kingfisher* (1977). His books include two autobiographies: *Mr. Home Pronounced Hume: An Autobiography* (1979), and *Old Men Remember* (1991). He was survived by his wife, the former Rachel Brand, Lady Dacre. (d. Winchester, England; September 28, 1992)

FURTHER READING

Obituary. *Variety*, Oct. 5, 1992.
Obituary. *The Times* (of London), Sep. 30, 1992.
Obituary. *New York Times*, Sep. 30, 1992.
Obituary. *Independent*, Sep. 30, 1992.

Downey, Robert, Jr.

(1965–) Young film star Robert Downey, Jr., emerged as a major figure in 1992, with his starring role as the legendary Charles Chaplin in Richard Attenborough's biofilm *Chaplin*. In the film, based on Chaplin's *My Autobiography* and David Robinson's *Chaplin: His Life and Art*, Downey portrays Chaplin from the ages of 18–83, from his start in London's East End to his acceptance of a 1972 honorary Academy Award, after having been driven away from the United States for 20 years because of McCarthy-era witch-hunting by FBI head J. Edgar Hoover. Co-starring were Dan Aykroyd as Mack Sennett; Geraldine Chaplin as her own grandmother Hannah Chaplin; Kevin Dunn as Hoover; Kevin Kline as Douglas Fairbanks, Moira Kelly as Hetty Kelly and Oona O'Neill; Diane Lane as Paulette Goddard; Penelope Anne Miller as Edna Purviance; Anthony Hopkins as George Hayden; and Paul Rhys as Sydney Chaplin.

Downey was also the narrator in the Marc Levin-Mark Benjamin documentary *The Last Party*, about the 1992 presidential election campaign. Forthcoming was a starring role in Ron Underwood's film *Heart and Soul*, a comedy-fantasy ghost story.

New York City-born Downey, the son of filmmaker Robert Downey, made his screen debut at the age of five, in his father's film *Pound* (1970), and played in several other children's roles. He emerged as a star in his late teens, in such films as *Baby, It's You* (1983), *Firstborn* (1984), *Tuff Turf* (1985), *Back To School* (1986), *Less Than Zero* 1987), *Johnny Be Good* (1988), *Chances Are* (1989), *True Believer* (1989), *Air America* (1990), and *Too Much Sun* (1991). He is married to actress Deborah Falconer.

FURTHER READING

"20 questions. . . ." *Playboy*, Aug. 1991.
"Cinema Scion." KENNETH TURAN and KAREN KUEHN. *Interview*, Apr. 1989.
"Hollywood's newest golden boy." PHOEBE HOBAN. *Premiere*, Apr. 1989.
"Arresting appeal. . . ." BETSY BORNS. *Harper's Bazaar*, Feb. 1989.

Drake, Alfred

(Alfred Capurro; 1914–92) New York City-born singer and actor Alfred Drake began his career while still a student at Brooklyn College. Graduating in 1935, he played in supporting roles until his breakthrough starring role came, as Curly in the classic *Oklahoma*, with such songs as "People Will Say We're in Love," "The Surrey With the Fringe on Top," and "Oh, What a Beautiful Morning." He won his first Drama Critics award for the role. In 1948, he created the Fred Graham role in Cole Porter's *Kiss Me Kate*, and went on to win a Tony and a second Drama Critics award for his Hadj in *Kismet* (1953). He also starred in a 1973 revival of *Gigi*, as well as in several non-singing roles, as in Richard Burton's *Hamlet* (1963), and opposite Katharine Hepburn in *Much Ado About Nothing* (1957). Drake also appeared in several television films, and in the film *Tars and Spars* (1948). He received a lifetime achievement Tony in 1990. He was survived by his wife, Esther Harvey Brown, and two daughters. (d. New York City; July 25, 1992)

FURTHER READING

Obituary. *Variety*, Aug. 3, 1992.
Obituary. *The Times* (of London), July 27, 1992.
Obituary. *New York Times*, July 26, 1992.

Dreyfuss, Richard

(Richard Stephan Dreyfuss; 1947–) For veteran film star Dreyfuss, 1992 brought a Broadway play; he starred opposite Glenn Close and Gene Hackman as Close's husband in Ariel Dorfman's play *Death and the Maiden*, about a woman's revenge on her former Latin-American police torturer. Mike Nichols directed the play, which received mixed reviews. Forthcoming was another play, but this one a screen adaptation of a Broadway hit: Dreyfuss will star opposite Mercedes Ruehl in Martha Coolidge's film version of *Lost In Yonkers*, adapted by Neil Simon from his play. On television, Dreyfuss starred as the voice of General William T. Sherman in the four-hour PBS television documentary *Lincoln*, co-starring Jason Robards as Lincoln, Glenn Close as his wife, Ossie Davis as Frederick Douglass, Rod Steiger as General Ulysses S. Grant, and Frank Langella as John Wilkes Booth. Dreyfuss also narrated the twelve-part Arts & Entertainment documentary series "The Class of the 20th Century."

New York-born Dreyfuss became a leading film star of the 1970s, with his roles in *American Graffiti* (1973), *The Apprenticeship of Duddy Kravitz*, (1974), *Jaws* (1975), *Close Encounters of the Third Kind* (1977), and *The Goodbye Girl* (1977), for which he won a Best Actor Oscar. He went on the star in such films as *Whose Life Is It Anyway?* (1981), *Down and Out in Beverly Hills* (1986), *Tin Men* (1987), *Always* (1989), *Rosencrantz and Guildenstern Are Dead* (1991), *Once Around* (1991), and *What About Bob?* (1991). On television he coproduced and starred in the HBO telefilm *Prisoner of Honor*. Dreyfuss attended San Fernando Valley State College (1965–67). In 1992, he filed for divorce from Jeramie Rain; they have three children.

FURTHER READING

"Against all odds." SUSAN SCHINDEHETTE. *People*, Mar. 4, 1991.
"Richard Dreyfuss, . . ." DIGBY DIEHL. *Cosmopolitan*, Nov. 1990.

Dubcek, Alexander

(1921–92) Slovakian-born Alexander Dubcek, the son of Slovak Communist leader Stefan Dubcek, was a highly respected old-style Communist leader for much of his career. He fought in the anti-Nazi resistance during World War II, rose to head the Slovak Communist Party (1962–68), and in January 1968 became first secretary of the Czech Communist Party and head of the Czech government. From January to August 1968, he initiated a series of major democratic reforms, all abolished after the Soviet invasion of his country. He was expelled from his party in 1970.

After twenty years out in the cold, Dubcek in 1989 emerged as one of the leaders of the new reform movement that swept away the Communist government. He began to speak out again in the spring of 1989, much to the dismay of the then-hardline Czech government, and on November 23 and 24, at massive Bratislava and Prague rallies, put his enormous prestige behind the new democratic movement. He announced his presidential candidacy on December 10, but a week later withdrew in favor of Vaclav Havel, and on December 28, 1989 the new Czech parliament unanimously elected him as its chairman. On June 27, 1990, he was re-elected to the post. In 1991, with Andras Sugar, he published a book, *The Soviet Invasion*. Dubcek attended Communist Party schools and Comenius University. He was survived by three sons. (d. Prague; November 7, 1992)

FURTHER READING

"The Gardener of Bratislava." *New Yorker*, Dec.7, 1992.

"Alexander Dubcek." Harry Hanak. *Independent*, Nov. 9, 1992.

Obituary. *The Times* (of London), Nov. 9, 1992.

Obituary. *New York Times*, Nov. 8, 1992.

"Dubcek, hero. . . ." Tony Allen-Mills and Andrew Alderson. *Sunday Times* (of London), Nov. 8, 1992.

Alexander Dubcek. Ina Navazelskis. Chelsea House, 1991.

After the Velvet Revolution: Vaclav Havel and the New Leaders of Czechoslovakia Speak Out. Tim D. Whipple. Freedom House, 1991.

" 'After a long darkness.' " Renee Krausova. *World Press Review*, May 1990.

"Metamorphosis in Prague. . . ." Leonid Shinkarev. *World Press Review*, May 1990.

Alexander Dubcek. Ina Navazelskis. Chelsea House, 1989.

"Czech former prime minister. . . ." Peter Hebblethwaite. *National Catholic Reporter*, Nov. 18, 1988.

Duke, David Ernest (1950–) After his upset second-place win in the October 19, 1991 Louisiana gubernatorial contest, ex-Ku Klux Klan leader and ex-Nazi Duke had attracted a

great deal of attention, and still drew news coverage even after his decisive defeat by Edwin W. Edwards in the November 1991 election, although he and his only-slightly-veiled racist views had been disowned by the Republican Party. But Duke's presidential candidacy, announced on December 4, went nowhere at all. With the entry of Pat Buchanan into the Republican primaries, most of Duke's possible right-wing support left him, going instead to Buchanan. Duke ran in several primaries, but won only 9 percent of the small Republican primary vote in Louisiana, showed best in Mississippi with 11 percent of the Republican primary vote, and elsewhere showed in the 0–3 percent range. He withdrew his candidacy on April 22, and disappeared from the national political scene. He later sent fundraising appeals to his former supporters, citing large debts. In August, Duke began a new career, as a health insurance agent.

Duke was associated with the Ku Klux Klan from his youth; he joined the Klan while still in high school, and was active throughout the late 1960s and 1970s, becoming Grand Wizard of the Louisiana Knights of the Ku Klux Klan after the 1975 murder of his Klan leader, James Lindsay. He was also openly associated with American Nazi movements, becoming a follower of Nazi leader George Lincoln Rockwell while a college student in the late 1960s.

In the late 1970s, he moved from the raw, open bigotry that had until then characterized his career toward the more sanitized racism that marked his later political development, in an attempt to appeal to the White middle class. He continued that approach after he had officially left the Klan in 1979, then forming the National Association for the Advancement of White People. He was elected as a Republican to the Louisiana legislature in 1989, although he had been denounced by the Republican Party. In 1990, he was defeated in a bid for the United States Senate by three-time Democratic Senator J. Bennett Johnston. Duke attended Louisiana State University. He was once married, and has two children.

FURTHER READING

"Eight for the prize." Steven Manning. *Scholastic Update*, Feb. 7, 1992.

"All the Duke's men." Victor Gold. *American Spectator*, Feb. 1992.

The Emergence of David Duke and the Politics of

Race. DOUGLAS ROSE, ed. University of North Carolina Press, 1992.

Cross to Bear: Louisiana Politics 1991 from David Duke to Edwin Edwards. John Maginnis. Darkhorse Press, 1992.

"Deconstructing Duke. . . ." JOE KLEIN. *New York,* Dec. 2, 1991.

"The hazards of Duke. . . ." JOHN MAGINNIS. *New Republic,* Nov. 25, 1991.

"The real. . . ." BILL TURQUE. *Newsweek,* Nov. 18, 1991.

"An ex-Klansman. . . ." BILL HEWITT et al. *People,* Nov. 18, 1991.

"Hate with a pretty face." JULIA REED. *Vogue,* Nov. 1991.

David Duke: Evolution of a Klansman. MICHAEL ZATARAIN. Pelican, 1990.

Dunaway, Faye (Dorothy Faye Dunaway; 1941–)

Moving into her 50s in a film world that generates few leading roles for women past 40, Dunaway is still finding some starring roles, though not recently in major commercial films. In 1992, she starred in an Israeli film set in modern Jerusalem, *Double Edge,* in which she plays an American reporter on a short-term assignment to Israel, who refuses to pass her stories through the Israeli censors and has her press card taken away by the Israelis. The film was written and directed by Israeli Amos Kollek, who also co-stars; also appearing as himself is Kollek's father, Teddy Kollek, mayor of Jerusalem. Dunaway also starred opposite Johnny Depp in Emil Kusturica's film *Arizona Dream,* which opened in Paris in November 1992, and opposite Timothy Hutton and Lara Flynn Boyle in the forthcoming thriller *The Temp.*

Florida-born Dunaway became a film star in 1967, with her portrayal of 1930s midwestern outlaw Bonnie Parker in *Bonnie and Clyde.* She went on to become a leading Hollywood star, in such films as *The Thomas Crown Affair* (1968), *Chinatown* (1974), *Network* (1976; she won a Best Actress Oscar), as Joan Crawford in *Mommie Dearest* (1981; she decribed the role as "career suicide"), *Barfly* (1987), and *The Handmaid's Tale* (1990). On television, she appeared as revivalist preacher Aimee Semple McPherson in *The Disappearance of Aimee* (1976) and in the title role of *Evita Peron* (1982), going on to roles in *Cold Sassy Tree* (1990), *Silhouette* (1990), and as the disembodied voice of Gaia, the mother goddess of the Earth, in the five-part, ten-hour epic miniseries "Voice of the Planet" (1991). Dunaway attended Boston University. She was formerly married to Peter Wolf, is married to Terrence O'Neill, and has one child.

FURTHER READING

"Faye Dunaway." TINA JOHNSON. *Harper's Bazaar,* Sep. 1989.

Faye Dunaway. ALLAN HUNTER. St. Martin's, 1986.

Dunne, Philip (1908–92)

New York City-born Dunne, the son of political humorist Finley Peter Dunne, was a leading screenwriter and a director. He was also a leading Hollywood liberal, who was a founder of the Screen Writers Guild, a speechwriter for and prominent supporter of presidents Roosevelt and Kennedy, and a leader in the unsuccessful fight against the blacklist during the McCarthy era. An anticommunist, he nonetheless in 1947 took a leading role, with John Huston and William Wyler, in the Committee for the First Amendment, unsuccessfully lobbying on behalf of the Hollywood Ten. Dunne received an Oscar nomination for John Ford's Oscar-winning *How Green Was My Valley* (1941), and another nomination for *David and Bathsheba* (1951). His more than 30 other screenplays included *Suez* (1938), *The Rains Came* (1939), *Stanley and Livingstone* (1939), *The Ghost and Mrs. Muir* (1947), and *The Agony and the Ecstasy* (1965). Among the several films he directed was *Ten North Frederick* (1958). In 1992 he published a revised edition of his *Take Two: A Life in Movies and Politics* (1980). He was survivedby his wife, actress Amanda Duff Dunne, and three daughters. (d. Malibu, California; June 2, 1992)

FURTHER READING

Obituary. *Variety,* June 8, 1992

Obituary. *The Times* (of London), June 8, 1992.

Obituary. *New York Times,* June 4, 1992.

Durning, Charles (1923–)

During 1992, much of veteran character star Durning's work was in television, as a key supporting actor in the hit series "Evening Shade," and in several television films. He won an Emmy nomination for best supporting actor in a comedy series for

"Evening Shade." Durning also starred in the television film *The Water Engine*, directed by Steven Schachter, adapted by David Mamet from his play. Mamet's work, his view of the fate of dissenters in American society, is set in 1934, and is about a machine operator who invents an engine powered by only water, who is attacked by business interests. Durning also starred as one of the 1930s antifascist refugee Hollywood intellectuals and artists in Christopher Hampton's telefilm adaptation of his own 1982 play *Tales From Hollywood*, co-starring Alec Guinness, Jeremy Irons, Elizabeth McGovern, and Sinead Cusack. On stage, Durning starred opposite Tyne Daly in a Long Beach Civic Light Opera production of a musical version of *Queen of the Stardust Ballroom*, in the role he originated in the 1975 television drama.

Durning has been a strong character actor for over 30 years, creating a wide range of notable roles on stage, screen, and television. In the theater he memorably played the governor in *Best Little Whorehouse in Texas*, and won a Tony as best featured actor in a play for his role as Big Daddy in the 1990 Broadway revival Tennessee Williams's *Cat on a Hot Tin Roof*. On film, he was especially notable as Jessica Lange's father and Dustin Hoffman's would-be suitor in *Tootsie* (1982). Among his other films are *The Sting* (1973), *Mass Appeal* (1984), *The Rosary Murders* (1987), *Far North* (1988), *Dick Tracy* (1990), and *V.I. Warshawski* (1991). He and Mary Ann Amelio married in 1974. He was born in Highland Falls, New York, and attended New York University and Columbia University.

FURTHER READING

"Playing a fiery big daddy. . . ." TOBY KAHN. *People*, June 4, 1990.

Duvall, Robert (1931–) Screen star Robert Duvall created a major role in 1992, that of Soviet dictator Joseph Stalin in Ivan Passer's HBO television film *Stalin*. Co-starring were Julia Ormond as Nadya Alliluyeva, Jeroen Krabbe as Bukharin, Maximilian Schell as Lenin, Joan Plowright, Frank Finlay, and Daniel Massey. The film, shot in Moscow in the fall of 1991, used many historical locations, including Lenin's original office, now a museum.

Duvall also starred in Luis Puenzo's film *The Plague*, adapted from the Albert Camus novel, which opened at the Venice Film Festival in August 1992. A third starring role was in the poorly received Disney musical *Newsies*. Forthcoming were starring roles in Joel Schumaker's film *The Fall* opposite Michael Douglas, and in the Randa Haines film *Wrestling Ernest Hemingway*, co-starring Shirley MacLaine, Richard Harris, and Piper Laurie.

San Diego-born Duvall was recognized as a powerful supporting actor in such films as *To Kill a Mockingbird* (1963), *True Grit* (1969), *M*A*S*H* (1970), the first two *Godfather* films (1972, 1974), *Network* (1976), and *Apocalypse Now* (1979). He went on to win a Best Actor Oscar for his lead in *Tender Mercies* (1983), while continuing to play strong supporting roles and sometimes leads in such films as *Colors* (1988), *Days of Thunder* (1990), *The Handmaid's Tale* (1990), *Rambling Rose* (1991), and *Convicts* (1991). On television, he played a notable Dwight D. Eisenhower in the mini-series *Ike* (1979). A graduate of Principia College, Duvall is married to Gail Youngs.

FURTHER READING

"Robert Duvall." LAURA DERN. *Interview*, Oct. 1991.
Robert Duvall: Hollywood Maverick. JUDITH SLAWSON. St. Martin's, 1985.

Dylan, Bob (Robert Alan Zimmerman; 1941–) His peers honored Dylan in in a very special way in 1992; on October 16, a wide range of celebrity performers paid tribute to him at a soldout Madison Square Garden concert. Among those who came to sing and play were Willie Nelson, Stevie Wonder, Tracy Chapman, George Harrison, Johnny Cash, June Carter, Roseanne Cash, Eric Clapton, and Kris Kristofferson. Sinead O'Connor came, too, but was unfortunately booed off the stage for having torn up a picture of Pope John Paul II two weeks earlier on "Saturday Night Live." In 1992, Dylan also did his first solo acoustic recording in 28 years; released in November, his *Good As I Been To You* album included thirteen standard blues and folk songs, which he accompanied with harmonica and guitar.

Duluth-born Dylan was one of the leading countercultural figures of the early 1960s, an enormously popular folk-rock singer and composer known to millions for many of his own songs, such as "The Times They are A-Changin" (1963) and "Blowin' in the Wind" (1963). Later in the 1960s, and through the 1970s and 1980s, he was much more a rock than a folk-rock musician. Although he continued to be a very popular figure in concert and on records, his impact was greatest in the early years, when he burst upon the scene as a 1960s emblem of protest. Dylan made a substantial comeback on records and in performance, starting in 1989, with his album *Oh Mercy* and a world tour. In 1990, his new album *Under the Red Sky*, was very well received, as was his second *Traveling Wilburys* album, made with George Harrison, Tom Petty, Jeff Lynne, and Roy Orbison. In 1991, he released *The Bootleg Series, Volumes 1–3 (Rare and Unreleased) 1961–91*, a three-CD boxed set carrying 58 Dylan tracks, approximately a quarter of which had never before been released on records. Dylan attended the University of Minnesota, in 1960.

FURTHER READING

Bob Dylan: A Bio-Bibliography. WILLIAM MCKEEN. Greenwood, 1993.

"Bringing folk back home. . . ." JAY COCKS. *Time*, Oct. 26, 1992.

Alias Bob Dylan. STEPHEN SCOBIE. Empire Publication Services, 1992.

Bob Dylan: A Man Called Alias. RICHARD WILLIAMS. Holt, 1992.

Hard Rain: A Dylan Commentary. TIM RILEY. Knopf, 1992.

"Dylan, Bob." *Current Biography*, Oct. 1991.

"Bob Dylan. . . ." TOM PIAZZA. *New York Times Book Review*, May 26, 1991.

"Forever young. . . ." MARC ELIOT. *California*, June 1991.

"Subterranean half-century blues." *Economist*, May 25, 1991.

Bob Dylan Behind the Shades. CLINTON HEYLIN. Summit, 1991.

Wanted Man: In Search of Bob Dylan. JOHN BAULDIE, ed. Carol, 1991.

Dylan Companion: A Collection of Essential Writing about Bob Dylan. ELIZABETH THOMSON. Delacorte, 1991.

Bob Dylan: Portraits from the Singer's Early Years. DANIEL KRAMER. Carol, 1991.

Bob Dylan, Performing Artist: The Early Years 1960–1973. PAUL WILLIAMS. Underwood-Miller, 1991.

Positively Bob Dylan: A Thirty-Year Discography, Concert and Recording Session Guide, 1960–1989. MICHAEL KROGSGAARD. Popular Culture, 1991.

Bob Dylan: American Poet and Singer: An Annotated Bibliography and Study Guide of Sources and Background Materials, 1961–1991. RICHARD D. WISSOLIK et al, eds. Eadmer, 1991.

Dylan: A Biography. BOB SPITZ. McGraw-Hill, 1989.

Death of a Rebel. MARC ELIOT. Watts, 1989.

Eagle, Harry (1905–92) New York-born Harry Eagle, a leading medical research scientist, was best known by far for his 1959 development of "Eagle's growth medium," a substance that made it possible to reproduce mammalian cells, including human cells, in a laboratory; this was a critically important research tool for researchers worldwide. He made or participated in a wide range of other discoveries, as well, beginning with a 1940s test for syphilis and work on the use of penicillin when dealing with syphilis and gonorrhea. His work also contributed to the understanding of the causes and treatment of cancer. After his 1927 graduation from Johns Hopkins Medical School, Eagle taught and was head of the Johns Hopkins venereal disease research laboratory and laboratory of experimental therapeutics. His affiliations included the National Institutes of Health (1947–61), the National Cancer Institute (1947–49), the National Microbiological Institute (1949–59), the National Institute of Allergy and Infectious Diseases (1959-61), and the Albert Einstein College of Medicine (1961–91). He was survived by his wife, Hope, a daughter, and a sister. (d. Port Chester, New York; June 12, 1992)

FURTHER READING

Obituary. *The Times* (of London), June 29, 1992.
Obituary. *New York Times*, June 13, 1992.

Eastwood, Clint (1930–) Continuing to create his own unique body of work, Clint Eastwood in 1992 directed, produced, and starred as

Bill Munny in his hard-edged, offbeat western *Unforgiven*. Munny is a farmer who was once a notorious gunman, and who now becomes a bounty hunter, possibly to help support his family and possibly for his more private reasons. The film has something of a feminist theme: the $1,000 bounty is offered by a group of prostitutes for the murders of two men who have mutilated a prostitute. Co-starring in the well-received film are Gene Hackman as a brutal sheriff, Morgan Freeman as Eastwood's former criminal partner, and Richard Harris as another bounty-hunting gunman. Forthcoming for Eastwood was a starring role as a Secret Service agent, opposite John Malkovich and Rene Russo in Wolfgang Peterson's film *In the Line of Fire*.

San Francisco-born Eastwood was a star in television as the lead in the western series "Rawhide" (1958–65). He pursued the same western themes in the Italian-made Sergio Leone "spaghetti westerns" that made him a worldwide star, beginning with *A Fistful of Dollars* (1967). He then went on to become one of the most durable of all international action film stars. Beginning with *Play Misty For Me* (1971), he directed, produced, and starred in many of his films, such as *Honkytonk Man* (1982), *Bird* (1988; about jazz great Charlie Parker), *White Hunter, Black Heart* (1990), and *The Rookie* (1990). Eastwood attended Los Angeles City College. He is divorced and has one son, Kyle, who appeared in *Honkytonk Man*.

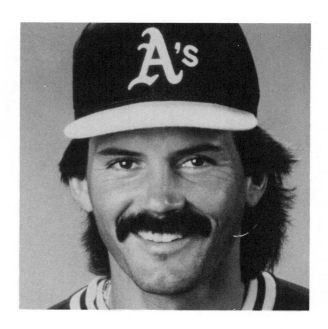

FURTHER READING

"Clint Eastwood. . . ." DAVID BRESKIN. *Rolling Stone*, Sep. 17, 1992.

"Shooting to kill. . . ." SEAN FRENCH. *Times*, Sep. 10, 1992.

"Scraps of hope. . . . ." HENRY SHEEHAN. *Film Comment*, Sep.–Oct. 1992.

"Play mayor for me. . . ." BENJAMIN SVETKEY. *Entertainment*, Apr. 3, 1992.

Clint Eastwood: Malpaso. FUENSANTA PLAZA. Ex Libris (CA), 1991.

"The man who would be Huston." GRAHAM FULLER. *Interview*, Oct. 1990.

"Clint Eastwood. . . ." *Film Quarterly*, Spring 1989.

"Eastwood, Clint." *Current Biography*, Mar. 1989.

The Films of Clint Eastwood. BORIS ZMIJEWSKY and LEE PFEIFFER. Carol, 1988.

Clint Eastwood. JEFFREY RYDER. Dell, 1987.

Clint Eastwood. FRANCOIS GUERIF. St. Martin's, 1986.

Eckersley, Dennis Lee (1954–) Oakland Athletics's right-handed relief pitcher Dennis Eckersley got double honors in 1992, winning the Cy Young Award as the best pitcher in baseball's American League (AL), and being named the AL's Most Valuable Player. In the history of the game, he is only the third relief pitcher and the ninth pitcher overall to capture both honors in the same season. During 1992, he set a major league record of 36 consecutive saves; counting the 4 that ended the 1991 season, that stretched his record to 40 consecutive saves. His 1992 total of 51 saves in 54 opportunities set a club record, and made him only the second pitcher in major league history to save 50 or more games in a season. His last save of the season, in the final game, gave him a career total of 239 career saves, breaking an American League record. Since Eckersley became Oakland's fulltime "stopper" in 1988, his record is 220 saves in 246 save opportunities, or 89 percent. In the All-Star game, he recorded the final out in the game, won by the American League. In July, Eckersley signed a two-year contract extension with Oakland, reportedly for a guaranteed $7.8 million, although he could have become a free agent and probably gained even more money elsewhere.

California-born Eckersley began his professional career in the minors at Reno (1972–73) and San Antonio (1974), then moving into the major leagues with Cleveland (1975–77), Boston (1978–1984), and Chicago (1984–86). He pitched a no-hitter in 1977 and posted 20 victories in 1978, but by 1986 he recognized that he had a severe alcohol problem and sought treatment, then winding up back in his hometown of Oakland in 1987. With his premier skill at "closing," Eckersley is regarded as one of the main reasons that the Oakland A's have been champions of the American League West four of the last five years, and he was a key player in winning the 1989 World Series. Eckersley is married to the former Nancy O'Neill and has one child.

FURTHER READING

"A saving grace." WILLIAM PLUMMER. *People*, Oct. 12, 1992.
"The paintmaster." STEVE WULF. *Sports Illustrated*, Aug. 24, 1992.
"By the numbers." TIM KURKJIAN. *Sports Illustrated*, June 17, 1991.
"Dennis Eckersley." KIT STIER. *Sporting News*, Apr. 1, 1991.
"Fall and rise of. . . ." KIT STIER. *Sporting News*, May 28, 1990.
"Yahoo! . . ." KIT STIER. *Sporting News*, Apr. 30, 1990.
"One Eck of a guy. . . ." PETER GAMMONS. *Sports Illustrated*, Dec. 12, 1988.

Edelman, Marian Wright (1939–)

The head and mainspring of the Children's Defense Fund, Marian Wright Edelman in 1992 published *The Measure of Our Success: A Letter to My Children and Yours*, a book that attracted great interest in a country that was then deeply involved in a watershed presidential campaign that focused in large part on education and other issues affecting the next generation. The depth of feeling generated by these issues had previously been indicated by the huge response to Jonathan Kozol's book *Savage Inequalities: Children in America's Schools* (1991). Edelman's Children's Defense Fund was very much in the news, too, as Hillary Clinton had worked for the Fund early in her career, was currently chairwoman of its Board of Directors, and had been attacked by some Republicans as being somehow "anti-family," because of that association. Edelman's 97-page book was a bestseller, achieving more than 200,000 hardcover copies in print. It was a booklength letter to her three sons, Joshua, Jonah, and Ezra, drawn from and joining many letters written to them while they were growing up, mainly on inspirational themes and including key lessons for life. With the paperback edition in preparation, Edelman continued her long career as a highly visible lobbyist on issues and legislation affecting children, with enhanced prospects of success during the Clinton years.

South Carolina-born Edelman, a lawyer, graduated from Spelman College in 1960. Her 1963 B.A. was from Yale Law School. After her graduation, she was a staff attorney with the New York City-based National Association for the Advancement of Colored People (NAACP) from 1963 to 1964, and then director of the NAACP's Legal and Defense Fund in Jackson, Mississippi (1964–68). She was the first African-American woman to be admitted to the Mississippi bar. In 1968, she founded the Washington Research Project, and from it in 1973 developed and became first and so far only president of the Children's Defense Fund. She is married to lawyer Peter Edelman, and has three children.

FURTHER READING

"Marian Wright Edelman. . . ." NORMAN ATKINS. *Rolling Stone*, Dec. 10, 1992.
"Edelman, Marian Wright." *Current Biography*, Sep. 1992.
"A mother's guiding message." ELEANOR CLIFT. *Newsweek*, June 8, 1992.
"The great defender." MATTHEW S. SCOTT. *Black Enterprise*, May 1992.
Marian Wright Edelman: Defender of Children's Rights. STEVE OTFINOSKI. Blackbirch/Rosen, 1991.
"On being uppity." ROGER WILKINS. *Mother Jones*, June 1990.
"The unraveling kids' crusade. " JOSEPH P. SHAPIRO. *U.S. News & World Report*, Mar. 26, 1990.
"I dream a world." BRIAN LANKER. *National Geographic*, Aug. 1989.
"A sense of urgency." CALVIN TOMKINS. *New Yorker*, Mar. 27, 1989.
"Who's behind the ABC?" *Christianity Today*, Mar. 17, 1989.
"Marian Wright Edelman." *U.S. News & World Report*, Feb. 13, 1989.
"By appointment only. . . ." DEREK SHEARER. *Mother Jones*, Oct. 1988.

Elders, Joycelyn

Elders, Joycelyn (1933–) President Bill Clinton's incoming Surgeon General is a leading Arkansas pediatrician, who became a resident in pediatrics at Little Rock's University of Arkansas Medical Center in 1961 and was chief pediatric resident at the center from 1963 to 1964. She continued to research, teach, and pursue her career as a clinical pediatrician in association with the center until 1987, and was an assistant professor of pediatrics (1967–71), associate professor (1971–76), and full professor (1976–87). She was appointed director of the Arkansas Department of Public Health in 1987 by governor Bill Clinton, leaving that post to become Surgeon General.

As chief public health official in Arkansas, Dr. Elders was a powerful advocate of preventive health care, and especially of care aimed at preventing unwanted teenage pregnancies. She strongly supported the development of sex education clinics in the schools, including the distribution of contraceptives to teenagers, on this and several other issues colliding head-on with anti-abortion and religious fundamentalist groups in her state; but she was fully supported by then-Governor Clinton, and her position prevailed.

Arkansas-born Elders's 1952 B.A. was from Philander Smith University, her 1960 M.D. from the University of Arkansas Medical Center, and her 1967 M.S. in biochemistry from the University of Arkansas Medical Center. Her publications include more than 100 professional articles. She is married to high school basketball coach Oliver B. Elders; they have two children.

FURTHER READING

"The crusade of. . . ." STEVE BARNES. *New York Times Magazine*, Oct. 15, 1989.

Elizabeth II

Elizabeth II (Elizabeth Alexandra Mary; 1926–) On February 6, Britain celebrated the 40th anniversary of Elizabeth's reign, with all the customary tributes and salutes, a new poem from Poet Laureate Ted Hughes, and a BBC documentary. Saying "It is a job for life," the Queen, now 66, made it clear she intended to stay on rather than abdicate in favor of her son, Prince Charles, as some had speculated. But in 1992, as it turned out, many in Britain began to question how long the life of the monarchy itself might be, as a series of highly publicized events concerning her children and their spouses turned much of public opinion sharply against the royal family.

In January, unrevealing published photos of "Fergie" (Sarah Ferguson, Duchess of York and wife of Elizabeth's son Andrew, Duke of York) holidaying with friend Steve Wyatt caused some embarrassment. In March, the Duchess of York filed for a legal separation, which caused a media storm. Also in March, Elizabeth's daughter Anne (the Princess Royal) sued for divorce from Captain Mark Phillips. In June, the book *Diana:*

Her True Story, by Andrew Morton, was serialized in London's *The Sunday Times*, and then became a best-seller; it alleged, among other things, that Princess Diana, the wife of her son, Charles, Prince of Wales and heir to the throne, had attempted suicide several times. Then, in late August, came the greatest media storm of all; British newspapers published photos of a topless "Fergie" on holiday with another friend, John Bryan, which created a huge scandal, and even generated the television film *Fergie and Andrew: Behind Closed Doors* (1992). In December, the palace announced that the Prince Charles and Princess Diana had separated, an event soon to be commemorated by at least three television films.

And that was not all. A November 20th fire destoyed substantial portions of Windsor Castle, the main royal family home; though most of the artworks in the castle were saved, repair costs were estimated at $100 million. The loss increased pressure on the monarchy, with many in Britain seriously questioning the need for its future existence, and many more calling for the royal family to help pay for repairs. The Queen responded by offering to pay taxes on her huge income, and suggesting that she might be willing to cut royal family costs, as well. It was not a good year for Elizabeth II and the British monarchy; no wonder she called it her "annus horribilis."

Elizabeth II is the daughter of George VI and Elizabeth Angela Marguerite, the Queen Mother. She succeeded her father to the throne in 1952, becoming Queen of the United Kingdom of Great Britain and Northern Ireland. She married Philip Mountbatten, the Duke of Edinburgh, in 1947, and is the mother of Prince Charles (1948–), Princess Anne (1950–), Prince Andrew (1960–), and Prince Edward (1964–).

FURTHER READING

"Separate lives." Martha Duffy. *Time*, Nov. 30, 1992.
"The rest of the mess." *First for Women*, Oct. 19, 1992.
"A royal mess." *First for Women*, Oct. 19, 1992.
"God save the Queen! " Robert K. Massie. *Vanity Fair*, Oct. 1992.
"The monarchy will prevail. " Hugo Young. *Newsweek*, June 22, 1992.
"The fall of. . . ." Stuart Reid. *American Spectator*, May 1992.
Queen Elizabeth II: 1952–1992: A Pictorial Celebration of Her Reign. Penny Junor. Longmeadow, 1992.

The Queen: A Revealing Look at the Private Life of Elizabeth II. Douglas Keay. St. Martin's, 1992.
"Windsor knot. . . ." Christopher Hitchens. *New York Times Magazine*, May 12, 1991.
Sovereign: Elizabeth II and the Windsor Dynasty. Roland Flamini. Delacorte, 1991.
Royal Sisters. Anne Edwards. Morrow, 1990.

Elliott, Denholm (1922–92)

London-born Elliott, a distinguished character actor, began his stage career following his release from three years in a German prisoner-of-war camp. Although much of his work was in strong supporting roles in the British and American theaters, he was best known by by far for his more than 80 screen roles, beginning with his 1949 debut in *Mr. Prohack* to his final role in the film version of *Noises Off* (1992). His breakthrough film role was in *The Cruel Sea* (1953). He went on to play notable roles in such films as *King Rat* (1965), a second breakthrough role in *Alfie* (1965), *The Sea Gull* (1968), *A Doll's House* (1973), *The Apprenticeship of Duddy Kravitz* (1974), *A Bridge Too Far* (1977), *The Hound of the Baskervilles* (1978), *Watership Down* (1978), *St. Jack* (1979), *Raiders of the Lost Ark* (1981), *Trading Places* (1983), *A Private Function* (1984; British Film Award), *Defence of the Realm* (1985; British Film Award), and *A Room With a View* (1986; Oscar nomination). His television work included several television miniseries, perhaps most notably Dennis Potter's "Blade on the Feather" (1980) and his role as George Smiley in "A Murder of Quality." He was survived by his second wife, Susan, a daughter, and a son. (d. Ibiza; October 7, 1992)

FURTHER READING

Obituary. *Variety*, Oct. 12, 1992.
Obituary. *The Times* (of London), Oct. 8, 1992.
Obituary. *New York Times*, Oct. 7, 1992.
Obituary. *Independent*, Oct. 7, 1992.

Enright, Dan (1918–92)

Television producer Dan Enright, with his partner, Jack Barry, was at the center of the massive television quiz show scandal of 1959. Enright and Barry, who had become partners in 1947, had by the late 1950s created many long-running hit television shows, including such game shows as

"Concentration," "Twenty One," "The Joker's Wild," and "Tic Tac Dough." On their "Twenty One" show, contestant Charles Van Doren had become a national celebrity, ultimately winning $129,000. But in 1959, Enright admitted before a Congressional investigating committee that "Twenty One" and "Tic Tac Dough" had been rigged, with contestants, including Van Doren, being given the answers before appearing, and with winners set up in advance. As no illegal act had been committed (the practice was only later made a federal crime), Enright and Barry escaped with some damage to their careers, and Van Doren with the loss of his job in television. Enright continued on in television, and Enright and Barry later successfully revived their partnership, even going back to producing game shows. He was survived by his wife, Stella, a daughter, and a son. (d. Los Angeles; May 22, 1992)

FURTHER READING

Obituary. *Variety*, June 1, 1992.
Obituary. *New York Times*, May 24, 1992.

Ephron, Henry (1912–92) New York City-born Ephron and his wife, Phoebe Ephron (d. 1971), were long-term stage and screenwriting partners, beginning with their play *Three's a Family* (1943). Their first screenplay, *Bride By Mistake* (1944), was followed by such works as *John Loves Mary* (1949), *The Jackpot* (1950), *There's No Business Like Show Business* (1954), *Daddy Long Legs* (1955), *Carousel* (1956; he also produced), the Tracy-Hepburn classic *Desk Set* (1957); and *Captain Newman, M.D* (1964). He also produced several other films. Their several plays included *Take Her, She's Mine* (1961). His autobiography was *We Thought We Could Do Anything* (1973). He was survived by four daughters, two of whom are the writers Nora and Delia Ephron. (d. Los Angeles; September 6, 1992)

FURTHER READING

Obituary. *The Times* (of London), Sep. 15, 1992.
Obituary. *Variety*, Sep. 14, 1992.
Obituary. *New York Times*, Sep. 7, 1992.

Ephron, Nora (1941–) Long established as a writer, Ephron expanded her role in films in 1992, cowriting and directing the well-received comedy *This Is My Life*, based on Meg Wolitzer's

1988 novel, *This Is Your Life*, a title that proved unacceptable to the owners of television's "This Is Your Life." In Ephron's film, Julie Kavner starred as a stand-up comedian juggling her growing career and her role as mother of two young girls; Carrie Fisher and Dan Aykroyd co-starred. The film was something of a family affair, as the script was cowritten by Ephron's younger sister, writer Delia Ephron, calling up echoes of the long and celebrated stage and screenwriting partnership between their parents Phoebe Ephron (d. 1971), and Henry Ephron (1912–92). Continuing on with this new stage in her career, Nora Ephron was to direct the forthcoming film *Sleepless in Seattle*, starring Tom Hanks and Meg Ryan.

New York City-born Ephron, the daughter of screenwriters Henry and Phoebe Ephron, began her career as a reporter for *New York Post* (1963–68), and then became a full-time writer for several years, becoming highly visible as a contributing editor to *New York Magazine* and *Esquire* in the early 1970s. She was an editor and columnist for *Esquire* (1974–78). Her books include *Wallflower at the Orgy* (1970), *Crazy Salad* (1975), *Scribble Scribble* (1978), *Heartburn* (1983), and *Nora Ephron Collected* (1991). Her screenplays include *Silkwood* (1983, with Alice Arlen; it won an Oscar nomination), *Heartburn* (1986; her adaptation of her 1983 book), *When Harry Met Sally. . .* (1989; Oscar nomination), and *My Blue Heaven* (1990). She also cowrote and was executive producer of *Cookie* (1989). Ephron's 1962 B.A. was from Wellesley College. She is married to Nicholas Pileggi, her third husband, and has two children. Her second husband was journalist Carl Bernstein; their relationship was the subject of *Heartburn*.

FURTHER READING

"Nora's arc." LESLIE BENNETTS. *Vanity Fair*, Feb. 1992.
"How to repossess a life. . . ." GARRY WILLS. *Time*, Jan. 27, 1992.
"Take one." LESLEY JANE NONKIN. *Vogue*, Jan. 1992.
"Ephron, Nora." *Current Biography*, Jan. 1990.

Espy, Mike (Alphonso Michael Espy; 1953–) President Bill Clinton's incoming Secretary of Agriculture, an attorney, worked with Central Mississippi Legal Services (1978–80),

moving into state government as a Mississippi assistant Secretary of State (1980–84) and as state Director of Consumer Protection (1984–85). He made a successful run for Congress in 1986, winning by a slim margin to become the first African-American since Reconstruction to represent Mississippi's Delta region. In office, he served on the House Agriculture Committee and several other committees central to the interests of his district, especially focusing on the needs of its agricultural poor. He helped pass the Lower Mississippi River Valley Development Act, which set up the Delta Commission.

Mississippi-born Espy's 1975 B.A. was from Howard University, and his 1978 J.D. from the University of Santa Clara. He was formerly married to Sheila Bell, and has two children.

FURTHER READING

"Black caucus weekend. . . ." *Jet*, Sep. 2, 1991.
"Mike Espy. . . ." LARKIN WARREN. *Esquire*, Dec. 1989.
"White and wrong." JOHN B. JUDIS. *New Republic*, Oct. 24, 1988.

Ewing, Patrick Aloysius (1962–) At the Summer Olympics, it was the "Harry and Larry" show—Larry being Bird and Harry (for unknown reasons) being Ewing. Formerly fierce competitors in the same conference, Bird and Ewing surprisingly became a comedy team, cracking up themselves and each other on the sidelines of the international basketball competition during the 1992 Olympics at Barcelona. Ewing played—and played well—on the U.S. "Dream Team," on the way to what was for him a second Olympic Gold Medal (the first coming in 1984), despite the fact that his thumb was dislocated and lacerated during training camp; but he seemed somewhat relieved to be able to relax, as other stars took their turn, especially with the media.

Earlier in the year, Ewing was anything but relaxed. Under coach Pat Riley, Ewing led his New York Knicks into the playoffs and all the way to the Eastern Conference finals of the National Basketball Association (NBA) for the 1991–92 season, where—to the surprise of most observers—they stretched the defending champion Chicago Bulls, starring Michael Jordan, to seven grueling games before finally succumbing. The team's performance was a testament to the series of moves designed—as Ewing wanted—to make the Knicks championship contenders. Not content, the Knicks management made several more trades for the 1992–93 season; though the revamped Knicks were at times on top in their division in the fall of 1992, it was unclear how the gamble would pay off by season's end. In January 1992, Ewing was for the third straight year voted starting center for the Eastern Conference squad of the NBA All-Stars.

Jamaica-born Ewing is one of the leading centers in modern basketball, which became apparent while he was still a college player at Georgetown University, where he took his team to three National Collegiate Athletic Association (NCAA) finals, winning the championship in 1984, when he was named Most Valuable Player of the Final Four. In his senior year, he won a host of "player of the year" awards, including the Kodak Award, Rupp Trophy, and Naismith Trophy. After his 1985 graduation, Ewing joined the New York Knicks, beginning a career that would take him to six all-star games (1986 and 1988–92, in the latter three as starting center) and international celebrity, even without a longed-for national championship. Ewing married Rita Williams in 1990; they have one daughter; Ewing also has a son.

FURTHER READING

Sports Great Patrick Ewing. JACK KAVANAGH. Enslow, 1992.
"Ewing, Patrick." *Current Biography*, May 1991.
"Patrick Ewing." SPIKE LEE. *Interview*, May 1990.
Patrick Ewing. MATTHEW NEWMAN. Macmillan, 1986.

Exley, Frederick (1929–92) Born in Watertown, New York, Frederick Exley wrote three novels, all of them critically notable and by some critics acclaimed, and all of them in a largely autobiographical form he called the "fictional memoir." The first, *A Fan's Notes* (1968), had as a central figure the author and football star Frank Gifford; it won a National Book Award nomination. The second, *Pages From a Cold Island* (1973), revolved around writer Edmund Wilson, and the third was *Last Notes From Home* (1988). Exley's novels, in sum an intensely introspective catalogue of his own concerns, achieved considerable popularity on American college campuses, and perhaps a kind of cult status, although they were far from becoming commercial successes. He was survived by two daughters and two sisters. (Alexandria Bay, New York; June 17, 1992)

FURTHER READING

"Fred Exley. . . ." PAUL SCANLON. *GQ—Gentlemen's Quarterly*, Sep. 1992.
Obituary. *The Times* (of London), July 2, 1992.
Obituary. *New York Times*, June 18, 1992.
"Exley, Frederick." *Current Biography*, Oct. 1989.
"Frederick Exley. . . ." JANE HOWARD. *People*, Nov. 14, 1988.

Fahd, Ibn Abd al-Aziz Al Saud

(1923–) Saudi Arabian king Fahd, his American alliance cemented by joint action during the Persian Gulf War and by American arms supplies afterward, in 1992 moved to somewhat modernize Saudi political and social life. But only somewhat; he also made it very clear that he had no intention of introducing democracy. Rather, his moves consisted of promoting the Saudi expression of the fundamentalist-moderate argument raging throughout the Muslim world, and positioning himself to remain a major conservative force in that world, while not sinking into the antimodern dead end of fundamentalism.

Announced on March 1, Fahd's reforms included the establishment of a Consultative Council, all member to be chosen by the king, which would recommend new laws, subject to final decision by the king; and formation of similar councils in every province, with provincial governments granted more legislative and spending autonomy. The reforms also included some safeguards against arbitrary government searches and arrests, thought by many to be an attempt to curb the ever-present Saudi religious police. The rules of succession were also altered; after confirming his brother Abdullah Ibn Abdul Aziz al-Saud as his heir, Fahd announced that future rulers would be chosen by the royal family rather than solely by hereditary right.

Abroad, Fahd continued to work with the members of the alliance against Iraq, and to bar Iraqi resurgence, strongly supporting extension of sanctions against Iraq and establishment of the southern Iraq "no-fly zone" in late August, to protect Iraqi Shiite Muslims from Iraqi government air attacks. He also withdrew all aid from the Palestine Liberation Organization and Jordan, which had backed Saddam Hussein, and in May offered to pay the cost of restoring Muslim holy sites in Jerusalem, estimated at $70 million, including repair work on Dome of the Rock; this was taken as an attempt to claim custody of the shrines, administered by Jordan since the 1940s.

Riyadh-born Fahd is the son of King Abdul al-Aziz Ibn Saud. He succeeded to the throne in 1982, after the death of his half-brother Khalid. He had previously been a member of the Saudi delegation to the San Francisco founding meeting of the United Nations in 1945, education minister in 1953, interior minister (1962–75), and a deputy prime minister (1962–82;). He became prime minister as well as king in 1982. He had been named Crown Prince in 1975, after the assassination of King Faisal.

FURTHER READING

"King Fahd's big gamble. . . ." PETER THEROUX. *Vanity Fair*, Apr. 1991.
"Who's sitting pretty. . . ." *Business Week*, Mar. 11, 1991.
"Lifting the veil. . . ." LISA BEYER. *Time*, Sep. 24, 1990.
"An exquisite balancing act. . . ." GEORGE J. CHURCH. *Time*, Sep. 24, 1990.
King Fahd and Saudi Arabia's Great Evolution. NASSER I. RASHID AND ESBER I. SHAHEEN. International Institute of Technology, 1987.

Faldo, Nick (1957–)

British golfer Faldo has had the reputation of being cold and unemotional—witness the nickname "Mechanical Man"—but that image was shed in July at the British Open at Scotland's Muirfield when he came back to retake the lead from American John Cook. After his last putt, Faldo shed tears of joy and nervous relief, for he had led after the second and third rounds, but then bogeyed three holes in the final round, clawing his way back in with two birdies in the final four holes, when Cook left him an opening. It was Faldo's fifth major championship, and his third British Open win, and put him back into first place in the Sony world rankings, ahead of Fred Couples, who had become first in April, but missed the cut at Muirfield. Acknowledging that his British Open performance was not pretty, Faldo croaked a bit from Frank Sinatra's song "My Way," with trophy in hand. Also in 1992, Faldo came in first at the Irish Open, in a playoff; the Scandinavian Masters; the European Open; World Match Play; and the Johnnie Walker World Championship, also in a playoff. Those wins, along with several other top-five finishes, all speak of his revival from a mediocre 1991. He attributes his success partly to his decision to rebuild his swing, coached by David Leadbetter, as he had done once before. Faldo has also said he is learning to be lighter in his approach to the game, sometimes even joking with the crowd and overall preferring—as he put it—to retire Mechanical Man in favor of "Monsieur Naturel." In 1992, Faldo also published a book, *Golf: The Winning Formula*.

Faldo became a leading junior British golfer in the mid-1970s, and turned professional in 1976. He was voted best new British golfer of the year in 1977, and went on to build a solid, unspectacular career, emerging as a major figure only a decade later, after rebuilding his entire game in 1985. His major wins include the 1987 British Open, the 1988 French Open, the 1989 and 1990 Masters, the French Open again in 1989, and a second British Open in 1990, a stunning win by five strokes, with a record-setting 18 strokes under par. Faldo attended the University of Houston. He is married, and has two children.

FURTHER READING

"Faldo, Nick." *Current Biography*, Sep. 1992.
"Nick Faldo." *Sporting News*, Apr. 15, 1991.
"Do you know me? . . ." Rick Reilly. *Sports Illustrated*, Apr. 8, 1991.

"What's next for Nick?" Michael McDonnell. *Golf*, Feb. 1991.

Fan Xueyan, Peter Joseph (1907–92)

Roman Catholic Bishop Fan was born in Hebei province. He was ordained a priest in 1934, and spent much of his subsequent career as a seminary teacher. In 1951, he was ordained Bishop of Baoding by Pope Pius XII. Like many other Catholics priests and laypeople, he refused to support the government-backed Catholic Patriotic Association, declaring his continuing religious allegiance to the Pope. He was arrested in 1958, and was imprisoned until 1979, becoming during his years of imprisonment a worldwide symbol of resistance to the government. Returning to Baoding, he re-entered his "underground" church activities, and in 1983 was again arrested, this time imprisoned for four years of a ten-year sentence, and then paroled, but kept under close control, and sometimes imprisoned again for short periods. In 1990, he was arrested again, although in very poor health. There were no survivors. (Died in detention somewhere in China; April 13, 1992)

FURTHER READING

Obituary. *The Times* (of London), June 6, 1992.
Obituary. *New York Times*, Apr. 25, 1992.

Farrow, Mia Villiers (1945–)

Mia Farrow's long relationship with Woody Allen came to an end in 1992, and with it also ended their long professional relationship. Their personal breakup was bitter, and its circumstances provided the media with an enormous story opportunity that was avidly seized upon, encouraged by lawyers seeking to fight the case very publicly.

Their relationship had started in 1980; they never married, but had three children, two of them adopted. Farrow has six other children as well, five of them adopted Vietnamese. The situation opened publicly when Allen sued for custody of their three children; Farrow opposed his suit. Soon afterward, Allen and Soon-Yi Farrow Previn, Farrow's 21-year-old adopted daughter, announced that they were in love. Though they were not related, the media implied that the relationship was incestuous. Farrow also caused child molestation charges involving one of the Farrow-Allen children to be filed in Connecticut. As the publicity grew immense, and after enormous damage had been done to all concerned, the judge in the case issued a "gag" order, forbidding the parties to discuss the case further anywhere but in court.

The year also saw the last two of the Allen-Farrow films. Farrow starred in *Shadows and Fog*, written and directed by Allen, and co-starring Allen, John Malkovich, Madonna, Jodie Foster, and Kathy Bates. She also starred in *Husbands and Wives*, written and directed by Allen, and co-starring Allen, Blythe Danner, Judy Davis, Sidney Pollack, Liam Neeson, and Lysette Anthony. In the latter film, Farrow is the wife of a college teacher, played by Allen, who becomes sexually involved with a 21-year-old student, played by Juliette Lewis, and breaks with his wife. The film opened earlier than planned, in a studio attempt to make money out of the obvious similarity between the story line and the specifics of the Allen-Farrow breakup, but did not do well commercially. Forthcoming in 1994 was Farrow's autobiography, to be published by Doubleday.

Los Angeles-born Farrow became a star in television as Alison Mackenzie in "Peyton Place" (1964–66). In movies, she became a star in *Rosemary's Baby* (1968), going on to such films as *John and Mary* (1969), *The Great Gatsby* (1973), *Death on the Nile* (1978), *Zelig* (1983), *Broadway Danny Rose* (1984), *Hannah and Her Sisters* (1986), *Radio Days* (1987), *Crimes and Misdemeanors* (1989), and *Alice* (1990). She also appeared in several leading stage roles in Britain during the mid-1970s, as a member of the Royal Shakespeare Company. The daughter of actress Maureen O'Sullivan and director John Farrow, she has been married twice, to Frank Sinatra and Andre Previn; Woody Allen was her long-time companion. She has nine children, five of them adopted Vietnamese.

FURTHER READING

"Mia's story." MAUREEN ORTH. *Vanity Fair*, Nov. 1992.

"Everything you always. . . ." PHOEBE HOBAN. *New York*, Sep. 21, 1992.

"A family affair." TOM GLIATTO. *People*, Aug. 31, 1992.

"Woody and Mia. . . ." ERIC LAX. *New York Times Magazine*, Feb. 24, 1991.

Mia: The Life of Mia Farrow. EDWARD Z. EPSTEIN. Delacorte, 1991.

Mia Farrow: Flower Child, Madonna, Muse. SAM RUBIN and RICHARD TAYLOR. St. Martin's, 1989.

Feinstein, Dianne (1933–   ) Former San Francisco mayor and California gubernatorial candidate Dianne Feinstein became a major national figure in "The Year of the Woman," defeating John Seymour, who had been appointed to fill out the unexpired term in the U.S. Senate of California's new governor, Pete Wilson. Two years remained of the Senate term, and she will be up for re-election in 1994. Democrat Feinstein led Republican Seymour throughout the campaign, running as a liberal on such issues as abortion rights, environmental protection, and military spending cuts, while Seymour, a moderate, did his best to distance himself from George Bush, whose popularity had plummeted so far in California that Bush hardly campaigned in the state, conceding it to Bill Clinton very early. In early August, some polls reported Feinstein with a 17–18 point lead, and that lead held, her November margin being 17 points. California also sent Barbara Boxer to the Senate, becoming the only state with two women Senators.

San Francisco-born Feinstein was a long-term member of her city's Board of Supervisors (1970–79). She was president of the Board of Supervisors on November 27, 1978, when Dan

White murdered San Francisco mayor George Moscone and supervisor Harvey Milk; she succeeded Moscone as acting mayor and then was elected mayor (1979–88). As mayor, she became one of the most influential and highly visible women in American politics. In 1990, she became the first woman to win a major party's gubernatorial nomination in her state, after winning a hotly contested Democratic primary race; but her run against Republican senator Pete Wilson was unsuccessful. Feinstein has been married three times, most recently to Richard Blum in 1980, and has one child. Her B.S. was from Stanford University, in 1955.

FURTHER READING

"Coastal dumping." Morton Kondracke. *New Republic*, Nov. 12, 1990.
"Dianne Feinstein." J.D. Reed. *People Weekly*, Oct. 8, 1990.
"A women of. . . ." Sidney Blumenthal. *New Republic*, Aug. 13, 1990.
"Charm is only. . . ." Jordan Bonfante. *Time*, June 18, 1990.
"Snow White's. . . ." Donald Baer. *U.S. News & World Report*, June 18, 1990.
"Feinstein's lost horizons." *Savvy*, Apr. 1988.

Fenwick, Millicent (1910–92) New York City-born Fenwick, a fiercely independent and free woman who was born to wealth, attended Columbia University and the New School for Social Research, broke away from her family in her youth to join a married man, whom she later married for several years. She then supported herself and her two children by working as an editor and writer. At the age of 59, she began a notable political career as a very liberal Republican, with a term in the New Jersey State Assembly. She became an activist first as New Jersey director of consumer affairs in 1972, and successfully ran for Congress in 1973, winning the first of her four terms in the House of Representatives. There she became a powerfully articulate and most unusual Republican, who spoke out on such issues as an end to the Vietnam War, for civil rights legislation, for gun control, for environmental legislation, and for a wide range of other matters that amounted to the basic liberal agenda of the time. In the process, she also emerged as one of the most colorful, quotable people in American life, whose

trademark was the pipe she adopted when she gave up cigarette smoking. She was the inspiration for Representative Lacey Davenport in Garry Trudeau's "Doonesbury" comic strip. Her Congressional career ended with a defeat in the 1982 New Jersey Senatorial race, but she served until 1987 as American representative to the Rome-based United Nations Food and Agriculture Organization. In 1982, she published *Speaking Up*. She was survived by a son. (d. Bernardsville, New Jersey; September 16, 1992)

FURTHER READING

Obituary. *The Times* (of London), Sep. 19, 1992.
Obituary. *Independent*, Sep. 19, 1992.
Obituary. *New York Times*, Sep. 17, 1992.

Fernández Ordóñez, Francisco (1930–92) Madrid-born Fernández Ordóñez, a lawyer, served in a series of Spanish government posts during the 1960s and early 1970s, but was one of the first high-ranking officials to break with the Franco dictatorship, going back to the private practice of law. After Franco's death, in 1975, he moved back into public life, and in 1977 was a elected to Spain's first post-Franco democratic parliament. He was Finance Minister (1977–79), there reforming the basic federal tax law, and Justice Minister (1981), there legalizing divorce in Spain despite Catholic Church opposition. In 1985, he became Foreign Mnister in the Socialist Felipe González government, then playing a major role in moving Spain into the European Community. He was survived by his wife, Maria Paz García Mayo. (d. Madrid; August 7, 1992)

FURTHER READING

Obituary. *The Times* (of London), Aug. 8, 1992.
Obituary. *New York Times*, Aug. 8, 1992.

Ferrer, José (José Vicente Ferrer y Cintrón; 1912–92) Puerto Rico-born Ferrer began his long stage and screen career in 1934; his first starring role was on Broadway, in *Charley's Aunt* (1940). His most notable Broadway roles were as Iago opposite Paul Robeson as *Othello* (1942); his Tony-winning *Cyrano de Bergerac*

(1946), which he repeated on screen in an Oscar-winning 1950 performance; and his Tony-winning lead in *The Shrike* (1951). His many screen appearances included starring roles as the artist Toulouse-Lautrec in *Moulin Rouge* (1953; he won Oscar nomination) and as composer Sigmund Romberg in *Deep in My Heart* (1954). He also appeared in such films as *Joan of Arc* (1948; for another Oscar nomination); *The Caine Mutiny* (1954), and *Lawrence of Arabia* (1962). He also appeared in television, and directed several plays and feature films. He was survived by his fourth wife, the former Stella Magee, three daughters, three sons, a sister, and a brother. Two of his wives were the actress Uta Hagen and the singer Rosemary Clooney. (d. Coral Gables, Florida; January 26, 1992)

FURTHER READING

"Adieu, king of anguish." *People*, Feb. 10, 1992.
Obituary. *Variety*, Feb. 3, 1992
Obituary. *The Times* (of London), Jan. 28, 1992.
Obituary. *Independent*, Jan. 28, 1992.
Obituary. *New York Times*, Jan. 27, 1992.

Ffrangcon-Davies, Gwen (1891–1992)

A leading figure in the British theater for half a century, Ffrangcon-Davies at 101 was a living link to the Victorian theater of Henry Irving and Ellen Terry. She made her stage debut in 1911 in *A Midsummer Night's Dream*, played in small roles for the balance of the decade, and was with the Birmingham Rep in 1921. In 1922, she played Eve in the world premiere of Shaw's *Back to Methuselah*, and in 1924 was Juliet to John Gielgud's first Romeo. She went on to play many of the classic theater roles, in the 1930s had a long run as Elizabeth Barrett Browning in *The Barretts of Wimpole Street*, and starred opposite Gielgud in several more plays, including his 1940 *The Importance of Being Earnest* and 1942 *Macbeth*. During the postwar period, she had a major success as Mary Tyrone in *A Long Day's Journey Into Night* (1958), and continued to play in a wide range of roles, her last stage appearance coming in the 1970 Royal Court Theater production of *Uncle Vanya*. There were no survivors. (d. Essex, England; January 17, 1992)

FURTHER READING

Obituary. *Variety*, Jan. 31, 1992.
Obituary. *The Times* (of London), Jan. 28, 1992.

Obituary. *New York Times*, Jan. 28, 1992.
Obituary. *Independent*, Jan. 28, 1992.

Finley, Karen (1956–)

The "NEA Four" case—the three-year-old National Endowment for the Arts censorship case that in 1990 catapulted performance artist Karen Finley onto the national scene—continued to develop in 1992. On June 10, 1992 Los Angeles federal judge Wallace Tashima ruled that the law under which their NEA grants had been refused was in violation of the First Amendment, setting the stage for a government appeal, if desired. With the end of the Bush Administration, there was considerable thought that new laws and different attitudes on the part of the incoming Clinton Administration would greatly change federal attitudes toward censorship of the arts.

Finley continued to produce performance art in 1992—and to shock the shockable, as clearly intended by her new work "A Certain Level of Denial." On July 24, at New York's Alice Tully Hall, she appeared wearing only a hat and shoes, to dramatize what was in fact a serious work of protest. A month earlier, her "Momento Mori" exhibit appeared at the Los Angeles Museum of Contemporary Art; it included paintings, text, and other inanimate objects, and also two tableux involving eight live people. "The Women's Room" was on abortion rights themes, and included a woman lying on a double bed; "The Memorial Room" was on AIDS themes, and included patients and their friends. Finley also ran into another censorship situation in July, when Tribune Entertainment cut her from "The Dennis Miller Show" because of some of her language.

Finley, who grew up in Chicago and Evanston, Illinois, attended the Art Institute of Chicago and the San Francisco Art Institute. Her *Shock Treatment* (1990) contains the text of some of her controversial performances, among other writings. She and three other artists, Holly Hughes, John Fleck, and Tim Miller, were denied NEA grants in 1990, on the basis of the alleged obscenity of their work, generating the NEA Four case. She was formerly married.

FURTHER READING

Performance art...." MARGOT MIFFLIN. *ARTnews*, Apr. 1992.

"Blood and chocolate. . . ." Luc Sante. *New Republic*, Oct. 15, 1990.

"Karen Finley. . . ." Richard Schechner. *Drama Review*, Spring 1988.

Finney, Albert (1936–)

Back in the theater for a major role on the London stage, Finney opened in April in Ronald Harwood's new play *Reflected Glory*, as the aggrieved older brother who takes great exception to being the centerpiece of a play written by his younger brother, played by Stephen Moore. Unfortunately, the work had an unexpectedly limited nine-week run; on June 5th, Finney pulled out because he had not been paid, for although the reviews had been good the box office was not, as hard times hit the London stage during the long, deep British and worldwide recession.

On screen, Finney starred in Gillies McKinnon's film *The Playboys*, set in modern Ireland. In the work, written by Shane Connaughton, Finney played Hegarty, a village police officer, opposite Robin Wright as a single mother and Aidan Quinn as a member of a traveling theater troupe. Forthcoming was a starring role in a family drama set in South Carolina in Bruce Beresford's film *Rich in Love*, opposite Jill Clayburgh as the mother and Kathryn Erbe as the troubled adolescent.

Born in Lancashire, Finney has been a major figure in the British theater for thirty years, from his appearance as *Billy Liar* (1960). He went on to star in such plays as *Luther* (1961), *A Day in the Death of Joe Egg* (1967), *Krapp's Last Tape* (1973), and in a wide range of classic works, including his National Theatre *Macbeth* (1978). At the same time, he became a film star, as *Tom Jones* (1963), as Hercule Poirot in *Murder on the Orient Express* (1974), and in such films as *Gumshoe* (1972), *Annie* (1982), *Under the Volcano* (1984), *Orphans* (1987), and *Miller's Crossing* (1990). In 1990, he made a highly acclaimed appearance on the London stage in Ronald Harwood's *Another Time*. Finney attended the Royal Academy of Dramatic Art. He has been married to Jane Wenham and Anouk Aimée, and has one child.

FURTHER READING

"The opportunity. . . ." Alvin Sanoff. *U.S. News & World Report*, Dec. 14, 1987.

Fischer, Bobby (1943–)

Legendary chess master Bobby Fischer came out of self-imposed seclusion in 1992, bringing with him trouble and turmoil, as of old. Fischer had not played chess publicly since 1972, when he beat Russian master Boris Spassky for the world chess championship. Retiring from public view, Fischer had refused to defend the title and had it stripped from him in 1975 by the International Chess Federation, when he would not play challenger Anatoly Karpov. His 1992 opponent was none other than 56-year-old Spassky, now a French citizen, in a $5 million match sponsored by Yugoslav millionaire Jezdimir Vasilijevic, who had originally challenged current world champion, Garry Kasparov, to play Fischer.

The problem was in the venue: The Fischer-Spassky rematch was held in the remains of the former Yugoslavia, which was under United States and United Nations trade sanctions for its human rights violations against other ethnic peoples, especially the Bosnians. Fischer derided the sanctions, and in a news conference even spat on the U.S. Treasury Department letter warning that if he played there, he could face charges, involving up to a $250,000 fine and up to 10 years imprisonment, on return to the United States. Fischer also noted that he had paid no income taxes since 1976, and had "no intention of paying them now;" and continued making the kinds of derogatory remarks about Jews (although his own mother, Regina Pustan, is Jewish), Blacks, and others that had alienated many people in the past.

In the end, Fischer played the match, which ran from early September to early November, on the Adriatic resort island of Sveti Stefan. After a first win followed by three consecutive losses, he steadied to win the match with an overall record of 10 wins to Spassky's 5, with 15 draws. Typically, in mid-match, he insisted on having a glass soundproof barrier installed. Often at Fischer's side was Zita Rajcsanyi, who won her country's junior women's chess championship shortly before her 19th birthday, in September, and who had helped draw him out of retirement.

Fischer's share of the prize money, as the first player to win 10 games (with draws not counted), was $3.35 million. Fischer had continued to regard himself as world champion, and this as his title defense, and afterward made derogatory remarks about official chess champion Kasparov, who during the match had criticized Spassky's play as "weak" and Fischer's as "very poor." As 1992 ended, Fischer's sponsor reported that Fischer would play another match in Yugoslavia early in 1993, though Fischer's precise whereabouts and plans were unknown. Typical for the times, two movies were being planned, by year's end one already in production, on Fischer's life.

Fischer was child chess prodigy, who studied with grandmaster Jack Collins from age 13, while still attending Brooklyn's Erasmus Hall High School. At 14, a school dropout, he became United States chess champion, and in 1958 the youngest grandmaster in history. Fischer became an international celebrity at age 29, when he ended decades of Soviet chess domination by defeating Spassky at Reykjavik, Iceland, becoming the first and so far only United States world chess champion. Fischer received $156,000 for his Reykjavik win, but turned down most promotional offers, though he did publish some books, including *My Sixty Memorable Games* (1972) and *Bobby Fischer Teaches Chess* (1981). He worked for a time as a cable television installer. Though he was contemptuous of the chess establishment, the U.S. Chess Federation had in recent years bought Fischer $10,000 worth of computer equipment, so he could work on his chess game, in hopes that he would return.

FURTHER READING

"Fischer, back. . . ." JULIE FLINT. *Observer*, Nov. 8, 1992.
Bobby Fischer: Complete Games of the American World Chess Champion. LOU HAYS. Hays, 1992.
Bobby Fischer: His Approach to Chess. ELIE AGUR. Macmillan, 1992.
Bobby Fischer: Profile of a Prodigy, rev. ed. FRANK BRADY. Dover, 1989.
Searching for Bobby Fischer: The World of Chess Observed by the Father of a Child Prodigy. FRED WAITZKIN. Random, 1988.

Fisher, Amy (1965–) On May 19, 1992, in Massapequa, Long Island, New York, 17-year-old high school student Amy Fisher assaulted and shot 36-year-old Mary Jo Buttafuoco. Buttafuoco, the wife of Joseph Buttafuoco, was seriously injured; a bullet that lodged in her head was inoperable, and she was left with partial paralysis of her face and partial hearing loss. Fisher claimed that she had been having an affair with Joseph Buttafuoco for more than a year, and that he was a co-conspirator in the shooting. He denied both allegations, and also denied a considerable number of related allegations that surfaced during the course of Fisher's trial and sentencing, including a formal statutory rape complaint against him brought by Fisher's lawyer, as well as charges that he had led Fisher into a life of prostitution. The Nassau County district attorney declined to press charges against Buttafuoco. Regarding Fisher, the district attorney and Fisher's defense ultimately struck a plea bargain; in return for the dropping of more serious charges, Fisher pleaded guilty to lesser charges and was on December 1, 1992 sentenced to 5–15 years in prison.

What distinguished the case was the attention it received in the media; calling Fisher "the Long Island Lolita," the media had a field day, giving the case enormous publicity day after day, from May to December. There were seemingly endless interviews with all concerned, media-generated charges piled on charges, the discovery of secret tapes, attempted Fisher suicides —and ultimately three made-for-television movies, with a promise of more of all of the above to come. Nor did public attention waver for a moment; it grew and grew. There were three highly successful television films on the case shown within a single week: On December 28, 1992, Noelle Parker played Fisher in the NBC version. On January 3, 1993, Drew Barrymore played Fisher in the ABC version; on the same night, Alyssa Milano played Fisher in the CBS version. The NBC film had a 19.4 rating, the highest television film of the season so far. The ABC and CBS films, even though shown on the same night, each had better-than-average ratings.

At year's end, Fisher was in prison; Mary Jo Buttafuoco was permanently damaged; the Buttafuoco's had filed civil suits against Fisher aimed at securing any monies that Fisher derived from the case; and much more seemed likely to occur.

FURTHER READING

"The three faces of Amy." BENJAMIN SVETKEY. *Entertainment*, Dec. 18, 1992.
"Sex, lies and videotapes." JOE TREEN. *People*, Oct. 12, 1992.
"Running wild. . . ." JEANIE KASINDORF. *New York*, Aug. 10, 1992.

Fisher, M. F. K.

Fisher, M. F. K. (Mary Francis Kennedy Fisher; 1908–92) Michigan-born Fisher, a writer, was best known for her cookbooks and other gastronomical works, although she also wrote novels, short stories, and a wide range of essays. Her interest in cooking began while she and her husband, Alfred Fisher, lived in Dijon, France (1929–31). Her first book was *Serve It Forth* (1937); her second *Consider the Oyster* (1941). Her best known works included *How to Cook a Wolf* (1942), *The Gastronomical Me* (1943), *Here Let Us Feast* (1946), *An Alphabet for Gourmets* (1949), *A Cordial Water* (1961), and *With Bold Knife and Fork* (1968). She was survived by two daughters and a sister. (d. Glen Ellen, California; June 22, 1992)

FURTHER READING

Conversations with M. F. K. Fisher. DAVID LAZAR, ed. University Press of Mississippi, 1993.

"M.F.K. Fisher: 1908–1992." CHARLES GANDEE. *House & Garden*, Nov. 1992.

"The gastronomical she." LAURA SHAPIRO. *Newsweek*, July 6, 1992.

Obituary. *The Times* (of London), June 29, 1992.

Obituary. *Independent*, June 24, 1992.

Obituary. *New York Times*, June 23, 1992.

Voice of One's Own: Conversations with America's Writing Women. MICKEY PEARLMAN. Houghton Mifflin, 1992.

Between Friends: M. F. K. Fisher and Me. JEANETTE FERRARY. Atlantic Monthly, 1991.

"The fine art of remembering." LAURA SHAPIRO. *Newsweek*, Sep. 24, 1990.

Inter-View: Talks with America's Writing Women. MICKEY PEARLMAN and KATHERINE U. HENDERSON. University Press of Kentucky, 1990.

" 'O Poor Cook!' . . . ." JEANNETTE FERRARY. *New York Times Book Review*, June 4, 1989.

"Native truths." *Architectural Digest*, May 1989.

Fitzwater, Marlin

Fitzwater, Marlin (Max Marlin Fitzwater; 1942–   ) The outgoing White House Press Secretary performed his normal functions as President Bush's spokesperson on a wide range of matters during 1992, issuing statements on matters as diverse as joblessness, the Middle East, and Japanese-American relations. He also undertook a highly controversial political role, sharply and very personally attacking the opposition candidates during the presidential campaign, with the unspoken but clear approval of President Bush. To those political ends, he again and again publicly called Governor Bill Clinton "Slippery Bill," and also accused Clinton of being "reckless" as regarded intervention in the Yugoslavian civil war. Fitzwater called Senator Al Gore "Mr. Sell Out America," for criticizing Bush environmental policies at the June 1992 Rio de Janeiro worldwide environmental summit meeting. He was reported to have called Ross Perot "a dangerous and destructive personality." He even blamed the April Los Angeles riots on "the social welfare policies of the '60s and '70s."

Kansas-born Fitzwater is a long-term Washington "insider," a writer and public relations professional who worked for the Department of Transportation, Environmental Protection Agency, and the Treasury before becoming deputy press secretary to the President in the mid-1980s. He was press secretary to Vice President George Bush (1985–87), became President Ronald Reagan's press secretary in 1987, and stayed on in the White House as press secretary to President Bush. Fitzwater's B.S. is from Kansas State University, in 1965. He has four children.

FURTHER READING

"The president's mouth. . . ." MARTIN FLETCHER. *Times*, Dec. 17, 1992.

"The art of the dodge." *Harper's*, May 1992.

"As the Gulf war rages. . . ." PAULA CHIN. *People*, Feb. 11, 1991.

"Fitzwater, Max Marlin." *Current Biography*, May 1988.

Foldes, Andor

Foldes, Andor (1913–92) A leading American pianist, Budapest-born Andor Foldes was a child prodigy in his native Hungary, making his concert debut at the age of eight, and the following year entering the Budapest Academy of Music. He also studied with several composers, most notably in the master class of Ernst von Dohnanyi. His most important influence came from Bela Bartok, whom he met in 1929; they became very close friends, and Foldes became a leading interpreter of Bartok's music. Foldes premiered Bartok's Second Piano Concerto in 1947, at Carnegie Hall, recorded it in 1948, and also made a complete and classic recording of Bartok's piano music. He was far from limited to Bartok, however, playing and recording a wide range of classical composers, very notably including

Schumann, Mozart, Brahms, Beethoven, Schubert, and Liszt. Foldes made his American debut on radio in 1940, and in concert at Town Hall in 1941. He also wrote several books, and with his wife, the Hungarian journalist Lily Rendy, wrote *Keys to the Keyboard* (1948). He was survived by his wife. (d. Zürich, Switzerland; February 9, 1992)

FURTHER READING

Obituary. *Variety*, Feb. 24, 1992.
Obituary. *New York Times*, Feb. 19, 1992.
Obituary. *The Times* (of London), Feb. 15, 1992.

Foley, Thomas Stephen

Foley, Thomas Stephen (1929–) Although John Sonneland, his Republican opponent, reportedly spent more than $500,000 in a bid to unseat him, Democratic Speaker of the House of Representatives Foley easily won reelection to a 15th House term from his eastern Washington State district in November, winning 55 percent of the vote. Foley seemed able to look forward to a less troubled further term as House Speaker, as well, although a year earlier his tenure had seemed very uncertain. By late 1992 the House bank overdraft scandals seemed safely behind him, the House post office scandals were no longer in the public eye, House perquisites had been sharply trimmed, and the powerful anti-incumbency mood that had seemed to dominate the country had resulted in the return to Congress of 93 percent of those incumbents who ran for office. Nor was his wife and chief and staff, Heather Foley, still under attack as in any way implicated in the post office scandal. Foley, who had publicly called the previous Congress a "Congress from Hell," seemed poised to function as Speaker in an entirely new situation, with a Democratic President and Congress breaking the "gridlock" that had characterized the Bush years.

Spokane-born Foley practiced law and was Washington state assistant attorney-general before going to Washington, D.C. as a lawyer in 1961. A liberal Democrat, he entered the House in 1965, and in 25 uninterrupted years rose to become chairman of the House Democratic Caucus in 1976, majority whip in 1981, and majority leader in 1987. He was elected 49th Speaker of the House on June 6, 1989, replacing James C. Wright, who had resigned while facing charges of ethics violations. Foley's 1951 B.A. and 1957 LL.B. were from the University of Washington. He married Heather Strachan in 1968; she is one of his key Congressonal aides.

FURTHER READING

"Mr. Nice Guy. . . ." BILL WHALEN. *Insight*, Aug. 19, 1991.
"Hill potatoes. . . ." FRED BARNES. *New Republic*, May 20, 1991.
"Foley's law." MICHAEL ORESKES. *New York Times Magazine*, Nov. 11, 1990.
"Foley, Thomas Stephen." *Current Biography*, Sep., 1989.

Foote, Emerson

Foote, Emerson (1906–92) Alabama-born Foote entered the world of advertising in San Francisco, in 1931. He moved to New York City in 1938 to work under legendary ad-person Albert D. Lasker, rose to supervision of the huge Lucky Strike account, and on Lasker's retirement in 1942 was one of three managers who bought the agency, then renamed for them Foote, Cone, and Belding, and one of the world's largest advertising agencies. Foote, however, became sharply criticial of cigarette advertising as cancer-promoting, and his agency resigned the very large American Tobacco account in 1948, Foote retiring as president in 1950. In 1952, he became executive vice president of McCann-Ericson; he was agency president (1960–63) and chairman 1962–64). He then resigned, once again because of his principled opposition to cigarette advertising, and serving on several federal commissions dealing with tobacco, cancer, heart disease, and related matters, and similarly campaigning throughout the world for population control. He was survived by three daughters and a son. (d. Carmel, New York; July 5, 1992)

FURTHER READING

Obituary. *New York Times*, July 8, 1992.

Ford, Gerald Rudolph, Jr.

Ford, Gerald Rudolph, Jr. (Leslie King, Jr.; 1913–) Former President Ford found an opportunity to play something of a political role in 1992, as an elder stateman supporting his party's presidential nominee. On August 20th, he addressed the Republican National Convention, supporting the nomination of then-President George Bush for a second term and, in a pointed reference to his own defeat by Jimmy Carter in 1976, attacking change as introducing a possible disaster for the country. Ford later campaigned with Bush in his home state of Michigan, but Bush was unable to win the state, receiving only 37 percent of the vote.

Omaha-born Ford, then Vice President, became the 38th President of the United States in August 1974, with the resignation of Richard Nixon, who faced impeachment because of his complicity in the Watergate affair. A month later, Ford pardoned Nixon. A year earlier, Ford had been appointed by Nixon to replace Vice President Spiro Agnew, who had resigned under fire.

The Ford presidency was relatively uneventful, seeming especially so after the turbulence of the 1960s, the Vietnam War, and the shock of Watergate. That shock did enable him to curb the excesses of the CIA and other national security organizations; beyond that, he began little new legislation, attempted with little success to mediate continuing Middle East crises, and furthered American relations with China. Ford defeated Ronald Reagan's bid for the Republican presidential nomination, but was himself defeated by Jimmy Carter in the 1976 presidential election. He wrote of his life and experiences in *A Time to Heal: The Autobiography of Gerald R. Ford* (1979).

Earlier, Ford had been an All-American college football player, a naval officer in World War II, and a lawyer in Grand Rapids (1941–49). He went to Washington as a Congressman in 1949, and became minority leader of the House (1965–73). His 1935 B.A. was from the University of Michigan, his LL.B from Yale in 1941. Ford married Elizabeth "Betty" Bloomer in 1948; they have four children.

FURTHER READING

Gerald R. Ford and the Politics of Post-Watergate America. BERNARD FIRESTONE and ALEXEJ UGRINSKY, eds. Greenwood, 1992.

The Limits of Power: The Nixon and Ford Administrations. JOHN R. GREENE. Indiana University Press, 1992.

"Kissinger's web." WALTER ISAACSON. *Vanity Fair*, Sep. 1992.

Farewell to the Chief: Former Presidents in American Public Life. RICHARD N. SMITH and TIMOTHY WALCH, eds. High Plains, 1990.

Gerald R. Ford's Date with Destiny: A Political Biography. EDWARD L. SCHAPSMEIER and FREDERICK H. SCHAPSMEIER. P. Lang, 1989

"Former presidents reflect . . ." MICHAEL DELON. *USA Today*, Nov. 1988.

Gerald R. Ford: President. SALLIE RANDOLPH. Walker, 1987.

Ford, Harrison (1942–) The versatile film star Harrison Ford returned in 1992 to the kind of film that had made him a worldwide celebrity in the late 1970s and throughout the 1980s, starring as CIA analyst Jack Ryan in the Philip Noyce action-adventure film *Patriot Games*, based on the best-selling Tom Clancy novel, a sequel to his *The Hunt for Red October*; co-starring were Anne Archer, Patrick Bergin, Sean Bean, Thora Birch, James Fox, James Earl Jones, and Richard Harris. The film was a summer blockbuster, and a worldwide hit, although at the same time criticized by many as an outdated Cold War glorification of mindless violence, and by some Irish Republican partisans as a vilification of their cause. In June, Joseph McBride wrote an angry review of film as anti-Irish in *Variety*; Paramount responded by pulling its advertising from the paper, and editor Peter Bart apologized to Paramount for the review, to the great dismay of many concerned about freedom of the press. Ford had taken the role after Alec Baldwin pulled out in favor of the classic Stanley Kowalski role in a Broadway revival of Tennessee Williams's *A Streetcar Named Desire*.

For Ford, the film was the first in a major three-picture Paramount commitment. Ford's 1991 film *Regarding Henry*, though not a box office smash, played to large home video audiences in 1992. And his "Indiana Jones" character continued to have a life of its own: in 1992, George Lucas created the hit series "The Young Indiana Jones Chronicles." Forthcoming were starring roles in Harold Becker's film *Night Ride Down*, and in Andrew Davis's *The Fugitive*.

Chicago-born Ford played largely in supporting roles, working part-time as a carpenter, for a decade before breaking through as Han Solo in *Star Wars* (1977) to become a leading movie actor. He completed the Star Wars trilogy with *The Empire Strikes Back* (1980) and *Return of the Jedi* (1983), meanwhile doing the blockbuster Indiana Jones trilogy: *Raiders of the Lost Ark* (1981), *Indiana Jones and the Temple of Doom* (1984), and *Indiana Jones and the Last Crusade* (1989). Among his other films are *Witness* (1985), *The Mosquito Coast* (1986), *Working Girl* (1988), *Presumed Innocent* (1990), and *Regarding Henry* (1991). Ford attended Ripon College. He has been married twice and has two children.

FURTHER READING

"Harrison Ford. . . ." MARTHA FRANKEL. *Movies USA*, May 1992.
"Harrison Ford. . . . ." NATALIE GITTELSON. *McCall's*, June 1991.
The Films of Harrison Ford. ED GROSS. Pioneer Books, 1990.
Harrison Ford. MINTY CLINCH. Trafalgar Square, 1988.
Harrison Ford. TOLEDO VARE. St. Martin's, 1988.

Foster, Jodie (Alicia Christian Foster; 1962–)
Now clearly a major international film star—at the advanced age of 30—Foster won her second Best Actress Oscar in 1992, for her starring role in Jonathan Demme's Oscar-winning *The Silence of the Lambs* (1991), opposite Anthony Hopkins as imprisoned psychopathic killer Dr. Hannibal "the Cannibal" Lecter, whom Starling consults in prison for help in finding a psychopathic killer still at large. Demme, Hopkins, and writer Ted Tally also won Oscars. Foster also won won a British Academy of Film & TV Arts Best Actress Award and a Golden Globe award for the role. The film was a worldwide hit; a sequel was planned.

Foster also costarred in Woody Allen's *Shadows and Fog*, in a cast that included Mia Farrow, John Malkovich, Madonna, and Kathy Bates. Her 1991 directorial debut, *Little Man Tate*, in which she also starred, did very well in 1992 home video release. Forthcoming was a starring role opposite Richard Gere in Jon Amiel's Civil War-era love story *Sommersby*, scheduled for 1993 release. Also forthcoming is *The Dinosaur Man*, based on Dr. Susan Baur's work with schizophrenics; Foster will direct and star in the film, and will also direct and star in the forthcoming *Jean Seberg*, based on the life of the American actress. She is working on several other projects as well, some of them through her own Egg Pictures production company.

Los Angeles-born Foster was a leading child actor in television, beginning with "Mayberry, R.F.D." in 1969. In her early teens, she played major roles in such films as *Alice Doesn't Live Here Any More* (1975) and *Taxi Driver* (1976). She then made the often extremely difficult transition to adult roles, in such films as *The Hotel New Hampshire* (1984), *Five Corners* (1986), and most notably *The Accused* (1988), for which she won a Best Actress Oscar. Her B.A. was from Yale in 1985.

FURTHER READING

"Foster, Jodie." *Current Biography*, Aug. 1992.
"Foster child. . . ." TOM GLIATTO et al. *People*, Nov. 18, 1991.
"Burden of the gift." JULIE CAMERON *American Film*, Nov.–Dec. 1991.
"What's driving Miss Jodie?" MICHAEL SEGELL. *Redbook*, Nov. 1991.
"Wunderkind." ARION BERGER. *Harper's Bazaar*, Nov. 1991.
"A screen gem turns director." RICHARD CORLISS. *Time*, Oct. 14, 1991.
"Jodie Foster." INGRID SISCHY. *Interview*, Oct. 1991.
"Jodie Foster." PHILLIP ZONKEL. *Seventeen*, Oct. 1991.
"Jodie Foster. . . ." BRIAN D. JOHNSON. *Maclean's*, Sep. 16, 1991.
"Jodie Foster." GEARI HIRSHEY. *Rolling Stone*, Mar. 21, 1991.
"Yet again. . . ." TRACY YOUNG. *Vogue*, Feb. 1991.
"Child of the movies." JONATHAN VAN METER. *New York Times Magazine*, Jan. 6, 1991.

Franjieh, Suleiman (1910–92)
Leader of a northern Lebanon Maronite Christian clan, Franjieh fielded anti-government forces of an estimated 5,000 fighters during the 1958 Lebanese

civil war. He entered the national assembly in 1960, held several cabinet-level posts during the 1960s, and in 1970 was a surprise parliamentary coalition choice for the Lebanese presidency. He held the presidency from 1970 to 1976, a period in which the country slid into its long civil war, as strong Palestine Liberation Organization forces entered the country, Lebanon's fragile Christian-Muslim balance was destroyed, and the prestige of the until-then neutral Lebanese Army disappeared. Franjieh's government was unable to stop the onset of the civil war in Beirut in 1975, and the quick spread of the fighting throughout the country. He was effectively driven from power in 1976, then allying his forces with the Syrians, and against the main body of the Maronite militias, an alliance that grew even firmer when his son Tony and his family were killed by a Christian raiding party in 1978. He was survived by his wife, Iris, three daughters, and a son. His grandson, also Suleiman, had succeeded him to leadership of his clan and private army in 1990. (d. Beirut, Lebanon; July 23, 1992)

FURTHER READING

Obituary. *Independent* , July 24, 1992.
Obituary. *The Times* (of London), July 24, 1992.
Obituary. *New York Times*, July 24, 1992.

Frankovich, Mike (1910–92) A quarterback at UCLA in the 1930s, Frankovich began his long entertainment career in radio, and worked in a wide range of film occupations from the late 1930s. He began producing with Republic Pictures and, after Air Corps service in World War II, became an independent film producer, with such films as *Decameron Nights* (1953) and *Footsteps in the Fog* (1955). He headed British and then European production operations for Columbia Pictures (1955–64), and world production for Columbia (1964–67), then once again becoming an independent producer. Some of his best known films were *Bob and Carol and Ted and Alice* (1969), *Cactus Flower* (1969), and *The Shootist* (1976). Frankovich was also a film industry and civic leader; he was a founder of the American Film Institute, as president of the Los Angeles Coliseum Commission took a leading role in attracting the 1984 Olympic and the Raiders football team to Los Angeles, and in

1984 received the Jean Hersholt Humanitarian Award of the Academy of Motion Picture Arts and Sciences. He was survived by his second wife, the actress Binnie Barnes, a daughter, two sons, a sister, and a brother. (d. Los Angeles; January 1, 1992)

FURTHER READING

Obituary. *Variety*, Jan. 13, 1992.
Obituary. *The Times* (of London), Jan. 8, 1992.
Obituary. *New York Times*, Jan. 4, 1992.

Freeman, Morgan (1938–) Building further on his late-career film success, Freeman starred during 1992 in two major films, on vastly different themes. In March, he starred as Geel Piet in John G. Avildsen's *The Power of One*, the story of the development of a young British boy who in the 1930s found himself among racist Africaaners in what is now Zimbabwe. Co-starring were John Gielgud, Stephen Dorff, Armin Mueller-Stahl, and Fay Masterson.

In August, he starred as Clint Eastwood's former criminal partner, now turned bounty-hunter with Eastwood, in Eastwood's hard-edged western *Unforgiven*; co-starring were Gene Hackman as a brutal sheriff and Richard Harris as another bountyhunting gunman. The film had something of a feminist theme: the $1,000 bounty is offered by group of prostitutes for the murders of two men who have murdered a prostitute.

Freeman also became a film director in 1992: in August he began filming in Harare, Zimbabwe, of *Bopha!*, starring Danny Glover; Arsenio Hall was executive producer. Based on a play by South African Percy Mtwa, the play is set in South Africa soon after the 1976 Soweto protests.

Freeman has spent most of his long career in the theater, winning a 1978 Tony nomination for his role in *The Mighty Gents*, and appearing in a considerable range of Shakespearean and other classical roles. He emerged as a leading screen and stage player late in his career, beginning with his lead off-Broadway as Hoke Colburn, the Black chauffeur in *Driving Miss Daisy* (1987), and in strong supporting roles in such films as *Street Smart* (1987) and *Clean and Sober* (1988). His major breakthrough came in 1989, with his film re-creation of the *Driving Miss Daisy* role, for which he won a 1990 Oscar nomination. In the same year, he appeared in *Glory*, and created the Joe Clark role in *Lean On Me*. In 1990, he appeared as Petruchio opposite Tracey Ullman in the New York production of *The Taming of the Shrew*. In 1991, he played Azeem in *Robin Hood: Prince of Thieves*. He has also appeared as a regular on two television series: public television's children's show "The Electric Company" (1971–76) and for a time in the early 1980s on "Another World," a daytime soap opera.

FURTHER READING

"Freeman, Morgan." *Current Biography*, Feb. 1991.
"In the driver's seat. . . ." JANICE C. SIMPSON. *Time*, Jan. 8, 1990.
"Two for the road." HENRY ALFORD and PAULA BULLWINKEL. *Interview*, Nov. 1989.
"Johnny Handsome. . . ." ROBERT SEIDENBERG. *American Film*, Oct. 1989.

Frohnmayer, John Edward (1921–)

On February 21, 1992, National Endowment for the Arts (NEA) chairman Frohnmayer was forced to resign, after right-wing Republican presidential candidate Pat Buchanan had attacked President George Bush for his support of Frohnmayer and the NEA, which Buchanan called part of "the arts and crafts auxiliary of the Eastern liberal establishment." Frohnmayer had been under attack by fundamentalist religious and conservative political groups since early 1991, when he began to support what he called freedom of expression, and what such groups as the Reverend Pat Robertson's Christian Coalition and Reverend Donald Wildman's American Family Association called pornography.

Frohnmayer had been appointed NEA head by President Bush in 1989, and earlier in his tenure had been involved in several controversies from quite the other side of the fence. In August 1990, he canceled grants to four artists, all accused of "obscenity;" these were Karen Finley, Holly Hughes, John Fleck, and Tim Miller, from then on known as the "NEA Four." Frohnmayer went on to deny several more grants, and to institute an "anti-obscenity oath," a pledge by those receiving federal grants through the NEA that they would not use the money to create "obscene" art. Joseph Papp of the New York Shakespeare Festival, among others, refused to take offered NEA grants as long as the oath was in effect. Ultimately, although the federal government denied that any political considerations were involved, government documents revealed that Frohnmayer had indeed cited political considerations in refusing the grants. He began to change his position in late 1990, and during 1991 emerged as a defender of several controversial NEA grants. Forthcoming in 1993 was Frohnmayer's book *Leaving Town Alive: Confessions of an Arts Warrior*.

Oregon-born Frohnmayer practiced law in Oregon (1972–89). He was also a member of the Oregon Arts Commission (1978–85), and has been a singer and active in the development of regional musical groups. His 1964 B.A. was from Stanford University, his 1969 M.A. from the University of Chicago, and his 1972 J.D. from the University of Oregon. He married Leah Thorpe in 1967; they have two children.

FURTHER READING

" 'The nature of the beast'. . . ." DANIEL GLICK. *Newsweek*, Mar. 16, 1992.
"Frohnmayer, John Edward." *Current Biography*, Apr. 1990.

Fujimori, Alberto (1938–)

In the early months of 1992, Peru's multiple crises intensified, as the Shining Path Maoist guerrilla army and the Tupac Amaru Revolutionary Movement gained strength throughout the country, and a deepening economic recession turned into a major depression. In November 1991, President Fujimori had issued decrees giving the Peruvian army virtually unlimited emergency powers, but little success resulted. On April 5, 1992, with the support of the military and in what he called a "self-coup," he seized dictatorial power, dissolving the federal Congress, the regional assemblies, and the courts, and ruling by decree. Fujimori seemed to have a good deal of popular support, as well as military support. He later promised a return to democracy and free elections in 1993, though his promises were greeted at home and abroad with understandable skepticism. Economic aid and relations were suspended by several countries.

On September 12, 1992, Fujimori scored a major Civil War victory, with the capture of Abimeal Guzmán Reynoso, head of the Shining Path, along with seven other leaders of his organization. Guzmán was quickly displayed to the world media in a steel cage and prison uniform, to demonstrate his powerlessness, and then sentenced by a military court to life imprisonment. The Shining Path responded by mounting several more guerrilla offensives against the government, demonstrating that the Civil War was far from over. Peru and the world waited to see if Fujimori really meant his promise to quickly restore democracy.

Peruvian-born Fujimori, the son of Japanese-Peruvian immigrants, attended La Molina, the National Agrarian University, graduating in 1961, and then taught at the university. His 1969 Masters degree was in mathematics, from the University of Wisconsin. He became dean of the science faculty at La Molina in 1984, was principal of the university (1984–89), and was president of the Peruvian National Council of Principals (1987–89). He scored an upset victory over novelist Mario Vargas Llosa in the 1990 presidential election. He married civil engineer Susana Higuchi in 1974; they have four children.

FURTHER READING

"Casting stones." Mike Moore. "Can Fujimori save Peru?" Michael Radu. *Bulletin of the Atomic Scientists*, July–Aug. 1992.

"Fujimori defends. . . ." Mariella Balbi et al. *World Press Review*, July 1992.

"Fujimori's plot: . . . ." Sarah Kerr. *New York Review of Books*, June 25, 1992.

"The 'Karate Kid' . . . ." Tom Vogel, Jr. *Commonweal*, Jan. 11, 1991.

"Fujimori, Alberto." *Current Biography*, Nov. 1990.

"Fujimori. . . ." Jeffrey Klaiber. *America*, Sep. 8, 1990.

"Who is. . ." Linda Robinson. *U.S. News & World Report*, Apr. 23, 1990.

"Engulfed by 'the Tsunami' . . . ." Frederick Ungeheuer. *Time*, Apr. 23, 1990.

"The man from nowhere." *Economist*, Apr. 14, 1990.

Gaines, William (1922–92) Heir to the family comic book publishing company, Gaines took over the company in 1947, after the untimely death of his father. He quickly turned to the production of "horror" comics with great commercial success, but he and other such horror comic publishers agreed to self-censorship after 1954 Congressional hearings and threats of legislative restraint. In 1955, he began publication of a series of comic books sharply attacking a wide and very diverse range of targets, and in 1955 began regular production of *MAD* magazine, which quickly grew to a circulation of more than one million, its then-shocking graphics and text very appealing to young people beginning the processes that would result in the counterculture of the 1960s. He was survived by his wife, Annie, a daughter, and two sons. (d. New York City; June 3, 1992)

FURTHER READING

Obituary. Robert Love. *Rolling Stone*, Aug. 6, 1992.
"The man who. . . ." Tim Appelo. *Entertainment*, June 19, 1992.
"Humor in a jugular vein." Charles Leerhsen. *Newsweek*, June 15, 1992.
"A perfect mad man." Kurt Andersen. *Time*, June 15, 1992.
Obituary. *Variety*, June 8, 1992.
Obituary. *The Times* (of London), June 6, 1992.
Obituary. *Independent*, June 5, 1992.

Galinski, Heinz (1912–92) A German Jew, whose father had been largely disabled by war wounds suffered while fighting for Germany during World War I, Galinski remained in Germany during the rise and rule of fascism. His father, his mother, and his wife were all murdered by the Germans during the Nazi era, with six million other Jews in the Holocaust. Galinski himself was imprisoned at the Auschwitz, Buchenwald, and Bergen-Belsen concentration camps, but survived. He then moved back to Berlin, where he had lived before the war, and set about his life's work, which involved attempting to rebuild Germany's very small surviving Jewish community, while demanding compensation for the victims of Nazism, clearly stating that these were by no means limited to Jews. While attempting to build bridges between Jewish and other Germans, he also consistently warned against the remnants of Nazism and Nazi thinking in Germany, and against the rise of new or "neo" Nazi movements. In recent years, he particularly warned that anti-foreign violence could very easily lead to the strengthening of Nazi forces and new attacks on German Jewish and other minority communities. Galinski became head of the Berlin Jewish community in 1949, and of the German Central Council of Jews in 1988. His second wife, Ruth, is the head of the German Federation of Jewish Women. He was survived by his wife and a daughter. (d. Berlin; July 19, 1992)

FURTHER READING

Obituary. *The Times* (of London), July 21, 1992.
Obituary. *Independent*, July 21, 1992.
Obituary. *New York Times*, July 20, 1992.

Gallo, Robert Charles (1937–) Seemingly settled in 1991, the bitter French-American dispute over who had discovered the AIDS virus exploded once again in 1992. Gallo, head of the U.S. National Cancer Institute's laboratory of tumor cell biology and a leading AIDS researcher at the U.S. National Institutes of Health, and French AIDS researcher Luc Montagnier had been jointly credited with discovery of the virus, both deriving enormous worldwide prestige and the prospect of Nobel Prizes from the discovery. But Montagnier had long claimed that Gallo did not really discover the virus, instead using samples that Montagnier had sent to him. Both claimed credit for the discovery in 1984, beginning a long controversy that ultimately generated a French lawsuit and a 1987 court settlement, though Montagnier and other French researchers continued to charge Gallo with misappropriation of the French specimens. In 1991, Montagnier suggested that Gallo had been sent a contaminated specimen which then grew to replace the different specimens both had been working on, a theory that Gallo seemed to generally accept. But several investigations continued.

In the spring of 1992, a National Institutes of Health (NIH) Office of Scientific Integrity report cleared Gallo of any wrongdoing. The report was immediately attacked by a National Academy of Sciences panel of experts asked to review it, and by the U.S. House of Representatives Subcommittee on Oversight and Investigations. On December 30, 1992, after a three-year-long investigation, the Federal Office of Research Integrity found that Gallo had been guilty of scientific misconduct, in "falsely reporting" a key research fact. Gallo continued to deny all wrongdoing.

Connecticut-born Gallo is one of the world's leading tumor cell biologists. He has been associated with the National Cancer Institute of the National Institutes of Health since 1965, in a series of increasingly responsible positions, and has been head of its tumor cell biology laboratory since 1972. He has also taught courses at Cornell and George Washington University, published numerous scientific works, and received many honors and awards for his work. A recent book is *Virus Hunting: Cancer, AIDS, and the Human Retrovirus: A Story of Scientific Discovery* (1991).

FURTHER READING

"AIDS' relentless adversary. . . ." SHANNON BROWNLEE. *U.S. News & World Report*, June 3, 1991.
"Taking credit for AIDS." JUDITH COLP. *Insight*, May 13, 1991.
"Profile: AIDS dispute. . . ." TIM BEARDSLEY. *Scientific American*, Jan. 1991.

Gardenia, Vincent (Vincent Scognamiglio; 1921–92) A leading character actor, Naples-born Gardenia was the son of Italian actor-manager Gennaro Gardenia Scognamiglio, who emigrated with his family to the United States in 1923, settled in Brooklyn, and formed an Italian-language theater company, with which Vincent Gardenia made his debut at age five. He continued to work with the company into his late 30s, while also developing his English-language career. Gardenia became a highly regarded character actor in stage, films, and television, winning awards in all three forms, including a Tony for his role in *The Prisoner of Second Avenue* (1971) and a Tony nomination for *Ballroom* (1978); Oscar nominations for his baseball manager in *Bang the Drum Slowly* (1972), and as Cher's father in *Moonstruck*(1987); two 1960s off-Broadway Obie awards, for *Machinal* (1960) and *Passing Through from Exotic Places* (1969); and an Emmy for *Age-Old Friends* (1990). His television work also included "All in the Family." A very recent film was *Glengarry Glen Ross* (1992). He was survived by a brother. (d. Philadelphia; December 9, 1992)

FURTHER READING

Obituary. *Variety*, Dec. 14, 1992.
Obituary. *The New York Times*, Dec. 10, 1992.

Garner, James (James Baumgarner; 1928–) A film and television star for almost four decades, Garner is a very familiar face on the world's television sets, as his popular series "The Rockford Files" continues to rerun. Even his early "Maverick" series is still in reruns. He will be appearing in a supporting role in the forthcoming *Maverick* film, based on his series; Mel Gibson will play the role that Garner originated.

Garner will also star in the long-awaited, probably controversial forthcoming HBO movie *Barbarians at the Gate*, as F. Ross Johnson, head of R.J.R. Nabisco, who lost his company in a highly publicized leveraged buyout organized by Kohlberg, Kravis, Roberts & Co. Co-starring are Jonathan Pryce as corporate takeover figure Henry Kravis and Peter Riegert as securities firm head Peter Cohen. Also forthcoming was a starring role in Robert Lieberman's *Fire in the Sky*, which started filming in mid-August 1992.

Oklahoma-born Garner began his long career in the mid-1950s, in a small, non-speaking role in *The Caine Mutiny Court Martial* (1954), and in bit parts in television. He quickly emerged as a major television series star, in the title role of the western "Maverick" (1957–61), and later as private investigator Jim Rockford in "The Rockford Files" (1974–80). His wide range of films included *Sayonara* (1957), *The Great Escape* (1963), *The Americanization of Emily* (1964), *Marlowe* (1969), *They Only Kill Their Masters* (1972), *Victor/Victoria* (1982), and *Sunset* (1987). He also starred in such telefilms as *Promise* (1986), which won five Emmys, including best drama; and *My Name Is Bill W* (1989), in the title role as the founder of Alcoholics Anonymous. Garner attended the University of Oklahoma. He married Lois Clarke in 1956; they have three children.

FURTHER READING

James Garner: A Biography. RAYMOND STRAIT. St. Martin's, 1985.

Garrison, Jim

(1922–92) Iowa-born Garrison, a lawyer, served as a New Orleans assistant district attorney before winning the first of his three terms as New Orleans District Attorney in 1962. In 1967, he quite suddenly emerged as a national figure, beginning an independent investigation of the assassination of President John F. Kennedy in Dallas four years earlier. His charges, which created an enormous controversy, were that Kennedy had been killed by a large body of conspirators, including CIA operatives and Dallas police officers, directed by the highest levels of the American government. In 1969, he brought New Orleans business figure Clay Shaw to trial; the jury acquitted Shaw in

50 minutes after a month-long trial, and the next day a federal judge threw out Garrison's attempt to charge Shaw with perjury. Garrison was later tried on unrelated corruption charges, lost his fourth district attorney election bid, and from 1978 until his death was an elected state court of appeals judge. But his Kennedy assassination charges and the speculations they generated had never been fully answered; his third book on the matter, *On the Trail of the Assassins* (1988), became much of the basis of Oliver Stone's highly controversial worldwide hit film *JFK* (1991), which starred Kevin Costner as Garrison, and in which Garrison played a small role as Chief Justice Earl Warren. Stone, attacked in the early 1990s much as Garrison had been in the late 1960s, created a film with great worldwide impact, ultimately forcing release of thousands of pages of previously "classified" documents, and giving the Kennedy assassination debate new life. Garrison was survived by his wife, the former Leah Ziegler, two daughters, a son, and a sister. (d. New Orleans; October 21, 1992)

FURTHER READING

"Shots in the dark." EDWARD JAY EPSTEIN. *New Yorker*, Nov. 30, 1992.

Obituary. *Independent*, Oct. 27, 1992.
Obituary. *Variety*, Oct. 26, 1992.
Obituary. *The Times* (of London), Oct. 23, 1992.
Obituary. *New York Times*, Oct. 22, 1992.
"The conspiracy. . . ." CARL OGLESBY. *Playboy*, Feb. 1992.
"The case against. . . ." NICHOLAS LEMANN. *GQ—Gentleman's Quarterly*, Jan., 1992.
"JFK—a new low. . . ." DAVID EHRENSTEIN. *Advocate*, Jan. 14, 1992.
JFK: The CIA, Vietnam and the Plot to Assassinate John F. Kennedy. L. FLETCHER PROUTY. Birch Lane/Carol, 1992.
Destiny Betrayed: JFK, Cuba, and the Garrison Case. JAMES DIEUGENIO. Sheridan Square Press, 1992.
"Conspiracy to. . . ." TOM BETHELL. *National Review*, Dec. 16, 1991.

Gaster, Theodor Herzl (1906–92)

London-born Gaster was the son of Moses Gaster, Chief Rabbi of the Sephardic Jews; he was named after Zionist leader Theodore Herzl, a family friend. Theodor Gaster taught at Columbia University after receiving his Ph.D. there in 1943, and later at several other American, European, and Australian universities and colleges. He headed the Hebraic division of the Library of Congress from 1944 to 1948. Gaster published many works on Near Eastern and Mediterraean mythology, including his very popular *Dead Sea Scriptures*, *The New Golden Bough*, *Myth, Legend, and Testament*, and *The Holy and the Profane: Evolutions of Jewish Folkways*. He was survived by his wife and a daughter. (d. Philadelphia; February 1, 1992)

FURTHER READING

Obituary. *The Times* (of London), Feb. 14, 1992.
Obituary. *New York Times*, Feb. 7, 1992.

Gates, Daryl F. (1927–)

Highly controversial Los Angeles police chief Gates resigned on June 26, 1992, ending a 14-year tenure greatly marred by the massive April 30-May 2, 1992 Los Angeles riots. These began on the night that four Los Angeles police officers were acquitted in the Rodney King beating case (except for one still-open count against one officer)—although their March 3, 1991 beating of King had been shown to a worldwide television audience every night for weeks after the beating.

After the beating, longstanding charges of Los Angeles police brutality began to be taken far more seriously, and Los Angeles mayor Tom Bradley and many other leaders called on Gates to resign, especially after the independent commission headed by Warren Christopher called for his resignation. Gates, who had attended a political fundraising event while the riot grew, disclaimed all responsibility. In September 1992, an independent commission headed by former FBI and CIA chief William Webster sharply criticized Gates and his police department; Gates responded by calling the authors of the report "liars." After his resignation, Gates became a Los Angeles radio talkshow host. He told his side of the story in his book *Chief: My Life in the LAPD* (1992). Gates's B.S. in Public Administration was from the University of Southern California.

FURTHER READING

"Daryl Gates. . . ." *Newsweek*, May 11, 1992.
"Law and disorder in LA." JOHN GREGORY DUNNE. *New York Review of Books*, Oct. 24, 1991.
"Gates's hell." FREDERIC DANNEN. *Vanity Fair*, Aug. 1991.
"Playboy interview. . . ." DIANE K. SHAH. *Playboy*, Aug. 1991.
"Gatesgate. . . ." HAROLD MEYERSON. *New Republic*, June 10, 1991.

Gates, John (1914–92) New York City-born Gates became a Communist in the early 1930s, leaving college to become a Communist organizer in the midwest. He joined the Abraham Lincoln Brigade, the United States section of the International Brigades, at the outbreak of the Spanish Civil War, becoming commissar, or political officer of the brigade; he fought with the Loyalists until their defeat in 1939, and then left Spain. After service during World War II, he resumed activity in the U.S. Communist Party, becoming a party leader and editor of the party newspaper, the *Daily Worker*. With other party leaders, he was arrested during the McCarthy period, and was imprisoned for five years. After the February 1956 Nikita Khrushchev speech to the 20th Soviet Communist Party congress, exposing some of the multifold crimes of the Stalin period, Gates and many other Communists around the world questioned their former allegiances. In the United States, he led an unsuccessful movement to reform his party, resigning when that movement failed. He later became a research assistant with the International Ladies Garment Workers Union. He was survived by his wife, the former Lillian Schwartz, three sisters, and a brother. (d. Miami Beach; May 23, 1992)

FURTHER READING

Obituary. *The Times* (of London), June 4, 1992.
Obituary. *New York Times*, May 25, 1992.

Gates, Robert Michael (1943–)
Shortly after the November presidential election, Director of Central Intelligence Gates announced his decision to resign. The Bush Administration appointee, long associated with White House National Security Advisor Brent Scowcroft and former CIA director George Bush, was not expected to be asked to stay on, although during his single year in office he had attempted to develop an impartial, nonpolitical image for himself and the "Agency." His attempt had been seriously compromised by very public CIA-Justice Department infighting over responsibility for long delays and cover-ups in the handling of the Bank of Credit and Commerce International (BCCI) affair, one of the most highly publicized bank scandals of the century.

Gates's nomination to be head of the U.S. Cen-

tral Intelligence Agency (CIA) was confirmed by the Senate on November 5, 1991, after a nomination process that had lasted almost six months, and that included a Senate Intelligence Committee investigation and three weeks of hearings. In 1987 then-President Ronald Reagan had nominated Gates for the same post, but had withdrawn his name from consideration in the face of very serious charges of complicity in the Iran-Contra Affair.

Born in Wichita, Kansas, Gates is a career intelligence officer. His B.A. was from the College of William and Mary, his M.A. from Indiana University, and his Ph.D. in Russian and Soviet history from Georgetown University. He joined the CIA as an intelligence analyst in 1966, and was assigned to the White House-based National Security Council (1974–79), where he worked for Brent Scowcroft. Gates returned to the CIA in 1979, and rose through a series of administrative positions, becoming deputy director in 1986. In 1988, he rejoined Scowcroft, then National Security Advisor, as Deputy National Security Advisor. Gates has a son and a daughter.

FURTHER READING

" 'We see a world. . . .' " BRUCE VAN VOORST. *Time*, Apr. 20, 1992.

"The arrogance of the clerks." ANGELO CODEVILLA. *National Review*, Nov. 4, 1991.
"Toughie, smoothy. . . ." DAN GOODGAME. *Time*, May 27, 1991.

Gaviria Trujillo, César (1947–)

Colombian President Gaviria Trujillo suffered a major setback on July 22, 1992, when Medellin drug cartel head Pablo Escobar Gaviria and several associates escaped from prison. The "prison" was the luxurious headquarters Escobar had built to his own specifications after his June 1991 plea bargain with the Gaviria Trujillo government. The "escape," as it turned out, was with the collusion of Colombian security forces, sent to Escobar's headquarters ostensibly to move him and his associates to a military prison. It was widely thought, however, that the projected move was intended to be much further, to a United States prison, and that the presence of U.S. agents on the scene indicated that Escobar had escaped from the kind of kidnap attempt recently sanctioned by the U.S. Supreme Court—or at least thought he was escaping such an attempt. The setback for Gaviria Trujillo was therefore major indeed, going far beyond Escobar, for Gaviria's *de facto* peace with his country's drug cartels, ending a very real civil war between the government and the drug traffickers, depended on a new constitutional amendment barring extradition to the United States and the ability to plead guilty to a single criminal charge, in essence a kind of mass plea bargain prior to surrender.

With those guarantees gone, a new government-drug cartel civil war began, joining and merging with the continuing civil war between the government and several left revolutionary organizations. A wave of bombings and guerrilla attacks swept the country, and on November 8th Gaviria declared a nationwide state of emergency, enabling him to prosecute the developing civil war by decree, bypassing Congress and the courts. On November 12th, the commanders of the air force, army, and navy were replaced, as Colombia's long civil war continued.

An economist, Gaviria entered politics at the age of 27, as mayor of his home town of Pereira. He later served several terms in the national assembly, and in 1986 became finance minister in the Barco Vargas government, later serving in other cabinet-level posts. He became campaign manager for Liberal Party presidential candidate Luis Carlos Galan Sarmiento in 1989; after Galan's August assassination, Gaviria became a candidate, was nominated by his party in March 1990, and was elected President of Colombia on May 27, 1990. He attended the University of the Andes.

FURTHER READING

"Colombia's bloodstained peace." *Economist*, June 6, 1992.
"Gavaria's gamble." JAMES BROOKE. *New York Times Magazine*, Oct. 13, 1991.
"Colombia's next president. . . ." LINDA ROBINSON. *U.S. News & World Report*, July 30, 1990.
"Colombia's elections." C. DOMINIQUE VAN DE STADT. *World Press Review*, July, 1990.
"President of last resort." *Time*, June 11, 1990.

Gephardt, Richard Andrew (1941–)

After taking himself out of the presidential race on July 17, 1991, powerful House Majority Leader Gephardt was widely reported to have come very close to re-entering the race in February 1992, if Bill Clinton had done badly in the New Hampshire primary. Ultimately, Gephardt decided once again to wait, though there was no doubt that his eye was still on the Presidency. He endorsed Bill Clinton on April 12, and addressed the Democratic National Convention on July 16 in favor of Clinton. Far more important than any of this, he remained throughout the year a key player in what came to be an election year "gridlock" between a Republican President and Democratic Congress. During 1992, he—and his colleagues—accomplished very little new legislation. Gephardt also remained a key Democratic Party spokesperson on some aspects of foreign affairs, notably attacking the U.S.-Canada-Mexico trade agreement that was one of the few specific agreements to emerge from the final year of the Bush Administration. Gephardt encountered some bad publicity because of his 28 overdrafts on the House bank when that scandal became news, but was in no way seriously damaged, as attested by his landslide re-election victory in November, with 66 percent of the vote to his opponent's 34 percent.

St. Louis-born Gephardt began his political career as a St. Louis alderman (1971–76), and his congressional career in 1979. His 1962 B.S. was from Northwestern University, and his 1965 J.D. from the University of Michigan. He married Jane Ann Byrnes in 1966; the couple have three children.

FURTHER READING

"Wanted. . . ." DOUGLAS HARBRECHT. *Business Week*, Nov .19, 1990.
"Gephardt speaks for the majority." BILL WHALEN. *Insight*, July 3, 1989.
"Man for all seasons. . . ." MORTON M. KONDRACKE. *New Republic*, July 3, 1989.

Gere, Richard (1949–) In Phil Joanou's psychological melodrama-murder film *Final Analysis*, Gere starred as Isaac Barr, a San Francisco psychiatrist who drifts into an affair with Heather Evans (Kim Basinger), the sister of one of his patients; murder, a murder trial, and post-trial plot twists follow. The film received mixed reviews, did badly at the box office, and quickly went into home video, where it did quite well, probably due to the enduring pull of Gere and Basinger.

Forthcoming were several substantial starring roles, one of them opposite Jodie Foster in Jon Amiel's Civil War-era love story *Sommersby*, scheduled for 1993 release. Another was as a manic-depressive psychiatric patient in Mike Figgis's film *Mr. Jones*, opposite Lena Olin as the psychatrist who falls in love with him; the film was originally scheduled for late 1992 release and then postponed to spring 1993. A third was in Mark Rydell's forthcoming film *Intersection*, a remake of Claude Sautet's 1970 film *Les Choses de la Vie*. A fourth was notable in social cause terms—a starring role opposite Lily Tomlin and Matthew Modine in Roger Spottiswoode's HBO film *And the Band Played On*, based on Randy Shilts's book about the early years of the AIDS epidemic, when recognition and action were very slow in coming.

Philadelphia-born Gere began his theater career in the early 1970s, and became a star in such films as *Report to the Commissioner* (1975), *Looking for Mr. Goodbar* (1977), *Yanks* (1979), *An Officer and a Gentleman* (1982), and *Internal Affairs* (1989). After several years in the doldrums, Gere's career received an enormous boost in 1990 from the unexpected popularity of *Pretty Woman*, the Pygmalion-like romantic comedy in which he co-starred with Julia Roberts. Long interested in Buddhism and Eastern philosophy, Gere is the founder and chairman of Tibet House. In October 1991, he met the Dalai Lama at Kennedy Airport, to begin 62 Tibet-related events organized into the International Year of Tibet. He attended the University of Massachusetts. He and model Cindy Crawford married in 1991.

FURTHER READING

"The model and. . . ." HERB RITTS and JULIA REED. *Vogue*, Nov. 1992.

Gibbons, John Howard (1929–) President Bill Clinton's incoming science advisor is a nuclear physicist and environmentalist, with especially strong credentials in the tremendously difficult and immensely important area of nuclear waste disposal. Gibbons worked at the Oak Ridge National Laboratory (1954–73); he was a physicist and group leader in nuclear geophysics (1954–69), and was director of the laboratory's environmental program (1973–74). He was director of the Office of Energy Conservation of the Federal Energy Administration (1973–74), and professor of physics and director of the University of Tennessee's Energy, Environment, and Resources Center (1974–79). From 1979 to 1992, he was director of the Office of Technology Assessment of the U.S. Congress, in that period fully emerging as one of the leading environmentalists of the day, with strong influence on many environmentally-minded lawmakers, including then-Senator Al Gore. Greatly critical of the Department of Energy record on nuclear waste disposal during the Reagan and Bush years, he was expected to focus on nuclear waste disposal and other environmenally sensitive issues, as well as on the whole range of technology.

Virginia-born Gibbons's B.S. was from Randolph-Macon College, as was his 1977 Sc.D. His 1954 Ph.D. in physics was from Duke University. He has published more than 50 books and articles. He is married to Mary Ann Hobart; they have four children.

FURTHER READING

"How John Gibbons. . . ." LAURA VAN DAM and ROBERT HOWARD. *Technology Review*, Oct. 1988.

Gibson, Mel (1956–) In 1992, Australian film star Gibson starred as Los Angeles police detective Martin Riggs, opposite Danny Glover as his partner, Roger Murtagh, in Richard Donner's *Lethal Weapon 3*, a high-budget violence-packed film that became one of the worldwide hits of the year, although many continued to deplore the unending string of shootings, explosions, and violent deaths that have characterized all three enormously popular "Lethal Weapon" films. The cast included Rene Russo, Joe Pesci, Steve Kahan, Darlene Love, Traci Wolfe, Damon Hines, Ebonie Smith, and Stuart Wilson. Gibson also starred as a cryogenically frozen 1930s test pilot who is reawakened in 1992, and is then a man-out-of-time in Steve Miner's film romance *Forever Young*; Jamie Lee Curtis and Elijah Wood co-starred.

For his 1990 film *Hamlet* and work on behalf of Shakespeare studies with young people, the very versatile and highly regarded actor received the fifth Will Award, from Washington's Shakespeare Theater, joining Joseph Papp, Kevin Kline, Christopher Plummer and Kenneth Branagh.

Forthcoming were several diverse new projects. One was a starring film role as murdered CBS correspondent George Polk, in *The Polk Conspiracy*, based on the Kati Marton book. Another was a feature film based on James Garner's classic western television series "Maverick," with Garner, who originated the role in 1957, playing a supporting role. Gibson was also scheduled to direct the forthcoming film *The Man Without a Face*, based on the Isabelle Holland novel.

Born in Peekskill, New York, Gibson emigrated to Australia with his family in 1968. He appeared on stage and screen in Australia from 1977, in South Australian regional theatre in the classics, in several television series, and most notably in the film *Tim* (1979). He soon became a popular worldwide film star, in such action films as *Mad Max* (1979), and its two sequels: *The Road Warrior* (1982) and *Mad Max Beyond Thunderdome* (1985); the dramas *Gallipoli* (1981) and *The Year of Living Dangerously* (1983); the *Lethal Weapon* films (1987, 1989); *Bird on a Wire* (1990); and *Air America* (1990). Gibson attended the Australian National Institute of Dramatic Arts. He married Robyn Moore in 1979; they have six children.

FURTHER READING

"Mel Gibson. . . ." JEANNE MARIE LASKAS. *Redbook*, Nov. 1992.
Mel Gibson. NEIL SINYARD. Outlet, 1992.
"Mel-o-drama. . . ." ROY SEKOFF . *Seventeen*, Jan. 1991.
"Mel Gibson. . . ." JOHN LAHR. *Cosmopolitan*, Dec. 1990.
"Road worrier. . . ." *Harper's Magazine*, Aug. 1990.
"Talking with. . . ." CARSON JONES. *Redbook*, Aug. 1990.
Mel Gibson: Australia's Restless Superstar. KEITH MCKAY. Doubleday, 1986.
Mel Gibson. DAVID RAGAN. Dell, 1985.

Gielgud, John (Arthur John Gielgud; 1904–) With Laurence Olivier, Ralph Richardson, and Michael Redgrave gone, Gielgud is one of the last of the great actors who dominated the British stage from the mid-1930s on. Now in his late 80's and beginning his eighth decade on stage and screen, his roles are in films and television, for a continuing theater run is far more physically demanding. In 1992, Gielgud starred as Sydney Cockerell, opposite Wendy Hiller as Laurentia McLachlan and Patrick McGoohan as George Bernard Shaw, in the television film version of Hugh Whitemore's *The Best of Friends*, based on Shaw's letters and journals. Gielgud also co-starred in David Seltzer's *Shining Through*, a romance-spy thriller set during World II. Michael Douglas and Melanie Griffith played the main roles; Liam Neeson, and Joely Richardson also co-starred. Gielgud also starred in John G. Avildsen's film *The Power of One*, the story of the development of a young British boy who in the 1930s found himself among racist Africaaners in what is now Zimbabwe. Costarring were Morgan Freeman, Stephen Dorff, Armin Mueller-Stahl, and Fay Masterson. With John Miller, Gielgud also in 1992 published *Acting Shakespeare*, an anecdotal work spanning his career in the theater.

One of the leading actors of the English-speaking theater for more than seven decades, and the grandnephew of the celebrated actress Ellen Terry, London-born Gielgud made his stage debut in 1921, and by 1929 had become a highly regarded Shakespearean actor at the Old Vic, going on to play major roles in Shakespeare for the next half century, perhaps most notably as *Hamlet*. He directed a legendary 1935 *Romeo and Juliet* in London, alternating with Laurence Olivier in the Mercutio and Romeo roles. Late in his career, he created several modern roles, among others in *Nude With Violin* (1956), *Tiny Alice* (1964), *Home* (1970), and *No Man's Land* (1970). Although Gielgud made his film debut in 1921 and played leads in the films *Secret Agent* (1936) and *Julius Caesar* (1970), he has for most of his career been primarily a theater actor. In recent years, however, he has played numerous strong supporting roles in such films as *Murder on the Orient Express* (1974), *Arthur* (1981; he won a Best Supporting Actor Oscar), and *Chariots of Fire* (1981) and in such television productions as *Brideshead Revisited* (1981) and *War and Remembrance* (1988). Among his writings are *Early Stages: A Theatrical Reminiscence* (1939), *Stage Directions* (1963), *An Actor in His Time* (1981), and *Backward Glances: Times for Reflection and Distinguished Company* (1990).

FURTHER READING

"A man for all seasons. . . ." GERALD C. LUBENOW. *Newsweek*, Mar. 21, 1988.

Gillespie, Dizzy (John Birks Gillespie; 1917–) In 1992, his 75th year, the great jazz trumpeter Dizzy Gillespie was once again honored by his peers, this time with a Large Jazz Ensemble Grammy for his 1991 record *Live at the Royal Festival Hall*, taped in London by Gillespie and his United Nations Orchestra. For the music world, it was a year-long 75th birthday celebration for Gillespie, which began with a month-long stay at Greenwich Village's Blue

Note, featuring more than a score of guest artists, as well his his United Nations Orchestra. Then it was back on the road again, on his perpetual world tour, in a year that was to have seen him once again perform on four continents. But major surgery in March made the balance of the year mainly a matter of recuperation, although the many tributes continued as planned.

Gillespie also appeared on screen in 1992, as band leader Bill Swann in Jose Antonio Zorrilla's *The Winter in Lisbon*, an international co-production set in Portugal. On December, the Alvin Ailey Dance Company premiered a new work dedicated to Gillespie, titled "That Night in Lisbon."

South Carolina-born Gillespie, a trumpeter, composer, arranger, bandleader, and recording artist, became a leading jazz figure in the mid-1940s; in that period, with Charlie Parker and others, he is credited with having originated "bop," also often called "be-bop." Gillespie became a trumpeter in the early 1930s, and played with Teddy Hill, Cab Calloway, Benny Carter, Duke Ellington, and others until he formed his first successful band, in 1946. Gillespie composed such jazz and popular standards as "Night in Tunisia" (1942), "Salt Peanuts" (1945), and "Manteca" (1947), and has toured widely and recorded for the past five decades. He has appeared in several films, most recently in the documentary, *A Night in Havana* (1990). In 1990, Gillespie received the first Duke Ellington Award, at Washington's Kennedy Center, and a National Medal of the Arts from President George Bush at the White House. An early autobiography was *To Be or Not to Bop: Memoirs of Dizzy Gillespie* (1955; written with Al Fraser). He married Lorraine Wills in 1940.

FURTHER READING

"Without you, no me." REGINA JONES. *American Visions*, Oct.–Nov. 1992.
"The candidate meets the press." *Down Beat*, July 1992.
"Diamond Dizzy." MICHAEL BOURNE. *Down Beat*, July 1992.
"Dizzy Gillespie. . . ." *Interview*, Jan. 1992.
Waiting for Dizzy. GENE LEES. Oxford University Press, 1991.
Dizzy Gillespie. TONY GENTRY. Chelsea House, 1991.
"Dizzy." WHITNEY BALLIETT. *New Yorker*, Sep. 17, 1990.
"Dizzy Gillespie. . . ." JAMES JONES, IV. *Down Beat*, Aug. 1990.

"Bebop's joyful pop. . . ." TIM POWIS. *Maclean's*, Mar. 20, 1989.
Dizzy Gillespie. BARRY MCRAE. Phaidon Universe, 1989.

Gingrich, Newt (Newton Leroy Gingrich; 1943–)

House Republican Whip Gingrich continued on his abrasive way during 1992, with all the scope offered by a presidential campaign year. In one of the most notably nasty attacks of a very nasty campaign, at a late-August Bush campaign rally in Georgia, he compared Governor Bill Clinton to Woody Allen, calling Allen "a perfect model of Bill Clinton's Democratic values," and going on to imply that the Democratic platform encouraged incest.

Gingrich himself was heavily criticized for his 22 overdrawn checks in the House of Representatives banking scandal, and for his expensive government-supplied limousine and driver, which he gave up during the primary campaign. He survived, however. In July, he won a primary fight against Herman Clark in a newly created Congressional district by a margin of less than 1,000 votes, and went on to easily win a Congressional seat by defeating Democratic nominee Tony Center by a 16-point margin. Gingrich, often critical of the Bush Administration, fully supported George Bush's re-election bid.

Pennsylvania-born Gingrich taught at West Georgia College before his election to the House of Representatives in 1979. He drew national attention in 1987 and 1988, as chief accuser of Democratic House Speaker Jim Wright, who ultimately resigned from the House. In August 1989, he urged ethics probes of seventeen other Congressional Democrats, as well. Gingrich himself was accused of earlier ethics violations in April 1989, soon after his March 1989 selection as House Republican Whip, and faced further ethics charges in October; but all charges against him were dropped in March 1990. Gingrich attended Emory and Tulane universities. In 1984, with David Drake and Marianne Gingrich, he published *Window of Opportunity: A Blueprint for the Future*. He has been married twice, and has two children.

FURTHER READING

"House revolutionary." ADAM CLYMER. *New York Times Magazine*, Aug. 23, 1992.
"A party's Newt testament. . . ." DANIEL WATTENBERG. *Insight*, Nov. 12, 1990.
"Having read George Bush's lips. . . ." BILL HEWITT. *People*, Nov. 12, 1990.
"New Newt news." DAVID BEERS. *Mother Jones*, Feb.–Mar. 1990.
"Master of disaster. . . ." DAVID BEERS. *Mother Jones*, Oct. 1989.
"Gingrich, Newton Leroy." *Current Biography*, July 1989.

Glass, Philip (1937–)

On October 12, 1992, the opera world saw a major event—the Metropolitian Opera premiere of the new Glass opera *The Voyage*. The work, its libretto by David Hwang, had been commissioned by the Met for introduction in 1992, the 500th centenary year of the Columbus voyage of discovery. The three-and-a-half-hour, $1.5 million production, its principal singers including Douglas Perry, Patricia Schuman, Tatiana Troyanos, Timothy Noble, Kaaren Erickson, and Julien Robbins, covered far more than the Columbus voyage, being in essence a meditation on the development of the worldwide human mosaic, the urge to explore, and the meeting of cultures.

The work was part of an extraordinarily productive period for Glass. His "Low" Symphony made its American premiere with the Brooklyn Philharmonic Orchestra at the Brooklyn Academy of Music on November 27; Dennis Russell Davies conducted. The work is based on the instrumental music in David Bowie's 1977 album *Low*. Forthcoming was the opera *Orphée*, an adaptation of the 1949 Jean Cocteau film; it was scheduled to premiere in May 1993 at the Cambridge, Massachusetts American Repertory Theater.

Also forthcoming was another major "voyage" opera, *The White Raven*, with libretto by Robert Wilson, scheduled for premiere in 1994. The opera was commissioned by the Portuguese government to commemorate the voyages of Portuguese explorer Vasco da Gama, who opened the East to Europeans by sailing around Cape Horn into the Indian Ocean, but it will undoubtedly become a far wider work.

In his developing body of work, Baltimore-born Glass has wiped out any "line" that might still be said to exist between modern classical and popular music. He emerged as a leading modern composer in the late 1960s, after a Paris period in which he worked with Ravi Shankar and studied with Nadia Boulanger, then weaving modernist and Indian themes and techniques into his music. He founded the Philip Glass Ensemble in 1968, and became a well-known figure on tour and a popular recording artist in the early 1970s, with such works as *Music in 12 Parts* (1971–74) and *Glassworks* (1982). He also began a major career as a classical composer in the 1970s, with *Einstein On the Beach*, still his best known classical work, and the other two parts of his celebrated "portrait opera" trilogy: *Akhnaten* (1980) and *Satyagraha* (1985). Among his other operas are *The Civil Wars* (1982–84), *The Making of the Representative for Planet 8* (1988), *One Thousand Airplanes on the Roof* (1988), *Mattogrosso* (1989), and *The Hydrogen Jukebox* (1990), produced in collaboration with poet Allen Ginsberg and visual artist Jerome Sirlin, starting from a cantata based on Ginsberg's anti-war poem, "Wichita Vortex Sutra." In 1987 he published the memoir *Music by Philip Glass*. Glass attended the University of Chicago and the Julliard School of Music. He was formerly married, and has two children.

FURTHER READING

"Glass plus." K. ROBERT SCHWARZ. *Opera News*, Oct. 1992.

"A persistent voyager. . . ." JAMES R. OESTREICH. *New York Times Magazine*, Oct. 11, 1992.

"Philip Glass. . . ." *Connoisseur*, Feb. 1991.

American Music Makers. JANET NICHOLS. Walker, 1990.

"Glass." TIM PAGE. *Opera News*, June 1988.

Glover, Danny (1947–)

Leading African-American actor Danny Glover starred in 1992 in the kind of action-adventure film that since 1985's *Lethal Weapon* has made him a familiar face to worldwide film audiences. He starred as Los Angeles police detective Roger Murtagh, opposite Mel Gibson as his partner, Martin Riggs, in Richard Donner's *Lethal Weapon 3*, a high-budget violence-packed film that became one of the worldwide hits of the year, although many continued to deplore the unending string of shootings, explosions, and violent deaths that characterized all three enormously popular "Lethal Weapon" films. The cast included Rene Russo, Joe Pesci, Steve Kahan, Darlene Love, Traci Wolfe, Damon Hines, Ebonie Smith, and Stuart Wilson.

During 1992, Glover also starred in the forthcoming Morgan Freeman film *Bopha!*, executive produced by Arsenio Hall. The movie, which began filming in August 1992 at Harare, Zimba-

bwe, is based on a play by South African Percy Mtwa, set in South Africa soon after the 1976 Soweto protests. Also forthcoming was a starring role as a homeless man opposite Matt Dillon in *The Saint of Fort Washington*, a film coproduced by Glover. He also narrated an audio version of Rudyard Kipling's classic story "How the Leopard Got His Spots."

San Francisco-born Glover, a civil rights activist during his late 1960s college years, entered the theater through appearances as an amateur in the works of such playwrights as Amiri Baraka and Athol Fugard, and worked as a professional in supporting roles on stage throughout the 1970s. In 1982, he appeared in a Yale Repertory Theater production of Fugard's *Master Harold and the Boys*. On screen, he appeared in such films as *Escape from Alcatraz* (1979), *Chu Chu and the Philly Flash* (1981), *Out* (1982), and *Iceman* (1984), before his breakthrough starring role as Moze opposite Sally Field in *Places in the Heart* (1984). In 1985, he starred opposite Whoopi Goldberg in *The Color Purple*, and also in *Witness* and *Silverado*. He then reached huge audiences in the thrillers *Lethal Weapon* (1985), *Lethal Weapon II* (1987), and *Predator II* (1990), also starring in such films as *To Sleep With Anger* (1990), *Flight of the Intruder* (1991), *Grand Canyon* (1991), and *A Rage in Harlem* (1991). His B.S. was from San Francisco State University. He is married to the former Asake Bomani, and has one child.

FURTHER READING

"Glover's leap." LISA SCHWARZBAUM. *Entertainment*, June 12, 1992.
"Danny Glover." MARJORIE ROSEN and LOIS ARMSTRONG. *People*, Feb. 10, 1992.
"An everyman. . . ." KITTY BOWE HEARTY. *Premiere*, Feb. 1992.
"Danny Glover." *Playboy*, Sep. 1991.
"Danny Glover. . . ." *GQ—Gentleman's Quarterly*, July 1989.

Gober, Hershel W: See Brown, Jesse.

Godfree, Kitty (Kathleen McCane Godfree; 1896–1992)

A leading British athlete of the 1920s, Godfree was an Olympic gold medalist in women's tennis doubles at the 1920 Antwerp summer games, and went on to win Wimbledon women's singles titles in 1924 and 1926, the first as Kitty McCane and the second as Kitty Godfree. In 1924, she defeated tennis great Helen Wills, and in 1926 defeated Lili de Alvarez. She also won in several doubles championships, one of them in 1926 with her husband Leslie Godfree. She was also a four-time all-England badminton champion. Although in her day the time of the big serve had not yet arrived, she was one of the first women players to develop a strong net game and powerful volley. She continued to be a familiar tennis figure and to play tennis well into her '90s, and as an historic figure was often called upon as a presenter of awards. She was survived by two sons. (d. London; June 19,1992)

FURTHER READING

Obituary. *The Times* (of London), June 20, 1992.
Obituary. *New York Times*, June 20, 1992.
Obituary. *Independent*, June 20, 1992.

Goldberg, Whoopi (Caryn Johnson; 1950–)

Now established as an international film star, Goldberg starred in 1992 as the teacher in Darrell James Roodt's film version of the stage musical *Sarafina*, filmed in Soweto and set in the modern Black South African civil rights struggle. Among her co-stars were Leleti Khumalo as Sarafina, and Miriam Makeba. While in South Africa, her presence was for a little while opposed by some fringe revolutionary groups, but she was so well received personally that all Black African opposition quickly vanished. She also taped interviews with such leaders as Nelson Mandela, Mangosuthu Gatsha Buthelezi, and Helen Suzman for use on her late-night television talk show, which premiered in autumn 1992. Elizabeth Taylor was Goldberg's first talk show guest, followed by Billy Crystal and Robin Williams, in a format providing for one celebrity guest per half hour show.

Goldberg starred opposite Maggie Smith and Harvey Keitel in Emile Ardolino's comedy *Sister Act*, as Deloris, a singer on the run from her gangster lover, played by Keitel. Smith played the Mother Superior of the convent in which Deloris hides, masquerading as a nun. Goldberg also joined many other stars playing small roles in *The Player*, Robert Altman's merciless, multistar lampoon of modern Hollywood. Forthcoming was a starring role opposite Ted Danson in Richard Benjamin's film *Made in America*, and a lead in Daniel Algrant's *Naked in New York*, co-starring Timothy Dalton, Kathleen Turner, Eric Stolz, and Mary Louise Parker.

New York City-born Goldberg, who had previously worked as a popular cabaret and stage entertainer, emerged as a film star in *The Color Purple* (1985; she received an Oscar nomination), and went on to such films as *Jumpin' Jack Flash* (1986), *Fatal Beauty* (1987), *Burglar* (1988), and *The Long Walk Home* (1990). In 1990, she scored a major success—including a Best Supporting Actress Oscar—as the Harlem-based psychic in the year's surprise top-grossing film, *Ghost*, opposite Patrick Swayze and Demi Moore. She also starred opposite Jean Stapleton in the short-lived television series "Bagdad Cafe" (1990). She had a one-woman show on Broadway in 1984, and toured in a second one-woman show in 1988. Goldberg was previously married, and has one child.

FURTHER READING

"Whoopi Goldberg." *People*, Dec. 28, 1992.
" 'I knew what I wanted to be.' " DOTSON RADER. *Parade*, Nov. 1, 1992.
"Witty, gritty. . . ." JAMIE DIAMOND. *Cosmopolitan*, Nov. 1992.
"Funny lady." MELANIE BERGER. *Ladies Home Journal*, Oct. 1992.

"Whoopi Goldberg." DAVID RENSIN. *US*, Oct. 1992.
"Whoopi Goldberg stars. . . ." ALDORE COLLIER. *Jet*, Sep. 28, 1992.
"The joy of being Whoopi." JOHN SKOW. *Time*, Sep. 21, 1992.
"Whoopi Goldberg." MATTHEW MODINE. *Interview*, June 1992.
"Whoopi Goldberg becomes. . . ." ALDORE COLLIER. *Jet*, June 1, 1992.
"The prayer. . . ." JESS CAGLE. *Entertainment*, May 29, 1992.
"Whoopi Goldberg. . . ." *Jet*, Apr. 22, 1991.
"Whoopi Goldberg. . . ." STEPHEN FARBER. *Cosmopolitan*, Mar. 1991.

Goldblum, Jeff (1952–) Focusing largely on films in 1992, Goldblum starred as a film director trying out a new life as a suburban bookstore owner, opposite Rory Cochrane as his son in the Paul Mones film *Fathers and Sons*. He also starred as a major drug dealer opposite Larry Fishburne as an undercover police officer in *Deep Cover*, Bill Duke's exploration of a vicious drug subculture. Goldblum also played a cameo as himself in *The Player*, Robert Altman's no-holds-barred look at Hollywood.

Forthcoming was a leading role in Stephen Spielberg's sci-tech special-effects blockbuster *Jurassic Park*, co-starring Sam Neill, Laura Dern, and Richard Attenborough, scheduled for release in the summer of 1993. The film, based on Michael Crichton's novel, is about modern genetically engineered dinosaurs that break free from a theme park and become a danger to humanity.

Pittsburgh-born Goldblum played in the New York theater in the early 1970s, most notably in *Two Gentlemen of Verona* (1971). His wide range of films includes *Invasion of the Body Snatchers* (1978), *The Big Chill* (1983), *The Right Stuff* (1983), *Silverado* (1985), *The Fly* (1986), *Beyond Therapy* (1987), *Earth Girls Are Easy* (1989; opposite Geena Davis, then his wife), *Twisted Obsession* (1990), *The Tall Guy* (1990), and *Mr. Frost* (1990). He also appeared in the television series "Tenspeed and Brownshoe" (1980), and in the telefilms *The Race for the Double Helix* (1987) as scientist James Watson, *Framed* (1990), and *The Favor, the Watch and the Very Big Fish* (1991). Goldblum attended the Neighborhood Playhouse. He was previously married to actress Geena Davis (1987–91).

FURTHER READING

"Married. . . . with chicken." JOHANNA SCHNELLER. *GQ—Gentlemen's Quarterly*, June 1989.

Gonzalez Márquez, Felipe (1942–) Spanish Prime Minister Gonzalez, secretary general of the Spanish Socialist Workers Party (PSOE), at 50 and in his tenth year in office continued to confront quite adverse economic problems at home, while at the same time bringing Spain even further forward into the European and world communities. It was unlikely to be his last year in office; in October, he announced that he would run for a fourth term, and he was thought quite likely to be re-elected, although his party seemed unlikely to win a clear majority, probably making a coalition government necessary.

For Gonzalez and Spain, 1992 was the year of the July Barcelona Olympics, symbolizing Spain's move out into the world, after the decades of Franco's dictatorship and the long revival that followed. Gonzalez continued to spearhead that move on many fronts, moving Spain further into the European Community (EC), actively supporting United Nations action in Bosnia-Herzogovina, pressing El Salvador toward its peace treaty, and attempting—without much success—to convince Fidel Castro to move toward democracy. But the move toward the European Community had economic and political costs. In April, planned unemployment insurance and welfare cuts aimed at bringing Spain's economic performance more in line with EC expectations, generated a general strike; Spain's unemployment rate was then 15 percent and continued high throughout the year. In the autumn of 1992, Gonzalez was also forced to devalue the Spanish currency and reinstate controls over the outflow of capital because of the European money system crisis, further damaging the Spanish economy and his own popularity.

Gonzalez became a member of the then-illegal Spanish Socialist Workers Party in 1964, having been a socialist youth group member since 1962. He rose to become his party's leader, and succeeded Adolfo Suarez González as prime minister with his party's victory in the 1982 elections. He was the first socialist prime minister of Spain since the Spanish Civil War; his election signaled the full emergence of a new Spain after the long night of the Franco period. In 1986, he took Spain into the European Common Market. He won a third term in the October 1989 elections, though only by one parliamentary seat; and on review that seat was lost by his party, leaving him without a clear parliamentary majority. Gonzalez attended the Catholic University of Louvaine. He is married to Carmen Romero; they have three children.

FURTHER READING

"Gonzalez vows. . . ." RICHARD OWEN. *Times*, Feb. 11, 1992.

Goodman, John (1952–) John Goodman

was honored by his peers in 1992, winnng an Emmy nomination as lead actor in a comedy series for his role in "Roseanne;" the long-running show was still a hit during the 1992–93 television season.

Goodman also moved into films very strongly during 1992, starring as legendary home-run hitter Babe Ruth in Arthur Hiller's *The Babe*, co-starring Kelly McGillis. The biofilm covered Ruth's life from the beginning of his interest in baseball in 1902 to his retirement from the game in 1935. Forthcoming was a starring role opposite Melanie Griffith in a new version of the film classic *Born Yesterday*, with Goodman in the wheeler-dealer role originated by Broderick Crawford and Griffith recreating the not-at-all-stupid Billie Dawn role originated by Judy Holliday. Also forthcoming was a starring role in Joe Dante's film *Matinee*.

Before his "Roseanne" role catapulted him to stardom, Missouri-born Goodman had played in strong character roles in the theater and in films, on Broadway in such plays as *Loose Ends* (1979) and *Big River* (1985), and in such films as *Eddie Macon's Run* (1983), *True Stories* (1986), *Raising Arizona* (1987), *Sea of Love* (1989), *Always* (1989), *Stella* (1990), *King Ralph* (1991), and *Barton Fink* (1991). Goodman attended Southwest Missouri State College. He married Anna Elizabeth (Annabeth) Hartzog in 1989; they have one daughter.

FURTHER READING

"Bat man." ALLEN BARRA. *Entertainment*, May 1, 1992.
"John Goodman." JAMES GREENBERG. *US*, Apr. 1992.
"The Babe." VIC ZIEGEL. *Life*, Apr.1992.
" 'The Babe' comes alive." ANDREA ZANI. *Sporting News*, Apr. 20, 1992.
"John Goodman is. . . ." PETE RICHMOND. *GQ—Gentleman's Quarterly*, Apr. 1992.
"Being the big guy. . . ." PETER DE JONGE. *New York Times Magazine*, Feb. 10, 1991.
"John Goodman." TOM GREEN. *Los Angeles*, Mar. 1991.
"John Goodman. . . ." ERIC SHERMAN. *Ladies Home Journal*, Feb. 1991.
"John Goodman. . . ." FRED ROBBINS. *Woman's Day*, May 1, 1990.
"Everybody's all American. . . ." RICHARD ZOGLIN. *Time*, Feb. 19, 1990.

Gorbachev, Mikhail Sergeyevich

(1931–) Out of power, former Soviet President Gorbachev returned to Moscow in January, moved with his wife Raisa into a Moscow apartment, and made his base the International Foundation for Social, Economic, and Political Research, the Moscow think tank founded by Alesandr Yakovlev. Although the great liberator of all of the countries of the former Soviet Union and Eastern Europe, he was in 1992 rather unpopular at home, for he had cautioned a careful—and for many too slow—approach to reform and independence. He was still enormously popular and respected throughout the world, however, and traveled widely, making an especially notable speaking tour of the United

States in May, en route visiting presidents Ronald Reagan and George Bush.

Gorbachev was highly critical of Russian President Boris Yeltsin as the year developed. As their longstanding animosity deepened, Yeltsin used his power against Gorbachev; in October Yeltsin banned Gorbachev from traveling abroad, a step that worldwide protests soon made Yeltsin reverse. Yeltsin also evicted Gorbachev's foundation from its government-supplied Moscow offices, using armed men to bar Gorbachev from entering, a move that contained a chilling message for the possible future prospects of Russian democracy. Gorbachev was later able to occupy part of his former offices. Despite his current unpopularity there, Gorbachev remained a major figure on the Russian scene.

Gorbachev's early career proceeded in orthodox Soviet fashion: he joined the Communist Party of the Soviet Union in 1952, and for the next 33 years moved up through the party and government. He became a member of his party's central committee in 1971 and later minister of agriculture (1978–85). In 1985, he became General Secretary of the Soviet Communist Party Central Committee and effectively leader of the Soviet Union. In power, he immediately began the processes of internal change. His two main slogans were *perestroika*, meaning a massive restructuring of the Soviet economy, away from central planning, bureaucracy, and full state ownership and toward a market economy, private enterprise, and even private ownership of land; and *glasnost*, or "openness," meaning a move toward basic democratic freedoms.

Abroad, Gorbachev also moved very quickly once in power. In a series of meetings with presidents Reagan and Bush, he initiated what became the end of the 45-year-long Cold War, beginning with the 1987 intermediate nuclear forces (INF) treaty, the first of a series of major Soviet-American peace moves, with planned troop pullbacks and, for the first time in decades, real progress on arms control. In the process, he and the American presidents also helped to negotiate the end of conflicts in Nicaragua, Cambodia, Angola, Mozambique, Namibia, Ethiopia, and several other countries, with both superpowers ending their long sponsorship of opposing parties in many regional conflicts. At the same time, he normalized relations with China, bringing that 30-year-old conflict to an end. And, during the late 1980s, he essentially agreed to set the peoples of Eastern Europe free, encouraging

the development of what became independent, non-communist governments in Poland, Czechoslovakia, Hungary, Bulgaria, Romania, and East Germany. The developments in East Germany led directly to the tearing down of the Berlin Wall and the 1990 unification of Germany.

On August 19, 1991 Gorbachev was placed under house arrest while vacationing in the Crimea, as part of an abortive right-wing coup that failed when he refused to sign away power, and when Boris Yeltsin led the massive resistance that developed in Moscow and several other cities. The coup collapsed on August 21st, after having generated a second Russian Revolution that swept away the remnants of Soviet communism—and ultimately swept away the Soviet state itself. As it turned out, Gorbachev's day was done; he failed to hold the Soviet state together, and Yeltsin and other leaders gained control of what became a set of successor countries. Gorbachev resigned; he is seen by many throughout the world as still by far the greatest Soviet leader of the 20th century.

In 1990, Gorbachev was awarded the Nobel Peace Prize. Among his recent works are *Perestroika and Soviet-American Relations* (1990), *At the Summit: A New Start in U. S.–Soviet Relations* (1988), and *Toward a Better World* and *Perestroika: New Thinking for Our Country and the World* (both 1987). Gorbachev attended Moscow State University and the Stavropol Agricultural Institute. He and Raisa Maximova Titorenko married in 1956; they have one child.

FURTHER READING

"My annus horribiliski." JONATHAN STEELE. *Guardian*, Dec. 24, 1992.

"Indignities pile up. . . ." MATTHEW CAMPBALL. *Sunday Times* (of London), Oct. 18, 1992.

"What's it all about, Gorby?" DAVID REMNICK. *Vanity Fair*, Aug. 1992.

" 'Yeltsin. . . .' " PAUL KLEBNIKOV. *Forbes*, June 8, 1992.

"Mikhail Gorbachev's. . . ." MASSIMO CALABRESI. *National Review*, Jan. 20, 1992.

Gorbachev, Yeltsin and the Last Days of the Soviet Empire. NEIL FELSHMAN. Thomas Dunne/St. Martin's, 1992.

The Sons of Sergei: Khrushchev and Gorbachev as Reformers. DONALD R. KELLY and SHANNON G. DAVIS, eds. Praeger/Greenwood, 1992.

Mikhail Gorbachev. ANNA SPROULE. Gareth Stevens, 1992.

The Gorbachev Version. RICHARD HUGO. Zebra, 1992.

Gorbachev: The Story of a Survivor. NEIL FELSHMAN. St. Martin's, 1991.

Gorbachev and After. STEPHEN WHITE. Cambridge University Press, 1991.

Gorbachev and His Reforms. RICHARD SAKWA. Prentice-Hall, 1991.

Mikhail Gorbachev. MICHEL TATU. Columbia University Press, 1991.

The Impact of Gorbachev. DEREK SPRING, ed. Columbia University Press, 1991.

Mikhail Gorbachev. JEROME MOGA. Bantam, 1991.

The Gorbachev Phenomenon: A Historical Interpretation, rev. ed. MOSHE LEWIN. University of California Press, 1991.

Mikhail Gorbachev. JOHN W. SELFRIDGE. Chelsea House, 1991.

Why Gorbachev Happened: His Triumphs and His Failure. ROBERT G. KAISER. Simon & Schuster, 1991.

Mikhail Gorbachev: Revolutionary for Democracy. ANNA SPROYLE. Gareth Stevens, 1991.

Gore, Al (Albert Gore, Jr.; 1948–) Incoming Vice President of the United States Al Gore is the son of longtime Tennessee Congressman and then Senator Albert Gore, and grew up in Washington, D. C. Like his father, he opposed the Vietnam War, and thought of leaving the country to avoid the draft, but in the end volunteered, seeing Army service in Vietnam (1969–71). He returned home to a job as an investigative reporter for Nashville's *The Tennessean* (1971–76). Turning to politics, he served four terms in the House of Representatives (1977–85), and was elected to the Senate in 1984. He made an unsuccessful presidential primary run in 1988, and in 1989 was positioning himself for a 1992 run when his youngest child, Albert Gore III, was seriously injured in an automobile accident. Gore spent much of his discretionary time after that focusing on his son's recovery and related family matters, and in 1991 declared himself out of the presidential race— only to find himself running with Bill Clinton in 1992.

Gore played a moderate's role during his Congressional career, voting for arms control, for only some defense cuts, for civil rights, and for education, child support, and welfare reform. While focusing on his son's recovery, Gore developed a very special interest in the environment, which resulted in the book *Earth in the Balance,* a 1992 best-seller. Also published under the names of Clinton and Gore was the campaign book *Putting People First.* Gore also spoke very strongly on environmental matters at the 1991 Rio de Janiero Earth Summit. His environmental commitment was unsuccessfully attacked by Republican leaders during the election campaign, but their attempt to depict him as a "radical environmentalist," labeling him "ozone man," seemed to have little adverse effect on the Clinton-Gore campaign.

During the campaign and after the election, Clinton and Gore established an unusual relationship. Rather than pushing Gore aside, as has been the fate of almost all previous Vice Presidents, President-elect Clinton included Gore at every step of the Cabinet appointment process, and also established Gore as the new adminstration's chief environmentalist. Clinton clearly stated that he wanted to include Gore in the whole range of presidential discussions and decisions; what remained to be seen was how that entirely nontraditional approach would work out during the Clinton years.

Gore attended Washington, D.C.'s St. Albans preparatory school. His 1969 B.A. was from Harvard University. He also attended the Vanderbilt University School of Religion (1971–72). He and Mary Elizabeth (Tipper) Aitcheson married in 1970; their four children are Karenna, Kristin, Sarah, and Albert III.

FURTHER READING

"The revenge of. . . .' " HILARY MACKENZIE. *Maclean's*, Nov. 16, 1992.

"Tennessee waltz." BILL HEWITT. *People*, Nov. 16, 1992.

"How to stay in the loop." BILL TURQUE. *Newsweek*, Oct. 26, 1992.

"Al Gore's double life." ALEX S. JONES. *New York Times Magazine*, Oct. 25, 1992.

"Quayle vs. Gore." STANLEY W. CLOUD. " 'We're not measuring the drapes.' " S.C. GWYNNE and ELIZABETH TAYLOR. *Time*, Oct. 19, 1992.

"Green giant." PHILIP SHABECOFF. "What it takes. . . ." FRED BARNES. "The other Al. . . ." MARTIN PERETZ. *New Republic*, Oct. 19, 1992.

"Captain Planet for veep." RONALD BAILEY et al. *National Review*, Sep.14, 1992. "Preserving God's 'very good' Earth." DAVID NEFF. *Christianity Today*. Sep. 14, 1992.

"Hard-Gore environmental issues." MICAH MORRISON. *Insight*, Aug. 31, 1992.

"The wonks. . . ." SIDNEY BLUMENTHAL. *New Republic*, Aug. 3, 1992.

"Gore. . . ." WALTER SHAPIRO. *Time*, July 20, 1992.

"Baby boom ticket. . . ." ANDREW BILSKI. *Maclean's*, July 20, 1992.

"Albert Arnold Gore Jr." *Facts on File*, July 16, 1992.

"Earth in the balance." *Christian Century*, Apr. 8, 1992.

Al Gore Jr.: His Life and Career. HANK HILLIN. Birch Lane/Carol, 1992.

Gore, Tipper

(Mary Elizabeth Aitcheson Gore; 1948–   ) Tipper Gore grew up in Virginia and attended a girl's school in Washington, D.C.. She met Al Gore at his high school prom, and that meeting was to color her entire future, for they soon decided to make their lives together. He went to Harvard, and she followed him to Boston, attending Garland Junior College and graduating with a major in psychology from Boston College in 1970. They married a month after her graduation. She also gained an M.A. in clinical psychology from Nashville's George Peabody College, but did not pursue a career in psychology. She did become a photographer with Nashville's *The Tennessean* in the mid-1970s, but gave up professional photography when Al Gore was elected to Congress in 1976.

In 1985, Tipper Gore became a national figure when, with a group of other Congressional wives, she led what became a national campaign

to label what she felt were morally objectionable records, because their lyrics were thought to promote sex, drugs, and violence. Her highly publicized campaign included testimony before one of her husband's Senate committees. The record industry soon responded to the pressure, and agreed to label some records, an action intensely distasteful to those in the entertainment industries and to civil libertarians. Tipper Gore, who was not also in favor of banning such record sales to minors—if such a ban were indeed constitutional—found herself hailed by many conservatives, who wanted to go much further, and actively disliked by many who saw her campaign as censorship. Although she went on to write *Raising PG Kids in an X-Rated Society* (1987), she ultimately pulled back from her crusade when it became clear that it was hurting her husband's 1988 Presidential campaign bid. During the 1992 campaign, Democratic strategists portrayed her as misunderstood on the matter, and she went to considerable lengths to point out that she had really loved rock music ever since her teenage years. The strategy seemed to work very successfully. Tipper and Al Gore have four children: Karenna, Kristin, Sarah, and Albert III.

FURTHER READING

"Tennessee waltz." BILL HEWITT. *People*, Nov. 16, 1992.

"First friends. . . ." HOWARD G. CHUA-EOAN. *People*, Nov. 16, 1992.

"The other partner. . . ." RICHARD LACAYO. July 20, 1992.

Running Mates. ANN GRIMES. Morrow, 1990.

"A new breed of Democratic wives. . . ." *People*, Feb. 22, 1988.

"Unfair labeling." GERALDINE A. FERRARO. *New Republic*, Jan. 18, 1988.

Gossett, Louis, Jr. (1936–   ) In the third film of the popular series, Gossett in 1992 starred once again as the "Iron Eagle" in John Glen's action film *Aces: Iron Eagle III*, the story of a group of over-age fighter pilots who go to Peru to fight drug traffickers. Gossett also starred as boxer Honey Roy Palmer opposite James Woods as boxing manager Gabriel Caine in Michael Ritchie's *Diggstown*, about a boxing scam that victimizes a villain.

On television, Gossett starred in the police procedural *Keeper of the City*, as a Chicago cop stalking a serial killer (Anthony LaPaglia), who is killing local mobsters. On a far more serious note, Gossett and Denzel Washington co-narrated the "American Experience" television series documentary *Liberators: Fighting on Two Fronts in World War II*, the story of African-American soldiers who were experiencing racism in their own segregated army while at the same time liberating Dachau and other German death camps. Gossett was also the voice of Frederick Douglass in the television documentary *Abraham Lincoln: A New Birth of Freedom.*

After over two decades as a highly regarded character actor in theater, films, and television, Brooklyn-born Gossett won an Emmy for his role as Fiddler in television's *Roots* (1977). He then went on to win a Best Supporting Actor Oscar in *An Officer and a Gentleman* (1982), and to appear in such films as *Iron Eagle* (1985), *The Principal* (1987), and *Toy Soldiers* (1991). On television, he had the title role in the miniseries *Sadat* (1983); his other telefilms include *A Gathering of Old Men* (1987), *Zora Is My Name!* (1990), *El Diablo* (1990), *Sudie and Simpson* (1990), *Carolina Skeletons* (1991), and *The Josephine Baker Story* (1991). Gossett's B.A. was from New York University, in 1959.

FURTHER READING

"Family business. . . ." MARK GOODMAN. *People*, May 6, 1991.

"Gossett, Louis, Jr." *Current Biography*, Nov. 1990.

Gotti, John (1941–   ) On April 2, 1992, after a ten-week trial, Mafia figure John Gotti was convicted by a Brooklyn, New York federal jury on all 13 counts brought against him in 1990. These included three counts of murder, four counts of conspiracy to murder, several other separate criminal acts, and a wide range of charges included in a racketeering count, among them the 1985 murder of Gambino crime family head Paul Castellano, whom Gotti then succeeded. Key elements in securing the conviction were the incriminating testimony of Gotti's former lieutenant Paul Gravano and a series of tapes of crime family discussions. Gotti's associate, Frank Locascio, was also convicted on several major counts, including murder and racketeering. On June 23, Judge I. Leo Glasser sentenced both men to life imprisonment without parole.

Until his conviction, Gotti had been termed in the media the "Teflon Don," to whom criminal charges would not stick, having survived three earlier attempts to convict him. His lawyers said that they would appeal the verdict, basing that appeal largely on the allegedly prejudicial actions of Judge Glasser, who had disqualified Bruce Cutler, Gotti's lawyer in the three earlier cases, and sequestered the jury from the start, also maintaining their anonymity.

FURTHER READING

"John Gotti and. . . ." PETER MAAS. *Esquire*, June 1992.

"After Gotti. . . ." MICHAEL STONE. *New York*, Feb. 3, 1992.

"The untouchable? . . . ." FREDRIC DANNEN. *Vanity Fair*, Jan. 1992

"Contrasts in hero worship." FRED BRUNING. *Maclean's*, Mar. 5, 1990.

Sleeping the Good Sleep: The Life and Times of John Gotti. DOUGLAS FEIDEN. Random, 1990.

"John Gotti. . . ." SELWYN RAAB. *New York Times Magazine*, Apr. 2, 1989.

"Cold-blooded king. . . ." KEN GROSS. *People*, Mar. 27, 1989.

Mob Star: The Story of John Gotti. GENE MUSTAIN and JERRY CAPECI. Watts, 1989.

Graf, Steffi (Stephanie Maria Graf;

1969–) Steffi Graf was back in 1992. She had lost her number-one world ranking to Monica Seles in early 1991, and did not succeed in her mission of regaining it. She did, however, play a solid year of tennis, with considerable more zest than in recent years. As defending champion, she had a notable win at Wimbledon, defeating Seles to take her fourth Wimbledon crown in five years and her eleventh Grand Slam title overall, and blocking Seles from a clean sweep of the Grand Slam titles for the year. After parting her longtime coach, Pavel Slozil, in late 1991, she began working with a new one, Heinz Gundhardt. A previously distracting lawsuit involving Graf's father was also settled during 1992; a model and her companion were convicted of extorting $484,000 from Peter Graf, to prevent them from publicly alleging that Graf had fathered the woman's baby, though blood tests later showed he had not.

Steffi Graf emerged as a leading under-14 tennis player in the early 1980s, turning professional at age 13. She won the German Open in 1986 and from 1987 was the world's dominant tennis player, with a string of 66 consecutive victories. She took the French Open in 1987, becoming World Champion in 1988, the year she won the U.S., Wimbledon, Australian, and French Opens, along with the Olympic championship. Among her succeeding major victories were the U.S., Wimbledon, and German Opens again in 1989; the Australian Open in 1990; and Wimbledon in 1991. During that period, she held the number one world ranking for a record 186

consecutive weeks, before losing it to Monica Seles in 1991, and regained it only temporarily later that year. Graf was coached from her earliest years by her father, Peter, and from 1987 to 1991 by Pavel Slozil.

FURTHER READING

"Dark star." HARM CLUEVER and PETER RIEBSCHLAEGER. *Tennis*, Nov. 1992.

"The spirit of '88." ANDREA LEAND. *World Tennis*, Feb. 1991.

Steffi Graf. JAMES R. ROTHAUS. Child's World, 1991.

Steffi Graf. Little, Brown, 1990.

"Serving her country." CURRY KIRKPATRICK. *Sports Illustrated*, June 26, 1989.

"Graf, Steffi." *Current Biography*, Feb. 1989.

Steffi Graf. JUDY MONROE. Crestwood House/Macmillan, 1988.

Greenspan, Alan (1926–) On February

27, 1992, the U.S. Senate confirmed another four-year term for Federal Reserve System head Alan Greenspan. As the year began, he was still expressing optimism about the economy and resisting further interest rate cuts as inflationary. On February 5th, he foresaw no need for further interest rate cuts, believing that the 1991 cuts would be enough to restimulate growth. On February 20th, he saw signs of accelerating growth. On April 18, he said that the 2 percent first quarter annualized rate of growth very strongly indicated growth, and that employment would rise as the economy continued its recovery.

None of those things happened; the deep recession worsened, unemployment grew, and by early September the Federal Reserve had lowered its discount rate and federal funds rate to 3 percent—and to little immediate avail, much to the discomfort of President George Bush, who lost the White House in November largely on economic issues. No longer quite as optimistic at year's end, Greenspan did not rule out further interest rate cuts.

Greenspan, a leading free-market economic conservative, was a key economic consultant to presidents Nixon and Ford, and was chairman of the national Council of Economic Advisors (1974–76). He moved into the center of national economic activity when he was appointed head of the Federal Reserve System by President Ronald Reagan. He was reappointed to a second term by President Bush in July 1991. A New Yorker,

Greenspan received his B.S. in 1948, his M.A. in 1950, and his Ph. D in 1977, all from New York University.

FURTHER READING

"The politician-economist. . . ." GLORIA BORGER. *U.S. News & World Report*, July 1, 1991.
"Alan Greenspan's." ROB NORTON. *Fortune*, Apr. 8, 1991.
"Is Alan Greenspan impotent?" ROBIN WRIGHT. *New Republic*, Apr. 9, 1990.
"Greenspan, Alan." *Current Biography*, Jan. 1989.

Griffith, Melanie (1957–) Continuing the long run of major films that started with her 1988 role opposite Harrison Ford in *Working Girl*, Griffith in 1992 starred opposite Michael Douglas in David Seltzer's *Shining Through*, a romance-spy thriller set in Germany during World II; Liam Neeson and Joely Richardson co-starred. Griffith also starred in Sidney Lumet's *A Stranger Among Us*, as case-hardened New York detective Emily Eden, assigned to a murder case in the Hassidic Jewish community; complete with a love affair, her cultural horizons are expanded by the experience. Forthcoming was a starring role opposite John Goodman in a new version of the film classic *Born Yesterday*; Griffith recreates the not-at-all-stupid Billie Dawn role originated by Judy Holliday, with Goodman in the wheeler-dealer role originated by Broderick Crawford

New York City-born Griffith got off to a quick start, playing strong young supporting roles in three 1975 films: *Night Moves*, *The Drowning Pool*, and *Smile*, but then encountered personal and professional problems. She re-emerged as a leading dramatic actress in the mid-1980s, in such films as *Something Wild* (1986), *The Milagro Beanfield War* (1988), and *Stormy Monday* (1988), scored a major hit opposite Harrison Ford in *Working Girl* (1988; she won an Oscar nomination), and followed up with starring roles in *Pacific Heights* (1990), *The Bonfire of the Vanities* (1990), and *Paradise* (1991). She is married to actor Don Johnson; they have one child.

FURTHER READING

"In the bedroom. . . ." MERYL GORDON. *Redbook*, Jan. 1992.
"Melanie Griffith. . . ." LAURIE WERNER. *Woman's Day*, Nov. 26, 1991.
"Melanie Griffith." BILL HIGGINS. *Los Angeles Magazine*, Oct. 1991.
"Griffith, Melanie." *Current Biography*, Oct. 1990.
"Melanie mellows out." BONNIE SIEGLER. *Ladies Home Journal*, Oct. 1990.
The New Breed: Actors Coming of Age. KAREN HARDY and KEVIN J. KOFFLER. Holt, 1988.

Grisham, John (1965–) Best-selling thriller author Grisham began his writing career with the courtroom drama *A Time to Kill* (1989). Published by the small Wynwood Press, it sold 10,000 copies in hardcover, a very modest success. In 1991, after Grisham's huge commercial success with subsequent books, Wynwood republished it as a trade paperback, and sold 200,000 copies. By mid-1992, the mass paperback edition of the book had sold 2.2 million copies, and was still going strong. Grisham by then had become a publishing phenomenon; he had gone on to publish *The Firm* and *The Pelican Brief*, both of them runaway bestsellers, and by the end of 1992 he had more than 10 million books in print.

By October 1992, Grisham was so "bankable" that his agents were able to sell the film rights to his forthcoming novel *The Client* for $2.5 million, long before its scheduled 1993 publication. Forthcoming was Alan Pakula's film version of *The Pelican Brief*, starring Julia Roberts as the law student who figures out who had planned the assassination of two Supreme Court justices. Also forthcoming was Sidney Pollack's film version of *The Firm*, starring Tom Cruise, scheduled for 1993 release.

Grisham's J.D. was from the University of Mississippi. He practiced law in Southaven, Mississippi, and was elected to the Mississippi House of Representatives in 1984, resigning before the conclusion of his second term, when his books began to be lucrative. He is married to Renee Grisham; they have two children.

FURTHER READING

"Tales out of court." KIM HUBBARD. *People*, Mar. 16, 1992.

Grishin, Viktor Vasilevich (1914–92)

Born at Serpukhov, near Moscow, Grishin was a longtime Communist Party official, who joined that organization in 1939, and became a full-time party worker in 1941. He became head of the Serpukhov party organization and then moved to Moscow. There he became a member of the Soviet Communist Party Central Committee in 1952, a nonvoting Politburo member in 1961, head of the Moscow party organization organization in 1967, and a voting and full member of the Politburo in 1971. A powerful old-line conservative bureaucrat, Grishin was also widely believed to be financially and morally corrupt, and a substantial contributor to the decline of the Soviet Union during the final years of the Cold War. In 1982, he was put forward by some conservatives as a possible successor to Leonid Brezhnev, and in 1985 as a possible successor to Constantin Chernenko. But all such moves failed, and one of Mikhail Gorbachev's first acts as Soviet leader was to replace Grishin as Moscow party leader, naming Boris Yeltsin to the post. Grishin lost all remaining positions in 1987, and retired. No information was available as to survivors. (d. Moscow; May 25, 1992)

FURTHER READING

Obituary. *The Times* (of London), May 29, 1992.
Obituary. *New York Times*, May 27, 1992.

Groves, Charles Barnard (1915–92)

London-born Groves, a leading British conductor and an exponent of British and especially new British music, began his career at the age of eight, as a boy chorister at St. Paul's Cathedral. After studying at the Royal College of Music, he was a chorus master with the BBC (1938–44), and then principal conductor of the BBC Northern Orchestra (1944–51). He moved to and helped save the Bournemouth Symphony Orchestra (1951–61), and then became the director of the newly formed Welsh National Opera (1961–63). Later he was music director of the Royal Liverpool Philharmonic (1963–77), also becoming a leading recording artist. He served briefly as head of the English National Opera (1977–78), but resigned to pursue a wide-ranging career as a freelance, much-sought-after conductor, continuing to be active through the 1980s. He was survived by his wife, Hilary, two daughters, and a son. (d. London; June 20, 1992)

FURTHER READING

Obituary. *New York Times*, June 23, 1992.
Obituary. *The Times* (of London), June 22, 1992.
Obituary. *Independent*, June 22, 1992.

Guare, John (1938–) Leading American playwright Guare scored another New York stage success in 1992, with the March opening at Lincoln Center's Vivian Beaumont Theater of his acclaimed new play *Four Baboons Adoring the Sun*, directed by Peter Hall. Stockard Channing starred as Penny McKenzie, opposite James Naughton as Peter McKenzie and Eugene Perry as Eros. The play is set in Sicily, where the McKenzies and their children are involved in an archeological dig; it soon moves into a fantasized mythological-modern mixed experience. The title is the name of an ancient granite sculpture. Guare's work won a Tony nomination for best play, as did Channing for best leading actress.

In July 1992, the London production of *Six Degrees of Separation* (1991) opened, with Channing starring in the role she had created on the New York stage in the 1990–91 season, to rave British reviews for Channing, Guare, and the play. The play began its national tour at the Los Angeles Doolittle Theater in October. Forthcoming was Fred Schepisi's movie version of the work, also starring Channing, to be adapted for film by Guare.

New York City-born Guare wrote the plays *Muzeeka* (1968) and *Cop-out* (1969) before emerging as a major modern playwright with his Tony-winning *House of Blue Leaves* (1971).

His later plays included *Landscape of the Body* (1977), *Bosoms and Neglect* (1979), *Lydie Breeze* (1982), and *Moon Over Miami* (1988). He scored a huge success with the Broadway production of *Six Degrees of Separation* (1990). Guare received an Oscar nomination for his 1981 *Atlantic City* screenplay. His 1961 B.A. was from Georgetown University and his M.A. from Yale. He is married to Adele Chatfield-Taylor.

FURTHER READING

"America's most. . . ." MICHAEL CHURCH. *Observer*, June 7, 1992.
"A dog day afternoon." PAUL TAYLOR. *Independent*, Apr. 25, 1992.
"The Guare facts. " TAD FRIEND. *Vogue*, Mar. 1992.

Gumbel, Bryant Charles (1948–)

After some rocky years following the replacement of long-time "Today" co-anchor Jane Pauley and her ill-fated successor Deborah Norville, Gumbel forged a new and successful on-screen partnership with Katie Couric, the fruits of which were shown in 1992 when NBC's morning show once again reached number one in the ratings. It was a year of celebration, as Gumbel and Couric hosted a primetime 40th-anniversary celebration of the "Today" show, in January, featuring their current colleagues plus previous hosts, including Tom Brokaw, Hugh Downs, Barbara Walters, Jane Pauley, and John Chancellor. Gumbel himself had, by late 1992, been in the anchor's seat for 11 years, the longest of any "Today" host, with two more years to go on his contract.

In August, while Couric was off doing the Olympics, Gumbel took the opportunity to go to sub-Saharan Africa, joined by his 13-year-old son Bradley, filming a series of broadcasts that were aired in November. His only mishap was a broken wrist in pursuit of a hippopotamus in Kenya. As part of "Today's" election coverage in a television-oriented campaign, then-candidates Bill Clinton and Ross Perot appeared for call-in segments, with Gumbel handling follow-up questions for Clinton, and Couric for Perot.

New Orleans-born Gumbel began his career as a writer and then editor (1971–72) of the magazine *Black Sports*. He moved into broadcasting as a California sportscaster (KNBC, Burbank, 1972–81), and was also a widely known NBC network sportscaster (1975–82), receiving 1976 and 1977 Emmy awards. He became a national figure as co-host of the "Today" show (1982–), a trailblazer as the first Black star of a television morning show, and still the leading African-American in network news. His 1973 B.A. was from Bates College. He married June Baranco in 1973; they have two children. Sportscaster Greg Gumbel is his brother.

FURTHER READING

"Questions, no doubt. . . ." JOANNE HARRIS. *American Visions*, Oct.–Nov. 1992.
"It's brother vs. brother. . . ." JANE MARION. *TV Guide*, July 14, 1990.
"The mourning anchor." RICK REILLY. *Sports Illustrated*, Sep. 26, 1988.

Guzmán Reynoso, Abimeal (1935–)

On September 12, 1992, Guzmán, head of the Peruvian Maoist revolutionary army the Shining Path (Sendoro Luminoso), was captured by Peruvian government forces in Lima, along with seven other leaders of his organization. On October 7, he was sentenced by a military court to life imprisonment. Before and after the trial, he was shown to the world media imprisoned in a steel cage and in a prison uniform, in an attempt to demonstrate his powerlessness. Guzmán responded with long speeches, affirming his defiant belief in his variety of Communism. His organization responded to his capture, display, and sentencing by mounting yet another guerrilla offensive against the government.

Born in the southern Peruvian town of Arequipa, Guzmán attended high school and college in Arequipa, and began his career a college teacher of philosophy, teaching and beginning to organize Communist groups at San Cristobal University of Huamango during the 1960s. In 1970, he led a Maoist group in a split-off from the Communist Party of Peru. His Shining Path moved into armed insurgency in 1980, in the next 12 years mounting an increasingly effective guerrilla war against the Peruvian government, taking control of much of the countryside in the southern provinces and growing strong enough in the poor neighborhoods of the cities to conduct bombings and assassinations seemingly at will. Guzmán, afflicted with skin problems of the kinds often found in the high mountains of the southern provinces and later afflicted with a serious kidney ailment, made his headquarters mainly in Lima from 1974. With his capture, the Shining Path had been dealt a serious blow, but its revolution was far from over; nor was it at all a foregone conclusion that he would spend the rest of life in prison, as the massive problems of poverty, disease, and population growth that had provided a fertile ground for revolution were apparently nowhere near solution.

FURTHER READING

"Some say Shining Path's. . . ." LUCIEN CHAUVIN. *National Catholic Reporter*, Oct. 30, 1992.
"Where the Shining Path leads." SIMON STRONG. *New York Times Magazine*, May 24, 1992.
"The war of. . . ." GUSTAVO GORRITI. *New Republic*, June 18, 1990.

H

Haakon, Paul (1914–92) Born in Denmark, Haakon studied ballet at Copenhagen's Royal Danish Ballet School before moving to New York. He made his debut in New York at the age of 13, with Michael Fokine's ballet company in *Harlequinade*. Returning to Europe for further study, he danced in Anna Pavlova's company, and in the United States as a guest in the opening season of George Balanchine's American Ballet Company. He became a well-known concert dance soloist from the mid-1930s, also appearing in Broadway musicals, as in *At Home Abroad* (1935), *The Show Is On* (1936), and *Mexican Hayride* (1944). He was also a star in variety, and later in television, turning largely to choreography from the mid-1940s. In the 1960s, he was ballet master of the José Greco Dance Company. Haakon was survived by his wife, Violet, two daughters, a son, a sister, and a brother. (d. New York City; August 16, 1992)

FURTHER READING

Obituary. *The Times* (of London), Sep. 3, 1992.
Obituary. *New York Times*, Aug. 21, 1992.

Habib, Philip Charles (1920–92) New York-born Habib studied forestry, and wrote his doctoral thesis on lumber industry economics, but instead of going on in that field joined the U.S. foreign service in 1949, and in the following 17 years held a wide range of appointments, becoming a State Department southeast Asia ex-

pert during the Vietnam War. He was chief assistant to U.S. ambassador Henry Cabot Lodge in Saigon in 1966, and a key negotiator at the U.S. Vietnamese peace talks (1968–70). He was ambassador to South Korea (1971–74), then becoming Assistant Secretary of State for Far Eastern Affairs. In 1976, then Undersecretary of State for Political Affairs, he became a key figure in the successful completion of the Camp David Egyptian-Israeli peace talks and treaty. Two heart attacks in two years forced him to retire in 1978, while still pursuing Middle East peace. But in retirement he remained a key American Middle East troubleshooter, most notably in Lebanon (1981–83), although in that instance without success. In 1985 he published *Diplomacy and the Search for Peace in the Middle East*, based on lectures at the Georgetown University School for Foreign Service. Habib was survived by his wife, Marjorie, and two daughters. (d. Puligny-Montrachet, France; May 26, 1992)

FURTHER READING

Obituary. *The Times* (of London), May 27, 1992.
Obituary. *New York Times*, May 27, 1992.

Hackman, Gene (1930–) For film star Gene Hackman, 1992 was a year to get his teeth into a solid stage role, starring in March on Broadway opposite Glenn Close and Richard Dreyfuss in Ariel Dorfman's play *Death and the*

Maiden. The play marked a move away from "good guy" roles as well, for he portrayed Latin American torturer Dr. Miranda, who had raped and tortured Pauline Salas (Close) 15 years earlier, and on whom Salas now takes her revenge. Dreyfuss played Salas's husband; Mike Nichols directed. The play received mixed reviews, but Hackman, Close, and Dreyfuss were all well received, and Close won a Tony in the role.

Hackman in 1992 also played a second villain, this time the brutal sheriff in Clint Eastwood's hard-edged western *Unforgiven*, co-starring Eastwood and Morgan Freeman as former criminal partners turned bounty hunters, and Richard Harris as a gunman. In a modern twist, the bounty was being offered by group of prostitutes for killing two men who had mutilated a prostitute.

California-born Hackman became a star in his Best Actor Oscar-winning role as Popeye Doyle in *The French Connection* (1971), a role he repeated in *The French Connection II* (1975). Among his other films are *The Poseidon Adventure* (1972), *The Conversation* (1974), *Night Moves* (1975), the notable *Mississippi Burning* (1988), *The Package* (1989), *Postcards from the Edge* (1990), *Narrow Margin* (1990), *Loose Cannons* (1990), *Class Action* (1991), and *Company*

Business (1991). He was previously married to Faye Maltese, and has three children.

FURTHER READING

"Hollywood's uncommon man." MICHAEL NORMAN. *New York Times Magazine,* Mar. 19, 1989.
"Fire this time. . . ." ELIZABETH L. BLAND et al. *Time,* Jan. 9, 1989.
"The last honest man. . . ." BEVERLY WALKER. *Film Comment,* Nov.–Dec. 1988.
Gene Hackman. ALLAN HUNTER. St. Martin's, 1988.

Hale, Clara (1905–92) The founder of Harlem's Hale House had retired when she began the main work of her life; she had worked as a cleaner and very successfully as a foster parent before her retirement. In 1969, she began to take into her own home the children of drug addicts, and to help their mothers, as well. Later, she also took in children who had inherited AIDS, and saw them through what for very many were terribly short lives. For decades known as Mother Hale, her work and great prestige grew throughout the rest of her life, and Hale House became a substantial institution, in its later years largely developed by Clara Hale's daughter Lorraine Hale. Her work drew even greater attention when it was lauded by President Ronald Reagan in his 1985 State of the Union Address. Clara Hale was survived by her daughter, two sons, several grandchildren, and all the children of Hale House. (d. New York City; December 18, 1992)

FURTHER READING

Obituary. *New York Times,* Dec. 19, 1992.
"When Mom's. . . ." SUSAN BIDEL. *Woman's Day,* May 22, 1990.
"I dream a world." BRYAN LANKER and MAYA ANGELOU. *National Geographic,* Aug. 1989.
"Clara McBride Hale." *U.S. News & World Report,* Feb. 13, 1989.

Haley, Alex Palmer (1921–92) A career journalist in the U.S. Coast Guard, Haley became a freelance writer on retirement in 1959. He began to find success with a series of interviews for the magazine *Playboy* in 1962, and later wrote for other magazines, as well. He worked with Malcolm X and largely wrote the best-selling *The Autobiography of Malcom X* (1965). Haley is best known by far for his exploration of his own African-American origins, which he developed in the best-selling and Pulitzer Prize-winning *Roots* (1976), the story of his family from Africa through slavery days to freedom after the Civil War. The book was adapted into the enormously popular 1977 12-hour television miniseries, with a huge cast led by Louis Gossett, Jr., LeVar Burton, Ben Vereen, Leslie Uggams, Madge Sinclair, Moses Gunn, and Cicely Tyson. It generated a 14-hour sequel, "Roots: The Next Generaton," with another large cast, led by James Earl Jones as Haley, Marlon Brando, Ruby Dee, Paul Winfield, Ossie Davis, Henry Fonda, and Stan Shaw. Haley was later an active lecturer. He was survived by his third wife, the former Myra Lewis, two daughters, and a son. (d. Seattle, Washington; February 10, 1992)

FURTHER READING

"In memoriam. . . ." MURRAY FISHER. *Playboy*, July 1992.
"Alex Haley's hometown burial." MAUREEN O'BRIEN. *Publishers Weekly*, Mar. 2, 1992.
"Deep roots." MARK GOODMAN. *People*, Feb. 24, 1992.
" 'A turtle atop a fence post.' " *U.S. News & World Report*, Feb. 24, 1992.
" 'Roots' author. . . ." *Jet*, Feb. 24, 1992.
Obituary. *Variety*, Feb. 13, 1992.
Obituary. *The Times* (of London), Feb. 13, 1992.
Obituary. *New York Times*, Feb. 11, 1992.

Hall, Arsenio (1955–)

In 1992's "Late Night Wars," following the retirement of Johnny Carson, Hall and new "Tonight Show" host Jay Leno fought hard for audience, especially younger viewers. The battle extended to guests: Various celebrities complained that after accepting an invitation to appear on "The Arsenio Hall Show," they were dropped from appearing on "The Tonight Show." Among Hall's visitors during 1992 were longtime Carson sidekicks Ed McMahon and Doc Severinsen. But both Hall and Leno were surprised to find themselves beaten at times by Ted Koppel's "Nightline," spurred to the top of the ratings initially during the riveting presidential campaign. By year's end, Hall's ratings were down 20 percent from 1991.

Hall had a notable coup when then-candidate Bill Clinton visited the show, sporting wrap-around shades and playing his saxophone for the late-night audience, a move that seemed to revive Clinton's temporarily flagging campaign by showing the candidate in a new light. Hall also sparked controversy with comments critical of George Bush, and was singled out by Press Secretary Marlin Fitzwater as one place where Bush would not appear, in the television-oriented campaign.

In January, Hall was honored with the NAACP's Key of Life Award for his work for the homeless and needy. In September, he produced the nonprofit AIDS-awareness home video *Time Out: The Truth About HIV, AIDS, and You*, hosted by Earvin "Magic" Johnson, and featuring such stars as Paula Abdul, Neil Patrick Harris, Kirstie Alley, and Bobby Brown. Through his production company, Hall also acted as executive producer of the forthcoming film *Bopha!*, on South Africa's 1976 Soweto uprisings, directed by Morgan Freeman and starring Danny Glover, which started shooting in Zimbabwe in August.

Cleveland-born Hall began his career as a standup comedian in the late 1970s, and moved to Los Angeles in the early 1980s. His first sustained talk show exposure was on the late-night "Thicke of the Night" (1983); he was also host of "Solid Gold," a rock and roll series. He was a guest host on Fox's "The Late Show" in 1987, and appeared in the film *Coming to America*, before breaking through with "The Arsenio Hall Show" in 1989. His B.A. was from Kent State University.

FURTHER READING

Arsenio Hall. NORMAN KING. Morrow, 1993.
"The big dis." ROD LURIE. *Los Angeles*, Nov. 1992.
"Claiming the late-night crown." LYNN NORMENT. *Ebony*, June, 1992.
"Arsenio Hall. . . ." MARK HARRIS. *Entertainment*, Apr. 17, 1992.
"Arsenio Hall dispels. . . ." ALDORE COLLIER. *Jet*, Jan. 27, 1992.
"Arsenio Hall talks. . . ." LAURA B. RANDOLPH. *Ebony*, Dec. 1990.
"The rise and rise. . . ." DIGBY DIEHL. *Cosmopolitan*, Mar. 1990.
" 'Let's get busy!' . . . ." RICHARD ZOGLIN. *Time*, Nov. 13, 1989.
"Alone at the top." PATRICK GOLDSTEIN. *Rolling Stone*, Nov. 2, 1989.
"Late-night cool." MICHAEL NORMAN. *New York Times Magazine*, Oct. 1, 1989.
"Hall, Arsenio." *Current Biography*, Sep. 1989.

Hall, Peter

Hall, Peter (Peter Reginald Frederick Hall, 1930–) It was yet another trans-Atlantic year—and a very busy one—for the celebrated British director and producer Peter Hall. Although the main body of his 1992 work was done on the British stage, his most notable single work was his production of John Guare's new play *Four Baboons Adoring the Sun*, which opened at New York Lincoln Center's Vivian Beaumont Theater in March. Set in a Sicilian archeological dig, the play starred Stockard Channing as Penny McKenzie, opposite James Naughton as Peter McKenzie and Eugene Perry as Eros.

In Britain, Hall's most notable work of 1992 was his production of Peter Shaffer's new play *The Gifts of the Gorgon*, which opened at London's The Pit theater in December. Set on a Greek island, the play stars Michael Pennington as playwright Edward Damson, opposite Judi Dench as his wife. Britain also saw several Hall revivals, including Oscar Wilde's *An Ideal Husband* at London's Globe Theater and his production of Shakespeare's *All's Well That Ends Well* at Stratford. He also made his television directing debut, with the five-part "Camomile Lawn," an adaptation of the Mary Wesley novel. Forthcoming in 1993 were several Peter Hall Company productions, including *Separate Tables*, *Lysistrata*, *She Stoops to Conquer*, and *Piaf*.

Hall has been one of the leading directors of the British theater since the mid-1950s; he directed the very notable first English-language production of Samuel Beckett's *Waiting For Godot* in London in 1955, and went on to direct scores of productions of the traditional classics, and to introduce such other modern classics as *The Homecoming* (1965; and the 1973 film version), *No Man's Land* (1975), and *Amadeus* (1979, and New York, 1980). He won directing Tonys for *The Homecoming* and *Amadeus*. He was managing director of the Royal Shakespeare Company (1960–68) and co-director of the National Theatre with Laurence Olivier (1973–88). He has also directed many operas, most of them at Covent Garden and the Glyndebourne Festival, and also at the Metropolitan Opera and other American houses, and was artistic director of the Glyndebourne Festival Opera (1984–90). He scored two notable trans-Atlantic critical and commercial successes in 1989–90, directing Vanessa Redgrave in Tennessee Williams's *Orpheus Descending* and Dustin Hoffman and Geraldine James in Shakespeare's *The Merchant of Venice*; both also appeared in television adaptations. In 1991, he directed a London revival of *The Homecoming*, and *Twelfth Night* and *The Rose Tattoo*, both also in London. He published *Peter Hall's Diaries* in 1984. Hall attended St. Catherine's College, Cambridge. He has been married three times, and has five children.

FURTHER READING

Peter Hall Directs Anthony and Cleopatra. TIRZAH LOWEN. Limelight, 1991.
"Weldon-Minskoff-Hall heat up. . . ." RICHARD HUMMLER. *Variety*, Oct. 4, 1989.

Hallinan, Vincent

Hallinan, Vincent (1897–1992) San Francisco-born Hallinan was a leading California lawyer for 70 years, from his graduation from Ignatius College in 1921 until shortly before his death. He was a noted criminal lawyer, who defended many accused of major crimes. He was best known by far for his 1950 defense of longshore union leader Harry Bridges, charged with perjury for having allegedly lied about Communist affiliations. Hallinan lost the case, but laid the basis for ultimate Supreme Court reversal of the conviction. Hallinan was sentenced to six months in prison for contempt of court in the aftermath of the case. He was also soon after sentenced to 18 months in prison for tax evasion, in a prosecution widely regarded as a government attempt to punish him for his role in the Bridges and other witch-hunt cases during the McCarthy era. While in prison, he ran as Progressive Party candidate for the Presidency in 1952, winning 140,000 votes. Hallinan was also a leading insurance claims lawyer, who campaigned successfully for reforms in San Francisco's judicial system, which for many years was notorious for its discrimination in favor of insurance companies wrongfully denying claims, through a combination of prejudicially selected juries and corrupt appellate judges. Hallinan was survived by his wife, the former Vivian Moore, and five sons. (d. San Francisco; October 2, 1992)

FURTHER READING

Obituary. *The Times* (of London), Oct. 9, 1992.
Obituary. *New York Times*, Oct. 4, 1992.

Hamburger, Jean (1909–92) Paris-born Hamburger was a major figure in modern medicine, who is often said to have originated the term "nephrology," to describe research into diseases of the kidney. A graduate in medicine from the Sorbonne, Hamburger taught at the University of Paris from 1956, and in 1958 began his great work as founder of the nephrology clinic at Paris's Necker Hospital. His group, working independently, performed the second artificial kidney transplant, and he contributed a large number of articles and several textbooks to the new field. He founded the International Society of Nephrology. He very successfully pursued a second career as a writer in literature and the humanities after his retirement from medicine, writing more than a dozen more works, from 1985 becoming a member of the French Academy, and becoming a Commander of the French Order of Arts and Letters. Hamburger was also a Grand Officer of the Legion of Honor. He was survived by three children. (d. Paris; February 1, 1992)

FURTHER READING

Obituary. *The Times* (of London), Feb. 18, 1992.
Obituary. *New York Times*, Feb. 6, 1992.

Hammer (Stanley Kirk Burrell; M.C. Hammer; 1962–) Now an established worldwide popular and rap music star, Hammer spent much of early 1992 on a *Too Legit to Quit* world tour, following the late-1991 issuance of his album of that name. The album, though popular, was not a smash hit, but several of its singles were, including the title song and "Addams Groove," which had a life of its own after becoming a hit in *The Addams Family*, one of the big Christmas-season films of the year. Hammer's earlier album *Please Hammer Don't Hurt 'Em* continued on its worldwide way, with more than 10 million copies sold, and continuing to be the most popular album of the 1990s so far.

In 1992, Hammer's honors included a Best Solo Rap artist Grammy nomination, a Best Dance Male Artist Billboard Music Video Award nomination for "Addams Groove," and a best video Soul Train award for "Too Legit to Quit" On April 3, he was the subject of the one-hour CBS biographical special *Hammer From the Heart*. He also continued his work with the organization USA Harvest, which provides food for a national network of shelters for the homeless.

Oakland-born Hammer became the Oakland A's batboy in the mid-1970s, and often traveled with the team, after he caught the attention of club owner Charles Finley, who saw him doing dance routines in the stadium parking lot. His start as a recording artist came with his own production of some of his songs, with the help of A's players Mike Davis and Dwayne Murphy (with whom he has since had financial disagreements). His first professional album was *Let's Get It Started*. He scored an enormous hit in 1990, with his second album, *Please Hammer Don't Hurt 'Em*, and had several hit singles, including "U Can't Touch This." *Please Hammer Don't Hurt 'Em—the Movie* won a 1991 Grammy as the best video of 1990. He became the first major rap artist to make a fully successful crossover to popular music. Hammer also runs his own studio and record company, Bust It Productions. He is married, and has one child.

FURTHER READING

"Hammer tells why. . . ." CLARENCE WALDRON. *JET*, May 25, 1992.
" 'Hammer' . . . ." LYNN NORMENT. *Ebony*, Mar. 1992.
Hammer: Two Legit Two Quit. LINDA SAYLOR-MARCHANT. Dillon/Macmillan, 1992.
"Hammer. . . ." BARBARA BAILEY KELLEY. *California*, June 1991.
"Hammer, M.C." *Current Biography*, Apr. 1991.
"What's next for. . . ." *Jet*, Feb. 18, 1991.
M.C. Hammer and Vanilla Ice. NANCY E. KRULIK. Scholastic, 1991.
" 'It's Hammer time!' . . . ." *Ebony*, Dec. 1990.
"M.C. Hammer says. . . ." CLARENCE WALDRON. *Jet*, Sep. 17, 1990.
"Hammer time. . . ." JEFFREY RESSNER. *Rolling Stone*, Sep. 6, 1990.
"M.C. Hammer. . . ." LISA RUSSELL. *People*, Aug. 6, 1990.

Hanks, Tom (1956–) Film star Hanks scored a major hit in 1992, as the crusty, highly individual ex-major league baseball player who becomes coach of an all-woman team in Penny Marshall's *A League of Their Own*. The film, a big-budget summer blockbuster, was a critical and commercial success, and a worldwide hit. It was the story of the first season of the Rockford, Illinois Peaches, a fictional midwestern World

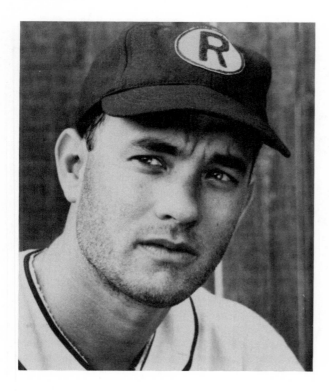

War II-era women's baseball team, in a newly formed women's league. Geena Davis co-starred as the team's catcher and star hitter, Lori Petty as her younger sister and the team's pitcher, and Madonna as the team's lively centerfielder.

Hanks also made his directorial debut in 1992, with the *None but the Lonely Heart* episode of the television series "Tales From the Crypt." Forthcoming were starring roles opposite Denzel Washington and Mary Steenburgen in Jonathan Demme's film *Philadelphia*; and opposite Meg Ryan in Nora Ephron's *Sleepless in Seattle*.

California-born Hanks appeared in the television series "Bosom Buddies" (1980–82), then emerged as a film star in the mid-1980s, with *Splash* (1984), and went on to star in such films as *Bachelor Party* (1984), *Volunteers* (1985), *The Man with One Red Shoe*, (1985), *The Money Pit* (1986), *Every Time We Say Goodbye* (1986), *Big* (1988), *Punchline* (1988), *Turner and Hooch* (1989), *Joe Versus the Volcano* (1990), and *The Bonfire of the Vanities* (1990). He attended California State University at Sacramento. He is married to Rita Wilson; they have two chldren.

FURTHER READING

" 'It's a cool gig' . . . ." CAROL TROY. *American Film*, Apr. 1990.

"Tom Hanks." NANCY ANDERSON. *Good Housekeeping*, May 1989.
"Tom Hanks, seriously." CHRISTOPHER CONNELLY. *Premiere*, Apr. 1989.
"Hanks, Tom." *Current Biography*, Apr. 1989.
"Hanks to you." BEVERLY WALKER. *Film Comment*, Mar.–Apr. 1989.
"Playboy interview. . . ." DAVID SHEFF. *Playboy*, Mar. 1989.
Tom Hanks. TRAKIN. St. Martin's, 1987.

Harkin, Thomas Richard (1939–)

For a little while in late 1991 and early 1992, Iowa Senator Harkin seemed a viable Democratic presidential candidate, campaigning as an old-fashioned New Deal Democrat, stressing his ties with labor and liberal voters, and calling for new public works and social service programs to fight a worsening recession and growing poverty, while attacking George Bush and the Republican Party as protectors of the rich and privileged. He declared his candidacy on September 15, 1991, went into the long series of primary campaigns, and emerged as the victor in the February 10th caucuses in his home state of Iowa. But he ran fourth in the February 18th New Hampshire primary, winning only 10 percent of the Democratic delegates, was still fourth in early March after several more primaries, and continued to decline, ending his campaign on March 9th. He full endorsed Bill Clinton on March 26th, and campaigned for Clinton, while in the Senate maintaining his position as a leading Democratic liberal, in a year of legislative "gridlock." He was not up for election, his term expiring in 1996.

Born in Cumming, Iowa, Harkin earned his 1962 B.S. from Iowa State University and his 1972 J.D. from the Catholic University of America. He was a U.S. Navy jet pilot (1962–67). He was a Congressional aide (1969–70), and a staff assistant to the House Select Committee on American Involvement in Southeast Asia (1970–72), then returning to Iowa as a lawyer with the Des Moines Legal Aid Society. Harkin served in the U.S. House of Representatives (1975–85), was then elected to the Senate, and was in 1991 in his second term. In 1990, with C.E. Thomas, he published *Five Minutes to Midnight: Why the Nuclear Threat Is Growing Faster Than Ever*. Harkin married Ruth Raduenz in 1968; they have a daughter and a son.

FURTHER READING

"Democratic disasters." RICHARD BROOKHISER. *National Review*, Feb. 17, 1992.

"Alone in the cockpit." ELEANOR CLIFT. *Newsweek*, Feb. 17, 1992.

"Tom Harkin's. . . ." JUDITH MILLER. *New York Times Magazine*, Feb. 9, 1992.

"Eight for the prize." STEVEN MANNING. *Scholastic Update*, Feb. 7, 1992.

"Harkin, Tom." *Current Biography*, Jan. 1992.

"Down-home Democrat. . . ." PAUL CLANCY. *National Catholic Reporter*, Sep. 27, 1991.

"The primal scream. . . ." SIDNEY BLUMENTHAL. *New Republic*, Oct. 21, 1991.

"The no bull campaign." HOWARD FINEMAN. *Newsweek*, Oct. 14, 1991.

"Liberal and. . . ." ELEANOR CLIFT and JOHN MCCORMICK. *Newsweek*, Aug. 26, 1991.

"GOP dream. . . ." MARK LAWRENCE RAGAN. *Insight*, July 8, 1991.

Harris, Neil Patrick (1973–)

Harris, 19 years old in 1992, continued to star in the title role of the television series "Doogie Howser, M.D." The show, renewed for a fourth season, continued to be popular, its recent emphasis on frank talk about AIDS, safe sex, and other serious matters still proving appealing to wide audiences. Harris also began a new show, as the voice of Max, a White House mouse, in the animated half-hour children's show "Capitol Critters," which began airing on Saturdays in February. In style and presentation, the show was much like the very successful animated "The Simpsons," although "Capitol Critters" tended to take up a wide range of serious matters, including political chicanery and the arms race.

Since the September 19, 1989 premiere of "Doogie Howser," Harris has starred in the imaginative role of a teenage doctor who graduated from medical school at the age of 14. Harris grew up in the little town of Ruidoso, New Mexico, acted in school productions, and was discovered by playwright Mark Medoff at a summer drama camp, then going into his first film, *Clara's Heart* (1988), and into such telefilms as *Cold Sassy Tree* (1989) and *Leave Her to Heaven* (1989). He has also appeared in guest roles in several television series.

FURTHER READING

"Three hot actors. . . ." KEVIN KOFFLER and CLAIRE CONNORS. *Seventeen*, Jan. 1992.

"Neil Patrick Harris. . . ." JOANNE KAUFMAN. *People*, Mar. 19, 1990.

"New teens on the tube." *Teen*, Jan. 1990.

Harris, Robert Alton (1953–92)

A convicted murderer, Harris was executed at San Quentin prison on the morning of April 21, 1992. He was the first person to be executed in California in 25 years, and his execution came only after 13 years of appeals and a frantic final night that saw four stays of execution by Ninth Circuit Court of Appeals judges reversed by the United States Supreme Court. The execution focused great attention on the sharp and continuing difference over the death penalty that continues to excite U.S. opinion. The case began with Harris's July 1978 murder of two teenage boys in San Diego; he was at the time on parole from a manslaughter conviction. He was convicted of the murders and sentenced to death in 1979, and his conviction was upheld by the California Supreme Court in 1981. Then followed eleven more years of unsuccessful state and federal habeas corpus convictions. In February 1990, a state judge set an execution date, and in March, an appeals judge granted a stay of execution, one of several in what had become a long battle between the two courts on the issue of the death penalty. The final stays of execution involved the claim that the use of cyanide gas in the execution was a form of cruel and unusual punishment.

FURTHER READING

"Entering gas chamber. . . ." KEVIN BAXTER. *National Catholic Reporter*, May 1, 1992.

"I cannot be destroyed." FRANK CLANCY. *California*, Sep. 1989.

Harrison, George (1943–)

Former Beatle George Harrison, an historic figure in world popular music and still a very popular songwriter and performer, won a literally unique award in 1992: he was the first recipient of Billboard's Century Award, for lifetime creative achievement. In October, he joined numerous other celebrities to salute another legend, Bob Dylan, with a special concert at Madison Square Garden.

Harrison also created an historic work in 1992. He toured for the first time since 1974, with Eric Clapton and his band, giving twelve performances in Japan, and in the summer of 1992 issued the two-CD set *George Harrison Live in Japan*, containing 19 songs that were in essence a retrospective drawn from his whole body of work. In an unusual move, Harrison appeared on a British stage in concert for the first time since 1969, in an April Albert Hall benefit for the Natural Law Party, before the general election.

Liverpool-born Harrison joined The Quarrymen as a guitarist in 1958, and in 1960, with Paul McCartney, John Lennon, and Pete Best (replaced by Ringo Starr in 1962) formed the Beatles; Harrison was lead guitarist and sometimes a singer. As a member of the group, he helped trigger a revolution in popular music and in the early 1960s emerged as a worldwide celebrity. He also played a special role, studying with Indian musician Ravi Shankar, learning the sitar and several other Indian instruments, and introducing Indian strains into the work of the Beatles and therefore helping to bring Indian music into the western popular music of his time. Harrison organized the 1971 *Concert for Bangla Desh*, the landmark first rock music international benefit for humanitarian goals.

Harrison's main work as a songwriter developed after the Beatles years. He also formed his own film production and rock management companies. He scored a substantial comeback with

the album *Cloud Nine* (1987), and was prime mover in the organization of The Traveling Wilburys, consisting of Harrison, Bob Dylan, Roy Orbison (until his death), Tom Petty, and Jeff Lynne, all long-time stars; for their first album, *The Traveling Wilburys* (1988), they won a surprising Grammy (1990) as best new group. Harrison has been married twice, and has one child.

FURTHER READING

Dark Horse: The Private Life of George Harrison. GEOFFREY GIULIANO. NAL-Dutton, 1990.
"Harrison, George." *Current Biography*, Jan. 1989.
"The rise of a craftsman." NICHOLAS JENNINGS. *Maclean's*, Oct. 17, 1988.
"Handmade man." ELAINE DUTKA. *Film Comment*, May–June, 1988.
It Was Twenty Years Ago Today. DEREK TAYLOR. Simon & Schuster, 1987.

Havel, Vaclav (1936–) Playwright and President of Czechoslavakia, Vaclav Havel had emerged as a symbol of dissent during the Communist era and of rebirth after the end of the Cold War and the dissolution of the Soviet Union. But the nationalist tide did not stop there; in 1992 it broke Czechoslavakia in two, as well, and brought an early end to Havel's presidency of the Republic. On July 3, 1992, Slovak members of parliament blocked Havel's re-election to the presidency, although he was the only candidate. On July 17th, the Slovak National Council passed a declaration of sovereignty. On that day, Havel resigned his presidency, saying that he could no longer function as President because he opposed the breakup of the country.

Perhaps to the disappointment of some of those in the arts, Havel announced in late November that he would run for the presidency of the new Czech republic, and that he would therefore continue his self-imposed ban on writing new plays. He did, however, publish a volume of essays: *Summer Meditations: On Politics, Morality and Civility In a Time of Transition.*

Havel has been a leading Czech playwright since the early l960s; such plays as *The Garden Party* (1963) and *The Memorandum* (1967) helped bring about the "Prague Spring" of 1968, and were repressed after the Soviet invasion that destroyed the new Czech government. Havel's plays were banned from the Czech stage for two decades, while he continued to be a leading dissenter. He was a leader of the Charter 77 organization in 1977, was under house arrest (1977–79), in prison (1979–1983), and was imprisoned again in early 1989.

On December 29, 1989, he became interim President, the first noncommunist President of his country since 1948. On July 5, 1990 he was re-elected to the presidency, for a full two-year term. In power, he dealt with the aftermath of the Communist decades, and began to move Czechoslavakia into the European and world economies. On June 21, 1991 the last Soviet troops left Czechoslovakia. On June 28, 1991 a Budapest meeting of Eastern European leaders disbanded the multinational Council for Mutual Economic Assistance (Comecon), a Soviet economic control instrument. On July 1, 1991 Havel hosted a Prague meeting of Eastern European leaders, which disbanded the Warsaw Pact, the last remaining instrument of Soviet military control.

In 1964, Havel married Olga Splíchalová, to whom he wrote *Letters to Olga* (1989) from prison. Among his other non-dramatic works were *Vaclav Havel; Or, Living in Truth* (1987) and *Open Letters; Selected Writings 1965–1990* (1990).

FURTHER READING

" 'I cherish a certain hope.' " LANCE MORROW. *Time,* Aug. 3, 1992.

"Crushed velvet." HENRIK BERING-JENSEN. *Insight,* June 1, 1992.

"A conversation with President Havel." ADAM MICHNIK. *World Press Review,* Mar. 1992.

"Scenes from 'Absurdistan.' " ROBERT ELIAS. *Humanist,* Jan.–Feb. 1992.

" 'Uncertain Strength' . . . ." DANA EMINGEROVA et al. *New York Review of Books,* Aug. 15, 1991.

"Havel's choice." STEPHEN SCHIFF. *Vanity Fair.* Aug. 1991.

" 'Parallels with a prison' . . . ." ANDREW NAGORSKI. *Newsweek,* July 22, 1991.

"Vaclav Havel." LINA WERTMULLER et al. *Interview,* May 1991.

Vaclav Havel: The Authorized Biography. EDA KRISEOVA. Atlantic Monthly, 1991.

After the Velvet Revolution: Vaclav Havel and the New Leaders of Czechoslovakia Speak Out. TIM D. WHIPPLE, ed. Freedom House, 1991.

Havers, Roger Michael Oldfield

(1923–92) Child of a family of British lawyers and judges, Havers attended Corpus Christi College, Cambridge, became a member of the bar in 1948, and "took silk"—that is, became a Queen's Counsel—in 1964. He also entered politics, from 1970 to 1987 as a Conservative Member of Parliament. From 1972, he was Solicitor-General in the Conservative government led by Edward Heath. From 1979 to 1987, he was Attorney General in the government of Margaret Thatcher, and was after that briefly Lord Chancellor, until retirement due to ill health. Havers was chief government prosecutor in several very notable modern British cases, including security cases involving alleged Irish Republican Army terrorists; his home was bombed in by the IRA in 1981. Two of those cases were those of the Maguire Seven and the Guildford Four, their convictions later reopened and reversed on appeal, allegedly because of prosecution concealment of evidence. In 1981, he prosecuted the case of 13-times-murderer Peter Sutcliffe, the "Yorkshire Ripper," as well as several highly visible espionage cases. He also prosecuted Peter Wright, author of *Spycatcher,* in an unsuccessful attempt to bar publication of the book abroad. Havers also coauthored several popular books. He was survived by his wife, Carol, and two sons, one of whom is the actor Nigel Havers. (d. London; April 1, 1992)

FURTHER READING

Obituary. *The Times* (of London), Apr. 3, 1992.

Obituary. *New York Times,* Apr. 3, 1992.

Hawking, Stephen William (1942–)

Becoming one of the most extraordinary "stars" in the history of cinema, physicist, mathematician, and author Hawking in 1992 became the real subject of Errol Morris's *A Brief History of Time*, a documentary film adaptation of Hawking's best-selling book of that name. Hawking narrated the main body of the film from his Cambridge office, in his wheelchair and at his computer, on the diverse body of scientific matters covered in his book and on his personal life; all through the film, his personal computer synthesizer was his only way of "speaking." The film premiered at the Sundance Film Festival, winning a best documentary award, and was put into general release in the summer of 1992.

Oxford-born Hawking has made key contributions to modern scientific theory, most notably as to the nature of black holes, gravitational theory, and the "big bang" theory of the origin of the universe. He was educated at University College, Oxford and Trinity Hall, Cambridge, and has been associated with Cambridge in a series of research and teaching positions since 1965. In 1988, he created a surprise best-seller with his *A Brief History of Time: From the Big Bang to Black Holes* (1988), a clearly written work on the nature of reality and the origins of the universe, which has been translated into more than 20 languages. He has also become a worldwide symbol of human ability to triumph over terribly adverse personal problems. He has

been progressively disabled by amytrophic lateral sclerosis (Lou Gehrig's disease) from the age of 20; by the early 1990s, he had left only the use of two fingers, which he used to successfully run a computer and motorized wheelchair, while he continued to teach and write. He has twice been married.

FURTHER READING

"Heart and mind." ARTHUR LUBOW. *Vanity Fair*, June 1992.
Unlocking the Universe: A Biography of Stephen Hawking. SHERIDAN SIMON. Dillon, 1991.
"Stephen Hawking and. . . ." CHET RAYMO. *Commonweal*, Apr. 6, 1990.
"Playboy interview. . . ." MORGAN STRONG. *Playboy*, Apr. 1990.
"Glimpses of God." RIC DOLPHIN. *Maclean's*, Sep. 19, 1988.
"Reading God's mind. . . ." JERRY ADLER. *Newsweek*, June 13, 1988.
"Roaming the cosmos." LEON JAROFF. *Time*, Feb. 8, 1988.

Hawn, Goldie (1945–)

Almost a quarter of a century after "Laugh-In," comedian and dramatic actress Hawn is still going strong. Her lead film in 1992 was Robert Zemeckis's dark comedy *Death Becomes Her*, a biting satire about the lifelong and post-death rivalry of two Hollywood beauties. Hawn played opposite Meryl Streep and Bruce Willis in a triangle story with a twist, as an aging beauty author competing with her husband's former lover for the affections of her surgeon husband.

Hawn also starred as a waitress who turns stripper to support herself and her 12-year-old son, played by Arliss Howard, in Chris Menges's film drama *Criss Cross*, set in 1969 Florida. Keith Carradine co-starred as her ex-husband, a demoralized former Vietnam War pilot. A third starring role was opposite Steve Martin in the Frank Oz comedy *Housesitter*, which was poorly received by the critics.

Hawn began her career as a dancer in the mid-1960s, and became a star comedian in television, in the "dumb blonde" role she created for Rowan and Martin's *Laugh-In* (1968–73). Her film career includes a Best Supporting Actress Oscar in *Cactus Flower* (1969), and starring roles in several popular film comedies, including *There's A Girl in My Soup* (1970), *Butterflies Are Free* (1972), *The Sugarland Express* (1973), *Shampoo* (1975), *The Duchess and the Dirtwater Fox* (1976), *Private Benjamin* (1980), *Best Friends* (1982), *Swing Shift* (1984), *Overboard* (1987), *Last Wish* (1988), *Bird on a Wire*, and *Deceived* (1991). Hawn attended American University. She has been married twice, and has four children.

FURTHER READING

"Hope I die before I get old." Teresa Carpenter. *Premiere*, Sep. 1992.
"Solid Goldie." Lynn Hirschberg. *Vanity Fair*, Mar. 1992.
"Goldie Hawn. . . ." Stephen Farber. *Cosmopolitan*, Aug. 1990.
"Pure Goldie." Kristine McKenna. *Harper's Bazaar*, July 1990.
"24-karat Goldie!" Jim Jerome. *People*, June 11, 1990.
Sweethearts of Sixties TV. Ronald L. Smith. St. Martin's, 1989.

Hayakawa, Samuel Ichiye (1906–92)

Vancouver-born Hayakawa graduated from the University of Manitoba in 1927, and emigrated to the United States in 1929. He received his Ph.D. in English from the University of Wisconsin in 1935, and taught English at several colleges and universities (1936–68), later becoming president of San Francisco State College (1968–73). He was the author or editor of several books and many articles on English usage, most notably *Language in Action* (1941). He became a national conservative spokesperson in 1968, when he led a faculty committee opposing a strike at San Francisco State; as acting president of the college, he banned student demonstrations and speeches, encouraging the mass arrests that followed, which were later overturned as First Amendment violations by the California Supreme Court. Hayakawa served a term as a U.S. Senator from California (1976–82), in that position pursuing the conservative agenda of the time. He was survived by his wife, the former Margedant Peters, a daughter, and two sons. (d. Greenbrae, California; February 17, 1992)

FURTHER READING

Obituary *The Times* (of London), Feb. 29, 1992.
Obituary. *New York Times*, Feb. 28, 1992.
"A conversation with. . . ." Roy F. Fox. *English Journal*, Feb. 1991.

Hayek, Friedrich August von (1899–1992)

Vienna-born Hayek, a leading free market economist and conservative political philosopher, was director of the Austrian Institute for Economic Research (1927–31) and a lecturer in economics at Vienna University (1928–31). Moving to Britain, he taught economics at London University (1931–50), and then taught social and moral science at the University of Chicago (1950–62) and economics at the University of Freiburg (1962–70). He shared the 1970 Nobel Prize for economics with Gunnar Myrdal. Hayek was a prolific writer, whose best known work by far was the book *The Road to Serfdom* (1944), which sharply stated the conservative case against central economic planning. With the advent of the conservative Margaret Thatcher government in Britain, Hayek's views, long out of the mainstream of western economic thinking, enjoyed a revival, as they did in the United States during the Reagan years. He was survived by his second wife, a daughter, and a son. (d. Breisgau, Germany; March 23, 1992)

FURTHER READING

"The road from serfdom." Thomas W. Hazlett. *Reason*, July 1992.
"The father of free markets." Brian Lee Crowley. *Canadian Business*, June 1992.
"The road from serfdom. . . ." John Gray et al. *National Review*, Apr. 27, 1992.

"Catallaxy, complexity and. . . ." LAWRENCE MINARD. *Forbes*, Apr. 13, 1992.

"In praise of Hayek." ECONOMIST, Mar. 28, 1992.

Obituary. *The Times* (of London), Mar. 25, 1992.

Obituary. *New York Times*, Mar. 24, 1992.

Irving Fisher 1867–1947, Arthur Hadley 1856–1930, Ragnar Frisch 1895–1973, Friedrich von Hayek b.1899, Allyn Young 1876–1929, Ugo Mazzola 1863–1899. MARK BLAUG. Ashgate, 1992.

Friedrich A. Hayek: Critical Assessments, in 4 vols. JOHN C. WOOD and RONALD WOODS. Routledge, 1991.

Ordered Liberty and the Constitutional Framework: The Political Thought of Friedrich A. Hayek. BARBARA M. ROWLAND. Greenwood, 1987.

Henreid, Paul (Paul George von Hernreid; 1908–92)

Austrian-born actor and director Henreid was "discovered" in Vienna in 1933 by Otto Preminger, then stage manager for Max Reinhardt's company, and quickly became a star on the Vienna stage. He also made two films in Germany in 1934–35. Strongly anti-Nazi, and listed as an "enemy of the Third Reich," he fled before the coming storm to England in 1935, playing roles as a German in *Goodbye Mr. Chips* (1939), *Madman of Europe* (1940), and *Night Train* (1940), before going on to America. Henreid is best known by far for two roles, as antifascist Victor Laszlo opposite Ingrid Bergman and Humphrey Bogart in the classic *Casablanca* (1942), and as Jerry Durrance opposite Bette Davis in the also-classic *Now, Voyager* (1942). Henreid also starred in several other Hollywood films until he was blacklisted for opposing the House Un-American Activities Committee. In the mid-1950s, however, he developed a second career, as a director and producer in films and television. In 1984, he published *Ladies' Man: The Autobiography of Paul Henreid*, written with Julius Fast. He was survived by his wife, the former Elizabeth Gluck, and two daughters. (Santa Monica, California; March 29, 1992)

FURTHER READING

"Here's looking at you, Paul." *People*, Apr. 20, 1992.

Obituary. *Variety*, Apr. 6, 1992.

Obituary. *The Times* (of London), Apr. 4, 1992.

Obituary. *New York Times*, Apr. 4, 1992.

Hepburn, Katharine (1907–)

Hepburn's autobiography *Me: Stories of My Life* continued to attract great interest during 1992; published in September 1991, it was a main selection of the Book-of-the-Month Club, went right to the top of the best-seller lists, and remained a best-seller in hardcover well into 1992. In the spring of 1992, a paperback edition also became a best-seller. And from late summer well into the fall, the book was also an audio best-seller. Understandably so: Hepburn, one of the greatest film stars of the century, was quite candid about her life, views, motives, screen and stage roles, and—probably what most readers wanted to see—about her now-legendary 27-year-long relationship with Spencer Tracy. Although it ended with his death 25 years ago, in 1967, it remains very much alive to the worldwide audiences who see the still extraordinarily popular Tracy-Hepburn films. In December, Hepburn starred opposite Ryan O'Neal in the CBS television film *The Man Upstairs*, as a smalltown spinster who plays host to an escaped convict on the run.

Hepburn's career spans over six decades; it began on stage, in 1928, but it is her work as a leading film actress that has made her a world figure. She has won four Best Actress Oscars—more than any other performer—and starred opposite Spencer Tracy in nine classic films. Her first film role was a lead opposite John Barrymore in *Bill of Divorcement* (1934). She went on to win Oscars for *Morning Glory* (1936); opposite Tracy in their last film together, *Guess Who's Coming to Dinner* (1967); *The Lion in Winter* (1968); and *On Golden Pond* (1981). Some of her other most notable films were *Little Women* (1933), *Stage Door* (1937), *Holiday* (1938), *The Philadelphia Story* (1940; also the 1939 Broadway play), *Woman of the Year* (1942), *Keeper of the Flame* (1942), *The Sea of Grass* (1947), *State of the Union* (1948), *Adam's Rib* (1949), *The African Queen* (1951), *Pat and Mike* (1952), *Summertime* (1955), *Desk Set* (1957), *Suddenly Last Summer* (1959), *Long Day's Journey Into Night* (1962), *A Delicate Balance* (1973), and *Rooster Cogburn* (1976). On Broadway, she also played the lead in *Coco* (1969). Hepburn attended Bryn Mawr College. She was honored for her lifetime achievement at the Kennedy Center in 1990. A previous book was *The Making of "The African Queen": Or How I Went to Africa with Bogart, Bacall and Huston and Almost Lost My Mind* (1987). She was formerly married, to Ludlow Ogden Smith.

FURTHER READING

"Katharine Hepburn. . . ." CHRISTINE REINHARDT. *McCall's*, Dec. 1992.

" 'My toughest moment.' " GLENN PLASKIN. *Ladies Home Journal*, Nov. 1992.

"A bad case of Hepburn." MARGARET CARLSON. *Time*, June 29, 1992.

"Kate on Kate." JOCELYN MCCLURG. *Saturday Evening Post*, Jan.–Feb. 1992.

Hollywood Royalty: Hepburn, Davis, Stewart and Friends Recall the Screen's Golden Years. GREGORY SPECK. Birch Lane/Carol, 1992.

Katharine Hepburn: Hollywood Legends. Outlet, 1992.

"Kate talks straight." MYRNA BLYTH. *Ladies Home Journal*, Oct. 1991.

"Kate the great." LIZ SMITH. *Vogue*, Sep. 1991.

"Katharine Hepburn." POPE BROCK. *People*, Nov. 5, 1990.

"Katharine Hepburn. . . ." SUSAN WARE. *History Today*, Apr. 1990.

"Katharine Hepburn. . . ." A. SCOTT BERG and JOHN BRYSON. *Architectural Digest*, Apr. 1990.

The Private World of Katharine Hepburn. JOHN BRYSON, PHOTOGRAPHER. Little, Brown, 1990.

The Films of Katharine Hepburn, rev. ed. HOMER DICKENS. Carol, 1990.

"Katharine Hepburn at 80." BARBARA LOVENHEIM. *McCall's*, Nov. 1989.

Katharine Hepburn. CAROLINE LATHAM. Chelsea House, 1989.

Young Kate: The Remarkable Hepburns and the Childhood That Shaped an American Legend. CHRISTOPHER ANDERSEN. Holt, 1988.

Tracy and Hepburn. GARSON KANIN. Fine, 1988.

A Remarkable Woman: A Biography of Katharine Hepburn. ANNE EDWARDS. Morrow, 1985.

Heston, Charlton (Charles Carter; 1923–)

Still literally one of the world's most familiar faces, Heston in 1992 seemed to spend rather less of his time in new stage and screen productions. He did star in a very familiar kind of role as Captain Al Haynes in the ABC television film *Crash Landing: The Rescue of Flight 232*, co-starring Richard Thomas and James Coburn. But as had been so in recent years, Heston emerged far more strongly as a conservative political figure, as in his highly visible television advertisements for the National Rifle Association and William Buckley's *National Review*, and his campaign against Ice-T's "Cop Killer." He was also highly visible as a campaigner in President George Bush's unsuccessful re-election run. Heston also was the narrator of the four-part documentary miniseries "Charlton Heston Presents the Bible," and plays a role in Ken Annakin's forthcoming film *Genghis Khan.*

Illinois-born Heston began his long stage and screen career in the late 1940s. On stage, his work has included three appearances as *Macbeth* (1954, 1959, 1976), and leads in *A Man for All Seasons* (1965 and 1987) and *The Caine Mutiny Court Martial* (1985). On screen, he has been a star since the early 1950s, in such films as *Julius Caesar* (1950 and 1970), *The Greatest Show on Earth* (1952), *The Far Horizons* (1955), *The Wreck of the Mary Deare* (1959), *Ben-Hur* (1959), *El Cid* (1961), *Diamond Head* (1962), *55 Days at Peking* (1962), *The Greatest Story Ever Told* (1965), *Khartoum* (1966), *Planet of the Apes* (1967; and the 1969 sequel), *Soylent Green* (1973), and *Midway* (1975). He has also worked extensively in television, as recently in *Treasure Island* (1990), produced and directed by his son, Fraser Heston, and as Sherlock Holmes in *Crucifer of Blood* (1991). Heston attended Northwestern University. He married Lydia Clark in 1944; the couple have one child, producer-director Fraser Heston.

FURTHER READING

"Charlton Heston." IVOR DAVIS. *Los Angeles Magazine*, Apr. 1988.

Charlton Heston: A Biography. MICHAEL MUNN. St. Martin's, 1986.

Hill, Anita Faye (1956–)

The spirit of Anita Faye Hill presided over the 1992 presidential election. Enraged by her treatment by the all-male Senate Judiciary Committee during the 1991 Clarence Thomas Supreme Court nomination hearings—when Senator Arlen Spector even directly and baselessly accused her of perjury at one point, before a worldwide audience—large numbers of women came forward to run for office, in many instances saying that they would not have run if not for Hill's treatment and her example. New Senators Patty Murray of Washington and Carol Moseley Braun of Illinois said that again and again; new Senators Barbara Boxer and Dianne Feinstein also tapped that wellspring of anger in their winning campaigns. Women candidates were supported by a revitalized women's movement, and by a great many women and men who were part of no movement, in what came to be known as "The Year of the Woman."

Hill herself took no direct part in politics, continuing on as a professor of law at the University of Oklahoma. In one of her rare public appearances, she spoke on April 25th to an audience of 2,100 women at New York's Hunter College. In another, she received an achievement award at an August 9th awards luncheon sponsored by American Bar Association's Commission on Women in the Professions, during the annual meeting of ABA, held in San Francisco; her audience of 1,200 women greeted her with a standing ovation. Hill did not speak on the Hill-Thomas confrontation, but on the role and problems of minority group law professors. Her tribute came in a speech by Hillary Rodham Clinton, who chaired the ABA Commission on Women from 1987 to 1991, and who made what amounted to a keynote speech in "The Year of the Woman." Hill did speak of her experience later in the year, while co-chairing an October 17th Georgetown University Law Center conference on "Race, Gender, and Power in America." Several books and television documentaries appeared on the first anniversary of the Judiciary Committee hearings.

Anita Faye Hill was born in Morris, Oklahoma, the youngest of 13 children. She attended Lone Tree Baptist Church and was valedictorian of her class at Morris High School, having been a straight-A student, secretary of the student council, member of the National Honor Society, and member of the Future Homemakers of America and the Pep Club. She attended Oklahoma State University, and graduated in 1977 with honors. She attended Yale Law School (1977–80), interned at the Washington, D.C. law firm of Ward, Harkrader, and Ross while in law school, and joined the firm after graduation. She became personal assistant to Clarence Thomas at the Office of Civil Rights of the U.S. Education Department in 1981, and moved with him to the U.S. Equal Employment Opportunity Commission. She left Washington to teach law at Oral Roberts University in 1983. Hill became a worldwide figure in the struggle for women's rights in 1991, when she charged then-Supreme Court nominee Clarence Thomas with sexual harassment during the years she worked for him; her confrontation with Thomas and the Senate Judiciary Committee came before a worldwide television audience. She has taught law at the University of Oklahoma since 1986, and became a tenured full professor in 1990.

FURTHER READING

"One year later. . . ." RONALD M. DWORKIN. *New York Times Book Review*, Oct. 25, 1992.

"The untold story." GLORIA BORGER and TED GEST. *U.S. News & World Report*, Oct. 12, 1992.

"The real Anita Hill." DAVID BROCK. *American Spectator*, Mar. 1992.

"Anita Hill: no regrets." JILL NELSON. *Essence*, Mar. 1992.

"Why Anita Hill lost." SUZANNE GARMENT. *Commentary*, Jan. 1992.

"Anita Hill: law professor." LAUREN HUTTON. *Interview*, Jan. 1992.

Capitol Games: Clarence Thomas, Anita Hill, and the Behind-the-Scenes Story of a Supreme Court Nomination. TIMOTHY M. PHELPS and HELEN WINTERNITZ. Disney, 1992.

"She could not keep silent." BILL HEWITT and BETH AUSTIN. *People*, Oct. 28, 1991.

"A question of character." RICHARD LACAYO. "An ugly circus." NANCY GIBBS. *Time*, Oct. 21, 1991.

"Thomas and Hill. . . ." ELOISE SALHOLZ. "Anatomy of a debacle." DAVID A. KAPLAN. "A moment of truth." *Newsweek*, Oct. 21, 1991.

"Judging Thomas." GLORIA BORGER. *U.S. News & World Report*, Oct. 21, 1991.

Hill, Benny (Alfred Hawthorn Hill; 1925–92)

Southampton-born Hill, child of a circus performer, began his career as a comic while in the British army during World War II, continuing on in variety and radio after the war. In the early 1950s, he became a star in British television, and had his own show from 1955, appealing to a public that liked his kind of sex jokes, pratfalls, and comedy bits featuring near-naked young women, in one kind of British music hall or American burlesque style. He called the women being displayed "Hill's Angels." He also appeared in several films, without great success. He was a star in British and American television into the 1980s, but changes in preferred styles and charges of sexism turned away much of his British audience, and his show was dropped in the mid-1980s. He remained popular in United States independent station and cable reruns on through the early 1990s. There were no survivors. (d. London; April 20, 1992)

FURTHER READING

Obituary. *Variety*, Apr. 27, 1992.

"Hill-arious. . . ." JAMES DALRYMPLE. *Sunday Times*, Apr. 26, 1992.

Obituary. *The Times* (of London), Apr. 22, 1992.
Obituary. *Independent*, Apr. 22, 1992.
Obituary. *New York Times*, Apr. 21, 1992.
Saucy Boy: The Life Story of Benny Hill. LEONARD HILL. Charnwood/ Ulverscroft, 1992.
The Benny Hill Story. JOHN SMITH. St. Martin's, 1989.

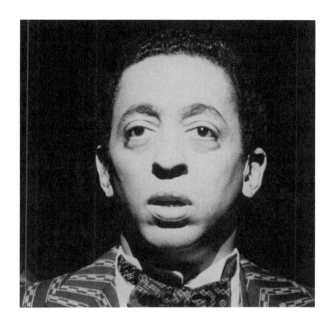

Hines, Gregory Oliver (1946–) As legendary jazz great Jelly Roll Morton, Hines had a tremendous success in 1992, as the star of *Jelly's Last Jam*, which opened at Broadway's Virginia Theater in late April. The musical was written and directed by George C. Wolfe, and co-starred Savion Glover as Young Jelly, Keith David, Ann Duquesnay, Staley Wayne Mathis, and Tonya Pinkins, with Morton's music adapted by Luther Henderson and lyrics by Susan Birkenhead. Hines won a Tony as leading actor in a musical in the role, and Pinkins a Tony as leading featured actress in a musical. In November, PBS presented a "Great Performances" segment on the making of the show: *Jammin': Jelly Roll Morton on Broadway*. Hines also starred in the television film *T Bone 'N Weasel*, co-starring Christopher Lloyd, Rip Torn, and Ned Beatty.

A leader of the tap revival of the 1980s, Hines is a multitalented tap dancer, actor, and variety entertainer. Born in New York City, he was on stage professionally at the age of five, with his brother Maurice touring as the Hines Kids (1949–55), the Hines Brothers (1955–63), and then with their father Maurice as Hines, Hines, and Dad (1963–73). On stage, he won Tony nominations in *Eubie* (1978), *Comin' Uptown* (1980), and *Sophisticated Ladies* (1981), and emerged as a film star in the 1980s, in such movies as *Wolfen* (1981), *The Cotton Club* (1984), *White Nights* (1985), *Running Scared* (1986), *Off Limits* (1988), *Eve of Destruction* (1990), and *A Rage in Harlem* (1991). He made his directorial debut in 1990, with the independently produced film *Gotta Dance*. He has been married twice, last to Pamela Koslow in 1981, and has three children.

FURTHER READING

" 'Jelly's Last Jam' . . . ." LAURA B. RANDOLPH. *Ebony*, Sep. 1992.
"Jelly on a roll." DINITIA SMITH. *New York*, June 8, 1992.
"The day I turned my life around." WALLACE TERRY. *Parade*, May 31, 1992.
"Former child stars. . . ." MICHELLE MCCALOPE. *Jet*, Apr. 15, 1991.
"Gregory Hines on. . . ." LAURA B. RANDOLPH. *Ebony*, Jan. 1991.
Black Dance in America: A History Through Its People. JAMES HASKINS. Harper, 1990.
"Hines on tap." SALLY SOMMER. *Dance Magazine*, Dec. 1988.

Hirsch, Judd (1935–) One of the leading actors of the American theater, Hirsch devoted 1992 to his long, extraordinarily successful run in *Conversations With My Father*, which opened at Broadway's Royale Theater in March. Written by Herb Gardner, the play is about cantankerous, bitter Eddie Ross, a New York Jewish immigrant, played by Hirsch, and his sons and acquaintances, as they move through the now-familiar phases of assimilation and rediscovery of their cultural heritage, and about what Gardner perceives as the inevitable war between the generations. Daniel Sullivan directed; co-starring were Tony Shalhoub, Gorda Rashovich, and David Margulies. Hirsch won a Tony as leading actor in a drama in the role, and an Outer Critics Circle award as best actor in a play, as well. On the personal side, Hirsch and Bonnie Chalkin married in New York City on December 24, 1992.

New York City-born Hirsch has had a long, varied, and very busy career on stage and screen. Much of his major work has been on stage, in such plays as *Barefoot in the Park* (1966), *Scuba Duba* (1967–69), *King of the United States* (1972), *Hot L Baltimore* (1972–73), *Knock Knock* (1975; he won a Drama Desk award), *Chapter Two* (1977–78), *Talley's Folly* (1979; he won an Obie award), and *I'm Not Rappaport* (1986; he won a Best Actor Tony award). To wider audiences, he is best known for his work in television, which includes his five-year run in "Taxi," for which he won two Best Actor Emmys (1981, 1983). He has also appeared in the "Delvecchio" series (1976–77), the "Dear John" series (1988), and in many television films. His films include *King of the Gypsies* (1978), *Ordinary People* (1980; he won an Oscar nomination), *The Goodbye People* (1984), and *Running on Empty* (1988). His 1960 B.S. was from New York's City College. He has one child.

FURTHER READING

"Dr. Jekyll or Mr. Hirsch?" ROY SEKOFF. *Redbook*, July 1991.
"Judd Hirsch. . . ." CAROL A. CROTTA. *TV Guide*, June 3, 1989.

Hobson, Harold (1904–92) Yorkshire-born Harold Hobson was the leading London theater critic of his day. A Christian Scientist, he began his long career in 1931, with reviews written for the American *Christian Science Monitor*, and became the *Monitor*'s London literary editor in 1946. He was also a television critic for *The Listener* (1947–51). Hobson was appointed assistant literary editor of the *Sunday Times* of London in 1944, in 1945 also becoming a theater reviewer for the newspaper, and in 1947 succeeded James Agate as theater critic, holding that post until 1976. In that period, he strongly supported new trends in the English-speaking theater, as in the work of Samuel Beckett, Harold Pinter, and the "angry young men" led by John Osborne. He also very strongly supported the modern French theater. Hobson's work included several books, most notably the anthology *Verdict at Midnight* (1952) and *The French Theatre of Today* (1953). There were no survivors. (d. Chichester, England; March 12, 1992)

FURTHER READING

Obituary. *Variety*, Mar. 30, 1992
Obituary. *The Times* (of London), Mar. 14, 1992.

Hoffman, Dustin Lee (1937–) During the early months of 1992, a Hoffman portrayal once again percolated out around the world; this time, it was as Captain Hook opposite Robin Williams as Peter Pan in Steven Spielberg's *Hook*, which became a worldwide hit. Much less of a hit was his 1991 big budget *Billy Bathgate*, a critical and box-office failure, which in video rental had not much more success than it had had in theatrical release.

During 1992, Hoffman also starred as small-time conman Bernie Laplante, opposite Geena Davis and Andy Garcia in Stephen Frears's film comedy *Hero*. In the film, Hoffman happens upon a just-occurred plane crash site, uncharacteristically and very bravely pulls some of the survivors out of the wreckage, including television interviewer Davis, and disappears. Garcia is the ex-Vietnam War soldier who takes credit for the act and collects the million-dollar reward and the love of Davis. The story line develops from there. The film was lukewarmly received, by the critics and at the box office.

Los Angeles-born Hoffman has been a major film star since his breakthrough role as *The Graduate* (1967), which he followed with such films as *Midnight Cowboy* (1969), *Little Big Man* (1971), *Lenny* (1974), *All the President's Men* (1976), *Marathon Man* (1976), *Kramer vs. Kramer* (1979; he won a Best Actor Oscar), *Tootsie* (1982), *Rain Man* (1988; and a second Best Actor Oscar), *Family Business* (1989), and *Dick Tracy* (1990). On stage, he was a notable Willy Loman in the 1984 revival of *Death of a Salesman* (televised in 1985), and in 1990 brought his Shylock from London to Broadway in Peter Hall's production of *The Merchant of Venice*. Hoffman attended Santa Monica City College. He was formerly married to Anne Byrne, married Lisa Gottsegen in 1980, and has five children.

FURTHER READING

"Acting his age. . . ." MARK ROWLAND. *American Film*, Dec. 1988.

Holm, Hanya (Johanna Eckert, 1893–1992) German-American dancer, choreographer, and teacher Hanya Holm began her very long career as a student of Mary Wigman, the leading modern dance teacher of Germany's Weimar Republic period, going on to tour and choreograph with Wigman throughout the 1920s. She toured the United States with Wigman (1930–31), and stayed on to found New York's Mary Wigman School, making it her own Hanya Holm Studio (1936–67), in those three decades becoming one of the central figures in modern dance. Two of her best known works are *Trend* (1937) and *Metropolitan Daily* (1939). She was best known to wide audiences for her later work in Broad-

way musicals, choreographing such works as *Kiss Me, Kate* (1948), *My Fair Lady* (1956), and *Camelot* (1960). Holm attended the Dalcroze Institute of Applied Rhythm and Mary Wigman's Dresden School. She was survived by a son. (d. New York City; November 3, 1992)

FURTHER READING

Obituary. *The Times* (of London), Nov. 10, 1992.
Obituary. *Variety*, Nov. 9, 1992.
Obituary. *The New York Times*, Nov. 4, 1992.
"Dance Magazine announces. . . ." ROBERT JOHNSON. *Dance*, Apr. 1990.

Holyfield, Evander (1962–) "Evander has the heart of a lion" was the new champion's tribute to the man he defeated. The championship bout took place on November 12, 1992, at the Thomas & Mack Center in Las Vegas, Nevada. Thirty pounds lighter and five years older, Holyfield was outclassed by the powerful, well-trained Riddick Bowe, but though he was knocked down once in the 11th round, he put forth a valiant effort for 12 rounds in the face of a relentless assault, battling back time and again with a courage that even had some of his team members in tears. Old fight hands said they had not seen a fight of this calibre since the first bout between Muhammad Ali and Joe Frazier 21 years before. Ironically, in what many people termed the magnificence of his defeat, Holyfield won the respect that had eluded him for the 25 months that he was undisputed heavyweight champion of the world. Earlier in the year, also in Las Vegas, Holyfield had made his third undistinguished, though successful defense of his title against Larry Holmes, a former champion (1978–85) but 13 years older than Holyfield. Even before the Bowe bout, Holyfield had talked of retiring, and immediately after the defeat said, "I think I'm finished. I don't want a rematch," though he later said he was reconsidering that decision.

Alabama-born Holyfield won a bronze medal in the 1984 Olympics and turned professional in 1986. For most of his career, he has been a light-heavyweight, rather than a heavyweight, and became World Boxing Association light-heavyweight world champion in 1986. He took the heavyweight championship from James "Buster" Douglas in October 1990, and defended it successfully three times, being undefeated until the loss to Bowe, with a record of 28–0, with 22 knockouts and estimated career earnings of $80 million. Holyfield was divorced in 1991, and has four children.

FURTHER READING

"The real deal. . . ." GARY CARTWRIGHT. *Texas*, June 1991.
"No joke: . . . ." PAT PUTNAM. *Sports Illustrated*, Apr. 29, 1991.
"Evander Holyfield. . . ." DOUGLAS C. LYONS. *Ebony*, Jan. 1991.
"Evander Holyfield. . . ." *Jet*, Nov. 19, 1990.
"At last!" David Miller. *Sport*, Nov. 1990.

Hooker, John Lee (1917–) At 75, now-legendary blues musician John Lee Hooker was honored by his peers in 1992 with a traditional blues Grammy nomination for last year's album *Mr. Lucky*. Still going strong, he toured in concert, taping a January concert with Bonnie Raitt, Ry Cooder, Albert Collins and Charlie Musselwhite for the BBC. The year also saw release of a two-volume compilation of his recordings, from his 1948 first hit "Boogie Chillen' " through 1990. Still forthcoming was the new Dennis Hopper movie *The Hot Spot*, starring

Don Johnson and Virginia Madsen with a soundtrack that features Hooker and jazz great Miles Davis.

Mississippi-born Hooker became a leading blues musician in the late 1940s, with such songs as "Boogie Chillen' " (1948) and "I'm in the Mood" (1951), and became a popular figure during the folk and blues revival of the 1960s, appearing often at the Newport and other jazz festivals, and recording scores of albums, such as *The Folklore of John Lee Hooker* (1962) and *The Big Soul of John Lee Hooker* (1964). He enjoyed yet another revival in the late 1980s, on tour again and with such albums as *Jealous* (1986). His album *The Healer* (1989) included a cut with Bonnie Raitt, "I'm in the Mood," which won the 1990 Grammy for best traditional blues recording.

FURTHER READING

John Lee Hooker: The Healer. H. Leonard, 1991.
"John Lee Hooker. . . ." STEVE DOUGHERTY. *People*, Oct. 29, 1990.
"John Lee Hooker. . . ." JOSEF WOODARD. *Down Beat*, Feb. 1990.
"John Lee Hooker. . . ." JAS OBRECHT. *Guitar Player*, Nov. 1989.

Hopkins, Anthony (1937–) Welsh stage and screen star Hopkins scored an extraordinary success as cannibal psychiatrist Hannibal Lecter in Jonathan Demme's 1991 *The Silence of the Lambs*. In 1992, Hopkins won a Best Actor Oscar for the role; Oscars were also won by the film, Demme, Jodie Foster, and Ted Tally. Hopkins also won a British Academy of Film and Television Arts Best Actor Award for the role. A sequel is planned.

During 1992, Hopkins continued to appear in a long and varied succession of films, among them some of the leading art films of the year. One such was James Ivory's film version of *Howard's End*, based on the 1910 E.M. Forster novel; co-starring were Vanessa Redgrave, Helena Bonham Carter, Emma Thompson, Prunella Scales, and Sam West; the screenplay was by Ruth Prawer Jhabvala. Another was Francis Ford Coppola's *Bram Stoker's Dracula*, co-starring Gary Oldham as Dracula, Winona Ryder, and Keanu Reeves. Working a great deal, Hopkins also starred in Geoff Murphy's futuristic sci-tech thriller *Freejack*; in the title role in Mark Joffe's Australian film comedy *The Efficiency Expert*; in a key role in Richard Attenborough's *Chaplin*; and in the television miniseries "To Be the Best," based on the Barbara Taylor Bradford novel, about a department store dynasty.

Forthcoming were several equally notable films, including John Schlesinger's *The Innocent*, co-starring Isabella Rossellini and Campbell Scott; David Jones's film *The Trial*, based on the Franz Kafka novel, screenplay by Harold Pinter, and co-starring Kyle MacLachlan, Jean Stapleton, and Juliet Stevenson; and James Ivory's film *Remains of the Day*, with another Pinter screenplay.

Wales-born Hopkins played in repertory during the early 1960s; he joined the National Theatre in 1967, the same year that he made his film debut in *The Lion in Winter*. A few of his most notable theater roles were in the title role of *Macbeth* (1972; National Theatre), *Equus* (1974–75; on Broadway); *Pravda* (1985; National Theatre), *King Lear* (1986; National Theatre), and *Anthony and Cleopatra* (1987; title role, at National Theatre). He has appeared in such films as *The Looking Glass War* (1967), *A Bridge Too Far* (1976), *Magic* (1978), *The Elephant Man* (1978), *The Bounty* (1984; as Captain Bligh), *84 Charing Cross Road* (1987), *Desperate Hours* (1989), and *Spotswood* (1991), and in a wide range of television roles, winning Emmys in *The Lindbergh Kidnapping Case* (1975) and *The Bunker* (1980), and playing such title roles as *Kean* (1980) and *Othello* (1981). Hopkins attended the Welsh College of Music and Drama and the Royal Academy of Dramatic Art. His second wife is the former Jennifer Lynton; he has one daughter.

FURTHER READING

" 'Call me Tony.' " Rita Gam. *World Monitor*. Apr. 1992.
"In step with. . . ." James Brady. *Parade*, Apr. 26, 1992.
" 'Anthony Hopkins'. . . ." Martha Frankel. *Movies USA*, Mar.–Apr. 1992.
"Anthony Hopkins." David Gritten. *M Inc.*, Aug. 1991.
"Anthony Hopkins. . . ." Jim Jerome. *People*, Mar. 4, 1991.
Anthony Hopkins: Too Good to Waste. Quentin Fack. Isis (NY), 1990.

Hopper, Grace Brewster Murray

(1906–92) A leading mathematician and pioneer computer scientist, Admiral Hopper began her long career after receiving her Ph.D. from Yale University in 1934. She taught mathematics at Vassar College (1931–43), and then joined the U.S. Navy, serving as a commander in the WAVES (1944–46), and from then until her retirement in 1986 was on active duty or active reserve, her appointment as a Rear Admiral coming in 1983. On her retirement, she was the oldest living officer in the U.S. armed forces. Hopper made several major contributions to computer science, working on the early ENIAC and UNIVAC computers, and developing the first compiler language. She was a co-inventor of the widely used COBOL programming language. While active in the Naval Reserve, she taught and participated in research at Harvard University and with several major computer development companies, and (with others) wrote a standard text *Understanding Computers*. She was survived by a sister and a brother. (d. Arlington, Virginia; January 1, 1992)

FURTHER READING

Obituary. *The Times* (of London), Jan. 4, 1992.
Obituary. *New York Times*, Jan. 3, 1992.
Grace Hopper: Navy Admiral and Computer Pioneer. Charlene W. Billings. Enslow, 1989.

Hoskins, Bob

(Robert William Hoskins; 1942–) British film star Bob Hoskins starred in 1992 in the central role of Johnny Scanlon in *Passed Away*, written and directed by Charlie Peters, and co-starring Jack Warden, Pamela Reed, William Petersen, Frances McDormand, Blair Brown, Maureen Stapleton, and Peter Riegert. Centered around a funeral, the work is a comedy-drama about a large Irish-American family. Hoskins also starred opposite Jeff Goldblum and Natasha Richardson in Ben Lewin's irreverent film comedy *The Favor, the Watch and the Very Big Fish*, set in Paris with an international cast, though all the characters in the film are French. He was also highly visible in his role as Smee in Steven Spielberg's 1991 *Hook*, which opened during the 1991 Christmas season and became a worldwide hit in 1992.

Forthcoming was a starring role in the new

Disney film *Super Mario Bros.* which filmed in the late summer of 1992. The film, directed by Rocky Morton and Annabel Jankel, co-stars John Leguizama and is scheduled for 1993 distribution. Still forthcoming was Andrei Konchalovsky's *The Inner Circle*, about Stalin's world as seen through the eyes of his film projectionist, with Tom Hulce, Lolita Davidovich, and Bess Meyer; and Lindsay Anderson's film version of Anton Chekhov's *The Cherry Orchard*, with Maggie Smith and Alan Bates.

From the mid-1980s, Hoskins emerged as a leading British film actor, making his debut in *National Health* (1974) and going on to such movies as *Royal Flash* (1975), *Zulu Dawn* (1980), *The Long Good Friday* (1980), *The Honorary Consul* (1984), *Lassiter* (1984), *The Cotton Club* (1985), *Sweet Liberty* (1986), *Mona Lisa* (1986), *A Prayer for the Dying* (1987), *The Lonely Passion of Judith Hearne* (1988), *Who Framed Roger Rabbit?* (1988), *Heart Condition* (1990), *Mermaids* (1990), *Shattered* (1991), and *Hook* (1991). He wrote, directed, and appeared in *The Raggedy Rawney* (1988). Hoskins has also appeared often on television, most notably in his powerful lead in the miniseries *Pennies from Heaven* (1979). His second wife is the former Linda Banwell; he has two daughters and two sons.

FURTHER READING

"Hoskins, Bob." *Current Biography*, Sep. 1990.

Houston, Whitney (1963–) Celebrity

singer Houston was honored by her peers again in 1992, most notably with a Grammy nomination for best female pop vocal; she was also nominated for best rhythm and blues female soul album for *I'm Your Baby Tonight*, and best female soul single for "Feels Like Another One," at the Soul Train Awards.

In her first leading film role, Houston starred opposite Kevin Costner in Mick Jackson's *The Bodyguard*, as popular singer Rachel Marron, who hires ex-Secret Service agent Frank Farmer, played by Costner, to protect her from a threatening insane fan; the situation generates a love affair between the stars. Notably, the interracial aspect of the relationship excited virtually no comment. The film received mixed reviews, but did very well at the box office. Its soundtrack generated several hit singles for Houston, most notably her rendition of the Dolly

Parton song "I Will Always Love You," which immediately climbed to the top of the pop singles chart, ultimately staying at number one a record-breaking 14 weeks.

On the personal side, Houston and singer Bobby Brown married in July and in the autumn announced that she was pregnant.

New Jersey-born Houston suddenly emerged as a leading popular singer in the mid-1980s, with her first album, the Grammy-winning *Whitney Houston* (1985), followed by *Whitney* (1986), and with such songs as "Didn't We Almost Have it All," "The Greatest Love of All," and "How Will I Know." In 1990, her single "I'm Your Baby Tonight," from the album of the same name, also hit number one, as did her 1991 "All the Man That I Need." Houston is the daughter of singer Cissy Houston, and the cousin of singer Dionne Warwick.

FURTHER READING

"Whitney Houston and. . . ." *Jet*, Dec. 14, 1992.
"Thoroughly modern Whitney." LYNN HIRSCHBERG. *Vanity Fair*, Nov. 1992.
"Whitney Houston and. . . ." *Jet*, Aug. 17, 1992.
"Whitney Houston talks. . . ." LYNN NORMENT. *Ebony*, May 1991.
"20 questions. . . ." *Playboy*, May 1991.
"Singer Whitney Houston. . . ." *Jet*, July 16, 1990.
"Whitney Houston." DAVID VAN BIEMA. *Life*, Oct. 1990.
"Whitney Houston." *Harper's Bazaar*, Sep. 1989.
The Picture Life of Whitney Houston. GENE BUSNAR. Watts, 1988.
Whitney Houston. KEITH E. GREENBERG. Lerner, 1988.

Howard, Ron (1954–) Film director Howard's major movie of 1992 was *Far and Away*, a highly textured epic of late-19th century emigrants from Ireland to the United States. Tom Cruise starred as young Irish tenant farmer Joseph Donnelly, who after various troubles in Ireland emigrates to America with his landlord's daughter, Shannon Christie, played by Cruise's real-life wife, Australian actress Nicole Kidman. Co-stars include Robert Prosky and Barbara Babcock, as Kidman's father and mother, who themselves ultimately emigrate to America and—with Cruise and Kidman—find themselves engaged in the Oklahoma land rush. Although box office and home video receipts were buoyed up by Cruise's box office appeal, critical response was mixed, for the film was essentially a very familiar kind of immigration epic. With Bob Dolman, Howard published *Far and Away: The Illustrated Story of a Journey from Ireland to America in the 1890s*. On the business side, Howard and his long-time associate Brian Glazer announced an 18-film, 6-year agreement with Universal Pictures.

Oklahoma-born Howard was a child star in television, as Opie in "The Andy Griffith Show" (1960–68), and later in "The Smith Family" (1971–72) and "Happy Days" (1974–80). He also appeared in such films as *The Music Man* (1962), *American Graffiti* (1973), and *The Shootist* (1976). As an adult, he directed, and in several instances cowrote and coproduced such films as *Splash* (1984), *Cocoon* (1985), *No Man's Land* (1987), *Clean and Sober* (1988), *Willow* (1988), *Parenthood* (1989), and *Backdraft* (1991). Howard was also (with Glazer) executive producer and writer of the television series spun off from *Parenthood*. He attended the University of Southern California. He married Cheryl Alley in 1975; they have five children.

FURTHER READING

"Ron Howard." JOHN CLARK. *Premiere*, Apr. 1991.

Howerd, Frankie (Francis Alick Howard; 1921–1992) British comic Howerd began his long stage, screen, and broadcasting career in 1946, after service in World War II. He became a celebrity in the late 1940s, in radio's *Variety Bandbox* and in variety, in the early 1950s entertaining troops during the Korean War. On stage, he scored hits in the revue *Pardon My French* (1953), and in Shakespeare as Bottom in *A Midsummer Night's Dream* at the Old Vic. His career sagged in the late 1950s, but he made a comeback in 1963, in television's "That Was the Week That Was," and on stage as Pseudolus in the London run of *A Funny Thing Happened on the Way to the Forum*. He also starred on Broadway in *Rockefeller and the Red Indians* (1968). He played in several films, as well, including *The Ladykillers* (1955), *The Great St. Trinian's Train Robbery* (1966), *Up Pompeii* (1970; derived from his television series), and *Sergeant Pepper's Lonely Hearts Club Band* (1978). There were no survivors. (d. London; Apr. 19, 1992)

FURTHER READING

Obituary. *Variety*, Apr. 27, 1992
Obituary. *The Times* (of London), Apr. 20, 1992.
Obituary. *Independent*, Apr. 20, 1992.

Hussein I (Hussein ibn Talal; 1935–) Jordan's King Hussein emerged from his support of Saddam Hussein during the Persian Gulf War greatly popular at home and greatly damaged abroad, with subsidies withdrawn by the rich Arab nations, led by Saudi Arabia; the United States relationship all but severed; and hundreds of thousands of Iraqi refugees and returning Jordanians to handle. Hussein began to regain some international recognition with his support of and participation in the mid-1991 Middle East peace talks, which continued through 1992. But the Arab nations kept their distance; when Hussein in early May 1992 offered $8.5 millon of his own money to pay the cost of restoring Muslim holy sites in Jerusalem, Saudi Arabian king Fahd immediately offered to pay an estimated $70 million, including repair work on Dome of the Rock, in a move taken as an attempt to claim custody of the shrines from Hussein. In spite of his support of the popular Palestinian and Iraqi causes, Hussein continued to face growing fundamentalist opposition at home, fanned by the ruin of Jordan's economy and soaring unemployment.

On the personal side, he was operated on for cancer at the Mayo Clinic in August, and in November announced that he would need further visits to the United States for treatment.

Hussein became the King of Jordan in 1953,

succeeding his father, Abdullah Ibn Hussein, himself the son of Hussein Ibn Ali, head of the 1916 Arab revolt against the Turks during World War I, the revolt assisted by British officer T. E. Lawrence ("Lawrence of Arabia"). For almost four decades, Hussein survived as a moderate in the turbulent politics of the Middle East, although he was drawn into the 1967 Third Arab-Israeli War, and lost control over the West Bank and Jerusalem, which Israel has occupied ever since. He gave up all territorial claims to these in 1988, during the Palestinian Intifada, to pave the way for a Palestinian declaration of independence. In 1970, he fought and won a war against the Palestine Liberation Organization (PLO), then headquartered in his country, although by 1990 the relatively large Palestinian population of Jordan strongly influenced his position on the Iraqi invasion of Kuwait, which was supported by most Palestinians. Hussein attended Britain's Victoria College and Sandhurst. He has been married four times, since 1978 to Lisa Halaby, now Queen Noor, and has eleven children.

FURTHER READING

" 'Trying to catch our breath'. . . ." CHRISTOPHER DICKEY. *Newsweek*, Aug. 19, 1991.

"The great survivor. . . ." JOHN STACKS and DEAN FISCHER. *Time*, July 22, 1991.

"Who's sitting pretty. . . ." *Business Week*, Mar. 11, 1991.

"Speech defect. . . ." MICHAEL KELLY. *New Republic*, Mar. 4, 1991.

"Divided loyalties." JOEL BRINKLEY. *New York Times Magazine*, Dec. 16, 1990.

"Facing a no-win. . . ." DEAN FISCHER and JAMES WILDE. *Time*, Nov. 5, 1990.

"Dangerous crossroads. . . ." *Maclean's*, July 9, 1990.

Hussein of Jordan: From Survivor to Statesman. JAMES LUNT. Morrow, 1989.

King Hussein and the Challenge of Arab Radicalism: Jordan, 1955–1967. URIEL DANN. Oxford University Press, 1989.

Hussein, Saddam (1937–) In 1992, in the continuing aftermath of the Persian Gulf War, Iraqi dictator Saddam Hussein managed to keep and to some extent to consolidate his power, although United Nations sanctions remained in place; UN inspectors still sought to identify and destroy his weapons of mass murder, and UN air power instituted a "no-fly" zone over southern Iraq. At the end of the Gulf War, American-led Allied forces had smashed his elite Republican Guard divisions, but then let large armored formations and some elements of his air force escape. Hussein no longer led a major military force, even a Middle Eastern regional one, but he had far more than enough left to easily defeat a subsequent Kurdish revolt in the north and a Shiite Muslim revolt in the south.

In 1992, while UN forces continued to protect Kurdish refugees in northern Iraq, the main military action shifted to the south, as Hussein's forces mounted genocidal attacks on Shiites, complete with aircraft, in violation of the Gulf War ceasefire agreements. Allied forces responded with establishment of a "no-fly zone" over southern Iraq in late August, aimed at stopping all military and civilian Iraqi flights over the area.

Another area of major contention was that of international inspection of Iraqi weapons facilities, which Iraq resisted throughout much of the year, giving in only when it became clear that the United States was willing to bomb Iraqi installations, including goverment offices in Baghdad, to enforce the right to inspection.

Hussein also survived a late June coup attempt by elements of the Republican Guard. At year's end, he was still very much in place, despite all efforts to depose him, though far from the threatening presence he had been before the Gulf War.

Takrit-born Hussein joined the Ba'ath socialist party in 1957, and went into Egyptian exile in 1958, after taking part in the failed attempt to assassinate general Karim Kassem, premier of the Iraqi republic. He returned to Iraq in 1963, after the army coup in which Kassem was killed. Hussein was a leader of the Ba'ath coup of 1968, and took full power in 1971, then surrounding himself with followers from his home village, instituting a reign of terror in his country, and becoming the dictator of Iraq. He also then began to develop a massive "cult of personality" around himself.

In 1980, Hussein's forces attacked Iran, beginning the Iran-Iraq war (1980–88); his forces used large amounts of poison gas against the Iranians, although such chemical warfare has been outlawed throughout the world. In the late 1980s, after the 1988 ceasefire with Iran, his forces continued to use poison gas, this time against Iraq's own rebellious Kurdish population, killing thousands of civilians, and forcing hundreds of thousands to flee into exile. With the end of the Iran-Iraq war, Hussein emerged as a Middle Eastern strongman. On August 2, 1990, his armies invaded and took oil-rich Kuwait. He then turned toward far richer Saudi Arabia, whether to invade or intimidate, and was met by the U.S.-led multinational response, coupled with UN action, that resulted in sanctions, blockade, and ultimately the Persian Gulf War.

Hussein attended Cairo University and Baghdad's al-Mujstanseriya University. He married Sajidal Khairalla in 1963, and has four children.

FURTHER READING

"Saddam's best ally." LESLIE COCKBURN and ANDREW COCKBURN. *Vanity Fair*, Aug. 1992.
" 'Back from the living dead' . . . ." RAY WILKINSON. *Newsweek*, Jan. 20, 1992.
"The stalking of Saddam." CHARLES LANE. *Newsweek*, Jan. 20, 1992.
Saddam Hussein. NITA RENFREW. Chelsea House, 1992.
Saddam Speaks on the Gulf Crisis: A Collection of Documents. OFRA BENGIO, ed. Syracuse University Press, 1992.
Rogues' Gallery: America's Foes from George III to Saddam Hussein. LARRY HEDRICK. Brasseys, 1992.
"How Saddam survived. . . ." GAIL SHEEHY. *Vanity Fair*, Aug. 1991.
"Getting even." URIEL DANN. *New Republic*, June 3, 1991.
"His war, his peace. . . ." *Economist*, Feb. 23, 1991.
"The man behind. . . ." PAUL GRAY. *Time*, Feb. 11, 1991.
"Saddam. . . ." LISA BEYER. *Time*, Jan. 7, 1991.
Saddam Hussein: A Political Biography. EFRAIM KARSH and INARI RAUTSI. Pergamon, 1991.
Outlaw State: Saddam Hussein's Quest for Power and the Gulf Crisis. ELAINE SCIOLINO. Wiley, 1991.
Saddam Hussein: A Political Biography. EFRAIM KARSH. Free Press, 1991.
Instant Empire: Saddam Hussein's Ambition for Iraq. SIMON HENDERSON. Mercury House, 1991.
Saddam Hussein and the Crisis in the Gulf. JUDITH MILLER and LAURIE MYLORIE. Random, 1990.

Huston, Anjelica (1952–) Late in 1992, as home video audiences were being introduced to her Morticia in *The Addams Family*, Huston was making the new Woody Allen film *Manhat-*tan Murder Mystery, opposite Allen, Diane Keaton, and Martin Landau. The film, scheduled for 1993 release, was to be Allen's first since the highly publicized Allen-Mia Farrow breakup; Keaton played the role originally designed for Farrow. Also forthcoming was a starring role in the four-hour ABC miniseries *Family Pictures*, based on the Sue Miller book; Huston was set to play the mother of a Chicago family that includes an autistic child. Another reportedly forthcoming film was a *The Addams Family* sequel, with Huston set to recreate her Morticia. Huston appeared as herself in Robert Altman's *The Player*, his merciless, multistar lampoon of modern Hollywood.

On the personal side, Huston and sculptor Robert Graham married in Los Angeles in May.

Born in Los Angeles but raised in Ireland, Huston took a critical pounding when her father, actor-director John Huston, cast the 15-year-old in his film, *A Walk With Love and Death* (1967). She retreated from film to the stage, emerging as a leading dramatic film actress in the mid-1980s, winning a Best Supporting Actress Oscar as Maerose Prizzi in John Huston's *Prizzi's Honor* (1985); and starring in *Gardens of Stone* (1987), *The Dead* (1987, screenplay by brother Tony Huston); *A Handful of Dust* (1988), John Huston's last film; *Enemies, A Love Story* (1989); *Crimes and Misdeameanors* (1989); *The Grifters* (1990); *The Witches* (1990), and *The Addams Family* (1991). The granddaughter of actor Walter Huston, she worked with acting coach Peggy Feury. In 1990, she ended a 17-year relationship with Jack Nicholson.

FURTHER READING

"Anjelica Huston." NANCY GRIFFIN. *Harper's Bazaar*, June 1992.
"Anjelica Huston. . . ." *People*, Dec. 30, 1991.
"Anjelica Huston." SUSAN MORGAN. *Interview*, Dec. 1991.
"Huston Addams." SUSAN MORGAN. *Interview*, July 1991.
"A bit of a coyote. . . ." DAVID THOMSON. *American Film*, Nov. 1990.
"Anjelica Huston. . . ." VICKI WOODS. *Vogue*, Nov. 1990.
"Huston, Anjelica." *Current Biography*, July 1990.
Anjelica Huston: The Lady and the Legacy. MARTHA HARRIS. St. Martin's, 1989.
The Hustons. LAWRENCE GROBEL. Macmillan, 1989.

Ice-T (Tracy Marrow; c. 1955–60–) Rap musician Ice-T organized the African-American, hardcore metal band Body Count in March 1992; its members also included Ernie-Cl, D-Roc, Mooseman, and Beatmaster V. The band's first album was *Body Count*, issued by Time Warner in later March, and one of the songs on that album was "Cop Killer," which included such lyrics as "I've got my 12-gauge sawed off . . . I'm 'bout to dust some cops off . . . die, pig, die;" and "I'm 'bout to kill me somethin . . . a pig stopped me for nuthin;" and "What do you want to be when you grow up? . . . Cop killer!"

The song generated a storm of protest from police associations all over the country, which claimed that it would literally encourage cop killing, and demanded that it be withdrawn. They were joined by such figures as President George Bush, actor Charlton Heston, many Time Warner stockholders, and a wide range of others, many of them (but far from all) far-right conservatives. Some defended the album on free speech grounds, questioning the credentials of such moralists as Oliver North, and some, like a southern regional African-American police officers' association, felt that the debate paid too little attention to the causes of urban violence. Ultimately, in late July, Ice-T and Time Warner folded, replacing the album with a version that did not include "Cop Killer."

The album, however, was extremely popular with Ice-T's young, mostly African-American audience, and although it brought him probably damaging celebrity, did not seem to harm his career. He won a Best Solo Rap Grammy nomination in 1992, and Home Box Office in August announced that he was to be the host of a 1993 talk and entertainment show. On the other hand, release of his next album, scheduled for November 1992, was postponed until an unspecified date in 1993.

During 1992, Ice-T also starred as King James in Walter Hill's action-thriller *Trespass*; Bill Paxton, William Sadler, and Ice Cube co-starred.

Newark-born Ice-T grew up in South Central Los Angeles, in the street gang culture that provides the setting for his music. His first recording was *The Coldest Rap* (1982), which led to work as a disc jockey and to a role in the film

Breakin' (1984). He emerged as a very popular rap musician in the late 1980s, with the appearance of his album *Rhyme Pays* (1987). Even more popular was his album *The Iceberg Freedom of Speech* (1989). He also scored a major success as an undercover police officer in the film *New Jack City* (1991). His companion is Darlene Ortiz; they have one child.

FURTHER READING

"Ice capades." MEREDITH BERKMAN. *Entertainment,* Dec. 18, 1992.
"Ice T. . . ." ALAN LIGHT. *Rolling Stone,* Aug. 20, 1992.

Iliescu, Ion (1930–) Romanian President Iliescu gained increased support in his country during 1992, even though he and other key government officials were Communist holdovers, and even though it was clear that he had encouraged the beating and dispersal of opposition groups protesting the organization and conduct of the 1990 elections by thousands of coal miners armed with clubs.

For many in Eastern Europe and the Soviet Union, 1992 was a year of Communist comeback, as a rapid turn away from central planning to a market economy brought enormous hardship and real questions as to whether the new systems were at all working. Iliescu profited from those concerns, promising a slowdown in the pace of change; he won re-election to the Romanian Presidency by a large majority in an October runoff election, with more than 60 percent of the vote. After the election, he spoke of listening to minority viewpoints, but his election and his alliance with hardline Communist and nationalist groups brought great concern as to the future of Romanian democracy, as Romania's problems continued to grow.

Iliescu had been associated with the Romanian Communist Party ever since joining its youth organization in 1944. He rose swiftly in the party hierarchy until the early 1970s, becoming a member of his party's central committee in 1967, and was youth minister (1967–72). But then he fell into disfavor with dictator Nicolae Ceausescu, and was sidetracked and demoted; he was head of a state-run publishing house in 1989, when Ceausescu fell. In that fall, Iliescu rose, on December 22, 1989, emerging as

a member of the revolutionary council, the National Salvation Front. On December 23, as president of the Front, he announced the arrest of Nicolae and Elena Ceausescu, who were executed on December 25. On December 26, Iliescu was named provisional president of Romania. He attended the Bucharest Polytechnic Institute and Moscow University, and is married to Elena Iliescu.

FURTHER READING

"Iliescu, Ion." *Current Biography,* June 1990.
"Between revolutions. . . ." VLADIMIR TISMANEANU. *New Republic,* Apr. 23, 1990.

Ireland, John (1914–92) Vancouver-born actor John Ireland grew up in New York City, and it was there that he began his stage career, making his debut in the 1941 Maurice Evans-Judith Anderson production of *Macbeth.* Although his career included many stage roles, his main work was in films, beginning with *A Walk on the Wild Side* (1945). Among his scores of films were *My Darling Clementine* (1946), *Red River* (1948), *All the King's Men* (1949; he won an Oscar nomination), *Outlaw Territory* (1953; he starred, codirected, and coproduced), *The Good Die Young* (1954), *Spartacus* (1960), and *Farewell, My Lovely* (1975). He also appeared in television. He was survived by his wife, the former Daphne Cameron, a daughter and two sons. His second wife had been the actress Joanne Dru, with whom he co-starred in several films. (d. Santa Barbara, California; March 21, 1992)

FURTHER READING

Obituary. *Variety,* Mar. 30, 1992.
Obituary. *The Times* (of London), Mar. 24, 1992.
Obituary. *New York Times,* Mar. 23, 1992.

Irons, Jeremy (1948–) British stage and screen star Jeremy Irons continued to build his career in a series of high quality art films during 1992. In another acclaimed role, he starred as high school history teacher Tom Crick in Stephen Gyllenhaal's *Waterland,* in which Crick takes his students through his own personal history in England's fen country, the film presented as a series of flashbacks; co-starring were Sinead

Cusack as Mary Crick (she is also Irons's real-life wife), and Grant Warnock and Lena Headey as the stars when they were teenagers.

Irons also starred in Louis Malle's controversial film *Damage*, based on the Josephine Hart novel, as adapted for film by playwright David Hare; Juliette Binoche, Miranda Richardson, Rupert Graves, Ian Bannen, and Leslie Caron co-starred. Irons also starred as one of the 1930s antifascist refugee Hollywood intellectuals and artists in Christopher Hampton's television film adaptation of his own 1982 play *Tales From Hollywood*, opposite Alec Guinness, Charles Durning, Elizabeth McGovern, and Sinead Cusack. He was also still seen in home video in his Best Actor Oscar-winning role as Claus von Bulow in *Reversal of Fortune*.

Forthcoming was a starring role in the film *House of the Spirits*, based on the Isabel Allende novel, set in Chile; co-starring were Meryl Streep, Winona Ryder, Glenn Close, and Anthony Banderas.

Irons emerged as a screen and stage star in the early 1980s. In 1981, he created the Charles Ryder role in the television miniseries "Brideshead Revisited," the celebrated adaptation of the Evelyn Waugh novel. In the same year, he played opposite Meryl Streep in *The French Lieutenant's Woman*. He went on to star in such films as *Moonlighting* (1982), *Betrayal* (1983), *The Wild Duck* (1983), *Swann in Love* (1984), *The Mission* (1986), *Dead Ringers* (1989), *Frankenstein Unbound* (1989), *A Chorus of Disapproval* (1989), and *Kafka* (1991). He won a Best Leading Actor in a Drama Tony for *The Real Thing* (1984). He and Sinead Cusack have two children.

FURTHER READING

"Fame is not exposure." IAN JOHNSTONE. *Sunday Times*, Aug. 16, 1992.
"Metamorphosis." HARLAN KENNEDY. *American Film*, Nov.–Dec. 1991.
"Claus encounters." ELLEN STERN. *GQ—Gentlemen's Quarterly*, Nov. 1990.
"Irons." DAVID DeNICOLO. *Interview*, June 1990.
Actors: A Celebration. RITA GAM. St. Martin's, 1988.

Ising, Rudolph (1910–92)

A pioneer film animator, Ising was hired as a cartoonist by Walt Disney in Kansas City, and moved to Los Angeles with Disney in 1925, as did Hugh Harman. Ising and Harman soon formed their own cartoon company, and in 1929, with partner Leon Schlesinger produced the first talking picture cartoon, *Bosko the Talk-Ink Kid*. In 1930, they took over the Looney Tunes series at Warner Brothers, and in 1931 created the Merrie Melodies series. Ising and Harman joined MGM in 1934, there creating the Happy Harmony series, and also creating Barney Bear, the forerunner of Yogi Bear. Ising's *The Milky Way* cartoon won a 1940 Oscar. During World War II, Ising headed the U.S. Air Force animation department, producing training films. After the war, he did not return to cartoons, instead working on commercials and later in television. He was survived by his wife, the former Alice Wagner, and a son. (d. Newport Beach, California; July 18, 1992)

FURTHER READING

Obituary. *The Times* (of London), Aug. 20, 1992.
Obituary. *Variety*, July 27, 1992.
Obituary. *New York Times*, July 23, 1992.

Ivory, James Francis (1928–)

Celebrated British director Ivory added yet another major art film to his long string of successes in 1991: the much-anticipated *Howard's End*, Ruth Prawer Jhabvala's adaptation of the 1910 E.M. Forster novel. The film, a Merchant-Ivory production, was set in an English country house of that name in class-dominated Edwardian Britain, immediately before World War I, which made much of that life and time obsolete. Its cast included Vanessa Redgrave, Anthony Hopkins, Emma Thompson, James Wilby, Helena Bonham Carter, Prunella Scales, Joseph Bennett, Adrian Ross Magenty, Jemma Redgrave, and Sam West. Forthcoming was another Merchant-Ivory production directed by Ivory: *Remains of the Day*, Harold Pinter's film adaptation of the Kazuo Ishiguro novel, starring Anthony Hopkins, Emma Thompson, James Fox, and Christopher Reeve.

Ivory and producer Ismail Merchant in 1992 did something unusual for them and for the movie industry; they signed a long-term agreement with Disney's Touchstone Pictures to release all Merchant-Ivory films not yet committed to other studios, with Disney to pay half of the cost of developing all such films. The agreement provided that Merchant-Ivory was to have complete creative control of all films costing less than $12 million. The first film announced was the forthcoming *Jefferson in Paris*, screenplay by Ruth Prawer Jhabvala. Given Disney's film industry reputation for creative control, many wondered how long the agreement would hold.

California-born Ivory began his long, fruitful collaboration with Merchant and Jahbvala in the early 1960s, with such films as *Shakespeare Wallah* (1965), *Bombay Talkie* (1970), and *Autobiography of a Princess* (1975), all of them largely set in India. His later films included *The Europeans* (1979), *Heat and Dust* (1983), *A Room with a View* (1986), *Maurice* (1987), *Slaves of New York* (1989), and *Mr. and Mrs. Bridge* (1990). Ivory's 1951 B.F.A. was from the University of Oregon, his M.A. from the University of Southern California.

FURTHER READING

"Doing it right the hard way. . . ." RICHARD CORLISS. *Time*, Mar. 16, 1992.

Films of Merchant Ivory. ROBERT E. LONG. Abrams, 1991.

"Mr. and Mrs. Bridge." GRAHAM FULLER. *Interview*, Nov. 1990.

J

Jackson, Glenda (1936–) The great British actress Glenda Jackson changed careers very sharply in 1992, winning election as a Labour Party Member of Parliament in London's Hampstead-Highgate constituency, as John Major's Conservative government was winning a surprise national victory over the Labour Party, then led by Neil Kinnock. The constituency had until recent years also been a reliable Conservative parliamentary seat, making her victory even more of a personal tribute. It was clearly more than a tribute to Jackson as a star, for she had made a full-scale, sober campaign for the seat, speaking on the key issues of the day, since announcing her candidacy in 1990, and had gone on to win the Labour selection poll for the seat over three other women candidates, with 60 percent of the vote. True to her campaign pledge, Jackson gave up acting on her election to Parliament, treating her new political career as a full-time occupation. Her worldwide audiences continued to hope for her return to stage and screen, whatever the course of her political career.

Jackson made her stage debut in 1957; she joined the Royal Shakespeare Company in 1964, and that year emerged as a powerful dramatic actress, as Charlotte Corday in *Marat/Sade*, a role she recreated on Broadway in 1965 and in the 1966 film. She went on to become a very notable stage and screen star, on stage as Ophelia in *Hamlet* (1965), Masha in *The Three Sisters* (1967), as *Hedda Gabler* (1975), as poet Stevie Smith in *Stevie* (1977; and in the 1977 film), and in such plays as *Rose* (1980), *Strange*

Interlude (1984), *Macbeth* (1988), and in Los Angeles in late 1989 in Edward Albee's production of his own *Who's Afraid of Virginia Woolf.* On screen, she was a notable Elizabeth I in the television miniseries "Elizabeth R" (1971), won Best Actress Oscars for *Women in Love* (1969) and *A Touch of Class* (1973), and also starred in such films as *Sunday Bloody Sunday* (1971), *The Abbess of Crewe* (1976), *The Return of the Soldier* (1982), *Turtle Diary* (1985), and *The Rainbow* (1989). Jackson attended the Royal Academy of Dramatic Art. She was formerly married, and has one child.

FURTHER READING

"Enter Glenda, state left." RITA GAM. *World Monitor*, July 1992.
"Glenda tackles. . . ." ANGELLA JOHNSON. *Guardian*, June 20, 1992.
"Labour pains. . . ." CHRISTOPHER SILVESTER. *Connoisseur*, July 1991.
Glenda Jackson: A Study in Fire and Ice. IAN WOODWARD. St. Martin's, 1985.

Jackson, Janet (1966–) Now established as a major popular singer, Jackson spent much of 1992 working on the first of the three albums covered by her March 1991, $40 million agreement with Virgin Records, which had made her one of the world's most highly paid performers. In February, she made a reportedly record-setting $3 million agreement with producers Jimmy Jam and Terry Lewis to produce and co-

write the album, and work began in early April; the three had collaborated on Jackson's tremendously successful 1989 breakthrough album *Rhythm Nation: 1814*. On March 10, Jackson won the Sammy Davis, Jr. Entertainer of the Year Soul Train award. Forthcoming was a starring role in John Singleton's film *Poetic Justice*, a film on African-American life in California, set in south central Los Angeles and Oakland.

On the personal side, the young singer was threatened in June by a man who tried to gain entry into her Encino, California home, claiming that he was her husband; he was arrested.

As a child, Jackson appeared with her brothers, then the Jackson Five. She made three albums in the early 1980s: *Janet Jackson* (1982), *Dream Street* (1984), and *Control* (1986); the latter introduced several hit singles, and suggested the major career that would blossom a few years later. She scored a major success in 1989, with the hit album *Rhythm Nation: 1814*. Singer and dancer Jackson began her first concert tour on March 1, 1990 in Miami, and from there went on to tour the United States, Japan, and Europe. In January, 1991, her "Love Will Never Do (Without You)" became a number one pop single. She was formerly married.

FURTHER READING

"Jackson, Janet." *Current Biography*, June 1991.
"Former child stars. . . ." MICHELLE McCALOPE. *Jet*, Apr. 15, 1991.

La Toya: Growing up in the Jackson Family. LA TOYA JACKSON and PATRICIA ROMANOWSKI. NAL-Dutton, 1991.
"Janet Jackson and Paula Abdul. . . ." *Jet*, May 7, 1990.
"Janet Jackson. . . ." ROBERT E. JOHNSON. *Ebony*, Feb. 1990.
"Free at last." ANTHONY DeCURTIS. *Rolling Stone*, Feb. 22, 1990.
My Family, The Jacksons. KATHERINE JACKSON. St. Martin's, 1990.
Janet Jackson. D.L. MABERY. Lerner, 1988.
Janet Jackson: In Control. NANCY ROBISON. Dillon, 1987.

Jackson, Jesse Louis (1941–)

What may have been good for the Democratic Party in 1992 was not necessarily good for Jesse Jackson's political career. Only four years earlier, he had emerged from the 1988 campaign as the outstanding African-American leader of his time. In 1992, he decided not to run for the Presidency, and run the risk of splitting his party, setting in motion a train of events that seemed to leave him very much out in the cold during and after the election. Later in the campaign, Jackson made it clear that he wanted the Democratic vice-presidential nomination; denied that, and at odds with Bill Clinton on a wide range of matters, he responded warmly to Jerry Brown's comment that he would welcome Jackson on his ticket. Jackson also refused to rule out supporting Ross Perot, until shortly before the Democratic Convention. In June, Clinton and Jackson

publicly disagreed, after Clinton, appearing before Jackson's Rainbow Coalition, criticized rap singer Sister Souljah, who was quoted as having said after the Los Angeles riots that Blacks should take a week off and kill Whites. Many, including Jackson, thought this a deliberate attempt by Clinton to distance himself from Jackson.

In the end, Jackson spoke to the July Democratic National Convention in support of Clinton, and then campaigned for Clinton all over the country. Jackson also in July spoke before a World Jewish Congress conference on anti-Semitism and prejudice, calling for a revitalization of the historic Jewish and African-American liberal coalition. Still a "shadow Senator" from the District of Columbia, Jackson also campaigned for D.C. statehood during 1992. A Clinton campaign promise, statehood might very well mean a U.S. Senate seat for Jackson.

Long active in the civil rights movement, Jackson directed the Southern Christian Leadership Operation Breadbasket (1967–71), and in 1971 founded Operation PUSH (People United to Save Humanity), and later the Rainbow Coalition. He made an unsuccessful bid for the Democratic presidential nomination in 1984, but emerged as a major figure. In 1988, he published *A Time to Speak: The Autobiography of the Reverend Jesse Jackson.* South Carolina-born Jackson received his 1964 B.A. from North Carolina Agricultural and Technical University. After postgraduate work at the Chicago Theological Seminary, he became a Baptist minister, in 1968. He married Jacqueline Brown in 1964; they have five children.

FURTHER READING

"America's great black hope." ALEXANDER COCKBURN and ANDREW KOPKIND. *New Statesman & Society,* July 10, 1992.

"The gift." Feb. 3, 1992. "History is upon us." Feb. 10, 1992. "Without portfolio." Feb. 17, 1992. Marshall Frady. *New Yorker.* (Parts I–III of *Outsider* series.)

I Am Somebody!: A Biography of Jesse Jackson. JAMES HASKINS. Enslow, 1992.

Keep Hope Alive: Super Tuesday and Jesse Jackson's 1988 Campaign for the Presidency. PENN KIMBALL. Joint Center for Political Studies, 1992.

Black American Politics: From the Washington Marches to Jesse Jackson, 2nd ed., MANNING MARABLE. Routledge Chapman and Hall, 1992.

"From Jim Crow. . . ." MARILYN BERLIN SNELL. *New Perspectives,* Summer 1991.

Jesse Jackson and Political Power. TERESA CELSI. Millbrook, 1991.

Jesse Jackson. ROBERT JAKOUBEK. Chelsea House, 1991.

Jesse Jackson: A Biography. PATRICIA C. MCKISSACK. Scholastic, 1991.

Jesse Jackson: Still Fighting for the Dream. BRENDA WILKINSON. Silver Burdett, 1990.

The Jackson Phenomenon: The Man, the Power, and the Message. ELIZABETH O. COULTON. Doubleday, 1989.

Jesse Jackson: A Voice for Change. STEVE OFFINOSKI. Fawcett, 1989.

Jackson, Michael Joseph (1958–   ) Pop superstar Jackson was as much a celebrity entertainer as ever in 1992, despite the somewhat disappointing peformance of his late-1991 album *Dangerous.* Even though the album did not rocket to the top of the charts and stay there, it did enjoy worldwide sale of some millions of records, and did provide the basis for his hit 1992 video "Remember the Time," and such 1992 hit singles as "In the Closet," "Jam," and "Heal the World," as well as the 1991 single "Black or White." He won a 1992 Billboard No. 1 worldwide single award for "Black or White," and a No. 1 worldwide album award for *Dangerous.*

In 1992, Jackson added another major commercial arrangement to his 1991 Sony contract, this one an 18-month contract with Pepsi-Cola International, for a series of commercials and a four-continent worldwide tour. His first major ad for Pepsi was the 60-second video "Dream," broadcast into an announced 165 countries. Forthcoming was Frito-Lay (a Pepsi subsidiary) sponsorship of Jackson's January 1993 Superbowl halftime show.

Jackson toured Europe from late June through mid-October, performing before soldout audiences, announcing that he was earmarking the concert proceeds for his new Heal the World foundation, to help underprivileged children. He canceled the balance of his trip after an appearance before 50,000–70,000 at Bucharest, citing throat problems, later in the year said to have been cured.

His honors in 1992 included a Best Male Dance artist Billboard music video award for "In the Closet." Jackson was named Billboard's top male pop singles artist, top male rhythm and blues artist, and top dance artist of the year.

Indiana-born Jackson began his extraordinary career in 1969, as the 11-year-old lead singer of his family singing group, The Jackson Five. He became a leading popular soloist in the late 1970s, with such albums as *Off the Wall* (1979), *Thriller* (1982), which sold over four million copies, *Bad* (1987), and such singles as "I Can't Stop Loving You," along with many popular videos. He starred opposite Diana Ross in the film version of *The Wiz* (1978), and in *Moonwalker* (1988).

FURTHER READING

"Ebony/Jet interview with. . . ." ROBERT E. JOHNSON. *Ebony*, Nov. 1992.

"Michael Jackson. . . ." ROBERT E. JOHNSON. *Ebony*, May 1992.

"Eyewitness report on. . . ." ROBERT E. JOHNSON. *Jet*, Mar. 16, 1992.

"Michael Jackson. . . ." MICHAEL GOLDBERG. *Rolling Stone*, Jan. 9, 1992.

The Michael Jackson Scrapbook. LES LEE. Citadel Press/Carol, 1992.

" 'Dangerous' album proves. . . ." *Jet*, Dec. 2, 1991.

"Former child stars. . . ." MICHELLE MCCALOPE. *Jet*, Apr. 15, 1991.

"Madonna and Michael." STEVE DOUGHERTY. *People*, Apr. 15, 1991.

Michael Jackson: The Magic and the Madness. J. RANDY TARABORRELLI. Carol, 1991.

La Toya: Growing up in the Jackson Family. LA TOYA JACKSON and PATRICIA ROMANOWSKI. NAL-Dutton, 1991.

Michael Jackson: A Life in Music. HAL SCHUSTER. Movie Publications, 1990.

My Family, The Jacksons. KATHERINE JACKSON. St. Martin's, 1990.

Sequins and Shades: The Michael Jackson Reference Guide. CAROL TERRY. Popular Culture, 1989.

Moonwalk. MICHAEL JACKSON. Doubleday, 1988; Writers Digest, 1989.

Michael Jackson Electrifying. GREG QUILL. Barron's, 1988.

Jackson, Phil (Philip Douglas Jackson; 1946–) In 1992, Chicago Bulls coach Phil Jackson did what few had done before him: he took his team to back-to-back National Basketball Association (NBA) championships. It wasn't that Jackson had the premiere player in the NBA, Michael Jordan, for 1991–92 was Jordan's eighth year with the Bulls. It wasn't that Jackson built the team, for most of the key players were in place before Jackson took over as head coach. It was that Jackson directed the team into championship-winning patterns. In particular, he developed the strategy of having Jordan score less and distribute the ball more to other members on the team, allowing all to become involved and making their opponents' defensive job that much harder. In fact, Jackson established the unusual pattern of giving almost all 12 players on the team regular playing time, where most coaches regularly use only 7–8 players. With his even-tempered manner, he also helped his players relax and enjoy the game more. What resulted were championship wins over the Los Angeles Lakers in 1991 and the Portland Trailblazers in 1992, when the team had a regular season won-lost record of 67–15. The Bulls' three-year playoff record of 40 wins to 15 losses under Jackson gives him the highest playoff winning percentage of any NBA head coach in history, at .727.

Because of his team's regular-season winning record, Jackson was coach of the 1992 Eastern Conference All-Star team. In March 1992, even before the second championship, Jackson signed a three contract extension. In the first half of the 1992–93 season, the team—with a somewhat new mix of players—had lost some of its edge, but it was clearly still going to be the team to beat going down the stretch toward the 1993 championships.

Montana-born Jackson was twice an All-American basketball player at the University of North Dakota in the mid-1960s. A strong defensive forward, he was drafted by the New York Knicks in 1967, and spent 11 years with the Knicks, missing the 1970 championship season because of an injury, but playing on the 1973 championship team. He ended his career with the New York Nets, but stayed on as an assistant coach and then television analyst. He compiled a winning record as coach of the Albany Patroons of the Continental Basketball Association (1982–87), capturing the CBA championship in 1984 and being named coach of the year in 1985, and then joined the Bulls as an assistant coach. He succeeded Doug Collins as head coach in 1989, and immediately emerged as a major figure in basketball, coaching the Bulls to an ensemble performance led by Michael Jordan that produced a 55–27 regular season record and took them as far as the Eastern Division finals. His second season brought a 61–21 winning record and the first Bulls NBA championship, making Jackson the only person ever to have coached championship teams in both the NBA and CBA. He wrote an early autobiography of himself and his Knick days, *Maverick* (1975). Jackson is married, and has five children.

FURTHER READING

"Jackson, Phil." *Current Biography*, July 1992.
"The age of Jackson." Jeff Coplon. *New York Times Magazine*, May 17, 1992.

"Phil Jackson's courtly attitude." *GQ—Gentleman's Quarterly*, Feb. 1992.
"For whom the Bulls toll." Jack McCallum. *Sports Illustrated*, Nov. 11, 1991.

Jacobs, Lou (Jacob Ludwig; 1903–92)

Born in Bremerhaven, Germany, Jacobs was an acrobat in variety as a child. He emigrated to the United States in 1923, and in 1925 was hired as a clown by Ringling Brothers. For 60 years, he was one of the greatest circus clowns of the century, traveling with the Ringling Brothers Barnum and Bailey Circus to play live for an audience that was ultimately measured in the millions. He was also seen in the film *The Greatest Show on Earth* (1952), and in 1966 his face, in clown makeup, was even seen on a U.S. stamp. In his later years, he taught the clown's art at Ringling's Clown College, at Venice, Florida. He was survived by his wife, the former star circus aerialist Jean Rockwell, and two daughters, both of whom were also aerialists. (d. Sarasota, Florida; September 13, 1992)

FURTHER READING

Obituary. *The Times* (of London), Sept. 19, 1992.
Obituary. *New York Times*, Sept. 15, 1992.

Jagger, Mick (Michael Philip Jagger; 1941–)

Historic rock superstar Jagger emphasized the acting, rather than the singing side of his career in 1992. He starred as Vacenkak opposite Emilio Estevez as Alex Furlong and Rene Russo as Julie, in a cast that included Anthony Hopkins as McCandless, in Geoff Murphy's science fiction action thriller *Freejack*, based on Robert Steckley's novel *Immorality, Inc.* The rather complicated plot, set in the year 2009, features Estevez and Russo playing lovers brought from the past by body-hunter Jagger, for mind-transfer purposes. The critics were not kind, the film fared rather poorly at the box office, and it was in home video release by May, having opened in January. On the musical side, Jagger's long-awaited *Wandering Spirit* album, scheduled for release late in 1992, was postponed once again; technical reasons were cited for the delay.

On the personal side, Jerry Hall, Jagger's

wife, gave birth in January, to a girl, whom they named Georgia May Ayeesha. The couple split temporarily during the summer, but later were reconciled.

Jagger was in 1962 the chief organizer of the Rolling Stones; he and Keith Richards were the group's main songwriters, and Jagger was its leading performer, playing the role of an angry, deeply alienated, uncontrollably violent, mythic sexual figure, a model for the scores of other such rock and popular music figures who would follow in the next three decades. Such albums as *The Rolling Stones* (1964; and two 1965 sequels), *Aftermath* (1966) and *Their Satanic Majesties Request* (1967), coupled with their worldwide tours, established them one of the leading popular musical groups of the century. In 1969, after a murder by their Hell's Angels security guards at an Altamont, California Stones concert, the group toned down their image somewhat. Although they continued to tour and record throughout the 1980s, their popularity lessened after the mid-1970s. Yet their very successful 1989–90 world tour showed that the 28-year-old rock group still had enormous vitality and drawing power. Jagger appeared in the film *Ned Kelly* (1969), and in the film of the Altamont concert, *Gimme Shelter* (1972). He has also done several solo recordings. Jagger attended the London School of Economics. He was married to Bianca Jagger (Bianca Pérez Morena de Macîas) from 1971–79, and married his longtime companion, model Jerry Hall, in 1990. Jagger has five children, the three youngest with Hall.

FURTHER READING

The Rolling Stones Album: Thirty Years of Music and Memorabilia. GEOFFREY GIULIANO. Viking/Studio Books, 1993.
"Mick's moves." STEPHEN SCHIFF. *Vanity Fair*, Feb. 1992.
Rolling Stones. DAVID CARTER. Outlet, 1992.
Time Is on My Side: The Rolling Stones Day-By-Day, 1962–1984. ALAN STEWART and CATHY SANFORD. Popular Culture, 1992.
The Rolling Stones' Rock and Roll Circus. MIKE RANDOLPH. Chronicle Books, 1991.
Rolling Stones Images. DAVID FRICKE. Simon & Schuster, 1991.
Blown Away: The Rolling Stones and the Death of the Sixties. A.E. HOTCHNER. Simon & Schuster, 1990.
The Pictorial History of the Rolling Stones. MARIE CAHILL. BDD Promo Books, 1990.

Rolling Stones Complete Recording Sessions. MARTIN ELLIOTT. Borgo Press/Sterling 1990.
The Rolling Stones Chronicle. MASSIMO BONANNO. Holt, 1990.
The Rolling Stones. TIM DOWLEY. Seven Hills, 1989.
It's Only Rock 'n' Roll: My On-the-Road Adventures with the Rolling Stones. CHET FLIPPO. St. Martin's, 1989.
The Life and Good Times of the Rolling Stones. PHILIP NORMAN. Outlet, 1989.
The Rolling Stone Interviews: The 1980s. St. Martin's, 1989.

Jaroszewicz, Piotr (1909–92) Former Polish premier Piotr Jaroszewicz and his wife, journalist Alicja Solska, were murdered in their home near Warsaw on September 1, 1992. Born at Nieswicz, in what was then the Russian-occupied portion of Poland, Jaroszewicz was a teacher and headmaster in the 1930s. During World War II, he fought with the Soviet-supported Polish army, ultimately fighting his way into Berlin. He ended the war a colonel and a top army political officer. A Communist, he rose during the postwar period to the rank of lieutenant general, and from 1952 to 1970 was deputy chairman of the Polish council of ministers, also holding several other key posts. He became premier of Poland in 1970, from then until 1980 pursuing a heavy industry-consumer subsidy policy that developed large foreign debts; then he attempted to right his failed policies by instituting an austerity program that included large food price increases. The resulting countrywide demonstrations toppled his government, and generated the Solidarity movement. In 1981, he was expelled from the Communist Party, and was imprisoned for a year, on his release retiring from politics. No information on survivors was available. (d. Warsaw; September 1, 1992)

FURTHER READING

Obituary. *The Times* (of London), Sep. 3, 1992.
Obituary. *New York Times*, Sep. 2, 1992.

Jenkins, Peter (1934–92) A leading British journalist, Jenkins began his career at the *Financial Times* in 1958, moved to *The Guardian* in 1960, and during the following 25 years

became a fixture there, first as a Labor reporter, then chief Labor correspondent, and then as a very widely read and authoritative political columnist. During the early 1970s, he was the Washington correspondent of *The Guardian*. In 1985, he moved to *The Sunday Times*, but stayed for only two years, that paper being far too right-wing in editorial policy for his comfort. From 1987 to 1992, he was associate editor of the more middle-of-the-road newspaper *The Independent*. His books included *The Battle of Downing Street* (1970) and *Mrs. Thatcher's Revolution: The Ending of the Socialist Era* (1987). Jenkins also wrote for the stage and for television. He was survived by his second wife, BBC editor Polly Toynbee, three daughters, and a son. (d. London; May 27, 1992)

FURTHER READING

Obituary. *The Times* (of London), May 28, 1992.
Obituary. *New York Times*, May 28, 1992.
Obituary. *Independent*, May 28, 1992.

Jennings, Peter Charles (1938–) In 1992, ABC news anchor Jennings continued to expand the bounds of his role, with emphasis on "long-form TV." In May 1992 he hosted an hour-long special, *Peter Jennings Reporting: Men, Sex and Rape*—focusing on the understanding that "forced sex originates in the minds of men," rather than being "caused" by women—followed by a 90-minute "news forum" on rape. In October 1992, he anchored a special on the 1962 Cuban missile crisis, called *The Missiles of October: What the World Didn't Know*, showing for the first time, he said, "how close we were to nuclear war." And in late December he did *The Cocaine War, Lost in Bolivia*.

During this political year, he moderated a Democratic presidential debate in March and then in June hosted a special *Who Is Ross Perot?*, followed by a town-meeting-style show, with Perot taking questions from viewers. His regular evening news show followed various "focus groups" of uncommitted voters throughout the campaign. For primary, convention, and election coverage, Jennings co-anchored with veteran newsman David Brinkley. Viewers noted with favor that Jennings was not deskbound, but rather was able to move around the two-tiered

election-night set housing various other colleagues.

Jennings also continued to reach out to young people. In February, he hosted a family-oriented live show, *Growing Up in the Age of AIDS*, which featured viewer call-ins, and in April a Saturday children's special, *Prejudice: Answering Children's Questions*. He was also scheduled to join in reading children's stories on "Mrs. Bush's Story Time," which began its third year on radio in November 1992.

Jennings's "World News Tonight" continued to be ranked number one, although CBS took the top spot once in early September, for the first time since December 1990, with its coverage of Hurricane Andrew. It was on Jennings's shows that Lt. Paula Coughlin first went public about the sexual harassment and assaults on women by Navy flyers, in what came to be known as the Tailhook Scandal.

Toronto-born Jennings worked in Canadian broadcasting before joining ABC News in 1964. During the next two decades, much of that time spent abroad, he rose to become chief London correspondent for ABC, and in 1983 became the anchor of "World News Tonight," and one of the three chief American reporters and interpreters of the news. Jennings attended Carleton University, and his LL.D. is from Rider College. Twice divorced, he is married to writer Kati Marton; he has two children.

FURTHER READING

"How 'Stanley Stunning'. . . ." ALAN EBERT. *Good Housekeeping*, Apr. 1991.
Anchors: Brokaw, Jennings, Rather and the Evening News. ROBERT GOLDBERG and GERALD J. GOLDBERG. Birch Lane/Carol, 1990.
"The kiss of the anchor man." E. JEAN CARROLL. *Playboy*, Dec. 1990.
"Peter Jennings gets no self-respect." ELIZABETH KAYE. *Esquire*, Sep. 1989.
"The A-B-Cs of Peter Jennings." NORMAN ATKINS. *Rolling Stone*, May 4, 1989.

John Paul II, Pope (Karol Wojtyla, 1920–) As the world moved into the post-Cold War period, Pope John Paul II continued to sound the main conservative themes of his papacy, at the same time focusing on the growth of the Catholic Church in the world's poorest and

highest population growth areas, as well as in the countries of newly free Eastern Europe and the former Soviet Union. A major focus continued to be the question of abortion, on which he gave absolutely no ground, although many within his own church continued to be advocates of population control and of women's choice in the matter of abortion. Another major focus also involved women; Pope John Paul steadfastly continued to oppose the ordination of women. Meeting with George L. Carey, the Archbishop of Canterbury on May, the Pope deplored the ordination of women in the Anglican Church, stating that it would hinder attempts at unity between their two churches. Carey continued to support the ordination of women. Underscoring his conservative commitment, the Pope on May 17th beatified Spanish priest Josemaria Escriva de Balaguer, founder of the the ultraconservative Opus Dei organization.

The Pope visited Angola in June, and on October spoke at Santo Domingo, capital of the Dominican Republic, on the 500th anniversary of the landing of Christopher Columbus in the Americas. He met with protesting Native American and Black groups on October 13th. On the personal side, on July 15th the Pope had a benign tumor removed from his colon and also had his gall bladder removed.

John Paul II is the first Pope of Polish origin, and the first non-Italian Pope of the past four centuries. He was ordained as a Catholic priest in 1946, and then moved steadily upward in the Polish Catholic Church, becoming a professor of theology in the 1950s, and ultimately archbishop of Crakow (1963–78). He became a Cardinal in 1967, and then Pope in 1978. He has been largely a very conservative Pope, strongly opposing abortion and strongly discouraging liberal social action on the part of the priesthood. He attended Cracow's Jagellonian University and Rome's Angelicum.

FURTHER READING

Pope John Paul Two. JAY WILSON. Chelsea House, 1992.
Portrait of John Paul II. ANDRE FROSSARD. Ignatius, 1990.
"The triumph of John Paul II. . . ." STEFAN KANFER. *Life*, Dec. 1989.
"John Paul's first decade. . . ." PETER HEBBLETHWAITE. *National Catholic Reporter*, Oct. 14, 1988.
"Television: the Papal medium." MICHAEL A. RUSSO. *America*, July 23, 1988.

"The post-modern Pope." NATHAN GARDELS. *New Perspectives Quarterly (NPQ)*, Fall 1988.
Pope John Paul II: Pilgrim of Peace. Crown, 1987.

Johnson, Earvin "Magic," Jr. (1959–)

For Magic Johnson, it was an extraordinary year, no matter how you looked at it. On November 7, 1991, Johnson had announced that he was infected with HIV, the virus that causes AIDS, and would be retiring from professional basketball. After a nationally televised ceremony in which his Los Angeles Lakers Jersey was retired, Johnson watched and cheered from the sidelines, while acting as sometime commentator on NBC's national basketball coverage.

Fans had other ideas, however, and voted him to the All-Star game. When Johnson indicated that he would like to play, National Basketball Commissioner (NBA) David Stern created an additional spot for him on the team; though some players before the February 9th game questioned whether Johnson should play, on the day all the other All-Stars embraced Johnson, one-by-one, in welcome. In the end, Johnson played one of his best games ever, scoring 25 points and making 9 assists in 29 minutes, and was voted the game's most valuable player—in the process doing much for AIDS education.

Johnson kept in shape through the following months, and then joined other NBA stars in the "Dream Team" which, after practice and exhibition games in the Americas, went to Barcelona, Spain, to compete in the Summer Olympics. Actually it was less a competition than a royal procession to the gold medal, to a large extent led by Johnson, with players from the opposing teams often gathering at the U.S. bench to be photographed with their basketball idols.

Feeling himself in good health, and obviously playing top basketball, Johnson announced on September 29th that he would rejoin the Lakers for the 1992–93 season, playing a limited schedule. He attended training camp and played in some exhibition games, but just before the season started retired again, this time for good. He later said it was because of the look of fear he saw on the faces of some players when he was being treated for a scratch, but beyond that some players were, privately or publicly, raising questions about whether Johnson should in fact be playing, and speculating on how he contracted HIV—all of which he felt took away from basketball, and certainly took away the joy that has always been so evident in Johnson's play. As NBC picked up its main basketball coverage in early 1993, Johnson once again joined the broadcasting team, as a commentator par excellence, bringing his own special magic to the viewing of the game.

Johnson—now using his given name, Earvin—continued active in AIDS education. His book (also audiocassette) *What You Can Do to Avoid AIDS*, with profits going to his AIDS Foundation, was given extraordinary publicity and distribution by the publishing and library communities, though some retail chains refused to carry it because of its frank language, descriptions, and illustrations. He hosted a nonprofit AIDS-awareness home video *Time Out: The Truth About HIV, AIDS, and You*, produced by Arsenio Hall, and featuring such stars as Paula Abdul, Neil Patrick Harris, Kirstie Alley, and Bobby Brown; and also a Nickelodeon special, fielding children's questions about AIDS. In September, Johnson resigned from the National Commission on AIDS, in protest over George Bush's lack of support for AIDS research and services; he indicated that he would rejoin the commission, if invited to do so by new president Bill Clinton.

On the personal side, Johnson's wife, Cookie, gave birth to Earvin Johnson, III, in June; both she and the child were healthy and HIV-negative. In 1992, Johnson also published an autobiographical work, *Magic Johnson: My Life*, written with William Novak, available in both book and audiocassette versions.

Michigan-born Johnson attended Michigan State University, leading his team to the 1979 NCAA championship. In his 12 professional seasons, he led the Los Angeles Lakers to the NBA finals nine times for five NBA titles (1980, 1982, 1985, 1987, 1988); was picked most valuable player in the playoffs three times (1980, 1982, 1987); and was named the league's MVP three times (1987, 1989, 1990). Twelve times an NBA All-Star, he was selected MVP for the first time in the 1990 All-Star Game, and again in the game played after his retirement, in 1992. Overall, Johnson amassed 17,239 points in 874 games, for an average of 19.7 a game; took down 6,376 rebounds; had 1,698 steals, second only to Maurice Cheeks's 2,197; and had 9,921 assists, in the 1990–91 season breaking the previous NBA record of 9,888. With his friend and rival, Larry Bird, and later with Michael Jordan as well, Johnson dominated the game of basketball in the 1980s. More than that, he revolutionized the way the game was played, being the first large player—at 6' 9"—to dominate as a point guard, with his astonishing versatility and skill, and with his magnetic personality, helping to make basketball popular worldwide. Johnson has also been a leader in establishing summer all-star games and other fund-raising events to benefit inner-city and minority youth. He has written two previous autobiographical works, *Magic* (1983; with Richard Levin) and *Magic's Touch* (1989; with Roy S. Johnson). He is married to retailer Earletha (Cookie) Kelly, who manages their Los Angeles sporting goods store, Magic 32. They have one child; he also has a son from a previous relationship.

FURTHER READING

"The two and only." BOB RYAN. *Sports Illustrated*, Dec. 14, 1992.
"In the shadow of AIDS. . . ." TODD GOLD. *People*, Oct. 19, 1992.
"My Life." MAGIC JOHNSON. *People*, Oct. 19, 1992.
" 'I'm still strong.' " JACK MCCALLUM. *Sports Illustrated*, Aug. 17, 1992.
"Magic Johnson seeks. . . ." *Jet*, July 20, 1992.
"A reason to believe." JEFF WEINSTOCK. *Sport*, June 1992.

"Magic and Cookie Johnson. . . ." Laura B. Randolph. *Ebony*, Apr. 1992.

"The importance of being Earvin." Roger Brigham. *Advocate*, Apr. 21, 1992.

"Magic Johnson: athlete." Paul Monette. *Interview*, Jan. 1992.

Sports Great Magic Johnson, rev. ed., James Haskins. Enslow, 1992.

Magic Johnson, Basketball Great. Sean Dolan. Chelsea House, 1992.

Magic Johnson. Bob Italia. Abdo and Daughters, 1992.

Magic Johnson: Hero on and Off Court. Bill Gutman. Millbrook Press, 1992.

Magic Johnson: Backcourt Wizard. Keith E Greenberg. Lerner, 1992.

Magic Johnson: Basketball's Smiling Superstar. Rick L. Johnson. Dillon/Macmillan, 1992.

"Magic Johnson. . . ." *Jet*, Nov. 25, 1991.

"It was Magic. . . ." Paul Attner. *Sporting News*, Nov. 18, 1991.

"Tragic Magic. . . ." James Deacon. *Maclean's*, Nov. 18, 1991.

"Unforgettable." Jack McCallum. *Sports Illustrated*, Nov. 18, 1991.

Magic Johnson. Scholastic, 1991.

Magic Johnson. Michael E. Goodman. Crestwood, 1988.

Jones, Allan (1908–92) A Hollywood musical film star of the 1930s, Jones appeared in several Broadway musicals before going to Hollywood. He starred as Gaylord Ravenal opposite Irene Dunne and Paul Robeson in James Whale's classic film version of *Show Boat* (1936). In 1937, he starred opposite Jeannette MacDonald in *The Firefly*, introducing the song "Donkey Serenade", which became his signature song. He also starred in two Marx Brothers films, *A Night at the Opera* (1935) and *A Day at the Races* (1937), and appeared in such films as *The Great Victor Herbert* (1939), *The Boys From Syracuse* (1940), and *Moonlight in Havana* (1942). He later appeared in several other films, and toured in several musicals. He was survived by his wife, Maria, and two sons, one of whom is the singer Jack Jones. (d. New York City; June 27, 1992)

FURTHER READING

Obituary. *Variety*, July 13, 1992.
Obituary. *The Times* (of London), July 3, 1992.
Obituary. *New York Times*, June 30, 1992.

Jones, James Earl (1931–) Although the much-honored American actor had won a 1991 Emmy for his creation of the ex-cop/ex-convict turned investigator hero of television's "Gabriel's Fire," the series was not a commercial success. Renamed "Pros and Cons," and with the addition of Richard Crenna for the 1991–92 season, its ratings did not improve enough to save it, and it was discontinued.

During 1992, Jones co-starred as U.S. admiral James Greer in Philip Noyce's hit political violence thriller *Patriot Games*, based on the best-selling Tom Clancy novel, which starred Harrison Ford as CIA analyst Jack Ryan. He also starred in a second action film, this one Phil Alden Robinson's well-received fast-paced comedy thriller *Sneakers*, featuring computer hackers, threats to national security, and assorted murders, in a cast that included Robert Redford, Ben Kingsley, Sidney Poitier, Mary McDonnell, and River Phoenix. Forthcoming was a role in Jon Hess's film, *Excessive Force*.

To his many awards, Jones added the 1992 National Medal of Arts, awarded by President George Bush. Jones also campaigned for unsuccessful California Democratic Senatorial candidate Mel Levine, whose major television ads featured Jones's voice, speaking on his behalf.

Mississippi-born Jones has been a leading figure in the American theater since his starring role as African-American heavyweight champion Jack Jefferson (inspired by the real-life

Jack Johnson) in *The Great White Hope* (1968; on film 1970). A classical actor of enormous range, Jones is highly regarded for such roles as *Macbeth* (1962), *King Lear* (1973), Hickey in *The Iceman Cometh* (1973), *Othello* (1982), and his starring role in *Fences* (1988), for which he won a Tony. He was the voice of Darth Vader in *Star Wars* (1977), played Alex Haley in television's miniseries "Roots II" (1979), and played major roles in such films as *Gardens of Stone* (1987), *Field of Dreams* (1989), *The Hunt for Red October* (1990), and *Convicts* (1991). Jones's 1957 B.A. was from the University of Michigan. He married Cecilia Hart in 1982. He is the son of actor Robert Earl Jones.

FURTHER READING

"James Earl Jones." JOHN CLARK. *Premiere*, June 1992.

Jones, Quincy (Quincy Delight Jones, Jr.; 1933–)

Celebrated pop music figure Quincy Jones tried something new in 1992, founding the rap magazine *Vibe*, stating that "Rappers need a home for themselves," and criticizing such rock magazines as *Rolling Stone* for inadequately covering rap musicians.

During 1992, Jones also stressed the social service and political participation side of his life, functioning as chairman of the Permanent Charities Committee of the Entertainment Industries, until succeeded by Warren Beatty late in the year. He was also active on behalf of the Clinton-Gore Presidential ticket. As the year ended, he was organizing the "A Call for Reunion" Lincoln Memorial concert that was to be the climax of the Clinton-Gore Monticello-to-Washington bus procession on the Sunday before the Clinton inaugural.

On the personal side, Jones and his wife, Nastassja Kinski, were expecting the birth of her first and his seventh child.

Chicago-born Jones has had a long and varied career, which in four decades has included arranging and working as a trumpeter with Lionel Hampton and Dizzy Gillespie in the mid-1950s; as an arranger for many of the leading singers of the 1950s and 1960s; in the 1960s as music director and producer for Mercury Records; and as composer and conductor of many film scores.

From 1969, he was a prolific recording artist, with such albums as *Walking in Space* (1969), *Smackwater Jack* (1971), and *Mellow Madness* (1975). He was most notably producer of the Michael Jackson records *Off the Wall* (1980), *Thriller* (1982), and *Bad* (1987). His 1989 album *Back on the Block*, sold over a million copies and in 1991 brought him six Grammy awards, making him the most honored pop artist in the history of the awards, with a total of 25 Grammys during his long career. His documentary *Listen Up: The Lives of Quincy Jones* was widely distributed in 1990. Jones attended the Berkeley College of Music and the Boston Conservatory.

FURTHER READING

"The piano next door. . . ." *Economist*, July 20, 1991.
"On Q." DIANE K. SHAH. *New York Times Magazine*, Nov. 18, 1990.
"Quincy Jones." STEVE DOUGHERTY. *People*, Oct. 15, 1990.
"Story of Q." BRENDAN LEMON. *Interview*, Sep. 1990.
"Playboy interview. . . ." ALEX HALEY. *Playboy*, July 1990.
"Quincy Jones." ELIOT TIEGEL. *Stereo Review*, June 1990.
"After 40 years. . . ." ALDORE COLLIER. *Ebony*, Apr. 1990.
"Back on the block. . . ." ROBERT L. DOERSCHUK. *Interview*, Jan. 1990.
"Herbie & Quincy. . . ." JOSEF WOODARD. *Down Beat*, Jan. 1990.
Quincy Jones. RAYMOND HORRICKS. Hippocrene, 1986.

Jordan, Michael (1963–)

On the court, things could hardly have gone better for Michael Jordan in 1992. At the end of the 1991–92 season, his Chicago Bulls won a second consecutive National Basketball Association (NBA) championship, over the Portland Trailblazers. Jordan himself was named most valuable player for both the regular season and the playoffs; he was also NBA scoring leader for the 6th season in a row, with an average of 30.1 points per game, and continued to hold the all-time record for highest career scoring average, at 32.2 points per game. Not only that, but he was a key (if initially reluctant) player in the extraordinary ensemble of basketball stars called the "Dream Team," which went to Barcelona for the Summer Olympics and brought back the gold medal,

cern that, at the gold medal ceremony, Jordan would not appear in the team uniform, since it displayed the name of a rival sponsor; in the end, he and several other players draped American flags over the sponsor's name, as a compromise.

Jordan is one the leading basketball players of the late 1980s and early 1990s. He starred at the University of North Carolina, and was on the team that won the Olympic gold medal in 1984. That same year he turned professional, and immediately emerged as a star for the Bulls. He was rookie of the year in the 1984–85 season, the NBA's best defensive player in the 1987–88 season, scoring leader six times (1987–92), and most valuable player three times (1987–88; 1990–91; and 1991–92). Jordan and his wife Juanita have two sons.

FURTHER READING

"Michael Jordan." *Playboy*, May 1992.

The Jordan Rules: The Inside Story of a Turbulent Season with Michael Jordan and the Chicago Bulls. SAM SMITH. Simon & Schuster, 1992.

Taking to the Air: The Rise of Michael Jordan. JIM NAUGHTON. Warner, 1992.

Michael Jordan. BOB ITALIA. Abdo and Daughters, 1992.

Michael Jordan: Basketball Camp. BILL GUTMAN. Millbrook Press, 1992.

Michael Jordan: Basketball Skywalker. THOMAS R. RABER. Lerner, 1992.

Sports Great Michael Jordan. NATHAN AASENG. Enslow, 1992.

Michael Jordan. JACK CLARY. Smithmark, 1992.

"Ten living legends: . . . ." STEVE WULF. *Sports Illustrated*, Dec. 23, 1991.

"For all his fame. . . ." CURRY KIRKPATRICK. *Sports Illustrated*, Dec. 23, 1991.

"Michael Jordan. . . ." JACK MCCALLUM. *Sports Illustrated*, Dec. 23, 1991.

"In pursuit of. . . ." JEFF WEINSTOCK. *Sport*, Dec. 1991.

"Show of shows. . . . " JACK MCCALLUM. *Sports Illustrated*, June 10, 1991.

"Michael Jordan. . . ." *Jet*, Apr. 29, 1991.

"Michael Jordan. . . ." BRUCE SHLAIN. *Sport*, Jan. 1991.

"Air to the throne." GEORGE CASTLE. *Sport*, Jan. 1991.

Michael Jordan. Scholastic, 1991.

Michael Jordan: A Biography. BILL GUTMAN. Pocketbook, 1991.

Michael Jordan. JAMES R. ROTHAUS. Child's World, 1991.

"Michael Jordan, king of style." BRUCE SHLAIN. *Sport*, Jan. 1991.

though he seemed happy to lay back a bit, and let others take the limelight. If, as the 1992–93 regular season started, the Bulls were not quite so dominant, Jordan's play was not at fault, and with him leading the team, they were still given a strong chance for a third league title.

Off the court was a different matter. There were stories of high-stakes gambling, in which Jordan paid over $100,000 to settle golf and poker debts; though Jordan himself was not the target of a legal investigation, the tales somewhat tarnished his public image. There was also the highly critical view of Jordan given by *Chicago Tribune* columnist Sam Smith in *The Jordan Rules*, though that was balanced by an opposing view in *Hang Time: Days and Dreams With Michael Jordan*, by another *Trib* columnist, Bob Greene. There were also more general allegations of excessive commercialism, which led him into arguments with both the NBA and the U.S. Olympics over licensing rights for his image. At Barcelona, there was for a time con-

Jordan, Vernon Eulion, Jr. (1935–)

On November 6, 1992, Jordan, a leading African-American lawyer and civil rights leader, was named by President-elect Bill Clinton to chair the Clinton transition team, which was to be responsible for developing recommendations for the key posts in the new administration.

Jordan practiced law in Atlanta (1960–61), and then plunged into the heart of the civil rights struggle of the time as a Georgia field director of the National Association for the Advancement of Colored People (1961–63) and then as director of the Voter Education Project of the Southern Regional Council (1964–68). He was executive director of the United Negro College Fund (1970–71), and then became the highly visible president of the National Urban League, in that position stressing job creation, training, and the development of ties between the civil rights movement and the American corporate world. It was as Urban League president that he began to sit on many corporate boards. He then moved to Washington to become a partner of the firm of Akin, Gump, Strauss, Hauer & Feld, his current affiliation, becoming one of Washington's most influential and well-connected corporate lawyers. Jordan was shot and seriously wounded in May 1980, outside a Ft. Wayne, Indiana hotel, while with a White woman Urban League employee. A self proclaimed racist, who had been convicted of murdering two African-Americans he saw with White women was arrested and tried in the shooting, but was acquitted.

Jordan's 1957 B.A. was from DePauw University, and his 1960 J.D. from Howard University. His second wife is Ann Dibble Cook; he has one child.

FURTHER READING

"Mister inside." J.D. PODOLSKY. *People*, Nov. 23, 1992.
"Vernon E. Jordan heads. . . ." *Jet*, Nov. 23, 1992.

Joseph, Helen Pennell (1905–92)

A leading White figure in South Africa's freedom movement for more than four decades, Helen Joseph spent more than three of those decades in some form of government restraint, often under house arrest, sometimes on trial, and sometimes in jail. Joseph taught in India before emigrating to South Africa in 1931, served in the armed forces during World War II, became a social worker after the war, and as apartheid was imposed in the late 1940s became a very early opponent of the systematic discrimination that was, in the next four decades, to tear South African society apart. Joseph was a founder of the African National Congress-affiliated Congress of Democrats, and led mass demonstrations against the new apartheid laws in the late 1940s and 1950s. From the late 1950s, she was under banning orders, aimed at silencing her; they did not succeed. She was also tried for treason, and in 1961 acquitted; her acquittal did nothing, however, to stop government persecution. In the mid-1980s, still campaigning even after a bout with cancer and a heart attack, she was a founder of the United Democratic Front, one of the major organizations that ultimately forced the government to free Nelson Mandela and other jailed freedom movement leaders. Helen Joseph lived long enough to see the beginning of serious negotiations toward the end of apartheid and the development of a new multiracial South African society. Her 1927 college degree was from the University of London. There were no direct survivors. (d. Johannesburg; December 25, 1992)

FURTHER READING

Obituary. *The Times* (of London), Dec. 26, 1992.
Obituary. *The New York Times*, Dec. 26, 1992.

Joyner-Kersee, Jackie (Jacqueline Joyner-Kersee; 1962–)

At Barcelona, in the summer of 1992, Jackie Joyner-Kersee did what no woman had ever done before: she won a second consecutive Olympic gold medal in the grueling seven-event heptathlon, which includes the 100-meter hurdles, the high jump, the shotput, the 200 meters, the long jump, the javelin, and the 800 meter. Not only that, but—at age 30—she led after every event, in a performance that many regarded as the greatest of her career, even though her total of 7044 points was her sixth-best career finish and far short of her 1988 Olympic heptathlon record of 7291 points, which still stands. In doing so, she gave support to those who had for years been saying that she was by far the world's greatest woman athlete—and perhaps the greatest athlete in the world, woman or man.

Also at the 1992 Summer Olympics, Joyner-Kersee won an Olympic bronze medal in the long jump. Earlier, in March, she had broken her own women's indoor record for the long jump. And she did all this after recovering from ankle and hamstring injuries, and from being out of competition during 1991 after having pneumonia. In October 1992, she was honored by the Women's Sports Foundation as amateur sportswoman of the year. Joyner-Kersee was already looking ahead to Atlanta in 1996, and the possibility of "ending her career on American soil."

East St. Louis-born Joyner-Kersee's win at Barcelona was only the most recent in a long string of wins, beginning with her four successive national junior pentathlon championships, starting at the age of 14, and including a 1987 world championship and then a 1988 Olympic gold medal in the long jump, and a silver heptathlon medal at the 1984 Olympics. With six of the only seven over-7,000 point heptathlon performances in history, she will be recognized as a preeminent athlete for at least decades to come. Her 1985 B.A. was from the University of California at Los Angeles. She is married to UCLA track and field coach—and her own coach—Bobby Kersee.

FURTHER READING

"Bound for glory." NEIL LEIFER. *Newsweek*, July 6, 1992.

"Defending her reign." RICHARD FINN. *Sporting News*, June 29, 1992.

"Cosmo talks to: . . . ." RALPH GARDNER, JR. *Cosmopolitan*, June 1989.

"Jackie Joyner-Kersee. . . ." DAN CHU. *People*, Jan. 30, 1989.

"Woman of the Year. . . ." DAVE NIGHTINGALE. *Sporting News*, Jan. 2, 1989.

"Jackie Joyner-Kersee. . . ." *Jet*, Nov. 21, 1988.

"Joyner-Kersee honored. . . ." *Jet*, Nov. 7, 1988.

"Wonder woman. . . ." PAT JORDAN. *Life*, Oct. 1988.

"Go, Jackie, go." MICHELE KORT. *Ms.*, Oct. 1988.

"Bound for glory." ALICE GABRIEL. *Rolling Stone*, Sep. 22, 1988.

"Regal masters. . . ." TOM CALLAHAN. *Time*, Sep. 19, 1988.

"Ghetto goddess." RIC DOLPHIN. *Maclean's*, Sep. 12, 1988.

"Jackie Joyner-Kersee. . . ." SUSAN REED. *People*, Aug. 29, 1988.

"Worldbeater." JOE MORGENSTERN. *New York Times Magazine*, July 31, 1988.

Judd, Wynonna (1964–), and Naomi Judd (1948–)

Country music star Wynonna Judd pursued a joint career with her mother Naomi Judd, as The Judds, until late in 1991. Then Naomi Judd retired, having contracted a so-far incurable case of chronic hepatitis; the last of their many shared awards was a Grammy as best duo or group country performers for their single "Love Can Build a Bridge."

In 1992, Wynonna Judd went on her own, quickly emerging as a major country music star in her own right. In April, she issued her first solo album, *Wynonna Judd*. It was acclaimed by critics and audiences alike; by October, only seven months later, it had sold more than 2 million copies, and Judd had issued several hit singles drawn from the album, including "She Is His Only Need," "I Saw the Light," and "My Strongest Weakness." She spent much of the rest of the year on a 110-city concert tour to promote the album, appearing before soldout houses throughout the country. At year's end, her voice appeared on the soundtrack of the Steve Martin-Deborah Winger film *Leap of Faith*, singing "Stone's Throw From Hurtin'," written by Elton John and Bernie Taupin. In 1992, she was honored by her peers for the first time on her own, with a Best Country Female Artist Billboard Music Video Award nomination for "No One Else on Earth." Judd's "I Saw the Light" was named Billboard's Number One country single of the year.

Naomi Judd was still in high school when Wynonna Judd was born. In 1984, after several moves that included a divorce, Naomi and Wynonna, as The Judds, began their joint recording career, with the album *The Judds—Wynonna and Naomi*. They very quickly emerged as country music stars, with a series of top-of-the-charts singles, and such number one albums as *Why Not Me* (1984), *Rockin' With the Rhythm* (1985), and *Heartland* (1987). Their many honors included four Grammys (1985, 1986, 1987, 1989), four Academy of Country Music Awards (1984, 1985, 1986, 1989), two Country Music Association Awards (1988, 1989), and a wide range of other awards. The Judds had a cross-country farewell tour in 1991 before Naomi retired—though not entirely, for she wrote an autobiography, *Love Can Build a Bridge*, published in November 1992.

FURTHER READING

" 'My toughest moment.'. . ." GLENN PLASKIN. *Ladies Home Journal*, Nov. 1992.
"Here comes the Judd." JAMES HUNTER. *US*, Oct. 1992.
"One for the road." STEVE DOUGHERTY and JANE SANDERSON. *People*, Dec. 9, 1991.
"The Judds." MARY MURPHY. *TV Guide*, Nov. 30, 1991.
"The Judds: . . . ." BOB ALLEN. *Country Music*, Nov.–Dec. 1991.
"The Judds' farewell song." KATHRYN CASEY. *Ladies Home Journal*, Nov. 1991.
"Making Music City listen." BOB MILLARD. *Country Music*, Sep.–Oct. 1989.
"The Judds' family ties." HOLLY GLEASON. *Ladies Home Journal*, Nov. 1988.
"Here come the Judds!" NANCY ANDERSON. *Good Housekeeping*. June 1988.
Behind Closed Doors: Talking with the Legends of Country Music. ALANNA NASH. Knopf, 1988.

Kang Keqing (1911–92) Born at Wan'am, Jiangsi, Kang was a lifelong revolutionary. She joined the Communist Youth League in 1927, and a year later joined the forces led by Zhu De in the Chingkang Mountains of western Jiangsi. She was a frontline fighter, a member of the Communist army during their historic Long March, the retreat from Jiangsi north to Yenan. She was also the fourth wife of Zhu De, who went on to head the Communist armies throughout the long anti-Japanese and civil wars. After Communist victory in 1949, Kang focused on women's organizations and social welfare work, largely through the All-China Women's Federation. Although she held many high positions, and was from 1977 to 1985 a Central Committee member, she was never a power-wielder in China; nor was she involved with any of the groups that struggled for power after the death of Mao. No information on survivors was available. (d. Apr. 22, 1992)

FURTHER READING

Obituary. *The Times* (of London), May 4, 1992.
Obituary. *New York Times*, Apr. 23, 1992.

Kantor, Mickey (1939–) President Bill Clinton's incoming United States Trade Representative is a veteran political campaigner and Los Angeles lawyer, who brings little international trade experience to his new job, but a great deal of political and negotiating experience.

Early in his legal career, Kantor was committed to representing those on the underside of American society. In 1967, he and Valerie Kantor, then his wife, founded the federally-funded South Florida Migrant Labor Services organization, and during the Carter years he served on the board of directors of the Legal Services Corporation, there meeting and becoming a friend of Hillary Rodham Clinton.

In 1975, Kantor became a partner in the Los Angeles law firm of Manatt, Phelps, Phillips, and Kantor, and in the years that followed became a leading California lawyer, with a strong corporate practice, also becoming active in California Democratic politics. He was a key aide to California Governor Jerry Brown in several campaigns, breaking with Brown during the 1992 presidential campaign.

Kantor was chairman of the Clinton/Gore presidential campaign; but considerable abrasion developed between Kantor and many others in the working campaign organization. He had been thought a logical candidate for the White House Chief of Staff job or some other major position in the new administration, and the trade representative's position, though an important one, was rather less than had been expected for him earlier in the year.

Kantor's 1961 B.A. was from Vanderbilt University, and his 1967 LL.B. from Georgetown University. He was a U.S. Navy officer from 1961 to 1965. He is married to Heidi Schulman; they have three children.

FURTHER READING

"FOB story." MICKEY KAUS. *New Republic*, Dec. 28, 1992.

Kaufman, Irving Robert (1910–92)

New York City-born Kaufman began his practice of law after his 1931 graduation from Fordham Law School. He was appointed to the federal bench by President Harry Truman in 1949, and to the U.S. Court of Appeals by President John F. Kennedy in 1961, became chief judge of the Second Circuit in 1973, was retired from that post in 1980, and stayed on as a judge until 1987. He was best known by far, and throughout the world, as the judge who on April 5, 1951 condemned Ethel Greenglass Rosenberg and Julius Rosenberg to death, after they had been convicted of espionage for the Soviet Union, at the height of the anti-communist hysteria of McCarthy period. The executions were carried out at Sing Sing Prison, on June 19, 1953, after a worldwide appeal for clemency had failed; the Rosenbergs were the first Americans to be executed in peacetime for espionage. Kaufman later presided over several other major cases, including several First Amendment cases, and also including the 1960 trial of alleged Mafia leaders after the Appalachin meeting, whose convictions were overturned on appeal. He was survived by his wife, the former Helen Rosenberg, and a son. (d. New York City; February 1, 1992)

FURTHER READING

Obituary. *The Times* (of London), Feb. 6, 1992.
Obituary. *New York Times*, Feb. 6, 1992.
Obituary. *Independent*, Feb. 5, 1992.
"Irving Kaufman" SIDNEY HOOK. *American Spectator*, Jan. 1989.

Kaysone, Phomvihane (1920–92)

Laotian Communist and nationalist leader Kaysone was recruited into the Vietnamese communist movement by Ho Chi Minh in the mid-1930s, while studying law at Hanoi University. He fought with North Vietnamese (Viet Minh) forces in the late 1940s, and then led Pathet Lao forces (1950–73), becoming defence minister in 1950 and commander in chief in 1955, also in 1955 becoming general secretary of the Lao Revolutionary Party (Communist Party). He led the Pathet Lao throughout the balance of the long civil war which, after the end of the brief 1960–62 period of peace in Laos, merged with the developing Vietnam War. After American withdrawal from Vietnam in 1973, Pathet Lao victory was assured, and Kaysone's forces took power in 1975, destroying the coalition government and ending the monarchy. Kaysone became prime minister and Communist dictator of Laos. In recent years, with the dissolution of the Soviet Union and freedom of Eastern Europe, Kaysone released many political prisoners, encouraged some private economic initiative, and invited foreign investment in Laos. Little information was available on his personal life, beyond that he was married. (d. Vientiane, Laos; November 21, 1992)

FURTHER READING

Obituary. *The Times* (of London), Nov. 23, 1992.
Obituary. *The New York Times*, Nov. 22, 1992.

Keating, Charles Humphrey, III

(1923–) Convicted of 17 state charges of securities fraud by a California jury on December 3, 1991, Keating was sentenced to a maximum 10-year prison term in April 1992. In July, a Tucson, Arizona federal jury awarded $3.3 billion in damage claims against Keating and $5 billion more against three co-defendants. A federal judge later substantially reduced the judgments, to approximately $1.9 billion against Keating and his co-defendants. Keating and four associates had also been indicted on a 77-count set of federal charges in December 1991, with trials still pending. In May 1992, a Keating son-in-law agreed to cooperate with federal prosecutors in the multiple federal and state investigation stemming from the Lincoln Savings and Loan Association case.

Keating emerged as a corporate takeover figure in the late 1970s, as executive vice president of the Cincinnati-based American Financial Corporation. He bought control of the Lincoln Savings Bank, in Irvine, California in 1984 for $51 million and began the process of building it into a $6 billion bank, heavily invested in junk bonds and heavily committed to what turned out to be very weak real estate loans, many of them to American Continental Corporation. Faced with opposition from the Federal Home Loan Bank Board, Keating engaged in a long-running battle with regulators, which included substantial contributions to many key Washington and state politicians, and set the stage for the investigations of five senators, known as the "Keating Five." Lincoln was taken over by federal bank regulators on April 14, 1990, as the national savings and loan crisis developed; the cost of the government bailout was estimated to be well over $2 billion. Keating was from the early 1970s also a substantial Cincinnati-based antipornography contributor; he founded an antipornography organization in the 1950s, and was a member of the 1969–70 Presidential Commission on Obscenity and Pornography.

Keating attended the University of Cincinnati and was a star swimmer, becoming 1946 national collegiate breast stroke champion. He married Mary Elaine Fette in 1941; they have six children.

FURTHER READING

"Profit without honor." JOE MORGENSTERN. *Playboy*, Apr. 1992.

"Mr. S & L. . . ." KATHLEEN KERWIN. *Business Week*, Nov. 25, 1991.

"The great banks robbery. . . ." JAMES K. GLASSMAN. *New Republic*, Oct. 8, 1990.

"Dirty bookkeeping. . . ." DAVID CORN. *New Republic*, Apr. 2, 1990.

"Money talks. . . ." MARGARET CARLSON. *Time*, Apr. 9, 1990.

"The man who shot. . . ." PHIL GARLINGTON. *California*, Mar. 1990.

"Seven sorry senators. . . ." MARGARET CARLSON. *Time*, Jan. 8, 1990.

The Greatest-Ever Bank Robbery: The Collapse of the Savings and Loan Industry. MARTIN MAYER. Macmillan, 1990.

Keating, Paul John (1944–) In his first full year in office, Australian Prime Minister Paul Keating faced the full impact of a massive and deepening worldwide recession, which hit Australia, a trading nation, especially hard. As federal Treasurer (1983–91), he had taken a very conservative anti-inflation, high-interest position. As candidate for Labor Party leadership, he had reversed course, calling for strong stimulative measures to combat the recession. As Prime Minister, he made a year-long series of stimulative moves, beginning with interest rate cuts in early January. His economic program included a wide range of public works, including a coast to coast Brisbane-to-Perth railway, a family allowance bonus, and many business and personal tax breaks, and was supplemented in May by additional proposals, including merger of two federally owned airlines. He also again and again throughout the year criticized international barriers to Australian exports, especially in the European Community and the United States.

On the direct political side, Keating was badly hurt when government minister, Graham Richardson, was forced to resign after a political scandal. With a worsening recession, which his economic reforms had not seriously dented, his popularity went into considerable decline, with a reversal needed if he was to survive the upcoming 1993 elections.

Sydney-born Keating began his long career in the Australian Labor Party while still in his teens, joining the party at the age of 15 and becoming president of the New South Wales youth council in 1966. He was elected to the federal House of Representatives in 1969, and was Minister for Northern Australia briefly in late 1975. With his party out of power, he became its spokesperson successively on agricultural, minerals and energy, and treasury matters (1975–83). He moved up in the party as well, becoming chairman of the New South Wales Labor Party (1979–83). With Labor victory in 1983, he became federal Treasurer, and Bob Hawke's heir-apparent, becoming Hawke's Deputy Prime Minister in April 1990. But Keating challenged Hawke for the Labor Party leadership in May 1991, and lost, in June resigning as Treasurer. He was not long out of power, though. In the factional fighting that followed, and in the context of a severely depressed Australian economy, Hawke lost support, resigned in December, and was succeeded by Keating. Keating attended Sydney's De La Salle College. He is married to the former Anita van Iersel, and has four children.

FURTHER READING

"Upsets down under. . . ." SCOTT STEELE. *Maclean's*, June 15, 1992.
"Keating, Paul." *Current Biography*, May 1992.
"Australia: when friends desert." *Economist*, Dec. 14, 1991.

Keaton, Diane (1946–) After the huge and rather unexpected commercial success of Charles Shyer's 1991 remake of Vincente Minnelli's *Father of the Bride* (1950), with Keaton as the mother in the Joan Bennett role, Touchstone Pictures in early 1992 announced a forthcoming remake of its sequel, *Father's Little Dividend*. Keaton will again star opposite Steve Martin as the father in the Spencer Tracy role, with Kimberly Williams again in the Elizabeth Taylor role as the bride.

In 1992, Keaton made her television film debut in the comedy *Running Mates*, as the reluctant-to-campaign, fish-out-of-water recent wife of a presidential candidate, played by Ed Harris. Forthcoming was a starring role in Woody Allen's film *Manhattan Murder Mystery*, opposite Allen, Anjelica Huston, and Martin Landau, in a role reportedly originally set for Mia Farrow, whose personal and professional relationship with Allen ended abruptly and very publicly in 1992.

California-born Keaton made the transition from the New York theater to Hollywood in Woody Allen's *Play It Again Sam*, starring opposite Allen on Broadway in 1971 and again in the 1972 film version. She was Michael Corleone's wife in the classic *Godfather* films (1972, 1974), won a Best Actress Oscar for Allen's *Annie Hall* (1977), and also starred in his *Interiors*

(1978) and *Manhattan* (1979). She went on to star in such films as *Reds* (1981), *The Little Drummer Girl* (1984), *Crimes of the Heart* (1986), *Radio Days* (1987), *The Godfather Part III* (1990) reprising her Kay Corleone role, and *The Lemon Sisters* (1990). In 1991, she directed *Wildflower*, her first full-length television film. She was a student at New York's Neighborhood Playhouse in 1968.

FURTHER READING

"Diane in La-La Land." PATRICK PACHECO. *Connoisseur*, Jan. 1992.
Diane Keaton: The Story of the Real Annie Hall. JONATHAN MOOR. St. Martin's, 1989.

Keaton, Michael (Michael Douglas; 1951–) For Keaton, it was another "Batman" year. In mid-June, he starred once again in the title role in the summer 1992 blockbuster film *Batman Returns*, which went on to become a worldwide commercial hit, though somewhat less than the original *Batman*, which was the top-grossing film of 1989, ultimately grossing over $400 million worldwide and selling a reported 13 million videocassettes. Tim Burton once again directed; Keaton's co-stars included Michelle Pfeiffer as the Catwoman (in a role originally set for Annette Bening), Danny DeVito as the Penguin, Christopher Walken, Michael Gough, Pat Hingle, and Michael Murphy.

Forthcoming was a considerable change of pace—a starring role as Dogberry in Kenneth Branagh's forthcoming film version of William Shakespeare's *Much Ado About Nothing*; co-starring are Branagh as Benedick; Emma Thompson as Beatrice, and Denzel Washington as Don Pedro.

Pittsburgh-born Keaton began his career as a comedian with the Los Angeles Second City group, appeared in television from the mid-1970s, and played in such films as *Night Shift* (1982), *Mr. Mom* (1983), and *Touch and Go* (1987). He emerged as a star in the film drama *Clean and Sober* (1988), and in the title role of *Batman* (1989), followed by *The Dream Team* (1989) and *One Good Cop* (1991). Keaton attended Kent State University. He married Caroline McWilliams in 1982; they have one child.

FURTHER READING

"Michael Keaton." *Playboy*, July 1992.
"Masked man. . . ." TRIP GABRIEL. *Entertainment*, June 19, 1992.
"Michael Keaton. . . ." DIGBY DIEHL. *Cosmopolitan*, Nov. 1991.
"Batman and the new world order." CAROL CALDWELL. *Esquire*, June 1991.
"Batguy." TERRI MINSKY. *Premiere*, July 1989.

Keillor, Garrison (1942–) Midwestern folk humorist and radio personality Keillor went home to Minnesota in late 1992. Ending his long-running "Prairie Home Companion" show in 1987, he had moved to New York City, from there broadcasting his widely syndicated "American Radio Company" syndicated show, which was very well received by his audiences. But cut off from his roots, he seemed unhappy; in October 1992, he took the "American Radio Company" show back to St. Paul, Minnesota, making it his broadcasting base once again.

During early 1992, Keillor toured, promoting his first novel, *WLT: A Radio Romance* (1991). He also continued to record in audio, making the two-cassette *Stories* tapes, reading a miscellaneous group of his own stories going back to 1976. He also issued the music record *Garrison Keillor and the Hopeful Gospel Quartet*.

Minnesota-born Keillor was creator, writer, and announcer of the enormously popular radio show "A Prairie Home Companion," which he hosted for 13 years (1974–87). After moving

briefly to Denmark, Keillor settled in New York City, there originating his "American Radio Company" show. His written works include *Happy to Be Here* (1982); *Lake Wobegon Days* (1985), which in its audio form received a 1987 Grammy for best non-musical recording; *Leaving Home* (1987); and *We Are Still Married* (1989). Keillor's B.A. was from the University of Minnesota in 1966. He married Ulla Skaeverd in 1985; he has one son and three stepchildren.

FURTHER READING

"The Hicksville boy. . . ." LESLEY WHITE. *Sunday Times*. Oct. 4, 1992.
"Garrison Keillor. . . ." PAUL ALEXANDER. *M Inc.*, Oct. 1991.
"Still mad." CHUCK BENDA. *MPLS-St. Paul*, Jan. 1991.
Garrison Keillor: A Voice of America. JUDITH Y. LEE. University Press of Mississippi, 1991.

Kelly, Petra (1947–92) and Gerd Bastian (1923–92) On October 19, 1992, the body of Petra Kelly, a founder of Germany's Green Party and a worldwide figure in the environmental movement, was found in her home at Bonn, Germany. She had been shot through the head. Also found was the body of her companion, former Major General Gerd Bastian, who had also been shot dead. The next day, October 20, the German police announced that she had been killed by Bastian, and that he had then committed suicide. Many of those close to Kelly and Bastian expressed extreme skepticism as to the police conclusion, pointing out that there had been no previous evidence of suicidal tendencies on the part of either, and that at the time of the police announcement autopsies had not even been concluded; nor had there been time to sift the mass of physical evidence adduced by any serious inquiry, much less enquire into related matters.

Born in Bavaria, Petra Kelly moved to the United States with her mother at the age of 13. In the 1960s, she became active in the anti-Vietnam War movement and an advocate of nonviolence, also working in the office of Senator Hubert Humphrey for two years. She later returned to Germany, and in 1979 cofounded the Green Party, quickly becoming a worldwide Green Movement leader, who campaigned on a wide range of social issues. Gerd Bastian was forced to resign from the German armed forces in 1980, after criticizing the deployment of new U.S. nuclear missiles in Europe. Kelly and Bastian served as Green Party representatives in the West German parliament (1983–90). Kelly had published several works, including *Fighting for Hope* (1984) and *Nonviolence Speaks to Power* (1992); Bastian wrote *Generals for Peace and Disarmament* (1984). At the time of their deaths, they were both leading antifascists, who actively opposed the new rise of Nazism in Germany, and likened the modern Nazi persecution of foreigners to the 1930s persecution of Germany's Jews, in what became the Holocaust.

FURTHER READING

"The death roll." *Maclean's*, Dec. 21, 1992.
" 'The Greens. . . .' " RUSSELL WATSON. *Newsweek*, Nov. 2, 1992.
"Petra: suicide—or murder?" TONY CATTERALL. *Observer*, Oct. 25, 1992.
"What killed Petra Kelly?" ISABEL HILTON. *Independent*, Oct. 24, 1992.
Obituary. *The Times* (of London), Oct. 21, 1992.
Obituary. *New York Times*, Oct. 21, 1992.

Kelly, Sharon Pratt Dixon (1944–)

In 1991, Washington, D.C. mayor Kelly became the first elected African-American woman mayor of a major city. She was elected in 1990 as Sharon Pratt Dixon, and changed her name to Kelly after her December 1990 marriage to James R. Kelly, 3rd. Succeeding Marion Barry, who had not run for re-election after his 1990 conviction on cocaine-posession charges, she won by a landslide 86 percent of the vote, and was widely expected to be the new broom that would sweep a corrupt administration clean and lead her city to long-overdue statehood.

But during her first two years in office, it did not quite work out that way; in spite of greater funding from Congress, she faced all the recession-related and federal neglect problems faced by other big city mayors, and was forced to cut into such central programs as drug treatment and education, areas in which her main electoral promises had been made. Nor did she make a full transition from the Barry Administration, moving far too slowly to replace Barry appointees who had left office and even leaving many Barry appointees in place. Late in 1992,

she even found Barry on the political scene again; having finished his jail term, he won election to the city council, and emerged as a renewed power in city politics. During 1992, Kelly also faced an embarrassing recall movement, as many became disenchanted with her limited progress in solving her city's many problems.

With the November 1992 election of Bill Clinton and Al Gore, Kelly faced what could become an entirely new situation, for Clinton had repeatedly stated his support for District of Columbia statehood. How that central issue would fare in the new Congress remained to be seen.

A third-generation Washingtonian, Dixon graduated from Howard University Law School in 1968. Three years later, after bearing two children, she joined her father's general practice law firm. In 1972 she began teaching public interest law at the innovative Antioch Law School in Washington. From 1976 she worked at the Potomac Electric Power company as a corporate lawyer, becoming vice president for consumer affairs. While still at PEPCO, she was elected D.C.'s delegate to the Democratic National Committee in 1977, and in 1984 became the first Black and first woman to be treasurer of the Democratic National Committee. Now married to James R. Kelly, III, she was formerly married to Arrington L. Dixon, chairman of the D.C. Council under ex-mayor Marion Barry. They had two daughters.

FURTHER READING

"Trust me." HARRY JAFFE et al. *Washingtonian*, May 1991.
"Sharon Dixon. . . ." GLORIA BORGER. *U.S. News & World Report*, Dec. 31, 1990.

Kemeny, John George (1926–92)

Budapest-born Kemeny, a distinguished American computer scientist, mathematician, and educator, emigrated from Hungary to the United States with his family in 1940. While in the Army, he was an assistant in the theoretical division of the Los Alamos atom bomb project (1945–46). His 1947 B.A. was from Princeton University, as was his 1949 Ph.D. in mathematics. He was a research assistant to Albert Einstein at Princeton's Insitute For Advanced Study (1948–49). Kemeny went on to a long career in education; he became a full professor of mathematics at Dartmouth in 1953, and was head of the Dartmouth mathematics department (1953–67), then president of the college (1970–81), returning to teaching until 1990. As president, he became a strong voice for interracial and intercultural understanding at the college, which was itself a focus of conservative-liberal antagonisms during much of his tenure.

Kemeny was widely known as a co-inventor of the BASIC computer language, the most used of all the early computer languages and central to the development of much of the computer software that followed. He also published numerous works, including *Philosopher Looks at Science* (1959), *The Accident at Three Mile Island: The Need for Change, the Legacy of TMI* (1980; as editor), *Back to BASIC: The History, Corruption, and Future of the Language* (1985), and numerous works on mathematics and computers. He was survived by his wife, the former Jean Alexander, a daughter, and a son. (d. Lebanon, New Hampshire; December 26, 1992)

FURTHER READING

Obituary. *The Times* (of London), Jan. 6, 1993.
Obituary. *New York Times*, Dec. 27, 1992.

Kemp, Jack French (1935–) Outgoing Secretary of Housing and Urban Development Kemp spent much of his final year in office positioning himself for a probable 1996 presidential candidacy. Indeed, there was little else to do, for no major new housing or urban development programs were funded by Congress, his buy-and-own proposals for existing urban rental housing made little progress, and his proposed tax-cutting plank for the 1992 Republican platform did not become a major initiative. Kemp emerged briefly as chief administration spokesperson on urban problems in early May, after the Los Angeles riots, but remained an outsider in the Bush years. He did continue to deplore the condition of America's inner cities throughout the year, and continued to do so in his well-received speech in support of George Bush at the Republican National Convention, but little practical help for the inner cities was accomplished.

California-born Kemp is a former star football player, who moved into politics after a 13-year professional football career, and was a Republican Congressman from western New York

(1971–89). He made an unsuccessful run for his party's 1988 presidential nomination and became a member of the Bush cabinet in 1989. He spent much of 1989 and 1990 on internal department cleanup matters, as the full size and scope of the huge HUD scandals emerged, though he was able to help develop the modest 1990 housing bill. Kemp's 1957 B.A. was from Occidental College. He is married to the former Joanne Main; they have four children.

FURTHER READING

"Kemp vs. Dole." FRED BARNES. *New Republic*, Dec. 14, 1992.
"An enterprising war on poverty." *New Perspectives*, Summer 1991.
"Party politics." GLORIA BORGER. *U.S. News & World Report*, Dec. 24, 1990.
"Bleeding-heart conservative. . . ." ROBERT KUTTNER. *New Republic*, June 11, 1990.
"Sure, he'd rather be president. . . ." JAMES S. KUNEN. *People*, June 18, 1990.
"Prince of poverty." FRED BARNES. *New Republic*, Oct. 8, 1990.

Kendal, Laura (Laura Liddell; 1908–92) A touring Shakespearean actress throughout her career, Laura Liddell Kendal was made famous in James Ivory's 1965 film *Shakespeare Wallah*, the story of the touring Shakespearean troupe she and her husband took throughout post-independence India, often in near-impossible conditions. Laura Liddell and Geoffrey Kendal married in 1933, and from then on always worked together, comanaging their touring troupe throughout Britain and Ireland, and then taking it to India and southeast and east Asia, staying on in India after independence. Their daughters, the actresses Felicity Kendal and Jennifer Kendal, grew up on tour, apprenticed to the theater with them, and later emerged as leading figures, Jennifer in India and Felicity in Britain. Laura Kendal was survived by her husband Geoffrey and her daughter Felicity. Jennifer Kendal died in 1984. (d. February 5, 1992)

FURTHER READING

Obituary. *The Times* (of London), Feb. 8, 1992.

Kendricks, Eddie (1939–92) Birmingham-born Kendricks and his high school friend and singing partner Paul Williams moved to Detroit at the age of 17, there forming The Primes. In

1960, they merged with The Distants; the resulting group signed with Berry Gordy's Motown in 1961, and became The Temptations. The group became popular in 1964, with "The Way You Do the Things You Do," which they followed with the 1965 smash hit "My Girl." In the six years that followed they continued to be a very popular group, with such hits as "It's Growing," "Since I Lost My Head," "It's Raining," and "Just My Imagination." Kendricks began a solo career in 1971, and scored major successes with "Keep on Truckin" (1973) and "Boogie Down" (1974). Kendricks returned to The Temptations for a reunion album and tour in 1982, and then toured and recorded during the 1980s with former Temptations star David Ruffin, who died in 1991. Kendricks was survived by his parents, a sister, and three brothers. (d. Birmingham, Alabama; October 5, 1992)

FURTHER READING

Obituary. *Rolling Stone*, Nov 26, 1992.
"Singer Eddie Kendricks. . . ." *Jet*, Oct. 26, 1992.
Obituary. *Billboard*, Oct. 17, 1992.
Obituary. *Variety*, Oct. 12, 1992.
Obituary. *The Times* (of London), Oct. 7, 1992.
Obituary. *New York Times*, Oct. 7, 1992.

Kennedy, Anthony McLeod (1936–)

Justice Kennedy, earlier viewed mainly as a conservative member of a very conservative Court, emerged during the 1991–92 term, with Justices O'Connor and Souter, as part of a new Court center. That became quite clear with the joint O'Connor-Kennedy-Souter majority opinion in the landmark abortion rights case, *Planned Parenthood of Southeastern Pennsylvania v. Casey*, in which a slim 5–4 majority upheld the essence of *Roe v. Wade* (which in 1972 had established the right of a woman to choose to have an abortion) while at the same time upholding most of the restrictive 1989 Pennsylvania abortion law and giving the states broader powers to restrict abortion. Kennedy also joined all of his colleagues in a rare, unanimous landmark sexual harassment decision; in *Franklin v. Gwinnett County Public Schools*, the Court unanimously ruled that Title IX of the 1972 education act allowed a sexually harassed student to collect damages from a school district, where a teacher-coach had sexually harassed Christine Franklin

and ultimately succeeded in pressing her to have sexual intercourse with him.

Kennedy wrote the majority opinions in *Lee v. Weisman*, barring nonsectarian or any other prayers at public high school graduations; and in *Freeman v. Pitts*, ruling that schools being operated under court-supervised desegregation orders could be released from those orders step by step. He also voted with the majority in a wide range of cases, including *Georgia v. McCollum*, ruling that criminal case defendants could not bar prospective jurors solely because of their race; *Nordlinger v. Hahn*, upholding the right of California to enact Proposition 13, with its unequal property taxes on newcomers; *Hudson v. McMillian*, ruling that the excessive use of force by prison guards was an Eighth Amendment violation even if the prisoner was not seriously hurt; *Riggins v. Nevada*, ruling that the state could not force an insane criminal defendant to take medication during a trial; *U.S. v. Fordice*, ruling that Mississippi had not fulfilled its obligation to desegregate its public colleges and universities; *Lujan v. Defenders of Wildlife*, ruling that the plaintiff, an environmental organization, had no standing to bring suit because no determinable specific interest was at issue; *U.S. v. Alvarez Machain*, upholding the 1990 U.S. kidnapping of a Mexican doctor suspected of a role in the torture of a U.S. drug enforcement agent; *Lechmere Inc. v. National Labor Relations Board*, ruling that companies did not have to allow union organizers access to such company-owned lands as parking lots and shopping malls; *New York v. U.S.*, which invalidated a federal law forcing states to handle their own radioactive waste; and *International Society for Krishna Consciousness v. Lee*, ruling that airports could ban groups from soliciting money. Kennedy also joined the majority in ruling that the Coast Guard could continue to intercept at sea and return Haitian refugees to Haiti; and in the decision barring return of RU-486 pills to Leona Benten, a pregnant woman who tried to import them into the U.S. for her personal use, in a challenge to their ban.

California-born Kennedy was appointed to the Sacramento-based 9th Circuit U.S. Court of Appeals in 1975; he had been recommended for the post by then-California governor Ronald Reagan. Thirteen years later, in 1988, President Reagan appointed him to the Supreme Court, after his nomination of Robert Bork was rejected by the Senate. Kennedy's 1958 B.A. was from

Stanford, his 1961 LL.B. from Harvard. He is married to Mary Davis; they have three children.

FURTHER READING

Anthony Kennedy. BOB ITALIA. Abdo and Daughters, 1992.
Turning Right: The Making of the Rehnquist Supreme Court. DAVID G. SAVAGE. Wiley, 1992.
"A new day in court." LAUREN TARSHIS and JAMES EARL HARDY. *Scholastic Update,* Nov. 1, 1991.
Reshaping the Supreme Court: New Justices, New Directions. ANNE B. RIERDEN. Watts, 1988.
Packing the Courts: The Conservatives' Campaign to Rewrite the Constitution. HERMAN SCHWARTZ. Macmillan, 1988.
"Kennedy, Anthony McLeod." *Current Biography,* July 1988.

Kennedy, Ted (Edward Moore Kennedy; 1932–)

During 1992, Senator Kennedy's personal problems greatly receded, and he was far more freely able to "fight the good fight," as he put his role in his self-critical October 1991 Harvard University speech. For Kennedy, that meant emerging once again as a leading liberal voice in the Senate; in January, he called for the use of money saved on military spending for pressing educational and social needs, the so-called "peace dividend." As chairman of the Senate Labor and Human Resources Committee, it also meant pressing for a comprehensive education bill, health care reforms, the 1990 Civil Rights Act, abortion rights, and all the other items on the Democratic liberal agenda. Little legislation resulted, in a year dominated by the "gridlock" between a Republican President and Democratic Congress, but Kennedy's regained voice was a considerable Democratic Party asset, and one used on behalf of Governor Bill Clinton at the July Democratic National Convention. Kennedy himself was not up for reelection in 1992, his term running until 1994. In March, during the controversy over the Oliver Stone film *JFK,* he backed full release of all government files bearing on his brother's 1963 assassination.

On the personal side, Ted Kennedy and Washington lawyer Victoria Reggie married on July 3, 1992.

Boston-born Kennedy is the fourth son of Joseph and Rose Fitgerald Kennedy, and the brother of President John Fitzgerald Kennedy, assassinated in 1963, and Senator Robert Francis Kennedy, assassinated while a presidential candidate in 1968. He has represented Massachusetts in the Senate since 1963. He probably would have been his party's presidential candidate in 1972 and in later elections, as well, but for the Chappaquidick incident of 1969, in which he left the scene of a fatal accident. Kennedy's B.A. was from Harvard, in 1956, his LL.B. from the University of Virginia, in 1959. He was formerly married to Virginia Joan Bennett, and has a daughter and two sons; Ms. Reggie has a daughter and a son.

FURTHER READING

"Tales of Ted." SHARON ISAAK. *Entertainment,* Oct. 30, 1992.
"Time to marry?" TOM GLIATTO. *People,* Mar. 30, 1992.
"The K-list. . . ." DEBRA WISE. *Mademoiselle,* Feb. 1992.
"Sobering times." EVAN THOMAS and MARK STARR. *Newsweek,* Dec. 9, 1991.
"The two faces of Ted." LESTER DAVID. *Ladies Home Journal,* Sep. 1991.
"The end of the line. . . ." ELIZABETH KAYE. *Esquire,* Aug. 1991.
"The end of the dream. . . ." JAMES CARROLL. *New Republic,* June 24, 1991.
"A question of survival. . . ." GLORIA BORGER and MISSY DANIEL. *U.S. News & World Report,* May 27, 1991.
"Boys' night out in. . . ." MICHELLE GREEN. *People,* Apr. 22, 1991.
"Ted Kennedy. . . ." MICHAEL KELLY. *GQ— Gentlemen's Quarterly,* Feb. 1990
Chappaquiddick Revealed. KENNETH R. KAPPEL and JOHN H. DAVIS. Shapolsky, 1989.
Senatorial Privilege: The Chappaquiddick Coverup. LEO DAMORE. Regnery, 1988.

Kennedy, William Joseph (1928–)

One of the literary events of 1992 was publication of *Very Old Bones,* another in William Kennedy's cycle of "Albany" novels and the third in the "Phelan" subgroup of Albany novels. In this work, Kennedy takes as his setting most of one day, a Saturday in July 1958, and in that day has Orson Phelan, born in the mid-1930s, cast back to the 1930s of his father's generation, re-examining many of the same people and events that had figured in *Ironweed.* Orson is the nephew of Francis Phelan, the central figure in

Ironweed. The "very old bones" examined here are pieces of family history, back as far the late 1880s; the men in Phelan's family are plagued by the alcoholism and madness Kennedy seems to see as an inescapable part of their family heritage, combined with a concept of Celtic mysticism shared by some Irish and Irish-American writers. Some have compared Kennedy's choices of subjects to those of Eugene O'Neill and his language and sensibility to that of James Joyce; others have questioned what they see as a false equation of alcoholism with the Irish-American heritage.

Albany-born Kennedy began his writing career as a journalist, starting with his first job after graduating from Siena College in 1949, as a sports editor for the *Glens Falls Post Star* (1949–50). He then worked as a reporter for the *Albany Times Union* (1952–56), for several newspapers in Puerto Rico until 1961, and then back at the *Times Union* (1963–70). He is best known for the "Albany" novels *Legs* (1975), *Billy Phelan's Greatest Game* (1978), and his Pulitzer Prize-winning *Ironweed*, all following the fortunes of the Phelan family in 1930s Albany. Meryl Streep and Jack Nicholson starred in Kennedy's adaptation of *Ironweed* into the 1987 film, directed by Hector Babenco. Kennedy also co-wrote, with Francis Ford Coppola, the screenplay of *The Cotton Club* (1984), as well as several other novels and stories. Kennedy has taught English at the Albany campus of the State University of New York since 1974. He is married to the former Ana Segarra, and has three children.

FURTHER READING

"In his new novel, ..." JAMES ATLAS. *Vogue*, May 1992.
Understanding William Kennedy. J.K. VAN DOVER. University of South Carolina Press, 1991.
"The responsibility of. . . ." KIM HERON. *New York Times Book Review*, May 22, 1988.

Kerrey, Bob (Joseph Robert Kerrey; 1943–) Nebraska Senator Kerrey made a highly visible early run for the Democratic presidential nomination in 1991–92, gaining a good deal of media recognition. He declared his candidacy on September 30, 1991, and in early 1992 entered into the long series of primary debates that characterized the Democratic nominating process. Running as a liberal, he stressed job creation, sharply criticized the Bush Administration for weakness in Japanese-American international trade disputes, called for deep military cuts and a "peace dividend," favored abortion rights and civil rights, and generally pursued the agenda he and other liberal Democrats had advocated during the Reagan and Bush years. But for Kerrey the votes were just not there. He scored a respectable 11 percent of the vote in the February 18th New Hampshire primary, and won the South Dakota primary with a 40 percent plurality in a field of five serious candidates, but then faded quickly. After achieving no better than fourth place in any of the March 3rd primaries, he quit the race on March 5, later supporting Bill Clinton. He was not up for re-election to the Senate in 1992, his term running until 1994.

Nebraska-born Kerrey went into the U.S. Navy right out of college. He served as a commando during the Vietnam War, and was wounded in action in 1969, then spending many months in a naval hospital, an experience he has often alluded to during his political career. He was awarded the Congressional Medal of Honor. After the war, Kerrey went into business, developing the Grandmother's restaurant chain and several other enterprises until he entered politics. He was governor of Nebraska (1983–87), and has been a first-term U.S. senator since

1989. Kerrey was formerly married, and has two children. He has also had a highly publicized friendship with actress Debra Winger.

FURTHER READING

"The uncanny candidate." JAMES TRAUB. *GQ—Gentleman's Quarterly*, Mar. 1992.
"Kerrey reflects. . . ." HOWARD FINEMAN. *Newsweek*, Feb. 10, 1992.
"Bob Kerrey's odyssey." PETER BOYER. *Vanity Fair*, Jan. 1992.
"Careless Kerrey." MORTON KONDRACKE. *New Republic*, Jan. 20, 1992.
"The politics of self. . . ." SIDNEY BLUMENTHAL. *New Republic*, Jan. 20, 1992.
"Is he ready for the big leagues?" JON D. HULL. *Time*, Dec. 9, 1991.
"Primed for combat." KIM HUBBARD and LINDA KRAMER. *People*, Nov. 25, 1991.
"The no bull campaign." HOWARD FINEMAN. *Newsweek*, Oct. 14, 1991.
"Introducing 'present man.' " GLORIA BORGER. *U.S. News & World Report*, Oct. 7, 1991.
"Looking back. . . ." JOSEPH L. GALLOWAY. *U.S. News & World Report*, July 15, 1991.
"The unfinished politician." ROBIN TONER. *New York Times Magazine*, Apr. 14, 1991.
"Kerrey, Bob." *Current Biography*, Feb. 1991.
"A senator of candor most rare." HAYS GOREY. *Time*, Oct. 29, 1990.

Kerry, John Forbes (1943–) Senator Kerry, the junior Democratic Senator from Massachusetts, voted a largely liberal agenda during 1992, on such issues as military spending cuts, abortion rights, civil rights, and capital gains taxes. His chief public focus continued to be the American prisoners of war thought by many to have been left in Vietnam after American withdrawal from the Vietnam War. As chairman of the Senate Select Committee on POW-MIA Affairs, he said publicly in June that as many as 80 Americans had been left behind in Vietnam, though he did not assert that any were still alive, the question remaining open as new hearings opened on June 26th. On September 24th, Henry Kissinger testified before Kerry's committee, taking sharp exception to criticism of himself and President Richard Nixon, contending that they had made every effort to get a full accounting from the Vietnamese, and criticizing Kerry, who was an anti-Vietnam War activist, for his questioning of the Nixon Administration record. Kerry continued to press for more information throughout the balance of the year.

Denver-born Kerry served as a young, front-line naval lieutenant in Vietnam (1966–69), winning a Silver Star and a Bronze Star with an Oak Leaf Cluster, and was wounded three times. In 1969, he became a founder and national coordinator of Vietnam Veterans Against the War. He was an assistant county district attorney (1976–79), practiced law in Boston (1979–82), and was state Lieutenant Governor (1983–85). Kerry won election to the Senate in 1985. In 1987, while investigating international drug trading, as chairman of Senate Foreign Relations Subcommittee on Terrorism, Narcotics, and International Operations, he discovered the secret $20 million Bank of Credit and Commerce International (BCCI) account of Panamanian general Manuel Noriega, starting the trail of events that led to exposure of the massive BCCI-First American Bankshares scandal. He is the author of *The New Soldier* (1971). Kerry's B.A. was from Yale University, and his J.D. from Boston College. He is married to the former Julia Stimson Thorne; they have two children.

FURTHER READING

"Kerry, John Forbes." *Current Biography*, June 1988.

Kesey, Ken (1935–) In 1992, Kesey published his third novel, *Sailor's Song*. Like his acclaimed first novel, *One Flew Over the Cuckoo's Nest*, it continued to explore what he saw as the essential madness of modern America—and perhaps all technologically-based human society—and the essential sanity of what he perceives as a more nature-based approach to life. In *Sailor's Song*, published 30 years on, he sees the end of current human society as much, much closer, and sets it 30 years more into the future to allow his apocalypse to develop a little further. This book is set in a small Alaskan fishing village, its (and Earth's) temperature warmed by the Greenhouse Effect, the place literally and figuratively the endplace of an American culture deep into dissolution and ecological disaster. His vehicle is a movie company, come to make a film, and then to use the sets to make the village over into a

theme park, symbolizing for Kesey the end of hope. Ultimately, Earth—or presumably Earth—responds with a huge storm, which destroys all that technology, and perhaps promises the hope of a better future. A fable for our times.

Colorado-born Kesey emerged as a major author with his novel *One Flew Over the Cuckoo's Nest* (1962), about a free-spirited, sane person trapped in an insane asylum. For the 1975 Milos Forman film version of his book, actor Jack Nicholson as that free spirit, actress Louise Fletcher, director Forman, the screenwriters, and the film itself all won Oscars. Kesey also wrote *Sometimes a Great Notion* (1964), which was adapted into the 1971 Paul Newman film. He has also published several nonfiction works, short stories, and children's stories. Since 1974, Kesey has been the publisher and editor of the magazine *Spit in the Ocean*. His 1957 B.A. was from the University of Oregon, and was followed by postgraduate work at Stanford University (1958–59). He is married to the former Norma Faye Haxby and has three children.

FURTHER READING

"Ken Kesey kisses no ass." CHIP BROWN. *Esquire*, Sep. 1992.
A Casebook on Ken Kesey's: One Flew over the Cuckoo's Nest. GEORGE J. SEARLES. University of New Mexico Native American Studies, 1992.
On the Bus: The Legendary Trip of Ken Kesey and the Merry Pranksters. PAUL PERRY and KEN BABBS. Thunder's Mouth, 1990.
Ken Kesey. STEPHEN L. TANNER. Twayne/Macmillan, 1990.
Ken Kesey. BARRY H. LEEDS. Ungar/Continuum, 1986.
The Contemporary American Comic Epic: The Novels of Barth, Pynchon, Gaddis, and Kesey. ELAINE B. SAFER. Wayne State University Press, 1988.

Kessler, David Aaron (1952–)

In his first full year in office, Food and Drug Administration (FDA) chairman Kessler continued to revitalize his agency. Perhaps his most spectacular and lifesaving success came early in the year: On January 6, the FDA declared a 45-day moratorium on silicone gel breast implants, while a safety review was conducted, thereby calling into question the approximately 2 million silicone gel breast implants done since the early 1960s. On April 16th, the moratorium was lifted and implants were once again permitted, but only on very limited bases, and with the kind of follow-up and monitoring that had never before been done. Kessler also continued the work started in 1991 on many fronts, in such areas as improved food labeling, the subject of a major controversy between the FDA and the Department of Agriculture late in 1992; contaminated food imports; generic drug manufacturing violations; and speeded-up review and release of AIDS-fighting medications.

Kessler was highly qualified to take on the massive task of turning around the FDA. A magna cum laude graduate of Amherst College, his 1978 LL.B. was from the University of Chicago and his 1979 medical degree from Harvard University Medical School. He also took courses at the New York University Graduate School of Business Administration. His residency was in pediatrics at Johns Hopkins, while in the same period he was a consultant to the Senate Labor and Human Resources Committee (1981–84). He was attached to New York's Montefiore Medical Center (1984–91), the last six years as director of the Jack D. Weiler Hospital, part of the Montefiore-Albert Einstein Hospital complex. He also taught food and drug law at Columbia Law School (1986–90), and served on a Health and Human Services commission set up to review the operation of the FDA before taking over as its chairman. He is married to lawyer Paulette Steinberg: they have two children.

FURTHER READING

"Under a microscope. . . ." MAGGIE MAHAR. *Barron's*, Mar. 2, 1992.

"An apple a day." MARLENE CIMONS. *Runner's World*, Feb. 1992.

"The best public service." *Business Week*, Jan. 13, 1992.

"Kessler, David Aaron." *Current Biography*, Sep. 1991.

"A shot in the arm. . . ." HERBERT BURKHOLZ. *New York Times Magazine*, June 30, 1991.

"Food fight! . . . ." DAVID GROGAN. *People*, June 24, 1991.

"The enforcer. . . ." *Newsweek*, May 27, 1991.

Kevorkian, Jack (1928–)

Still called by the media "Dr. Death," during 1992 Kevorkian continued his campaign for physician-assisted suicide, which he calls *medicide*, and for which he has invented suicide devices. On February 3, 1992, a Michigan grand jury indicted Kevorkian for murder, in assisting in the October 1991 suicides of two Michigan women, Sherry Miller and Marjorie Wanz. On May 15th, while awaiting trial, Kevorkian assisted another Michigan woman to commit suicide. On July 22nd, both murder charges were discussed by a state judge, who called Kevorkian's action legal in Michigan, but also urged Kevorkian to stop assisting suicides in the state, because his actions might well trigger a new state law prohibiting assisted suicides. In most states, assisting suicides is illegal. Kevorkian was reportedly planning to next test the state of Massachusetts, by assisting a suicide in that state.

On December 15, Kevorkian assisted Michigan residents Marguerite Tate and Marcella Lawrence to commit suicide, a few hours before Michigan governor John Engler signed a law making it illegal for a doctor to assist a suicide in Michigan for 15 months, while the legislature considered the matter more fully.

Kevorkian first came to public attention in April 1990, when he appeared on the *Donahue* show, describing his suicide machine. In June 1990, Janet Adkins, a 54-year-old English professor who had seen the show and was suffering from early stages of Alzheimer's disease, used his machine to kill herself. First degree murder charges were brought against Kevorkian, but then dropped.

Born and educated in Michigan, Kevorkian was licensed as a physician in 1953, interned in Michigan hospitals, and then worked as a pathologist at the Pacific Hospital in Long Beach, California, until 1982. An advocate of euthanasia throughout his medical career, Kevorkian has published various books and articles on the subject. His 1991 book, *Prescription: Medicine: The Goodness of Planned Death*, received considerable public attention in the United States, as part of the continuing "right-to-die" debate. Kevorkian has been unemployed since 1982, he believes because of his upsetting ideas.

FURTHER READING

"Mercy's friend or foe?" NANCY GIBBS. *Time*, Dec. 28, 1992.

"The paradoxes of 'rational' death." ROBERT BARRY.

"Assisted suicide and professional responsibilities." WILLIAM J. WINSLADE and KYRIAKOS S. MARKIDES.

"Masks of autonomy." JOHN J. CONLEY. "The suicide machine." NORMAN K. DENZIN. *Society*, July–Aug. 1992. Special *Medicide: New Humanism or Old Euthanasia?* coverage.

"The odd odyssey of. . . ." GLORIA BORGER. *U.S. News & World Report*, Aug. 27, 1990.

"The right to die. . . ." D'ARCY JENISH. *Maclean's*, June 25, 1990.

"A vital woman. . . ." BONNIE JOHNSON et al. *People*, June 25, 1990.

"The doctor's suicide van. . . ." MELINDA BECK. *Newsweek*, June 18, 1990.

Khamenei, Mohammed Ali (1940–)

During 1992, Ayatollah Khamenei, Iran's most powerful fundamentalist leader, continued to support Iranian President Ali Rafsanjani's new, relatively moderate economic and political policies, which in 1991 had included a call for much stronger economic ties with the West and other Persian Gulf nations, and autumn 1991 moves to release American and other hostages held in Lebanon by the Iranian-controlled Hezbollah (Party of God). Even the May 1992 electoral defeat of Islamic fundamentalist forces by Rafsanjani supporters did not bring him into renewed open conflict with Rafsanjani, although he did express great concern about several trends in Iranian society, including newly-rampant corruption of epidemic proportions. But solving

Iran's deepening economic crisis, which was accompanied by runaway inflation, mass poverty, and in April and May by urban riots, seemed to be central for Khameini and Rafsanjani during 1992, and Khameinei proposed no new self-isolating return to hardline fundamentalism—yet.

Khamenei was a disciple and political ally of Ayatollah Ruhollah Khomenei; he was imprisoned in Iran on several occasions during the 1960s and 1970s, and exiled in 1978, returning to Iran when Khomeini came to power in 1979. He was president of Iran (1981–89), and became supreme Iranian Shiite Muslim religious leader and a competitor in the internal struggle for state power after Khomeini's death in 1989. He is married, and has five children.

FURTHER READING

"Iran without Khomeini." MICHAEL LEDEEN.
  American Spectator, Aug. 1989.
"Change in Teheran. . . ." *National Review*, June 30, 1989.
"Burying the passions. . . ." BILL HEWITT. *Newsweek*, June 19, 1989.

Khoei, Ayatollah Seyed Abul-asim al- (1899–1982)

Born in Khoi, in Iranian Azerbaijan, Khoei was sent to the holy city of Najaf, in Iraq, at the age of 13, and remained there all his life, ultimately becoming a highly respected Islamic scholar and one of the six grand ayatollahs of the Shiite Muslim faith, which claims an estimated 200 million members throughout the Muslim world. Unlike Iran's Ayatollah Khomeini, Khoei was a nonpolitical Muslim cleric, who did not takes sides in any of the wars and others disputes that have convulsed Near East since he became a major leader in the 1960s. But in 1991, after the Persian Gulf War, when Iraqi forces accompanied their suppression of the Shiite rebellion in southern and central Iraq with mass killings, Khoei publicly appealed to the world for aid to the Shiites. Saddam Hussein then arrested many of Khoei's aides, including his eldest son, and probably under threat of death forced Khoei to publicly praise Hussein. Khoei, carefully watched by the Iraqi police, was long under effective house arrest. No information on survivors was available. (d. Kurfah, Iraq; August 8, 1992)

FURTHER READING

Obituary. *The Times* (of London), Aug. 10, 1992.
Obituary. *New York Times*, Aug. 9, 1992.

Kidman, Nicole (1967–   )

Up-and-coming Australian film star Nicole Kidman's major 1992 film was Ron Howard's romantic drama *Far and Away*. She starred as the Irish landlord's daughter who marries a rebellious young Irish tenant farmer, played by her real-life husband, Tom Cruise. They emigrate to America, and much of the story is that of their immigration and subsequent move into American life. The film did well at the box office, in spite of generally unfavorable reviews and perhaps because of Cruise's great box office appeal.

Kidman also appeared as the head girl of an Australian school in John Duigan's film *Flirting* (1991), which opened to good reviews in the United States in 1992. Forthcoming was a starring role opposite Alec Baldwin in Harold Becker's film *Damages*.

Kidman made her film debut at age 14, in the film *Bush Christmas* (1980), and in the same year appeared in *BMX Bandits*. In 1983, she starred in the Disney miniseries *Five Mile Creek*, and in 1984 in the film *Windrider*. Her breakthrough role came in the Australian television miniseries *Vietnam* (1986). She also starred in the television miniseries *Bangkok Hilton*. Her American theatrical film debut came in *Dead Calm* (1987); she went on to such films as *Days of Thunder* (1990) and *Billy Bathgate* (1991). She and Tom Cruise met while making *Days of Thunder*, and married in 1990.

FURTHER READING

"Nicole Kidman." *Playboy*, July 1992.
"No kidding." WILLIAM NORWICH. *Vogue*, June 1992.
"Crazy for each other." ELIZABETH SPORKIN. *People*, June 8, 1992.

King, Albert (Albert Nelson; 1923–92) Mississippi-born King, a classic blues guitarist and singer, began his career in the Midwest, at Gary, Indiana and then at St. Louis, where he formed a highly regarded band. He began recording in 1953, and scored his major breakthrough in the late 1960s and early 1970s, with such albums as *Born Under a Bad Sign, Jammed Together, I'll Play the Blues for You,* and *Live Wire/Blues Power.* From the mid-1970s, he also added other musical elements to his blues, as well, becoming a very popular touring artist, playing to appreciative White audiences as well as the African-American audiences that had earlier been his whole focus. His style and sound were thought by many to have influenced a whole generation of rock-and-roll performers. He was survived by his wife, Glendle King, two daughters, a son, and a sister. (d. Memphis, Tennessee; December 21, 1992)

FURTHER READING

Obituary. *Billboard*, Jan. 9, 1993.
Obituary. *Variety*, Jan. 4, 1993.
Obituary. *The New York Times*, Dec. 23, 1992.

King, Larry (1933–) CNN's "Larry King Live" was the "in" place to be for political candidates in 1992. It all began on February 20th, when guest Ross Perot—at King's prompting—allowed that he would run for president if drafted. That began a dizzying year in which the whole presidential campaign took on the air of a televised town meeting, and all the major candidates—one by one—made their pilgrimage to King's show, especially after Perot announced his *re*-entrance into the race at the beginning of October. It was on King's show that George Bush questioned by innuendo Clinton's visit to Mos-

cow as a student; that Dan Quayle softened his position regarding abortion, at least as hypothetically applied to his own daughter; and that Perot defended his charges that the Republicans had a dirty tricks campaign against him. Detractors charged that the campaign process was being degraded, since King and his call-in viewers were not asking the really hard, probing questions, that journalists would ask. King himself said he did not profess to be a journalist, but that he has always asked what "the man in the street" would ask. In any case, many observers noted that the King phenomenon had begun an unprecedented opening of the presidential debates beyond the circumscribed confines of traditional news and presidential debates, and helped to create a much greater sense of public interest and involvement. King reported that he was bemused to find himself "on the front pages day after day, just for doing what he's always done." In September, King was even brought in as a guest to talk about the phenomenon on NBC's "Meet the Press." Earlier in the year, in January, King had hosted an "American Town Meeting" on CNN, in which unemployed blue- and white-collar workers were able to question government officials.

King's show remained wider than the political spectrum, however, including celebrities of all sorts and people involved in controversial issues, such as the chairman of Dow Corning speaking on breast implants. In February, King held the first live interview ever given by Barbra Streisand, and he remains the only talk-show host to have been visited by the wary Frank Sinatra. Late in 1992, it was announced that King's syndicated radio show on the Mutual Broadcasting Network, then on at night, would be shifted to afternoon "drive time," 3–6 P.M., at least in some areas of the country. In 1992, King also published his memoirs, *When You're from Brooklyn, Everything Else Is Tokyo*, written with Marty Appel.

Brooklyn-born King spent his early career as a broadcaster in Miami, working as a disc jockey for various radio stations (1957–71), then—at first still in the Miami area—developing a wider broadcasting career, while also working as a writer, as for the *Miami Herald, USA Today*, and *Sporting News*. He began "The Larry King Show" on radio in 1978, and began "Larry King Live" on the Cable News Network (CNN) in 1985, there winning various cable industry awards from 1987 and being awarded a reported $8 million, 5-year contract in 1990. The International Radio and TV Society honored him as Broadcaster of the Year in 1989. King has also appeared in the movies *Ghostbusters* (1984) and *Lost in America* (1985); acted as host for the Goodwill Games (1990); and written several books, including *Larry King* (1982) with Emily Yoffe; *Tell It to the King* (1988) with Peter Occhiogrosso; *Mr. King, You're Having a Heart Attack* (1989) with B.D. Colen. He has been married six times to five women, and has two children.

FURTHER READING

"Larry King." *People*, Dec. 28, 1992.
"A King who can listen." STANLEY CLOUD. *Time*, Oct. 5, 1992.
"Larry King." DAVID RENSIN. *TV Guide*, July 25, 1992.
"King vs. King. . . ." LISA DePAULO. *Philadelphia*, May 1991.
"The maestro of. . . ." THOMAS MEYER. *New York Times Magazine*, May 26, 1991.
"Playboy interview: . . . ." DAVID RENSIN. *Playboy*, Aug. 1990.
"All alone. . . ." LYNN ROSELLINI. *U.S. News & World Report*, Jan. 15, 1990.
"Cosmo talks to. . . ." SANDRA McELWAINE. *Cosmopolitan*, Nov. 1988.

King, Rodney Glenn (1966–) The

March 1991 beating of African-American Rodney King set in motion a chain of events that grew into the massive April 30–May 2, 1992 Los

Angeles riots. On the night of March 3, 1991, King was dragged from his car by police officers and subjected to a brutal beating by White Los Angeles police officers. Unknown to them, the beating was videotaped by a nearby resident— and was then broadcast on television, night after night, to the whole world. Ultimately, charges were filed against four police officers, who were tried in March and April 1992 in neighboring Ventura County, by a jury that included no African-Americans. On April 30, all four officers were acquitted on all but one count against one officer, on which the jury could not make a decision. That night, the Los Angeles riots began. Rodney King, who had seen his assailants acquitted, pleaded for calm and an end to the riots, at one point asking poignantly, "Can't we all get along?" King was arrested twice more in 1991 and 1992; in both instances, no prosecutions resulted. On August 3, 1992, a Los Angeles grand jury indicted the same four police officers—Sergeant Stacey C. Koon, and officers Laurence M. Powell, Theodore J. Brisoneno, and Timothy E. Wind—on federal charges of violating King's civil rights. Trials were pending at year's end.

FURTHER READING

"The selling of Rodney King." PETER BOYER. *Vanity Fair*, July 1992.
"Following orders." BARRY SCHECK. *New Republic*, May 25, 1992.
"How the defense. . . ." BOB COHN and DAVID KAPLAN. *Newsweek*, May 11, 1992.
"Anatomy of an acquittal." RICHARD LACAYO. *Time*, May 11, 1992.
Understanding the Riots: Los Angeles and the Aftermath of the Rodney King Verdict. LOS ANGELES TIMES STAFF. Los Angeles Times, 1992.
Presumed Guilty: The Tragedy of the Rodney King Affair. STACEY C. KOON and ROBERT DEITZ. Regnery Gateway, 1992.
Rodney King and the L.A. Rebellion: Analysis and Commentary by 13 Independent Black Writers. RAS M. COLLIER et al. Untd Brothers, 1992.
" 'Damn! They gonna lynch us!' " MIKE SAGER. *GQ—Gentleman's Quarterly*, Oct. 1991.

King, Stephen (1947–) Once again, the

prolific American writer Stephen King had a two-novel year, while at the same time also moving strongly into screenwriting. In June, he published the novel *Gerald's Game*, about a woman handcuffed to a bed, prey to psychological and physical terrors; it was thought by some to be a metaphor for womens' condition in modern society, by others to be part of a continuing body of King horror-and-degradation exploitation works. His second 1992 novel was *Doris Claiborne*, published in December, a Maine-set work focused on two deaths, one current and one long ago.

King also wrote his first original screenplay, for the film *Stephen King's Sleepwalkers*, directed by Mick Garris, a vampire horror film that was a major summer 1992 commercial hit. Forthcoming was his first television screenplay, for a projected ABC miniseries based on his best-selling novel *The Stand*, which King will also co-produce. His novel *Needful Things* is the basis of a forthcoming Fraser Heston film.

On the legal front, King unsuccessfully sued to block release of the film *Stephen King's Lawnmower Man*, based on a King short story, claiming that the title was misleading, in that he had nothing to do with the production; the defense claimed that he had sold rights to the story that included the use of his name.

Maine-born King received his 1970 B.S. from the University of Maine, then taught English at the Hampden Academy (1971–73), before embarking on his writing career. Among his many novels, are *Carrie* (1974), *Salem's Lot* (1975), *The Shining* (1976), *The Stand* (1978; republished uncut, 1990), *Firestarter* (1980), *Danse Macabre* (1981), *Cujo* (1981), *Pet Sematary* (1983), *The Talisman, Cycle of the Werewolf* (1985), *Skeleton Crew* (1986), *The Eyes of the Dragon* (1987), *Misery* (1987), *The Tommyknockers* (1987), *The Dark Half* (1989), *Four Past Midnight* (1990), *Needful Things* (1991), and the *Dark Tower* series: *The Gunslinger* (1982), *The Drawing of the Three* (1987), and *The Waste Lands* (1991). He has also published many short stories and short screenplays, as well as novels under the name of Richard Bachman, including *Rage* (1977), *The Long Walk* (1979), *Roadwork* (1981), *The Running Man* (1982), and *Thinner* (1984). Many of King's works have been adapted for the screen, among them *Carrie* (1976), *The Shining* (1980), *Christine* (1983), *The Dead Zone* (1983), *Stand By Me* (1986; based on *The Body*), *The Running Man* (1987), *Pet Sematary* (1989), and *Misery* (1990); King himself directed from his own scripts *Children of the Corn* (1984) and *Maximum Overdrive* (1986). King married Tabitha Jane Spruce in 1971; they have three children.

FURTHER READING

"Digging up stories. . . ." W.C. STROBY. *Writer's Digest*, Mar. 1992.

Stephen King: Master of Horror. ANNE SAIDMAN. Lerner, 1992.

Stephen King's America. JONATHAN DAVIS. Starmont House, 1992.

In the Darkest Night: The Student's Guide to Stephen King. TIM MURPHY. Starmont House, 1992; Borgo Press, 1992.

The Stephen King Short Story Concordance. CHRIS THOMSON. Starmont House, 1992.

More Stephen King and Clive Barker: The Illustrated Guide to the Masters of the Macabre. JAMES VAN HISE. Movie Pubs Services, 1992.

Stephen King A to Z: A Dictionary of People, Places and Things in the Works of the King of Horror. STEPHEN SPIGNESI. Popular Culture, 1992.

Stephen King: The Second Decade: Danse Macabre to the Dark Half. TONY MAGISTRALE. Twayne/Macmillan, 1992.

The Work of Stephen King: An Annotated Bibliography and Guide. MICHAEL R. COLLINGS. Borgo Press, 1992.

The Dark Descent: Essays Defining Stephen King's Horrorscape. TONY S. MAGISTRALE, ed. Greenwood, 1992.

"Stephen King." MARK MARVEL. *Interview*, Oct. 1991.

The Shape under the Sheet: The Complete Stephen King Encyclopedia. STEPHEN SPIGNESI. Popular Culture, 1991.

Stephen King: Man and Artist, rev. ed. CARROL F. TERRELL. North Lights, 1991.

The Stephen King Story. GEORGE BEAHM. Andrews & McMeel, 1991.

The Stephen King Companion. GEORGE BEAHM, ed. Andrews & McMeel, 1989.

Feast of Fear: Conversations with Stephen King. TIM UNDERWOOD and CHUCK MILLER, eds. Underwood-Miller, 1989; McGraw-Hill, 1989; Carroll and Graf, 1992.

Stephen King: The First Decade, Carrie to Pet Sematary. JOSEPH REINO. Macmillan, 1988.

Bare Bones: Conversations on Terror with Stephen King. TIM UNDERWOOD and CHUCK MILLER, eds. McGraw-Hill, 1988; Warner, 1989.

Kingsley, Gregory (1980–81–) Twelve-year-old Gregory Kingsley was the central figure in a very unusual case during 1992. He had been given into foster care three times by his mother, Rachel Kingsley. In October 1991, he had gone to live with foster parents George and Elizabeth Russ, who then moved to adopt him. His mother, then an unemployed waitress, op-

posed adoption, and asserted her rights as a natural parent to have him come back to her. But he wanted to be adopted by his foster parents, and went to juvenile court to assert his right to live with whom he chose, and to have his mother's parental rights nullified; such suits had sometimes been brought before, but this was the first brought in the child's own name. The case drew national attention, as a children's rights versus parents' rights matter. Gregory testified that his mother had not been in touch with him during years of foster care, that he felt that she had no real interest in him, and that he wanted to join the Russ family. Florida state circuit court judge Thomas S. Kirk, after a hearing in Orlando, found for Gregory Kingsley and against his natural mother, allowing the adoption into the Russ family to go forward. His mother's attorney announced that they would appeal the decision, and the basic issues involved remained to be settled by higher courts.

FURTHER READING

"Gregory K." *People*, Dec. 28, 1992.
"The home of his choice." BILL HEWITT. *People*, Oct. 12, 1992.
"The mother of all divorces." ANDREW STEPHEN. *Observer*, Sep. 27, 1992.

Kinison, Sam (1954–92) Peoria-born Kinison, who began his career as a preacher, moved to Los Angeles and into show business as a standup comic in his early 20s. His act included a great deal of abuse, often directed at women, gays, and lesbians, and delivered, as was most of his material, in very loud, abrasive style, which generated major protests from those so abused and others concerned about bigotry. One characteristic Kinison approach was to punctuate his act with periods of screaming. For much of his career, Kinison was greatly troubled by drug and alcohol abuse problems. He became a popular comedian in cabaret, television, films, and records in the mid-1980s, with career highlights including an appearance in the film *Back to School* (1986), a television special, the comedy series "Charlie Hoover," and appearances on several television variety shows. He died in an automobile accident, in which his wife, Malika, was injured. He was survived by his wife, his mother, and a brother. (d. Needles, California; April 10, 1992)

FURTHER READING

"The last laugh." TOM HEDLEY. *Esquire*, Dec. 1992.
"Sam Kinison. . . ." JANE WOLLMAN RUSOFF. *Entertainment*, June 12, 1992.
Obituary. *Rolling Stone*, May 28, 1992.
"In with a howl. . . ." TOM GLIATTO. *People*, Apr. 27, 1992.
Obituary. *Variety*, Apr. 20, 1992.
Obituary. *New York Times*, Apr. 12, 1992.
"The comedy of hate." GERRI HIRSHEY. *GQ—Gentleman's Quarterly*, Aug. 1989.
"Why I wear. . . ." *GQ—Gentleman's Quarterly*, June 1989.
"The devil and. . . ." DAVID HANDELMAN. *Rolling Stone*, Feb. 23, 1989.
"Stand-up from hell. . . ." KIM MASTERS. *Premiere*, Feb. 1989.
"One more time. . . ." SUSAN SCHINDEHETTE. *People*, Nov. 28, 1988.

Kinnock, Neil Gordon (1942–) During the first few months of 1992, British Labour Party leader Neil Kinnock seemed headed for power. During the run-up to the April general elections, every early poll showed Labour comfortably ahead of John Major's Conservative Party, and the late polls showed only a narrowing of the Labour Party's lead. Kinnock's strategy was thought to have worked, with Labour capturing enough of the much-needed center to win, after Kinnock had fully supported the Persian Gulf War, supported the controversial European Community Maastricht Treaty, and attacked the left within his own party. Every poll was wrong; Labour lost, with 271 House of Commons seats and 34 percent of the vote; the Conservatives won 42 percent of the vote and 336 seats, down 39 seats from the 1987 general elections, but not enough to save Kinnock. Having lost two successive general elections, he announced his resignation as leader of the Labour Party, and was succeeded by John Smith in July. Kinnock was elected to the Labour Party executive committee in September.

Kinnock began his political career in the mid-1960s, in Labour Party educational work, became a Labour Member of Parliament in 1970, and has remained in Parliament for two decades, while steadily moving up in his party. He became party leader and leader of the parliamentary opposition in 1983. In 1987, he published *Making Our Way: Investing in Britain's Future.* Kinnock attended the University College of

Cardiff. He married Glenys Elizabeth Parry in 1967; they have two children.

FURTHER READING

"Waiting for a call. . . ." LESLEY WHITE. *Sunday Times*, Nov. 15, 1992.
"Next stop. . . . " DANIEL PEDERSEN. *Newsweek*, Mar. 30, 1992.
"The rewards of Labour. . . ." HUGO YOUNG. *New Republic*, May 27, 1991.
"A coal miner's son." MARY NEMETH. *Maclean's*, May 14, 1990.

Kirsten, Dorothy (1910–92) For three decades a leading lyric soprano at the Metropolitian Opera, New Jersey-born Dorothy Kirsten began her career as a popular radio singer in the mid-1930s. Sponsored by soprano Grace Moore, she studied with Astolfo Pescia in Italy (1937–38), and returned to the United States to a wide-ranging musical career in opera, radio, film, and recital. She made her operatic debut with the Chicago Grand Opera in 1940, sang leading roles with the San Carlo Opera Company in 1942, and then with other companies in the early 1940s. She also had her own radio show (1943–44). In 1945, she began her 30-year-long association with the Metropolitan Opera, making her debut as Mimi in *La Boheme*. She went on to sing many major roles, and was especially well regarded for her roles in such Puccini works as *The Girl of the Golden West*, *Tosca*, and *La Boheme*. She also continued to work in radio, and was probably best known to wide audiences for her co-starring role in the film *The Great Caruso* (1951), opposite Mario Lanza in the title role. She also appeared in several other films. In 1982, she published *A Time to Sing*, written with Rasponi Lanfracno. She was married twice, and was survived by two sisters and a brother. (d. Los Angeles; November 18, 1992)

FURTHER READING

Obituary. *Variety*, Nov. 23, 1992
Obituary. *The Times* (of London), Nov. 21, 1992
Obituary. *New York Times*, Nov. 19, 1992.

Kite, Tom (1949–) American golfer Tom Kite has long been been tagged as the "Greatest Player Who Never Won a Major Championship." But that all ended in 1992, when he won the U.S. Open at California's Pebble Beach by two

strokes. The lack of a major win was even more surprising because Kite had had numerous victories over the previous two decades; by the end of 1992, his career tally was 17 wins, starting with his 1980 win at the European Open and including the 1992 BellSouth Classic. He is also the Professional Golfers' Association (PGA) all-time leading money winner, with over $7.5 million, nearly $1 million in 1992 alone. But time and again, in the major championships, he had been overtaken at the end, most notably at the 1984 Masters and the 1989 U.S. Open.

Kite joined the PGA Tour in 1972, but did not make major impact until 1980 when he won the European Open. In 1981 he was named Golfer of the Year by two organizations, won the Vardon Trophy (again in 1982), and headed the PGA Tour money list. He was a member of the World Cup Team (1984 and 1985) and the Ryder Cup Team (1981, 1983, 1985, 1987, and 1989), and was PGA Player of the Year and leading money winner in 1989, when he won the Players Championship. Kite attended the University of Texas. He and his wife, Christy, have a daughter and twin sons.

FURTHER READING

"Major accomplishment." DAVID BARRETT. *Golf*, Aug. 1992.
"Different kinds of dreamers." DAVD KINDRED. *Sporting News*, June 29, 1992.
"Tom Kite. . . . " MIKE BRYAN. *Golf*, Nov. 1989.

Kline, Kevin Delaney (1947–) Stage

and screen star Kevin Kline starred in 1992 as Douglas Fairbanks opposite Robert Downey, Jr., in Richard Attenborough's *Chaplin*, the film autobiography of the legendary Charlie Chaplin. Co-starring were Dan Aykroyd as Mack Sennett; Geraldine Chaplin as her own grandmother, Hannah Chaplin; Kevin Dunn as J. Edgar Hoover; Moira Kelly as both Hetty Kelly and Oona O'Neill; Diane Lane as Paulette Goddard; Penelope Anne Miller as Edna Purviance; Anthony Hopkins as George Hayden; and Paul Rhys as Sydney Chaplin.

Kline also starred as Richard Parker opposite Mary Elizabeth Mastrantonio as Priscilla Parker and Kevin Spacey as their murderous, psychotic neighbor in Alan J. Pakula's *Consenting Adults*. Forthcoming was a starring role opposite Sigourney Weaver in Ivan Reitman's *Dave*, about an American Presidential lookalike called in to impersonate the President and fool all those around him, including his wife, played by Weaver.

St. Louis-born Kline became a star on Broadway in the late 1970s, winning a Tony for *On the Twentieth Century* (1978), starring in *Loose Ends* (1979), and winning a second Tony for *Pirates of Penzance* (1980), a role he repeated in the 1983 film version. He also appeared off-Broadway in the early 1970s, and as *Richard III* (1983), *Henry V* (1984), and *Hamlet* (1986). On screen, he also played in such films as *Sophie's Choice* (1982), *The Big Chill* (1983), *Silverado* (1985), *A Fish Called Wanda* (1988; he won a Best Supporting Actor Oscar), *I Love You to Death* (1990), *Soapdish* (1991), and *Grand Canyon* (1991). In 1990, he also starred in and directed *Hamlet* for PBS's "Great Performances" series. Kline's B.A. was from Indiana University, and he also attended the Julliard School. He married Phoebe Cates in 1989; they have one child.

FURTHER READING

"Kevin Kline. . . ." SHARI ROMAN. *Video*, Dec. 1991.
"Kevin's choice." JOE MORGENSTERN. *Connoisseur*, July 1991.

Kohl, Helmut (1930–) As a horrified

world watched the rise of a new Nazism in Germany, German Chancellor and Christian Democratic Party leader Kohl found himself coping

with several very difficult problems, of which Nazism was only the most highly visible. Chief among the other problems, and quite related to the rise of Nazism, was the far-greater-than-expected cost and difficulty of converting former East Germany into a modern, competitive economy, as Kohl freely admitted in speeches before parliament and his own party in September, when calling for new taxes to finance the conversion and predicting slower than usual economic growth.

Kohl also found long-planned European unification, which he strongly favored, in great difficulty, as the Maastricht Treaty foundered late in the year. Germany's economic problems contributed to that: Germany continued to pay high interest rates to attract foreign capital, triggering a crisis in the European Monetary System (EMS), ultimately forcing British withdrawal from the EMS in September, after considerable damage to many already-weak European economies.

As massive anti-Nazi rallies throughout Germany made it clear that very many Germans had no sympathy at all for Nazism, and as massive world pressure grew, Kohl's government began to take serious steps to curb the new Nazis, setting up special police units, banning several Nazi organizations and distribution of the songs of several Nazi singing groups, and to some extent meeting the Nazis in the streets. The world watched as the new rise of Nazism in Germany became in 1992 an overriding question for Kohl, for Germany, for Europe, and for the world.

Kohl began his political career in the Rhineland, becoming Christian Democratic Party chairman in the Rhineland (1966–73) and deputy national chairman of his party in 1969; he has been national chairman since 1973. He was opposition leader in the West German parliament (1976–82), and then succeeded chancellor Helmut Schmidt. Throughout his career he has been a rather careful centrist, much concerned with the development of the European Community and pursuing a Western-oriented, but also independent course. Kohl attended the University of Frankfurt and the University of Heidelberg. He married Hannelore Renner in 1960; the couple have two children.

FURTHER READING

"Kohl. . . ." ROBERT J. DOWLING et al. *Business Week*, May 18, 1992.
"King Kohl." T.S. ALLMAN. *Reader's Digest* (Canadian), May 1991.
"Who's sitting pretty. . . ." *Business Week*, Mar. 11, 1991.
"Helmut Kohl. . . ." BRUCE W. NELAN. *Time*, Jan. 7, 1991.
"Herr Klutz. . . ." ANNE MCELVOY. *New Republic*, Dec. 10, 1990.
"Driving toward. . . ." HENRY MULLER and KARSTEN PRAGER. *Time*, June 25, 1990.
"Kohl power." EDWARD M. STEEN. *Inc.*, Nov. 1990.
"Helmut Kohl. . . ." DAVID GOW. *World Press Review*, Oct. 1990.

Koppel, Ted (1940–) In the late night television wars that emerged with the retirement of Johnny Carson—expected to be largely a contest between talk show hosts Jay Leno and Arsenio Hall—Ted Koppel emerged a surprising winner. This was partly because events during the year were in themselves riveting, including the selection of a president, the eruption of Los Angeles after the Rodney King verdict, and massacres and starvation in Somalia and the former

Yugoslavia. But it was more than that: Koppel was widely commended for the excellence of his handling of these and other events, and audiences responded as well. Observers noted a change in emphasis to more investigative reports and features, and an increased willingness to break away from his show's standard format for special stories. During the week after the Los Angeles events and the week of the United States armed forces arrival in Somalia, Koppel was there, reporting from the front lines and interviewing the combatants. At the end of the presidential campaign, he scored a major coup, spending the day *before* the election with Bill Clinton, and having the first televised interview with the president-elect the day after the election.

"Nightline"'s ratings achievement was even more remarkable because, as late as June, Koppel himself was concerned about the program's future, since many ABC affiliates were not supporting the program, with less than two-thirds showing "Nightline" live; the rest were delaying the broadcast for more profitable syndicated programming. Indeed, in an interview, Koppel said he would leave the program rather than "go through a slow dance of death." But by year's end, "Nightline's" fourth-quarter ratings were up an astonishing 13 percent over 1991. Koppel was personally honored by induction into the Academy of Television Arts and Sciences' Hall of Fame.

British-born Koppel emigrated to the United States with his German refugee family in 1953. He began his broadcasting career at New York's WMCA Radio in 1963, in that year moving to ABC News, where he has spent his entire career. He went to Vietnam as an ABC correspondent, worked in Hong Kong and Miami as an ABC bureau chief, was ABC's chief diplomatic correspondent (1971–80), and anchored the "ABC Saturday Night News" (1975–1977). In March 1980, he emerged as a leading figure in American broadcast journalism, as ABC turned its nightly reports on the Iran hostage crisis into the Koppel-anchored Monday-to-Friday "Nightline," identified with him ever since. With Marvin Kalb, he wrote *In the National Interest* (1977). Koppel's B.A. in journalism was from Syracuse University, his M.A. in journalism from Stanford. He is married to Grace Anne Dorney; they have four children.

FURTHER READING

"Anchor monster. . . ." JOHN KATZ. *Rolling Stone*, Jan. 10, 1991.
"Ted Koppel." RICHARD M. COHEN. *Life*, Oct. 1988.
"Ted Koppel's edge." MARSHALL BLONSKY. *New York Times Magazine*, Aug. 14, 1988.

Kravchuk, Leonid Makarovich

(1934–   ) In his first full year as the President of Ukraine, Kravchuk moved very cautiously on the economic side, the pace of privatization moving hardly at all, while Ukraine's economy remained largely centrally planned, but from Kiev, rather than Moscow. Prices, however, were allowed to rise, the net result being a high rate of inflation coupled with all the old ills of central planning—and without some of the Ukraine's old markets in the countries of the former Soviet Union and in Eastern Europe. In September, the year-old government of premier Vitold P. Fokin fell over the economic issues, to be replaced by the more reform-oriented government of premier Leonid Kuchma

In August, Kravchuk and Russian President Yeltsin settled their sharp dispute over ownership of the former Soviet Black Sea fleet, agreeing to split the fleet in three years, holding it jointly until then. He also faced conflicting Russian and Ukrainian territorial ambitions in the Crimea; Russia claimed the Crimea, part of the

Ukraine since 1954; encouraged by Russia, the Crimean parliament in May voted independence from Ukraine, but rescinded that vote when Kravchuk threatened miltary action to hold the Crimea.

Kravchuk also brought Ukraine onto the world stage, visiting several countries in 1992. Most notably, he visited the United States in May; after meeting with President George Bush, he reaffirmed Ukraine's intention to become a nuclear-free zone, but once again demanded U.S. security guarantees before giving up Ukraine's nuclear weapons to Russia, as previously agreed. There was considerable question as to whether Kravchuk actually intended to give up much more than tactical nuclear weapons, given the instability of neighboring Russia.

Ukraine-born Kravchuk began his career as a political economy teacher at the city of Chernovtsy, then moving into Communist Party work; he joined that party in 1958. Most of his career was spent as a party ideology secretary in a series of minor posts. But with the rise of Mikhail Gorbachev, and the wholly new situation Gorbachev created in the Soviet Union, Kravchuk in the late 1980s became a reform leader, and in due course a leader of the powerful movement to secede from the Soviet Union. He was elected President of the Ukraine by its parliament on July 23, 1990, and elected directly by popular vote on December 2, 1991. Kravchuk attended Kiev University. He is married to political economist Antonina Kravchuk; they have one son.

FURTHER READING

"The end of the U.S.S.R." GEORGE J. CHURCH. *Time*, Dec. 23, 1991.
"Divided they fall. . . ." DOUGLAS STANGLIN. *U.S. News & World Report*, Dec. 30, 1991.
"A house of cards." MALCOLM GRAY. *Maclean's*, Dec. 16, 1991.
"Europe's new state: Ukraine." *Economist*, Dec. 7, 1991.
"Your pace or mine?" *Economist*, June 22, 1991.

Kristofferson, Kris (1936–   ) Country music artist and actor Kris Kristofferson went on the road again in the spring of 1992, touring with his friends Johnny Cash, Waylon Jennings, and Willie Nelson, as The Highwaymen. With Nelson and Jennings, he also played at Farm

Aid V, organized at Irving, Texas by Nelson. For much of the year, Kristofferson also toured at the head of his own country music group. On April 29, 1992, Kristofferson presented the Pioneer Award to Willie Nelson at the 27th annual Country Music Awards, held in Los Angeles.

On the acting side of his career, he starred opposite Dyan Cannon, Richard Roundtree, and Tony Curtis in Arnold Schwarzenegger's film comedy *Christmas in Connecticut*, a remake of the 1945 Peter Godfrey film, which starred Barbara Stanwyck and Dennis Morgan. Forthcoming was a starring role opposite Lance Henriksen in the film *Knights*, a fantasy set in the wake of a cataclysm.

The Christmas season also saw release of a two-disc CD set presenting Kristofferson as a singer of his own songs, and as a songwriter. The first disc contains his own recordings of 17 of his own songs, the second the same songs sung by such music headliners as Willie Nelson, Waylon Jennings, Janis Joplin, Johnny Cash, and Bob Dylan. Kristofferson was also one of many celebrities to perform in a special 50th-birthday tribute to Dylan, at Madison Square Garden in October.

Texas-born Kristofferson has appeared in such films as *Cisco Pike* (1972), *Blume in Love* (1973), *Alice Doesn't Live Here Anymore* (1974), *The Sailor Who Fell From Grace With The Sea* (1976), *Heaven's Gate*, (1981), *Rollover* (1981), and *Welcome Home* (1990). He has also appeared in such telefilms as *Stagecoach* (1986), *Amerika* (1987), *Pair of Aces*. (1990; and the 1991 sequel), and *Miracle in the Wilderness* (1991). His singing career has produced numerous albums, starting with *Kristofferson* (1980). Kristofferson attended Pomona College and was a Rhodes Scholar at Oxford University. He has been married three times, and has three children.

FURTHER READING

"Kristofferson." ROSA JORDAN. *Progressive*, Sep. 1991.
"Kris Kristofferson. . . ." PATRICK CARR. *Country Music*, Jan.–Feb. 1988.
Written in My Soul: Rock's Great Songwriters . . . Talk about Creating Their Music. BILL FLANAGAN. Contemporary, 1986.

Kurosawa, Akira (1910–) Now a legend,

as well as one of the world's most celebrated film directors, Kurosawa created yet another new work in 1992; scheduled for 1993 release, *Mada Do Yo* (*Not Ready Yet*) was his third film in three years. The film, based on the life of essayist Hyakken Uchida during the post-World War II period, stars Tatsuo Matsumura as Uchida, Kyoko Kagawa, Hisasha Igawa, George Tokoro, Masayuki Yui, and Akora Terao, many of whom have appeared in earlier Kurosawa films. Kurosawa described the film, largely the story of the relationship by Uchiki and some of his former students, as a biography; some others in Japan have thought it to be a celebration of lost Japanese values, and especially of student-teacher relationships.

Kurosawa's awards continued. On March 14, while he was shooting *Mada Da Yo* in Japan, his son accepted the Directors Guild of America D. W. Griffith lifetime achievement award for him. In October, he accepted a corporate-financed Japanese Imperial award. On the legal side, Kurosawa sued Japan's Toho Company, producer of many of his films, claiming unpaid royalties on 21 of his films.

Kurosawa was an assistant director (1936–43); his first film as a director was *Sugata Sanshiro* (1943). He emerged as a major figure during the postwar period, bringing Japanese films to a world audience in the 1950s, with such films as *Rashomon* (1950; Best Foreign Film Oscar); *The Seven Samurai* (1954); and *Throne of Blood* (1957; his adaptation of *Macbeth*). His later films included such classics as *Yojimbo* (1961), *Redbeard* (1964), *Derzu Uzala* (1976), *Kagemusha* (1980), *Ran* (1984; his adaptation of *King Lear*), *Akira Kurosawa's Dreams* (1990), and *Rhapsody in August* (1991). In 1982, he published *Something Like an Autobiography*. He attended the Doshusha School of Western Painting.

FURTHER READING

"Moments with. . . ." SHAWN LEVY and JAMES FEE. *American Film*, Jan.–Feb. 1992.
"Kurosawa, Akira." *Current Biography*, July 1991.
The Warrior's Camera: The Cinema of Akira Kurosawa. STEPHEN PRINCE. Princeton University Press, 1991.
"A. Kurosawa." RALPH RUGOFF. *Interview*, Sep. 1990.
"Akira Kurosawa." JOHN CLARK. *Premiere*, Aug. 1990.
"Japan's emperor. . . ." IAN BURUMA. *New York Times Magazine*, Oct. 29, 1989.
"Akira Kurosawa." GERALD PEARY. *American Film*, Apr. 1989.

Laettner, Christian (1969–) It was truly a dream year for basketball star Christian Laettner. In his senior year, as co-captain, he led the Duke University Blue Devils to their second

straight National Collegiate Athletic Association (NCAA) championship. In the process he became the only player ever to start in four Final Four teams, and the all-time NCAA basketball tournament scoring leader, passing the record of 407 points set by the great Elvin Hayes, while also tying the record for steals at 32. Laettner had an extraordinary sweep of college basketball's major awards in 1992, receiving the Wooden Award, the Naismith Award, and the Adolph F. Rupp Trophy; topping the college basketball players' list of the Associated Press, UPI, Basketball Times, Basketball Weekly, and Scripps-Howard; and being unanimously named National Player of the Year by Kodak/NABC. His jersey #32 was retired by Duke, only the sixth to be retired in that school's illustrious basketball history.

Laettner was then honored by being the only college player selected to play on what was called the U.S.A.'s "Dream Team," including some of the world's greatest basketball players. Laettner held his own in heady company and, with them, came home from the 1992 Barcelona Olympics with the gold medal for basketball. In the National Basketball Association (NBA) draft of college players, Laettner was selected second (after Shaquille O'Neal) by the Minnesota Timberwolves, an expansion team sorely in need of his many skills. After signing a multimillion-dollar six-year contract, he began his professional career and, by the end of 1992, was averaging 19 points and over 8 rebounds a game.

Born in upstate New York, Laettner emerged

as a nationally recognized prep school player at Buffalo's Nichols School, and, as a leading scorer and rebounder, was sought by many colleges before choosing Duke. His first three years of college basketball established him as a national figure; he had an outstanding freshman year and then went on to become a three-time All-American, as a leading scorer, shot-blocker, and rebounder, equally promising on offense and defense. He led Duke to the 1991 NCAA championship, and was named most valuable player of the Final Four.

FURTHER READING

"Devilishly different." CURRY KIRKPATRICK. *Sports Illustrated*, Nov. 25, 1991.

Lake, Anthony (1939–) President Bill Clinton's incoming National Security Advisor brings three decades of foreign affairs experience and teaching with him into the White House. Lake was a Foreign Service Officer in the U.S. State Department from 1962, joining as a strong believer in the foreign policy of President John F. Kennedy and staying on until the Cambodian invasion of 1970 and disillusion with American policy in Vietnam. He served in a series of Vietnam postings (1962–65), and acted as Henry Kissinger's Special Assistant to the Assistant to the President on National Security Affairs (1969–70). Lake returned to the White House during the Carter years, as State Department director of policy planning (1977–81). From 1981 to 1992, he was a Professor of International Relations at Mt. Holyoke College. He was a Senior Foreign Policy Advisor to the Clinton/Gore campaign. Lake's 1961 A.B. was from Harvard College, and his 1974 Ph.D. from Princeton University's Woodrow Wilson School of Public and International Affairs. His works include *The "Tar Baby" Option: American Policy Toward Southern Rhodesia* (1976), *The Legacy of Vietnam: The War, American Society, and the Future of American Foreign Policy* (1976; as editor), *Our Own Worst Enemy: The Unmaking of American Foreign Policy* (1984; written with I.M. Destler and Leslie Gelb), *Third World Radical Regimes: U. S. Policy under Carter and Reagan* (1985), *Somoza Falling* (1989), and *After the Wars: Reconstruction in Afghanistan, Indochina, Central America, Southern Africa, and the Horn of Africa* (1990). He is married and has three children.

FURTHER READING

"A foreign policy puritan." J.F. MCALLISTER. *Time*, Nov. 30, 1992.

Landsbergis, Vyatautas (1932–) For newly independent Lithuania, 1992 was a sobering year. With independence came severe economic problems, chief among them inability to pay Russia full world market prices for the absolutely essential oil supplies that the Soviet Union had previously supplied at very low subsidized prices. The Landsbergis government refused to pay the much higher prices, Russia sharply curtailed its supply of oil, and in Lithuania homes went unheated and business ground to a near-halt. Unable to handle the economy for this and other reasons, the government floundered—and to the majority of Lithuanians some of the old Communist leaders became attractive once again, a trend not at all limited to Lithuania, but apparent in many countries of Eastern Europe and the former Soviet Union as the second post-Soviet winter came on.

In the October 25, 1992, parliamentary elections and the November 8 runoffs, Landsbergis's Sajudis party lost to the Democratic Labor Party, headed by former Lithuanian Communist leader Algirdas Brazaukas, which won a decisive victory. Although Landsbergis charged Russia with having manipulated the election by use of its economic power, there was no real question of election fraud; the Lithuanian people had voted the ex-Communists in and the nationalists out. Landsbergis and his party, however, remained a power to be reckoned with in Lithuanian life, and he was thought a major contender for the presidency in the upcoming 1993 elections.

Landsbergis is a very recent politician, who spent most of his working life as a distinguished Soviet musicologist, teaching at the Vilnius Conservatory. He began to emerge as a major Lithuanian and Soviet political figure in 1989, at the head of Sajudis, the leading noncommunist Lithuanian nationalist organization. In May 1989 he was a highly visible Lithuanian nationalist delegate to the first session of the Soviet Congress of People's Deputies. On March

11, 1990, the Lithuanian parliament scored a historic "first," seceding from the Soviet Union; it elected Landsbergis the first President of independent Lithuania. He led his country to fully recognized independence in 1991. Divorced, then remarried, Landsbergis has three children.

FURTHER READING

"Orchestrating freedom." JOHN BUDRIS. *World Monitor*, Dec. 1991.
"Landsbergis, Vytautas." *Current Biography*, July 1990.
"Landsbergis talks tough. . . ." *U.S. News & World Report*, Dec. 17, 1990.
"The meddlesome musicologist. . . ." JEFF TRIMBLE. *U.S. News & World Report*, May 14, 1990.

lang, k. d. (Kathy Dawn Lang; 1962–   ) After a two-year break with recording, popular singer k. d. lang returned with a complete change of direction. In April, she issued the album *Ingenue*, and with it broke from country music, at least for the moment, moving over to a wholly mainstream cabaret style that some critics compared to that of French singer Edith Piaf, and that she described as much influenced by show tunes, movie musicals, and such singers as Billie Holiday. The album was a hit, as were such singles drawn from it as "Constant Craving," "The Mind of Love," and "Miss Chatelaine." Lang won a 1992 Billboard music video award as best female artist for "Constant Crav-

ing." She toured widely in the United States and Europe during 1992.

During her two year break, lang starred in Percy Adlon's film *Salmonberries*, in large part a lesbian love story. In June 1992, she also for the first time publicly declared her lesbian sexual preferences, although she had long since made her preferences clear, and had attracted a focused lesbian audience in addition to her much larger country and crossover popular music audiences.

Born in the small town of Consort, Alberta, Canada, lang began her career as a performance artist singing country music while still at Alberta's Red Deer College. She made her professional singing debut in cabaret in Edmonton, Alberta, and in 1984 formed her first group, the Reclines. Moving to Toronto and gaining in popularity as she toured, she also cut her first country music album, *A Truly Western Experience* (1984). She made her U.S. debut in New York City in 1985, and from that appearance came her association with Sire Records, which issued her albums *Angel With a Lariat* (1986) and *Shadowland* (1988), neither of them a great commercial hit, but both critically acclaimed. Lang won a 1990 Best Female Country Vocalist Grammy award for her fourth album *Torch and Twang*. An activist in many social causes, including animal rights, she has sparked considerable controversy, most notably with her anti-meat ads.

FURTHER READING

"K.D. gets real." PETER GODDARD. *Chatelaine*, Sep. 1992.
"Lang, K.D." *Current Biography*, Sep. 1992.
"Virgin territory. . . ." BRENDAN LEMON. *Advocate*, June 16, 1992.
"Midnight cowgirl." KRISTINE MCKENNA. *US*, May 1992.
"Torch and twang. . . ." DON GILLMOR. *Reader's Digest (Canadian)*, Oct. 1990.
"Lesley Gore on. . . . " LESLEY GORE. *Ms.*, July–Aug. 1990.
"The amazing k.d. lang." CHARLA KRUPP. *Glamour*, Feb. 1990.
"Another country." HOLLY GLEASON. *Harper's Bazaar*, Oct. 1989.
"Out of the corral. . . ." RICHARD FLOHIL. *Canadian Composer*, Oct. 1988.
"Quirky k.d. Lang. . . ." STEVE DOUGHERTY. *People*, July 4, 1988.
"Is k.d. Lang. . . ." TIM APPELO. *Savvy*, July 1988.
"A bracing breeze. . . ." NICHOLAS JENNINGS and ANNE GREGOR. *Maclean's*, May 30, 1988.

Lange, Jessica (1949–) Film star Lange made a major move to Broadway in 1992, starring in the classic Blanche DuBois role in a hit revival of Tennessee Williams' *A Streetcar Named Desire*, opposite Alec Baldwin as Stanley Kowalski, Amy Madigan, and Timothy Carhart; Gregory Mosher directed. On screen, she starred as Helen Nassaros opposite Robert De Niro as Harry Fabian, a small-time New York ambulance-chasing lawyer, in Irwin Winkler's *Night and the City*, a remake of Jules Dassin's 1950 *Night and the City*. In 1992 Lange also made her television drama debut, in the Hallmark Hall of Fame adaptation of Willa Cather's 1913 novel *O Pioneers!*, the story of a Swedish family in late 19th century Nebraska, produced and directed by Glenn Jordan. Still forthcoming was *Blue Sky*, the story of a nuclear engineer and his family enmeshed in a military coverup situation, in which she starred opposite Tommy Lee Jones. The film had been scheduled for 1992 release, but was postponed.

Minnesota-born Lange became one of the leading movie stars of the late 1970s and of the 1980s, with such films as *All That Jazz* (1979), *The Postman Always Rings Twice* (1981), *Frances* (1982), *Tootsie* (1982), *Crimes of the Heart* (1986), *Music Box* (1989), *Men Don't Leave* (1990), and *Cape Fear* (1991). She attended the University of Minnesota. She was formerly married to Paco Grande, and has three children, one from a former relationship with ballet star

Mikhail Baryshnikov, two from her relationship with actor-playwright Sam Shepard. (For additional photo, see DeNiro, Robert.)

FURTHER READING

"Full-tilt Jessica." NANCY COLLINS. *Vanity Fair*, Oct. 1991.
"Jessica." VALERIE MONROE. *Harper's Bazaar*, Jan. 1991.
"Jessica Lange." *American Film*, Aug. 1990.
"The enigmatic allure. . . ." LINDA BIRD FRANCKE. Cosmopolitan, Feb. 1990.
Jessica Lange. J.T. JEFFRIES. St. Martin's, 1986.

Lansbury, Angela Brigid (1925–) As Cabot Cove mystery writer and detective Jessica Fletcher, stage and screen star Lansbury was once again a major television star in 1992, as her "Murder, She Wrote" continued to show strongly in its 8 P.M. Sunday night slot into the 1992–93 season. Reruns of earlier shows on the USA cable channel also drew substantial audiences. As she had promised in 1991, she opened out the show somewhat, choosing a New York setting that allowed her much greater plot and ethnic variety. In 1992, Lansbury won an Emmy nomination as lead actress in a drama series and a Golden Globe award as best actress in a drama series. She also won an honor of a quite a different kind, being chosen Grand Marshal of the 104th Tournament of Roses. In a change of pace, Lansbury starred opposite Omar Sharif and Diana Rigg in the CBS television film *Mrs. 'Arris Goes to Paris*, about a working-class British woman who goes to Paris to buy a Christian Dior original, in fulfillment of her dream.

British-born Lansbury began her long film and theater career with a supporting role in *Gaslight* (1944), and played competently in over a score of substantial film roles during the following 25 years. But it was on Broadway and in television, both much later, that she became a major star. She won four Tony Awards on Broadway, for *Mame* (1966), *Dear World* (1969), *Gypsy* (1973), and *Sweeney Todd* (1979). Then, quite late in her career, she became a major television star with "Murder, She Wrote" (1984–), also starring in such television films as *The Shell Seekers* (1989) and *The Love She Sought* (1989). She starred in the animated film *Beauty and the Beast*, one of the hits of the 1991 Christmas season. She has published *Angela Lansbury's Posi-*

tive Moves (1991). Lansbury married Peter Shaw in 1949; they have two children.

FURTHER READING

"Auntie Angela." KEVIN ALLMAN. *Advocate*, Sep. 22, 1992.
"Gardens, she wrote." SUSAN SWIMMER. *Ladies Home Journal*, July 1992.
"She's conquered movies. . . ." RICHARD ALLEMAN. *Vogue*, Dec. 1991.
"Angela Lansbury has. . . ." SUZANNE ADELSON. *People*, Nov. 7, 1988.
"Solving the case of. . . ." PHYLLIS BATTELLE. *Woman's Day*, Sep. 13, 1988.
Angela Lansbury: A Biography. MARGARET W. BONNANO. Thomas Dunne/St. Martin's, 1987.

Laubenstein, Linda (1947–92) Boston-born Dr. Linda Laubenstein played a major early role in the recognition and treatment of AIDS and related diseases. A paraplegic who was confined to a wheelchair from age five because of poliomyelitis, and asthmatic as well, she graduated from New York University Medical School, became an oncologist and a hematologist, and was a clinical professor at the New York University Medical Center. In 1981, she and Dr. Alvin Friedman-Klein wrote the first paper published in a medical journal on formerly rare Karposi's sarcoma, and by 1982 she was treating scores of AIDS cases, and predicting an epidemic. In 1983, she and Friedman-Klein organized a pioneering medical conference on AIDS at New York University. She also became a leader in the fight for enlightened societal response to AIDS patients, and in 1989 co-organized the nonprofit organization Multitasking, which provided office services work for AIDS patients. A very sharp critic of inadequate government research and help on AIDS, she also called for public health measures to prevent its spread, as in the closing of bathhouses. She inspired the Dr. Emma Brookner character in Larry Kramer's play *The Normal Heart*. She was survived by her parents and a brother. (d. Chatham, Massachusetts; August 15, 1992)

FURTHER READING

Obituary. *The Times* (of London), Aug. 22, 1992.
Obituary. *New York Times*, Aug. 17, 1992.

Lee, Spike (Shelton Jackson Lee; 1957–) Filmmaker Spike Lee was once again a focus of controversy and publicity in 1992, most of it generated by the filming and distribution of his film *Malcolm X*, which opened in mid-November. Lee began filming in late 1991; by late spring 1992, he was $5 million over budget, and highly publicized arguments involving Lee, Warner Brothers, and the Completion Bond Company were in progress. In late May, Lee announced that a group of moneyed African-Americans had saved the film by contributing an unspecified sum of money. In late October, nearing distribution, Lee publicly announced that he preferred to be interviewed by African-American journalists, setting off another round of controversy and publicity.

Ultimately, *Malcolm X* opened; the film biography of the African-American leader ran three hours and nineteen minutes, and was the epic treatment that Lee had wanted to make. Denzel Washington starred as Malcolm X, leading a large cast that included Angela Bassett as his wife, Al Freeman, Jr., as Elijah Muhammad, Delroy Lindo, Albert Hall, Theresa Randle, Kate Vernon, Lonette McKee, Tommy Hollis, James McDaniel, Ernest Thompson, Jean LaMarre, Christopher Plummer, Karen Allen, Peter Boyle, Bobby Seale, Al Sharpton, and William Kunstler. Lee directed, co-produced, and co-wrote the screenplay, based on the book *The Autobiography of Malcolm X*, as told to Alex Haley.

Far from being incendiary, the film was generally reviewed as a rather sober, reverential biographical epic, with reviewer responses ranging from generally favorable to quite negative, some reviewers calling the work dull and slow and others liking its pace and content. There was also an accompanying book: *By Any Means Necessary: The Trials and Tribulations of the Making of Malcom X*, by Spike Lee and Ralph Wiley.

Atlanta-born Lee has made several films, including *She's Gotta Have It* (1986) and *School Daze* (1988); with Lisa Jones, he wrote books about the making of both films. He became a notable and very controversial filmmaker in 1989, with release of his film *Do the Right Thing*, a fictional story that sharply explored racial tensions in his home area of Bedford-Stuyvesant, in Brooklyn. Denzel Washington starred in Lee's equally controversial 1990 film *Mo' Better Blues*, attacked by many as anti-Semitic for its story of the exploitation of African-American artists, in this instance by two Jewish club owners. His 1991 film was *Jungle Fever*, an interracial love story. Lee's 1979 B.A. was from Morehouse College, and his 1983 M.A. in filmmaking from New York University.

FURTHER READING

" 'I'm for truth,'. . . ."ANNE THOMPSON. *Entertainment*, Nov. 27, 1992.

"Words with Spike." JANICE C. SIMPSON. *Time*, Nov. 23, 1992.

"X, lies and videotapes?" PLAYTHELL BENJAMIN. *Guardian*, Nov. 18, 1992.

"Great Xpectations." RALPH WILEY. *Premiere*, Nov. 1992.

"Spike goes the extra mile. . . ." *Scholastic Update*, Oct. 23, 1992.

"Spike Lee hates. . . ." BARBARA GRIZZUTI HARRISON. *Esquire*, Oct. 1992.

"Movies. . . ." DAVID DENBY. *New York*, Sep. 14, 1992.

"Black and white movies." RICHARD BROOKS. *Observer*, May 17, 1992.

"The battle to film. . . . " JANICE C. SIMPSON. *Time*, Mar. 16, 1992.

Spike Lee. ALEX PATTERSON. Avon, 1992.

"Spike Lee. . . ." DAVID BRESKIN. *Rolling Stone*, July 11, 1991.

"Spike Lee. . . ." ELVIS MITCHELL. *Playboy*, July 1991.

"Spiking a fever. . . ." JACK KROLL. *Newsweek*, June 10, 1991.

"Spike's peak. . . ." GERRI HIRSHEY. *Vanity Fair*, June 1991.

Five for Five: The Films of Spike Lee. TERRY McMILLAN. Stewart Tabori & Chang, 1991.

Lehrer, Jim (James Charles Lehrer; 1934–) Veteran journalist Lehrer was selected by the Commission on Presidential Debates to be the moderator of not one but two of the three presidential debates in the 1992 campaign—an honor not significantly diminished by the fact that CBS and NBC refused to participate, because the candidates had a say in choosing the moderators. In the first of the October 1992 debates, Lehrer moderated with a panel of journalists; in the third, Lehrer was the sole questioner at first, then joined by three other journalists. With his colleague Robert MacNeil, Lehrer in January also moderated the third of the nationally televised debates among the major Democratic presidential candidates. Meanwhile, the pair continued with PBS's highly respected "MacNeil/Lehrer NewsHour," offering an unparalleled summary of the day's events and in-depth exploration of what lies behind both current events and longer-ranging concerns—a rarity in a world where news elsewhere seems to be coming in ever shorter "sound-bites." During the Democratic and Republican conventions in the political year of 1992, in a break with tradition, Lehrer and MacNeil were joined on PBS by NBC news anchor Tom Brokaw.

On a different front, Lehrer published two books in 1992: a book of memoirs called *A Bus of My Own*, and *Short List*, the fifth of his comedic novels about the fictional Oklahoma-born "one-eyed Mack," the grossly underqualified lieutenant governor who this time almost becomes Vice-

President, after giving an impromptu keynote address at the Democratic National Convention.

Kansas-born Lehrer was a reporter for the *Dallas Morning News* (1959–61), then moving to the *Dallas Times Herald* as reporter and later city editor (1961–70). He moved into broadcast journalism as a correspondent and producer for KERA-TV, Dallas (1970–72). He joined the Public Broadcasting System in 1972, and in 1973 began his long association with Robert MacNeil; they won an Emmy for their live coverage of the Senate Watergate hearings. The "Robert Mac-Neil Report," with Lehrer as Washington correspondent, began in 1975, and became their award-winning "MacNeil/Lehrer Report" in 1976 and 'The MacNeil/Lehrer NewsHour" in 1983. His many awards include several Emmys, a George Polk Award, and a Peabody award. Lehrer has also hosted several PBS specials. His novels include *Viva Max* (1966), *We Were Dreamers* (1975), *Kick the Can* (1988), *Crown Oklahoma* (1989), and *The Sooner Spy* (1990). His plays include *Chili Queen* (1986) and *Church Key Charlie Blue* (1987). His 1956 journalism degree was from the University of Missouri. He is married to author Kate Staples, and has three children.

FURTHER READING

"MacNeil/Lehrer. . . ." MORGAN STRONG. *Playboy*, June 1991.
"Inside TV's finest. . . ." MALCOLM McCONNELL. *Reader's Digest* (Canadian), July 1988.

Leiber, Fritz Reuter, Jr. (1910–92)

Chicago-born Leiber, a graduate in biology of the University of Chicago, began his career as an actor in his family's touring company, and played a small role in Greta Garbo's *Camille* (1937). In the late 1930s, he turned to writing, becoming a leading fantasy and science fiction author. He was best known for his enduring "Fafhrd and the Grey Mouser" series of stories, which began with his first published story, "Two Sought Adventure," in 1939. Leiber went on to write such works as the classic science fiction novel *Gather, Darkness* (1943), which prefigured many later works on the rise and rule of fundamentalist religious cults. His work included such genre classics as *Conjure Wife*, *The Black Gondolier*, *Green Millenium*, and *The Wanderer*. He

was survived by his second wife, Margo Skinner, and a son. (d. San Francisco; September 5, 1992)

FURTHER READING

Obituary. *The Times* (of London), Sept. 28, 1992.
Obituary. *New York Times*, Sept. 11, 1992.
Fritz Leiber. GORDON BENSON, JR. Borgo Press, 1990.
"SF's dean of sci-fi. . . ." HARRY MOSS. *San Francisco*, Dec. 1988.

Leigh, Jennifer Jason (Jennifer Morrow; 1962–)

Film star Jennifer Jason Leigh appeared in 1992 in another intensely dramatic role as very troubled and deadly roommate Hedra Carlson in Barbet Schroeder's sex-and-murder film *Single White Female*, starring opposite Bridget Fonda as threatened Allison Jones, and Steven Weber. The film was a surprise summer hit, as one of the several commercially successful extremely violent "women's" films of the period. Leigh also starred opposite Andras Jones in Steven Shainberg's film *The Prom* as a talk-but-don't-touch sex parlour worker with a heart of gold.

Leigh appeared in quite another kind of film as well, starring in Vincent Ward's *Map of the Human Heart*, a large-canvas multigenerational and crosscultural (English Canadian, French Canadian, and Inuit Eskimo) romantic drama set largely in the Canadian Arctic from the 1930s through the 1960s. She was also widely seen in the United States and abroad in her late-1991 film *Rush*, in which she and Jason Patric starred as undercover narcotics officers who become drug addicts. Forthcoming was a starring role opposite Paul Newman and Tim Robbins in Joel Coen's film *The Hudsucker Proxy*.

Los Angeles-born Leigh, the daughter of actor Vic Morrow and screenwriter Barbara Turner, began her career with guest appearances in television while in her mid-teens. Leaving high school shortly before graduation, she made her film debut in the horror film *Eyes of a Stranger* (1981), in the first of a long series of roles portraying physically and psychologically battered women. Her breakthrough role came a year later, in *Fast Times at Ridgemont High* (1982). She went on to star in such films as *Easy Money* (1983), *Grandview U.S.A.* (1984), *Flesh + Blood* (1985), *The Hitcher* (1986), *The Men's Club* (1986), *Sister, Sister* (1987), *Under Cover* (1987),

Heart of Midnight (1988), *Last Exit to Brooklyn* (1989), *Miami Blues* (1990), and *Crooked Hearts* (1991). In television, she starred as an anorexic teenager in *The Best Little Girl in the World* (1981), and on stage off-Broadway in *Sunshine* (1989).

FURTHER READING

"Not the girl next door." JEFFREY RESSNER. *US*, Sep. 1992.
"Leigh, Jennifer Jason." *Current Biography*, Aug. 1992.
"Jennifer Jason Leigh." TRISH DEITCH ROHRER. *Entertainment*, June 26, 1992.
"Jennifer Jason Leigh." *Playboy*, Feb. 1992.
"The devil and Miss Leigh." JOSEPH HOOPER. *Esquire*, Jan. 1992.
"Jennifer Jason Leigh. . . ." TOM GREEN. *Cosmopolitan*, May 1991.
"Jennifer Jason Leigh." JEFF YARBROUGH. *Interview*, Apr. 1991.
"Jennifer Jason Leigh." LANCE LOUD. *Interview*, May 1990.
"Jennifer Jason Leigh. . . ." PHILIP WEISS. *Rolling Stone*, May 17, 1990.
Midnight heart." GAVIN SMITH. *Film Comment*, Mar.–Apr. 1990.
"Leighway." CAROL BLUE. *Interview*, Oct. 1989.

teen years later, he won a Best Actor Oscar for *Save the Tiger* (1973). Among his other films, a few of the most notable were *Bell Book and Candle* (1958), *Some Like It Hot* (1959), *The Apartment* (1960), *Days of Wine and Roses* (1962), *Irma La Douce* (1963), *The Odd Couple* (1968), *The Prisoner of Second Avenue* (1975), *The China Syndrome* (1978), *Missing* (1981), *Mass Appeal* (1984), and *Dad* (1989). Lemmon's B.A. and B.S. are from Harvard. He was formerly married to Cynthia Boyd Stone, married Felicia Farr in 1962, and has two children.

FURTHER READING

"Jack Lemmon." JOHN CLARK. *Premiere*, Nov. 1992.
"An everyman in a class of his own." PHILIP FRENCH. *Observer*, Oct. 25, 1992.
"Laughing on the outside." TOM JUNOD and MICHAEL O'NEILL. *Life*, Oct. 1992.
"Lemmon, Jack." *Current Biography*, Aug. 1988.
"Jack of all trades." BURT PRELUTSKI. *American Film*, Mar. 1988.
Actors: A Celebration. RITA GAM. St. Martin's, 1988.
The Films of Jack Lemmon. JOE BALTAKE. State Mutual, 1987.
Jack Lemmon. MICHAEL FREEDLAND. St. Martin's, 1985.

Lemmon, Jack (John Lemmon III; 1925–) In a Hollywood film world with less and less powerful dramatic roles available, a really fine role is very hard to come by. Jack Lemmon found one in 1992, starring as failing, shady Chicago real estate boiler room salesman Shelley Levene in James Foley's film adaptation of David Mamet's dark drama *Glengarry Glen Ross* (screenplay by Mamet). Co-starring in equally appealing roles were Al Pacino, Alec Baldwin, Ed Harris, Alan Arkin, Kevin Spacey, and Jonathan Pryce. Lemmon's superb portrayal immediately made him a prime 1993 Academy Award contender. His first Best Actor award for the role came in September 1992, at Italy's 49th Venice Film Festival. On film, Lemmon also appeared as himself in Robert Altman's merciless, multistar lampoon of modern Hollywood, *The Player*. On television, he starred in the far less successful television film comedy *For Richer, For Poorer*.

Boston-born Lemmon played in early television, and began his long film career by winning a Best Supporting Actor Oscar for his portrayal of Ensign Pulver in *Mister Roberts* (1954). Nine-

Leno, Jay (James Douglas Muir Leno; 1950–) Leno took the hot seat in 1992, when "The Tonight Show Starring Johnny Carson"—a fixture in late-night television for 30 years, with a format dating back to 1954—became "The Tonight Show With Jay Leno." Leno's face was not new to late-night audiences. He had been a frequent guest on both the "Tonight Show" and the then-following "Late Night with David Letterman" from 1977, and was a guest host on the "Tonight Show" from 1986—the exclusive guest host from 1987.

But taking over from an icon is never easy. Ratings were initially high, starting with the first show, on May 25th, featuring Billy Crystal, with many viewers being drawn by all the publicity surrounding the change. Later the show's ratings dropped off, especially as political and social events plus pre-emption during the Barcelona Summer Olympics drew attention elsewhere. "Tonight" got unwelcome publicity when some celebrities charged that their appearances had been cancelled because they refused to break dates with the competing "Arsenio Hall Show." The policy was associated with executive producer Helen Kushnick, Leno's longtime manager, who was eventually fired by NBC. As Leno settled into his new role, ratings grew stronger.

Even so turbulence once again swirled, when David Letterman—passed over as Carson's replacement and unhappy with his late slot—received an attractive offer from CBS and presented NBC with a dilemma: to let him go or give him Leno's spot. While Leno expressed dismay over the network's refusal to guarantee his position, NBC dithered for weeks before finally, in mid-January 1993, releasing Letterman to CBS. Leno and Letterman were expected to go head-to-head in a new ratings war in 1993.

Born in New York's suburbs and raised in Massachusetts, Leno began his career as a stand-up comic at Boston nightclubs while studying for a speech degree at Emerson College. He later worked New York clubs and wrote for television's "Good Times." He has toured widely, hosted two of his own NBC Specials, made numerous guest appearances, and published four books of odd or absurd newspaper cuttings, many sent by fans. Leno married scriptwriter Mavis Nicholson in 1980.

FURTHER READING

"Why is everybody. . . . " MARK HARRIS.
  Entertainment, Aug. 14, 1992.
"Jay Leno: the early years." STEVE BUCKLEY. Boston,
  May 1992.
"Hosts of trouble." FRANK SWERTLOW. Entertainment,
  Apr. 10, 1992.

"Midnight's mayor. . . . " RICHARD STENGEL. Time,
  Mar. 16, 1992.
The World of Jay Leno: His Humor and His Life.
  BILL ADLER and BRUCE CASSIDAY. Birch Lane/Carol,
  1992.
"Wipe that smirk. . . . " PETER W. KAPLAN and PETER
  STEVENSON. Esquire, Sep., 1991.
"The funniest man. . . . " SEAN PICCOLI. Insight, July
  22, 1991.
"Playboy interview. . . . " DICK LOCHTE. Playboy, Dec.
  1990.
"He-e-ere's Jay Leno." GRAYDON CARTER. Reader's
  Digest, Feb. 1990.
"The joker." GRAYDON CARTER. Rolling Stone, Nov. 2,
  1989.
"He-e-e-e-e-e-r-e's Jay Leno!" STU SCHREIBERG.
  Cosmopolitan, Sep. 1989.
"Jay Leno." MERRILL SHINDLER. Los Angeles, Aug. 1989.
"Jawing with Jay Leno." MARY BILLARD. GQ—
  Gentleman's Quarterly, Aug. 1989.
"Meet the millionaire comic. . . . " JOANMARIE KALTER.
  TV Guide, June 10, 1989.
"Jay Leno. . . . " PETER TAUBER. New York Times
  Magazine, Feb. 26, 1989.

Lerner, Max (1902–92)

Lerner, Max (1902–92) Born in Minsk, Russia, Max Lerner emigrated to the United States with his family in 1907. He graduated from Yale University in 1923 and received his Ph.D. from the Brookings School in 1927, then embarking on a career that in the 1930s included several college teaching jobs, including five years at Williams College (1938–43). He left teaching in 1943 to become editorial director of the liberal New York newspaper *PM*, then emerging as one of the leading liberal spokespersons of his day. After *PM* failed in 1948, he moved to the *New York Post* as a syndicated columnist, and wrote for the *Post* until shortly before his death. He was a prolific writer; in addition to his column he wrote many articles for other periodicals, and several books, including *It's Later Than You Think* (1938), *Ideas Are Weapons* (1939), the very popular *America as a Civilization: Life and Thought in the United States Today* (1957), and *The Age of Overkill* (1959). He was survived by his second wife, the former Edna Albers, two daughters, and two sons. (d. New York City; June 5, 1992)

FURTHER READING

"Sane Max. . . . " MARTIN PERETZ. New Republic, June
  29, 1992.
Obituary. New York Times, June 6, 1992.

Levinson, Barry L. (1932–) Distin-

guished director Barry Levinson and his film *Bugsy* came very, very close to major wins at the 1992 Academy Awards ceremonies. He won a nomination as best director, Warren Beatty as best actor, Allen Daviau for cinematography, Harvey Keitel and Ben Kingsley as supporting actors, and Ennio Morricone for best original song. But the Oscars went elsewhere, with *Bugsy* winning Oscars only for art direction and costume design. The film was, however, a worldwide box-office hit, and the Los Angeles Film Critics gave Levinson Best Director and the film Best Picture awards. Levinson's major 1992 film was the comedy-fantasy *Toys*, starring Robin Williams, Michael Gambon, Joan Cusack, Robin Wright, and Donald O'Connor. The film, about a toymaking factory gone mad in the hands of a mad general, had echoes of *Babes in Toyland* and *Dr. Strangelove*.

On the legal front, Levinson and writer David Simon, author of the 1991 nonfiction book *Homicide: A Year on the Killing Streets,* charged the writer and producer (Warner Television) of the new CBS television series "Polish Hill" with plagiarizing facts and plot lines from the Simon book. The matter was settled after considerable publicity by Warner's agreeing to make changes. Levinson's own television series based on the book, starring Daniel Baldwin, Richard Belzer, and Ned Beatty, was scheduled for 1993 release.

Baltimore-born Levinson worked as a writer and comedian in television, and as a screenplay writer, before turning to directing feature films. His early screenplays include *Silent Movie* (1976) and *High Anxiety* (1977) (both co-written with Mel Brooks), *And Justice for All* (1979), *Inside Moves* (1980), and *Best Friends* (1982). He made his directorial debut with the well-received *Diner* (1982), and went on to direct and in some instances co-write such films as *The Natural* (1984), *Good Morning Vietnam* (1987), *Tin Men* (1987), *Rain Man* (1988; Best Director Oscar), and *Avalon* (1990). In 1990 he published *Avalon, Tin Men, and Diner: Three Screenplays.* Levinson attended American University.

FURTHER READING

"Levinson, Barry." *Current Biography*, July 1990.
"Storyteller." GAVIN SMITH. *Film Comment,*
   Nov.–Dec. 1990.
"Baltimore. . . ." BEN YAGODA. *American Film*, Nov.
   1990.

"Barry in Baltimore." ALEX WARD. *New York Times Magazine*, Mar. 11, 1990.

Lindros, Eric (1973–) Hockey fans

thought they saw the future in 1991—but they had to wait a year. Eric Lindros, the most highly touted hockey star in years, was the number one pick overall in the 1991 National Hockey League (NHL) amateur entry draft, selected by the Quebec Nordiques. There was only one problem: Lindros did not want to play for the Nordiques. He resisted all blandishments, including a reported ten-year, $50 million contract. Various other teams attempted to obtain the rights to Lindros, and both the New York Rangers and the Philadelphia Flyers claimed to have made a deal with the Nordiques. Finally in June 1992, after a controversial arbitration hearing to decide which team's deal was made first, Philadelphia acquired the rights to Lindros in exchange for six current players, the Flyers' first round draft picks in the 1993 and 1994 drafts, and $15 million—a measure of the expectations they have for the tall, swift, powerful rookie center. Philadelphia hockey fans were beside themselves with joy and anticipation, treating Lindros like a teenage idol. Lindros himself became one of the four highest-paid players in the NHL, with a six-year contract of reportedly $16–18 million, plus a bonus for signing.

In his early professional games, the 19-year-old Lindros showed strength and occasional brilliance, but not yet dominance of the game. Few expected Lindros alone to lift his team into play-off contention, but future promise still glistened. In late November, Lindros lost nine games with a knee sprain, but on his return helped his team break a six-game losing streak.

Ontario-born Lindros was a member of the Canadian national junior team (1989–92), leading the team to the world championships in 1990 and 1991. Though drafted by the Ontario Hockey League (OHL) in 1989, he played for Detroit Compuware Junior A team of the United States Hockey League in 1989, before his rights were traded to the OHL's Oshawa Generals. There he set an OHL record with 19 game-winning goals in the 1990–91 season and led the Generals to the Memorial Cup, being named most valuable forward of the Cup Tournament. Lindros was also a member of the 1991–92 Canada Cup team and the Canadian team that won the silver medal in the 1992 Winter Olympics at Albertville. Lindros published *Fire on Ice* in 1991. He has attended Toronto's York University.

FURTHER READING

"Lucky Lindros." BRUCE WALLACE. *Maclean's*, Sep. 9, 1991.
"A sporting price tag. . . ." JOHN DALY and JAMES DEACON. *Maclean's*, May 6, 1991.
"Eric Lindros." RICHARD REGEN. *Interview*, Mar. 1991.
"Big, tough and turbocharged, . . ." *People*, Feb. 4, 1991.

Ling Ling (1969–92) Ling Ling was the famous female giant panda at the Washington Zoo; along with her male companion Hsing Hsing, she was a gift from China to the United States soon after President Richard M. Nixon's 1972 "opening to China" visit to the Peoples Republic of China. It had been hoped that the two pandas would produce offspring in captivity, but, although Ling Ling had five cubs, none survived infancy, dying due to natural causes. Much loved, Ling-Ling was seen during her 20 years of captivity by more than 63 million visitors to the zoo. She was survived by Hsing Hsing, also 23. (d. Washington, D.C.; December 30, 1992)

FURTHER READING

"Bye-bye, Ling-Ling." *People Weekly*, Jan. 18, 1993.

Li Peng (1928–) Chinese Premier Li Peng, with his leader Deng Xiaoping, during 1992 continued to develop the highly unstable combination of economic liberalization and political repression that had resulted in the the 1989 Tiananmen Square massacre. In his March 1992 policy-setting speech to the National People's Congress, he carried forward the themes developed a year earlier, citing low productivity, low quality, waste, and poor morale as adding up to an ailing centrally planned economy that needed transformation into a market economy—but accompanied by continuing repression of all political dissent. Part of the new emphasis on economic growth was a go-ahead on the controversial Three Gorges Dam on the Yangtse River, focus of worldwide environmentalist concern. What remained to be seen was whether or not the two mutually contradictory approaches could work, and especially whether they would be able to work once Deng, now 88 and in poor health, left power.

On the international side, Li Peng continued to build trade relations, while resisting all pressure to improve China's human rights record. China's "most favoured nation" trading status with the United States was restored in February 1992, and during the rest of the year the Bush administration successfully resisted all Congressional efforts to alter that status; many thought that the incoming Clinton adminstration might be less accommodating.

Li Peng began his long, steady rise in the Chinese Communist bureaucracy as a young protégé of premier Zhou En-lai. He emerged as a major figure in the 1980s, serving as minister of power in 1981 and as a Politburo member in 1985. In the late 1980s, as great tension developed between the liberal and conservative wings of the Chinese leadership, he became a conservative faction leader. Throughout the world, he is viewed as the chief architect of the 1989 Tiananmen Square massacre. Li attended the Moscow Power Institute. He married Zhu Lin in 1958; the couple have three children.

FURTHER READING

Tiananmen Square. SCOTT SIMMIE and BOB NIXON. University of Washington Press, 1989.
"Li Peng." *Current Biography*, Nov. 1988.

Lithgow, John Arthur (1945–) American stage and screen star John Lithgow had ample opportunity to display all his talent and versatility in Brian De Palma's 1992 film *Raising Cain*, for in the film he played five roles: the central role of child psychologist Carter, his twin brother Cain, his father Nix, his seven-year-old son Josh, and a woman named Margo, the last a resonant echo of his Oscar-nominated role as a transvestite in *The World According to Garp*. The film was well received as a vehicle for Lithgow, but was not a critical or commercial success. Lolita Davidovich, Steven Bauer, and Frances Sternhagen co-starred. Lithgow's 1991 crime-and-cops thriller *Ricochet*, co-starring Denzel Washington, with a cast that included Ice-T, did well in home video during 1992. In 1992, Lithgow also narrated an audio version of Dr. Seuss's "Yertle the Turtle and Other Stories." Forthcoming was a return to the Broadway theater in a starring role in the David Williamson play *Money and Friends*, scheduled to open in April 1993.

Rochester-born Lithgow began playing substantial roles on the New York stage in the early 1970s, in such plays as *The Changing Room* (1972), *Beyond Therapy* (1982), *Requiem for a Heavyweight* (1985), and *M. Butterfly* (1988). His most notable films include *The World According to Garp* (1982; he received an Oscar nomination), *Terms of Endearment* (1983; and a second Oscar nomination), *The Manhattan Project* (1986), *Memphis Belle* (1990), and *At Play in the Fields of the Lord* (1991). He has also appeared in several television films, including *The Day After* (1983), *Amazing Stories* (1987; he won an Emmy), and *The Boys* (1991). Lithgow is a 1967 Harvard University graduate, and also attended the London Academy of Music and Dramatic Art (LAMDA). He has been married twice, last to Mary Yeager in 1981, and has two children.

FURTHER READING

"John Lithgow. . . ." MEGAN ROSENFELD. *American Baby*, Aug. 1988.

Little, Cleavon (1939–92) Oklahoma-born Cleavon Little played in a wide range of stage, film, and television roles from the mid-1960s. On the New York stage, he appeared in several off-Broadway plays, made his Broadway debut in *Jimmy Shine* (1968), appeared at the New York Shakespeare Festival, and won a Tony and a Drama Desk award for his role in the musical *Purlie* (1970). He also appeared in many supporting film roles, and is best known to wide audiences for his role as the African-American sheriff in Mel Brooks' *Blazing Saddles* (1974). His work in television included roles in the series "Temperature's Rising," "Bagdad Cafe," and "True Colors," as well as many guest appearances and television film roles. He won an Emmy for his guest appearance in the series "Dear John." A very recent role was as a lawyer opposite Sidney Poitier as Thurgood Marshall in the 1991 television miniseries "Separate But Equal." Little's 1965 B.A. was from San Diego College; he was also a graduate of New York's American Academy of Dramatic Arts. He was survived by a daughter, his father, stepmother, two sisters, and two brothers. (d. Sherman Oaks, California; October 22, 1992)

FURTHER READING

"Star of 'Blazing Saddles,'. . . ." *Jet*, Nov. 9, 1992.
Obituary. *Variety*, Oct. 26, 1992.
Obituary. *New York Times*, Oct. 23, 1992.

Li Xiannian (1909–92) A Chinese Republican soldier while still in his teens, Li joined the Communist Party in 1927, fighting with Communist forces throughout the long Civil War. He

quickly rose to command positions, leading Fourth Front Red Army units on the Long March, and in 1938 becoming a corps commander in the New Fourth Army. After Communist victory in 1949, he rose steadily, becoming governor of Hubei Province in 1949, a vice-premier in 1954, and a Politburo member (1956–87). He was finance minister (1954–75) and held many other key positions during and after the Mao period, even surviving the Cultural Revolution without losing power as one of the key central managers of the Chinese economy. A supporter of Deng Xiaoping in the 1980s, he held the largely ceremonial post of President of China (1983–88), then becoming chairman of the Chinese People's Consultative Assembly. An economic and political conservative, he resisted decentralizing economic reforms and accompanying democratic political reforms, and strongly urged the 1989 army attacks on the Tiananmen Square student demonstrators. He was survived by his wife, Lin Jiamei, three daughters, and a son. (d. Beijing; June 21, 1992)

FURTHER READING

Obituary. *The Times* (of London), June 23, 1992.
Obituary. *New York Times*, June 23, 1992.

Lloyd Webber, Andrew (1948–)

While such Lloyd Webber hit musicals as *Cats* and *Phantom of the Opera* continued to play and pay worldwide, the celebrated composer and producer continued to generate more revivals of old hits and major new works. Early in 1992, a revival of his musical *Joseph and the Amazing Technicolor Dreamcoat* was a smash hit at London's Palladium. The play toured North America in the summer and fall of the year, and was set to open on Broadway in 1993. Lloyd Webber's major new work was his musical theater version of the film *Sunset Boulevard*, with Patti LuPone in the Norma Desmond role. The work premiered at his Sydmonton Festival in 1992, and was scheduled to open in London in late June 1993 and in New York soon after. Still forthcoming were several major projects, including a collaboration with Steven Spielberg on a film version of *Cats*; a film version of *Evita*, with Madonna in the title role; and a new night-time water spectacular, *Noah's Ark*, for Disney World, in Orlando, Florida, with an original symphonic score for the pageant.

On the personal side, Lloyd Webber's wife, Madeleine Gordon, gave birth to their first child, Alistair Adam.

Lloyd Webber emerged as a leading musical theater composer in 1968 with *Joseph and the Amazing Technicolor Dreamcoat*, lyrics by Tim Rice; he then wrote the trailblazing rock opera *Jesus Christ Superstar* (1970), with lyrics again by Rice. He won Tonys for the musicals *Evita* and *Cats*. His compositions also include the *Requiem Mass* (1975) and *Variations on a Theme by Pagannini* (1977), as well as the film scores for *Gumshoe* (1971), *Jesus Christ Superstar* (1973), and *The Odessa File* (1974). Lloyd Webber attended Oxford University and the Royal Academy of Music. He married fashion entrepreneur Madeleine Gordon in 1991; he has been married twice before, until 1990 to singer-actress Sarah Brightman, and has three children. He is the brother of cellist Julian Lloyd Webber.

FURTHER READING

"Andrew Lloyd Webber leaves. . . ." TOM GLIATTO. *People*, July 23, 1990.
Andrew Lloyd Webber: His Life and Works. MICHAEL WALSH. Abrams, 1989.
"The changing face of Broadway. . . ." MARILYN STASIO. *Life*, Feb. 1988.
"Magician of the musical. . . ." MICHAEL WALSH. *Time*, Jan. 18, 1988.

Lozano, Paul: See Bean-Bayog, Margaret.

Lorentz, Pare (1905–92) A leading documentary filmmaker, West Virginia-born Lorentz was a film critic in the late 1920s and early 1930s. In 1936, for the New Deal's Resettlement Administration, he wrote, directed, and produced his first film, the classic documentary *The Plow That Broke the Plains*, about the impact of soil erosion on Dust Bowl farmers. The highly praised film, with a score by Virgil Thompson, was made for $10,000, and was the first federal film to have a general release. In 1938, for the Farm Security Administration, he made *The River*, another classic documentary about the Mississippi in flood, again with a score by Virgil

Thompson. Lorentz became head of the U.S. Film Service in 1939. In 1940, he made a third classic, *The Fight for Life*, about the struggle to reduce infant mortality. He served as an armed forces filmmaker during and immediately following World War II. His final major work was the documentary *The Nuremberg Trials* (1946). He was later a lecturer and film consultant. Among his written works are *Lorentz on Film: Movies 1927 to 1941* (1968) and *FDR's Moviemaker: Memoirs and Scripts* (1992). He was survived by his wife, Elizabeth, a daughter, and a son. (d. Armonk, New York; March 5, 1992)

FURTHER READING

Obituary. *Variety*, Mar. 9, 1992.
Obituary. *The Times* (of London), Mar. 6, 1992.
Obituary. *New York Times*, Mar. 5, 1992.

Louis, Victor (1928–92)

Moscow-born Louis, a journalist, was something of a mystery to foreign observers during much of his lifetime. He had attended Moscow University, and had worked for several western embassies in Moscow before his arrest and imprisonment by Soviet authorities (1949–56). He then became an independent journalist in Moscow, one apparently very well placed to secure otherwise-secret information and breaking news stories, as demonstrated in his 1964 "scoop" about the political end of Nikita Khrushchev and his 1980 "scoop" on the death of Leonid Brezhnev. He is also said to have been responsible for the smuggling out of Alexander Solzhenitsyn's book *The Cancer Ward*, and several other proscribed works. Louis worked as a Moscow-based freelancer for several Western publications, wrote guides to the Soviet Union and other books, and also published a directory of otherwise hard-to-get Soviet telephone numbers. Whether or not he also worked for the Soviet government was at the time of his death still a matter of conjecture. He was survived by his wife, the former Jennifer Stratham, and three sons. (d. London; February 28, 1992)

FURTHER READING

Obituary. *The Times* (of London), Feb. 20, 1992.
Obituary. *New York Times*, Feb. 20, 1992.

Ludwig, Daniel Keith (1897–1992)

Child of a Great Lakes shipping family, Michigan-born Ludwig went into the shipping business at the age of 19, converting an old paddle steamer into a freight-hauling barge. In the 1920s, he went into the oil tanker business, building and operating a growing tanker fleet, and prospered even during the Great Depression of the 1930s. He made massive profits during World War II, emerging from the war as operator of the fifth largest U.S. tanker fleet. In 1951, he began building large oil tankers in Japan, and in the 1950s, as sole owner, developed the multibillion dollar National Bulk Carriers company. During the 1960s, he diversified into a considerable range of other areas, including banking, insurance, and mining. In 1967, he began a massive development project in the Brazilian Amazon, and in the next fifteen years lost $850–900 million while pursuing the unsuccessful project. Still a billionaire, he continued to operate his other businesses, selling some foreign operations to fund the Ludwig Institute for Cancer Research, which he founded in 1971. He was survived by his second wife and a daughter. (d. New York City; August 27, 1992)

FURTHER READING

Obituary. *The Times* (of London), Aug. 31, 1992.
Obituary. *New York Times*, Aug. 29, 1992.
No guts, no glory. STANLEY H. BROWN. *Forbes*, Oct. 21, 1991.
The Alexander Complex: Six Businessmen and the Empires They Built. MICHAEL MEYER. Random, 1989.
The Invisible Billionaire, Daniel Ludwig. JERRY SHIELDS. Houghton Mifflin, 1986.

Lund, John (1913–92)

A Hollywood film star of the 1940s and 1950s, Lund began his career in local productions in his hometown of Rochester, New York. He made his Broadway debut in *As You Like It* (1941), and worked in radio as an actor and writer. He wrote the book and lyrics for the stage musical *New Faces of 1943*. His breakthrough Broadway lead came in 1945, in *The Hasty Heart*, and brought a film contract and a move to Hollywood. He made his film debut in *To Each His Own* (1946), opposite Olivia De Havilland, and went on to star in such films as *A Foreign Affair* (1948), opposite Marlene Dietrich and Jean Arthur; *The Night Has a Thousand Eyes* (1948), opposite Edward G. Robinson; and *My Friend Irma* (1949). He continued to star in several 1950s films, mostly Westerns, but his career was in decline, and ended with *If a Man Answers* (1962). He was survived by a sister.

FURTHER READING

Obituary. *Variety*, June 22, 1992.
Obituary. *The Times* (of London), June 22, 1992.
Obituary. *New York Times*, June 19, 1992.
Obituary. *Independent*, May 13, 1992.

Lynch, David (1946–) Film director Lynch revisited his "Twin Peaks" television series themes and characters in 1992, directing and co-authoring the film *Twin Peaks Fire Walk With Me*, a retelling of the Laura Palmer story featured in Lynch's television series. Sheryl Lee, Ray Wise, and Kyle MacLachlan starred. In the film, he and Robert Engels told the Laura Palmer story as a chronological "prequel"; the series had told it in flashback form. The film was very poorly received, critically and commercially. *Twin Peaks Fire Walk With Me* was the first film in a three-picture financing and co-producing contract between Lynch and French entrepreneur Francis Bouygues. Lynch also created a new half-hour television comedy series, "On the Air," a slapstick farce.

Montana-born Lynch directed four films before 1990: *Eraserhead* (1977); *The Elephant Man* (1980), adapted from the stage play; the science fiction epic *Dune* (1984); and *Blue Velvet* (1986), a film about American small town life that is widely regarded as an earlier approach to the themes of his recent works. He emerged as a celebrity director with the April 1990 premiere of his offbeat nighttime soap opera television series "Twin Peaks" (1990–91). Lynch's next large work was the film *Wild at Heart* (1990), which starred Nicolas Cage and Laura Dern. The film won the grand prize at the Cannes Film Festival, although it was not as well received in the United States. Lynch attended the Corcoran School of Art, the Boston Museum School of Fine Arts, and the Pennsylvania Academy of Fine Arts. He has been married twice, and has two children.

FURTHER READING

David Lynch. KENNETH KALETA. Twayne/Macmillan, 1992.
"You are now. . . ." STEVE POND and MARCIA COBURN. *Playboy*, Feb, 1991.
"The Rolling Stone interview, . . ." DAVID BRESKIN. *Rolling Stone*, Sep. 6, 1990.
"David Lynch." JIM JEROME. *People*, Sep. 3, 1990.
"David Lynch." JOHN CLARK. *Premiere*, Sep. 1990.
"Weird America." JOSEPH SOBRAN. *National Review*, Oct. 1, 1990.
"Czar of Bizarre. . . ." RICHARD CORLISS. *Time*, Oct. 1, 1990.
"Lynch-time." BART BULL. *Vogue*, Feb. 1990.

M

McCartney, Paul

McCartney, Paul (1942–) Paul McCartney's fiftieth year was in career terms largely a year of preparation for the former Beatle and founder of Wings. After his immensely successful 1989 tour and his 1991 *Liverpool Oratorio*, he spent much of late 1991 and 1992 in his studio on England's Sussex coast, composing and creating the new album *Off the Ground*, scheduled for February 1993 release, and preparing for the projected world tour that would accompany it. Scheduled for release in January was the first single from the album, "Hope of Deliverance." Also scheduled was an MTV special titled *Up Close*, which McCartney taped in New York City in mid-December 1992.

He and his wife, Linda McCartney, continued to be very active in social causes, speaking out on environmental issues and against blood sports; Linda McCartney continued to express their shared vegetarian beliefs with her line of frozen vegetarian products as an alternative to meat dishes. One major effort was to raise the money to fund the conversion of Paul's old school, the Liverpool Institute, into a school for the performing arts; another was to raise the money to save nearby Rye Memorial Hospital.

In May 1992 McCartney became the first to be awarded the Polar Music Prize by the Swedish Academy of Music; he said that he would use the approximately $173,000 prize to help the performing arts and hospital projects. He was also honored by his peers with an Emmy nomination for best classical program in the performing arts, for *Paul McCartney's Liverpool Oratorio*, broadcast as part of the PBS "Great Performances" series.

Liverpool native McCartney is a major figure in popular music. From 1960 to 1970, with John Lennon, George Harrison and Ringo Starr, he was a member of the Beatles, as rhythm guitarist and then bass guitarist. He and John Lennon wrote a great many of the Beatles' songs, such as "Yesterday," "Strawberry Fields Forever," and "Sgt. Pepper's Lonely Hearts Club Band," and he was often the group's lead singer. In 1970, he went on his own, and in 1971 formed Wings, continuing to compose, perform, and record for worldwide audiences during the next two decades. In 1989, he went on the road for the first time in 13 years, with a highly successful world tour, which also produced a live album, *Tripping the Live Fantastic*, released in November 1990. *The Liverpool Oratorio*, his first classical work, premiered in 1991. In 1984, McCartney published *Give My Regards to Broad Street*. He married Linda Eastman in 1969; they have four children.

FURTHER READING

"Winged Beatle. . . ." *Economist*, June 13, 1992.
"Rock meets classical." DENNIS POLKOW. *Musical America*, Jan.–Feb. 1992.
Blackbird: The Life and Times of Paul McCartney. GEOFFREY GIULIANO. NAL-Dutton, 1991.
Strange Days: The Music of John, Paul, George and Ringo Twenty Years On. WALTER PODRAZIK. Popular Culture, 1991.
"Paul McCartney." TOM MULHERN. *Guitar Player*, July 1990.

Yesterday: The Biography of a Beatle. CHET FLIPPO. Doubleday, 1988.

It Was Twenty Years Ago Today. DEREK TAYLOR. Simon & Schuster, 1987.

McCartney: The Definitive Biography. CHRIS SALEWICZ. St. Martin's, 1986.

The Beatles, 2nd ed. HUNTER DAVIES. McGraw-Hill, 1985.

McClintock, Barbara (1902–92) Nobel

Prize-winner Barbara McClintock was one of the world's leading geneticists. After receiving her Ph.D. at Cornell University in 1927, she taught and researched at Cornell until 1936, taught at the University of Missouri (1936–41), and in 1941 settled down for a 51-year tenure at the Cold Spring Harbor Laboratory of the Carnegie Institution. There she pursued her pathbreaking and dedicated studies of the genetic constitution of maize, usually twelve hours a day and six days a week, keeping the outside world at bay, and until 1986 not even installing a telephone. As early as the 1930s, she had discovered that chromosomes and the movement of DNA fragments were at the basis of heredity, four decades before the structure of DNA had been discovered. Her discovery of transposable genetic elements, presented in 1951, was so ill-received that she withdrew from further publication in the area, while continuing her work. In the late 1970s, when those in her field had finally caught up to her, she was recognized for her pioneering

work. Her Nobel Prize in Physiology or Medicine came in 1983. Recipient of many other honors, McClintock refused to be distracted to the end, working in her laboratory until shortly before her death. She was survived by a sister and a brother. (d. Huntington, New York; September 2, 1992)

FURTHER READING

Obituary. *The Times* (of London), Sep. 5, 1992.
Obituary. *New York Times*, Sep. 4, 1992.
The Dynamic Genome: Barbara McClintock's Ideas in the Century of Genetics. NINA FEDOROFF and DAVID BOTSTEIN, eds. Cold Spring Harbor, 1992.
Barbara McClintock. CHARLOTTE KENT. Chelsea House, 1991.

McEntire, Reba (1955–) Country singer

McEntire was honored often by her peers in 1992. At the 27th annual Country Music Awards, she was named top female vocalist for the sixth time and won video of the year honors for "Is There Life Out There?" She also won a Best Female Country Singer Grammy nomination, and a Best Country Female Artist Billboard Music Video Award nomination for "Is There Life Out There?" McEntire was also named Billboard's Top Female Country Artist of The Year, for the eighth straight year.

In August 1992, she released the single "The

Greatest Man I Never Knew," from her 1991 hit album *For My Broken Heart*, which had also generated several other hit singles, including the single, "Is There Life Out There?," and "The Night the Lights Went Out in Georgia." In late December, she released her latest album, *It's Your Call*, preceded by release of the single "Take It Back." Forthcoming in 1993 was a 125-city North American tour in support of the album.

Oklahoma-born McEntire began her career as a recording artist in 1978 with the debut album *Reba McEntire*, and emerged in 1984 as one of the leading country music singers of her time with the album *My Kind of Country*, a hit that brought the first of her many major awards, as Country Music Association female vocalist of the year, an award repeated in 1985, which saw release of her album *Have I Got a Deal for You*. Her albums include *Whoever's In New England* and *What Am I Gonna Do About You*, both released in 1986; *The Last One to Know* and *Reba McEntire's Greatest Hits*, both in 1987; *Reba* (1988); *Reba Live!* and *Sweet 16*, both in 1989; *Rumor Has It* (1990); and *For My Broken Heart* (1991). She has also appeared in the film *Tremors* (1990), and opposite Kenny Rogers in the television miniseries "The Gambler IV." In March 1991, her tour manager and seven members of her band were killed in an airplane accident. She is married to Narvel Blackstock, and has one child.

FURTHER READING

"Reba rising." SUSAN ELLIOTT. *Woman's Day*, Nov. 3, 1992.
Reba: Country Music's Queen. DON CUSIC. St. Martin's, 1991.
"Reba McEntire. . . ." BOB ALLEN. *Country Music*, Nov.–Dec. 1990.
"Talking with. . . ." LAURA FISSINGER. *Redbook*, Jan. 1990.
"Reba McEntire. . . ." TIM ALLIS. *People*, Sep. 18, 1989.
"Reba takes the reins." HOLLY GLEASON. *Ladies Home Journal*, Nov. 1988.

McGowan, William (1927–92)

Pennsylvania-born McGowan, a chemical engineer and consultant, was engaged as a financial consultant by Microwave Communications Inc. in 1968. The company, then engaged in an effort to secure Federal Communications Commission approval of its microwave communications system, had encountered massive opposition from the U.S. telephone monopoly, American Telephone and Telegraph (AT&T). McGowan bought half of the company, reorganized it into MCI Communications Corporation, and entered the long fight that ultimately resulted in the breakup of AT&T. In 1974, MCI filed an antitrust suit against AT&T, winning a multimillion dollar 1980 jury award that was settled by the two companies in 1985. The U.S. Justice Department's simultaneous case against AT&T, which McGowan aided, ended in a 1982 consent decree; AT&T agreed to spin off its local telephone companies by 1984. Able to compete equally, McGowan then built MCI into a multibillion dollar company. He was survived by his wife, Sue Ling Gin, a sister, and three brothers. (d. Washington, D.C.; June 8, 1992)

FURTHER READING

Obituary. *The Times* (of London), June 17, 1992.
Obituary. *New York Times*, June 9, 1992.
"'Make some damn mistakes!'. . . ." KEN ADELMAN. *Washingtonian*, Oct. 1990.
"Out of chaos: MCI." EDMUND L. ANDREWS. *Business Month*, Dec. 1989.
"Together apart." LESLIE WAYNE. *New York Times Magazine*, Mar. 27, 1988.

MacGrath, Leueen (1914–92)

London-born Leueen MacGrath, an actress and writer, studied at the the Royal Academy of Dramatic Arts, and made her stage debut in a London production of *Beggars in Hell* (1933). An early major role was in Terence Rattigan's *French Without Tears* (1936). She later appeared in such plays as *Edward, My Son* (London and New York, 1948, and in the 1949 film); *The Enchanted* (1950); *The Potting Shed* (1957); *A Voyage Around My Father* (1966); and *A Bequest to the Nation* (1970). She also appeared in several films. With her third of five husbands, George S. Kaufman, she wrote three plays: *The Small Hours* (1951), *Fancy Meeting You Again* (1952), and the book of the musical *Silk Stockings* (1955). She was survived by a sister and a stepdaughter. (d. London; March 27, 1992)

FURTHER READING

Obituary. *The Times* (of London), Apr. 14, 1992.
Obituary. *Variety*, Apr. 6, 1992.
Obituary. *New York Times*, Mar. 31, 1992.

McInerney, Jay (1955–)

In 1992, nine years after publication of his first novel, *Bright Lights, Big City*, which established him as one of the "in" novelists of the 1980s, McInerney published his fourth novel, *Brightness Falls*. The earlier novel was a cocaine-and-New-York-highlife story of the decline and decay of some of the bright young acquisitors of the period, which to some extent moralized about their decline and fall, while at the same time quite glamorizing them, their big money, and their life style. In McInerney's new novel, set in 1987, the year of the stock market crash and the beginning of the unraveling of the purely selfish money ethic, the novelist's characters are older and have failed. For New York stockbroker Corinne Makepeace, the bloom is off career and highlife; for her husband, editor Russell Calloway, a grandiose takeover scheme involving his publishing company fails, and he is fired; for both, their marriage is nearly over. And cocaine has ruined their best friend, Jeff.

McInerney was widely thought in this novel to be expressing many of his own recent observations and concerns. With it, he certainly said goodbye to his New York period and to the 1980s. Personally, he also made a great change, marrying Tennessee society figure Helen Bransford, and settling in Nashville, far from his "wild" New York lifestyle of the '80s.

Hartford-born McInerney held several writing and publishing jobs early in his career, starting with a brief period as a reporter for the *Hunterdon County Democrat*, a Flemington, New Jersey newspaper. He lived in Japan (1978–79), worked as a fact checker for *The New Yorker* in 1980, and as a reader at Random House (1980–81). He became established as a bestselling novelist with *Bright Lights, Big City* (1983). Michael J. Fox starred in James Bridges' 1988 film version of the book. McInerney's work also includes the novels *Ransom* (1985) and *Story of My Life* (1988). He has also published several short stories. His 1976 B.A. was from Williams College, and he did some postgraduate work at Syracuse University. Helen Bransford is his third wife.

FURTHER READING

"Jay walks." BENJAMIN SVETKEY. *Entertainment*, July 10, 1992.
"Stop the presses. . . ." LESLEY WHITE. *Sunday Times*, May 24, 1992.
"A new Jay dawning." MICHAEL SHNAYERSON. *Vanity Fair*, May 1992.
Spy Notes on McInerney's Bright Lights, Big City. . . . SPY MAGAZINE EDITORS. Doubleday, 1989.
"Promoting his new book. . . ." ANDREA CHAMBERS. *People*, Sep. 19, 1988.
"Slave of New York." DAVID BLUM. *New York*, Sep. 5, 1988.
"Bright lights. . . ." DEBRA GOLDMAN. *American Film*, Jan.–Feb. 1988.

McKellen, Ian (1939–)

Celebrated British actor McKellen won his fifth British Olivier award for his 1991 portrayal of Shakespeare's *Richard III*. In June 1992, he brought Richard Eyre's extraordinary Royal National Theatre production of the play to Brooklyn's Academy of Music, to rave reviews. After a limited New York run, the company went on a national tour, ending in late September in Los Angeles, where the UCLA School of Theater, Film, and Television set up a new Ian McKellen theater scholarship. Forthcoming was a starring role in Maggie Greenwald's film *The Ballad of Little Jo*, costarring Suzy Amis, Bo Hopkins, David Chung, and Carrie Snodgress.

A leading British actor since the early 1960s, McKellen has played on stage in a wide range of leading roles. He made his stage debut in 1961, joined the National Theatre Company in 1965, made his Broadway debut in 1966 in *The Promise*, and was a founder of the Actor's Company in 1972. His debut with the Royal Shakespeare

Company came in 1974, with his role in *Dr. Faustus*. He further developed his international reputation with *Bent* (1979) and *Amadeus* (1980), for which he won a Tony on Broadway. He toured in his one-man show *Acting Shakespeare* in 1984, played in a series of major roles with the National Theatre during the 1980s, and was an associate director of the National Theatre (1984–86). His films include *Alfred the Great* (1965), *Plenty* (1985), and *Scandal* (1988). He has also appeared often on television. In 1991, he was Cameron Mackintosh professor of contemporary theatre at Oxford University.

In 1991, McKellen accepted a knighthood, becoming Sir Ian. The honor was especially notable because he had been openly working on behalf of gay rights in Britain since announcing his own homosexuality on a BBC program three years earlier. Some fellow gay activists criticized him for accepting the honor from a Conservative government they felt was anti-gay. But he was publicly defended by many other gay artists, who felt that the honor "was a significant landmark in the history of the British gay movement."

FURTHER READING

"Out and about with Sir Ian." BEN BRANTLEY. *Vanity Fair*, June 1992.
"Sympathy for the devil." LAWRENCE O'TOOLE. *New York Times Magazine*, Apr. 5, 1992.
"McKellen. . . ." JACK PITMAN. *Variety*, Jan. 7, 1991.

MacLaine, Shirley (Shirley MacLean Beaty; 1934–) Entertainer, film star, and author MacLaine starred as the recently bereaved Pearl, beginning to make a new life, in Beeban Kidron's 1992 comedy-melodrama film *Used People*. Set in 1960s New York City, the film co-starred Kathy Bates and Marcia Gay Harden as her daughters, Jessica Tandy as her mother, Sylvia Sidney as Tandy's best friend, and Marcello Mastroianni as MacLaine's long-adoring Italian-American suitor. MacLaine toured in the spring of 1992, and in the autumn appeared in joint concert with Frank Sinatra; their three October Radio City Music Hall concerts were sell-outs.

MacLaine was scheduled to reprise her Oscar-winning role in *Terms of Endearment* in a 15-years-later sequel *The Evening Star*, based on the Larry McMurtry novel. Also forthcoming were starring roles in Hugh Wilson's film *Guarding Tess*; and opposite Robert Duvall, Richard Harris, and Piper Laurie in Randa Haines' film *Wrestling Ernest Hemingway*.

Virginia-born MacLaine, the sister of actor Warren Beatty, became a Hollywood star in the 1960s in such light films as *The Apartment* (1960), *Two for the Seesaw* (1962), *Irma La Douce* (1963), and *Sweet Charity* (1969). Later in her career, she became a leading dramatic actress, in such films as *The Turning Point* (1977), *Being There* (1979), *Terms of Endearment* (1983; she won a Best Actress Oscar), *Madame Souszatska* (1988), *Steel Magnolias* (1989), *Waiting for the Light* (1990), and *Postcards from the Edge* (1990). She also produced, co-directed, and appeared in the documentary film *The Other Half of the Sky: A China Memoir* (1975), and has written several very popular books, including *Many Happy Returns* (1984), *Dancing in the Light* (1985), *Don't Fall Off the Mountain* (1987), and *Dance While You Can* (1991). She was previously married, and has one child.

FURTHER READING

"Still kicking over the traces." VALERIE GROVE. *Times*, Jan. 31, 1992.
"Write while you can. . . ." BILL GOLDSTEIN. *Publishers Weekly*, Aug. 8, 1991.
"The real MacLaine." NANCY COLLINS and ANNIE LEIBOVITZ. *Vanity Fair*, Mar. 1991.
"Shirley MacLaine lives." PAT DOWELL. *Washingtonian*, Oct. 1988.

Shirley MacLaine and the New Age Movement.
JAMES W. SIRE. Inter-Varsity, 1988.
Shirley MacLaine. MICHAEL FREEDLAND. Salem House, 1986.
Shirley Maclaine. ROY PICKARD. Hippocrene, 1985.

McLarty, Thomas "Mack" (Thomas F. McLarty III; 1946–) President Bill Clinton's incoming White House Chief of Staff is one of Clinton's oldest friends. He was born in Hope, Arkansas, went to kindergarten with Clinton, and attended Boys State with Clinton while both were in high school. McLarty went into his family's automobile dealership business in Hope after his 1968 graduation from the University of Arkansas. In 1984, he became chairman and chief executive officer of rkla, Inc. (Arkansas Louisiana Gas Company), a natural gas distribution firm. He has also long been a Little Rock civic leader. McLarty became a key figure in the organization of Clinton's presidential campaign, and then a member of his transition team. He was expected as Chief of Staff to be less a "power broker" than some recent occupants of the job, and more a quiet, trusted aide. He is married to Donna McLarty; they have two children.

FURTHER READING

"They call him Mack. . . ." MICHAEL DUFFY. *Time,* Dec. 28, 1992.
"Bill and Mack. . . ." DAVID DODSON. *Business Week,* Nov. 23, 1992.

MacMillan, Kenneth (1929–92) Scotland-born MacMillan, a leading ballet choreographer, studied with Ninette de Valois and joined her company as a dancer in 1945, then moving to the Sadler's Wells Opera Ballet. He made his professional debut as a choreographer with the very well-received *Dances Concertantes,* first performed in January 1955 by the Theatre Ballet, and went on to create such works as *Noctambules* (1956), *The Burrow* (1958), *The Invitation* (1961), and in 1965 his full-length breakthrough ballet *Romeo and Juliet,* which established him as a major figure. He was associated with the American Ballet Theater (1957–90), and became artistic director of the company (1984–90). He later became the ballet director of the West Berlin Opera company (1966–69), and from 1970 to 1977 was artistic director of the Royal Ballet, then becoming that company's choreographer. MacMillan was survived by his wife, Deborah MacMillan, and a daughter. (d. London; October, 30, 1992)

FURTHER READING

"Kenneth MacMillan's legacy." CLIVE BARNES.
Obituary. MARILYN HUNT. *Dance.* Jan. 1993.
Obituary. *Variety,* Nov. 2, 1992.
"Virtuoso of. . . ." DAVID DOUGILL. *Sunday Times,* Nov. 1, 1992.
Obituary. *The Times* (of London), Oct. 31, 1992.
Obituary. *Independent,* Oct. 31, 1992.
Obituary. *New York Times,* Oct. 30, 1992.
Kenneth MacMillan: The Man and the Ballets.
EDWARD THORPE. Trafalgar Square, 1986.

MacNeil, Robert Breckenridge (1931–) Robert MacNeil is the senior member of America's longest-lasting television news duo, paired with Jim Lehrer since 1973 in what is now called the "MacNeil/Lehrer NewsHour," on PBS. As original sole anchor of the show, MacNeil—generally known to friends and colleagues as Robin—developed the approach of summarizing the day's events, and then concentrating on one or two stories in substantial depth each night, often with panelists from a range of views. He points out that this allows viewers to hear directly from the kinds of sources reporters would contact when researching a story. In January 1992, MacNeil and Lehrer moderated the third of the nationally televised debates among

Report," began in 1975, and became "The Mac-Neil/Lehrer Newshour" in 1983. MacNeil was co-author and host of the Emmy and Peabody-winning nine-part series "The Story of English," and co-author of the accompanying book. He has also hosted several PBS specials. His published works also include *The People Machine, The Influence of Television on American Politics* (1968), *The Right Place at the Right Time* (1982), *The Way We Were: 1963, the Year Kennedy Was Shot* (1988), and *Wordstruck* (1989). A graduate of Ottawa's Carleton University, MacNeil is married and has four children.

FURTHER READING

"Stranger to fiction." BRUCE HEADLAM. *Saturday Night*, Mar. 1992.
"MacNeil/Lehrer. . . ." MORGAN STRONG. *Playboy*, June 1991.
"Inside TV's finest. . . ." MALCOLM MCCONNELL. *Reader's Digest* (Canadian), July 1988.

the major Democratic presidential candidates. In an unusual break with tradition, MacNeil and Lehrer were joined on PBS during the early evening coverage of the 1992 Democratic and Republican nominating conventions by NBC news anchor Tom Brokaw, who then did late-evening coverage on NBC.

In 1992, MacNeil published a new novel, *The Burden of Desire*, about the relationships of an unconventional young woman and two men attracted to her, set in Nova Scotia, against the backdrop of World War I, particularly the 1917 Halifax munitions ship explosion, regarded as the largest manmade explosion before the atomic bomb. MacNeil also prepared a revised edition of his book, *The Story of English*, scheduled for January 1993 publication.

Montreal-born MacNeil began his broadcasting career as an actor in radio and a radio and television announcer in Halifax, Nova Scotia (1951–55). He moved into journalism as a Reuters editor in London (1955–60), and was an NBC news correspondent (1960–67), successively based in London, Washington, and New York. From 1967 to 1971, he was a London-based BBC correspondent with the "Panorama" series, also in that period working in U.S. public television, which became a full-time affiliation in 1971. He and Jim Lehrer began their long association in 1973 with their Emmy-winning daily live coverage of the Senate Watergate hearings on PBS. Their award-winning "MacNeil/Lehrer Report," originally named the "Robert MacNeil

Madonna (Madonna Louise Ciccone; 1958–) Massive worldwide media coverage of Madonna continued during 1992, as the entertainer continued on her highly publicized way.

She generated a large commercial set of events in October, with issuance of her album *Erotica*, preceded by a single and accompanied by a music video, both also named "Erotica." These were accompanied by the simultaneous Time Warner publication of her shrink-wrapped $49.95 picture book titled *Sex*, which proceeded to sell more than 500,000 copies worldwide, although many were defectively manufactured (the front cover came off). Book purchasers seemed attracted by a combination of Madonna's celebrity, the nude shots of Madonna and others in the book, and the book's attempt to convey not-very-hard-core but conscientiously degenerate attitudes toward sex, women, and men. Earlier in the year, she had concluded a lucrative long-term contract with Time Warner. She won a Best Music Long-Form Video Grammy for *Madonna: Blond Ambition World Tour Live*, and a Best Female Artist Billboard Music Video Award nomination for "This Used to Be My Playground."

During 1992, Madonna appeared in several films, including Penny Marshall's *A League of Their Own*, as centerfielder on a World War II-era women's baseball team; Woody Allen's *Shadows and Fog*; and Robert Altman's *The Player*. Forthcoming were appearances in Clint Eastwood's *In the Line of Fire* and opposite Willem Dafoe in Uri Edel's *Body of Evidence*.

Michigan-born Madonna is one of the best-known celebrities of her time, in concert and for such albums as *Madonna* (1983), *Like a Virgin* (1983), *True Blue* (1986), *You Can Dance* (1987), and *Like a Prayer* (1989). She is also a competent actress, as demonstrated in such films as *Desperately Seeking Susan* (1985) and *Who's That Girl?* (1987), and in her Broadway stage debut in *Speed-the-Plow* (1988). In 1990, she played Breathless Mahoney in Warren Beatty's *Dick Tracy*, which sparked her "Blond Ambition" international concert tour, the album *I'm Breathless* (1990), and the documentary film *Truth or Dare: In Bed With Madonna*. She also released a collection of her previous work, *The Immaculate Collection* (1990); both albums spawned best-selling singles. Her video of "Justify My Love" was judged so steamy that MTV refused to air it; the single became an immediate bestseller. Madonna was formerly married to actor Sean Penn (1985–89). She attended the University of Michigan (1976–78).

FURTHER READING

"Madonna." *People*, Dec. 28, 1992.

"Madonna. . . ." JAMIE MALANOWSKI. *Esquire*, Dec. 1992.

"Madonna revealed." JOANNE KAUFMAN and PAMELA GUTHRIE O'BRIEN. *Ladies Home Journal*, Nov. 1992.

"Sex and money." GISELLE BENATAR et al. *Entertainment*, Nov. 6, 1992.

"Talking with Madonna. . . ." DAVID ANSEN. *Newsweek*, Nov. 2, 1992.

" 'Sex' is the latest lode. . . ." D.T. MAX. *Variety*, Oct. 26, 1992.

"Sex and Romance." LAURENCE ROMANCE. *Guardian*, Oct. 16, 1992.

"Madonna in wonderland." MAUREEN ORTH and STEVEN MEISEL. *Vanity Fair*, Oct. 1992.

"Weekend in the material world." NEAL RUBIN. *Entertainment*, Aug. 28, 1992.

Material Girl: Madonna in the 90s. TIM RILEY. Disney, 1992.

Madonna: The Book. NORMAN KING. Morrow, 1992.

Madonna Revealed: The Unauthorized Biography. DOUGLAS THOMPSON. Dorchester, 1992.

Madonna: Blonde Ambition. MARK BEGO. Harmony/Crown, 1992.

The Madonna Scrapbook. LEE RANDALL. Citadel Press/Carol, 1992.

"Madonna revealed." DOUGLAS THOMPSON. *Cosmopolitan*, Nov. 1991.

"Single sex and the girl. . . ." JOSEPH SOBRAN. *National Review*, Aug. 12, 1991.

"True confessions. . . ." CARRIE FISHER and STEVEN MEISEL. *Rolling Stone*, June 13 and 27, 1991. (Two parts.)

"Madonna in bloom. . . ." CARL WAYNE ARRINGTON. *Time*, May 20, 1991.

"Unmasking. . . ." BRIAN D. JOHNSON. *Maclean's*, May 13, 1991.

"Madonna and Michael." STEVE DOUGHERTY. *People*, Apr. 15, 1991.

"The misfit." LYNN HIRSCHBERG and STEVEN MEISEL. *Vanity Fair*, Apr. 1991.

"Playgirl of the western world." MICHAEL KELLY. *Playboy*, Mar. 1991.

Madonna Revealed. DOUGLAS THOMPSON. Carol, 1991.

Madonna, Unauthorized. CHRISTOPHER ANDERSEN. Simon & Schuster, 1991.

Madonna: Her Complete Story. NAL-Dutton, 1991.

Madonna. WILLIAM RUHLMANN. Smithmark, 1991.

Major, John (1943–) In the first few months of his second full year in office Conservative British Prime Minister Major faced growing unpopularity, as the British economy sank

further into a deep recession, unemployment rose, and Labour Party strength grew. There was also sharp opposition to his commitment to the European political and financial union within his own party—opposition led by former Conservative Prime Minister Margaret Thatcher. All the polls showed him headed toward defeat in the April 1992 general elections. But all the polls were wrong. The Conservatives won, with 336 seats in the House of Commons and 42 percent of the popular vote, to Labour's 271 seats and 34 percent of the vote. Major formed a new government, and Labour Party leader Neil Kinnock resigned, after his second general election defeat.

The election was a great personal victory for Major, but his problems remained and deepened. The long recession worsened, and increasingly sharp criticism of government inaction came from British industry as well as Labour. The key European Community Maastricht treaty ran into serious difficulty on the continent, and, although Major was able to win a narrow vote in support of the treaty in the House of Commons, he announced in early November that British ratification would be delayed, probably until mid-1993. The treaty faltered even more in Britain after Major was forced to pull Britain out of the European monetary system in mid-September, after full-scale Bank of England support of the currency had failed to stop its free fall against the high-interest-paying German mark. Nor did the highly publicized multiple troubles of the British royal family help his position. Overwhelmingly, though, it was the economy that clearly had to be addressed if he and his government were to long remain in power.

London-born Major's first career was with the Standard Chartered Bank (1965–79). He joined the Conservative Party in 1960, was a Lambeth Borough Councillor (1968–71), and became a member of Parliament in 1979, after two unsuccessful tries. His rise in the Thatcher government was very rapid; by 1985, he was a junior minister at the department of health, and by 1986 social security minister. He became Treasury chief secretary in 1987, foreign secretary in July 1989, Chancellor of the Exchequer in October 1989, and then at 47 the youngest British Prime Minister of the 20th century, succeeding Margaret Thatcher on November 27, 1990. In office, he quickly canceled the enormously unpopular poll tax, and developed a more moderate Conservative government than that of Thatcher. He supported the Persian Gulf War without reservation, sending British heavy armor into the ground offensive when it came, to join the air and sea forces already in place. Major married Norma Johnson in 1970; they have two children.

FURTHER READING

"When niceness. . . ." JULIA LANGDON. New Statesman & Society, Nov. 6, 1992.
"Major says. . . ." MICHAEL JONES. Sunday Times, July 12, 1992.
"Major's hour." Economist, Apr. 11, 1992.
"John Major at bat." CRAIG WHITNEY. New York Times Magazine, Mar. 29, 1992.
"Major. . . ." DANIEL PEDERSEN. Newsweek, Mar. 23, 1992.
"Major looks. . . ." MICHAEL WHITE. Guardian, Jan. 2, 1992.
John Major: The Making of the Prime Minister. BRUCE ANDERSON. Trafalgar Square, 1992.
"Major player. . . ." EDWARD PEARCE. New Republic, Jan. 21, 1991.
John Major: Prime Minister. PRESS ASSOCIATION STAFF and JOHN JENKINS. Trafalgar Square, 1991.
"A quiet dropout. . . ." BILL HEWITT. People, Dec. 10, 1990.
"Thatcher's favorite." ANDREW BILSKI. Maclean's, Dec. 3, 1990.
"John Major." Economist, Nov. 24, 1990.
"Major, John." Current Biography, Oct. 1990.

Malkovich, John

Malkovich, John (1953–) For stage and screen star Malkovich, 1992 was yet another very busy year. He starred as Lennie opposite Gary Sinise as George in Sinise's film version of John Steinbeck's *Of Mice and Men*, screenplay by Horton Foote. He also starred in Woody Allen's *Shadows and Fog*, in a cast that included Allen, Mia Farrow, Madonna, Jodie Foster, and Kathy Bates; the film had been scheduled for 1991 release, but was delayed. A third starring film role was in Bruce Robinson's film thriller *Jennifer Eight*, co-starring Uma Thurman, Lance Henriksen, and Kathy Baker. Malkovich also starred on the London stage in the very topical Dusty Hughe's play *A Slip of the Tongue*, about an Eastern European writer who becomes a political leader. Several films were forthcoming, including a starring role opposite Clint Eastwood and Rene Russo in Wolfgang Peterson's film *In the Line of Fire*; and another as a voice in the Dick and Ralph Zontag animated film *We're Back*.

Before becoming a New York stage player, Illinois-born Malkovich was from 1976 a leading member of Chicago's Steppenwolf theater company. He won an Obie off-Broadway for his role in *True West* (1982), appeared as Biff opposite Dustin Hoffman's Willy Loman in the 1984 Broadway revival of *Death of a Salesman*, and took his highly praised stage performance in Lanford Wilson's *Burn This* from New York to London late in 1990, making his British stage debut. He began his film career in 1984 with *Places in the Heart*, and went on to strong dramatic roles in such films as *The Killing Fields* (1984), *Eleni* (1985), *The Glass Menagerie* (1987), *Empire of the Sun* (1987), *Dangerous Liaisons* (1988), *The Sheltering Sky* (1990), and *The Object of Beauty* (1991). Malkovich has also acted and directed in regional theater, and appeared on television. He is married to actress Glenne Headly.

FURTHER READING

"What is. . . ." DAVID GRITTEN. *Cosmopolitan*, Nov. 1992.
"Life, art and Malkovich." JOE MORGENSTERN. *Playboy*, May 1990.
"Wild card." BECKY JOHNSTON and BRIGITTE LACOMBE. *Interview*, Mar. 1989.
"Malkovich, John." *Current Biography*, May 1988.

Mamet, David Alan

Mamet, David Alan (1947–) Playwright and screenwriter Mamet adapted his dark stage drama *Glengarry Glen Ross* into the 1992 James Foley film, starring Al Pacino, Jack Lemmon, Alec Baldwin, Ed Harris, Alan Arkin, Kevin Spacey, and Jonathan Pryce as an unscrupulous group of Florida real estate boiler room salesmen. The film was very well received by most critics, although it was only moderately successful at the box office.

For television, Mamet adapted his play *The Water Engine*. The telefilm, starring Charles Durning and directed by Steven Schachter, is set in 1934; it is about a machine operator who invents an engine powered by only water, and is attacked by business interests who see their profits threatened.

But most controversial was Mamet's new play, *Oleanna*, which premiered regionally as the first production of Mamet's Boston Back Bay Theater Company, and off-Broadway in late October. The play was about two fictional characters: a very sweet, decent, blameless male professor, who is victimized by a vicious, man-hating woman student, who files false charges of sexual harassment against him. In a period dominated by the Anita Faye Hill-Clarence Thomas sexual harassment confrontation before a worldwide audience, and in an election year widely described as "The Year of the Woman," Mamet and his play were immediately and widely attacked as bitterly sexist. Some, however, saw the confrontation as more ambiguous, involving human conflicts beyond the purely sexual. In an interesting twist, the woman's role was played by Mamet's wife, Rebecca Pidgeon.

In 1992, Mamet also published an autobiographical work, *The Cabin*. Forthcoming was a screenplay for the Philip Kaufman film *The Rising Sun*, based on the Michael Crichton novel and starring Sean Connery.

Chicago-born Mamet emerged as a substantial playwright in the 1970s with such works as *Sexual Perversity in Chicago* (1973), *American Buffalo* (1976), *A Life in the Theater* (1976), *The Woods* (1977), *Edmond* (1983), *Glengarry Glen Ross*, (1984; Pulitzer Prize for drama), and *Speed-The-Plow* (1987). His screenplays include *The Postman Always Rings Twice* (1981), *The Verdict* (1982), *The Untouchables* (1987), *We're No Angels* (1989), and *Homicide* (1991). He co-wrote and directed the film *House of Games* (1987), and wrote and directed *Things Change* (1988). Among his nonfiction works are *Writing in Restaurants: Essays and Prose* (1986) and *On Directing Film* (1990). Mamet's B.A. was from Goddard College. Previously married to actress Lindsay Crouse, Mamet is married to actress-singer-songwriter Rebecca Pidgeon.

FURTHER READING

"Theater. . . ." RICHARD DAVID STORY. *New York*, Sep. 14, 1992.
David Mamet: Language As Dramatic Action. ANNE DEAN. Fairleigh Dickinson, 1990.
"Mamet on the make." BOB DAILY. *Chicago*, May 1988.
"The prophet of Broadway." JONATHAN LIEBERSON. *New York Review of Books*, July 21, 1988.
American Voices: Five Contemporary Playwrights in Essays and Interviews. ESTHER HARRIOTT. McFarland, 1988.
David Mamet. DENNIS CARROLL. St. Martin's, 1987.
David Mamet. C.W. BIGSBY. Routledge Chapman & Hall, 1985.

Mandela, Nelson Rolihiahia (1918–)

During 1992, Mandela continued to lead the African National Congress (ANC) and its allies toward the goals of coalition government and majority rule in South Africa—but not without grave difficulties. While complicated negotiations proceeded, the civil war between the Zulu Inkatha and the ANC continued in the Black

townships, as did killings organized and in some instances carried out by South African security forces and White extremists. By mid-June, an estimated 1,500–2,000 had died. After the June 17th massacre of more than 40 unarmed Blacks at Boipatong, near Johannesburg, the ANC on June 21st broke off negotiations with the government, charging police and military complicity in the continuing murders; the ANC then went over to a policy of mass demonstrations. Mandela addressed a special sesson of the United Nations Security Council in July, calling for UN intervention to stop the violence in the townships.

Mass murder was also committed by Black militants; in late November, members of a splinter group, the Azanian Peoples Liberation Army, began a series of terrorist attacks on Whites, murdering four and wounding 17 at a winetasting party in King William's Town. The attacks were immediately condemned by Mandela and other ANC leaders.

Codesa (Convention for a Democratic South Africa) talks restarted in late September, after major government concessions, among them a promise to disarm Inkatha by prohibiting the carrying of weapons in public (Zulu militants usually carried clubs and spears in their attacks within the townships). Although Inkatha leader Mangosuthu Gatsha Buthelezi then boycotted the talks and moved toward alliance with the White rightwing, the talks went forward. In late November, Mandela offered a major concession, the sharing of power with the White minority after the coming of majority rule.

On the personal side, Nelson Mandela in April announced that he and Winnie Mandela would separate, an act urged on him by his ANC associates, who felt that her recent legal and personal problems might harm the ANC. Nelson Mandela's autobiography was in preparation.

Early in his career, Mandela was a leading advocate of non-violence (1944–60), but both he and the previously nonviolent ANC turned to violence after the Sharpeville Massacre of 1960. He was imprisoned in 1962, sentenced to life imprisonment for sabotage. During his 28-year-long imprisonment, he became a worldwide symbol of the long fight against South African racism. On February 11, 1990, his release by De Klerk's new South African government ushered in a new period in South African history, leading to a full ceasefire after 30 years of guerrilla warfare. Mandela was elected President of the ANC in 1991. Mandela attended the University College of Fort Hare and the University of the Witwatersrand, and practiced law in Johannesburg in the early 1950s. He married Winnie Mandela, his second wife, in 1958; they have two daughters. Among his autobiographical writings are *No Easy Walk to Freedom* (1986) and *Nelson Mandela: The Struggle Is My Life* (rev. ed., 1986). With Fidel Castro, he also wrote *How Far We Slaves Have Come!* (1991).

FURTHER READING

" 'We understand white's fears.' " *Newsweek*, Mar. 2, 1992.

Nelson Mandela: The Fight Against Apartheid. STEVEN OTFINOSKI. Millbrook Press, 1992.

Nelson Mandela. BENJAMIN POGRUND. Gareth Stevens, 1992.

Nelson Mandela: Voice of Freedom. LIBBY HUGHES. Macmillan, 1992.

Nelson Mandela: The Man, the Struggle, the Triumph. DOROTHY HOOBLER and THOMAS HOOBLER. Watts, 1992.

"Mandela. . . ." SCOTT MACLEOD. *Time,* Jan. 7, 1991.

Nelson Mandela: Strength and Spirit of a Free South Africa. BENJAMIN PROUND. Gareth Stevens, 1991.

Nelson Mandela: Symbol of Resistance and Hope for a Free South Africa. E.S. REDDY, ed. Apt Books, 1991.

Nelson Mandela. BRIAN FEINBERG. Chelsea House, 1991.

Nelson Mandela. RICHARD TAMES. Watts, 1991.

Mandela, Tambo, and the African National Congress: The Struggle Against Apartheid, a Documentary Study, 1948–1990. SHERIDAN JOHNS and R. HUNT DAVIS, JR., eds. Oxford University Press, 1991.

Nelson Mandela: "No Easy Walk to Freedom." BARRY DENENBERG. Scholastic, 1991.

Nelson Mandela. BRIAN FEINBERG. Chelsea House, 1991.

Nelson Mandela. RICHARD TAMES. Watts, 1991.

Nelson Mandela: A Voice Set Free. REBECCA STEFFOF. Fawcett, 1990.

Mandela: Echoes of Era. ALF KUMALO and MPHAHLELE ES'KIA. Viking Penguin, 1990.

The Struggle: A History of the African National Congress. HEIDI HOLLAND. Braziller, 1990.

Higher Than Hope: The Authorized Biography of Nelson Mandela. FATIMA MEER. HarperCollins, 1989.

Nelson Mandela: South Africa's Silent Voice of Protest. J. HARGROVE. Childrens, 1989.

Mandela, Winnie (Winnie Nomzano; 1934– ）

As a symbol and leader of the South African freedom movement, and the wife of imprisoned South African leader Nelson Mandela, Winnie Mandela has been one of the world's leading women. Her situation changed greatly in 1989, when she was publicly censured by the leadership of the African National Congress (ANC) and other leaders, after her alleged involvement in the beating and murder of a young boy and the beatings of several other young boys in Soweto. Two of her bodyguards were convicted of murder in May 1990; she was charged with kidnapping and assault in September 1990 and convicted in May 1991. Sentenced to a six-year prison term, her case is on appeal. Although Nelson Mandela supported her throughout the trial, there were apparently other problems, and in April 1992, Nelson Mandela announced that he and Winnie Mandela would separate. In September, she resigned from the last of her ANC positions. While new charges against her continued to surface within the ANC, she denied them all.

Winnie Mandela was a social worker before becoming active in the ANC in 1956. She married Nelson Mandela in 1958; the couple then joined their work in the South African freedom movement. She, too, became a worldwide symbol of resistance to racism, as she pressed for his release during his 28 years in prison and at the same time continued her anti-apartheid work. She was forced into silence for long periods by the South African government, and internally exiled in 1977. From 1985, however, she was able to defy the government, due to growing worldwide condemnation of apartheid and of the imprisonment of Nelson Mandela. Among her writings is *A Part of My Soul Went with Him* (1985). Winnie and Nelson Mandela have two daughters.

FURTHER READING

"Nelson Mandela. . . ." BARBARA GRIZZUTI HARRISON. *Mademoiselle,* Aug. 1992.

"Blood soccer. . . ." JOHN CARLIN. *New Republic,* Feb. 18, 1991.

"The ordeal and. . . ." D. MICHAEL CHEERS and JESSE JACKSON. *Ebony,* May 1990.

" 'Mother of the nation.' " ANDREW BILSKI. *Maclean's,* Feb. 12, 1990.

Nelson and Winnie Mandela. JOHN VAIL. Chelsea House, 1989.

Winnie Mandela: Life of Struggle. JAMES HASKINS. Putnam, 1988.

Nelson and Winnie Mandela. DOROTHY HOOBLER and THOMAS HOOBLER. Watts, 1987.
Winnie Mandela. NANCY HARRISON. Braziller, 1986.
Winnie Mandela: The Soul of South Africa. MILTON MELTZER. Viking Child, 1986.

Marsalis, Branford (1960–) In a highly publicized move, leading jazz saxophonist Branford Marsalis succeeded Doc Severinsen as bandleader of the NBC "Tonight Show," joining Jay Leno after Johnny Carson retired in May 1992. His move brought him much increased public visibility, but as it worked out little opportunity to display his accomplishments, for most of what he did on the show had little need of his great talents.

Aside from the "Tonight Show," Marsalis issued a blues album, in which he explored a wide range of blues works from early New Orleans to complex modern blues. His guest stars included John Lee Hooker, B. B. King, and Linda Hopkins. In 1992 Marsalis was also the subject of Donn Pennbaker-Chris Hegedus documentary, *The Music Tells You.*

New Orleans-born Marsalis is the son of teacher and jazz pianist Ellis Marsalis, and the older brother of trumpeter Wynton Marsalis and trombonist Delfeayo Marsalis. He joined Wynton's band as a saxophonist at the age of sixteen, and while still at school played summers and holidays with the Art Blakey and Lionel Hampton bands. He recorded with Art Blakey in 1981 and from 1982 toured with Wynton's band. In 1985, he toured with Sting, and in 1986 formed his own band. His albums include *Scenes in the City* (1984), *Romances for Saxophone* (1986), *Royal Garden Blues* (1986), *Renaissance* (1987), *Random Abstract* (1988), *Trio Jeepy* (1989), *Music from Mo' Better Blues* (1990), *Crazy People Music* (1990), and *The Beauty Ones Are Note Yet Born* (1991). Branford Marsalis is a perennial Grammy nominee for his solo jazz instrumental performances. He has also appeared in several films. He attended Southern University, and studied at the Berklee College of Music (1979–81).

FURTHER READING

"The revolution might. . . ." JOSEF WOODARD. *Down Beat,* Sep. 1992.
"The prime of. . . ." JOSEPH HOOPER. *Esquire,* June 1992.
"Here's Branford." PETER WATROUS. *New York Times Magazine,* May 3, 1992.
"Heeere's Branford." MICHAEL BOURNE. *Down Beat,* May 1992.
"Gang of 2 . . . ." BILL MILKOWSKI. *Down Beat,* Jan. 1992.
"Marsalis, Branford." *Current Biography,* Sep. 1991.
"Marsalis and Pine." DIMITRI EHRLICH. *Interview,* Nov. 1990.
"Branford Marsalis. . . ." DAVE HELLAND. *Down Beat,* Nov. 1989.
"Wynton and Branford. . . ." A. JAMES LISKA. *Down Beat,* Sep. 1989.
"Branford Marsalis . . . ." CLARENCE WALDRON. *Ebony,* Feb. 1989.
"Branford Marsalis. . . ." ERIC LEVIN and BARBARA ROWES. *People,* Jan. 18, 1988.
"Branford's two worlds. . . ." CATHLEEN McGUIGAN. *Newsweek,* Jan. 4, 1988.

Marsalis, Wynton (1961–) Celebrated jazz composer and musician Wynton Marsalis had a varied and productive 1992. Most visibly, he and Kathleen Battle issued a classical album, *Baroque Duet,* which was a commercial hit. Their partnership also won them an Emmy nomination for best classical program in the performing arts. Peter Gelb and Albert Maysles created a 90-minute documentary about the making of the album, *Kathleen Battle and Wynton Marsalis: Baroque Duet,* broadcast as part of the PBS "Great Performances" series.

Marsalis premiered a major composition at Lincoln Center's Avery Fisher Hall on May 27th, *In This House On This Morning*, a gospel-music work based on many jazz historical and religious music themes and touching on several jazz styles. The Marsalis jazz septet also issued the very well-received album *Blue Interlude*, which included Marsalis's own 40-minute title composition, subtitled "The Bittersweet Saga of Sugar Cane and Sweetie Pie." The septet also toured widely during 1992, pursuing their campaign to revitalize jazz and return it to its classic roots. Forthcoming were several albums and books, as well as more major pieces for Lincoln Center.

New Orleans-born Marsalis is the son of pianist and teacher Ellis Marsalis, younger brother of saxophonist Branford Marsalis, and older brother of trombonist Delfeayo Marsalis. After briefly playing with Art Blakey's Jazz Messengers, Wynton Marsalis emerged as one of the leading trumpet soloists of his time, functioning equally well in the classics and in jazz, although he has focused on jazz in the late 1980s and early 1990s. A few of his many notable albums are *Fathers and Sons* (1982), *Wynton Marsalis* (1982), *Trumpet Concertos* (1983), *Black Codes from the Underground* (1985), *Standard Time* (Vol. 1, 1987; Vol. 2, 1990; Vol. 3, 1991, *The Resolution of Romance*), *Majesty of the Blues* (1989), and *Soul Gestures in Southern Blue* (1991). He studied at the Juilliard School of Music (1979–81).

FURTHER READING

"The cool world." ERIC POOLEY. *New York*, Dec. 21, 1992.
"Wynton's decade." HOWARD REICH. *Down Beat*, Dec. 1992.
"Wynton Marsalis." JAMES BRADY. *Parade*, Aug. 16, 1992.
"Horns of plenty. . . ." THOMAS SANCTON. *Time*, Oct. 22, 1990.
"Wynton. . . ." DAVE HELLAND. *Down Beat*, Sep. 1990.
Outcats: Jazz Composers, Instrumentalists, and Singers. FRANCIS DAVIS. Oxford University Press, 1990.
"Wynton and Branford. . . ." A. JAMES LISKA. *Down Beat*, Sep. 1989.

Marshall, Penny (1942–) Film director

Penny Marshall emerged as a major figure in 1992, with *A League of Their Own*, a film that she directed and executive produced, and whose

screenplay was written by Lowell Ganz and Babaloo Mandel. The film, a big-budget summer blockbuster, was a critical and commercial success, and a worldwide hit. It was the story of the first season of the Rockford, Illinois, Peaches, a fictional midwestern World War II-era women's baseball team playing in a newly formed women's league. The light, warm, funny film could not have come at a better time for its makers, as it provided a moment of relaxation during a period of renewed focus on women's rights, with the Anita Faye Hill-Clarence Thomas confrontation still evoking white-hot reactions and the "Year of the Woman" election campaign at the top of the news. The multi-star cast included Geena Davis as the team's catcher and star hitter, Lori Petty as her younger sister and the team's pitcher, Madonna as the team's lively centerfielder, and Tom Hanks as their ex-major leaguer coach. *A League of Their Own* was the first film in Marshall's three-picture deal with Columbia, signed in 1990. The second was to be the comedy *Calendar Girl*, co-produced with Elliott Abbott.

New York City-born Marshall emerged first as an actress in television, making her television debut in "The Danny Thomas Show." During the early 1970s, she appeared as a guest and regular on a considerable range of shows, most notably "The Odd Couple" (1972–74), "Saturday Night Live" (1975–77), "The Mike Douglas Show" (1975–77), and in her starring role as Laverne in "Laverne and Shirley" (1976–83), which made her a celebrity. She also appeared as an actress in several films, including *1941* (1979). She began her second major career by directing several episodes of "Laverne and Shirley," and moved into film direction with the successful *Jumpin' Jack Flash* (1986), followed by the highly successful *Big* (1988), and *Awakenings* (1990). She attended the University of New Mexico. She was twice married, the second time to director Rob Reiner, and has two children. She is the sister of producer-director Garry Marshall.

FURTHER READING

"Marshall, Penny." *Current Biography*, May 1992.

"Making it in the majors." PEGGY ORENSTEIN. *New York Times Magazine*, May 24, 1992.

"The Marshall plan." CAROL CALDWELL. *Interview*, Jan. 1991.

"Penny from heaven." JOE MORGENSTERN. *Playboy*, Jan. 1991.

"Penny Marshall. . . ." TOM CUNNEFF. *People*, Aug. 15, 1988.

Martin, Paul James Joseph (1903–92)

Ottawa-born Martin, a victim of spinal meningitis at the age of four, lived to help create the Canadian social welfare system, one of the world's best. Child of a French-Canadian mother and Irish father, he was fluent in both of Canada's major languages. A lawyer, he was first elected to parliament in 1935, beginning a long political career that included posts as Secretary of State of Canada (1945–46), Minister of National Health and Welfare (1946–57), Secretary of State for External Affairs (1963–68), Senior Minister and Leader of the Government in the Senate (1968–74), and Canadian High Commissioner in the United Kingdom (1974–80). He headed several Canadian delegations to the United Nations during the 1950s. Martin lost three bids to head the Liberal Party, his 1968 resignation from parliament coming after his third loss to Pierre Trudeau. He was survived by his wife, the former Eleanor Adams, a daughter, a son, and three sisters. (d. Windsor, Ontario; September 14, 1992)

FURTHER READING

"The death roll." *Maclean's*, Dec. 21, 1992.

"A Canadian hero." RAE CORELLI. *Maclean's*, Sep. 28, 1992.

Obituary. *The Times* (of London), Sep. 17, 1992.

Obituary. *New York Times*, Sep. 17, 1992.

"Into the final stretch." *Maclean's*, May 14, 1990.

Martin, Steve (1945–)

In Richard Pearce's film *Leap of Faith*, which opened during the 1992 Christmas season, Martin starred as fraudulent faith healer Jonas Nightengale, whose traveling road show finds itself stranded in little Rustwater, Kansas, when its bus breaks down, and who does a tent show there, with ultimately surprising results. Debra Winger co-starred as his manager, in a cast that included Lolita Davidovich, Liam Neeson, and Lukas Haas. Martin also starred opposite Goldie Hawn in the Frank Oz comedy *Housesitter*, which was very badly received by the critics. In 1991, he had starred in the Spencer Tracy role in Charles Shyer's film remake of the classic *Father of the Bride*; in 1992, the film was a hit in home video. A sequel was planned.

Texas-born Martin was a television comedy writer and comedian in cabaret before emerging as a leading television, film, and recording comedian in the late 1970s, most notably as a prominent guest and sometimes host on "Saturday Night Live," and with his Grammy-winning albums *Let's Get Small* (1977) and *A Wild and Crazy Guy* (1978). He became a leading comedy film star with *The Jerk* (1979), and went on to such films as *Pennies from Heaven* (1981), *Dead Men Don't Wear Plaid* (1982), *The Man With Two Brains* (1983), *The Lonely Guy* (1984), *All of Me* (1984), *Three Amigos* (1986), *Little Shop of Horrors* (1986), *Planes, Trains and Automobiles* (1987), *Roxanne* (1987; he also wrote and produced), *Dirty Rotten Scoundrels* (1988), *Parenthood* (1989), *My Blue Heaven* (1990), *L.A. Story* (1991), and *Grand Canyon* (1991). On stage in 1989, he and Robin Williams starred in an acclaimed New York revival of *Waiting for Godot*. Martin attended the University of California. He and actress Victoria Tennant married in 1986.

FURTHER READING

"Cool jerk." PETER DE JONGE. *New York Times Magazine*, May 31, 1992.

"The king of. . . ." ELVIS MITCHELL. *GQ—Gentlemen's Quarterly*, July 1990.

"Steve Martin. . . ." CORK MILLNER. *Saturday Evening Post*, Nov.–Dec. 1989.

Icons: Intimate Portraits. DENISE WORRELL. *Atlantic Monthly*, 1989.

"I'm just a White guy. . . ." ELVIS MITCHELL. *American Film*, Nov. 1988.

Mastroianni, Marcello (1923–) Italian and international film star Mastroianni played in 1992 in one of his rare English-language film roles. In Beeban Kidron's comedy-melodrama film *Used People*, he starred as Shirley MacLaine's Italian-American suitor, who had introduced her to her now-dead husband decades earlier and comes forward after the husband's death. Set in 1960s New York City, the film co-starred Kathy Bates, Marcia Gay Harden, Jessica Tandy, and Sylvia Sidney.

Mastroianni also starred opposite Julie Andrews in Gene Saks film *A Fine Romance*; the Ronald Harwood screenplay was based on the Francois Billetdoux play *Tchin Tchin*, a Paris-based romantic comedy about two people whose spouses have just run off together. The film opened at the 1991 Cannes Film Festival, and in the United States in 1992.

Mastroianni began his film career in 1947, and emerged to world prominence in the late 1950s in such films as *White Nights* (1957), *La Dolce Vita* (1960), *The Night* (1961), *Divorce Italian Style* (1961), *8½* (1963), *Yesterday, Today, and Tomorrow* (1963), and *Marriage Italian Style* (1964). His later work includes such films as *Down the Ancient Stairs* (1974), *City of Women* (1980), *Dark Eyes* (1987), *Splendor* (1989), *What Time Is It?* (1989), *Everything's Fine* (1990), and *The Suspended Step of the Stork* (1991). Mastroianni attended the University of Rome. He was formerly married, and has one child.

FURTHER READING

"Marcello? . . ." MARCELLE CLEMENTS. *Premiere*, June 1991.

"The 35-second seduction. . . ." GEORGINA HOWELL. *M Inc.*, Apr. 1991.

Masur, Kurt (1927–) In his first full year as music director of the New York Philharmonic, German conductor Kurt Masur continued in his attempts to bring the orchestra more fully into the life of the city, while at the same time continuing to work toward harmony within the orchestra as an organization. Such innovations as the Young Peoples' Concerts; the Philharmonic Forums, in which he met directly with the public to discuss changes and plans; and the brief "rush hour" and Saturday afternoon concerts all proved popular—and, perhaps even more significant, began to convince the wider public that the orchestra was not meant to serve a small elite, but rather a large, diverse metropolitan area, occupying a central position in world music. To many people, Masur seemed to refocus much of the orchestra's approach to its music, stressing simplicity and directness of address and achieving more warmth and less hard, only sometimes brilliant personal virtuosity.

Masur's second season, the 150th anniversary season for the orchestra, opened with a series of events, one of them a gala tribute to one of Masur's predecessors, Leonard Bernstein. Many new works had also been commissioned, some destined to be introduced very near the turn of the century. In July 1992, the Philharmonic visited Argentina, playing three concerts at Buenos Aires' Colón. A European tour was planned.

Masur is one of Germany's leading conductors, developing the bulk of his career in East Germany before unification. He was an opera company director in Erfurt and Leipzig, conductor of the Dresden Philharmonic (1955–58), directed the Mecklenburg State Opera (1958–60), was music director of Berlin's Komische Opera (1960–64), went back to Dresden as music director of the Philharmonic (1967–72), and was director of the Leipzig Gewandhaus (1972–90). He has also toured widely, and is principal guest conductor of the London Philharmonic. In April 1990, he was named to succeed Zubin Mehta as music director of the New York Philharmonic, one of the most prestigious posts in the world of classical music.

Masur was a major figure in events that led to the peaceful East German revolution of 1990, intervening on several occasions to avert civil war and bring a peaceful revolution. Afterward, his prestige was so great that there was talk of making him head of the new government, much like the writer Vaclav Havel in Czechoslovakia—but Masur chose to stay with his musical career.

Masur attended the National Musical School at Breslau and the Leipzig Conservatory. He is married to singer Tomoko Sakurai, and has five children.

FURTHER READING

"Kurt Masur." HERBERT KUPFERBERG. *Stereo Review*, May 1992.
"New York's new maestro." ROBERT ANGUS. *Audio*, Dec. 1991.
"New Philharmonic maestro. . . ." PETER G. DAVIS. *New York*, Sep. 23, 1991.
"Maestro of the moment." JOHN ROCKWELL. *New York Times Magazine*, Sep. 8, 1991.
"From Leipzig. . . ." WILLIAM H. YOUNGREN. *World Monitor*, Apr. 1991.
"Masur, Kurt." *Current Biography*, Sep. 1990.

Matlin, Marlee Beth (1965–) Still breaking new ground for hearing-impaired people and by extension for all those who are physically disadvantaged, Matlin starred in 1992 as the deaf prosecutor in the popular television series "Reasonable Doubts," opposite Mark Harmon as her detective and prosecutor partner. For her role in the series, Matlin won the House Ear Institute's Media Award. Still appealing to wide audiences, Matlin's classic *Children of a Lesser God* continued to appear on home screen reruns, and she continued to be a very familiar face, signaling a widening—though still far from ideal—role for deaf and hearing-impaired people in American life.

On screen, Matlin played herself in Robert Altman's *The Player*, a merciless, multi-star lampoon of modern Hollywood. Forthcoming was a starring role in Robert Greenwald's film *Hear No Evil*. She was also scheduled to sign the national anthem to Garth Brooks' singing at the Super Bowl in January 1993.

Born in Morton Grove, Illinois, near Chicago, Matlin became deaf as a result of a childhood illness. She began to work on stage as a child in productions done by Chicago's Center for Deafness, and at the age of 21 was cast as the hearing impaired student opposite William Hurt as her teacher in the Randa Haines film version of the Mark Medoff play *Children of a Lesser God*. In 1987, she won a Best Actress Oscar for her portrayal. She also appeared in the film *Walker* (1988).

FURTHER READING

"In step with. . . ." JAMES BRADY. *Parade*, May 3, 1992.
"Matlin, Marlee." *Current Biography*, May 1992.
"The nerve of Marlee!" MICHAEL SEGELL. *Redbook*, Apr. 1992.

"Actress Marlee Matlin. . . ." PATRICIA FREEMAN. *People*, Apr. 10, 1989.
"Marlee Matlin. . . ." MICHAEL LEAHY. *TV Guide*, Apr. 8, 1989.

Mayes, Wendell (1920–92) Missouri-born Mayes began his writing career in the 1950s, scoring a success with his first television script, *No Riders*. His first screenplay was *The Spirit of St. Louis* (1957), co-written with Billy Wilder. In 1959, he wrote the screenplay to *Anatomy of a Murder* (1959), which won him an Oscar nomination and a New York Film Critics Best Screenplay award. He went on to write many other screenplays, including *Advise and Consent* (1962), *In Harm's Way* (1965), *Hotel* (1969; he also produced), *The Poseidon Adventure* (1973), and *Death Wish* (1974). Late in his career, he also returned to television scriptwriting. He was survived by his wife, the former Phyllis Channing. (d. Santa Monica, California; March 28, 1992)

FURTHER READING

Obituary. *Variety*, Apr. 6, 1992.
Obituary. *New York Times*, Apr. 2, 1992.

Menchú, Rigoberta (1959–) On October 16th, Guatemalan peace activist Menchú was awarded the 1992 Nobel Peace Prize. She is a Quiché Indian, whose family was caught up in the long and continuing Guatemalan civil war, which began in June 1954, when the elected government of Jacobo Arbenz Guzmán was overthrown by the United States-backed forces of Carlos Castillo Armas. As detailed in her autobiography *I, Rigoberta Menchú: An Indian Woman in Guatemala* (1983), her father Vicente, a leader of the Committee for Peasant Unity, was killed in a fire that consumed the Spanish embassy in Guatemala City, after it had been occupied by his group in a demonstration. Her 16-year-old brother was tortured and publicly burned to death by the Guatemalan military. Her mother was repeatedly raped by government soldiers and left to die. She fled into Mexican exile to escape the same kind of fate in 1981, herself becoming a leader of the Committee for Peasant Unity, and at the same time be-

coming a spokesperson for Indian peoples throughout Latin America. As the Norwegian Nobel Committee made clear, the fact that her award coincided with the 500th anniversary of the first Columbus voyage was intentional and meant to focus attention on the dark side of the European conquest of the Indian peoples of the Americas.

FURTHER READING

"Rigoberta Menchu's. . . ." EVELYN BLANCK. *World Press Review*, Dec. 1992.
"Menchu's prize. . . ." MARY JO MCCONAHAY. *National Catholic Reporter*, Oct. 30, 1992.
"Strike against racism." BRUCE W. NELAN. *Time*, Oct. 26, 1992.
"Roots and culture." LAURIE CRITCHLEY. *Guardian*, Oct. 17, 1992.
"1992 will be no party. . . ." DOROTHY VIDULICH. *National Catholic Reporter*, Apr. 19, 1991.
You Can't Drown the Fire: Latin American Women Writing in Exile. ALICIA PARTNOY, ed. Cleis Press, 1988.

Menem, Carlos Saul (1935–) For Argentinian President Menem, 1992 was a relatively quiet year, without riots in the streets over his economic policies, an army revolt, or a massive government scandal, all of which he had survived in 1991. There were, however, still major economic problems, chief among them a continuing ruinous inflation, although the January 1, 1992 introduction of a new peso-based currency put a very temporary brake on it. Far more beneficial was the April 7, 1992 agreement between Argentina and its major bank creditors that included new terms of payment and forgiveness of more than one third of Argentina's $23 billion external debt.

Menem continued to come to grips with some unhappy aspects of Argentina's modern history as well. On February 3, 1992 he ordered release of secret files covering Nazi war criminals harbored in Argentina for decades after World War II; these included files on such infamous Nazis as Adolf Eichmann and Josef Mengele.

Menem spent almost all of his long career in law and politics in his home province of Rioja, beginning with his Peronist youth group activities of the mid-1950s and association with the provincial labor confederation. He became president of the Rioja Justicialist party in 1963, and

was three times elected provincial governor (1973, 1983, 1987). He was elected president of Argentina in May 1989, and succeeded President Raul Foulkes Alfonsin on July 8, 1989, four months before his scheduled December inauguration, because of Argentina's economic problems. He took office following food riots and the declaration of a state of siege, soon losing his early popularity as the economic crisis continued.

Menem attended Cordoba University. He was married to Zulema Fatima Yoma Menem in 1966; the highly publicized breakup of their marriage ultimately resulted in her June 1990 eviction from the presidential mansion by an army contingent. They have two children.

FURTHER READING

"A talk with. . . ." LINDA ROBINSON. *U.S. News & World Report*, May 7, 1990.
"Menem, Carlos Saul." *Current Biography*, Nov. 1989.

Merriam, Eve (1916–92) Philadelphia-born Merriam, a leading feminist poet, worked in a variety of writing jobs in the 1940s, publishing her first poetry collection, *Family Circle*, in 1946. Her poetry included *Tomorrow Morning* (1951), *The Double Bed from the Feminine Side* (1958), *The Trouble With Love* (1961), *It Doesn't Always Have to Rhyme* (1964), *Independent Voices* (1968), *The Inner City Mother Goose* (1969), *The Nixon Poems* (1970), *Growing Up Female in America* (1971), *Rainbow Writing* (1976), *The Birthday Cow* (1978), *Blackberry Ink* (1985), and *Halloween ABC* (1986). She also wrote the stage musicals *Inner City* (1971), *The Club* (1976; it won an Obie award), and *At Her Age* (1979). She was survived by two sons, a brother, and a sister. Her fourth husband was the writer Waldo Salt. (d. New York City; April 11, 1992)

FURTHER READING

Obituary. *New York Times*, Apr. 13, 1992.

Messiaen, Olivier (1908–92) Avignon-born Messiaen, a leading 20th-century composer, began to compose at the age of 7, and entered the Paris Conservatory at the age of 9,

in 1919. He completed his studies in 1930, and in 1931 became chief organist of the Church of the Trinity in Paris, beginning a lifelong affiliation. He taught at the Schola Cantorum (1936–39), and at the École Normale de Musique in Paris (1941–78), after a break for World War II service, including capture and two years of imprisonment by the Germans. During his imprisonment, he composed his best-known work, *Quartet for the End of Time* (1940). As a composer, teacher, and organist, he powerfully influenced the development of 20th-century music. His very large body of work reflected his devout Catholicism, later merged with love themes and the bird themes that for a considerable period dominated his work. His later work, much of it massive, included the choral piece *The Transfiguration* (1969) and the opera *St Francis of Assisi* (1983). His final work was the eleven-movement *Reflections on the Hereafter* (1991), not yet performed at his death. He was survived by his wife, Yvonne Loriod. (d. Paris; April 28, 1992)

FURTHER READING

"Olivier Messiaen. . . ." GEORGE FLYNN. *Christian Century*, July 1, 1992.
"Olivier Messiaen. . . ." ARVED ASHBY. *American Record Guide*, July–Aug. 1992.
"Of hopelessness and hope." PETER PLAGENS. *Newsweek*, May 11, 1992.
"When time stands still." BAYAN NORTHCOTT. *Independent*, May 2, 1992.
Obituary. *Variety*, May 4, 1992.
Obituary. *The Times* (of London), Apr. 29, 1992.
Obituary. *New York Times*, Apr. 29, 1992.
Obituary. *Independent*, Apr. 29, 1992.

Michener, James Albert (1907–) Still

going strong in his 85th year, Michener reached far back to publish what may be his last "big" novel. It was *Mexico*, largely written in the 1960s, but abandoned with two thirds done. Michener's agent, Owen Laster, had found the book contract in the late 1960s, but not the mislaid manuscript; it was finally found in a box in Michener's Bucks County, Pennsylvania, home, and was then completed. In 1992, Michener also published *My Lost Mexico*, describing the process of writing *Mexico*. Michener's really current 1992 work was autobiographical: *The World Is My Home: A Memoir*. As with all his books, it

immediately found wide readership, as had his 1991 work *The Novel*, a shorter-than-usual novel set in the world of publishing. In 1992, *The Novel* became a paperback bestseller. Continuing their gift-giving, the Micheners in 1992 donated $15 million to a University of Texas writers' program.

Michener was a teacher and editor during the late 1930s and 40s. He emerged as a major U.S. popular author in 1947, with his Pultizer Prize-winning first novel *Tales of the South Pacific*; the book was adapted into the musical *South Pacific* in 1949. He went on to write many bestsellers, many of them historical novels and several of them adapted into hit movies. Some of his best known novels are *The Bridges at Toko-ri* (1953), *Sayonara* (1954), *The Bridge at Andau* (1957), *Hawaii* (1959), *The Source* (1965), *Iberia* (1968), *Centennial* (1974), *Chesapeake* (1978), *The Covenant* (1980), *Space* (1982), *Texas* (1985), *Alaska* (1988), and *Caribbean* (1989). He has also written several volumes of essays and edited several art books. Michener attended Swarthmore College. He has been married three times, since 1955 to Mari Yoriko Sabusawa.

FURTHER READING

"Novel approach." HELEN THOMPSON. *Texas*, Oct. 1992.
"The man who. . . ." LYNN ROSELLINI. *U.S. News & World Report*, June 17, 1991.
"The continuing sagas of. . . ." JIM SHAHIN. *Saturday Evening Post*, Mar. 1990.

Midler, Bette (1945–)

Midler won an Oscar nomination and a Golden Globe award for her portrayal of Dixie Rydell opposite James Caan as Eddie Sparks in *For the Boys* (1991), the show business story of two USO performers going through three wars. She also produced the film, which in spite of her fine personal reviews and honors was not a critical or commercial success. For her appearance on "The Tonight Show Starring Johnny Carson," Midler also won a 1992 Emmy for best performance in a variety or music program.

Forthcoming was a starring role as Gypsy Rose Lee in a television film version of the Broadway musical *Gypsy*, and another in the Disney film *Hocus Pocus*, a comedy about three time-traveling Salem witches in modern Salem, co-starring Sarah Jessica Parker and Kathy Najimy. Filming started in October 1992.

On the legal front, Midler won a major victory for herself and for many other celebrity performers. In late March, the U.S. Supreme Court ruled that she could collect a lower-court-awarded $400,000 judgment from an advertising agency that had used an imitation of her voice in a 1986 television commercial, upholding a California law that defined such taking as illegal.

Hawaii-born Midler, on stage and screen from 1965, was in the early 1970s the long-running lead singer at New York's Continental Baths, a gay men's health club. She began her recording career with the album *The Divine Miss M* (1973), also recording such albums as *Bette Midler* (1973), *Thighs and Whispers* (1979), *Divine Madness* (1980), and *Some People's Lives* (1990), as well as the soundtrack album for *The Rose* (1980), her first starring film role. Her single "Wind Beneath My Wings" won a 1990 Grammy award for best song. Midler went on to play in such films as *Jinxed* (1982), *Down and Out in Beverly Hills* (1986), *Ruthless People* (1986), *Outrageous Fortune* (1987), *Beaches* (1989), *Stella* (1990), and *Scenes From a Mall* (1991), and has also appeared in television. She published *A View from a Broad* (1980). Midler attended the University of Hawaii. She married Martin von Haselberg in 1984; they have one child.

FURTHER READING

"La belle Bette." KEVIN SESSUMS. *Vanity Fair*, Dec. 1991.

"A fashion fairy tale extravaganza." JONATHAN VAN METER. *Vogue*, Dec. 1991.

"Bette Midler and. . . ." EMILY YOFFE. *Newsweek*, Nov. 25, 1991.

"Bette." VERNON SCOTT. *Good Housekeeping*, Mar. 1991.

"The best Bette yet." CLIFF JAHR. *Ladies Home Journal*, Jan. 1990.

Bette Midler. ACE COLLINS. St. Martin's, 1989.

Bette Midler: Outrageously Divine. MARK BEGO. NAL-Dutton, 1987.

Mikulski, Barbara (1936–)

In the "Year of the Woman," Maryland Democratic Senator Mikulski was elected for a second term, by a landslide 71–29 percent majority. Given the strength of her support, she probably would have won by some such majority in any year. Long the only woman Democrat in the Senate, Mikulski was in 1992 joined by Barbara Boxer, Carol Moseley Braun, Dianne Feinstein, and Patty Murray. A leading liberal in the Senate, Mikulski was faced by "gridlock" in 1992, as a Republican President and Democratic Congress jockeyed for political position in a presidential election year. Little was accomplished on either side, although Mikulski voted with other liberals on such issues as health care reform, education, military spending cuts, abortion rights, and civil rights.

A social worker, Baltimore-born Mikulski moved into local politics as a community organizer. She served on the Baltimore City Council (1971–76), making an unsuccessful run for the U.S. Senate in 1974. She served five terms in the House of Representatives, (1976–86), and was elected to her first Senate term in 1986. Her 1958 B.A. was from Mt. St. Agnes College and her 1965 M.S.W. from the University of Maryland.

FURTHER READING

Women in Power: The Secrets of Leadership. DOROTHY W. CANTOR. Houghton Mifflin, 1992. "Nancy Kassebaum and. . . ." *Ms.,* Sep. 1988.

Milken, Michael (1946–) On August 5, 1992, jailed financier Michael Milken benefited from a major reduction in his sentence. Judge Kimba Wood, who had originally sentenced Milken to a ten-year prison term, cut his term to less than three years, making him eligible for release in March 1993, and probably for prison release to a halfway house much earlier. The reduction was hailed by Milken's attorney and friends. Senator Edward M. Kennedy and many regulators deplored the action, Kennedy calling it hypocrisy to reduce the sentence of someone who has robbed "billions of dollars." That was not the only good news for Milken: An advantageous settlement of federal claims left him and his family with assets reportedly in the $500 million range.

Milken was the central figure in the massive Drexel Burnham Lambert stock scandals of the late 1980s that brought multiple indictments of the Drexel firm in 1988, after a two-year investigation aided by convicted stock market manipulator Ivan Boesky. Drexel pleaded guilty to six felony counts in 1988 and agreed to pay $650 million. Milken was indicted on 98 counts in March 1989, resigned from Drexel in June 1989, and in April 1990 pleaded guilty to six felony counts and agreed to pay $600 million.

Milken's entire career had been with Drexel, Burnham, Lambert. He worked part-time with the firm while in college and joined its bond department in 1970. During the 1970s, he began his long career as a high-yield bond trader, developing the "junk bond" concept. He moved the firm's bond department to Beverly Hills, California in 1978, and vastly expanded junk bond operations throughout the 1980s, using it as a financing technique that raised tens of billions of dollars and earned billions in fees for the firm. He personally earned over $1 billion. But in the mid-1980s, allegations of insider trading and other securities frauds began to surface, and a

long series of federal investigations and prosecutions began.

Milken's B.B.A. was from the University of California, and his M.B.A. from the Wharton School of the University of Pennsylvania. He is married to Lori Anne Hackett.

FURTHER READING

"Prose and con. . . ." JOE QUEENAN. *Barron's,* Nov. 30, 1992.
"My story. . . ." JAMES W. MICHAELS and PHYLLIS BERMAN. *Forbes,* Mar. 16, 1992.
"Den of thieves. . . ." JAMES B. STEWART. *Cosmopolitan,* Feb. 1992.
Fall from Grace: The Untold Story of Michael Milken. FENTON BAILEY. Birch Lane/Carol, 1992.
Highly Confident: The True Story of the Crime and Punishment of Michael Milken. JESSE KORNBLUTH. Morrow, 1992.
The Junk Bond Revolution: Michael Milken, Wall Street and the Roaring Eighties. FENTON BAILEY. Fourth Estate/Trafalgar, 1992.
"Insider reporting." JUDE WANNISKI. *National Review,* Dec. 2, 1991.
"A reversal of misfortune? . . ." MICHELE GALEN. *Business Week,* Nov. 11, 1991.
"Michael Milken. . . ." TAD FRIEND. *Esquire,* May 1991.
Den of Thieves: The Untold Story of the Men Who Plundered Wall Street and the Chase That Brought Them Down. JAMES B. STEWART. Simon & Schuster, 1991.

Miller, Arthur (1915–) As in every year, Miller's plays were seen in revival in 1992 in many countries and languages. One notable revival was the New York Roundabout Theater production of his play *The Price,* starring Hector Elizondo, Debra Mooney, Eli Wallach, and Joe Spano. Another very notable revival of *The Crucible* ended its run at New York's National Actors' Theater, starring Martin Sheen and Maryann Plunkett. Miller was scheduled to direct a Swedish-language production of *Death of a Salesman* at Stockholm's Royal Dramatic Theater in early 1993.

Miller's most recent play, *The Last Yankee,* was scheduled to run from January 5 to February 7, 1993, at the Manhattan Theater Club. *The Ride Down Mt. Morgan* (1991), Miller's first play to premiere outside the United States, ended its London run on February 15, 1992, six weeks earlier than scheduled, as the London theater continued to reel under the impact of Britain's long, deep recession. On January 15, 1992, Miller received a Medal of Honor for Literature from the National Arts Club.

Miller has been a leading American playwright since the 1947 production of *All My Sons*, which won a New York Drama Critic Award. He became a world figure with his Pulitzer-Prize winning *Death of a Salesman* (1949), in which Lee J. Cobb created the memorable Willy Loman. His most notable further work included the Tony-winning *The Crucible* (1953), the Pulitzer-winning *A View from the Bridge* (1955), *After the Fall* (1963), *Incident at Vichy* (1965), *The Price* (1968), and *The American Clock* (1979). He wrote the screenplay for *The Misfits* (1961), which starred his second wife, Marilyn Monroe, who committed suicide in 1962. His second screenplay was for Karel Reisz's *Everybody Wins* (1990), starring Nick Nolte and Debra Winger. Miller's recent work also includes an Americanized adaptation of Ibsen's *An Enemy of the People* (1990), done in a televised production for PBS's "American Playhouse." In 1987 he published *Timebends: A Life*. Miller attended the University of Michigan. He has been married three times, since 1962 to photographer Inge Morath, with whom he has collaborated on two travel books; he has two children.

FURTHER READING

Marilyn's Men: The Private Life of Marilyn Monroe. JANE E. WAYNE. St. Martin's, 1992.
"Miller's crossing." JAMES KAPLAN. *Vanity Fair*, Nov. 1991.
Miller the Playwright. DENNIS WELLAND. Heinemann, 1988.
Conversations with Arthur Miller. MATTHEW C. ROUDANE, ed. University Press of Mississippi, 1987.

Miller, Roger Dean (1936–92)

Texas-born country singer, composer, and instrumentalist Roger Miller began his professional career after Korean War service; his recording debut came in 1958 with the song "Invitation to the Blues," recorded by Ray Price. He wrote such early-1960s country hits as "When Two Worlds Collide" (1961), "Dang Me" (1964), and "Chug-a-Lug" (1964), and then scored a huge breakthrough with by far his best-known song, "King of the Road" (1965), followed in the same year by a string of hit songs, including "Engine No. 9" and "England Swings." Miller won six Grammy Awards for his 1965 songs, and went on to win five more in the years that followed, although his career sagged during the 1970s. He made a strong comeback in 1985, writing the score for the long-running Broadway musical *Big River*, for which he won a Best Musical Score Tony. He was survived by his third wife, Mary Miller, and seven children. (d. Los Angeles; October 25, 1992)

FURTHER READING

Obituary. *Billboard*, Nov. 7, 1992.
Obituary. *Variety*, Nov. 2, 1992.
Obituary. *The Times* (of London) Oct. 27, 1992.
Obituary. *New York Times*, Oct. 27, 1992.

Mills, Wilbur Daigh (1909–92)

Born in Kensett, Arkansas, Mills was a powerful figure in the U.S. House of Representatives for more than three decades. He began his long political career a year after receiving his degree from Harvard Law School, when elected as a county judge, and at 29 became the second youngest member of the House. He was appointed to the powerful House Banking and Currency Committee in 1939, then to the centrally important tax law-writing Ways and Means Committee in 1943, in 1957, as the most senior member, becoming its chairman. For the next 17 years, he was responsible for much of the shape and content of the American federal tax system. A conservative Southern Democrat, Mills was until the 1960s anti-civil rights and segregationist, and sharply opposed to social welfare legislation, but later moderated his views somewhat. An alcoholic, Mills' career effectively ended after a highly publicized 1974 drunken driving incident near the Jefferson Memorial, also involving other addictive substances and the strip dancer Annabel Battistella, who performed as Fanne Fox. Mills was survived by his wife, Clarine, two daughters, a sister, and a brother. (d. Kensett, Arkansas; May 2, 1992)

FURTHER READING

Obituary. *The Times* (of London), May 4, 1992.
Obituary. *New York Times*, May 3, 1992.

Milosevic, Slobodan (1941–) Serbian

President Milosevic became widely known as "The Butcher of the Balkans" during 1992, as Serbian forces turned Bosnia-Herzegovina into a slaughterhouse, with hundreds of thousands dead, millions in flight, and the world once again faced with the reality of genocide, called by the mass murderers of this time and place "ethnic cleansing." Milosevic steadfastly denied all responsibility for events in Bosnia-Herzegovina, but nobody believed him, as it was perfectly clear that Serbian forces were using Serbian army tanks, artillery, and other heavy ordnance, and were supported by the Serbian air force. In December, Milosevic was re-elected, defeating Yugoslav premier Milan Panic in an election widely described as shot through with fraud. At year's end, the killing continued, while yet another round of peace talks were scheduled in Geneva, Switzerland in early January and the whole world watched, waited—and did nothing effective to stop the slaughter.

Born in Pozarevac, near Belgrade, Milosevic followed a very orthodox career path in Tito's Communist Yugoslavia. He became a member of the League of Communists of Yugoslavia in 1959, attended Belgrade University, and moved up as a protégé of Serbian Communist leader Ivan Stambolic. Milosevic worked in the Belgrade city administration during the 1960s, and then became deputy director of the government industrial gas monopoly Technogas (1969–73). He ran a state bank (1978–83) and headed the Belgrade Communist organization (1984–86), then becoming president of the League of Communists of Serbia in 1986. In 1987, resurgent Serbian nationalism created an opportunity for him to take a hard line, and gain massive popular and armed forces support. He is married to League of Communists leader Marjana Markovic.

FURTHER READING

"Mob rule. . . ." CHARLES LAN. New Republic, Dec. 28, 1992.

"The butcher of the Balkans." JAMES GRAFF. Time, June 8, 1992.

"Conman of the Balkans." IAN TRAYNOR. Guardian, June 1, 1992.

"Carving out a greater Serbia." STEPHEN ENGELBERG. New York Times Magazine, Sep. 1, 1991.

"Milosevic, Slobodan." Current Biography, Apr. 1990.

"Sloba 0, Stipe 1." Economist, Oct. 22, 1988.

"O nationalism! . . ." DAVID AIKMAN. Time, Oct. 24, 1988.

"Dreams and nightmares of Greater Serbia." Economist, Sep. 17, 1988.

Milstein, Nathan (1903–92) Odessa-born

Milstein, one of the century's greatest violinists, was a child prodigy who began his study of the violin at age four, was admitted to the Odessa Conservatory at eleven, and a year later commenced his study in St. Petersburg with the great teacher Leopold Auer, who also taught Mischa Elman, Jascha Heifetz, and many others who became central figures in world music. Milstein made his debut in recital at 15, soon becoming a well known figure in Russian music. In 1926, he emigrated to the West, making his debut in Paris and then in 1929 with the Philadelphia Orchestra. He became an American citizen in 1942. Milstein continued his long worldwide recital career well into his eighties, his final public performance being with the New York Philharmonic in 1987. He also made a large number of recordings, many of them long out of print, though reissues of his works on CD are reportedly planned. In 1990 he published *From Russia to the West: The Musical Memoirs & Reminiscences of Nathan Milstein*, written with Solomon Volkov. He was survived by his wife, Therese Kaufman Milstein, and a daughter. (d. London; December 21, 1992)

FURTHER READING

Obituary. Billboard, Jan. 9, 1993.

Obituary. The Times (of London), Dec. 26, 1992.

Obituary. New York Times, Dec. 22, 1992.

Mitchell, George John (1933–) Senate

Majority Leader George Mitchell continued to play a key role in the growing Democratic attack on President George Bush in 1992. In 1991, he and his party had developed the themes that would take them through the 1992 presidential campaign, calling Bush a do-nothing president and demanding action on such issues as joblessness and the growing recession, the health care crisis, and the ballooning deficit. In 1992, their message taking hold so well as to propel Bill Clinton into the Presidency, they continued the attack, as election year "gridlock" developed between a Republican President and Democratic Congress. Beyond political advantage, very little was accomplished by Congress or the Bush administration in 1992, although Mitchell and others continued to push very hard and very publicly on such issues as abortion rights, job creation, civil rights, and comprehensive education and health care reforms. Meanwhile, the Democratic Congressional leadership and the White House escalated their war of words throughout 1992, each calling the other responsible for the gridlock situation. Mitchell was reelected Senate Majority Leader in November.

Maine-born Mitchell began his career in Washington as a Justice Department attorney (1960–62) and as an assistant to Maine Democratic Senator Edmund Muskie (1962–65). He went home to practice law and politics in Maine, became a U.S. attorney and then U.S. district judge in the late 1970s, and was elected as a Maine Democratic Senator in 1981, succeeding Muskie. Mitchell rose quickly in the Senate and in his party, becoming majority leader of the Senate in 1988. With fellow Maine senator William S. Cohen, a Republican, Mitchell has published *Men of Zeal: A Candid Story of the Iran-Contra Hearings* (1988) and *World on Fire: Saving an Endangered Earth* (1991). His 1954 B.A. was from Bowdoin College, and his 1960 LL.B. from Georgetown University. He has one child.

FURTHER READING

"Clinton and Congress. . . ." ERIC FELTEN. *Insight*, Nov. 23, 1992.
"Hill potatoes. . . ." FRED BARNES. *New Republic*, May 20, 1991.
"Mitchell, George John." *Current Biography*, Apr. 1989.
"A hardball player. . . ." HAYS GOREY. *Time*, Dec. 12, 1988.

Mitchell, Peter (1920–92)

A leading biochemist, Peter Mitchell was awarded the 1978 Nobel Prize for chemistry, for his trailblazing work in the electrochemistry involved in the conversion of food by animals and light by plants into energy that was then used in life processes. His discoveries, although resisted by most other scientists when introduced, ultimately became regarded as basic. Mitchell received his Ph.D. at Cambridge University in 1950, teaching there until moving to the University of Edinburgh in 1955. Leaving his teaching career for health reasons in the early 1960s, he set up a small research institute at his home in Bodmin, proceeding to develop his major work to increasing acclaim. He was survived by his second wife, Helen, a daughter, and three sons. (d. Bodmin, England; Apr. 10, 1992)

FURTHER READING

Obituary. *Independent*, Apr. 16, 1992.
Obituary. *The Times* (of London), Apr. 15, 1992.

Mitterrand, François Maurice Marie

(1916–) French President Mitterrand faced a considerable number of problems during 1992. Although comparatively strong, the French economy in 1992 was not immune to the effects of the deepening worldwide recession, and unemployment and declining real wages continued to fuel discontent. With unemployment high, antiforeign feelings were successfully exploited by rival parties. There were financial scandals affecting members of his government as well. Most highly visible of all were the massive farmer protests that had grown in 1991 and extended into 1992 as European Community (EC) pressures brought in meat and other products from Eastern Europe. French President Mitterrand's popularity continued to decline and his Socialist Party suffered severe electoral defeats in March, winning only a little more than 18 percent of the vote in the regional elections, only half of its 1988 vote.

Mitterrand fired highly controversial premier Edith Cresson in the aftermath of the elections. But his situation did not greatly improve: what came next was a long fight for French approval of the European Community's Maastricht Treaty. Unfortunately for Mitterrand, the treaty vote came on September 20, only a few days after the start of the major European Monetary System crisis. The treaty won in France, but barely, ran into great trouble in Britain and other countries, and seemed unlikely to survive. A third major crisis and massive farmer demonstration developed when the outgoing U.S. Bush administration brought longstanding trade negotiation problems to a head by placing punitive duties on some European imports, most notably French white wines and soybeans. Although Mitterrand continued to be a strong foreign policy figure, his situation at home in France had greatly deteriorated by year's end.

On the personal side, Mitterrand was reported in September to have treatable prostate cancer. His wife Danielle narrowly escaped death in a terrorist attack while on a humanitarian visit to Kurdish communities in northern Iraq.

A soldier during World War II, Mitterrand was captured early, but escaped from the Germans and became an active Resistance fighter. He entered politics after the war and was a Socialist Deputy in the national assembly (1946–58; 1962–81), holding many cabinet positions in the early years, when his party held power. At the same time, he rose within the Socialist Party and was its First Secretary (1971–81), while also becoming a vice-president of the Socialist International (1972–81). In 1981, he was elected President of France, and was reelected to a second seven-year term in 1988. Mitterrand attended the University of Paris. He married Danielle Gouze in 1944; the couple have two children. His brother is general Jacques Mitterrand.

FURTHER READING

"France turns tetchy." *Economist*, Mar. 7, 1992.
Mitterrand: A Political Biography. Wayne Northcutt. Holmes & Meier, 1992.
Seven Years in France: François Mitterrand and Unintended Revolution, 1981–1988. Julius W. Friend. Westview, 1988.
The Black and the Red: François Mitterrand and the Story of an Ambition. Catherine Nay. Harcourt Brace, 1987.
Mitterrand's France. Sonia Mazey and Michael Newman, eds. Routledge Chapman & Hall, 1987.

Miyazawa, Kiichi (1919–)   Japan's Miyazawa government, like several previous governments formed by his ruling Liberal Democratic Party (LDP), was deeply tainted by scandal in 1992. Leader of the strongest faction of the LDP, Miyazawa had taken office on November 6, 1991, succeeding Toshiki Kaifu, whose proposed reform program had been rejected by the LDP. On November 6, the day he took office, Miyazawa named a new Cabinet that included many politicians previously forced from power after their involvement in major scandals, including the Recruit stock scandal.

During 1992, the scandals continued and multiplied. In January, one of Miyazawa's closest assistants, Fumio Abe, was arrested on charges of receiving bribes in the Kyowa Corporation scandal, that later was found to involve several other politicians. In February, the Tokyo Sagawa Kyubin Company scandal broke, which involved $4–7 billion dollars, Japanese organized crime, and many of Japan's leading politicians, including LDP kingmaker Shin Kanemaru, Japan's most powerful politician, who resigned his LDP positions on August 28, though keeping his seat in parliament. More revelations were expected to follow.

In office, Miyazawa continued his criticism of the United States, though moderating it somewhat after generating a firestorm of U.S. criticism when in February he criticized the American work ethic. Japanese-American trade relations continued to be strained throughout the year, as Japan resisted opening its domestic markets, and were not expected to improve during the first year of the Clinton presidency and while Japan's deep recession continued.

There were two very notable echoes from the past in 1992. In January, Miyazawa apologized for the Japanese army's forced use of thousands of Korean women as prostitutes during World War II. On June 15, Miyazawa won Diet approval of his plan to send up to 2,000 Japanese troops abroad to participate in United Nations peacekeeping missions, the first time Japanese troops were to be used abroad and for anything but self-defense since World War II. The highly controversial move was attacked by several Asian nations and by opponents in Japan as a first step toward rearmament.

Tokyo-born Miyazawa, the child of a prominent Japanese political family, is a graduate of Tokyo Imperial University. He began his five-decades-long political career during World War II, and was with the Finance Ministry (1942–52) through the war and the postwar American occupation of Japan. He became secretary to the Minister of Finance in 1949. A powerful leader of the ruling Liberal Democratic Party (LDP), he became an elected official in 1953, and then Vice Minister of Education (1959–69), holding a series of Cabinet-level posts for the following three decades. He was chairman of the Executive Council of the LDP (1984–86), and became a key leader of the most powerful of the three LDP factions during that period. He is married to Yoko Miyazawa; they have two chldren. He also has two brothers, both active in government.

FURTHER READING

"Miyazawa, Kiichi." *Current Biography*, Feb. 1992.
"Miyazawa unravels." *Economist*, Dec. 14, 1991.
"Raw and fishy...." JOANNA PITMAN. *New Republic*, Nov. 4, 1991.

Moore, Demi (Demi Guynes; 1962–) In 1992, film star Demi Moore starred as Lieutenant Commander Joanne Galloway, a Navy lawyer who is special counsel in a military murder

trial in Rob Reiner's film *A Few Good Men*, adapted by Aaron Sorkin from his own long-running play. Co-starring were Tom Cruise, as the young Navy lawyer trying the case, who she presses to do the best possible job, and Jack Nicholson, as the Guantanamo Bay base commander who is their chief antagonist. The courtroom drama co-stars Kevin Bacon, Kiefer Sutherland, and Kevin Pollak. Forthcoming was a starring role opposite Robert Redford in Adrian Lyne's film *Indecent Proposal* as a losing gambler's wife who is paid $1 million to sleep with top Las Vegas gambler Redford.

Having created quite a stir by appearing nude and nine months pregnant on the August 1991 cover of the magazine *Vanity Fair* (though she was not really entirely nude), Moore in August 1992 again appeared on the magazine's cover, this time looking fully clothed, although on this occasion actually nude and wearing a body-painted pin-striped suit.

New Mexico-born Moore played reporter Jackie Templeton in television's "General Hospital," and appeared in such 1980s films as *Choices* (1981), *Parasite* (1982), *St. Elmo's Fire* (1985), *Wisdom* (1986), and *We're No Angels* (1989). Her breakthrough came in 1990 with a starring role opposite Patrick Swayze and Whoopi Goldberg in the fantasy *Ghost*, which became the surprise top-grossing film of the year, thus making her a bankable star. She married Bruce Willis in 1987; they have two daughters.

FURTHER READING

"Demi's body language." JENNET CONANT and ANNIE LEIBOVITZ. *Vanity Fair*, Aug. 1992.
"Demi Moore." JOE RHODES. *Harper's Bazaar*, June 1992.
"What she did. . . ." JEFF ROVIN. *Ladies Home Journal*, June 1992.
"Demi's big moment." NANCY COLLINS and ANNIE LEIBOVITZ. *Vanity Fair*, Aug. 1991.
"The haunting magic of. . . ." TOM BURKE. *Cosmopolitan*, Dec. 1990.
"They heard it through. . . ." JEANNIE PARK. *People*, Nov. 12, 1990.
"Bruce, Demi, and. . . ." NANCY ANDERSON. *Good Housekeeping*, Nov. 1988.

Moreau, Jeanne (1928–) French actress Moreau starred in 1992 in Didier Martiny's film *À Demain* (*See You Tomorrow*), a family story set in 1960's Paris. She is the mother of nine-year-old Pierre, played by Laurent Lavergne, who tells him much about life and prepares him for the concept of death before she dies that year. He tells the story as an adult in voiceovers, while the movie proceeds in flashbacks. Moreau also appeared in Vincent Ward's *Map of the Human Heart*, a large-canvas multigenerational and crosscultural (English Canadian, French Canadian, and Inuit Eskimo) romantic drama set largely in the Canadian Arctic from the 1930s through the 1960s. In a third notable appearance, Moreau narrated the Jan-Jacques Annaut film *L'Amant* (*The Lover*), based on the Marguerite Duras novel, a sexual memoir that was a bestseller in France.

Paris-born Moreau has been a leading actress on the French stage and screen since 1948. She became an international film star in the 1950s and has appeared in such films as *Frantic* (1957), *The Lovers* (1958), *Les Liaisons Dangereuses* (1959), *Jules and Jim* (1961), *Diary of a Chambermaid* (1964), *Viva Maria* (1965), *The Bride Wore Black* (1967), *Lumière* (1976; she also directed), *The Trout* (1982), *Lillian Gish* (1984), *The Miracle* (1986), *Calling the Shots* (1988), *La Femme Nikita* (1990), *Till the End of the World* (1991), *The Old Lady Who Wades in the Sea* (1991), and *The Suspended Step of the Stork* (1991). Moreau attended the National Conservatory of Dramatic Art. She has been married twice and has one son.

FURTHER READING

"Failed ballerina. . . ." *Economist*, Aug. 1, 1992.
"La lumière." MOLLY HASKELL and ANDREA R. VAUCHER. *Film Comment*, Mar.–Apr. 1990.

Morley, Robert (1908–92) Actor and writer Robert Morley studied at the Royal Academy of Dramatic Art, making his stage debut in 1928 in *Dr. Syn*, and his London stage debut in 1929. He scored his first major London success as the lead in *Oscar Wilde* (1936), taking the play to Broadway in 1938. Another great success was his role as Sheridan Whiteside in the London production of *The Man Who Came to Dinner* (1941). He also co-wrote and starred in *Edward My Son* (1947, Broadway 1948), and continued to star on stage for decades. He won an Oscar nomination for his film debut in *Marie Antoinette*, and went on to appear in scores of films during the following four decades, as in *Major Barbara* (1940), *Outcast of the Islands* (1951), *The African Queen* (1951), *Beat the Devil* (1953), *Around the World in 80 Days* (1956), and *Oscar Wilde* (1960; in the title role), continuing to appear on stage and screen through the 1980s. Late in his career, he was a very familiar face in television commercials, and played in several television films, including "War and Remembrance" (1989). He also wrote several plays and autobiographical works, including *Pleasures of Age* (1990) and *Around the World in Eighty-One Years* (1991). He was survived by his wife, a daughter, and two sons, one of whom is the drama critic Sheridan Morley. (d. Berkshire, England; June 3, 1992)

FURTHER READING

Obituary. *Variety*, June 8, 1992.
"One life's performance." SHERIDAN MORLEY. *Sunday Times*, June 7, 1992.
Obituary. *The Times* (of London), June 4, 1992.
Obituary. *Independent*, June 4, 1992.
Obituary. *New York Times*, June 4, 1992.

Morrison, Toni (Chloe Anthony Wofford; 1931–) African-American writer Toni Morrison published three books in 1992. By far the most popular and attention-getting was her novel *Jazz*, published in April, set in Harlem in

the mid-1920s, with flashbacks back to the turn-of-the-century South and personal histories that include the great post-World War I African-American northward migration. The "jazz" of Morrison's title is an attempt to relate the new jazz rhythms to the culture of African-American city life, so different from rural African-American country life. Morrison's chief characters are middle-aged Joe, who murders his young lover Dorcas, and Joe's wife, Violet, who attempts to slash Dorcas' corpse at her funeral. Morrison explores their lives, motives, history, and setting. Morrison also published a work of literary criticism in 1992, *Playing in the Dark: Whiteness and the Literary Imagination.* She also collected and edited *Race-ing Justice, En-Gendering Power*, a book of essays on the Anita Faye Hill-Clarence Thomas confrontation.

Ohio-born Morrison taught English and the humanities at Texas Southern University (1955–57), and at Howard University (1957–64). Making a major career and location change, she then joined Random House as an editor in 1965, becoming a substantial figure in the New York publishing world during the decades that followed. But it is for her novels that she is by far best known, her focus on the lives of African-American women placing her at the center of the emerging feminist and African-American movements of her time. Her works include *The Bluest Eye* (1969), *Sula* (1973), *Song of Solomon* (1977), *Tar Baby* (1981), and her Pulitzer-Prize winning *Beloved* (1987), which also won several other prizes. Morrison's 1953 B.A. was from Howard University, and her 1955 M.A. from Cornell University. She has two children.

FURTHER READING

Toni Morrison: Critical Perspectives Past and Present. HENRY L. GATES, JR., and K.A. APPIAH. Amistad Press, 1993.
"Black and right. . . ." CLIVE DAVIS. *Times*, Apr. 28, 1992.
The Voices of Toni Morrison. BARBARA RIGNEY. Ohio State University Press, 1992.
Fiction and Folklore: The Novels of Toni Morrison. TRUDIER HARRIS. University of Tennessee Press, 1991.
Toni Morrison. HAROLD BLOOM, ed. Chelsea House, 1991.
"The divining Ms. Morrison." MAYA ANGELOU. *Savvy Woman*, Aug. 1989.
"Toni Morrison." MARCIA ANNA GILLESPIE. *Ms.*, Jan. 1988.
The World of Toni Morrison: Explorations in Literary Criticism. BESSIE W. JONES and AUDREY L. VINSON. Kendall-Hunt, 1985.

Mubarak, Hosni (Mohammed Hosni Mubarak; 1928–) Egyptian President Mubarak received massive infusions of foreign aid as a result of his support of the Persian Gulf War alliance against Iraq. Egypt had sent 45,000 troops to Iraq and received back almost two million Egyptians working abroad; in return, Western nations forgave approximately $25 billion of Egypt's $50 billion in outstanding foreign debt, also providing interest rate reductions, payment stretchouts, and probably future forgiveness of more debt. They also guaranteed at least $8 billion more in foreign aid. Continually faced with Egypt's mounting economic problems and huge rate of population growth, the relatively large amounts of money and credit gained greatly strengthened Mubarak's government, at least for a time. His position in the Arab world was greatly improved as well. Egypt had been cast out by hardline anti-Israeli Arab nations after the 1979 Camp David Accords with Israel, had regained some prestige in the late 1980s, and after the Gulf War resumed a major position at the center of the Arab world.

Mubarak continued to be faced with large-scale Muslim fundamentalist extremism in 1992. The Egyptian government, which had long refused to legalize several fundamentalist political parties, responded by intensified harassment, mass arrests of fundamentalist leaders, and new laws making membership in several banned organizations punishable by death. Starting in the spring of 1992, violence escalated, and Muslim fundamentalists began a long terrorist campaign against tourists in southern Egypt aimed at cutting into national revenues from the lucrative tourist trade. They fired on tourist buses and ships, made individual attacks on tourists, and bombed historic sites; the government responded with riot police and troops.

Mubarak was a career air force officer who moved up to direct the Air Academy (1967–69), became Air Force chief of staff (1969–72), and was commander in chief (1972–75). He became Anwar Sadat's vice president in 1975 and moved into the presidency in 1981, after Sadat's assassination. He won a second term in the 1987 elections. In 1988, the Mubarak government moved against the fundamentalists, beginning a period of widespread arrests under emergency decrees in effect since the Sadat assassination. Mubarak has been a moderate within the Arab world throughout his presidency, as well a considerable force in the search for Middle East and Arab-Israeli peace. As president of the Organization of African Unity (1989–90), he tried to help settle such regional conflicts as those in Ethiopia, Chad, and Namibia. After the August 1990 Iraqi attack on Kuwait, he led moderate Arab response, convening an Arab summit meeting on August 8th and attempting to convince Saddam Hussein to withdraw. When the Iraqis would not do so, Mubarak led in the formation of the multinational Arab army sent to Saudi Arabia. Mubarak attended the Egyptian military and air academies. Little is known of his private life, except that he is married to Suzanne Mubarak and has at least two children.

FURTHER READING

"Who's sitting pretty. . . ." *Business Week*, Mar. 11, 1991.
Hosni Mubarak. JOHN SOLECKI. Chelsea House, 1991.
"A call to negotiate. . . ." DEAN FISHER. *Time*, Sep. 10, 1990.
"The view from Cairo." MORTIMER B. ZUCKERMAN. *U.S. News & World Report*, Apr. 16, 1990.

Muldoon, Robert David (1921–92) New

Zealand National Party leader Muldoon entered electoral politics in 1954 with an unsuccessful run for parliament. He was elected on his third

try in 1960, served as a parliamentary undersecretary in the finance ministry (1960–63), and was finance minister (1967–72). His party was defeated by Labour in 1972, and he became party leader in 1974, becoming Prime Minister with National Party victory in 1975. While Prime Minister, he held several key international financial posts. Competent but sharply criticized during his tenure for his abrasive personal style, he lost power in the 1984 elections, and was not returned to the cabinet when his party regained power in 1990. He was survived by his wife, Thea, two daughters, and a son. (d. Auckland, New Zealand; August 5, 1992)

FURTHER READING

Obituary. *The Times* (of London), Aug. 6, 1992.
Obituary. *Independent*, Aug. 6, 1992.
Obituary. *New York Times*, Aug. 5, 1992.

Mulroney, Brian (Martin Brian Mul-

roney; 1939–) Canadian Prime Minister Mulroney again had a very, very bad year, as the same two issues that had destroyed much of his early support continued to plague his country, with no resolution in sight. As in earlier years, the overriding day-to-day issue continued to be Canada's greatly depressed economy, with growing unemployment accompanied by bitterly resented cuts in government-funded social welfare, health, and education programs. Although the deepening Canadian recession was tied to the worldwide recession, many Canadians felt that it had been exacerbated by the 1988 Canada-U.S. free trade agreement, which they believed to be siphoning off desperately needed Canadian income. They blamed Mulroney, the chief Canadian architect of the pact. Government attempts to stimulate the economy during 1992 had no visible effects.

The overriding long-term issue was also the same as in previous years—the question of Quebec separatism and of the continuing existence of a united Canada. After the 1990 failure of the 1987 Meech Lake agreements, Mulroney and other leaders, including Quebec premier Robert Bourassa, had tried again and came up with the August 28, 1992 Charlottetown Accord, providing for recognition of a "distinct society" for Quebec within Canada, as part of a considerable range of concessions to Quebec; major federal and provincial government changes; and "aboriginal" self-government for the nation's Native Canadians. In an October 26th referendum, the accords were decisively rejected, and at year's end the issue remained unresolved, as was the future of the Canadian nation.

Mulroney practiced law in Montreal (1965–76), and then moved into industry, as executive vice president and then president of the Iron Ore Company of Canada (1976–83). He became Progressive Party leader and a Member of Parliament in 1983, and Prime Minister in 1984. He was returned to power in the general election of November 1988, after having made the election a virtual referendum on the recently concluded 1988 Canada-U.S. trade pact. Mulroney attended St. Francis Xavier and Laval Universities. He married Mila Pivnicki in 1973; they have four children.

FURTHER READING

"Mulroney and Bush. . . ." *U.S. News & World Report*, May 25, 1992.

" 'The basics are right.' " KEVIN DOYLE and ANTHONY WILSON-SMITH. *Maclean's*, Jan. 6, 1992.

"Life of Brian. . . ." JOHN SAWATSKY. *Saturday Night*, Oct. 1991.

"Mulroney revealed. . . ." ANTHONY WILSON-SMITH. *Maclean's*, Oct. 1991.

"Mulroney vs. the unions." ANTHONY WILSON-SMITH. *Maclean's*, Sep. 23, 1991.

"Mulroney up close. . . ." ANTHONY WILSON-SMITH. *Maclean's*, June 10, 1991.

"Under the gun. . . ." BRUCE WALLACE. *Maclean's*, Sep. 24, 1990.

" 'Off to the races.' " KEVIN DOYLE and ANTHONY WILSON-SMITH. *Maclean's*, June 25, 1990.

Sacred Trust: Brian Mulroney and the Conservative Party in Power. DAVID BERCUSON. Doubleday, 1987.

Murdoch, Rupert (Keith Rupert Murdoch; 1931–) As the worldwide recession deepened in 1992, Murdoch's media empire continued to suffer cash drains because of diminished advertising revenues. He continued to hold his head above water with further sales of assets, stock sales, and new borrowings, some of them in the form of promissory notes that needed no cash paybacks immediately and were to be later convertible into stock. That the general level of interest rates was down helped his ability to meet scheduled repayments, although the restructuring and stretchout of loan repayments negotiated in 1991 included bonuses and higher interest rates for his creditors. His situation was also helped by a lesser drain from the British Sky Television operation. The net of it all was that, although his total debts continued to be in the $8 billion range, with total cash flow still less than total expenditure, and although he held a smaller proportion of the stock in his companies, News Corporation stock rose considerably during 1992 and borrowing became easier for Murdoch.

On February 24, Murdoch announced that he was taking over the chairmanship and hands-on management of Fox Inc., owner of 20th Century Fox films and the Fox television network. Critics sharply criticized the quality of Fox television programming during 1992 and especially of such sex-filled programs as "Studs" and of such violence-filled "reality" programs as "A Current Affair" and "America's Most Wanted." Murdoch, a political conservative, responded that they were good business. In July, Murdoch fired Fox television executive Stephen Chao for bringing a male strip act in to make a point about censorship during a Murdoch-organized Aspen seminar attended by many prominent conservatives.

Australian-American publisher Murdoch started with a small Australian family newspaper in 1952 and by 1990 had built a large worldwide communications company, controlling such publications and companies as Fox Television, 20th Century Fox Films, *The Times* of London,

HarperCollins Publishers, Sky Television, *The Australian* and many other publications in Australia, *New York* magazine, and Triangle Publications, purchased for $3 billion in 1988, until then the largest acquisition in publishing history. He became dangerously overextended in 1990, as worldwide advertising revenues fell in a growing recession, existing assets realized less money on sale, and interest rates remained high for a time. His debts exceeded $8 billion by late 1990, and, in the changed atmosphere of the early 1990s, he quickly ran into major problems. Murdoch attended Oxford University. He married Anna Maria Torv in 1967; they have two children.

FURTHER READING

"Uppers and downers." HELEN KAY. *Management Today*, Oct. 9, 1991.
"Murdoch's map maker." *Economist*, Jan. 26, 1991.
"A chastened man." *Economist*, Jan. 19, 1991.
Outfoxed: Marvin Davis, Barry Diller, Rupert Murdoch and the Inside Story of America's Fourth Television Network. ALEX B. BLOCK. St. Martin's, 1990.
Rupert Murdoch. JEROME TUCCILLE. Donald I. Fine, 1989.
Citizen Murdoch: The Unexpurgated Story of Rupert Murdoch—The World's Most Powerful and Controversial Media Lord. THOMAS KIERNAN. Dodd, Mead, 1986.
Arrogant Aussie: The Rupert Murdoch Story. MICHAEL LEAPMAN. Carol, 1985.

Murphy, Eddie (1961–) Still a film star

in the 1990s but far from the superstar he was in the mid-1980s, Murphy in 1992 starred in the sex comedy *Boomerang*, based on his own story. In the film, directed by Reginald Hudlin and co-starring Robin Givens and Halle Berry, Murphy played Marcus Berry, a successful, sex-obsessed, rich yuppie business executive in an affluent corporate world, a fantasy figure whom no woman can deny—except Jacqueline, who works with Berry and rejects his advances, making him unhappy. The film was poorly received by the critics. Murphy also starred as larcenous congressman Thomas Jefferson Johnson in Jonathan Lynn's film comedy *The Distinguished Gentleman*, a lampoon of corrupt federal government practices and people. Forthcoming was a starring role in *Beverly Hills Cop 3*, a big-budget Paramount film intended for Christmas 1993 release.

On the legal front, the long-running Art Buchwald lawsuit continued. In March, a Los Angeles judge ordered Paramount Pictures to pay $900,000 to humorist Buchwald and his partner; they had charged that Murphy's film *Coming to America* (1988) was based on a Buchwald treatment. In August, Paramount filed an appeal, and the case dragged on. On the personal side, Murphy's companion, model Nicole Mitchell, gave birth to a baby boy in early November, their second child.

Brooklyn-born Murphy became one of the leading entertainment celebrities of the 1980s, beginning with his regular featured role on television's "Saturday Night Live" (1980–84). His recording career began with the album *Eddie Murphy* (1982), and included *Eddie Murphy Comedian* (1983) and *So Happy* (1989). He began a spectacular film career with *48 Hours* (1982), moving on to such other films as *Trading Places* (1983), *Beverly Hills Cop* (1983; *Beverly Hills Cop II*, 1987), *Harlem Nights* (1989), and *Another 48 Hours* (1990). He and model Nicole Mitchell have a daughter and a son.

FURTHER READING

"The second coming. . . ." MEREDITH BERKMAN. *Entertainment*, Dec. 18, 1992.
"Eddie Murphy cons. . . ." *Jet*, Dec. 7, 1992.
"Eddie Murphy." JOHN CLARK. *Premiere*, Aug. 1992.
"Eddie Murphy plays ladies' man. . . ." *Jet*, July 13, 1992.
"Do you still love Eddie?" RICHARD CORLISS. *Time*, July 6, 1992.

"Trading places." PETER RICHMOND. *GQ—Gentleman's Quarterly*, July 1992.

"The taming of Eddie." JILL NELSON. *Essence*, June 1992.

"Eddie Murphy. . . ." WALTER LEAVY. *Ebony*, Jan. 1990.

Films of Eddie Murphy. EDWARD GROSS. Movie Publications, 1990.

"Eddie Murphy. . . ." BILL ZEHME. *Rolling Stone*, Aug. 24, 1989.

Eddie Murphy. TERESA KOENIG and RIVIAN BELL. Lerner, 1985.

Eddie: Eddie Murphy from A to Z. MARIANNE RUTH. Holloway, 1985.

Murphy, George (1902–92) New Haven-born Murphy began his career as a dancer in cabaret, partnered from the late 1920s with Juliette Henkel, his first wife, with whom he also danced on Broadway. He made his film debut in *Kid Millions* (1934), and went on to appear in more than forty films, including *Broadway Melody of 1938* (1938), *Little Nelly Kelly* (1938), *This Is the Army* (1943), *Having Wonderful Crime* (1945), and *Walk East on Beacon* (1952). Murphy, originally a Democrat, became a Republican in 1939 and was a founder of the Hollywood Republican Committee in 1947. He served twice as president of the Screen Actor's Guild during the 1940s, and was closely associated with Ronald Reagan. After his 1952 retirement from acting, he became a film industry consultant and a leading Republican Party conservative, chairing the 1954 Republican National Convention. He served one term as a U.S. Senator from California (1964–70), losing his bid for a second term. He was survived by his second wife, a daughter, and a son. (d. Palm Beach, Florida; May 3, 1992)

FURTHER READING

Obituary. *Variety*, May 11, 1992.
Obituary. *Independent*, May 8, 1992.
Obituary. *The Times* (of London), May 6, 1992.
Obituary. *New York Times*, May 5, 1992.

Murray, Patty (1950–) Like so many other women in the "Year of the Woman"—perhaps better called the "Year of the Angry Woman"—Murray decided to run for high national office after witnessing the treatment of Anita Faye Hill and her sexual harassment charges by the all-male Senate Judiciary Committee during the 1991 Clarence Thomas Supreme Court nomination hearings. Running as a liberal strongly advocating abortion rights choice—and as the ultimate outsider, "a mom in tennis shoes"—Washington State Senator Murray easily won the Democratic primary contest for the seat vacated by Democratic Senator Brock Adams, who retired amid charges of sexual harassment. During the campaign that followed, Murray led Republican candidate Rod Chandler by as much as 24 points. Chandler closed the gap somewhat late in the race, but on November 3rd Murray won a landslide victory, with 55 percent of the vote to Chandler's 45 percent.

Murray's 1972 B.A. was from Washington State University. She began her political career in 1983, as a member of the Shoreline, Washington school board, and served in the State Senate (1989–92). She is married and has two children.

FURTHER READING

"Capitol Hill's newcomers speak." *Fortune*, Jan. 25, 1993.
"Ms. Mom." JOHN G. WEST. *National Review*, Nov. 2, 1992.
"The outsiders." RICHARD LACAYO. *Time*, Nov. 2, 1992.

Naughton, Bill (1910–92) Ireland-born Naughton, who grew up and survived the Great Depression in England's industrial Lancashire, used that era and setting in northern England for his first novel *A Roof Over Your Head* (1945). His early work included many radio plays and short stories, and the novel *One Small Boy* (1957). His best-known work was the film *Alfie* (1966), which he adapted from his 1963 play, itself based on his earlier novel and two earlier radio plays. Terence Stamp starred in the play, and Michael Caine in the film; Naughton won an Oscar nomination for his screenplay, as did Caine and the film's theme song. Naughton also wrote the long-running play *Spring and Port Wine* (1965), which was adapted into the 1970 Peter Hammond film, starring James Mason. He adapted his play *All in Good Time* (1962) into the film *The Family Way* (1967). He also wrote several other plays and screenplays, and three autobiographical works. He was survived by his second wife, the former Ernestine Piroit, a daughter, and a son. (d. Isle of Man; January 9, 1992)

FURTHER READING

Obituary. *Variety*, Jan. 20, 1992.
Obituary. *New York Times*, Jan. 11, 1992.
Obituary. *The Times* (of London), Jan. 10, 1992.

Navratilova, Martina (1956–) In 1992, tennis great Martina Navratilova broke the previous record (shared with Chris Evert) for women's singles tournament wins with her 158th title at the Chicago Virginia Slims in February 1992, and by year's end had extended that record to 161, with three more wins. Though in her mid-30's tennis great Martina Navratilova lags a bit behind some younger players, she still has formidable power, ranking among the top five in the world. As an unaccustomed underdog, she also enjoys crowd support that she never had in her younger years. This support was most notable at the Virginia Slims tournament in November, where she lost the finals in straight sets to half-her-age Monica Seles, but not before heroic efforts that won her a wild post-match ovation. After the match, Navratilova said that 1993 might well be her last year playing singles, and that her appearance there would probably be her last with long-time doubles partner Pam Shriver, with whom she has won 79 titles.

Earlier in the year, Navratilova had reached the semifinals at Wimbledon before losing to Seles. But at Eastbourne, England, where she was defending champion, she exited in the first round in her first-ever loss to a player outside the world's top 50, and her earliest tournament loss since 1981. In September, Navratilova played a $500,000 pay-per-view televised "battle-of-the-sexes"-type match against Jimmy Connors in Las Vegas, in which Connors had the handicap of covering part of the doubles alley and getting only one serve, though Navratilova had to return to the court from which he had served. She lost the match, 7–5, 6–2, but only after giving Connors a run, especially in the first set.

Personally, Navratilova was active in politics in 1992, supporting the Clinton-Gore ticket over the Republicans. As an open lesbian, she was active against the anti-gay-rights amendment that eventually passed in Colorado, later working with the ACLU to overturn it through legal action and stating that she would move out of Colorado if the amendment were not repealed. In March Navratilova reached an out-of-court settlement with her former lover, Judy Nelson, with whom she split acrimoniously in 1991. Terms were not disclosed, but included a $1.3 million home in Aspen, Colorado for Nelson and apparently cleared the way for Nelson to write a book about their relationship, though Navratilova wanted it otherwise.

Prague-born Navratilova emerged as a leading Czech tennis player while still in her early teens and was Czech national champion (1972–75). She was a notable defector to the West in 1975, and then went on to become the top-ranked woman tennis player in the world for four years in a row (1982–85), enjoying 271 weeks as number one—a record for men *or* women—as well as having a Grand Slam (1983–84). She continued to win major tournaments throughout the later 1980s as well, and in all has won the U.S. Open four times (1983–84, 1986–87) and Wimbledon an unprecedented nine times (1978–79, 1982–1987, 1990), with a record six consecutive titles. Navratilova has also been a notable doubles player. She and Pam Shriver won three doubles Grand Slams (1983–84; 1984–85; 1986–1987) and a record 109 consecutive doubles matches (April 24, 1983–July 6, 1985). Navratilova and Gigi Fernandez won the U.S. Open doubles championships in 1990, sweeping the main doubles championships for the year. In that same year, Naratilova had both knees surgically rebuilt. Navratilova also holds the all-time earning record, at over $17 million through 1992. In 1985 she published *Martina: Autobiography*, written with George Vecsey. Navratilova became a U.S. citizen in 1981.

FURTHER READING

"Courting costs." DANA RUBIN. *Texas*, May 1992.
"Martina. . . ." DAVID HIGDON. *Tennis*, Mar. 1992.
Martina Navratilova: Tennis Star. Blackbirch, 1992.
Three Female Myths of the 20th Century: Garbo-Callas-Navratilova. IRIS BUNSCH. Vantage, 1992.
"Ten living legends. . . ." STEVE WULF. *Sports Illustrated*, Dec. 23, 1991.
" 'Not obsessed about. . . .' " JIM MARTZ. *Sporting News*, July 2, 1990.
"Postscript to. . . ." ANN SMITH and LEWIS ROTHLEIN. *Women's Sports and Fitness*, Mar. 1990.
Martina Navratilova: Tennis Power. R. R. KNUDSON. Viking, 1986; Puffin, 1987.
Martina Navratilova. JANE M. LEDER. Crestwood House, 1985.

Nazarbayev, Nursultan Abishevich

(1940–) In his first full year as the President of Kazakhstan, Nazarbayev seemed to encounter far less economic transition problems than those facing Russian President Boris Yeltsin, although his newly independent country was poor, thinly populated, and arid. An economist, Nazarbayev was also an economic radical, who quickly and effectively moved toward a market economy with the aid of foreign advisors. He also made the most of his country's assets, in May 1992 entering into a joint venture with the Chevron Oil Company to exploit the huge Tengiz oilfield in western Kazakhstan.

Nazarbayev in 1992 continued to hold major nuclear weapons installations. Before independence, he had very strongly supported U.S. and Soviet weapons cuts, closed a nuclear testing range, and demanded that Kazakhstan be made a nuclear-free zone. Late in 1991, he began hedging, and during 1992 made it clear that he was determined to keep nuclear weapons capability, pointing out that several of his Asian neighbors, at least Russia, China, and India, had nuclear arsenals. He did agree to accept the weapons-cutting Strategic Arms Reduction Treaty during a May 1992 meeting with President George Bush in Washington, but the matter of Kazakh nuclear capability remained a matter of great concern, as was the whole matter of nuclear weapons proliferation and the possible sale and theft of nuclear weapons out of the former Soviet arsenal.

Kazakhstan-born Nazarbayev, who joined the Communist Party in 1962, worked as an economist at the Karaganda Metallurgical Combine (1960–69), and then moved into party work. After holding a series of local posts, he emerged as Kazakh central committee secretary (1979–84), was leader of his party in Kazakhstan from 1984, and was a member of Soviet Communist Party central committee from 1986. He became President of the Soviet republic of Kazakhstan in 1990. While he supported the continued existence of the Soviet Union, he opposed the August 1991 attempted coup, quickly resigning all his Communist Party positions and then leading his country to independence.

FURTHER READING

"The end of the U.S.S.R." GEORGE J. CHURCH. *Time*, Dec. 23, 1991.
"Warily seeking sovereignty." ROBIN KNIGHT. *U.S. News & World Report*, Sep. 23, 1991.
"The khan of Kazakhstan...." CARROLL BOGERT. *Newsweek*, July 8, 1991.
"The war within the corridors...." MARY NEMETH. *Maclean's*, Apr. 1, 1991.

Nelson, Ruth (1905–92)

Born in Saginaw, Michigan, Nelson grew up in vaudeville, travelling with her mother, variety star Eva Mudge. She made her acting debut in 1926, and in 1931 became one of the original members of the Group Theater, the theater of leftist political commitment organized by Harold Clurman, Lee Strasberg, and Cheryl Crawford as a breakaway from the Theater Guild. Nelson appeared in many Group Theater productions, perhaps most notably as the wife in Clifford Odets' Depression-era classic *Waiting For Lefty* (1935). She went on to appear in many stage roles during a career that spanned 56 more years. Her film career, which began in 1943, included such films as *Three Women* (1977) and *Awakenings* (1990), in which she played Robert De Niro's mother. She was survived by two sisters and a stepson. Her second husband was director John Cromwell. (d. New York City; September 12, 1992)

FURTHER READING

Obituary. *Variety*, Sep. 21, 1992.
Obituary. *The Times* (of London), Sep. 18, 1992.
Obituary. *New York Times*, Sep. 14, 1992.

Nelson, Willie (1933–)

Still on the road, and playing more than 200 shows in his 59th year, the great country singer Willie Nelson once again spent much of 1992 on tour with his own band, the Family, although he also toured again with Johnny Cash, Kris Kristofferson, and Waylon Jennings as The Highwaymen in the spring. Very good news was that he was working on a new album with Paul Simon and producer Don Was. Nelson continued to work for a wide range of social causes in 1992, with Jennings and Kristofferson organizing the Farm Aid V concert, and backing Ross Perot's presidential bid until Perot's withdrawal from the race. He was honored with the Pioneer Award at the April 27th annual Country Music Awards ceremony in Los Angeles.

Nelson was still plagued by tax problems in 1992. But friends helped, some buying his Texas ranch at auction and holding it for later return to him, others buying his Austin recording studio and golf course, and renting it back to him. In 1992, Nelson filed a $45 million lawsuit against accounting firm Price Waterhouse for allegedly causing many of his tax problems by advising him to make bad tax shelter investments; the firm denied that it had done so. He also continued to sell his "The IRS Tapes" album by mail, raising more than $1 million; CBS then took over commercial distribution.

Texas-born Nelson began composing and recording in the early 1960s, emerging as a country music star in the mid-1970s, then crossing over to become a major popular music star as well on records, in concert, and on screen. His first national hit was the song "Blue Eyes Cryin' in the Rain," from his *Redheaded Stranger* album (1975). He went on to become one of the most popular musicians of the the 1970s and 1980s with such songs as "Georgia on My Mind," "Stardust," "On the Road Again," "Always on My Mind," and "Blue Skies," and such albums as *Waylon and Willie* (1978), *Stardust* (1978), and *Honeysuckle Rose*, the soundtrack album of his 1980 film of that name. He has also appeared in such films as *Barbarossa* (1982), *Red-Headed Stranger* (1986), and *Pair of Aces* (1990). In 1990, he, Johnny Cash, Waylon Jennings, and Kris Kristofferson began touring as The Highwaymen. Nelson ran into severe tax difficulties in 1990, and much of what he owned was seized and auctioned off by the U. S. Internal Revenue Service, generating his album *Who'll Buy My Memories (The I.R.S. Tapes)*. In 1988 he published his autobiographical *Willie*. Nelson attended Baylor University. He has been married three times and has five children, one of whom, Billy, was a probable suicide late in 1991.

FURTHER READING

"Willie Nelson." MICHAEL BANE. *Country Music*, Mar.–Apr. 1992.
"Willie Nelson's heartbreak." *People*, Jan. 13, 1992.

"The ballad of. . . ." RON ROSENBAUM. *Vanity Fair*, Nov. 1991.

"Willie the actor. . . ." GARY CARTWRIGHT. *Texas*, May 1991.

"Poor Willie. . . ." ROBERT DRAPER. *Texas*, May 1991.

Country Musicians . . . Other Great American Artists—Their Music and How They Made It. JUDIE EREMO, ed. Grove-Weidenfeld, 1987.

Heart Worn Memories: A Daughter's Personal Biography of Willie Nelson. SUSIE NELSON. Eakin Press, 1987.

Newell, Allen (1927–92)

San Francisco-born Newell was a leading computer scientist and a founder of the study of artificial intelligence. He was the founder and first president of the American Association for Artificial Intelligence, and with John McCarthy, Marvin Minsky, and Herbert Simon was generally regarded as one of the four originators of the field. A 1949 graduate of Stanford University, with his 1957 doctorate from Carnegie-Mellon University, Newell began working on the creation of thinking processes while at the Rand Corporation during the 1950s and later went on to develop the General Problem Solver software system, continuing to seek computer programs that could simulate and then become at least equal to human thought processes. His most complex system was *Soar*, which he felt was capable of replicating human problem-solving processes. A prolific writer, Newell produced hundreds of articles and ten books in his field. He was survived by his wife, the former Noel McKenna, a son, and a daughter. (d. Pittsburgh; July 19, 1992)

FURTHER READING

Obituary. *The Times* (of London), July 28, 1992.
Obituary. *New York Times*, July 20, 1992.

Newell, Joe (Joseph Dwight Newman; 1922–92)

New Orleans-born Newman began his career as a jazz trumpeter while still at Alabama State College. He began his professional career in 1941 as a replacement trumpeter with Lionel Hampton's big band and stayed with Hampton until 1943, then moving to Count Basie's band until 1946. He then went on his own, often playing with tenor saxophonist Illinois Jacquet and drummer J. C. Heard, and recording with Billie Holiday in 1952. He rejoined Basie (1952–61), becoming a soloist with Basie and a major jazz figure. In 1962, he joined the Benny Goodman band that toured the Soviet Union and in 1975 toured the Soviet Union again, this time with the New York Jazz Repertory Orchestra. In the 1970s, he and his wife joined in developing Jazz Interactions, a nonprofit educational organization, while Newman also continued to record his own albums, play in the recording sessions of other artists, play in cabaret, and tour. He was survived by his companion, Keiko Kimura, three daughters, and two sons. (d. New York City; July 4, 1992)

FURTHER READING

Obituary. *The Times* (of London), July 14, 1992.
Obituary. *New York Times*, July 8, 1992.

Newman, Paul (1925–)

Celebrated film star, director, and philanthropist Newman, now 67 and spacing his films further apart than earlier in his career, was still far from inactive in 1992. He continued to be a very active race car driver—and reportedly came rather close to serious injury on July 25th, while racing his Lotus Esprit Turbo at Lime Rock Park, Connecticut. In the SCCA World Challenge race, his car went out of control and crashed. Fortunately, Newman walked away from the wreck unharmed.

Philanthropist Newman, through his Newman's Own food company, continued to be a very active contributor to hundreds of charities throughout the world in 1992. One very notable new contribution was announced in October; Newman established the PEN/Newman's Own First Amendment Award—a $25,000 annual award to a U.S. resident who has made a courageous fight for the First Amendment, each yearly award also including a limited edition Louise Bourgeois sculpture.

Newman and his wife, Joanne Woodward, themselves received awards, among them John F. Kennedy Center for the Performing Arts awards, given at a White House ceremony. Newman presented awards as well, joining Elizabeth Taylor to present major awards before a worldwide audience at the 64th annual Academy Awards ceremonies. Forthcoming was a starring role opposite Tim Robbins and Jennifer Jason Leigh in Joel Coen's film *The Hudsucker Proxy*.

Cleveland-born Newman has been a film star for 35 years, breaking through in *Somebody Up There Likes Me* (1956) and *Cat on a Hot Tin Roof* (1958). A few of his many major films were *Exodus* (1960), *The Hustler* (1961), *Sweet Bird Of Youth* (1962; he had starred in the Broadway play in 1959), *Hud* (1963), *Harper* (1966), *Cool Hand Luke* (1967), *Butch Cassidy and the Sundance Kid* (1969), *The Sting* (1973), *Absence of Malice* (1981), *Harry and Son* (1984; he also wrote and directed), *The Color of Money* (1986; he won a Best Actor Oscar), *Fat Man and Little Boy* (1989), *Blaze* (1990), and *Mr. and Mrs. Bridge* (1990; he co-starred with his wife, Joanne Woodward). Newman's B.A. was from Kenyon College in 1949; he also attended Yale Drama School. Previously married to Jacqueline Witte, he married Joanne Woodward in 1958. He has had six children; his son Scott's death (1980) was drug-related, and Newman founded an anti-drug education foundation in his memory.

FURTHER READING

"Paul Newman and. . . ." MAUREEN DOWD. *McCall's*, Jan. 1991.

"Mr. and Mrs. Bridge." GRAHAM FULLER. *Interview*, Nov. 1990.

"Joanne Woodward. . . ." BETH WEINHOUSE. *Redbook*, Jan. 1990.

Paul Newman. ELENA OUMANO. St. Martin's, 1989.

Icons: Intimate Portraits. DENISE WORRELL. *Atlantic Monthly*, 1989.

No Tricks in My Pocket: Paul Newman Directs. STEWART STERN. Grove-Weidenfeld, 1989.

Paul and Joanne: A Biography of Paul Newman and Joanne Woodward. JOE MORELLA and EDWARD Z. EPSTEIN. Delacorte, 1988.

Nichols, Mike (Michael Igor Pechowsky; 1931–) Stage and screen director and producer Nichols returned to Broadway in 1992, in a year that saw many film stars trying their hands in the New York theater. In March, Nichols directed three of those stars in the New York version of Ariel Dorfman's play *Death and the Maiden*, which had been a hit in London the year before. Glenn Close starred as Paulina Salas, a woman who takes revenge on the Latin American police officer who raped and tortured her 15 years earlier, opposite Gene Hackman as her tormentor, Dr. Miranda, and Richard Dreyfuss as her husband. The play received mixed reviews, but the stars were very well received—Close won a Tony for the role—and the play was a box-office hit, probably because of the stars' "bankability."

On the film side, *Regarding Henry*, which was a critical and commercial failure, went into release in home video, where it did moderately well. Early in 1992, Nichols and his Icarus Productions signed a two-picture development and production agreement with Columbia Pictures, the first film to be *Wolf*, scheduled for production in 1993. Nichols also paid a reported $2.1 million for an option on the Scott B. Smith novel *The Simple Plan*.

Berlin-born Nichols appeared in cabaret during the late 1950s, and was partnered with Elaine May on Broadway in 1960 in *An Evening with Mike Nichols and Elaine May*. He received a Best Director Tony for *The Odd Couple* (1965), and has directed five Tony-winning plays: *Barefoot in the Park* (1963), *Luv* (1964), *Plaza Suite* (1968), *The Prisoner of Second Avenue* (1971), and *The Real Thing* (1984). In 1989, he directed a notable revival of Samuel Beckett's *Waiting for Godot*, starring Robin Williams and Steve Martin. He has also directed such films as *Who's Afraid of Virginia Woolf* (1966), the Oscar-winning *The Graduate* (1967), *Carnal Knowledge* (1971), *Silkwood* (1983), *Biloxi Blues* (1987), *Working Girl* (1988), and *Postcards from the Edge* (1990). In 1988 he published *Life, and Other Ways to Kill Time*. Nichols attended the University of Chicago (1950–53). He was formerly married to Patricia Scott and Margot Callas, and married Diane Sawyer in 1988.

FURTHER READING

"Mike Nichols. . . ." STEPHEN GRECO. *Advocate*, May 5, 1992.

"Nichols, Mike." *Current Biography*, Jan. 1992.

"Without cutaways. . . ." GAVIN SMITH. *Film Comment*, May–June 1991.

"Waiting for Mike." STEPHEN FARBER. *Connoisseur*, June 1991.

"Mr. Success." ALICE ARLEN. *Interview*, Dec. 1988.

"The happiest couple. . . ." LISA GRUNWALD. *Esquire*, Dec. 1988.

Nicholson, Jack (1937–) Late in December 1992, Nicholson opened in the title role of Danny DeVito's *Hoffa*, a biographical film about the rise of corrupt Teamsters Union president

Jimmy Hoffa, who disappeared in 1975 and was thought to have been kidnapped and murdered, probably by criminals who were former associates. Nicholson's Hoffa is a strong, unscrupulous union leader, his criminal exploitation of his own union members and his own criminal associations quite underplayed. DeVito also co-produced and appeared as Hoffa associate Bobby Ciaro, in a cast that included Armand Assante, J. T. Walsh, John C. Reilly, and Robert Prosky.

Nicholson also starred as the Guantanamo Bay base commander who is Tom Cruise's chief courtroom antagonist in Rob Reiner's well-received military courtroom hit film *A Few Good Men*. Demi Moore co-starred in a cast that included Kevin Bacon, Kiefer Sutherland, and Kevin Pollak. Nicholson also starred as a dog trainer opposite Ellen Barkin as an opera singer in Bob Rafelson's comedy *Man Trouble*, which was not so well received.

New Jersey-born Nicholson played strong supporting roles beginning in the late 1950s, most notably in *Easy Rider* (1969), and then moved into the powerful dramatic roles that made him a major figure for the next two decades in such films as *Five Easy Pieces* (1970), *Chinatown* (1974), *One Flew Over the Cuckoo's Nest* (1975; he won a Best Actor Oscar), *The Postman Always Rings Twice* (1981), *Reds* (1981), *Terms of Endearment* (1983; he won a Best Supporting Actor Oscar), *Prizzi's Honor* (1985), *Heartburn* (1986), *Ironweed* (1987), and

Batman (1989). In 1990, he directed and starred in *The Two Jakes*, a sequel to *Chinatown*. Nicholson was formerly married to Sandra Knight; they had one daughter. He had a 17-year relationship with actress Anjelica Huston that ended in 1990. He and actress Rebecca Broussard have two children, a daughter born in 1990 and a son born in 1992; the couple reportedly split in autumn 1992.

FURTHER READING

"The sexy legend. . . ." MICHAEL SEGELL. *Cosmopolitan*, Aug. 1992.
"Happy Jack." NANCY COLLINS. *Vanity Fair*, Apr. 1992.
Jack Nicholson: An Unauthorized Biography. DONALD SHEPERD. St. Martin's, 1991.
Jack Nicholson: The Unauthorized Biography. BARBARA SIEGEL and SCOTT SIEGEL. Avon, 1991.
"The myth that Jack built." STEVE ERICKSON. *Esquire*, Sep. 1990.
"Hollywood's wild card." BRIAN D. JOHNSON. *Maclean's*, Aug. 20, 1990.
"Jake Jake. . . ." JULIAN SCHNABEL. *Interview*, Aug. 1990.
"Forget it, Jack. . . ." JAMES GREENBERG. *American Film*, Feb. 1990.
The Films of Jack Nicholson. DOUGLAS BRODE. Carol, 1990.

Nie Rongzhen (1899–1992) Born in Sichuan province, Nie studied in Europe and the Soviet Union before returning to China in 1925. A Communist soldier, he taught at the Whampoa Military Academy in the mid-1920s and fought in several unsuccessful campaigns, going to the countryside in 1930 to join Zhu De and Mao Zedong. He was part of the Long March, the Communist retreat north (1934–35), and commanded major Red Army units during the anti-Japanese war, in 1945 turning to fight the Kuomintang. He commanded large Communist forces in the north and was chief negotiator for the surrender of Beijing. Marshal Nie was the last of the ten Marshals who led the Communist armies in the Chinese Civil War. After 1949, he was mayor of Beijing and head of the army's General Staff. He became a deputy prime minister in 1956 and from 1957 was responsible for the development of the Chinese atom bomb. A supporter of Deng Xiaoping, Nie resigned from the Chinese Politburo in 1985. He was survived by his wife and two children. (d. Beijing; May 15, 1992)

FURTHER READING

Obituary. *Independent*, May 18, 1992.
Obituary. *The Times* (of London), May 16, 1992.
Obituary. *New York Times*, May 16, 1992.

Nixon, Richard Milhous (1913–) Although former President Nixon continued in his role as Republican "elder statesman" in 1992, the disgrace of Watergate was still never far away. The year brought the 20th anniversary of the scandal and also the death of the incorruptible Judge John J. Sirica, who brought Nixon down. Nixon did not attend the August Republican National Convention, but did play a small political role in March by criticizing President George Bush for providing inadequate help to the new Russian democracy and in June by meeting with Ross Perot. He even hosted a black tie dinner for Bush, climaxing a conference sponsored by the Nixon Library. He also published a new book, *Seize the Moment*.

In November 1992, Nixon won his 18-year-long action for compensation for the White House tapes and documents seized during the course of the Watergate investigation. The District of Columbia federal Court of Appeals then sent the case back to the District Court for determination of the size of the award to be made.

California-born Nixon became the 37th President of United States in 1969 and resigned to avoid impeachment in 1974, after his complicity in the Watergate scandal was exposed. He had previously been a leading member of the House Un-American Activities Committee while a California Congressman (1947–51), senator from California in the early 1950s, and Dwight D. Eisenhower's vice-president (1953–61). He was defeated for the presidency by John F. Kennedy in 1960, but came back to defeat Hubert Humphrey in 1968 and George McGovern in 1972. He presided over the last stages of his country's defeat in Vietnam and played a key role in re-establishing U.S.-Chinese relations, but is in the long run chiefly notable for his multiple illegal attacks on domestic political opponents, which climaxed with the Watergate Democratic National Committee break-ins by his "plumbers," ultimately destroying his career and reputation.

His written works include *RN: Memoirs of Richard Nixon* (1978); *The Memoirs of Richard Nixon* (2 vols.; 1978–79); *1999: Victory Without War* (1988); and *In the Arena: A Memoir of Victory, Defeat, and Renewal* (1990). Nixon's 1934 B.A. was from Whittier College, and his 1937 LL.B. from Duke. Nixon and Thelma Patricia "Pat" Ryan married in 1940; they had two children.

FURTHER READING

Cold War Patriot and Statesman: Richard M. Nixon. LEON FRIEDMAN and WILLIAM F. LEVANTROSSER, eds. Greenwood, 1993.
"How Nixon came in. . . ." MICHAEL BESCHLOSS. *Vanity Fair*, June 1992.
"He's back again." DAVID POSTMAN. *New Republic*, Apr. 6, 1992.
George Wallace, Richard Nixon, and the Transformation of American Politics. DAN T. CARTER. Baylor University Press, 1992.
The Limits of Power: The Nixon and Ford Administrations. JOHN R. GREENE. Indiana University Press, 1992.
The Great Cover-up: Nixon and the Scandal of Watergate. BARRY SUSSMAN. Stephanus, 1992.
The Nixons. CASS R. SANDAK. Crestwood House/Macmillan, 1992.
Watergate and Afterward: The Legacy of Richard M. Nixon. LEON FRIEDMAN and WILLIAM F. LEVANTROSSER, eds. Greenwood, 1992.
Richard M. Nixon Oral History Project. CALIFORNIA STATE UNIVERSITY—FULLERTON ORAL HISTORY OFFICE STAFF, ed. Meckler, 1992.
Nixon: Ruin and Recovery, 1973–1990, 1991. *Nixon: The Triumph of a Politician, 1962–1972*, 1989. *Nixon: The Education of a Politician, 1913–1962*, 1987. STEPHEN E. AMBROSE. Simon & Schuster.
Silent Coup: The Removal of Richard Nixon. LEN COLODNY and ROBERT GETTLIN. St. Martin's, 1991.
Richard M. Nixon: Politician, President, Administrator. LEON FRIEDMAN and WILLIAM F. LEVANTROSSER, eds. Greenwood, 1991.
One of Us: Richard Nixon and the American Dream. TOM WICKER. Random, 1991.
Richard Nixon. RICHARD M. PIOUS. Silver Burdett, 1991.
The Great Stream of History: A Biography of Richard M. Nixon. LAURIE NADEL. Macmillan, 1991.
Richard Nixon: The Making and Unmaking of a President. REBECCA LARSEN. Watts, 1991.
Richard Nixon and His America. HERBERT S. PARMET. Little, Brown, 1990.

Richard M. Nixon, President. SALLIE RANDOLPH. Walker, 1989.

Richard Milhous Nixon: The Rise of an American Politician. ROGER MORRIS. Holt, 1989.

Nolan, Sidney Robert (1917–92)

Melbourne-born Nolan, one of Australia's leading artists, began his career in the late 1930s, continued painting during his World War II service, and from 1945 to 1947 showed his first "Ned Kelly" series, the work for which he became a world figure, its subject being Australian outlaw folk hero Kelly. His second "Ned Kelly" series (1954–55) added to his worldwide stature. His Australian work also included the late 1940s "Elisa Frazer" and "Eureka Stockade" series. His "Galippoli" series was completed after his 1953 move to Europe, as was his "Paradise Garden" (1970). Nolan was also a prolific set designer, beginning with his designs for Serge Lifar's *Icarus* (1940). He was survived by his third wife, Mary Nolan, and a daughter. (d. London; November 27, 1992)

FURTHER READING

Obituary. *New York Times*, Dec. 1, 1992.

Obituary. *The Times* (of London), Nov. 30, 1992.

Obituary. *Independent*, Nov. 30, 1992.

Sidney Nolan: Landscapes and Legends. JANE CLARK. Cambridge University Press, 1988.

Nolte, Nick (1942–)

In 1992, Nolte was honored by his peers, winning a Best Actor Oscar nomination for his role in *The Prince of Tides.* He also won a Best Actor Golden Globe award for the role. In late December, Nolte played Augusto Odone opposite Susan Sarandon as his wife in *Lorenzo's Oil*, George Miller's study of a couple who successfully struggle to save their five-year-old son from what was considered incurable ALD (adrenoleukodystrophy). Nolte also appeared as himself in *The Player*, Robert Altman's merciless, multistar lampoon of modern Hollywood. Forthcoming was a starring role opposite Tracy Ullmann, Joely Richardson, and Albert Brooks in James L. Brooks's forthcoming film *I'll Do Anything.*

Nebraska-born Nolte spent years in regional theater before emerging as a film star in the mid-1970s in *The Deep* (1977), and went on to star in such films as *Who'll Stop the Rain* (1978), *North Dallas Forty* (1979), *Cannery Row* (1982), *48 Hours* (1982), *Under Fire* (1983), *Down and Out in Beverly Hills* (1986), *Three Fugitives* (1989), *Everybody Wins* (1990), *Another 48 Hours* (1990), *Q&A* (1990), *Cape Fear* (1991), and *The Prince of Tides* (1991). He has also appeared in television, most notably in *Rich Man, Poor Man* (1976). Nolte attended Pasadena College. He has been married three times, since 1984 to Rebecca Linger; they have one child.

FURTHER READING

"The time of Nick Nolte." SUSAN SCHINDEHETTE. *People*, Mar. 16, 1992.

"Nick's time." LISA SCHWARZBAUM. *Entertainment*, Jan. 24, 1992.

"Nick Nolte." TRIP GABRIEL. *US*, Jan. 1992.

"Off-balance heroes." PETER DE JONGE. *New York Times Magazine*, Oct. 27, 1991.

"Nick Nolte. . . ." STEPHANIE MANSFIELD. *GQ— Gentlemen's Quarterly*, Oct. 1991.

"Prince of Hollywood." MEREDITH BRODY. *Connoisseur*, Sep. 1991.

"Nick Nolte." PETER BECKER. *M Inc.*, Sep. 1991.

"The passions of. . . ." ERIC GOODMAN. *McCall's*, Sep. 1991.

Noriega Morena, Manuel Antonio

(1938–) After a seven-month trial that began on September 15, 1991, a federal jury in Miami on April 9, 1992 found former Panamanian dictator Noriega guilty on eight counts of money laundering, drug trafficking, and racketeering; he was acquitted on two drug trafficking counts. On July 10, Judge William M. Hoeveler sentenced him to 40 years imprisonment; he will be eligible for parole in the year 2002. Hoeveler rejected Noriega's contention that he was a prisoner of war and therefore not subject to U.S. laws. Noriega was the first foreign head of state to be convicted in a U.S. court. However, on December 8, Judge Hoeveler ruled that Noriega *was* a prisoner of war and that, although he could be sent to a federal prison because of his U.S. law violation convictions, he might be entitled to prisoner of war, rather than ordinary U.S. prison treatment.

Noriega was a career Panamanian military intelligence officer. As head of Panamanian intelligence (1970–82) and dictator (1982–89), he was deeply involved with U.S. military and intelligence activities in Latin America and was on the CIA payroll for many years. He was also even more profitably associated with one or more drug cartels during the same period. In 1988, while still in power, Noriega was indicted in Florida on drug trafficking charges. After the November 20, 1989 U.S. invasion of Panama, a period in hiding, and a period of asylum in the Vatican's Panama City diplomatic mission, Noriega surrendered to U.S. forces. On January 3, 1990, he was flown to Miami and arraigned on drug trade-related charges, although he claimed the status of a political prisoner. Then began a very long set of pre-trial preparations, jury selection processes, and many months of hearings on disputed pre-trial matters. Ultimately, in August 1991, Judge Hoeveler acceded to defense requests for previously withheld government documents, clearing the way for the trial to begin. Noriega attended Panama University. He is married to Felicidad Sieiro and has three children.

FURTHER READING

The Noriega Mess. LUIS MURILLO. Video Books, 1993.
"Canned pineapple. . . ." CATHY BOOTH. *New Republic*, Mar. 30, 1992.
Our Man in Panama: The Shrewd Rise and Brutal Fall of Manuel Noriega. JOHN DINGES. Random, 1991.
"Our man in Panama. . . ." SEYMOUR M. HERSH. *Life*, Mar. 1990.
"Noriega on ice. . . ." RICHARD LACAYO. *Time*, Jan. 15, 1990.
"The Noriega files." FREDERICK KEMPE. *Newsweek*, Jan. 15, 1990.
"Lifestyle of a dictator." RAE CORELLI. *Maclean's*, Jan. 1, 1990.
Divorcing the Dictator: America's Bungled Affair with Noriega. FREDERICK KEMPE. Putnam, 1990.
"Noriega Morena, Manuel Antonio." *Current Biography*, Mar. 1988.

North, Oliver (1943–) During 1992, former Marine officer, White House aide, and Iran-Contra scandal figure Oliver North, now acquitted of all charges, began trying to develop a political career. His early moves included an address to a highly receptive state convention and a fundraising letter to 25,000 Republicans, in which he attacked the Virginia state government as holding "more than six million people . . . in virtual bondage to tyrannical government," and attacked Governor L. Douglas Wilder as "King Douglas, the Wilder," singling out Wilder's support of abortion rights. In late August, North announced his possible interest in a 1994 U.S. Senate run, opposite Virginia Democratic Senator Charles S. Robb.

North, a career Marine officer, was on active service in Vietnam (1968–69). From 1981 to 1986, he was deputy director of the military affairs bureau of the U.S. National Security Council, working directly out of the White House; he became a Marine lieutenant-colonel in 1983. North was involved in developing several covert operations during his White House years. One of them blew up in late 1986, becoming the Iran-Contra affair, a set of scandals that resulted in North's dismissal from his White House post, though not from the Marines, in November 1986. North then became an international figure, testifying on television before congressional committees. He was indicted on Iran Contra-related charges on March 14, 1988 and convicted on three felony counts in May 1989. He had one of three counts overturned and two sent back to the trial court on appeal in 1990. All charges against North were dropped on September 16, 1991, after testimony by former National Security Advisor Robert C. McFarlane made it clear that the Iran-Contra hearings had fatally tainted the prosecution's case. North has published the best-seller *Under Fire: An American Story* (1991), written with William Novak. He is a graduate of the U.S. Naval Academy at Annapolis. He is married to Betsy (Frances Elizabeth) Stuart; they have three children.

FURTHER READING

"North, Oliver." *Current Biography*, Mar. 1992.
"Oliver North. . . ." *Christianity Today*, Nov. 25, 1991.
"The unsinkable. . . ." BARRETT SEAMAN. *Time*, Oct. 28, 1991.
Opening Arguments: A Young Lawyer's First Case: United States v. Oliver L. North. JEFFREY TOOBIN. Viking Penguin, 1991.
Guts and Glory: The Oliver North Story. BEN BRADLEE, JR. Fine, 1988.
The Secret Government. BILL MOYERS. Seven Locks, 1988.
Men of Zeal: A Candid Story of the Iran-Contra Hearings. WILLIAM S. COHEN and GEORGE J. MITCHELL. Viking Penguin, 1988.
Defiant Patriot: The Life and Exploits of Lieutenant Colonel Oliver North. PETER MEYER. St. Martin's, 1987.

*Taking the Stand: The Testimony of Lieutenant
Colonel Oliver L. North.* DANIEL SCHORR, ed. Pocket
Books, 1987.

Northrop, F. S. C. (Filmer Stuart

Cuckow Northrop; 1893–1992) Wisconsin-born
Northrop began his long teaching career as a
philosophy instructor at Yale University in
1923, a year before he received his Ph.D. in the
philosophy of science from Harvard University.
He remained at Yale for four decades, ultimately
as Stirling professor of philosophy and law, pursuing a wide range of interests that involved
many other disciplines as well. He was a leading
20th-century student of comparative cultures
and of the philosophy of science, best known for
his book *The Meeting of East and West* (1946).
His other books include *Science and First Prin-
ciples* (1931), *The Logic of the Sciences and Humanities* (1947), *The Taming of the Nations*
(1952), *European Union and United States Foreign Policy* (1954), *The Complexity of Legal and
Ethical Experience* (1959), *Philosophical An-
thropology and Practical Politics* (1960), and
Man, Nature and God (1962). He was survived
by two sons. (d. Exeter, New Hampshire; July
21, 1992)

FURTHER READING

Obituary. *The Times* (of London), July 28, 1992.
Obituary. *New York Times*, July 23, 1992.

Nunn, Sam (Samuel Nunn, Jr.; 1938–) In

1992, as the deep recession worsened and the
threat of civilization-destroying nuclear war receded somewhat, Senate Armed Forces Committee chairman Nunn played a major role in a
developing national debate about military
spending cuts and the future shape of the American military. The Georgia Democrat, a moderate with strong ties to the military, was at odds
with many in his own party on several important issues. For example, he opposed the Strategic Defense Initiative (SDI) cuts favored by
many liberal Democrats, and in September finally cast a compromise vote that split the difference between the two opposing positions and
made it possible to pass the whole 1993 defense
bill. On issues like the B-2 bomber and NATO

funding, he also parted with his liberal colleagues. He declared himself in favor of major
post–Cold War defense cuts, however, carrying
through the position he had adopted in 1990,
proposing in March 1992 cuts amounting to $85
billion spread over five years, while opposing the
steep "peace dividend" cut proposed by other
Democrats. He was not up for re-election in
1992, his term running until 1996.

Georgia-born Nunn was a Georgia state legis-
lator (1968–72) and began his long career in the
Senate in 1973. He became chairman of the Senate Armed Services Committee in 1986, was regarded as a possible 1988 Democratic
presidential and then vice-presidential candidate during the run-up to the Dukakis nomination, but refused the vice-presidential
nomination when it was offered. During the late
1980s, as the Cold War wound down, Nunn
moved from general support of military spending plans toward a call for large cuts in spending, armaments, and force levels. In late July
1990, his committee reported out the first large
Senate defense-cuts bill in decades. Nunn's B.A.
and LL.B. were from Atlanta's Emory University.

He married Colleen O'Brien in 1964; they
have two children.

FURTHER READING

"The mystique of. . . ." SIDNEY BLUMENTHAL. *New
Republic*, Mar. 4, 1991.
"Wanted. . . ." DOUGLAS HARBRECHT. *Business Week*,
Nov. 19, 1990.
"Born to be mild. . . ." TIMOTHY NOAH. *Washington
Monthly*, Dec. 1989.
"Smart, dull and very powerful." MICHAEL KRAMER.
Time, Mar. 13, 1989.

Nureyev, Rudolf Hametovich

(1938–) The great dancer, his work becoming
legendary in the first year after his retirement
from dancing, turned to conducting in 1992, as
he had promised. He made his conducting debut
in July 1991, leading a Vienna chamber orchestra, and continued on in the year that followed,
conducting in Europe, making his American debut with the American Ballet Theater in May,
and leading the University of California at San
Francisco Orchestra in July. But as the year progressed, it became clear that Nureyev was very
ill, and then desperately so. He was widely re-

ported to have AIDS, but did not comment on the rumors.

At the Paris Opera, on October 8, 1992, the company premiered a full-length version of *La Bayadere*, which he had choreographed. Afterward, in a private ceremony, he was made a French Commander of Arts and Letters.

Nureyev joined the Leningrad-based Kirov Ballet as a soloist in 1958, and quickly became a leading Soviet dancer. Three years later, in 1961, he defected to the West, becoming within a year a world figure in the ballet, most notably as Margot Fonteyn's partner at London's Royal Ballet. During the next quarter century, he danced as a guest artist in many countries, and also became a leading choreographer of such works as *Tancredi* (1966), *Romeo and Juliet* (1977), and *Wash-ington Square* (1985). He was artistic director of the Paris Opera Ballet (1983–89), and became its principal choreographer in 1989, while continuing to dance throughout the world. In 1989–90, he starred on stage in musical theater for the first time in a U.S. tour of *The King and I*. He has also appeared in several films, including *Valentino* (1977) and *Exposed* (1982).

FURTHER READING

"At the bedside of. . . ." ETTORE MO. Dec. 8, 1992.
"And now, superstar?" IRIS M. FANGER. *World Monitor*. June 1991.
"Nureyev. . . ." ELIZABETH KAYE. *Esquire*, Mar. 1991.
"Nureyev Now!" PAUL H. LEMAY. *Dance*, May 1990.
"Nureyev resigns. . . ." ROBERT JOHNSON. *Dance*, Feb. 1990.

O'Connor, Sandra Day (1930–) In the 1991–92 term, Justice O'Connor emerged, with Justices Kennedy and Souter, as part of a new Court center. That became quite clear with the joint O'Connor-Kennedy-Souter majority opinion in the landmark abortion rights case, *Planned Parenthood of Southeastern Pennsylvania v. Casey*, in which a slim 5–4 majority upheld the essence of *Roe v. Wade* (which had in 1972 established the right of a woman to choose to have an abortion), while at the same time upholding most of the restrictive 1989 Pennsylvania abortion law and giving the states broader powers to restrict abortion. She also joined all of her colleagues in a rare, unanimous landmark sexual harassment decision; in *Franklin v. Gwinnett County Public Schools*, the Court unanimously ruled that Title IX of the 1972 education act allowed a sexually harassed student to collect damages from a school district where a teacher-coach sexually harassed Christine Franklin and ultimately succeeded in pressing her to have sexual intercourse with him.

O'Connor wrote the majority opinions in *Hudson v. McMillian*, ruling that the excessive use of force by prison guards was an Eighth Amendment violation even if the prisoner was not seriously hurt; in *Riggins v. Nevada*, ruling that the state could not force an insane criminal defendant to take medication during a trial; and in *New York v. U.S.*, which invalidated a federal law forcing states to handle their own radioactive waste. She also ruled with the majority in such key cases as *Nordlinger v. Hahn*, upholding

the right of California to enact Proposition 13 with its unequal property taxes on newcomers; *Lee v. Weisman*, barring nonsectarian or any other prayers at public high school graduations; *U.S. v. Fordice*, ruling that Mississippi had not fulfilled its obligation to desegregate its public colleges and universities; *Lechmere Inc. v. National Labor Relations Board*, ruling that companies did not have to allow union organizers access to such company-owned lands as parking lots and shopping malls; *Freeman v. Pitts*, ruling that schools being operated under court-supervised desegregation orders could be released from those orders step by step; and *International Society for Krishna Consciousness v. Lee*, ruling that airports could ban groups from soliciting money. She also joined the majority in ruling that the Coast Guard could continue to intercept at sea and return Haitian refugees to Haiti; and in the decision barring return of RU-486 pills to Leona Benten, a pregnant woman who tried to import them into the U.S. for her personal use, in a challenge to their ban. O'Connor wrote a dissenting opinion in *Georgia v. McCollum*, ruling that criminal case defendants could not bar prospective jurors solely because of their race; and in *Jacobson v. U.S.*, ruling that the federal government had illegally entrapped a defendant into buying child pornography through the mail. She wrote a concurring opinion in the landmark *R.A.V. v. St. Paul*, overturning a St. Paul, Minnesota ordinance making sexist, racist, or otherwise bigoted speech or behavior a crime; in *Lujan v. Defenders of Wildlife*, ruling that the plaintiff, an environmental orga-

297

nization, had no standing to bring suit because no determinable specific interest was at issue; in *U.S. v. Alvarez Machain*, upholding the 1990 U.S. kidnapping of a Mexican doctor suspected of a role in the torture of a U.S. drug enforcement agent; and in *Keeney v. Tamayo-Reyes*, which sharply limited the federal habeas corpus appeals of state prisoners.

El Paso-born O'Connor made history in 1981 when she became the first woman Supreme Court justice, the climax of long careers in law and politics. She had moved from private practice to become Arizona assistant attorney general (1965–69), into politics as an Arizona state senator (1969–75), and then back into a series of Arizona judicial posts, ultimately becoming a state court of appeals judge (1979–81). O'Connor's 1950 B.A. and 1952 LL.B. were from Stanford. She married John Jay O'Connor in 1952; they have one child.

FURTHER READING

Sandra Day O'Connor: American Women of Achievement. PETER HUBER. Chelsea House, 1992.

Sandra Day O'Connor. PAUL DEEGAN. Abdo & Daughters, 1992.

Sandra Day O'Connor. NORMAN L. MACHT. Chelsea House, 1992.

"A new day in court." LAUREN TARSHIS and JAMES EARL HARDY. *Scholastic Update*, Nov. 1, 1991.

Sandra Day O'Connor: A New Justice, a New Voice. BEVERLY BERWALD. Fawcett, 1991.

Sandra Day O'Connor. BEVERLY GHERMAN. Viking Penguin, 1991.

Sandra Day O'Connor. PETER HUBER. Chelsea House, 1990.

Eight Men and a Lady. HERMAN SCHWARTZ et al. National Press, 1990.

counting firm before entering federal energy regulation with the Department of Energy during the Ford administration. She also worked in the U.S. Department of Energy during the Carter administration. In 1981, she joined O'Leary Associates, a consulting firm in the energy field operated by her husband, John O'Leary, now deceased, who was a deputy Energy Secretary during the Carter administration. She became executive vice president of the Minneapolis-based Northern States Power Company in 1989. She has one son.

FURTHER READING

"Clinton picks. . . ." *Jet*, Jan. 11, 1993.

"Words of advice. . . ." *MPLS-St. Paul*, Apr. 1991.

O'Leary, Hazel Rollins (1947–) President Bill Clinton's incoming Secretary of Energy has been a federal regulator and an energy company executive. She is the first energy secretary to have been directly employed by the industry she now regulates.

Virginia-born O'Leary's 1959 B.A. was from Nashville's Fisk University, and her 1966 J. D. from New Jersey's Rutgers University. She was a New Jersey assistant attorney general, an assistant Essex County, New Jersey prosecutor, and a partner in the Coopers and Lybrand ac-

O'Neal, Frederick (1905–92) Mississippi-born O'Neal made his stage debut in St. Louis in 1927 and his New York stage debut with the Civic Repertory Theater in 1936. In 1940 he was a founder of the American Negro Theater. In 1944, he made his Broadway debut as Frank in *Anna Lucasta*, winning the Clarence Derwent, Drama Critics, and Donaldson awards for the role, which he repeated in London in 1945. His long career included many other stage, screen, and television roles. O'Neal was President of Actor's Equity (1964–73), and then president emeritus, as well as president of Associated Actors and Artists (1970–88). O'Neal was a vice-president of the AFL-CIO and an executive council member (1969–88), and was also active in labor, civil rights, and other civic organizations. He was named to the Black Filmmakers Hall of Fame in 1975, and received its Special Tribute award in 1990. With Gary Null, he wrote *Black Hollywood: The Negro in Motion Pictures* (1975). He was survived by his wife, Charlotte Talbot Hainey. (d. New York City; August 25, 1992)

FURTHER READING

"Actor, Equity president. . . ." *Jet*, Sep. 14, 1992.
Obituary. *Variety*, Aug. 31, 1992.

O'Neal, Shaquille (1972–) In a year when Earvin "Magic" Johnson and Larry Bird both retired, basketball fans were looking for new stars, and they seem to have found one in Shaquille O'Neal. By lottery, the Orlando Magic won the rights to pick first in the April 1992 National Basketball Association (NBA) draft; the team hesitated not at all before selecting O'Neal, and by August had signed him to a reported seven-year, $40 million contract. With his 7′1″, 300 pound body, his strength matched with agility, and his skill at rebounding, blocking shots, and scoring, "Shaq" quickly became a

dominant force in basketball. By mid-season, at the end of 1992, O'Neal was not only on track to be rookie of the year, averaging over 20 points and 15 rebounds a game, but was also leading the early All-Star balloting in the Eastern Conference, ahead of such highly regarded veterans as Patrick Ewing. Nor was O'Neal's a purely individual effort. He lifted the playing level of the Orlando Magic, a recent expansion team with a weak record. At some points early in the year, the team even led their division, admittedly the league's weakest. O'Neal's long-term impact remains to be seen, but many observers continue to see stars in their crystal ball.

An "Army brat," New Jersey-born O'Neal and his family lived in various places, including Germany twice, where Louisiana State University (LSU) coach Dale Brown spotted him in a basketball clinic. He attended Cole High School in San Antonio, Texas, then moved on to LSU, where he was named national player of the year by AP, UPI, and Sports Illustrated after his sophomore season, during which he broke his leg and was a two-time consensus first-team All-American. O'Neal left LSU after his junior season in 1992.

FURTHER READING

"The next superstar." *New York Times Magazine*, Nov. 15, 1992.
"Shaq attack!" WILLIAM PLUMMER and RON RIDENHOUR. *People*, Dec. 16, 1991.
"College's biggest deal? . . ." BRUCE SCHOENFELD. *Sporting News*, Feb. 4, 1991.
"Shack attack." CURRY KIRKPATRICK. *Sports Illustrated*, Jan. 21, 1991.

O'Rourke P. J. (Patrick Jake O'Rourke; 1947–) Satirist O'Rourke became a bestselling author with his 1991 *Parliament of Whores: A Lone Humorist Attempts to Explain the U.S. Government*, a wide-ranging, irreverent, largely anti-liberal set of mostly political essays that found large audiences in an anti-Establishment, anti-politician time; the book remained a bestseller well into 1992. In 1992, he published *Give War a Chance: Eyewitness Accounts of Mankind's Struggle Against Tyranny, Injustice, and Alcohol-Free Beer*, another collection of satirical essays. Some of these were reprints of the arti-

cles he had written for *Rolling Stone* while covering the Persian Gulf War for the magazine and for ABC Radio; a considerable range of unrelated articles were also included. During 1992, O'Rourke also covered the Republican and Democratic national conventions for Fox Broadcasting.

Ohio-born O'Rourke was an "underground press" writer, editor, and poet (1968–71), and a features editor for the *New York Herald* (1971–72). He joined New York's *National Lampoon* in 1973, as executive and managing editor, and was editor-in-chief of the magazine from 1978 to 1981. He then worked as a freelance writer, publishing articles in a wide range of magazines, one of them *Rolling Stone*, for which he became foreign affairs desk chief. His books also include *Modern Manners: Etiquette for Very Rude People* (1983), *Republican Party Reptile* (1987), and *Holidays in Hell* (1988). O'Rourke's 1969 B.A. was from Miami University of Ohio, and his 1970 M.A. from Johns Hopkins University. He is married to Amy Lumet, daughter of film director Sidney Lumet.

FURTHER READING

"White mischief." Bob Ickes. *New York*, Dec. 21, 1992.

"Another holiday in hell. . . ." Lesley White. *Sunday Times*, Sep. 6, 1992.

"P.J. O'Rourke. . . ." Chris Goodrich. *Publishers Weekly*, Mar. 16, 1992.

"Of cows, scuds and scotch. . . ." Michael Riley. *Time*, Apr. 15, 1991.

"Is P.J. O'Rourke . . .?" Andrew Sullivan. *Esquire*, Aug. 1990.

"Serving up Emily Post. . . ." Kim Hubbard. *People*, July 3, 1989.

Ortega Saavedra, Daniel (1945–)

Secretary-General of the Sandinist National Liberation Front (FSLN) and former President of Nicaragua, Ortega in 1992 continued to abide by his country's election of Violetta Chamorro to the Presidency, and continued to cooperate on many matters with Chamorro in the aftermath of Nicaragua's civil war. But he only cooperated so far; many of the issues of the civil war were left unresolved, and continued to generate strong feelings and even armed clashes, including the very difficult issue of who owned property taken by the Sandinistas while they were in power, and of how to dispose of thousands of claims by those from whom land and other property was taken. In September, when Chamorro bowed in some matters to United States pressure in hopes of freeing $104 million in economic aid frozen by the Bush administration in June, Ortega sharply warned of renewed civil war if she went too far along that path, making it clear that her freedom of action in continuing U.S.-Sandinista and Contra-Sandinista disputes was quite limited.

Ortega in 1992 seemed to seek a centrist position, though many Sandinistas defined it as going to the right as part of the run-up to the 1994 Presidential elections. But he too had limited freedom of action, for his moves generated a reaction within his own party. For Ortega and Chamorro, much depended on the views of the new Clinton administration.

Ortega became active in the movement to overthrow the Anastasio Somoza dictatorship while a teenager, became a Sandinista guerrilla fighter in 1963, and was a national leader of the Sandinista movement (1966–67). He was imprisoned (1967–74), and in the late 1970s became a major leader of the successful rebellion against Somoza. In 1979, he and Violeta Chamorro were two of the five leaders of the coalition that ruled Nicaragua after Somoza fled. Ortega became the Marxist leader of Sandinista-ruled Nicaragua (1981–90), and its president (1985–90). After the ceasefire of March 1988 effectively ended the 8-year-long Nicaraguan civil war, he negotiated a series of agreements with the Contras that paved the way for the transition to democracy. Ortega's then-surprising agreement to allow free elections was one of the notable features of the period. With Daniel Sheehan, he wrote *Assault on Nicaragua: The Untold Story of the U.S. "Secret War"* (1987). Ortega attended Managua's Centralamerican University. He is married to Rosario Murillo; the couple have seven children.

FURTHER READING

Daniel Ortega. JOHN STOCKWELL. Chelsea House, 1991.

"Crisis of the clans. . . ." ARTURO CRUZ, JR., and CONSUELO CRUZ SEQUEIRA. *New Republic*, May 21, 1990.

Life Stories of the Nicaraguan Revolution. DENIS L. HEYCK. Routledge Chapman and Hall, 1990.

O'Toole, Peter Seamus (1932–) Stage and screen star O'Toole returned to London's West End in a new play in 1992. In November, he opened opposite Tara Fitzgerald in Keith Waterhouse's *Our Song*, adapted from the 1988 Waterhouse novel and directed by Ned Sherrin. O'Toole, Waterhouse, and Sherrin had successfully collaborated on Waterhouse's 1989 hit play *Jeffrey Bernard Is Unwell*, and the new play was eagerly anticipated in an otherwise very weak London season, buffeted by Britain's long, deep recession. But it was not to be; the play was a critical and commerical failure. O'Toole's autobiography, *Loitering with Intent*, was published by Macmillan in 1992. Forthcoming were several previously announced films, including Alexandro Jodorowsky's *The Rainbow Thief*, Ian Pringle's *Isabelle Eberhardt*, and *Rebecca's Daughters*, a comedy-love story set in 19th-century Wales at the time of the "Rebecca riots" of farmers against oppressive English road tolls.

Galway-born O'Toole began his long theater career in the mid-1950s in repertory with the Bristol Old Vic Theatre, and went on to play in a wide range of stage roles for the next three decades with such companies as the Old Vic, the National Theatre, and Dublin's Abbey Theatre. He is best known for his films, quickly emerging as a major international star in the title role of *Lawrence of Arabia* (1960), and going on to such films as *Becket* (1964), *The Lion in Winter* (1968), *Man of La Mancha* (1972), *Zulu Dawn* (1978), *My Favorite Year* (1982), *The Last Emperor* (1986), and *King Ralph* (1991). O'Toole attended the Royal Academy of Dramatic Art. He was formerly married to actress Sîan Phillips, and has three children.

FURTHER READING

"Revival for the golden boy." *Observer*, Oct. 18, 1992.

P

Pacino, Al (Alfredo Pacino; 1940–) Celebrated screen and stage star Pacino starred in 1992 as Ricky Roma, the most successful of the unscrupulous group of real estate boiler room salesmen in James Foley's film adaptation of David Mamet's Pulitzer Prize-winning play, the dark drama *Glengarry Glen Ross*, adapted for the screen by Mamet. The film was an outstanding artistic success, particularly notable in a very lean period for high quality dramatic films. Jack Lemmon, Alec Baldwin, Ed Harris, Alan Arkin, Kevin Spacey, and Jonathan Pryce co-starred. Pacino also starred as blind lieutenant colonel Frank Slade opposite Chris O'Donnell as

a teenager who acts as his eyes during a visit to New York, in Martin Brest's film *Scent of a Woman*.

In 1992, Pacino also starred in two notable stage roles, played in repertory at New York's Circle-in-the-Square Theater in June and July. In one, he played an arresting King Herod in Oscar Wilde's *Salome*, opposite Sheryl Lee (who was Laura Palmer in David Lynch's "Twin Peaks") as Salome; Robert Allan Ackerman directed. In the other, he starred opposite Charles Cioffi in the Ira Lewis two-character play *Chinese Coffee*, directed by Arvin Brown.

New York-born Pacino is one of the leading alumni of the Actor's Studio, beginning his long association with the group in 1966 and becoming one of its artistic directors (1982–84). He worked in the theater through the 1960s, and in the early 1970s emerged as a major film star, breaking through as Michael Corleone in *The Godfather* (1972). He went on to star in such films as *Serpico* (1973), *The Godfather, Part II* (1974), *Dog Day Afternoon* (1975), *Cruising* (1980), *Scarface* (1983), *Sea of Love* (1989). *Dick Tracy* (1990), *The Godfather, Part III* (1990), and *Frankie and Johnny in the Clair De Lune* (1991). He also continued to work in the theater, in such plays as *Camino Real* (1973), *Richard III* (1973), and *American Buffalo* (1981).

FURTHER READING

"Conquest of space." DAVID DENBY. *New York*, Dec. 21, 1992.
"Al alone." MAUREEN DOWD. *GQ—Gentleman's Quarterly*, Sep. 1992.

Bomb: Interviews. Betsy Sussler, ed. City Lights, 1992.

"Al Pacino." Julian Schnabel. *Interview*, Feb. 1991.

"Pacino powers. . . ." John Podhoretz. *Insight*, Jan. 14, 1991.

Life on the Wire: The Life and Art of Al Pacino. Andrew Yule. Fine, 1991.

Al Pacino: A Life on the Wire. Andrew Yule. Shapolsky, 1992.

Paglia, Camille (1947–) Always highly controversial, Paglia became a celebrity after publication of her book *Sexual Personae: Art and Decadence from Nefertiti to Emily Dickinson* (1990). In that work, Paglia discussed aspects of culture and education, attacking many current trends in both areas and calling for a classics-based curriculum. Her rather familiar postions, however, were stated very combatively—and she drew even more media coverage with her attacks on many feminists and current feminist issues, which were applauded by many conservatives. Ironically, Paglia denies that she is a conservative and describes herself as "anti-establishment." Paglia also became a widely seen lecturer, whose abrasive personal style drew large audiences. In 1992, she published a new book of essays, *Sex, Art and American Culture*, in which she continued to explore many of the same themes, expressing her opinions on a great many current issues, including astrology, Madonna, disco dancing, the Hill-Thomas confrontation, rape, and current trends in philosophy.

Paglia graduated from the State University of New York at Binghamton in 1968, and began teaching at Bennington College in 1972, the same year that she completed her Ph.D. at Yale University. Always flamboyantly abrasive, she reportedly engaged in several fistfights and other physical and verbal battles with students and other faculty members while a teacher at Bennington (1972–80), and later while teaching at Wesleyan and Yale. She began teaching at the Philadelphia University of the Arts in 1984.

FURTHER READING

"Paglia's power trip." James Wolcott. *Vanity Fair*, Sep. 1992.

"Paglia, Camille." *Current Biography*, Aug. 1992.

"CP, feminist firebrand. . . ." Lesley White. *Sunday Times*, June 7, 1992.

"Undressing Camille." Susie Bright. *OUT-LOOK*, Spring 1992.

"Feminist fatale. . . ." Naomi Wolf. *New Republic*, Mar. 16, 1992.

"Who is. . . ." Steven Petrow. *Advocate*, Feb. 11, 1992.

"Camille Paglia. . . ." *Working Woman*, Mar. 1992.

"Camille Paglia. . . ." Laurence R. Stains. *Philadelphia*, Jan. 1992.

"A scholar and. . . ." *Cosmopolitan*, Nov. 1991.

"20 questions. . . ." *Playboy*, Oct. 1991.

Panetta, Leon (1938–) President Bill Clinton's incoming Office of Management and Budget Director Panetta accepted the job after 12 years on the House of Representatives Budget Committee, four of them as committee chairman. During the Reagan and Bush administrations, he was a key Congressional critic of the often understated budgets submitted to Congress, and a leading liberal who was especially concerned about the environmental threats posed by offshore oil drilling in his California coastal district. He sponsored the establishment of a national marine sanctuary at Monterey Bay.

California-born Panetta began his political career as a Congressional assistant after his

1964–66 Navy service. He was director of the U.S. Office of Civil Rights in the Department of Health, Education, and Welfare (1969–70), but was fired by the Nixon administration for his strong civil rights advocacy. From 1970 to 1971, he served as executive assistant to New York mayor John Lindsay. After practicing law (1971–76), he successfully ran for Congress, and was an eight-term California Democratic congressman (1976–92), leaving to accept the Budget Director's post. His 1960 B.A. was from the University of Santa Clara, and his 1963 J.D. from the University of Santa Clara Law School. He is married to the former Sylvia Marie Varni; they have three sons.

FURTHER READING

"Clinton team. . . ." THOMAS FRIEDMAN. *New York Times*, Dec. 11, 1992.

"Clinton's team. . . ." DAVID WESSEL and JEFFREY H. BIRNBAUM. *Wall Street Journal*, Dec. 10, 1992.

"To omb or not to omb?" PAUL HOUSTON. *Los Angeles Times*, Nov. 30, 1992.

Parks, Bert (1914–92) Atlanta-born Parks

began his long career in his teens as a singer in radio on "The Eddie Cantor Show," and was a CBS radio announcer from 1933 to 1939. His breakthrough job came as host of the "Break the Bank" radio quiz program, which led to his host-ing of "Stop the Music" in 1948. His television career began as host of the quiz show "Party Line," and he became a well-known television figure as host of television's "Stop the Music" (1949–56). He went on to host a wide range of television shows, also working as a guest actor in many series episodes. Parks was best known for his 25 years (1955–80) as television host of the Miss America pageant, and for the song "There She Is, Miss America" that became his signature song. He was survived by his wife, Annette, a daughter, and two sons. (d. La Jolla, California; February 2, 1992)

FURTHER READING

"Last song for Bert." MARK GOODMAN. *People*, Feb. 17, 1992.

"A career of. . . ." JESSE CAGLE. *Entertainment*, Feb. 14, 1992.

Obituary. *Variety*, Feb. 10, 1992.

Obituary. *New York Times*, Feb. 4, 1992.

"And the winner. . . ." MARJORIE ROSEN. *People*, Sep. 10, 1990.

Parnis, Mollie (1905–92) New York City-

born Parnis informally began her career as a designer while selling clothing in New York's garment district in the 1920s. She and Leon Livingston, whom she married in 1930, went into business together in 1933, and until his death in 1962 built their dress business together, she as an increasingly prominent designer, he on the business side. She left the business briefly after his death, but then reopened it, continuing to design and operate her company until 1984, afterward still doing some designing. Parnis was also a considerable collector of artworks—and of people in the arts, politics, journalism, and other highly visible occupations. She was one of the leading New York hostesses of her day, her Park Avenue apartment a salon to which came some of the leading intellectuals and artists of her time. She was also a considerable philanthropist, funding park projects in New York City and Jerusalem, and also funding the Livingston Awards for journalists after the 1979 death of her son, Robert Livingston. She was survived by a nephew. (d. New York City; July 18, 1992)

FURTHER READING

Obituary. *New York Times*, July 19, 1992.

Perkins, Anthony (1930–92) New York City-born Perkins, the son of actor Osgood Perkins, toured on stage while still in his teens, and made his 1954 Broadway debut in *Tea and Sympathy*. In 1957, he emerged as a star on Broadway, creating the Eugene Gant role in *Look Homeward, Angel*. He continued to work in the theater throughout his career, as in *The Star Spangled Girl* (1956) and *Equus* (1966), though he is best known worldwide for his films. His film debut came in 1953, opposite Jean Simmons in *The Actress*. He won a Best Supporting Actor Oscar nomination for *Friendly Persuasion* (1956), and went on to such films as *Fear Strikes Out* (1957), *Desire Under the Elms* (1958), *The Matchmaker* (1958), *On the Beach* (1959), and his starring and by far best known role as psychopathic killer Norman Bates in *Psycho* (1960), a role that he later felt greatly damaged his career by defining him far too narrowly. His career sagged considerably after *Psycho*, though it included roles in such films as *Phaedra* (1962), *Pretty Poison* (1968), and *Murder on the Orient Express* (1974). He later returned to horror film themes, most notably in the three *Psycho* sequels (1983, 1986, 1990). Perkins, who died of AIDS-related illnesses, was survived by his wife, Berinthia Berenson, and two sons. (d. Hollywood, California; September 12, 1992)

FURTHER READING

"Anthony Perkins, ..." DAVID THOMSON. *Film Comment*, Nov.–Dec. 1992.
"One final mystery." MARK GOODMAN. *People*, Sep. 28, 1992.
"The outsider." LAWRENCE O'TOOLE. *Entertainment*, Sep. 25, 1992.
Obituary. *Variety*, Sep. 21, 1992.
Obituary. *The Times* (of London), Sep. 14, 1992.
Obituary. *New York Times*, Sep. 14, 1992.
Osgood and Anthony Perkins: A Comprehensive History of Their Work. . . . LAURA K. PALMER. McFarland, 1991.
"Live Bates." MIM UDOVITCH. *Interview*, Nov. 1990.
"Janet Leigh and. . . ." ROD LURIE. *Los Angeles*, July 1990.

Perot, H. Ross (Henry Ross Perot, 1930–) For a few months in 1992, it seriously looked as if Texas billionaire Ross Perot might possibly revolutionize American politics by winning a three-way Presidential race against the Republican incumbent and Democratic challenger—and all from a standing start without primaries, a patiently built national campaign organization, fundraising, or any of the other things that have become commonplace for major Presidential candidates. All Perot had was two billion dollars worth of assets, the willingness to spend a couple of hundred million dollars of his own money—and tremendous national disaffection with the politicians of both parties in very hard economic times.

Perot began his "unannounced" candidacy on February 20th during an appearance on "Larry King Live"; by late March, he had opened headquarters in Dallas, named John Stockdale as his probable running mate, and had started a nationwide petition drive, promising that he would run if his fast-growing army of volunteers succeeded in putting his name on the ballot in all 50 states. On June 3, he hired political professionals Hamilton Jordan and Ed Rollins to run his unorthodox campaign. He continued to build strength throughout the spring and early summer, relying largely on media exposure through talk-show interviews, and by mid-June was running ahead of both George Bush and Bill Clinton in many states. Some analysts saw a historic upset in the making; most predicted that Perot would fade in the fall, as had so many other American third party candidates—but all admitted that the situation was unprecedented and unpredictable.

There were signs of strain, though, as disarray was reported within his campaign organization and attacks against him mounted in the media. In early July, his support began to fade as Clinton's support grew. Perot charged a Republican "dirty tricks" campaign, and on July 16, in an extraordinary turnaround, announced that he had decided to withdraw from the race, shocking and dismaying thousands of active campaigners and millions of supporters. Even while withdrawing, though, he urged his supporters to keep on gathering petition signatures to place him on the ballot, and to maintain their voice through the organization they had developed (with his funding), named after his 1992 book *United We Stand*, which became a bestseller.

On October 1, Perot reversed course again, announcing that he was once again a Presidential candidate. He then proceeded to actively campaign, spending tens of millions of dollars on television advertising, and becoming a full participant in the Clinton-Bush-Perot televised Presidential debates. There he performed effectively, and was widely regarded as having "won" one of the debates. But his candidacy had been fatally compromised by his earlier withdrawal, and although he won 19 percent of the popular vote on November 3, he won no electoral votes. His possible future role in American politics was unclear.

Texarkana-born Perot graduated from the U.S. Naval Academy in 1953, afterwards serving four years in the navy. He worked as an IBM salesperson (1957–62), then founded Electronic Data Systems in 1962, and in the decades that followed built it into a major company, selling it to General Motors for $2.5 billion in 1984, so becoming GM's major stockholder. He resigned from the GM board of directors in 1986, and in 1988 founded Perot Systems. He has long been associated with attempts to secure more information and possible release of U.S. prisoners of war thought to be held in Vietnam. He and Margot Birmingham married in 1956; they have five children.

FURTHER READING

"Ross Perot." *People*, Dec. 28, 1992.

"Citizen Perot." TOM MORGANTHAU. *Newsweek*, Nov. 9, 1992.

"Big D, little H.R.P." LAWRENCE WRIGHT. *New Yorker*, Oct. 26, 1992.

"Perot's final days. . . ." MARIE BRENNER. *Vanity Fair*, Oct. 1992.

"Ross II. . . ." STANLEY BING. *Esquire*, Oct. 1992.

"The man from nowhere." HADLEY ARKES. *National Review*, Aug. 3, 1992.

"The quitter. . . ." TOM MORGANTHAU. " 'I just wanted. . . .' " MAYNARD PARKER. *Newsweek*, July 27, 1992.

"Roots. . . ." ALAN BRINKLEY. *New Republic*, July 27, 1992.

"Retro man." MARK SEAL. *Esquire*, July 1992.

"Perot in '92. . . ." PAUL BURKA. *Texas*, June 1992.

"The other side of Perot." GEORGE J. CHURCH. *Time*, June 29, 1992.

"Perot on Perot." DAVID R. GERGEN et al. *U.S. News & World Report*, June 29, 1992.

"The man from Texarkana." LAWRENCE WRIGHT. *New York Times Magazine*, June 28, 1992.

"How he might govern." JONATHAN ALTER. "The man and the myth." HOWARD FINEMAN. "President Perot?" TOM MATHEWS. *Newsweek*, June 15, 1992.

"And now. . . ." ALAN FARNHAM. "What business. . . ." THOMAS STEWART. *Fortune*, June 15, 1992.

"Enter Perot." *Economist*, June 6, 1992.

"Perot and his presidents." MARGARET CARLSON. "He's ready. . . ." WALTER SHAPIRO and PRISCILLA PAINTON. " 'Working folks say. . . .' " HENRY MULLER and RICHARD WOODBURY. *Time*, May 25, 1992.

"Perot on the podium." Richard S. Dunham and Wendy Zellner. *Business Week*, Apr. 27, 1992.

" 'It's up to you, folks.' " GINNY CARROLL. "The wild card." TOM MORGANTHAU. *Newsweek*, Apr. 27, 1992.

"Cow-country Cuomo." CHRISTOPHER BYRON. *New York*, Apr. 6, 1992.

The Big Bio of Ross Perot. CAROLE MARSH. Gallopade, 1992.

Ross Perot: the Candidate: A Portrait of the Man and His Views. CECIL JOHNSON. Summit (TX), 1992.

Ross Perot: In His Own Words. TONY CHIU. Warner, 1992.

Ross Perot Speaks Out: In His Own Words. JAMES W. ROBINSON. Prima, 1992.

Ross Perot: The Man Behind the Myth. KEN GROSS. Random, 1992.

Irreconcilable Differences: Ross Perot Versus General Motors. DORON LEVIN. Little, Brown, 1989.

The Alexander Complex: Six Businessmen and the Empires They Built. MICHAEL MEYER. Random, 1989.

Pesci, Joe (1944–) Emerging film star Joe Pesci had a very busy 1992, starring in two films and appearing in strong supporting roles in two of the year's commercial blockbusters. In March, he starred as Vinny in Jonathan Lynn's very well-received comedy-drama *My Cousin Vinny*, a farce about a very new lawyer from Brooklyn defending a case in Alabama. In October, he starred opposite Barbara Hershey in Howard Franklin's *The Public Eye* as a 1940s New York City photographer who explores the seamy side of the nighttime city. Pesci was also highly visible in the high-budget summertime violence-thriller hit *Lethal Weapon 3*, starring Mel Gibson and Danny Glover. And he once again played a bumbling villain in Chris Columbus' *Home Alone 2*, starring Macaulay Culkin.

Newark-born Pesci began his long career at four years of age, appearing on television's "Star Time Kids." He made his film debut in *The Death Collector* (1975). His breakthrough role came as Joe, brother to Robert De Niro's Jake La Motta, in *Raging Bull* (1980), a role that won him a Best Supporting Actor Oscar nomination. Pesci went on to appear in such films as *I'm Dancing As Fast As I Can* (1981), *Dear Mr. Wonderful* (1983), *Easy Money* (1983), *Once Upon a Time in America* (1984), *Man on Fire* (1987), *Moonwalker* (1988), *Lethal Weapon II* (1989), *Backtrack* (1990), *Betsy's Wedding* (1990), *Goodfellas* (1990; he won a Best Supporting Actor Oscar), *Home Alone* (1990), *JFK* (1991), and *The Super* (1991).

FURTHER READING

" 'It was like a grip that let go.' " Tom Seligson. *Parade*, Oct. 18, 1992.
"Smokin' Joe. . . ." Donald Chase. *Entertainment*, Apr. 3, 1992.
"Joe Pesci." *Playboy*, Dec. 1991.
"Mighty Joe Pesci." David Patrick Stearns. *Cosmopolitan*, Jan. 1991.

Petty, Richard (1937–) The King pulled over to the side of the road in 1992. After 35 years as the king of stock-car racing, Richard Petty decided to call it quits in 1992, taking what he called a Fan Appreciation Tour around the country. Everywhere, he found himself mobbed by well-wishers and autograph-seekers, many of whom have visited the Richard Petty Museum near his home in Level Cross, North Carolina, which houses many of the handmade gifts given to him over the years. Petty momentos sold on the 1992 tour netted millions, over half a million of which is being donated to charities. The only thing that did not go quite as planned was that, in his 1,185th and final race at Georgia's Atlanta Motor Speedway on November 15, 1992, Petty was caught in a wreck and his car burst into flames. Petty was unhurt, reportedly commenting, "I went out in a blaze. Forget the glory." The car survived, too, his old #43, and he later came back out to the track for a final lap, behind the winners. In a December White House ceremony, Petty received the Presidential Medal of Freedom from President George Bush, who had visited Petty in his final Daytona appearance in July. Petty remains active in the sport as a team-owner.

Petty will not have to worry about his name fading from memory, for his records are likely to stand for decades. In particular, Petty has an astounding 200 NASCAR victories (second-best is 84), along with seven Winston Cup championships, seven victories at the Daytona 500, nine times being named most popular driver, and ten consecutive wins (August–September 1967). Petty's first win, in his third season, was in 1960, and his last in 1984 at the Daytona International Speedway; the car he drove in that 200th win is on display at the Smithsonian Museum. In 1971, he became the first stock-car racer to have career earnings topping $1 million. North Carolina-born Petty graduated from Randleman High School in 1955. He and his wife Lynda have three daughters and one son, Kyle, also a stock-car racer.

FURTHER READING

"Black Sunday." MIKE ZIZZO. *Sporting News*, Nov. 16, 1992.
"The king kicks back. . . ." KATHERINE RUSSELL RICH. *People*, Nov. 16, 1992.
"The King." ED HINTON. *Sports Illustrated*, Oct. 19, 1992.
A Farewell to the King: A Personal Look Back at the Career of Richard Petty, Stock Car Racing's Winningest and Most Popular Driver. FRANK VEHORN. Down Home (NC), 1992.

as one of the leading film players of the 1980s, starring in such films as *Grease 2* (1982), *Scarface* (1983), *Into the Night* (1984), *Ladyhawke* (1985), *Sweet Liberty* (1986), *The Witches of Eastwick* (1987), *Married to the Mob* (1988), *Tequila Sunrise* (1988), *Dangerous Liaisons* (1989), *The Fabulous Baker Boys* (1989; she won an Oscar nomination), *The Russia House* (1990), and *Frankie and Johnny* (1991). In the summer of 1989, she appeared as Olivia in *Twelfth Night* at the New York Shakespeare Festival. She was formerly married to actor Peter Horton.

FURTHER READING

"The bat's meow. . . ." GERRI HIRSHEY. *Rolling Stone*, Sep. 3, 1992.
"The two lives of Catwoman." MICHAEL LIPTON. *People*, July 13, 1992.
"What she did. . . ." JEFF ROVIN. *Ladies Home Journal*, June 1992.
"Tough guise." JONATHAN VAN METER. *Vogue*, Oct. 1991.
"Queen for a decade." MARC ELIOT. *California*, Sep. 1991.
"The fabulous Pfeiffer girl." ROBERT SEIDENBERG. *American Film*, Jan. 1991.
"Michelle Pfeiffer as. . . ." HAL HINSON. *Esquire*, Dec. 1990.
"Pfeiffer, Michelle." *Current Biography*, Mar. 1990.

Pfeiffer, Michelle (1959–) In 1992 film star Pfeiffer played a leading role as Catwoman, opposite Michael Keaton as Batman and Danny DeVito as Penguin, in Tim Burton's *Batman Returns*, the summer-blockbuster high-budget sequel to *Batman*; like the original, the film became a worldwide hit. She also starred opposite Dennis Haysbert in one of the year's leading dramatic films, Jonathan Kaplan's long-deferred *Love Field*, which opened during the Christmas season. Set in 1963, the film tells the story of an interracial Deep South friendship, struck up on a bus ride from Dallas to Washington; Pfeiffer plays an innocent on her way to Washington to attend the Kennedy funeral. Forthcoming was a starring role in Martin Scorsese's *The Age of Innocence*, co-starring Daniel Day-Lewis and Winona Ryder. Filmed in the spring of 1992, the movie was originally scheduled for Christmas 1992 release but was rescheduled for the autumn of 1993.

California-born Pfeiffer very quickly emerged

Picon, Molly (1898–1992) New York City-born Picon, a star of the American Yiddish theater, made her stage debut at the age of six in a Philadelphia Yiddish-language repertory company. She went on the road in Yiddish repertory at 15 in *Uncle Tom's Cabin*, and, while still in her teens, played in vaudeville. She married writer Jacob Kalich in 1919; they lived in Eastern Europe until 1923, returning to New York to do his play *Yankele*, in which she played her first and most enduring starring role. She went on to become a leading figure in the American Yiddish theater, and, as that theater waned, moved more into English-language roles, in 1940 starring on Broadway in *Morning Star*. On Broadway, she also starred in the long-running musical *Milk and Honey* (1961), and in several other plays, including *Paris Is Out* (1970) and *Something Old, Something New* (1977). She also appeared in several films. Picon returned to the Yiddish theater in the musical *The Kosher Widow* (1959), also writing the show's lyrics.

Her autobiography was *Molly!* (1960), written with Jean Grillo. She was survived by a sister. (d. Lancaster, Pennsylvania; April 5, 1992)

FURTHER READING

Obituary. *Variety*, Apr. 13, 1992.
Obituary. *New York Times*, Apr. 7, 1992.
Molly Picon: A Gift of Laughter. LILA PERL. JPS (Philadelphia), 1990.

Pinter, Harold (1930–) It was another busy year for the celebrated playwright, screenwriter, and actor. Harold Pinter. He starred as Hirst in a November 1992 London revival of his now-classic 1975 play *No Man's Land*, in a cast that included Paul Eddington as Spooner, Douglas Hodge, and Gawn Grainger. (Hirst had originally been played on stage by Ralph Richardson, opposite John Gielgud as Spooner.) The year also saw two Pinter screenplays. He wrote the screenplay for David Jones' forthcoming *The Trial*, based on the Franz Kafka novel and starring Kyle MacLachlan, Anthony Hopkins, Jean Stapleton, and Juliet Stevenson. He also wrote the screenplay for James Ivory's forthcoming *Remains of the Day*, based on the novel by Japanese author Kazuo Ishiguro and starring Anthony Hopkins, Emma Thompson, and James Fox.

London-born Pinter began his career as an actor, from 1949 working largely in repertory. He moved into playwriting in the late 1950s, scoring his first major success with *The Caretaker* (1960; he also adapted it into the 1964 film), and went on to such works as *The Homecoming* (1965; and the 1973 film), *Old Times* (1970), *No Man's Land* (1975), *Family Voices* (1980), and *Party Time* (1991). He has also directed such plays as *Exiles* (1970), *Butley* (1971; and the 1973 film), *Otherwise Engaged* (1975), and *The Common Pursuit* (1984), and has written many screenplays, including *The Servant* (1962), *The Quiller Memorandum* (1965), *The Go-Between* (1969), *The French Lieutenant's Woman* (1980), *The Turtle Diary* (1984), *The Handmaid's Tale* (1990), *The Heat of the Day* (1990), *Reunion* (1991), and *The Comfort of Strangers* (1991). Pinter has been married twice, first to actress Vivien Merchant and since 1980 to the writer Antonia Fraser. He has one child.

FURTHER READING

"The Pinter principle." DONALD CHASE. *American Film*, Oct. 1990.
Harold Pinter, 2nd ed. BERNARD F. DUKORE. St. Martin's, 1990.
Harold Pinter. LOIS GORDON, ed. Garland, 1990.
Pinter the Playwright, 4th ed. MARTIN ESSLIN. Heinemann, 1988.
Harold Pinter. HAROLD BLOOM, ed. Chelsea House, 1987.
Pinter: The Player's Playwright. DAVID T. THOMPSON. Schocken, 1985.

Piper, John (1903–92) A multifaceted British visual artist, designer for the theater, and writer, John Piper began his six-decades-long career after studying at the Royal College of Art in the late 1920s. His early paintings were highly abstracted and Cubist-influenced, but he turned in the late 1930s to the English structures and settings that were the focus of the main body of his work, perhaps most notably expressed in his group of wartime watercolors of Windsor Castle. He was a theater and art critic in the 1930s, and in the 1940s also became a leading theater designer, as seen in his costumes and set designs for the premieres of several Benjamin Britten works from the mid-1940s through the early 1970s. Piper worked in stained glass from the 1960s and in ceramics from the 1970s. He was also a printmaker, book illustrator, and photographer. He was survived by his wife and collaborator, Myfanwy Evans, two daughters, and a son. (d. Henley, England; June 28, 1992)

FURTHER READING

Obituary. *New York Times*, July 1, 1992.
Obituary. *Independent*, June 30, 1992; July 2, 1992.
Obituary. *The Times* (of London), June 30, 1992.
John Piper: A Painter's Camera: Building and Landscapes in Britain 1935–1985. DAVID F. JENKINS. University of Washington Press, 1987.

Poiret, Jean (1926–92) Paris-born Poiret, an actor, playwright, and director, was best known by far as the writer and co-star of the farce *La Cage Aux Folles* (1973). He and Michel Serrault starred in the original Paris production as the aging gay couple at the center of the piece.

He also co-wrote the 1978 Edouard Molinaro film version starring Serrault and Ugo Tognazzi, as well as the two film sequels. Harvey Fierstein adapted his work into the Tony-winning 1984 Broadway musical. Long a leading character actor, Poiret made his film debut in the Brigitte Bardot vehicle *Mam'zelle Pigalle* (1955), going on to appear in more than 50 films and in many stage roles. His directorial debut came in 1992 with *Le Zebre*. He was survived by his wife, the actress Caroline Cellier, and a son. (d. Paris; March 14, 1992).

FURTHER READING

Obituary. *Variety*, Mar. 23, 1992.
Obituary. *The Times* (of London), Mar. 17, 1992.
Obituary. *New York Times*, Mar. 15, 1992.

Poitier, Sidney (1924–)

On March 12, 1992, Poitier became the 20th—and the first African-American—recipient of the American Film Institute's Life Achievement Award, one of the highest of cinema honors, whose previous recipients included such luminaries as Gregory Peck, Bette Davis, Orson Welles, and Billy Wilder. Poitier, the first breakthrough African-American film star, paid tribute to many who had broken ground for him, including Paul Robeson, Lorraine Hansberry, Jackie Robinson, Rosa Parks, and Canada Lee. Late in 1992, Poitier starred in Phil Alden Robinson's well-received fast-paced comedy thriller *Sneakers*, complete with computer hackers, national security risks, and assorted murders, in a cast that included Robert Redford, Ben Kingsley, Dan Aykroyd, Mary McDonnell, River Phoenix, and James Earl Jones.

Miami-born Poitier grew up in the Bahamas, retaining his West Indian accent in a 45-year-long stage and screen career that included appearances in such plays as *Anna Lucasta* (1948) and *A Raisin in the Sun* (1959). He became Hollywood's first major African-American movie star in the late 1950s. His most notable films were *The Defiant Ones* (1958), *Porgy and Bess* (1959), the film version of *A Raisin in the Sun* (1961), *Lilies of the Field* (1963; he was the first Black actor to win a Best Actor Academy Award), *In the Heat of the Night* (1967), and *Guess Who's Coming to Dinner* (1967). Poitier also directed such films as *Buck and the Preacher* (1972; he also starred), *Uptown Saturday Night* (1982), *Hanky Panky* (1984), and *Ghost Dad* (1990). He starred as U.S. Supreme Court Justice Thurgood Marshall in the television film *Separate But Equal* (1991). In 1980 he published the autobiographical *This Life*. He has been married twice and has six children.

FURTHER READING

"Sidney Poitier." FRANK SPOTNITZ. *American Film*, Sep.–Oct. 1991.
"Poitier's stellar career. . . ." *Jet*, Mar. 20, 1989.
"Poitier thanks. . . ." RALPH TYLER. *Variety*, Mar. 8, 1989.
Sidney Poitier. CAROL BERGMAN. Chelsea House, 1989.

Pol Pot (Tol Saut; Saloh Sar; 1928–)

At the beginning of 1992, peace seemed near in Cambodia. The October 23, 1991 Treaty of Paris had provided for an immediate cease fire in the long civil war; the return home of an estimated 350,000 refugees, and the posting of thousands of United Nations troops and civilian personnel to keep the peace helped set up a new government and prepare for free elections to be held in 1993. But there was great worldwide concern as well, for the strongest single force in Cambodia, and seemingly an essential part of the new government, was the Khmer Rouge (Red Khmer) organization, which under Pol Pot's leadership had been directly responsible for the Cambodian Holocaust (1975–78), a series of mass murders in which an estimated one to three million Cambodians died, until the Vietnamese took the country after their 1978 invasion.

By the end of 1992, it was clear that those concerns had been justified, and peace seemed once again far away in Cambodia, as the Khmer Rouge proved unwilling to abide by the terms of the peace treaty. In mid-March, Khmer Rouge forces attacked in central Cambodia, seeking territorial gains before UN forces arrived; a UN-brokered ceasefire went into effect two weeks later. In mid-June, Khmer Rouge forces attacked again in central Cambodia, and at the same time refused to give up their arms and go into demobilization camps as provided by the treaty. As the year progressed, the Khmer Rouge proved no more tractable, in November and December beginning to take groups of UN peacekeepers as hostages, as Cambodia seemed on the brink of a return to full-scale civil war.

Pol Pot has spent his whole life as a Communist activist, beginning as a teenager in the Indochinese Communist Party in the 1940s. After World War II, he moved up in the Cambodian communist party, and in 1963 emerged as party general secretary and organizer of the Khmer Rouge army. He became prime minister of Cambodia, then renamed Kampuchea, in 1976, after the 1975 Khmer Rouge victory, but resumed his career as a guerrilla leader after the successful Vietnamese invasion of Cambodia in 1978. His wife is Khieu Ponnary.

FURTHER READING

"Pol Pot, cobra. . . ." JAMES PRINGLE. *Times*, Nov. 14, 1992.
Cambodia, Pol Pot, and the United States: The Faustian Pact. MICHAEL HAAS. Greenwood, 1991.
Pol Pot: A Political Biography. DAVID P. CHANDLER. Westview, 1991.
"Skeletons in the closet. . . ." STEPHEN J. MORRIS. *New Republic*, June 4, 1990.
Leftism: From de Sade and Marx to Hitler and Pol Pot. ERIK LEDDIHN. Regnery Gateway, 1990.
Pol Pot. REBECCA STEFOFF. Chelsea House, 1989.
Pol Pot Plans the Future: Confidential Leadership Documents from Democratic Kampuchea, 1976–1977. DAVID P. CHANDLER, ed. Yale University, Southeast Asia, 1989.
Beyond the Horizon: Five Years with the Khmer Rouge. LAURENCE PICQ. St. Martin's, 1989.
How Pol Pot Came to Power. BEN KIERNAN. Schocken, 1985.

Powell, Colin Luther

(1937–) Lieutenant General Powell, the chairman of the Joint Chiefs of Staff, continued in 1992 to urge caution before committing to military action, as he had before the Persian Gulf War. In the spring of 1992, for example, he did not favor military action against Iraq when others wanted to attack Iraq to force compliance with nuclear and chemical weapons destruction; and in autumn, he opposed quick armed intervention in the Yugoslavian civil war. At the same time, he urged continued U.S. military strength, in February and throughout the year joining Defense Secretary Cheney in defending Pentagon-proposed defense cuts as deep enough, and resisting Congressional proposals for deeper cuts. Powell

Colin Powell (right) and George Bush.

stayed clear of the presidential race, except for supporting George Bush's statement that all concerned had agreed on the timing of the decision to stop fighting the Gulf War; General Norman Schwarzkopf had declared his own opposition to the decision, though later Schwarzkopf retracted his statement.

New York-born Powell began his long military career in 1958. He has held a series of line and staff posts in Europe and the United States, including command posts in the 101st Airborne and 4th Infantry divisions. He was National Security Affairs assistant to President Reagan (1987–89). Powell was appointed chairman of the Joint Chiefs of Staff by President George Bush on August 10, 1989; it was a historic "first," as he was the first African-American to hold the post. One of his earliest major tasks was the organization of the December 1989 Panama invasion. He has also sent American forces into El Salvador, Liberia, and The Philippines. Powell's 1958 B.S. was from the City University of New York, and his 1971 M.B.A. from George Washington University. Most unusually for one who has gone so far in the U.S. Army, he is not a West Point graduate, instead having become an officer through the Reserve Officer Training Corps (ROTC). He married Alma Johnson in 1962; they have three children.

FURTHER READING

Colin Powell: Soldier-Statesman—Statesman-Soldier. HOWARD MEANS. Fine, 1992.

Colin Powell: A Man of War and Peace. CARL SENNA. Walker, 1992.

Colin Powell. CATHERINE REEF. Twenty-First Century Books (MD), 1992.

Colin Powell: A Biography. JAMES HASKINS. Scholastic, 1992.

Colin Powell. WARREN BROWN. Chelsea House, 1992.

Story of Colin Powell and Benjamin Davis. KATHERINE APPLEGATE. Dell, 1992.

Colin Powell: Straight to the Top. ROSE BLUE. Millbrook, 1992.

"Colin Powell." *People,* Summer 1991.

" 'Nobody knows my politics' " TOM MATHEWS. *Newsweek,* May 13, 1991.

"The reluctant warrior. . . ." EVAN THOMAS. *Newsweek,* May 13, 1991.

"Another Ike?" VICTOR GOLD. *Washingtonian,* Apr. 1991.

"America's Black Eisenhower. . . ." JOHN RANELAGH. *National Review,* Apr. 1, 1991.

"What next. . . ." STEVEN V. ROBERTS. *U.S. News & World Report,* Mar. 18, 1991.

"In the footsteps. . . ." BRUCE B. AUSTER. *U.S. News & World Report,* Feb. 4, 1991.

Colin Powell. JONATHAN EVERSTON. Bantam, 1991.

Colin Powell: Four Star General. ELAINE LANDAU. Watts, 1991.

Price, Sammy (1908–92) Texas-born Price began his career as a jazz pianist on the road with several groups in the Southwest during the 1920s, and cut his first record, *"Blue Rhythm Stomp,"* in Dallas in 1929. During the 1930s, he lived and played in Kansas City, Chicago, and Detroit, arriving in New York City and becoming a Decca Records staff musician in 1937, and also organizing his own group, the Texas Blusicians. Price made many records on his own in the decades that followed, and also recorded with such jazz greats as Mezz Mezzrow, Sidney Bechet, Doc Cheatem, and Lester Young. He toured Europe with Mezzrow in the late 1940s, and with his own Blusicians in the 1950s, a decade in which he moved back to Dallas to run two clubs. Later in his career, he became widely recognized as a soloist in cabaret and in festivals, also working with the group Two Tenor Boogie. Price was also active in musical education and New York politics, campaigning for several Democratic presidential candidates. In 1990, he published *What Do They Want: A Jazz Autobiography.* He was survived by two daughters. (d. New York City; Apr. 14, 1992)

FURTHER READING

"Blues for the blues." HANK BORDOWITZ. *American Visions,* Aug.–Sep. 1992.

Obituary. *Variety,* Apr. 27, 1992

Obituary. *The Times* (of London), Apr. 18, 1992.

Obituary. *Independent,* Apr. 17, 1992.

Obituary. *New York Times,* Apr. 16, 1992.

Pryce, Jonathan (1947–) British stage and screen actor Pryce starred in 1992 as a victimized real estate purchaser in James Foley's acclaimed film adaptation of David Mamet's Pulitzer Prize-winning play, the dark drama *Glengarry Glen Ross,* adapted for the screen by Mamet. Al Pacino, Jack Lemmon, Alec Baldwin, Ed Harris, Alan Arkin, and Kevin Spacey co-starred, as an unscrupulous group of real estate boiler room salesmen. Pryce also starred in the forthcoming HBO movie *Barbarians at the Gate* as financier Henry Kravis, who organized the 1980s leveraged buyout of R.J.R. Nabisco by Kohlberg, Kravis, Roberts & Co.; James Garner co-stars as F. Ross Johnson, head of R.J.R. Nabisco, and Peter Riegert as securities firm head Peter Cohen. Pryce was also the voice of Trilby in the British animated film *Freddie and F.R.O.7.,* written and directed by Jon Acevski and co-starring Ben Kingsley and Jenny Agutter.

A leading British actor, Pryce has played in a series of major stage roles from the mid-1970s. He won a Tony for *The Comedians* (1976), a production originating in England that transferred to New York. His 1980 *Hamlet* won Britain's Olivier Award. His plays include *The Caretaker* (1981), *Accidental Death of an Anarchist* (1984), *The Seagull* (1985), *Macbeth* (1986; title role), and *Uncle Vanya* (1988). Pryce was widely acclaimed for his portrayal of the Eurasian pimp in the musical *Miss Saigon* (1989), with which he moved from London to Broadway, where he won a 1991 Tony as leading actor in a musical. He has also appeared in such films as *The Ploughman's Lunch* (1983), *Brazil* (1985), *The Doctor and the Devils* (1986), *Consuming Passions* (1988), *The Adventures of Baron Munchausen* (1988), *The Rachel Papers* (1989), and *The Man from the Pru* (1991); in several television films; and in the television series "Roger Doesn't Live Here Any More" (1981). He attended the Royal Academy of Dramatic Art.

FURTHER READING

"Mr. Saigon." MICHAEL BILLINGTON. *Interview*, Apr. 1991.
"Mr. Saigon . . . ." CHRIS SMITH. *New York*, Mar. 11, 1991.

Pucci, Emilio (1914–92) Fashion designer Pucci was an Italian Air Force bomber pilot (1938–47), and was an Allied prisoner of war during World War II. He reportedly entered the fashion industry accidentally in 1947, after being photographed in ski clothing of his own design. He opened a clothing shop on Capri on 1948, and in 1950 founded Emilio, his firm in Rome. He became a major worldwide fashion industry figure of the 1950s and 1960s, as his colorful silk sports clothes became extremely popular. He also diversified into a wide range of other businesses, including cosmetics and other clothing lines. In his native Florence, he developed several handicraft projects. Pucci also pursued a career in politics, becoming a Liberal Party deputy in the national assembly in 1963 and serving two terms. He attended the University of Milan, the University of Georgia, Oregon's Reed College (M.A., 1939), and the University of Florence (Ph.D., 1941). He was survived by his wife, Cristina Pucci, a daughter, and a son. (d. Florence, Italy; November 29, 1992)

FURTHER READING

Obituary. *New York Times*, Dec. 1, 1992.
Obituary. *The Times* (of London), Dec. 1, 1992.
Obituary. *Independent,* Dec. 1, 1992.

Qaddafi, Muammar Muhammed al-

(1942–) Faced with increasingly difficult economic problems and Islamic fundamentalist challenges to his rule, Libyan President Qaddafi continued to try to build his opening to Arab world moderates and to the West in 1992. It was a very difficult task, as he had essentially supported Saddam Hussein during the Persian Gulf War, though making some gestures toward neutrality as the scope of Hussein's defeat became apparent.

Compounding his international problems was the continuing case of the Lockerbie airplane bombing. In November 1991, an international investigation of the 1989 bombing resulted in charges that two Libyans, allegedly government secret service operatives, were responsible; their extradition to the United States to stand trial was demanded, along with the questioning of four other suspects. Qaddafi refused. The net result was the March 1991 passage of a United Nations Security Council resolution calling for limited sanctions against Libya that went into effect on April 15, 1992, after Qaddafi's government had organized demonstrations against foreign embassies in Tripoli and the World Court had refused to postpone the sanctions. Qaddafi remained defiant, while his problems at home and abroad continued to multiply.

A career military officer, Qaddafi led the 1969 military coup in Libya, and quickly seized power for himself, holding it as a dictator ever since; he had himself named president in 1977. He has made repeated, largely unsuccessful attempts to establish himself as a major radical leader of the Arab world, fanning anti-western Islamic fundamentalism, supporting terrorist activities, and supporting Iraq during the Persian Gulf Crisis. His long direct intervention in the Chadian civil war (1975–87) was no more successful, as he was finally forced to sue for peace after defeat on the battlefield, the loss of large air bases, and the Chadian invasion of southern Libya. He has stopped just short of going to war with Egypt on several occasions. There have also been several armed clashes with the United States. In the most serious of these, U.S. warplanes and ships bombarded Libya, in April 1986. Qaddafi attended Libya University. He is married and has five children.

FURTHER READING

"Gadaffi goes back. . . ." Marie Colvin. UL1/*Sunday Times.* May 10, 1992.

"Qaddafi, Muammar al-." *Current Biography*, Mar. 1992.

Qaddafi on the Edge. Camelia Sadat. HarperCollins, 1991.

Qaddafi, Terrorism, and the Origins of the U. S. Attack on Libya. Brian L. Davis. Greenwood, 1990.

Muammar El-Qaddafi. Ted Gottfried. Chelsea House, 1987.

Qaddafi and the Libyan Revolution. David Blundy and Andrew Lycett. Little, Brown, 1987.

The Making of a Pariah State: The Adventurist Politics of Mummar Quaddafi, Martin Sicker. Greenwood, 1987.

Qaddafi: His Ideology in Theory and Practice. Mohamed El-Khawas. Gordon, 1987.

Libya: Qadhafi's Revolution and the Modern State. Lillian C. Harris. Westview, 1986.

Quayle, Dan

Quayle, Dan (James Danforth Quayle, III; 1947–) The outgoing Vice President spent 1992 deeply involved in the presidential campaign. There were some early doubts as to whether or not George Bush would pick him once again as his running mate, but these soon faded, and Quayle quickly emerged as a campaigner designed to appeal to the most conservative wing of the Republican Party. Stressing adherence to "family values," he attacked the "cultural elite," abortion, rap music, pornography, gays and lesbians, and the characters and personal histories of Bill Clinton, Al Gore, and Ross Perot. But, although Quayle proved appealing to the Republican right, which was useful to a Bush campaign attacked from the right by Pat Buchanan, Quayle's own popularity remained very low, far lower than any of the other candidates, and his family values theme failed to make real headway with voters concerned with the worsening economic crisis. Actually, his family values campaign provided one of the Bush campaign's greatest setbacks, for Quayle quite imprudently on May 19 and 20 attacked Candice Bergen, her hit television show "Murphy Brown," and Hollywood in general for encouraging "illegitimacy" and thereby attacking "family values." President Bush at first endorsed his remarks, and then backed away at full speed as the depth and virulence of the national reaction to Quayle's attacks became apparent. The firestorm Quayle created continued right through to election day, contributing to a record vote of working women for the Clinton-Gore ticket.

Indiana-born Quayle worked in his family's newspaper business for several years before becoming an Indiana state employee in 1971. He became a Congressman in 1977, was a U.S. senator from Indiana (1981–89), and was chosen by George Bush to be his running mate in the 1988 presidential campaign. Quayle's B.S. was from DePauw University, and in 1969, his J.D. from Indiana University in 1974. He married Marilyn Tucker in 1972; they have three children.

FURTHER READING

" 'People vote. . . .' " MICHAEL DUFFY. "Quayle vs. Gore." STANLEY CLOUD. *Time*, Oct. 19, 1992.

"The boy in the bubble. . . ." Michael Lewis. *New Republic*, Oct. 19, 1992.

"Biographies of the Republican candidates." *Facts on File*, Aug. 20, 1992.

"Dan's big plan." SIDNEY BLUMENTHAL. *Vanity Fair*, Sep. 1992.

"Being Dan Quayle." MIMI SWARTZ and DAVID BURNETT. *Life*, Sep. 1992.

"Airhead apparent." PAUL SLANSKY and STEVE RADLAUER. *Esquire*, Aug. 1992.

"I'm here. . . ." HOWARD FINEMAN and CLARA BINGHAM. *Newsweek*, Aug. 24, 1992.

"Quayle's moment." ANDREW ROSENTHAL. *New York Times Magazine*, July 5, 1992.

"But seriously folks. . . ." LANCE MORROW. *Time*, June 1, 1992.

The Dan Quayle Dictionary. JAMES WYNBRANDT. Berkley, 1992.

Imperial Caddy: The Rise of Dan Quayle in America and the Decline and Fall of Practically Everything Else. JOE QUEENAN. Disney, 1992.

What a Waste It Is to Lose One's Mind: The Unauthorized Autobiography of Dan Quayle. DEBORAH WERKSMAN, et al. Quayle Quarterly, 1992.

"Quayle alert." FRED BARNES. *New Republic*, May 27, 1991.

"The right's point man." TOM MORGANTHAU. "Why Quayle is doomed." JONATHAN ALTER. "The Quayle handicap. . . ." EVAN THOMAS. "Rx for the veep." *Newsweek*, May 20, 1991.

"Why not the best? . . ." DAN GOODGAME. "Is he really that bad?" MICHAEL DUFFY. *Time*, May 20, 1991.

"A talk with. . . ." LEE WALCZAK and DOUGLAS HARBRECHT. *Business Week*, Apr. 1, 1991.

"Quayle so far." DAVID BROCK. *Commentary*, Jan. 1991.

The Official Unauthorized Biography of J. Danforth Quayle. Electric Strawberry, 1991.

"Quayle, (James) Dan(forth)." *Current Biography* June 1989.

Quayle Droppings: The Politics of J. Danforth Quayle. ARTHUR F. IDE. Liberal Press, 1988.

Rabin, Yitzhak (1922–) On February 19, 1992, Israeli general and former prime minister Rabin defeated Shimon Peres for leadership of the Labor Party. His country was ready for a change after the ultra-conservative hard-line seven years of the Yitzhak Shamir government, and Rabin was widely seen as a military-minded leader who could also be somewhat flexible, providing much-wanted security while at the same time moving toward real negotiations on Arab-Israeli matters. In the June 23rd general election, Labor won enough of a plurality to form a coalition government without the Likud Party, and Rabin once again became prime minister.

His early months in office seemed to bear out expectations, as he made clear his desire to pursue meaningful peace talks with the Palestinians and Arab states, making several gestures of conciliation. With Rabin's initiatives, Israel and Syria together made it possible to resume the stalled Arab-Israeli peace talks in Washington in late August. Earlier in August, Rabin had visited Washington to discuss the whole range of outstanding issues with President Bush and Secretary of State Baker, and had come away with loan guarantees that had been denied the Shamir government. But the Palestinian Intifada (Uprising) continued, as did conservative Israeli opposition to conciliation, and Rabin still faced a task that had frustrated Israeli, Arab, and western leaders for more than four decades.

Rabin suffered a considerable setback late in 1992, after his decision to expel more than 400 Arab fundamentalists into Lebanon, for Lebanon, with the approval of Syria, refused to accept the exiles, leaving them in a sort of no-man's-land between the countries. They became martyrs, their situation triggering new Palestinian disturbances, the killings of many demonstrators by Israeli forces, and great internal and international pressure on Rabin to solve the problem, which had not been cleared up by year's end.

Jerusalem-born Rabin has spent all of his adult life involved in war and politics. He was an officer in the Israeli frontline fighting force, the Palmach, from 1943 to 1948, through the Israeli War of Independence (First Arab-Israeli War), and remained a soldier, rising to become commander in chief of the Northern Command (1956–59), Deputy Chief of Staff (1960–64), and Chief of Staff (1964–68), achieving the rank of major-general. He was later Israeli ambassador to the United States (1968–73). Rabin entered the Knesset (parliament) in 1974, in that year briefly serving as Minister of Labour, and then becoming head of the Labour Party and Prime Minister, holding both posts until 1977. He became Defense Minister in the 1984 coalition government, taking personal responsibility for the repression of the Palestinian Intifida (Uprising) that began in 1988. He has published *The Rabin Memoirs* (1979) and, with Uri Lubrani, *Israel's Lebanon Policy: Where To?* (1984). He was educated at the Kadoorie Agricultural School and at military colleges. He is married to the former Leah Schlossberg, and has two children.

FURTHER READING

"Rabin offers. . . ." MARIE COLVIN. *Sunday Times*, Dec. 6, 1992.
"Yitzhak Rabin. . . ." *Time*, Nov. 30, 1992.
"Hawk with an olive branch." *Observer*, June 28, 1992.
"Talk of peace from. . . ." SARAH HELM and DAVID HOROWITZ. *Independent*, Apr. 17, 1992.
"The view from Jerusalem." *U.S. News & World Report*, Apr. 16, 1990.

Rackmil, Milton R. (1903–92) New York City-born Rackmil, a leading American entertainment industries figure, began his career in the late 1920s, as an accountant with the Brunswick Radio Corporation. In 1934, he was a founder of Decca Records, rising to the company presidency in 1949. At Decca, he and his colleagues created a massive catalog of low-priced popular records, featuring many of the top entertainers of the day. Decca was one of the first of the major record companies to move into unbreakable longplaying records. In 1951–52, Rackmil acquired Universal Pictures for Decca, and was also president of Universal (1952–62), a period in which Universal, previously a B-picture maker, became a major movie company. After the acquisition of Universal by MCA in 1962, Rackmil stayed on as president of Universal and Decca, also becoming vice-chairman of MCA. After his 1972 retirement, he became president of the Record Industry Association. He was survived by his wife, the former Joan Crane,

a daughter, and a brother. (d. New York City; Apr. 2, 1992)

FURTHER READING

Obituary. *The Times* (of London), Apr. 20, 1992.
Obituary. *Variety*, Apr.13, 1992.
Obituary. *New York Times*, Apr. 5, 1992.

Rafsanjani, Ali Akbar Hashemi

(1934–) Iranian President Rafsanjani won a major electoral victory in May, when his supporters, organized as the Society of Combatant Clergymen, won a decisive majority in the Iranian parliament, displacing the majority held by hard-line Islamic fundamentalists. Rafsanjani, who had greatly changed his stance after the Persian Gulf War, continued to reach out to other Islamic nations and to some extent also to the West in 1992, attempting to encourage foreign investment in Iran and to portray himself as a stable, reliable national leader. At the same time, he made a series of large-scale armaments purchases, rearming Iran, and very clearly attempted to acquire atomic weapons and delivery systems. He also did not move to lift his death sentence on author Salman Rushdie for writing *The Satanic Verses* (1988). International human rights organizations continued to call attention to his government's multiple abuses of human rights.

Although Rafsanjani's opponents had been defeated during 1992, the always-strong threat of a return to full-scale Islamic fundamentalism remained. Iran faced enormous economic problems, that generated riots in several cities in April and May 1992, as poverty and misery deepened, widespread official corruption grew, and ever-increasing populations created what seemed to be unsolvable problems. Rafsanjani's political survival—and in Iran that has often meant physical survival, as well—was far from assured as 1992 closed.

Rafsanjani was long associated with Ayatollah Ruhollah Khomeini. He became a key figure in Iranian politics as speaker of the national assembly during the 1980s. As speaker, he sometimes played the role of hard-line Iranian politician, as in 1989 when he called for the assassination of the author Salman Rushdie for writing *The Satanic Verses*, but sometimes functioned as a relative moderate, who made very tentative overtures to the West in a bid to re-establish broken relationships. He became president of Iran in August 1989, during the period of maneuvering that followed the death of Ayatollah Khomeini. Facing a mounting economic crisis at home and growing American power in the Middle East, he took a markedly conciliatory attitude after the Persian Gulf War defeat of Iraq, calling for economic ties with the West and other Gulf nations. This also extended to the American and other European hostages held in Lebanon by the Iranian-controlled Hezbollah (Party of God). In the autumn of 1991, following a September 10–13 Tehran meeting between United Nations Secretary-General Javier Pérez de Cuéllar and Rafsanjani, 9 of the 11 remaining Lebanon Western hostages were released. Rafsanjani's personal life has been kept very private, but it is known that he is married and has several children.

FURTHER READING

"Who's sitting pretty. . . ." *Business Week*, Mar. 11, 1991.

"Rafsanjani, Ali Akbar Hashemi." *Current Biography*, Nov. 1989.

" 'Rafsanjani would have. . . .' " ALFRED BALK. *World Press Review*, Aug. 1989.

"Iran without Khomeini." MICHAEL LEDEEN. *American Spectator*, Aug. 1989.

"Burying the passions. . . ." BILL HEWITT. *Newsweek*, June 19, 1989.

"Santa satan?. . . ." MAGGIE MAHAR. *Barron's*, Jan. 16, 1989.

Raitt, Bonnie (Bonnie Lynn Raitt; 1949–)

In June 1992, singer-composer Bonnie Raitt and her father, singer John Raitt, now 75, did their first-ever concert together. She joined him before a sold-out Boston Pops audience in "They Say It's Wonderful" from *Annie Get Your Gun* and "Hey There" from *The Pajama Game,* and he joined in her 1975 "I'm Blowin' Away."

Their joint concert was a highlight in a year full of highlights for Bonnie Raitt. Building even further on the hugely successful comeback achieved in 1989 with her hit and award-winning album *Nick of Time*, and carried even further by her 1991 hit album *Luck of the Draw*, 1992 brought yet another hit album, *Something to Talk About*. Raitt won a female pop vocal single Grammy for "Something to Talk About," the title song of that Grammy-nominated album, and a solo rock vocal Grammy for the title song "Luck of the Draw." She also shared a duo or group rock vocal Grammy with Delbert McClinton for "Good Man, Good Woman." Her work also continued to sell very well, *Luck of the Draw* joined *Nick of Time* at the 3 million sales level early in 1992, and *Something to Talk About* was clearly headed into the same range.

California-born Raitt became a popular folk and blues figure in the early 1970s with such albums as *Bonnie Raitt* (1971), *Give It Up* (1972), *Streetlights* (1974), and *Sweet Forgiveness* (1977). Far less popular in the late 1970s and throughout the 1980s, she was dropped by her old record company, Warner. She scored a phenomenal success in February 1990 with a sweep of the Grammy awards, winning Best Album, Best Female Pop Vocal, and best female rock vocal for her *Nick of Time* album and its title song, and best traditional blues recording for "I'm in the Mood," a duet with John Lee Hooker on Hooker's album, *The Healer*. Raitt attended Radcliffe College. She married actor Michael O'Keefe in 1991.

FURTHER READING

"Raitt, Bonnie." *Current Biography*, Aug. 1990.

"Bonnie Raitt. . . ." JAMES HENKE. *Rolling Stone*, May 3, 1990.

"20 questions. . . ." PAUL ENGLEMAN and JOHN REZEK. *Playboy*, Nov. 1989.

"Veteran rocker. . . ." KIM HUBBARD. *People*, Apr. 24, 1989.

Ramaphosa, Cyril (1953–) Widely regarded as Nelson Mandela's political heir, labor leader Cyril Ramaphosa became secretary-general of the African National Congress (ANC) in July 1991. As such, he is the chief day-to-day operating officer of the organization, ultimately responsible for all the specifics, from office administration to negotiation. As a practical matter, Ramaphosa is the key ANC negotiator in the long, off-and-on Codesa (Convention for a Democratic South Africa) talks with the South African government, aimed at leading to an interim government and a constitutional convention. During 1992, he also spoke for the ANC on the whole range of matters affecting the South African freedom movement. He is expected to play a major role in a new multi-racial South Africa.

Johannesburg-born Ramaphosa became a South African anti-apartheid leader while at the University of Turfloop as chair of the South African Students' organization. He was imprisoned for his activities for 17 months while a law student. He earned his law degree at the University of South Africa. In 1981, he became a legal advisor to the Council of Unions of South Africa. In 1982, he became General Secretary of the National Union of Mineworkers, and in the decade that followed helped build the union into a powerful force with more than 275,000 members. Ramaphosa led the union through the 1987 mine strike; its failure did not break the union or end his leadership.

FURTHER READING

"A younger generation. . . ." ROBIN KNIGHT. *U.S. News & World Report*, Dec. 30, 1991.

Ramos, Fidel V. "Eddie" (1928–)
The new President of The Phillippines was elected on May 11, 1992 for a single six-year term, with 24 percent of the popular vote. He succeeded Corazon Aquino, who supported his candidacy, and whose last great accomplishment in office was to see her country through a free, democratic, and relatively orderly election without a right-wing coup or a great step-up in guerrilla warfare from the left.

Ramos recognized that he was taking office in a greatly troubled country, which still faced all the problems of massive population increase, 20–25 percent unemployment figures, deepening poverty, and official corruption that had plagued Aquino. Inaugurated on June 30, he called for an end to the long civil war with the left and the more recent right-wing military insurgency, attempting to negotiate ceasefires and amnesties with both groups. He also called for an end to government corruption and for a new focus on foreign investment, especially from Japan, though at the same time stressing traditional ties with the United States. A very early right-wing response was a series of bombings on the day of his inauguration. During the early months of his administration he moved forward on several major power plant projects.

A career soldier, Ramos is a member of a highly placed family, the son of former Foreign Minister Narcisco Ramos, and the brother of Senator Leticia Ramos Shahani. As a young soldier, he saw service in Korea, and later in Vietnam. When Ferdinand Marcos took full power in 1972, thereafter ruling by martial law and decree, Ramos became head of the Philippine Constabulary, a key instrument of government repression. Under Marcos, Ramos became Army Deputy Chief of Staff in 1981. In February 1986, then Army Chief of Staff, he became a key figure in the Philippine revolution that toppled Marcos, with Defense Minister Juan Ponce Enrile going over into support of Corazon Aquino, taking decisive sections of the armed forces with them. Ramos became Secretary of National Defense in 1988. He was educated at the National

University of Manila, the United States Military Academy at West Point, and the University of Illinois. He is married and has five children.

FURTHER READING

"An olive branch. . . ." *Economist*, Aug. 1, 1992.
"Fast Eddie. . . ." ALAN BERLOW. *New Republic*. June 15, 1992.

Tony Randall (right) and Lynn Redgrave.

Randall, Tony (Leonard Rosenberg; 1920–) The year 1992 saw the balance of the first season of Randall's National Actors Theater. The theater's second production (the first was *The Crucible*, opening in November 1991) was Georges Feydeau's farce *A Little Hotel on the Side*, starring Maryann Plunkett, Lynn Redgrave, Rob Lowe, and Randall, which received mixed reviews. The third, directed by Randall, was Henrik Ibsen's *The Master Builder*, starring Earle Hyman, Redgrave, and Plunkett, which also received mixed reviews. In both productions, Plunkett and Redgrave were singled out for critical praise. For the theater's second season, the company moved to Broadway's Lyceum Theater. Its first production was a revival of Anton Chekhov's *The Seagull*, starring Tyne Daly and Jon Voight, which opened in November to mixed reviews. Forthcoming were a production of George Bernard Shaw's *St. Joan*, starring Maryann Plunkett in the title role, and a revival of *Three Men on a Horse*, starring Randall and Jack Klugman.

Tulsa-born Randall has played in a wide variety of stage and screen roles during his five-decades-long career. He is best known by far for his role as Felix opposite Jack Klugman in the long-running television series "The Odd Couple" (1970–74) developed from Neil Simon's 1965 play of that name; Randall won a 1975 Emmy award for his performance in the series. He also starred in "Mr. Peepers" (1952–55), "The Tony Randall Show" (1976–77), and "Love Sydney" (1981–83). Much of his work on stage was in the 1940s and early 1950s. His many films include *Oh Men Oh Women* (1957), *Pillow Talk* (1959), *Send Me No Flowers* (1964), and *The Alphabet Murders* (1966). His autobiographical reminiscences were published in *Which Reminds Me* (1989). Randall attended Northwestern University, Columbia, and the Neighborhood Playhouse. Randall's wife, Florence Mitchell, died in 1992.

FURTHER READING

"Tony Randall. . . ." JOHN HEILPERN. *Vogue*, Jan. 1992.
"A bargain on Broadway. . . ." *U.S. News & World Report*, Dec. 16, 1991.

Rao, P.V. Narasimha (Pamulaparti Venkate Narasimha Rao; 1921–) Named Indian Prime Minister on June 20, 1991, after the assassination of Indian Prime Minister Rajiv Gandhi, Rao was initially expected to serve as a caretaker, governing until an orderly new election could be assured. It did not happen that way; once in power, Rao held on to it, introducing major economic changes that changed India's socialist and central planning commitment to one focused on the development of a market economy. He greatly cut the national budget, devalued the currency, welcomed multinational corporations, and moved toward closure of many state-owned industries. There were great adverse impacts on the great masses of India's poor, who lost some of what was already a very slim social services support network; Rao felt that these were acceptable human costs of his austerity and rebuilding program.

It is not clear whether Rao's austerity measures contributed to the rise of India's Hindu fundamentalist parties, or whether a more substantial reason was the loss of powerful secular leadership when the last of the Gandhi-Nehru prime ministers was assassinated; but what is clear is that during Rao's stewardship the Hindu fundamentalist movement flared throughout India, generating the Hindu destruction of the historic Ayodhya mosque on December 6, 1992. The attack ignited Hindu attacks on Muslims throughout India, and answering attacks on Hindus in Pakistan and other Muslim countries, while the Rao government hesitated; when Rao moved, much of the damage had been done. India's ethnic and religious problems continued to destabilize the country and to threaten Indian democracy; they would have to be addressed by Rao or his successor.

Uttar Pradesh-born Rao is a long-time Congress Party leader, who supported Indira Gandhi during her rise to power, and went with her faction when the party split in 1969. He was chief minister of the state of Andra Pradesh (1971–73), and held several cabinet positions thereafter, including four years as Indian foreign minister (1980–84) . He is also a well known translator and writer. Rao attended the universities of Bombay and Nagpur. He has eight children.

FURTHER READING

"Doing the splits: India." *Economist*, Aug. 22, 1992.
"The accidental prime minister." Subrata Chakravarty. *Forbes*, July 20, 1992.
"Rao, P.V. Narasimha." *Current Biography*, Jan. 1992.
Prime Minister P. V. Narasimha Rao: The Scholar and the Statesman. South Asia Books, 1991.

Rather, Dan (1931–) Though still generally ranked second behind Peter Jennings' "World News Tonight" on ABC, Dan Rather and the "CBS Evening News" made something of a comeback during 1992. During one week in September, CBS's news show was—for the first time since December 1990—ranked number one, largely because of Rather's strong coverage of the damage caused by Hurricane Andrew, followed up with a "48 Hours" primetime special. But even without the emphasis on disaster coverage that has made some observers jokingly call him "Hurricane Dan," CBS made a stronger showing. Rather got a strong boost from CBS's coverage of the Winter Olympics in February, which highlighted the presidential primaries between Olympics events, and built on that with more emphasis on personal issues, like money and health. In late spring, Rather also gained ground with strong coverage of the aftermath of the Los Angeles riots, as part of a wider plan to provide more coverage of West Coast news. On election night, CBS nearly tied ABC in ratings, and indeed surpassed it in the last half-hour of evening coverage. Earlier in the year, Rather found his evening news bumped to an earlier hour and CBS's convention coverage preempted by baseball's All-Star game.

During 1992, Rather also continued the prime-time news series "48 Hours," including specials on the Kennedy assassination and Malcolm X, both triggered by current movies, and "Crazy About Elvis" in August, for the 15th anniversary of Presley's death. In December, Rather traveled to Somalia, reporting live as U.S. forces moved to intervene.

Texas-born Rather became CBS news anchor in 1981, climaxing a long career that began in Houston in the early 1950s. His breakthrough came when, as a young CBS correspondent in Dallas, he reported live to the nation on the November 22, 1963, assassination of President John F. Kennedy. After working as a CBS White House correspondent in 1964, and then abroad, he returned to Washington as CBS White House correspondent (1966–74), playing a substantial role as an investigative reporter during the unfolding Watergate affair and the resignation of Richard Nixon, before succeeding Walter Cronkite as one of the three chief American reporters and interpreters of the news. His written works include *The Palace Guard* (1974), with Gary Gates; *The Camera Never Blinks* (1977), with Mickey Herskowitz; and his personal memoirs *I Remember: Fifty Years Ago in America* (1991), with Peter Wyden. Rather's B.A. was from Sam Houston State College, in 1951. He is married to Jean Goebel; they have two children.

FURTHER READING

"Dan Rather is. . . ." ROBERT DRAPER. *Texas*, Nov. 1991.
Anchors: Brokaw, Jennings, Rather and the Evening News. ROBERT GOLDBERG and GERALD J. GOLDBERG. Carol, 1990.
Dan Rather and Other Rough Drafts. MARTHA A. TURNER. Eakin, 1987.

Rauh, Joseph Louis (1911-92)

Cincinnati-born Rauh graduated from Harvard University magna cum laude, from Harvard Law School first in his class, and went to Washington as clerk to Justice Benjamin Cardozo and then to Justice Felix Frankfurter. During the late 1930s, he was also a counsel to several government agencies. After World War II service, he returned to Washington to practice law. In 1947, he was a founder of Americans for Democratic Action, a liberal organization that stressed anti-communism during the McCarthy period. As a lawyer, he represented several civil rights organizations and labor unions, including the United Auto Workers, the Brotherhood of Sleeping Car Porters, and the Leadership Conference on Civil Rights, and was for some years a board member of the National Association for the Advancement of Colored People (NAACP). During the McCarthy period, he represented several prominent people before Congressional committees, including Arthur Miller and Lillian Hellman. With Clyde W. Summer and Herman Benson, he published *Union Democracy and Landrum Griffin* (1986). He was survived by his wife, the former Olie Westheimer, and two sons. (d. Washington, D. C.; September 3, 1992)

FURTHER READING

Obituary. *The Times* (of London), Sep. 7, 1992.
Obituary. *New York Times*, Sep. 5, 1992.

Ray, Satyajit (1921–92)

Calcutta-born Ray, the child of Bengali intellectuals, was by far the greatest of Indian filmmakers, and a major figure in world cinema. He introduced modern Indian film to a world audience with his first film, *Pather Panchali* (1955), based on the Bibhuti Bhusan Banerji novel about village life in Bengal, with music by Ravi Shankar. The film, which he made on a budget of less than $40,000, shooting on weekends over a three-year period, won a special jury prize at Cannes. He followed it with *Aparijito* (1956) and *The World of Apu* (1959), the three films together forming his celebrated "Apu Trilogy." Ray wrote and directed all three, and did so for all the rest of his films, later also creating costumes and writing the music for many of his works. His films included such classics as *The Goddess* (1960), *The Lonely Wife* (1964), *Days and Nights in the Forest* (1970), *Distant Thunder* (1973), *The Chess Players* (1977), and *The Home and the World* (1984). His last film, *The Stranger*, opened in New York in May 1992. He was survived his wife, Bijoya, and a son, the director Sandip Ray. (d. Calcutta; April 23, 1992)

FURTHER READING

"Farewell and hail." STANLEY KAUFFMANN. *New Republic*, June 15, 1992.
"To western audiences. . . ." GOWRI RAMNARAYAN. *Interview*, June 1992.
Obituary. *Variety*, Apr. 27, 1992.
Obituary. *New York Times*, Apr. 24, 1992.
Obituary. *Independent*, Apr. 24, 1992.
Obituary. *The Times* (of London), Apr. 24, 1992.
Satyajit Ray: The Inner Eye. ANDREW ROBINSON. University of California Press, 1990.
Satyajit Ray: A Film. SHYAM BENEGAL. South Asia Books, 1988.
Satyajit Ray: A Study of His Films. BEN NYCE. Praeger/Greenwood, 1988.

Reagan, Ronald Wilson (1911–)

In a very real sense, the Reagan era did not end until November 3, 1992, with the defeat of his successor, President George Bush. The $4 trillion federal deficit, health care crisis, worsening economy, anti-abortion rights stand—all the key issues hammered home by the Clinton campaign to the detriment of Bush—were products of the Reagan years and the Reagan policies that Bush had inherited and been unable or unwilling to change. Ironically, the Iran-Contra scandal, which damaged Bush so greatly in the final days of the campaign, was a scandal that had tainted the latter Reagan administration years; but in August 1992, two months before it hit Bush hard, Iran-Contra prosecutor Lawrence Walsh sent a letter to Reagan, finally ending any investigation of Reagan for possible complicity in the affair.

Still enormously popular, however controversial some of his actions and policies might have been while in office, Reagan injected a fresh, upbeat note into an otherwise rather sour and negative August Republican National Convention. He supported George Bush without visible reservation, appearing with him and attacking Democratic presidential candidate Bill Clinton.

Reagan continued to pursue a moderately busy schedule in retirement, speaking, taping messages in lieu of personal appearances and for broadcast, and receiving visitors, including some visiting heads of state. On April 13, he narrowly escaped injury in Las Vegas, when a man rushed the stage as he was speaking, and smashed a crystal honorary statue that Reagan had just received from the National Association of Broadcasters. On December 4, in a speech to the Oxford Union, Reagan urged NATO action in Bosnia-Herzegovina, including air strikes against Greater Serbia. He also urged use of military force to ensure the distribution of humanitarian aid in Somalia and Sudan.

For Illinois-born Ronald Reagan, the presidency was the culmination of his second major career. After briefly working as a sportscaster in the Midwest, he had became a film actor in the late 1930s and early 1940s playing in such movies as *Knute Rockne—All American* (1940) and *King's Row* (1942). He headed the Screen Actors Guild (1947–52). He was governor of California (1967–75), and after two unsuccessful runs for the Republican presidential nomination was ultimately nominated and defeated Jimmy Carter in the 1980 election. He notably began his presidency with the hardline anti-communism of his "evil empire" speech and ended with the series of treaties and Reagan-Gorbachev meetings that, under his successor George Bush, brought the long Cold War to a close. Reagan also presided over the build-up of a national debt that approached two trillion dollars by the time he left office.

After leaving office, Reagan was largely able to put the Iran-Contra affair behind him, successfully claiming executive privilege as to his diaries during the trial of John Poindexter, and limiting his involvement to videotaped testimony at that trial. November 1990 saw publication of his bestselling autobiography *An American Life*; his wife had published her view in 1989 in *My Turn: The Memoirs of Nancy Reagan*. The Reagan Presidential library at Simi Valley, California, opened on November 4, 1991.

Reagan's B.A. was from Eureka College in 1932. He was previously married to actress Jane Wyman (1940–48); they had two children. He married Nancy Davis Reagan in 1952; they had two more children.

FURTHER READING

"The Real Reagan Record." *National Review*. Aug. 31, 1992. Special Issue.
Reckoning with Reagan: America and Its President in the 1980s. MICHAEL SCHALLER. Oxford University Press, 1992.
The Reagan Presidency: An Actor's Finest Performance. WILBUE EDEL. Hippocrene, 1992.
The Bully Pulpit: The Presidential Leadership of Ronald Reagan. WILLIAM K. MUIR. ICS Press, 1992.
Ronald Reagan: The Great Communicator. KURT RITTER and DAVID HENRY. Greenwood, 1992.
"Ronald Wilson Reagan." A. ROYCE DALBY. *Ad Astra*, July–Aug. 1991.
"Ronald and. . . ." DANIEL WATTENBERG. *Insight*, July 22, 1991.
President Reagan: A Role of a Lifetime. LOU CANNON. Simon & Schuster, 1991.
A Shining City on a Hill: Ronald Reagan's Economic Rhetoric, 1951–1989. AMOS KIEWE and DAVIS W. HOUCK. Greenwood, 1991.
Ronald Reagan. RENEE SCHWARTZBERG. Chelsea House, 1991.
Ronald Reagan. JOHN DEVANEY. Walker, 1990.
Reagan As President: Contemporary Views of the Man, His Politics, and His Policies. PAUL BOYER, ed. I. R. Dee, 1990.
The Reagan Years. HODDING CARTER. Braziller, 1988.
Early Reagan: The Rise to Power. ANNE EDWARDS. Morrow, 1987.

Redford, Robert (Charles Robert Redford, Jr.; 1937–) Celebrated actor, director, and producer Redford scored a major hit late in 1992, with release of his film *A River Runs Through It*, which he directed and produced, a process he described in a book released at the same time. The family drama, set in Montana from 1910 to 1935, centered around fly fishing; it starred Tom Skerritt, Craig Sheffer, Brad Pitt, and Brenda Blethn; Richard Friedenberg wrote the screenplay, adapted from the Norman Maclean story. In 1992, actor Redford also starred in Phil Alden Robinson's well-received fast-paced comedy thriller hit *Sneakers*, a film complete with computer hackers, national security risks, assorted

murders, in a cast that included Dan Aykroyd, Ben Kingsley, Sidney Poitier, Mary McDonnell, River Phoenix, and James Earl Jones.

Redford also co-produced and narrated Michael Apted's *Incident at Oglala*, a documentary about the 1975 Pine Ridge reservation armed encounter that left two FBI agents dead and Native American leader Leonard Pelletier serving two consecutive life prison terms; it premiered at the Sundance film festival in February 1992. Forthcoming was a starring role opposite Demi Moore in Adrian Lyne's film *Indecent Proposal*, about a Las Vegas gambler who pays $1 million to sleep with Moore, cast as the wife of another gambler.

California-born Redford began his spectacular film career in the late 1960s. His first starring role was in *Barefoot in the Park* (1967), a role he had played on Broadway in 1963. He went on to star in such classics as *Butch Cassidy and the Sundance Kid* (1969), *Jeremiah Johnson* (1972), *The Way We Were* (1973), *The Sting* (1973), and *All the President's Men* (1976). He later directed the Oscar-winning *Ordinary People* (1980), directed and starred in *The Natural* (1984), starred in *Out of Africa* (1985), directed and produced *The Milagro Beanfield War* (1988), and starred in *Havana* (1990). During the 1980s and early 1990s, his film institute at Sundance, Colorado, became a mecca for moviemakers from all over the world. Redford attended the University of Colorado, Pratt Institute, and the American Academy of Dramatic Arts. He married Lola

Jean Van Wagenen in 1958; they later separated. They have two children.

FURTHER READING

"Robert Redford." GABRIEL TRIP. *US*, Nov. 1992.
"Robert Redford. . . ." PHILIP CAPUTO. *Esquire*, Sep. 1992.
"Redford talks. . . ." NEIL GABLER. *New York*, Dec. 10, 1990.
"Hollywood goes. . . ." MERLE LINDA WOLIN. *New Republic*, Apr. 16, 1990.
Robert Redford. BRUCE CROWTHER. Hippocrene, 1985.

Redgrave, Lynn (1943–) For British stage and screen star Lynn Redgrave, 1992 was another diverse year in the theater. In January, she starred opposite Tony Randall, Maryann Plunkett, and Rob Lowe, in the National Actors Theater revival of the Georges Feydeau farce *A Little Hotel on the Side*. The production received mixed reviews, but Redgrave and Plunkett were generally praised for their performances. In March, she starred in a second National Actors Theater production, this one a revival of Henrik Ibsen's *The Master Builder*, with Earle Hyman in the title role and co-starring Plunkett; Tony Randall directed. Again, Redgrave and Plunkett were generally well reviewed in a production that was not. In July, Redgrave starred opposite John Clark in A. R. Gurney's play *Love Letters*, in Santa Barbara. Redgrave spent much of the balance of 1992 and was projected to go into 1993 touring in her one-woman show *Shakespeare for My Father*.

London-born Redgrave quickly emerged as a star in the film *Georgy Girl* (1966; she was nominated for an Oscar), and went on to pursue a very diverse career on both sides of Atlantic, in theater, films, and television, acting in such works as *Tom Jones* (1963) and *The Happy Hooker* (1975) on screen; *St. Joan* (1977) and *Sweet Sue* (1987) on stage; and "Centennial" (1978), "House Calls" (1984) and "Chicken Soup" (1989) in television. She appeared on stage in a notable 1990–91 London production of *The Three Sisters*. In 1992 she published *This Is Living: How I Found Health and Happiness*.

Redgrave attended London's Central School of Speech and Drama. She married director John Clark in 1967; they have three children. She is the daughter of actress Rachel Kempson and actor Michael Redgrave, the sister of actress Vanessa Redgrave and actor-director Corin Redgrave, and the aunt of actresses Natasha Richardson, Joely Richardson, and Jemma Redgrave. (For photo, see Randall, Tony.)

FURTHER READING

"Fuming over. . . ." KAREN S. SCHNEIDER. *People*, Mar. 11, 1991.
"The Redgrave sisters." RODDY McDOWALL. *Interview*, Feb. 1991.
"Catching up with. . . ." LEE RANDALL. *Weight Watchers Magazine*, Aug. 1990.
Life among the Redgraves. RACHEL KEMPSON. NAL-Dutton, 1988.

Redgrave, Vanessa (1937–)   Once again, celebrated stage and screen star Vanessa Redgrave scored a major success, this time performing in James Ivory's 1992 *Howard's End*, Ruth Prawer Jhabvala's adaptation of the 1910 E.M. Forster novel. The film, set in an English country house of that name in pre-World War I Britain, co-starred Anthony Hopkins, Emma Thompson, James Wilby, Helena Bonham Carter, Prunella Scales, Joseph Bennett, Adrian Ross Magenty, Jemma Redgrave, and Sam West. In 1992 Redgrave also starred as Sister Crucifix in Beppe Cino's film *Di Ceria dell'Unore (The Plague Sower)*, opposite Franco Nero and Fernando Rey. The film was set in 1946 in a sanitorium for the terminally ill, thought by some to represent defeated war-torn Italy. An-

other 1992 film in which Redgrave starred was Yevgeny Yevtushenko's film *Stalin's Funeral*.

Vanessa Redgrave is one of the most celebrated stage and screen actresses of her time, emerging in the early 1960s in the classics and then in her very notable starring role in the stage version of Muriel Spark's *The Prime of Miss Jean Brodie* (1966). She reached world audiences on screen in such films as *Isadora* (1968), *Julia* (1977), *Agatha* (1978), and in television's *Playing For Time* (1979), *The Bostonians* (1983), and *Comrades* (1986). Her recent work includes Peter Hall's acclaimed revival of Tennessee Williams's *Orpheus Descending* (1989; on Broadway and on television in 1990); and a London stage version of *The Three Sisters* (1990–91). Active in far left politics for many years, and notably as a supporter of the Palestine Liberation Organization, she also produced and narrated *The Palestinians* (1977).

Vanessa Redgrave attended the Central School of Speech and Drama (1955–57). She was formerly married to director Tony Richardson, and has a son and two daughters, the actresses Natasha Richardson and Joely Richardson. She is the daughter of actor Michael Redgrave and actress Rachel Kempson, and the sister of Lynn Redgrave and actor-director Corin Redgrave, father of Jemma Redgrave.

FURTHER READING

"A woman of conscience." NICHOLAS WROE. *New Statesman and Society*, Oct. 4, 1991.
"Who's afraid of. . . ." STEPHEN SCHIFF. *Vanity Fair*, July 1991.
"Fuming over. . . ." KAREN S. SCHNEIDER. *People*, Mar. 11, 1991.
"The Redgrave sisters." RODDY McDOWALL. *Interview*, Feb. 1991.
"Vanessa ascending. . . ." WILLIAM A. HENRY, III. *Time*, Oct. 9, 1989.
Life among the Redgraves. RACHEL KEMPSON. NAL-Dutton, 1988.

Reed, Robert (Robert Reitz, Jr.; 1933–92) Illinois-born Reed, a versatile American actor, attended Northwestern University, the University of London, and the Royal Academy of Dramatic Art. He began his career in the American theater, beginning to do television series guest appearances in 1959. From 1961 to 1965, he starred opposite E.G. Marshall as the father-

and-son team of lawyers in the classic television series "The Defenders." He was by far best-known, however, for his starring role as Mike Brady, the father in "The Brady Bunch" (1969–74), a very popular television series that is still seen regularly in syndicated reruns. He also appeared in several other television series, including "Mannix" (1969–75) and "Nurse" (1981–82), and in many television and several theatrical films. He received Emmy nominations for his roles in "Roots," "Rich Man, Poor Man," and a segment of "Medical Center." He was survived by a daughter and his mother. (d. Pasadena, California; May12, 1992)

FURTHER READING

"An actor's last wish." TOM GLIATTO. *People*, May 25, 1992.
Obituary. *Variety*, May 18, 1992.
Obituary. *New York Times*, May 14, 1992.

Reeve, Christopher (1952–) Still Superman to mass worldwide audiences, Reeve continues to pursue a varied stage and screen career. In 1992, he starred on screen in Peter Bogdanovich's farce *Noises Off*, based on the Michael Frayn play, in a cast that included Carol Burnett, Michael Caine, Denholm Elliott, Julie Hagerty, Marilu Henner, Mark Linn-Baker, and Nicollette Sheridan. He also starred as a problemed Boston architect opposite Roxanne Hart as his wife in the television family drama *The Last Ferry Home*. Another starring television movie role was as a Roman Catholic priest who hears a murderer's confession and then solves the murder in *Mortal Sins*. He played a third role on television opposite Jaclyn Smith in *Nightmare in the Daylight*. Reeve also narrated Jill Janow's documentary *Fear and the Muse: The Story of Anna Akhmatova*, a biographical work featuring readings from the Russian poet's works. Forthcoming was a starring role in James Ivory's film *Remains of the Day*, Harold Pinter's screenplay adaptation of the Kazuo Ishiguro novel, co-starring Anthony Hopkins, Emma Thompson, and James Fox.

New York City-born Reeve has appeared on Broadway in *A Matter of Gravity* (1978) and *Fifth of July* (1980), and has played a wide range of roles in regional theater, also working in London opposite Vanessa Redgrave and Wendy

Hiller in *The Aspern Papers* (1984). His recent work in the theater includes a New York Shakespeare Festival production of Shakespeare's *Winter's Tale* (1989) and a London stage production of Chekhov's *The Three Sisters* (1990–91), with Lynn and Vanessa Redgrave. He has also appeared in such films as *Somewhere in Time* (1980), *Deathtrap* (1982), *Monsignor* (1982), *The Bostonians* (1984), and *Switching Channels* (1988), as well as in several television films, including *The Great Escape* (1988), *Bump in the Night* (1991) and *Death Dreams* (1991). Reeve attended the Juilliard School; his B.A. is from Cornell University. He has two children.

FURTHER READING

Caught in the Act: New York Actors Face to Face. DON SHEWEY and SUSAN SHACTER. NAL-Dutton, 1986.

Rehnquist, William Hubbs (1924–) Ultraconservative Supreme Court Chief Justice Rehnquist, his position strengthened by the replacement of Justice Thurgood Marshall by Justice Clarence Thomas, was widely expected to finally succeed in erasing *Roe v. Wade* and a wide range of other Warren and Burger Court decisions during the 1991–92 term. That did not happen; although a very conservative Court became even more conservative on some matters, a new centrist group emerged, composed of Justices O'Connor, Souter, and Kennedy, which refused to destroy *Roe v. Wade*, and accepted many Warren and Burger Court decisions as precedents.

Rehnquist wrote the majority opinions in *International Society for Krishna Consciousness v. Lee*, ruling that airports could ban groups from soliciting money; and in *U.S. v. Alvarez Machain*, upholding the 1990 U.S. kidnapping of a Mexican doctor suspected of a role in the torture of a U.S. drug enforcement agent. He also voted with the majority in such key cases as *Georgia v. McCollum*, ruling that criminal case defendants could not bar prospective jurors solely because of their race; *Nordlinger v. Hahn*, upholding the right of California to enact Proposition 13, with its unequal property taxes on newcomers; *Hudson v. McMillian*, ruling that the excessive use of force by prison guards was an Eighth Amendment violation even if the prisoner was not seriously hurt; *Riggins v. Nevada*, ruling that the state could not force an insane criminal defendant to take medication during a trial; *U.S. v. Fordice*, ruling that Mississippi had not fulfilled its obligation to desegregate its public colleges and universities; *Lujan v. Defenders of Wildlife*, ruling that the plaintiff, an environmental organization, had no standing to bring suit because no determinable specific interest was at issue; *Lechmere Inc. v. National Labor Relations Board*, ruling that companies did not have to allow union organizers access to such company-owned lands as parking lots and shopping malls; *Keeney v. Tamayo-Reyes*, which sharply limited the federal habeas corpus appeals of state prisoners; *New York v. U.S.*, which invalidated a federal law forcing states to handle their own radioactive waste; and *Freeman v. Pitts*, ruling that schools being operated under court-supervised desegregation orders could be released from those orders step by step. He also joined all of his colleagues in a rare, unanimous landmark sexual harassment decision; in *Franklin v. Gwinnett County Public Schools*, the Court unanimously ruled that Title IX of the 1972 education act allowed a sexually harassed student to collect damages from a school district where a teacher-coach sexually harassed Christine Franklin and ultimately succeeded in pressing her to have sexual intercourse with him. Rehnquist also ruled with the majority that the Coast Guard could continue to intercept at sea and return Haitian refugees to Haiti; and in the decision barring return of RU-486 pills to Leona Benten, a pregnant woman who tried to import them into the U.S. for her personal use, in a challenge to their ban.

Rehnquist wrote the dissenting opinion in the landmark abortion rights case, *Planned Parenthood of Southeastern Pennsylvania v. Casey*, in which a 5–4 majority upheld the essence of *Roe v. Wade*, (which had in 1972 established the right of a woman to choose to have an abortion), while at the same time upholding most of the restrictive 1989 Pennsylvania abortion law and giving the states broader powers to restrict abortion. He also dissented in *Lee v. Weisman*, barring nonsectarian or any other prayers at public high school graduations; *Jacobson v. U.S.*, ruling that the federal government had illegally entrapped a defendant into buying child pornography through the mail; and in *R.A.V. v. St. Paul*, overturning a St. Paul, Minnesota ordinance making sexist, racist, or otherwise bigoted speech or behavior a crime.

During 1992, Rehnquist also published a new book, *Grand Inquests: The Historic Impeachments of Justice Samuel Chase and President Andrew Johnson*.

Milwaukee-born Rehnquist clerked with Supreme Court Justice Robert Jackson (1952–53), and then practiced law in Phoenix until 1969. He was a Washington-based assistant attorney-general (1969–71), was named to the Supreme Court by then-president Nixon in 1971, and was confirmed only after a sharp Senate battle over his allegedly extremely conservative views. President Reagan appointed him Chief Justice in 1986; he was confirmed after another Senate battle. Rehnquist's 1948 B.A. was from Stanford, his 1949 M.A. from Harvard, and his 1952 LL.B. from Stanford. In 1987, he published *The Supreme Court: The Way It Was—the Way It Is*. He married Natalie Cornell in 1953; the couple have two children.

FURTHER READING

"Dead end. . . ." JOHN TUCKER. *New Republic*, May 4, 1992.

Chief Justice William Rehnquist. BOB ITALIA. Abdo & Daughters, 1992.

Turning Right: The Making of the Rehnquist Supreme Court. DAVID G. SAVAGE. Wiley, 1992.

"A new day in court." LAUREN TARSHIS and JAMES EARL HARDY. *Scholastic Update*, Nov. 1, 1991.

Original Intent: Chief Justice Rehnquist and the Course of American Church State Relations. DEREK DAVIS. Prometheus, 1991.

Eight Men and a Lady. HERMAN SCHWARTZ et al. National Press, 1990.

Packing the Courts: The Conservatives' Campaign to Rewrite the Constitution. HERMAN SCHWARTZ. Scribner/Macmillan, 1988.

Reich, Robert Bernard (1946–) President Bill Clinton's incoming Secretary of Labor is a leading political economist, author, and commentator. He and Clinton became close friends while both were Rhodes Scholars at Oxford in the late 1960s and then classmates at Yale Law School. Reich went on to a career in government and education. He was an assistant solicitor general in the U.S. Justice Department (1974–76), and during the Carter years served as director of policy planning for the Federal Trade Commission (1976–81). From 1981 to 1992, he taught at Harvard University's John F. Kennedy School of Government. He was a Senior Advisor to the

Clinton-Gore campaign and was transition team Director of Economic Policy.

Pennsylvania-born Reich's 1968 B.A. was from Dartmouth College, his 1970 M.A. from Oxford University, and his 1973 J.D. from Yale University. His books include *Minding America's Business: The Decline and Rise of the American Economy* (1982, with Ira C. Magaziner), *The Next American Frontier* (1983), *New Deals: The Chrysler Revival and the American System* (1985, with John D. Donahue), *Tales of a New America* (1987), *The Power of Public Ideas* (co-author, 1987), *Public Management in a Democratic Society* (1989), *Resurgent Liberal and Other Unfashionable Prophecies* (1989), and *The Work of Nations: Preparing Ourselves for 21st Century Capitalism* (1991). He has been a contributing editor of *The New Republic* since 1982, and chairman of the editorial board of *The American Prospect* since 1990. He is also a widely seen television commentator, whose work includes hosting and co-authoring the PBS series "Made In America" (1992). He is married to Clare Dalton; they have two children.

FURTHER READING

"The policy hustler. . . ." MICKEY KAUS. *New Republic*, Dec. 7, 1992.

"Clinton's economic idea man." DAN GOODGAME. *Time*, Nov. 23, 1992.
"In education, he trusts." VICTORIA LYTLE. *NEA Today*, Nov. 1991.
"25 who help. . . ." LOUIS KRAAR. *Fortune*, Spring–Summer 1991.
"Harnessing human capital. . . ." SUSAN DENTZER. *U.S. News & World Report*, Apr. 22, 1991.
"American society in a global economy." RICHARD SMITH and DEBORAH SINGER. *Society*, Nov.–Dec. 1990.

Reilly, William Kane (1940–   ) In his final year as Bush administration Environmental Protection Agency (EPA) Administrator, former environmentalist leader Reilly met with a series of major setbacks on a wide range of key issues, as Vice President Dan Quayle, with the approval of President Bush, led a prolonged attack on environmental protection. One of the most striking examples of that attack occurred on June 25, when the EPA issued a new rule that allowed companies to sharply increase their ouput of pollutants without notice or regulatory approval. Another, greatly embarrassing to Reilly, was administration introduction of legislation that would have allowed the logging of millions of acres of old forest on the eve of the Rio de Janiero Earth Summit. At that meeting, Reilly attempted to defend Bush administration policies, but met with worldwide hostility, even from closely allied nations. Perhaps in response, Reilly criticized administration preparation for the summit in a post-meeting evaluation prepared for all EPA employees. In November, after Bush's electoral defeat, the EPA activated new vehicle emission standards for most-polluted American cities.

Illinois-born Reilly has held a series of key environmental posts, including the presidency of the Conservation Fund from 1973, presidency of the World Wildlife Fund (1985–89), and several federal government positions. Reilly's 1962 B.A. was from Yale, his 1965 J.D. from Harvard, and his 1971 M.S. in urban planning from Columbia. He is married to Elizabeth Bennett Buxton; they have two children.

FURTHER READING

"It's lonely being green. . . ." TED WILLIAMS. *Audubon*, Sep.–Oct. 1992.
"Eco-man." WILLIAM L. SHARFMAN. *Self*, Jan. 1992.

"Voice in the wilderness." KEN GROSS and JANE SIMS. *People*, Dec. 23, 1991.
"Reilly, William Kane." *Current Biography*, July 1989.

Reiner, Rob (1945–) Actor, writer, and director Reiner focused on the directing side in 1992. His major film of the year was the military courtroom drama *A Few Good Men*, which he also co-produced, with screenplay by Aaron Sorkin from his own long-running play. Tom Cruise, Demi Moore, and Jack Nicholson starred in a cast that also included Kevin Bacon, Kiefer Sutherland, Kevin Pollak, James Marshall, and Wolfgang Bodison. Cruise played a young Navy lawyer, Lt. J.G. Kaffee, who defends two Marines (Marshall and Bodison) accused of murder while disciplining a private at the Guantanomo Bay Cuban naval base. Moore is Lieutenant Commander Joanne Galloway, the special counsel who presses Cruise to fight the case hard. Nicholson is Marine Colonel Nathan Jessup, the base commander who acts as their chief courtroom antagonist. Reiner was still a familiar face on the world's television screens, appearing in reruns of his early role as Meathead in "All in the Family" (1974–78); he won 1974 and 1978 Emmys for the role.

New York City-born Reiner became a television scriptwriter in the late 1960s. He moved into film direction in the mid-1980s with the documentary *This Is Spinal Tap* (1984), and then directed several well-received feature films, including *The Sure Thing* (1985), *Stand By Me* (1986), and *The Princess Bride* (1987). His breakthrough film was *When Harry Met Sally. . .* (1989), which he directed and co-produced; the film starred Billy Crystal, Meg Ryan, and Carrie Fisher. He also directed *Misery* (1990) and the television series "Morton and Hayes" (1991). Reiner attended the University of California at Los Angeles. He has been married twice, first to actress-director Penny Marshall, then to Michele Singer in 1989. He is the son of actor-writer-directer Carl Reiner.

FURTHER READING

"Pals." ROBERT LLOYD. *American Film*, July–Aug. 1989.
"Reiner's reason." APRIL BERNARD and MICHELLE SINGER. *Interview*, July 1989.
"Reiner, Rob." *Current Biography*, May 1988.

Reshevsky, Samuel (Samuel Herman Rseszewski; 1911–92) A child chess prodigy while still living in his native Poland, Reshevsky first appeared competitively in Vienna at the age of six, and played in competitions throughout Europe before his family emigrated to the United States in 1920. From 1920 to 1922, he was a major American celebrity, touring the country and playing scores of games at once. He "retired" at the age of ten, re-entering the world of competitive chess after his 1933 graduation from the University of Chicago. He won the first of his seven U.S. chess championships in 1936, became a major figure in world chess, and—although falling short of winning the world chess championship—won many tournaments. Reshevsky "retired" again in 1948, but soon returned to action, in 1955 even defeating world champion Mikhail Botvinnik in non-championship play. In 1958, he was defeated at the American championship by Bobby Fischer, then fourteen years old. Reshevsky defeated Fischer once in 1961, when Fischer walked out of a tied match, but never again seriously contended for the world title, though he did win a final U.S. title in 1971. Among his written works are *Reshevsky's Best Games of Chess* (1960), *Reshevsky Teaches Chess* (1974), *Great Chess Upsets* (1975), and *How Chess Games Are Won* (1978).

He was survived by his wife, two daughters, and son. (d. Suffern, New York; April 4, 1992)

FURTHER READING

Obituary. *The Times* (of London), Apr. 9, 1992.
Obituary. *New York Times*, Apr. 7, 1992.

Reso, Sidney J.: See **Arthur Seale**

Reynolds, Burt (1936–) For veteran stage and screen star Burt Reynolds, 1992 brought an Emmy nomination as leading actor for a series, and yet another successful year in his highly successful television series "Evening Shade," heading a cast that included Ossie Davis, Elizabeth Ashley, Charles Durning, Hal Holbrook, Marilu Henner, and Jay R. Ferguson. He also appeared as himself in *The Player*, Robert Altman's merciless, multi-star lampoon of modern Hollywood. Forthcoming was a starring role as a police detective in Henry Winkler's film *Cop and a Half*, co-starring eight-year-old Norman Golden II, as a boy who wins the right to work with him as a cop.

On the personal side, Reynolds revealed that he had become addicted to the prescription drug Halcion while taking it as a pain killer after injuries suffered while making the film *City Heat* in 1984, but that with the help of his wife he had finally been able to conquer his addiction.

Georgia-born Reynolds became a very popular film star in the 1970s, acting in such films as *Deliverance* (1972), *The Man Who Loved Cat Dancing* (1973), *White Lightning* (1973), *The Longest Yard* (1974), *W.W. and the Dixie Dance Kings* (1975), *Nickelodeon* (1976), the two *Smokey and the Bandit* films (1977, 1980), *Hooper* (1978), *Sharkey's Machine* (1981), the two *Cannonball Run* films (1981, 1984), *Physical Evidence* (1989), and *Breaking In* (1989). On television, he appeared in many episodes of "Gunsmoke" (1965), and starred in the series "Hawk" (1966), "Dan August" (1970–71), "ABC Mystery Movie" (1988–89; as B. L. Stryker), and "Evening Shade" (1990–). Reynolds attended Palm Beach Junior College and Florida State University. Formerly married to Judy Carne, he married Loni Anderson in 1988; they have one child.

FURTHER READING

"Burt Reynolds." MARY MURPHY. *TV Guide*, Apr. 25, 1992.
"Reynolds unwrapped." JESS CAGLE. *Entertainment*, Mar. 27, 1992.
Burt Reynolds. LISA SMITH. Magic Light, 1992.
"What's hot. . . ." DAVID WALLACE. *Ladies Home Journal*, Sep. 1991.
Burt Reynolds: Superstar. CAROLINE LATHAM. Putnam, 1986.

Rice, Jerry Lee (1962–) San Francisco 49ers Jerry Rice continues to win adherents to the proposition that he could be the greatest wide receiver in the history of football. On November 29, 1992, in a game against the Philadelphia Eagles, Rice caught his 100th touchdown pass, tying the record set by Steve Largent, who did so in 14 years as compared to Rice's 8. A week later, against Miami, Rice broke the record with his 101st touchdown catch, and by season's end had built the record to 103. Still relatively early in his career, Rice is also looking down the road to other records; at year's end he was ninth on the all-time National Football League (NFL) list in career catches (with 593 as of his recordbreaking day), and had become the ninth player to surpass 10,000 receiving yards.

Even so, Rice was not particularly happy about his playing situation. Though he had 84 receptions in the 1992–93 season, with Steve Young as quarterback following the coach's game plan of spreading the ball around, Rice remembers the 1980s when he and the legendary Joe Montana were so closely knit and successful a duo that they took their team to three Super Bowl wins. Good as Young is—and he was named most valuable player in the league in 1992—he had not yet replaced Montana in Rice's estimation.

Mississippi-born Rice was a football, basketball, and track star at Crawford Moor High School before moving on to Mississippi Valley State, where he was a consensus All-American, with over 100 receptions in both his junior and senior years and over 1000 yards in three consecutive years; he set numerous National Collegiate Athletic Association (NCAA) records. A first-found draft pick in 1985, Rice exploded in 1986 to lead the league with 86 receptions, 15 receiving touchdowns, and 1,570 receiving yards; he was named *Sports Illustrated's* NFL Player of the Year. The next year he became the league's most valuable player, leading the NFL with 138 points and setting NFL records with 22 receiving scores and receiving scores in 13 consecutive games. In 1988, he was MVP of Super Bowl XXIII, tying league records for postseason touchdowns (6) and most receiving touchdowns in a single game (3); he equaled the latter in Super Bowl XXIV in 1989. In 1989 and 1990 Rice was again league leader in number of receptions, and in 1990 in receiving yardage. Also in 1990 he tied the NFL record for most career touchdowns (12), and was named *Sports Illustrated*'s NFL Player of the Year. Rice has been named to eight consecutive Pro Bowls, has had seven consecutive years of over 1000 reception yards, and has helped win three Super Bowls (1985, 1989, and 1990). He and his wife, Jackie, have a son and a daughter.

FURTHER READING

"Rice, Jerry." *Current Biography*, Apr. 1990.
"Why I wear. . . ." STEVE KETTMANN.
   GQ—Gentleman's Quarterly, Oct. 1989.
"The 49er with golden hands. . . ." PETE AXTHELM.
   Newsweek, Jan. 11, 1988.
"The San Francisco treat. . . ." TOM FITZGERALD.
   Sporting News, Jan. 4, 1988.

Riley, Pat (Patrick James Riley; 1945–) Who would have believed that the rebuilt New York Knicks would not only make the National Basketball Association (NBA) playoffs and get to the Eastern Conference finals, but also stretch the defending champion Chicago Bulls to a grueling seventh game before finally losing? But that is exactly what Pat Riley accomplished in his first full year as head coach of the team, reconstructed around Patrick Ewing to have championship *potential*, though few anticipated current competitive ability. In fact, the New York Knicks grew stronger as the 1991–92 season progressed, under Riley's tough, hard-driving, meticulous tutelage that stressed physical defense, and were the surprise of the playoffs. By the end of the regular 1991–92 season, Riley had posted a career won-lost record of 584–225, or .722; and he remained the only NBA coach in history to win more than 100 playoff games, his total after the Knicks' post-season run resting at 108. Not content with that, the Knicks management made a number of additional trades for the 1992–93 season. Though the team was understandably uneven at first, Riley welded them together so that, by year's end, they were at the top of their division. Personally, Riley continued involvement in charitable and community service programs, and sat on the board of directors of the Magic Johnson AIDS Foundation.

Born in Schenectady, New York, Riley has spent his whole career in and around basketball. During his eight-year career as a professional basketball player, he was a guard with the San Diego Rockets (1967–70), the Los Angeles Lakers (1970–75), and the Phoenix Suns (1975–76). He was an assistant coach of the Lakers (1979–81), and then began his extraordinarily successful nine-year run as Laker head coach (1981–90). Under Riley, the Lakers had a won-lost record of 533–194, and won four National Basketball Association (NBA) championships (1982, 1985, 1987, and 1988). In 1990 he was for the first time named NBA Coach of the Year. In June 1990, after a winning season but an early elimination in the playoffs, Riley resigned from the Lakers. At that point, he led all coaches in NBA history, including the legendary Red Auerbach, in percentage of regular-season games won, at .733, and total number of playoff victories, at 102. Riley had broadcast Laker games (1977–79), and returned to broadcasting, at NBC television for the 1990–91 season, after resigning his coaching job. In 1988 he published *Show Time: Inside the Laker's Breakthrough Season.* He is married to Chris Riley; they have two children.

FURTHER READING

"Character study." DAVID HALBERSTAM. *New York,* Dec. 21, 1992.
"Pat Riley. . . ." JOE McDONNELL. *Sport,* Oct. 1992.
"The life of Riley." KEN AULETTA. *Vanity Fair,* Apr. 1992.
"A whole new ball game. . . ." MICHAEL STONE. *New York,* Nov. 25, 1991.
"Coach Pat Riley brings. . . ." ERIC POOLEY. *New York,* Sep. 23, 1991.
" 'Call me Mister Riley.' " AL STUMP. *Los Angeles Magazine,* Oct. 1989.
"The transformation. . . ." DIANE K. SHAH. *GQ—Gentlemen's Quarterly,* Jan. 1989.

Clinton had long worked together in the National Governors Conference on matters affecting education, Clinton as Arkansas governor and Riley as South Carolina governor.

Greenville-born Riley began his law practice in his family's law firm in 1961, triumphing over rheumatoid spondylitis, a form of arthritis that ultimately left him with a rounded back and damaged, immobile neck. He continued to practice law as his political career simultaneously developed. He served in the South Carolina House of Representatives (1962–66), in the state Senate (1966–76), and as governor (1979–87). As governor, he developed a series of educational initiatives, financed by tax increases, also focusing on such issues as affordable health care and nuclear waste disposal.

Riley's B.A. was from Furman University, and his J. D. from the University of South Carolina School of Law. He is married to the former Ann Osteen Yarborough; they have four children.

FURTHER READING

"Watchman. . . ." JOHN W. DONOHUE. *America,* Nov. 10, 1990.

Riley, Richard Wilson (1935–) President Bill Clinton's incoming Secretary of Education brings with him to Washington a strong reputation as an education reformer. He and

Rivlin, Alice Mitchell (1931–) President Bill Clinton's incoming Deputy Director of Management and Budget is a distinguished economist, who was the President of the Amer-

Roach, Hal (Harold Eugene Roach; 1892–1992) Elmira-born Roach, a film producer, director, and writer whose work was central to the development of American film comedy, began his long screen career in 1912 as an extra in cowboy movies. One of his early stars was comedian Harold Lloyd, produced by Roach from 1916. In 1922, Roach also conceived and for 16 years produced hundreds of the enormously popular "Our Gang" comedies, later continued by MGM and syndicated in television as the "The Little Rascals." Roach also developed the Laurel and Hardy films, from 1927 to 1940 producing a series of worldwide comedy hits. In the late 1930s, he also produced the three "Topper" films, and in that period also produced *Of Mice and Men* (1939) and *One Million B.C.* (1940). After World War II filmmaking service, he moved into television, producing such classic early television series as "My Little Margie" and "The Life of Riley." The third of his Academy Awards was an honorary one, given to him in 1984; and in 1992, at the age of 100, he was lauded once again at the Oscar ceremonies. He was survived by his second wife, Lucille Prin, and by three daughters. (d. Bel-Air, California; October 2, 1992)

FURTHER READING

Obituary. *Variety*, Nov. 9, 1992.
Obituary. *The Times* (of London), Nov. 4, 1992.
Obituary. *Independent*, Nov. 4, 1992.
Obituary. *New York Times*, Nov. 3, 1992.
"Hal Roach. . . ." RICHARD W. BANN. *Architectural Digest*, Apr. 1990.

ican Economic Association in 1986. She began her long Washington career as a member of the staff of the Brookings Institution (1957–66), moved to the Department of Health, Education, and Welfare (1966–69), and in 1975 founded and became first director of the Congresssional Budget Office. She left that post to return to the Brookings Institution as director of economic studies (1983–87). She is Hirst Professor of Public Policy at George Mason University and a Senior Fellow in Economic Studies at the Brookings Institution.

Philadelphia-born Rivlin's 1952 B.A. was from Bryn Mawr College, and her 1958 Ph.D. from Radcliffe College. Her works include *The Role of the Federal Government in Financing Higher Education* (1961), *Caring for the Disabled Elderly: Who Will Pay?* (1988), and *Reviving the American Dream* (1992). She co-authored *Microanalysis of Socioeconomic Systems* (1961), *Systematic Thinking for Social Action* (1971), *Economic Choices* (1987), *The Swedish Economy* (1987), and *Understanding Economic Policy: A Citizen's Handbook* (1990). Her second husband is Sidney Graham; she has three children.

FURTHER READING

"No longer home alone." *Time*, Dec. 21, 1992.
"Tipping the balance. . . ." VIVA HARDING. *U.S. News & World Report*, Nov. 30, 1992.
"Shifting power. . . ." SUNEEL RATAN. *Fortune*, June 29, 1992.

Robards, Jason, Jr. (Jason Nelson Robards, Jr.; 1922–) Celebrated stage and screen star Robards had another varied and productive year. In January, he starred as corrupt New Orleans Congressman Clifford Fowler opposite James Spader, Joanne Whalley-Kilmer, and Piper Laurie in Mark Frost's New Orleans-set political crime melodrama *Storyville*. In a major work for television, Robards was the voice of Abraham Lincoln in the four-hour ABC documentary *Lincoln*, opposite Glenn Close as Mary Todd Lincoln, Ossie Davis as Frederick Douglass, Rod Steiger as General Ulysses S. Grant, Richard Dreyfuss as General William T. Sherman, and Frank Langella as John Wilkes Booth. Forthcoming was a starring role in the Stephen

Sommers film *The Adventures of Huck Finn*, which began filming in August 1992.

Chicago-born Robards became a leading player on the American stage in 1956 as Hickey in Eugene O'Neill's *The Iceman Cometh*, a role he repeated in 1976 and 1988. His work in O'Neill included *Long Day's Journey Into Night* (1956, 1976, 1986), *A Moon for the Misbegotten* (1973), and *A Touch of the Poet* (1977). He won a Tony in *The Disenchanted* (1958), and also starred in such plays as *A Thousand Clowns* (1962; and the 1965 film), *After the Fall* (1964), *The Country Girl* (1972), and *Park Your Car in Harvard Yard* (1991). On screen, he appeared in many films, largely in strong supporting roles. His most notable films include *The Loves of Isadora* (1969), *All the President's Men* (1976; he won a Best Supporting Actor Oscar), *Julia* (1977; and a second Best Supporting Actor Oscar), *Melvin and Howard* (1979), *Parenthood* (1989), *Black Rainbow* (1990), and *Reunion* (1990), as well as many telefilms, most notably in *The Iceman Cometh* (1961), *One Day in the Life of Ivan Denisovitch* (1963), *Haywire* (1980), *The Day After* (1983), *Sakharov* (1984), *Inherit the Wind* (1988), *Chernobyl: The Final Warning* (1991), *The Perfect Tribute* (1991), and *Mark Twain and Me* (1991). Robards attended the American Academy of Dramatic Arts. He has been married four times and has seven children. He is the son of actor Jason Robards.

FURTHER READING

"Robards. . . ." WILLIAM E. GEIST. *New York Times*, May 22, 1983.

Robbins, Tim (1958–) Until 1992 regarded as a highly promising young actor, Robbins became far more than that in 1992, writing, directing, writing the songs for, and appearing in the title role of one of years' most acclaimed films, *Bob Roberts*. Robbins starred as the child of 1960s dissenters, who grew up in a commune, but emerged as an utterly corrupt ultraconservative singer and songwriter, who becomes a right-wing dirty-tricks American senatorial candidate. The writer Gore Vidal, in a great change of pace, plays Senator Brickley Paiste, Roberts' intended victim, in a cast that includes Giancarlo Esposito, Brian Murray, Ray Wise, and several stars in cameos, including Robbins' companion, Susan Sarandon.

Robbins "arrived" twice in 1992. Playing utterly detestable film executive Griffin Mill, he was the star of *The Player*, Robert Altman's highly acclaimed merciless, multi-star lampoon of modern Hollywood. He starred opposite Greta Scacchi in a very large cast that included Whoopi Goldberg, Fred Ward, and more than a score of major stars appearing in cameos as themselves. Robbins won the Best Actor Award at the 1992 Cannes Film Festival for his performance in *The Player*.

Robbins also ventured into radio in 1992, writing, co-directing, and starring in the satire *Mayhem: The Invasion*, about the Columbus expedition to the Americas. Forthcoming were starring roles as a Los Angeles police officer with marital problems in Altman's film *Short Cuts*; and a starring role opposite Paul Newman and Jennifer Jason Leigh in Joel Coen's film *The Hudsucker Proxy*.

California-born Robbins grew up in New York's Greenwich Village, the child of a theater family (his father, Gil Robbins, was a folksinger and cabaret manager). He made his stage debut in his early teens, studied theater at the Plattsburgh campus of the State University of New York and the University of California at Los Angeles, and while still in school was a founder of the Actors' Gang; he is still artistic director of the group. He has written several experimental plays. He made his film debut in *No Small Affair* (1984), and went on to roles in such films as *The Sure Thing* (1985), and *Five Corners* (1987), his breakthrough role coming in *Bull Durham* (1988), followed by such films as *Eric the Viking* (1989), *Cadillac Man* (1990), and *Jacob's Ladder* (1990). Robbins and Sarandon have two children, one born in 1992.

FURTHER READING

"A dangerous man." STEPHANIE MANSFIELD.
   GQ—Gentleman's Quarterly, Oct. 1992.
"Tim Robbins." *Playboy*, Oct. 1992.
"Renaissance radical." JONATHAN ALTER. *Vogue*, Sep.
   1992.
"Tim Robbins." MARK HARRIS. *Entertainment*, June
   26, 1992.
"Two-coast man." JACK KROLL. *Newsweek*, Nov. 12,
   1990.
"The John and Tim show." BILL FLANAGAN. *Rolling
   Stone*, Nov. 3, 1988.

Roberts, Julia (Julie Roberts; 1967–)

Film star Roberts, who had emerged as a major
figure during 1990 and 1991, was highly visible
on the world's screens in 1992 as Tinker Bell in
Hook, Stephen Spielberg's version of the *Peter
Pan* story. She was also one of more than a score
of stars who appeared as themselves in cameos
in the film *The Player*, Robert Altman's merciless, multi-star lampoon of modern Hollywood.

After completing *Hook*, Roberts took a year off
from the business of making films, and re-
emerged again in mid-1992 with new films and
talk of new films swirling around her. One firm
commitment was a starring role in Alan Pakula's forthcoming film *The Pelican Brief*, the
movie version of John Grisham's bestselling
novel; she was set to play the astute and then
greatly threatened law student who identifies
and exposes the corrupt businessman behind the
assassination of two U.S. Supreme Court justices. Another near-commitment, Tom Stopp-
ard's new comedy *Shakespeare in Love*, was
postponed and seemed to have fallen through,
although Roberts expressed continuing interest.

Georgia-born Roberts began her acting career
with a small role as sister to her actor-brother,
Eric, in the western *Blood Red* (1986; released
in 1989). After a single 1986 guest role on the
television series "Crime Story," followed by a
role in the HBO telefilm *Baja, Oklahoma* (1987),
she very quickly moved into feature films, in
Satisfaction (1988) playing guitar in an all-
female rock band; in her breakthrough role as
the highly sexual waitress in *Mystic Pizza*
(1988); and in *Steel Magnolias* (1989) as diabetic
Shelby, winning a Golden Globe award and an
Oscar nomination for best supporting actress.
Her starring role in *Pretty Woman* (1990) won
her a 1991 Academy Award nomination and a
Golden Globe Award as best actress. She has
also starred in *Flatliners* (1990), *Sleeping With
the Enemy* (1991), and *Dying Young* (1991). She
is the sister of actor Eric Roberts and actress
Lisa Roberts.

FURTHER READING

"Julia Roberts. . . ." ANN TREBBE. *McCall's*, Sep.
   1992.
"Julia Roberts." JOHN CLARK. *Premiere*, Dec. 1991.
"Hooked on Julia!" *Teen*, Nov. 1991.
"20 questions. . . ." *Playboy*, Nov. 1991.
"Queen for a decade." MARC ELIOT. *California*, Sep.
   1991.
"Miss Roberts regrets." LOUISE LAGUE. *People*, July 1,
   1991.
"Julia Roberts. . . ." SALLY OGLE DAVIS. *Ladies Home
   Journal*, July 1991.
"Roberts, Julia." *Current Biography*, May 1991.
"Bare-foot girl. . . ." JOHANNA SCHNELLER.
   GQ—Gentlemen's Quarterly, Feb. 1991.
"The jewel who's Julia." SUSAN SCHINDEHETTE. *People*,
   Sep. 17, 1990.
"Suddenly, Julia." ROBERT PALMER. *American Film*,
   July 1990.
"The barefoot principessa. . . ." MICHAEL REESE.
   Newsweek, Mar. 26, 1990.
"Julia Roberts." CATHERINE SEIPP. *Harper's Bazaar*,
   Sep. 1989.
"Family ties. . . ." DOUG GARR. *Harper's Bazaar*, Feb.
   1989.

Robinson, Mary (Mary Bourke; 1944–)

Ireland's first woman President made some more
history in 1992, as she continued to build the
Irish Presidency into more than a figurehead position, speaking out on the issues that had animated her entire parliamentary career; ending
the war in Northern Ireland, the legalization of
divorce, equal employment, the legalization of
contraceptives, day care for the children of working mothers, repeal of laws discriminating
against homosexuals and making homosexuality a criminal offense, and increased abortion
information. On February 4, she made the first
state visit of an Irish President to Northern Ireland since 1921, strongly speaking against terrorism during her visit. Later that month, she
joined those demanding that a 14-year-old rape
victim be allowed to go to England for an abortion, an issue that convulsed Ireland after the
Irish courts had banned her trip (later reversed).
In July, Robinson made history again, address-

ing both houses of the Irish parliament on the question of European unity. She supported the very modest proposals on abortion taken up in the November 25 Irish referendum; although mainly defeated, she made it clear that the issue was very far from being closed.

Mary Robinson has for two decades been a leading Irish liberal and human rights lawyer. She received her B.A. and LL.B. from Trinity College, Dublin, and her LL.M. from Harvard Law School. Returning to Ireland from the United States in 1968, she became the youngest-ever law professor at Trinity. A year later, in 1969, she ran as a Labour candidate, and won election to the Irish Senate, going on to serve for 20 years in the Senate, until 1989. Robinson scored an upset victory in the 1990 Irish presidential election, winning by a narrow margin what had until then been a powerless ceremonial post. She is married to lawyer Nicholas Robinson; they have three children.

FURTHER READING

"Proud Mary." MAUREEN ORTH. *Vanity Fair*, July 1992.
"Symbol of the new Ireland." MARTHA DUFFY. *Time*, June 29, 1992.
"Robinson, Mary Bourke." *Current Biography*, Apr. 1991.
Mary Robinson: A President with a Purpose. FERGUS FINLAY. Dufour, 1991.
"Here's to you Mrs. Robinson. . . ." RON ARIAS. *People*, Nov. 26, 1990.

Roh Tae Woo (1932–) During his last full year in office, South Korean President Roh Tae Woo continued to try to normalize relations with North Korea, still pursuing a long overdue Korean War peace treaty, free trade and free access for the citizens of both Koreas, and an end to the North Korean atomic arms program, all as part of an overall North and South Korean unification process. But it was not to happen on his watch; as he pointed out in a September 1992 United Nations speech, the active North Korea nuclear weapons program barred much progress toward those goals. He did, however, normalize relations with China and Russia, and sign a Russia-South Korea trade agreement in October that provided the basis for a late November state visit to South Korea by Russian President Boris Yeltsin. The visit resulted in reinstatement of

an earlier economic assistance pact that aimed at further increasing trade between the two countries.

As the worldwide recession deepened, South Korea encountered economic problems, as least partly accounting for Roh's loss of his legislative majority in the March National Assembly elections. During the run-up to the December 18 national elections, Roh resigned from the Liberal Democratic Party and replaced many of his cabinet ministers in a move aimed at creating a transition government that would not be involved in partisan politics during the election campaign.

Roh Tae Woo was a career military officer who fought in the Korean War, in the late 1970s rose to divisional command, and retired in 1981 as a four-star general. He held several appointive cabinet level posts in the early 1980s, then entering electoral politics as a national assembly-man and chairman of the National Justice Party in 1985. He became president of the Republic of Korea in February 1988. He attended the Korean Military Academy. He is married to Kim Ok Sook; they have two children.

FURTHER READING

"Roh. . . ." BRADLEY MARTIN. *Newsweek*, June 18, 1990.
"Roh faces. . . ." LAXMI NAKARMI. *Business Week*, Dec. 19, 1988.
"Roh Tae Woo." *Current Biography*, Feb. 1988.

Romanov, Vladimir Kirillovich (Grand Duke Vladimir; 1917–92) Born in Finland, Romanov was the son of Kirill Romanov, a first cousin of Czar Nicholas II, and a Grand Duke. After the murders of the Russian imperial family, Kirill Romanov claimed to be the legitimate heir to the Russian throne, and settled in France as a leader of the Russian emigré community. Kirill Romanov died in 1938, and Vladimir Romanov then took over his claim, thereafter being known as a "pretender to the throne." He remained in France during World War II, on good terms with the Nazis, though he apparently declined a Nazi suggestion that he become puppet ruler of the Ukraine. After the war, he fled, ultimately settling in Spain, then ruled by Francisco Franco. Vladimir Romanov visited Russia for the first time in 1991, at the

337

invitation of the St. Petersburg city government, on the occasion of the city's renaming from Leningrad to St. Petersburg. He was survived by his wife and a daughter. (d. Miami; April 21, 1992)

FURTHER READING

Obituary. *The Times* (of London), Apr. 23, 1992.
Obituary. *Independent*, Apr. 23, 1992.
Obituary. *New York Times*, Apr. 22, 1992.
"A Tsar is born?" MARY H.J. FARRELL and PETER MIKELBANK. *People*, Oct. 21, 1991.

Ronstadt, Linda Marie (1946–) Popular music star Ronstadt continued to exlore her Latin-American roots in 1992. Her rendition of the 1950s hit "Perfidia" on the soundtrack of the film *The Mambo Kings* became a hit Latin single. She also recorded "Quiereme Mucho" for the film, which starred Armand Assante and Antonio Banderas in an adaptation of Oscar Hijuelos' Pulitzer Prize-winning novel, *The Mambo Kings Play Songs of Love*, and featured performances by Tito Puente and Celia Cruz.

Ronstadt also issued the album *Frenesi*, a mambo record in which she sang many Afro-Cuban-influenced Mexican popular songs of the 1940s and 1950s; her renditon of "Alma Adentro" was especially noted in reviews, as were "Piensa En Mi," and "Cuandos Me Querías Tú." In November, she also released the single "Entre Abismos." Forthcoming in 1993 was a country music album that some thought would bring her back to the much larger audiences she had enjoyed at the height of her popularity.

Tucson-born Ronstadt began her recording and touring career in the late 1960s, and emerged in mid-1970s as a very versatile popular and country star. Her first hit album was *Heart Like a Wheel* (1974), containing two of her most popular songs: "You're No Good" and "I Can't Help It if I'm Still in Love with You." She went on to record such albums as *Different Drum* (1974), *Prisoner In Disguise* (1975), *Hasten Down the Wind* (1976), *Blue Bayou* (1977), *Living in the U.S.A* (1978), *Mad Love* (1980), *Lush Life* (1984), *Trio* (1986; with Dolly Parton and Emmylou Harris), *'Round Midnight* (1987), *Canciones de Mi Padre* (1987), *Cry Like a Rainstorm—Howl Like the Wind*(1989), and *Warm Your Heart* (1991). On stage, she starred in *Pirates of Penzance* (1981; on film, 1983), and off Broadway in *La Bohème* (1984).

FURTHER READING

Linda Ronstadt. Chelsea House, 1993.
"Skylark." JONATHAN SCHWARTZ. *GQ—Gentlemen's Quarterly*, Feb. 1990.
Linda Ronstadt. MARK BEGO. Eakin, 1990.

Ross, Steven Jay (1927–92) A leading American entertainment and media figure, Ross began his career in the early 1950s, as an employee in his father-in-law's New York City undertaking business, The Riverside. He started and acquired several related and unrelated businesses in the 1950s and early 1960s, in 1962 issuing stock in the Kinney corporation, into which he had merged them all. In 1969, he became a major player in the entertainment business with Kinney's acquisition of Warner-Seven Arts, in 1971 renamed Kinney Warner Communications. He then proceeded to grow Warner into a large, diverse music, television, and film company. In 1989, near the end of the merger boom of the 1980s, he made his largest corporate move, purchasing Time, Life for $14 billion after structuring a debt-free merger that went sour when Paramount made an attractive purchase offer that Ross decided to top. The purchase put the merged Time Warner company into $11 billion of debt, creating problems that had not been resolved at the time of his death. Partly due to heavy stockholder criticism of the merger, and partly because of the post-financial-orgy climate of the early 1990s, Ross was sharply criticized for his enormous salaries; his 1990 salary and bonus take, for example, was more than $78 million. Ross attended Paul Smith's College. He was survived by his third wife, Courtney Sale Ross, two daughters, and a son. (d. Los Angeles; December 20, 1992)

FURTHER READING

Obituary. *Billboard*, Jan. 9, 1993.
Obituary. *Variety*, Jan. 4, 1993.
Obituary. *The Times* (of London), Dec. 22, 1992.
Obituary. *The New York Times*, Dec. 21, 1992.
"Steve Ross. . . ." ROGER COHEN. *New York Times Magazine*, Mar. 22, 1992.
"Just call him Steve." RICHARD M. CLURMAN. *Vanity Fair*, Jan. 1992.

Rostropovich, Mstislav Leopoldovich (1927–) Celebrated cellist and conductor Rostropovich, for seventeen years director of Washington's National Symphony Orchestra, announced in June 1992 that he would retire from that post in 1994 and become the orchestra's lifetime laureate conductor, conducting it four weeks each season. He said that he would continue to record and tour, but wanted to spend more time at home in Russia, involved in the humanitarian and national rebuilding work he and his wife, singer Galina Vishnevskaya, began in the Gorbachev era. In September 1991, he and Vishnevskaya had announced plans to create a foundation for the purpose of building a modern children's hospital in Moscow; in 1992, their fundraising work went forward. On December 6, 1992 Rostropovich received a John F. Kennedy Center for the Performing Arts award at a White House reception. In 1992, he also received the Freedom of Speech Award of the Franklin and Eleanor Roosevelt Institute.

Born in Baku, cellist, pianist, and conductor Rostropovich was a child prodigy, making his debut as a cellist at the age of 13. During the 1950s, he was generally recognized as one of the world's leading cellists, and became a greatly honored Soviet musician, winner of two Stalin Prizes and a Lenin Prize. Disillusioned with the Soviet system of the time, especially after incurring official displeasure for aiding dissident Alexander Solzhenitsyn, he and Vishnevskaya left for the West in 1974. Both were stripped of their Soviet citizenships in 1978. In the Gorbachev era, their citizenships was restored, as were their medals and honors, and Rostropovich made a triumphant return to Moscow in February 1990 with the Washington National Symphony Orchestra. On hearing of the attempted August 1991 rightwing Soviet coup, Rostropovich immediately flew from Paris to Moscow, went directly to the Russian parliament building, and joined the resistance. There he stayed, with one three-hour break, until the coup collapsed, calling those three days "the best days of my life."

Rostropovich studied at the Moscow Conservatory, graduating in 1948, and taught at the Moscow and Leningrad Conservatories. He became music director of Washington, D.C.'s National Symphony Orchestra in 1977. He and Vishnevskaya have two children.

FURTHER READING

The Great Cellists. MARGARET CAMPBELL. Trafalgar Square, 1989.
"Rostropovich, Mstislav." *Current Biography*, Nov. 1988.

Rubin, Robert Edward (1938–) President Bill Clinton's incoming National Economic Council chairman is a lawyer and Wall Street investment banker. After his graduation from Yale Law School, he worked for two years (1964–66) as a lawyer at the New York City firm of Cleary, Gottlieb, Steen, and Hamilton. In 1966, he began his long career at the Wall Street investment banking firm of Goldman, Sachs & Co. He became a partner in 1971 and a member of the firm's management committee in 1980, then becoming vice chairman and co-chief operating officer (1987–90), and co-senior partner and co-chairman (1990–92).

He also advised New York City and New York State on financial matters, and served on a wide range of other government advisory boards and for-profit and nonprofit organization boards of directors. He was also a key Democratic Party fundraiser throughout the 1980s and early 1990s, and was chairman of the New York committee that hosted the 1992 Democratic National Convention.

New York City-born Rubin's 1960 A.B. was from Harvard University. He did postgraduate work at the London School of Economics (1960–

61). His 1964 LL.B. was from Yale Law School. He is married to Judith Leah Oxenberg; they have two children.

FURTHER READING

"Is Mr. Rubin. . . . " LEAH NATHANS SPIRO. *Business Week*, Nov. 23, 1992.

Rushdie, Salman (Ahmed Salman Rushdie; 1947–)

For a fourth year, British writer Rushdie, author of *The Satanic Verses* (1988), remained in hiding, under Scotland Yard protection, as Islamic fundamentalist assassins continued to hunt him. For good reason: In July, Britain ordered three Iranians suspected of plotting his assassination out of the country, and on November 2 an Iranian government-operated religious foundation announced that it was raising the price for his murder to more than $2 million. In 1991, the Japanese translator of his book had been murdered, and the Italian translator of his book had been knifed by an Iranian who said that he was seeking Rushdie. But Rushdie did not simply hide; he continued to write and publish, and during 1992 appeared more and more in public, campaigning to persuade governments to condemn the Iranian death sentence and to impose sanctions if it is not withdrawn. He made a surprise public appearance in London in February, on the third anniversary of his death sentence; spoke at a March Washington, D.C. conference on freedom of expression; and also spoke in Spain, Denmark, and Norway in June; at the University of Colorado in September, and in Toronto in December. In Washington, he also met with several supportive Senators, though the Bush administration refused to see or support him.

On the creative side, he wrote an analysis and personal evaluation of the film *The Wizard of Oz*, as part of the British Film Classics series published by Indiana University Press. It included his story "At the Auction of the Ruby Slippers," previously published in *Granta*. Forthcoming was his next novel *The Moor's Last Sigh*, to be published by Pantheon Books; it is scheduled for delivery to the publisher in December 1993 and publication in the autumn of 1994. After much delay and hesitation, a paperback edition of *The Satanic Verses* was finally released in 1992 by a consortium of publishers, writers, and human-rights organizations.

Rushdie's *The Satanic Verses* became a worldwide bestseller in 1988, after many fundamentalist Muslims protested its publication, rioting, publicly burning the book, and threatening the life of its author and publishers. In February 1989, Iran's Ayatollah Khomeini publicly sentenced Rushdie to death and offered $1 million to anyone who would murder him, a threat since repeated by others and taken very seriously indeed, then and now. Ayatollah Khamenei repeated the death threat in February 1990. Rushdie continued to deny any intent to insult those of Muslim faith, while calling for free speech for those would murder him; he also publicly apologized to any who may have been offended by his book, opposed its issuance in paperback, and affirmed his allegiance to Islam, all to no immediate avail.

Bombay-born Rushdie is a leading novelist, whose works also include *Midnight's Children* (1981), which won a Booker Prize, and *Shame* (1983). His *Haroun and the Sea of Stories* was named best children's novel of 1990 by the Writers' Guild of Great Britain. During 1991, Rushdie published *Imaginary Homelands: Essays and Criticisms 1981–1991*. He attended King's College, Cambridge. He has been married twice, and has one child.

FURTHER READING

"Salman Rushdie. . . . " GERALDINE BROOKS. *New Republic*, July 27, 1992.
" 'Free speech is life itself.' " KARSTEN PRAGER. *Time*, Dec. 23, 1991.
"The fugitive. . . . " MARK ABLEY. *Saturday Night*, May 1991.
"Keeping up with. . . . " JAMES FENTON. *New York Review of Books*, Mar 28, 1991.
Bomb: Interviews. BESTY SUSSLER, ed. City Lights, 1992.
Salman Rushdie. JAMES HARRISON. Macmillan, 1991.
A Satanic Affair: Salman Rushdie and the Rage of Islam. MALISE RUTHVEN. Trafalgar Square, 1991.
The Novels of Salman Rushdie. R.K. DHAWAN and G.R. TANEJA, eds. Advent (NY), 1991.
Salman Rushdie: Sentenced to Death. W.J. WEATHERBY. Carroll & Graf, 1990.
The Rushdie Affair: The Novel, the Ayatollah, and the West. DANIEL PIPES. Carol, 1990.
The Rushdie File. SARA MAITLAND, ed. Syracuse University Press, 1990.
The Salman Rushdie Controversy in Inter-Religious Perspective. DAN COHN-SHERBOK, ed. E. Mellen, 1990.
Salman Rushdie and the Third World: Myths of the Nation. TIMOTHY BRENNAN. St. Martin's, 1989.

Ryder, Winona

Ryder, Winona (Winona Laura Horowitz; 1971–   ) Young film star Winona Ryder played two roles in *Bram Stoker's Dracula*, Francis Ford Coppola's big budget 1992 Christmas season hit. She was young Transylvanian knight Dracula's wife Elizabeta in the late 15th century, and Mina Murray, the reincarnation of Elizabeta in 1897 London, who is courted by the then-vampire Dracula. Ryder starred opposite Gary Oldham as Dracula, Anthony Hopkins, and Keanu Reeves in Coppola's arresting film, a highly sexual and quite bloody retelling of Stoker's 1897 novel. Forthcoming was a starring rle in Martin Scorcese's *The Age of Innocence*, co-starring Daniel Day-Lewis and Michelle Pfeiffer; filmed in the spring of 1992, the movie was originally scheduled for Christmas 1992 release but was rescheduled for the autumn of 1993. Also forthcoming was a starring role in *House of the Spirits*, based on the Isabel Allende novel and set in Chile; co-starring are Meryl Streep, Glenn Close, Jeremy Irons, and Anthony Banderas.

Minnesota-born Ryder became a teenage film star in the late 1980s, making her debut in *Lucas* (1986). She appeared in *Beetlejuice* (1988), played a breakthrough role as Veronica in *Heathers* (1989), and went on to star in such films as *Great Balls of Fire* (1989), *Welcome Home Roxy Carmichael* (1990), *Mermaids* (1991), and *Edward Scissorhands* (1991). She studied at the American Conservatory Theater.

FURTHER READING

"Winona among the grown-ups." MICHAEL HIRSCHORN. *Esquire*, Nov. 1992.
"Winona." *Harper's Bazaar*, Jan. 1991.
"Winona Ryder. . . ." JULIA REED. *Vogue*, Dec. 1990.
"Winona." CLAIRE CONNORS. *Seventeen*, Dec. 1990.
"Winona Ryder. . . ." JEFF GILES and MICHEL HADDI. *Interview*, Dec. 1990.
"Wise child." PHOEBE HOBAN. *Premiere*, June 1989.
"Hot actress. . . ." DAVID HANDELMAN. *Rolling Stone*, May 18, 1989.

Rypien, Mark

Rypien, Mark (1962–   ) For Washington Redskins' quarterback Mark Rypien, 1992 started on a high. After compiling a 17–2 won-lost record in the 1991 regular season, he led his team through the playoffs to victory in Super Bowl XXVI, and was named most valuable player. In that stellar season, he led the league

in touchdown to interception ratio (28 TDs/11 INTs) and the conference in passing yards, and had the second-highest quarterback rating in the league. Not surprisingly, he was selected for the Pro Bowl.

Rypien's contract—paying him less, sometimes significantly less, than 11 other quarterbacks in the league—was up in February, and his Super Bowl success gave him some bargaining power for a new contract. Unfortunately, contract negotiations dragged on so long that Rypien missed training camp. When he did join the team, he was rusty and out of synch with the rest of the players; and by the time he had worked himself back into shape, injuries had sidelined many of the team's key players, especially on the offensive line that protects the quarterback. Without the protection, Rypien's passing game was in trouble, and at mid-season he was at the bottom of the quarterback rankings. Rypien and the team rallied a bit toward the end of the season, barely squeaking into the playoffs and finally being knocked out of contention by the San Francisco 49ers. It was not the way Rypien had envisioned the season's end.

Born in Calgary, Alberta, Rypien was raised in Spokane Washington, where he broke football passing records at Shadle Park High School, while also leading his school's basketball team to a state title and being named the tournament's outstanding player. His college football career at Washington State showed promise, but Rypien was hampered by injuries, including a broken collarbone in his sophomore year, and was a sixth-round draft pick of the Washington Redskins in 1986. His first two years as a pro were also marred by injuries to knee and back; he won the backup quarterback spot in 1988, and then became an occasional starter in 1989. He moved firmly into the starting spot only in 1990, but again lost crucial weeks to injuries. A professional-level golfer, Rypien holds an annual tournament benefiting cystic fibrosis and is a national spokesperson for spina bifida. He and his wife Annette, a former "Redskinette," have two daughters.

FURTHER READING

"Mark Rypien." RICK WEOMBERG. *Sport*, Aug. 1992.
"City of stars." STEVE RUSHIN. *Sports Illustrated*, July 27, 1992.
"Rypien's last chance. . . ." RANDY RIELAND. *Washingtonian*, Sep. 1991.

Sabah, Jabir al-Ahmed al-Jabir al-

(1928–   ) In the long, continuing aftermath of the Persian Gulf War, Kuwait continued its massive clean-up. Although the estimated 500 oil well fires set by the Iraqis had all been extinguished by mid-November 1991, thousands of land mines, unexploded ordinance, and a ruined physical structure remained. To finance clean-up and reconstruction, estimated to cost in the $60–70 billion range, the government of Kuwaiti Emir Sabah sold substantial portions of its foreign assets, and incurred a large budget deficit. But, as the huge Kuwaiti oil industry began to produce again, massive amounts of money started to flow into Kuwait, which was expected to quickly cancel out all debts and deficits.

The aftermath of the war brought calls for more democracy in Kuwait. On October 5, 1992, long-delayed parliamentary elections were held, the first in six years; they had been announced more than a year earlier, in June 1991. Very limited numbers of Kuwaitis were allowed to vote, and women were denied the vote—but the somewhat surprising result was still a clear victory for the opposition parties, some of them democratic and some made up of Islamic fundamentalists, which together won 31 of 50 seats. Sabah immediately showed his disregard for the results, on October 12 naming his son and heir, Sheikh Saad al-Abdallah al-Salim Al-Sabah as Prime Minister, a move toward autocratic, secretive Kuwaiti ruling family business-as-usual that left the future of Kuwaiti democracy very much in question.

Sabah is the head of the Kuwaiti royal family, in a government that includes many members of the ruling family. He fled Kuwait during the Iraqi invasion and returned to a looted country on March 14, 1991. He was educated primarily through private tutoring.

FURTHER READING

"After the liberation." Milton Viorst. *New Yorker*, Sep. 30, 1991.
"Rolls-Royce revolutionaries." Michael Kelly. *New Republic*, Apr. 8, 1991.
"Who's sitting pretty. . . ." *Business Week*, Mar. 11, 1991.

Salerno, Anthony "Fat Tony"

(1911–92) New York City-born Salerno began his criminal career as a numbers runner in his own East Harlem neighborhood. He emerged as a powerful figure in New York's Mafia Genovese family in the 1950s, and in the 1960s was reportedly running a $50–60 million yearly numbers operation based in East Harlem. His earliest conviction came for tax evasion in 1968; represented by Roy Cohn, he was sentenced to a six-month term. He reportedly succeeded to the leadership of the Genovese family in the early 1980s, becoming one of the most powerful criminals in the United States. In 1986, he and seven others were convicted on racketeering charges, and he was sentenced to 100 years in prison. In 1988, he was also sentenced to 70 years in prison on several other charges. He died in a prison hospital. No information was available as to survivors. (d. Springfield, Missouri, July 27, 1992)

FURTHER READING

Obituary. *The Times* (of London), July 30, 1992.
Obituary. *New York Times*, July 29, 1992.

Salinas de Gortari, Carlos (1948–)

Mexican President Salinas faced continuing massive problems during 1992. Pollution-caused school and business closings in Mexico City throughout the year again demonstrated that his capital city had become an extraordinarily dangerous place to live. Meanwhile new studies showed how much human damage had already been done by pollution in an area with nearly 20 million people crowded into a small area of near-permanent air inversion, most of those people living in wholly unsanitary, barely livable conditions in the shantytowns surrounding the city itself. In the country as a whole, massive unemployment continued, despite the creation of some jobs by runaway American firms in Mexican-U.S. border areas, where pollution also grew rapidly. Mexico's enormous population growth continued, guaranteeing even greater problems for future generations.

Salinas pinned great hopes on the Mexican-U.S.-Canadian North American Free Trade Agreement, completed on August 12, 1992, which provided for elimination of a wide range of tariff barriers, some immediately and some over a fifteen-year period, and which contained many other provisions aimed at essentially merging the economies of the three countries. Were the pact to be ratified by the U.S. Congress, Mexico stood to gain hundreds of thousands of low-paying jobs. But powerful opposition developed in Congress, and with the election of the Clinton-Gore ticket and impending retirement of George Bush the agreement seemed to be unlikely to pass in its original form, although it was signed by Presidents Bush and Salinas before Bush left office. Clinton had expressed environmental and job-loss reservations during the election campaign; his election was a blow to Salinas, as it might bring with it most only loss of the free trade agreement, but also new restirctions on runaway American companies.

Salinas has spent his whole career in a series of increasingly responsible Mexican federal goverment financial planning posts, beginning with his term as Assistant Director of Public Finance in the finance ministry (1971–74). Before his 1987 presidential nomination, he was minister of planning and the federal budget (1982–87). Salinas attended the National University of Mexico and Harvard. He is married to Yolanda Cecilia Occelli González; they have three children.

FURTHER READING

"Salinas speaks. . . ." MARSHALL LOE. *Fortune*, Dec. 28, 1992.
" 'We are talking about our children.' " JONATHAN FISHER. *International Wildlife*, Sep.–Oct. 1992.
"Interview with. . . ." ALFREDO J. ESTRADA. "A man for all seasons." MICHELE HELLER. *Hispanic*, Sep. 1992.
"Salinas's Mexican standoff." DEIRDRE McMURDY. *Maclean's*, Sep. 7, 1992.
"Behind Mexico's 'economic miracle'. . . ." *Reader's Digest*, Aug. 1992.
" 'We had to react quickly.' " MALCOLM S. FORBES, JR. and JAMES W. MICHAELS. *Forbes*, Aug. 17, 1992.
" 'We have to get together.' " *Newsweek*, Feb. 3, 1992.
"President Salinas. . . ." STEPHEN B. SHEPARD. *Business Week*, Aug. 12, 1991.
"Mexico according to. . . ." MORTIMER B. ZUCKERMAN. *U.S. News & World Report*, July 8, 1991.
"North American. . . ." NATHAN GARDELS. *New Perspectives*, Winter 1991.
"The man behind the mask. . . ." JOHN MOODY. *Time*, Nov. 19, 1990.
"Salinas takes a gamble. . . ." ROBERT A. PASTOR. *New Republic*, Sep. 10, 1990.
"Salinas de Gortari, Carlos." *Current Biography*, Mar. 1989.

Salk, Lee (1926–92)

New York City-born Salk, a child psychologist whose 1954 Ph.D. in psychology was from the University of Michigan, began his career in research, and went on to an early career that included teaching, employment by several hospitals and psychiatric institutions, consulting, and private practice. In 1960, he published research indicating that holding babies so that they could hear their mothers' heartbeats might have some calming and other beneficial effects. From the late 1960s, he became a highly visible popular psychologist as a writer and television personality. In 1972,

he began his long-running "You and Your Family" column for *McCall's* magazine. He also appeared as a syndicated television commentator on family matters, and also frequently as a guest on television talk and news shows. Salk also published several books on parenting, concluding with *Familyhood: Nurturing the Values That Matter*. He was survived by his wife, Mary Jane, a daughter, a son, and his brother, polio vaccine inventor Jonas Salk. (d. New York City; May 1, 1992)

FURTHER READING

Obituary. *The Times* (of London), May 6, 1992.
Obituary. *New York Times*, May 6, 1992.

Salvadori, Max (1908–92) London-born Salvadori, a leading antifascist, teacher, and author, grew up in Italy. He and his father went into exile in Switzerland (1924–29), after battles with Mussolini's Blackshirts. He returned to Italy in 1929, functioning as an underground antifascist organizer until his capture. Sentenced to 10 years imprisonment, he was freed due to British intervention after one year, and again went into exile in Africa, Europe, and then the United States, where he taught at St. Law-

rence University, and began his writing career. During World War II, he worked for British Intelligence in Africa and then in Italy as a key operative from 1943 to 1945. After the war, he returned to teaching, first at Bennington College, and then teaching history at Smith College until his retirement. He was survived by wife, Joyce Pawle Salvadori, a daughter, a son, and two sisters. (d. Northhampton, Massachusetts; August 6, 1992)

FURTHER READING

Obituary. *The Times* (of London), Aug. 29, 1992.
Obituary. *New York Times*, Aug. 11, 1992.

Sarandon, Susan (Susan Abigail Tomalin; 1946–) Highly regarded actress Sarandon was honored by her peers in 1992, winning a Best Actress Oscar nomination and a British Academy of Film & Television Arts Best Actress nomination for her role in the 1991 hit *Thelma and Louise*. During 1992, she starred as a drug dealer who is retiring from the trade, opposite Willem Dafoe as one of her drug deliverers in Paul Schrader's film *Light Sleeper*, which opened in January at the Sundance film festival. She also appeared as herself in *The Player*, Robert Altman's merciless, multistar lampoon of modern Hollywood, starring with her real-life companion, Tim Robbins. Another notable cameo was in Robbins' satirical film *Bob Roberts*. In

Susan Sarandon (right) and Willem Dafoe

late December, Sarandon opened as Michaela Odone opposite Nick Nolte as Augusto Odone in *Lorenzo's Oil*, George Miller's film study of a couple who successfully struggle to save their five-year-old son from what was considered incurable ALD (adrenoleukodystrophy).

On the personal side, Sarandon had a baby, Miles Guthrie Tomalin, in 1992. She also continued to be active on many social issues.

New York City-born Sarandon began her film career with *Joe* (1970), and went on to play a wide variety of roles in the next two decades, in such films as *The Rocky Horror Picture Show* (1974), *Pretty Baby* (1978), *Loving Couples* (1980), *Atlantic City* (1981), *The Hunger* (1983), *Compromising Positions* (1985), *The Witches of Eastwick* (1987), *Bull Durham* (1988), *A Dry White Season* (1989), and *White Palace* (1990). She has also appeared in several plays and on television. Her B.A. was from Catholic University of America. She and actor-director Tim Robbins have two children, one of whom was born in 1992; she also has a third child. She was formerly married to actor Chris Sarandon.

FURTHER READING

"Most of all. . . ." OVID DEMARIS. *Parade*, Mar. 1, 1992.
"Susan Sarandon. . . ." DONNA MINKOWITZ. *Advocate*, June 4, 1991.
"Susan Sarandon." GRAHAM FULLER. *Interview*, June 1991.
"The prime of. . . ." BEN YAGODA. *American Film*, May 1991.
"Susan Sarandon." ROD LURIE. *Los Angeles*, May 1991.
"Sarandon, Susan." *Current Biography*, Sep. 1989.

Savimbi, Jonas (1934–) For Savimbi, leader of the National Union for the Total Independence of Angola (UNITA), a quarter century of armed revolution and civil war seemed over in 1991. In May 1991, the long Angolan war and civil war had ended with a ceasefire, the withdrawal of Cuban forces, and on May 31 the formal signing of a peace treaty between Savimbi and President José Eduardo Dos Santos, leader of the opposing Popular Movement for the Liberation of Angola (MPLA).

The agreement had provided for multi-party free elections to take place in the autumn of 1992, preceded by partial demobilization of both armies and merger of the remaining forces into a new national army. However, only modest progress was reported; a new national army was formed, but by the summer of 1992 it was clear that both sides remained largely armed and ready for renewed hostilities. There were skirmishes in August and September, as the election approached and as Savimbi began to charge the government with fraudulent practices.

Savimbi lost the October 2–3 election, gaining 39 percent of the vote to Dos Santos' 51 percent and the MPLA also won a parliamentary majority. Charging massive fraud, Savimbi refused to accept the results and withdrew UNITA forces from the national army. On October 30, the civil war resumed, with heavy fighting between MPLA and UNITA forces in Luanda, the capital; UNITA forces resumed control of areas won before the 1991 ceasefire. More than 1,000 deaths were reported. Although the United Nations arranged a truce on November 2, fighting broke out again in December, and Angola's long wars seemed far from over.

Savimbi became active in the anti-Portuguese Angolan revolutionary movement in the early 1960s. In 1966, he founded UNITA, and has led it through 25 years of revolution and civil war. From 1975, he led a guerrilla war against the Soviet and Cuban-backed Angolan government of the MPLA, being substantially helped by Portuguese exiles from Angola and by the South African government. Savimbi attended the University of Lausanne. Though his personal life has been kept very private, it is known that he has been married and has several children.

FURTHER READING

The Cold War Guerrilla: Jonas Savimbi, the U. S. Media and the Angolan War. ELAINE WINDRICH. Greenwood, 1992.
Jonas Savimbi: A Key to Africa. FRED BRIDGLAND. Paragon House, 1987.

Scalia, Antonin (1936–) Justice Scalia continued to be one of the Court's leading conservatives during the 1991–92 Court term. The Court, though, did not move sharply to the right with the replacement of Justice Thurgood Marshall by Justice Clarence Thomas, and Scalia, though still part of a conservative majority, found himself in dissent in several landmark cases.

Scalia wrote the majority opinions in *R.A.V. v. St. Paul*, overturning a St. Paul, Minnesota ordinance making sexist, racist, or otherwise bigoted speech or behavior a crime; and in *Lujan v. Defenders of Wildlife*, ruling that the plaintiff, an environmental organization, had no stnading to bring suit because no determinable specific interest was at issue. He also ruled with the majority in such key cases as *International Society for Krishna Consciousness v. Lee*, ruling that airports could ban groups from soliciting money; *U.S. v. Alvarez Machain*, upholding the 1990 U.S. kidnapping of a Mexican doctor suspected of a role in the torture of a U.S. drug enforcement agent; *Nordlinger v. Hahn*, upholding the right of California to enact Proposition 13, with its unequal property taxes on newcomers; *Lechmere Inc. v. National Labor Relations Board*, ruling that companies did not have to allow union organizers access to such company-owned lands as parking lots and shopping malls; *Keeney v. Tamayo-Reyes*, which sharply limited the federal habeas corpus appeals of state prisoners; *New York v. U.S.*, which invalidated a federal law forcing states to handle their own radioactive waste; and *Freeman v. Pitts*, ruling that schools being operated under court-supervised desegregation orders could be released from those orders step by step. He also joined all of his colleagues in a rare, unanimous landmark sexual harassment decision; in *Franklin v. Gwinnett County Public Schools*, the Court unanimously ruled that Title IX of the 1972 education act allowed a sexually harassed student to collect damages from a school district where a teacher-coach sexually harassed Christine Franklin and ultimately succeeded in pressing her to have sexual intercourse with him. He also ruled with the majority that the Coast Guard could continue to intercept at sea and return Haitian refugees to Haiti; and in the decision barring return of RU-486 pills to Leona Benten, a pregnant woman who tried to import them into the U.S. for her personal use, in a challenge to their ban.

Scalia wrote dissenting opinions in *Riggins v. Nevada*, ruling that the state could not force an insane criminal defendant to take medication during a trial; and in *Lee v. Weisman*, barring nonsectarian or any other prayers at public high school graduations. He also dissented in such key cases as *Planned Parenthood of Southeastern Pennsylvania v. Casey*, in which a 5–4 majority upheld the essence of *Roe v. Wade* (which in 1972 had established the right of a woman to choose to have an abortion), while at the same time upholding most of the restrictive 1989 Pennsylvania abortion law and giving the states broader powers to restrict abortion; *Georgia v. McCollum*, ruling that criminal case defendants could not bar prospective jurors solely because of their race; *Hudson v. McMillian*, ruling that the excessive use of force by prison guards was an Eighth Amendment violation even if the prisoner was not seriously hurt; and *U.S. v. Forice*, ruling that Mississpippi had not fulfilled its obligatoin to desegregate its public colleges and universities.

New Jersey-born Sacalia taught law at the University of Virginia (1967–74), was an assistant attorney-general (1974–82), and taught law again at the University of Chicago (1977–82). He was appointed to the District of Columbia U.S. Court of Appeals by President Ronald Reagan in 1982, and to the Supreme Court by Reagan in 1986. Scalia's 1957 B.A. was from Georgetown University, and his 1960 LL.B. from Harvard Law School. He married Maureen McCarthy in 1960; they have nine children.

FURTHER READING

Antonin Scalia. BOB ITALIA. Abdo & Daughters, 1992.
"A new day in court." LAUREN TARSHIS and JAMES EARL HARDY. *Scholastic Update*, Nov. 1, 1991.
"Top gun on the high court." FRED BARNES. *Reader's Digest*, July 1991.
Eight Men and a Lady. HERMAN SCHWARTZ et al. National Press, 1990.
Packing the Courts: The Conservatives' Campaign to Rewrite the Constitution. HERMAN SCHWARTZ. Scribner/Macmillan, 1988.

Schmidt, Benno (1942–) Yale University President Schmidt rocked the world of American higher education in 1992, resigning his highly prestigious position after six years in the job, in favor of a job as president and chief executive officer of the Edison Project, an attempt to build a privately financed for-profit network of American schools. The project was founded in 1991 by Christopher Whittle, who heads Whittle Communications, best known as the developer of Channel One, a highly controversial commercial-carrying television news program aimed at classroom audiences. Whittle

FURTHER READING

"The Edison project. . . ." DANIEL F. HALLORAN. *America*, Oct. 3, 1992.
"Chris and Benno's. . . ." JESSE KORNBLUTH. *Vanity Fair*, Aug. 1992.
"The importance of. . . ." JOHN ANDERSON. *Town & Country Monthly*. June 1992.
"Knowledge for sale." DAVID ELLIS. *Time*, June 8, 1992.

Schrader, Paul Joseph (1946–) Celebrated screenwriter Schrader, whose writing credits include the classics *Taxi Driver*, *Raging Bull*, and *The Last Temptation of Christ*, has also directed many of his later films, though with somewhat mixed results. In 1992, he premiered his latest work, *Light Sleeper*, at the Sundance film festival. It starred Willem Dafoe as John LeTour, a drug deliverer and another of Schrader's highly moral, near-psychopathic outsiders, and Susan Sarandon as his drug dealer-supplier, the plot stemming from her decision to leave the drug business in favor of a cosmetics line. Schrader, who wrote and directed the film, saw his LeTour character as a later-years version of his taxi driver and his somewhat older key character in *American Gigolo*. Also featured in the film were Dana Delany, David Clennon, and Mary Beth Hurt.

Michigan-born Schrader emerged as a leading screenwriter with such films as *Taxi Driver* (1976), *Obsession* (1976), the classic *Raging Bull*

and Schmidt announced that they aimed to build a network of 1,000 private schools, 100 of them by 1996, with fees under $5,000 per year, made possible by such means as staff economies, computerized teaching, and the use of students for janitorial work. They also announced that a total of $60 million had been committed for project design by Whittle Communications, Time Warner, Phillips Electronics, and Associated Newspapers, and that real estate acquisition and staff hirings would soon begin. The project was from the start highly controversial, hailed by those seeking to privatize education and viewed with great doubt and alarm by those seeking to preserve and expand public education.

Washington, D.C.-born Schmidt began his legal career as a law clerk to U.S. Supreme Court Justice Earl Warren (1966–67). He then became a special assistant in the Justice Department (1967–69). Then began his teaching career; he taught law at Columbia University Law School (1969–86), and was Harlan Fiske Stone professor of constitutional law at Columbia. During his final two years at Columbia, he was the dean of the Law School. He became director of the National Humanities Center in 1985, and President of Yale University in 1986, also becoming a professor at Yale Law School. He has published *Freedom of the Press versus Public Access* (1976) and co-authored *The Judiciary and Responsible Government 1910–1921* (1984). His 1963 B.A. was from Yale University, his 1966 J.D. from Yale Law School. He is married to Helen Cutting Whitney, and has two children.

(1981), *The Mosquito Coast* (1986), and the highly controversial *The Last Temptation of Christ* (1988). He co-wrote the screenplays of *The Yakuza* (1974), *Rolling Thunder* (1977), and *Old Boyfriends* (1979), and wrote and directed *Hardcore* (1978) and *American Gigolo* (1979). He co-wrote and directed *Blue Collar* (1978) and *Mishima* (1985), and directed such films as *Cat People* (1982), *Light of Day* (1987), *Patty Hearst* (1988), and *The Comfort of Strangers* (1991). Early in his career, he was an editor of the magazine *Cinema* (1970), and in the same period wrote the book *Transcendental Style in Film: Ozu, Bresson and Dreyer* (1972). He has also published *Schrader on Schrader* (1990), co-written by Kevin Jackson. Schrader's B.A. was from Calvin College, his M.A. from the University of California at Los Angeles. He is married to actress Mary Beth Hurt.

FURTHER READING

"To hell with Paul Schrader." LAURA DE COPPET. *Interview*, Mar. 1992.
"Paul Schrader. . . ." *American Film*, July–Aug. 1989.
"Citizen Paul." RICHARD GEHR. *American Film*, Sep. 1988.

Schroeder, Patricia Scott (1940–)
Representative Pat Schroeder, a women's rights movement leader and liberal Democrat, won reelection to her eleventh Congressional term in 1992, with a landslide 69 percent to 31 percent victory, becoming part of the story of "The Year of the Woman"—although it is likely that she would have won handily in any event. During 1992, Schroeder and her colleagues were caught up in the "gridlock" generated by a Republican President and Democratic Congress, each seeking to portray the other as "do-nothing" in a presidential election year, and both succeeding in—doing nothing. One major accomplishment, though, was her participation in the development of the Women's Health Equity Act; it failed to pass, but provided a plan that many thought would become law in the next Congress.

Schroeder was also greatly involved in sexual discrimination issues, as in the aftermath of the 1991 Navy Tailhook scandal. A member of the House Armed Services Committee, she was unpopular with some in the military for this, and for advocating women's entry into combat functions. In one notable incident, three senior Navy fliers, all Fighter Squadron commanders, were relieved of command for not taking action when a group of fighter pilots put on a sexually offensive skit referring to Schroeder.

Portland-born Schroeder's 1961 B.A. was from the University of Minnesota, and her 1964 J.D. from Harvard Law School. She was a field attorney with the National Labor Relations Board (1964–66), and an attorney and teacher until her first election to the House of Representatives in 1972. Among her written works are *The Great American Family* (1988) and *Champion of the Great American Family: A Personal and Political Book* (1989), co-authored with Andrea Camp and Robyn Lipner. She is married to James White Schroeder; they have two children.

FURTHER READING

Women in Power: The Secrets of Leadership. DOROTHY W. CANTOR. Houghton Mifflin, 1992.
"Women of the House." MARIANNE WAIT. *Ladies Home Journal*, Nov. 1991.
"Watch Pat run." JANE O'REILLY and GLORIA JACOBS. *Ms.*, Feb. 1988.

Schuman, William Howard (1910–92)
New York City-born Schuman, a leading composer and educator, taught music at Sarah Lawrence College from 1935 to 1945, was briefly chief editor at the music publisher G. Schirmer in 1945, and later that year became president of the Juilliard School of Music. From 1962 to 1969,

he was the first president of New York's Lincoln Center for the Performing Arts, and also held several other administrative and board positions in the American music world, including that of chairman of the MacDowell Colony. His early work included the *American Festival Overture* (1939), the critically acclaimed *Third Symphony* (1943), and the cantata *A Free Song* (1943), for which he won the first Pulitzer Prize for music. Central to his work were the ten symphonies; he also composed several concertos, four string quartets, and wide range of ballet, operatic, choral, and band music. Among his many honors was a second Pulizer Prize, awarded in 1985 for his whole body of composition and administration. He was survived by his wife, the former Frances Prince, a daughter, and a son. (d. New York City; February 15,1992)

FURTHER READING

"William Howard Schuman." KARL F. MILLER. *American Record Guide*, July–Aug. 1992.
Obituary. *Variety*, Feb, 24, 1992.
Obituary. *The Times* (of London), Feb. 17, 1992.
Obituary. *New York Times*, Feb. 16, 1992.

Schwarzenegger, Arnold Alois

(1947–) Action-violence film star Schwarzenegger, a worldwide celebrity, was probably the world's most bankable film star after the success of his 1991 *Terminator 2: Judgment Day*, a worldwide hit that ultimately grossed in the $450–500 million range, its special effects and extraordinary violence highly prized by Schwarzenegger's huge audiences. Forthcoming was another massive blockbuster film, John McTiernan's *The Last Action Hero*, scheduled for summer 1993 release.

Schwarzenegger in 1992 continued to appear widely as an advocate of clean living and healthy lifestyles, most notably for President George Bush's Youth and Fitness Council. Due in 1993 were two books: *Arnold: The Education of a Bodybuilder*, written with Douglas K. Hall, and *Arnold's Fitness for Kids Ages Eleven to Fourteen: A Guide to Health, Exercise, and Nutrition*, with Charles Gaines. Schwarzenegger also was a prominent supporter of Bush's unsuccessful re-election bid.

Schwarzenegger in 1992 made his film directing debut with the comedy *Christmas in Con-* *necticut*, starring Dyan Cannon, Kris Kristofferson, Richard Roundtree, and Tony Curtis. It was a remake of the 1945 Peter Godfrey film, starring Barbara Stanwyck and Dennis Morgan.

Austrian-born Schwarzenegger was a champion bodybuilder (1969–75), then turning to films. He played in such films as *Stay Hungry* (1976) and *Pumping Iron* (1977), emerged as an action film star in *Conan, the Barbarian* (1982; and the 1983 sequel), and went on to such very popular films as *The Terminator* (1984), *Commando* (1985), *Raw Deal* (1986), *Predator* (1987), *Red Heat* (1988), *Twins* (1988), *Total Recall* (1990), *Kindergarten Cop* (1990), and *Terminator 2: Judgment Day* (1991). He has also written several bodybuilding books. He attended the University of Wisconsin. He married newscaster Maria Owings Shriver in 1986; the couple have two children.

FURTHER READING

"Fitness. . . ." JOHN WOOD. *Modern Maturity*, Dec.–Jan. 1992.
" 'Steroids don't pay off.' " KENNETH T. WALSH. *U.S. News & World Report*, June 1, 1992.
Arnold Schwarzenegger. SUE HAMILTON. Abdo & Daughters, 1992.
Arnold Schwarzenegger. BROOKS ROBARDS. Smithmark, 1992.
"Schwarzenegger, Arnold." *Current Biography*, Oct. 1991.
"Mr. Big Shot." BILL ZEHME. *Rolling Stone*, Aug. 22, 1991.
"Arnold Schwarzenegger. . . ." JEFF ROVIN. *Ladies Home Journal*, Aug. 1991.
"Rnld Schwzngr." PAT H. BROESKE and HERB RITTS. *Interview*, July 1991.
Schwarzenegger. NAL-Dutton, 1991.
"Box-office brawn. . . ." RICHARD CORLISS. *Time*, Dec. 24, 1990.
"Pumping. . . ." LYNN ROSELLINI. *U.S. News & World Report*, Nov. 26, 1990.
"Brand loyalty." SUZANNE MOORE. *New Statesman & Society*, Aug. 3, 1990.
Arnold Schwarzenegger: A Portrait. GEORGE BUTLER. Simon & Schuster, 1990.
Arnold: The Unauthorized Biography. WENDY LEIGH. Congdon & Weed, 1990.

Schwarzkopf, H. Norman (1934–)

With the focus of his country changed from victory in the Persian Gulf War to the worsening economy and the 1992 Presidential election, still-popular General Schwarzkopf, now retired, became a far less visible presence on the American scene. For many, the war itself also became somewhat tarnished, as Democrats mounting a successful Presidential campaign charged the Bush administration with having encouraged and supplied Saddam Hussein before the war. There was also criticism of the early termination of hostilities, which allowed much of the elite Iraqi Republican Guard to escape, with their weapons. Schwarzkopf did not take a very visible role in the presidential campaign, beyond supporting George Bush in the Florida primary and expressing reservations about Bill Clinton as a commander-in-chief because of his draft record; he also expressed similar doubts about Dan Quayle. He did assert that the Clinton and Perot campaign staffs had queried him as to his interest in a vice-presidential nomination, but that he was not interested.

Schwarzkopf became a broadcaster in 1992, as part of a CBS World War II series; in June 1992, CBS announced that Schwarzkopf had signed a three-year contract to host news documentaries and specials. October saw publication of his best-selling autobiography *It Doesn't Take a Hero*; the latter half of the book took up the Persian Gulf War, detailing the Desert Shield and Desert Storm operations. Some accompanying newspaper articles and reviews made much of his assertion that administration "hawks" insisted on an earlier start than he had favored for the land war against Iraq.

New Jersey-born Schwarzkopf is a career military officer. He is a 1956 graduate of West Point, later studying guided missile engineering at the University of Southern California. An infantry officer for much of his career, he joined the Army as a second lieutenant, was a paratroop advisor during his first Vietnam tour of duty, and was an infantry battalion commander during his second tour of duty. He was wounded twice in Vietnam, and won three Silver Stars. He commanded mechanized infantry divisions at home and in Germany during the 1970s and early 1980s, and was deputy commander of American forces during the 1983 Grenada invasion, becoming a leading field commander in the late 1980s. He married Brenda Holsinger in 1968; they have three children.

FURTHER READING

"Calm that followed. . . ." VALERIE GROVE. *Times*, Oct. 23, 1992.

"What Schwarzkopf's book. . . ." JERRY BARRY. "Schwarzkopf's autobiography . . . ." *Newsweek*, Sep. 28, 1992.

"Norman after the storm." JAMES ADAMS. *Sunday Times*, Sep. 27, 1992.

General H. Norman Schwarzkopf. BOB ITALIA. Abdo & Daughters, 1992.

Norman Schwarzkopf: Hero with a Heart. LIBBY HUGHES. Dillon/Macmillan, 1992.

Norman Schwarzkopf. REBECCA STEFOFF. Chelsea House, 1992.

"Desert Norm." C.D.B. BRYAN. *Reader's Digest* (Canadian), July 1991.

"Schwarzkopf, H. Norman." *Current Biography*, May 1991.

"Fierce loyalty. . . ." RICHARD MACKENZIE. *Insight*, Mar. 18, 1991.

"A general's cunning. . . ." RICHARD MACKENZIE and ERIC FELTEN. *Insight*, Mar. 18, 1991.

"Operation Desert Norm. . . ." C.D.B. BRYAN. *New Republic*, Mar. 11, 1991.

"Stormin' Norman. . . ." *People*, Mar 11, 1991.

"A soldier of conscience. . . ." TOM MATHEWS and C.S. MANEGOLD. *Newsweek*, Mar. 11, 1991.

"Sayings of Stormin' Norman." *Time*, Mar. 11, 1991.

"A bear leads the invasion." *Maclean's*, Mar. 4, 1991.

"Stormin' Norman. . . ." JESSE BIRNBAUM and DAN FISCHER. *Time*, Feb. 4, 1991.

"The Gulf. . . ." LINDA ROCAWICH. *Progressive*, Jan. 1991.

In the Eye of the Storm: The Life of General H. Norman Schwarzkopf. ROGER COHEN and CLAUDIO GATTI. Farrar, Straus & Giroux, 1991.

H. Norman Schwarzkopf. E.J. VALENTINE. Bantam, 1991.

H. Norman Schwarzkopf: Road to Triumph. M.E. MORRIS. St. Martin's, 1991.

Schwarzkopf: An Insider's View of the Commander and His Victory. ROBERT D. PARRISH. Bantam, 1991.

Schwarzkopf in His Own Words. RICHARD PYLE. NAL-Dutton, 1991.

In the Eye of Desert Storm. C.D. BRYAN. Abrams, 1991.

Scorsese, Martin (1942–)

Celebrated film director Scorsese was not immune to the wave of postponements and cancellations that plagued filmmakers in 1992, as the worldwide recession deepened. His major film of the year, the forthcoming *The Age of Innocence*, starring Daniel Day-Lewis, Michelle Pfeiffer, and Winona Ryder, completed filming in late spring, and was scheduled for Christmas 1992 release, with publication of an accompanying book. But

Paramount postponed release, rescheduling it for the autumn of 1993, almost a year later.

Scorsese did produce Irwin Winkler's 1992 remake of Jules Dassin's 1950 *Night and the City*, starring Robert De Niro and Jessica Lange. He was also to produce the forthcoming Daniel Algrant film *Naked in New York*, starring Timothy Dalton, Whoopi Goldberg, Kathleen Turner, Eric Stolz, and Mary Louise Parker. Another forthcoming Scorsese production was John Mac-Naughton's *Mad Dog and Glory*, starring Robert De Niro.

Scorsese continued his work of restoring old films to their original condition, and continued to fight for the right of creators of films to successfully resist their alteration, as by colorization and soundtrack alterations. In March, he was named to the French Order of Arts and Letters.

New York-born Scorsese scored his first major success with *Mean Streets* (1973), set on the underside of New York life. He went on to become one of the major directors of the modern period, with such films as *Alice Doesn't Live Here Anymore* (1974), *Taxi Driver* (1976), *New York, New York* (1977), the classic *Raging Bull* (1980), *The Color of Money* (1986), the highly controversial *The Last Temptation of Christ* (1988), *Good-Fellas* (1990), and *Cape Fear* (1991). He also appeared as an actor in a small but key role as Van Gogh in *Akira Kurosawa's Dreams* (1990). Scorsese's 1964 B.S. and 1966 M.A. in Film Communications were from New York University. He has been married four times and has two children.

FURTHER READING

The Scorsese Picture: The Art and Life of Martin Scorsese. DAVID EHRENSTEIN. Birch Lane/Carol, 1992.

Martin Scorsese. LESTER KEYSER. Twayne/Macmillan, 1992.

"Martin Scorsese." GRAHAM FULLER. *Interview*, Nov. 1991.

"Slouching toward Hollywood. . . ." PETER BISKIND. *Premiere*, Nov. 1991.

"Playboy interview. . . ." DAVID RENSIN. *Playboy*, Apr. 1991.

Martin Scorsese: A Journey. MARY P. KELLY. Thunder's Mouth, 1991.

The Future of the Movies: Interviews with Martin Scorsese, George Lucas, and Steven Spielberg. ROGER EBERT and GENE SISKEL. Andrews & McMeel, 1991.

"Martin Scorsese." ANTHONY DECURTIS. *Rolling Stone*, Nov. 1, 1990.

"Blood and pasta." AMY TAUBIN. *New Statesman & Society*, Nov. 9, 1990.

"Made men." KATHLEEN MURPHY and GAVIN SMITH. *Film Comment*, Sep.–Oct. 1990.

" 'God's lonely man'. . . ." RICHARD GEHR. *Video Magazine*, Mar. 1990.

Martin Scorsese: A Guide to References & Resources. MARION WEISS. G.K. Hall, 1987.

Martin Scorsese and Michael Cimino. MICHAEL BLISS. Scarecrow, 1985.

Scowcroft, Brent (1925–) In his final year as National Security Advisor, Lieutenant-General Scowcroft continued to assess and develop U.S. policy in the post-Cold War world, as the collapse of Soviet Union, the new balances in the Middle East after the Persian Gulf War, and the end of many regional conflicts—as well as the beginning of many new ones—generated new sets of problems and opportunities for the United States and its allies. But, although the world was just as large and just as problemed as it had been in earlier years, there was less scope for Scowcroft, for George Bush was locked in the electoral struggle that would in November end his career. Major focus was on the issues affecting that struggle, most notably the worsening U.S. economy, rather than on the global geopolitical issues that had for 45 years been Scowcroft's main concerns. Scowcroft in 1992 watched Iraq's Saddam Hussein, threatening military action if necessary on nuclear and chemical weapons questions, and in August setting up the "no-fly" zone in southern Iraq; continued to advise the President on a worldwide range of matters; and awaited the outcome of the elections. At one point, late in the campaign, he contested a Ross Perot assertion about pre-Persian Gulf War events; otherwise, he was not visibly part of the campaign.

Scowcroft is an old "Washington hand," a career military officer and strategic planner. He went to Washington as an Air Force strategic planner in the mid-1960s, after teaching at West Point and at the Air Force Academy, as well as serving in Belgrade as an Air Force attaché. He was a White House-based military assistant to President Nixon (1971–72), was deputy national security assistant (1973–75), and then became President Ford's national security assistant (1975–77). During the Carter and Reagan administrations, he served on several advisory committees, most notably as a member of the Tower Commission, joining in its adverse report on Reagan administration behavior during the Iran-Contra affair. Utah-born Scowcroft was a West Point graduate in 1947; his 1953 M.A. and 1967 Ph.D. were from Columbia. He married Marian Horner in 1951; they have one child.

FURTHER READING

"America can't afford to turn inward." *New Perspectives*, Summer 1992.
"What foreign policy? . . ." JOHN B. JUDIS. *New Republic*, Feb. 24, 1992.
"Brent Scowcroft. . . ." PRISCILLA PAINTON. *Time*, Oct. 7, 1991.
" 'We won't let. . . .' " KENNETH T. WALSH. *U.S. News & World Report*, Dec. 24, 1990.
" 'Even Saddam. . . .' " DOUGLAS HARBRECHT. *Business Week*, Sep. 10, 1990.
"Distrust, but verify. . . ." FRED BARNES. *New Republic*, Mar. 6, 1989.

Seale, Arthur (1947–) and Seale, Irene

On April 29, 1992, Irene and Arthur Seale kidnapped Sidney J. Reso, president of Exxon Company International, as he left his Morris Township, New Jersey, home on the way to his nearby office. Reso, who was shot and wounded during the kidnapping, was bound, gagged, blindfolded, and placed in a public storage box in Washington, New Jersey. He was given no food or water, and died a few days later. Meanwhile, the Seales, posing as "environmental" terrorists,

attempted to collect a multimillion-dollar ransom from Exxon. The Seales were captured on June 21st, after law enforcement agents, following their instructions, had tracked them and their rented car during their attempt to collect the ransom. The kidnappers at first denied all charges, but in late June Irene Seale changed her story, led investigators to Reso's grave, and pleaded guilty to much reduced charges of extortion, in return for testifying against her husband. Arthur Seale pleaded not guilty to all charges, but on September 8th pleaded guilty to seven counts of extortion and conspiracy, with life imprisonment in prospect. The nature of the crime, the false issue of terrorism, and the terrible death of the victim all contributed to the great public interest generated by the kidnapping.

FURTHER READING

"Death in a storage locker." KENNETH L. WOODWARD. *Newsweek*, July 13, 1992.
"Reso's last days." *Time*, July 13, 1992.

Seles, Monica (1974–) Young Monica Seles dominated the world of women's tennis in 1992. Martina Navratilova, who met Seles in several finals and semifinals, and who herself is no slouch in the power department, described her opponent variously as playing like a "big, bad wolf" or "a Mack truck." Seles had reached the finals of all 16 events she entered in 1991 and all but 1 of 15 in 1992, including a string of 22 consecutive finals, second only to Navratilova's earlier 23. In that two-year period Seles won an astonishing 10 tournaments, including six Grand Slam titles; she also became the first woman in 55 years (since Hilde Sperling) to win three consecutive French Open crowns. Her 1992 single-year earnings of over $2.6 million broke her own 1991 record—for male or female tennis player—of $2.4 million. With those statistics, she remained the world's top-ranked woman tennis player for the second consecutive year.

Not that she had things all her own way. Opponents complained about her widely discussed "grunting" when she hits the ball, saying that it prevents them from hearing the sound of the ball as it hits the racket. The media took up the question, and some newspapers even installed "gruntometers" to measure the courtside decibel level. At Wimbledon, Seles attempted to go silent; whether that distraction played a part in her loss to Steffi Graf in the finals of that Grand Slam event is unknown. Late in the year, Seles's grunting was even the subject of a comic skit on "Saturday Night Live." Certainly, some observers noted a double standard on noise production, since male grunters over the years, such as Jimmy Connors, have not been especially singled out or criticized.

Ethnically a Hungarian, Seles was born in the Serbian part of what was Yugoslavia, but had no love for the government there. On entering Wimbledon in 1992 she listed herself as from Sarasota, Florida, where she has lived since 1986.

A leading amateur tennis player in her native Yugoslavia and throughout Europe, Seles came to America with her family at age 11 to train at the Bradenton Tennis Academy in Florida under Nick Bollettieri; she was also coached by her father, cartoonist and documentary filmmaker Xarolj. Seles turned professional in 1989, and emerged in 1990 as a dominating presence on the women's tennis scene, winning the Italian and German Opens, and defeating then-No. 1 player Steffi Graf at the French Open, becoming the youngest player since 1887 to win a Grand Slam event. She won the French Open again in 1991 and 1992; her other Grand Slam titles include the U.S. Open (1991 and 1992) and the Australian Open (1991 and 1992).

FURTHER READING

"Women's tour '92. . . ." CINDY HAHN. *Tennis*, Feb. 1992.

"Mystery women or material girl?" PETER BODO. *Tennis*, Nov. 1991.

"Madonna is the model." PETER NEWCOMB. *Forbes*, Aug. 19, 1991.

"Steppin' out. . . ." CURRY KIRKPATRICK. *Sports Illustrated*, May 27, 1991.

"Monica Seles. . . ." PETER BODO. *Tennis*, Jan. 1991.

"Grunts, giggles. . . ." JIM MARTZ. *Sporting News*, Aug. 27, 1990.

"Hitting out in all directions." CINDY SHMERLER. *World Tennis*, Aug. 1990.

"Yiii! Can this be. . . ." SUSAN REED. *People*, July 2, 1990.

Selleck, Tom (1945–) Television and film

star Tom Selleck starred in 1992 as Jack Elliott, an aging American baseball player in Japan in Fred Schepisi's film *Mr. Baseball*, in an other-

wise Japanese cast. The highly controversial film had originally included some material critical of Japanese anti-foreign and specifically anti-American bias, emphasis on warlike spirit, group over individual dominance, and brutal workout practices. After the Matsushita Electric takeover of MCA, Universal Pictures' parent company, the original director was replaced and the script greatly reworked to show the Selleck character making great personal changes to conform to the "superior" Japanese ways, the critical material being greatly softpedaled. The much-discussed question of anti-Black bias in Japanese baseball was reportedly not even taken up. The film was a critical and commercial failure in the United States.

Selleck also starred as King Ferdinand, opposite Marlon Brando as Spanish Inquisition leader Torquemada, George Corraface as Columbus, and Rachel Ward as Isabella in John Glen's *Christopher Columbus: The Discovery*, produced by Ilya Salkind. Almost universally panned by the critics, the expensive film was a box-office disaster. Selleck also starred as Jon Aldrich in Ted Kotcheff's comedy *Folks*, with Don Ameche, Anne Jackson, Christine Ebersole, and Wendy Crewson as the rest of the Aldrich family; this film, too, was very badly received.

Detroit-born Selleck appeared on stage and screen during the 1970s, and emerged as a major star playing the title role of the television series "Magnum P.I." (1980–88). His films include *High Road to China* (1983), *Lassiter* (1984),

Runaway (1985), *Three Men and a Baby* (1987), *Her Alibi* (1989), *Three Men and a Little Lady* (1990), and *Quigley Down Under* (1990). Selleck attended the University of Southern California. He has been married twice, the second time to actress Jillie Mack in 1987, and has two children.

FURTHER READING

"Tom Selleck. . . ." CINDY PEARLMEN. *First for Women,* July 27, 1992.
"Three man and. . . ." JEFF ROVIN. *Ladies Home Journal,* Dec. 1990.
"Magnum. . . ." PAT JORDAN. *GQ—Gentlemen's Quarterly,* Oct. 1989.
"Tom Selleck." MERRILL SHINDLER. *Los Angeles Magazine,* Feb. 1989.

Sergeyev, Constantin Mikhailovich

(1910–92) A leading Russian dancer and choreographer of the Soviet period, Sergeyev emerged as a major figure after joining St. Petersburg's (then Leningrad) Kirov Ballet in 1930. Dancing largely in the classics, and often opposite prima ballerina Galina Ulanova, he was a leading dancer with the Kirov for three decades, retiring as a dancer in 1961. He began his career as a choreographer in 1946 with the Kirov's staging of Prokofiev's *Cinderella,* and went on to do new stagings of several ballet classics. Sergeyev, a conservative in dance, was the artistic director of the Kirov Ballet (1951–55), and again (1960–70), then being removed by the Soviet government after the defection to the West of ballerina Natalya Makarova. During his later years, he remained associated with the Kirov. He was survived by his wife, the ballerina and teacher Natalia Dudinskaya. (d. St. Petersburg; April 1, 1992)

FURTHER READING

Obituary. *Variety,* Apr. 20, 1992.
Obituary. *Independent,* Apr. 15, 1992.
Obituary. *The Times* (of London), Apr. 11, 1992.
Obituary. *New York Times,* Apr. 11, 1992.
"Two decades of Kirov danseurs. . . ." *Dance,* Apr. 1989.

Sevareid, Eric

(1912–92) South Dakota-born Sevareid, a leading broadcast and print journalist, began his career in 1936 with the *Minneapolis Journal.* In 1938, after studying in Europe, he became a newspaper reporter and then night editor for the Paris edition of the *New York Herald Tribune.* In August 1939, Edward R. Murrow asked him to join the CBS team he was assembling to cover the coming world war. Sevareid accepted, and began his broadcasting career at the center of world events, broadcasting from Paris just before it fell to the Nazis, announcing the coming French surrender, and joining Murrow in Britain during the Blitz. He returned to the United States in 1940, later going out again to cover the Far East, the invasion of Italy, the partisan war in Yugoslavia, and the fall of Germany. Sevareid went on to become a familiar and authoritative television news presence for the rest of his very long career, covering presidential campaigns, Cold War crises, and all the other major events of his time long after his retirement from CBS in 1977. He also wrote a syndicated column and several books. He was survived by his third wife, Susan St. Pierre, a daughter, and two sons. (d. Washington, D. C.; July 9, 1992)

FURTHER READING

"The philosopher-correspondent." CHARLES LEERHSEN. *Newsweek,* July 20, 1992.
Obituary. *The Times* (of London), July 14, 1992.
Obituary. *Variety,* July 13, 1992.
Obituary. *New York Times,* July 10, 1992.

Shalala, Donna Edna

(1941–) President Bill Clinton's incoming Secretary of Health and Human Services began her career in education as a Peace Corps teacher in Iran (1962–64). She worked at Syracuse University (1965–70), was assistant professor of political science at City University of New York (CUNY; 1970–72), and was an associate professor at Teachers College of Columbia University (1972–79). She was an assistant secretary for policy development and research at the Department of Housing and Urban Development (1977–80). Shalala emerged as a major figure as president of Hunter College (1980–88), and then as the highly visible chancellor of the University of Wisconsin (1988–92), in that position stressing multicultural education and ethnic and women's studies and rights. Among her many advisory board and board of director posts is that of chairman of the board of the Children's Defense Fund.

Cleveland-born Shalala's 1962 A.B. was from Western College, and her 1968 M.S.S.C. from Syracuse University, as was her 1970 Ph.D.

FURTHER READING

"Campus CEO." CEIL CLEVELAND. *Working Woman*, Dec. 1991.
"Shalala, Donna Edna." *Current Biography*, Mar. 1991.
"Big campus, big issues. . . ." BONNIE ANGEL. *Time*, Apr. 23, 1990.
"Tackling the Big Ten. . . ." LINDSY VAN GELDER. *Savvy Woman*, Dec. 1989.

Shamir, Yitzhak

Shamir, Yitzhak (Yitzhak Yzernitsky; 1915–) For the first five months of 1992, Israeli Prime Minister Shamir conducted business much as usual, steering Israel on an entirely hard-line ultraconservative course. That meant full support of settlement in the lands occupied by Israel, only token participation in the Middle East peace talks, and continually worsening relations with the United States, Israel's chief ally. That was so even though the Palestine Liberation Organization had emerged from its support of Iraq during the Persian Gulf War in much weakened condition, and even though the united anti-Israeli front of the Arab states had long since ceased to exist.

Shamir's constituency felt differently, however. The majority of Israelis were ready for more flexibility and a real attempt to bring a full-scale Middle East settlement. On June 23, Labor won enough of a plurality to form a coalition government without the Likud Party, and Yitzhak Rabin once again became prime minister. In defeat, Shamir continued on as leader of the opposition, although immediately after the election he had seemed to state that he would soon retire.

Shamir became a Zionist in his native Poland, emigrating to Israel in 1935. In 1937, he became a member of the terrorist group Irgun Zvai Leumi, and in 1940 left the Irgun with Abraham Stern to become a founder of the terrorist group Lehi, better known as the Stern Gang. In 1942, he became chief of operations of the Stern Gang, which was responsible for a great many terrorist operations, most notably including the assassinations of Lord Moyne in 1944 and of United Nations mediator Folke Bernadotte in 1948. He was a member of Israeli intelligence (1955–65). Shamir moved into politics with the Herut Party in 1970, was elected to the Israeli parliament in 1973, was foreign minister in the Menachim Begin government (1980–83), and succeeded Begin as prime minister in 1983. He served as foreign minister (1984–86), and again became prime minister in 1986. Shamir attended Warsaw University and the Hebrew University of Jerusalem. He is married, and has two children.

FURTHER READING

"Arguing Israel's case. . . ." MORTIMER B. ZUCKERMAN. *U.S. News & World Report*, Feb. 3, 1992.
"When Shamir blinked. . . ." ELIAHU SALPETER. *New Leader*, Aug. 12, 1991.
"The view from Jerusalem." *U.S. News & World Report*, Apr. 16, 1990.
"A talk with. . . ." J. ROBERT MOSKIN. *Present Tense*, May–June 1989.
"A talk with Dr. No." JACQUES AMALRIC and ALAIN FRACHON. *World Press Review*, Apr. 1989.
"Saying no to Arafat. . . ." SCOTT MACLEOD. *Time*, Jan. 2, 1989.
"Shamir stands his ground. . . ." *Newsweek*, Jan. 2, 1989.

Sharon, Ariel

Sharon, Ariel (1928–) Israeli political leader Sharon lost his early 1992 bid to replace Prime Minister Yitzhak Shamir as leader of the Likud Party, on February 20th winning only a little over 22 percent of the leadership vote in the Likud central committee. He remained housing minister in the Shamir government, and the leader of the very far right in Israeli politics, however, and moved up to third position on the Likud candidates list for the June 23rd general elections.

During the election campaign, the conduct of Sharon's housing ministry was criticicized in a government audit, which charged that much had been wasted, and also made serious fraud charges against some in the ministry. Although Sharon defended his ministry, the report was damaging to him and to his party, probably helping to defeat Likud at the polls. Labor won enough of a plurality to form a coalition government without the Likud Party. As a result, Yitzhak Rabin once again became prime minister, and Sharon was replaced as housing minister, going into opposition.

A career military officer, Sharon was active in the main Israeli fighting force, the Haganah, from the mid-1940s, and fought in the 1948 Israeli War of Independence and accompanying First Arab-Israeli War. He conducted anti-guerrilla actions in the low-level border war that followed, and rose to divisional command during the 1967 and 1972 Arab-Israeli wars. He went into politics in 1973, holding several cabinet-level posts during the 1970s. He was appointed defense minister by Menachem Begin in 1981 and was a chief architect of the 1982 Lebanon invasion, being forced to resign that post after the Sabra and Shatila massacres, but remaining in the cabinet through the 1980s. In 1986 he was involved in a notable libel suit with *Time* magazine. In 1990, he published *Warrior: An Autobiography*.

Sharon attended Hebrew University. He is married, and has two children.

FURTHER READING

"A place to call home. " DANIELLE PLETKA. *Insight*, Oct. 28, 1991.
"Destroy Iraq's military. . . ." NATHAN GARDELS. *New Perspectives*, Winter 1991.
"Never! Never! Never!" MURRAY J. GART. *Time*, Apr. 17, 1989.
Blood Libel: The Inside Story of General Ariel Sharon's History-Making Suit Against Time Magazine. URI DAN. Simon & Schuster, 1987.
Reckless Disregard: Westmoreland v. CBS et al.; Sharon v. Time. RENATA ADLER. Knopf, 1986.

Shawn, William (1907–92)

One of the leading magazine editors of his day, Chicago-born Shawn began his career in the mid-1920s as a reporter in Las Vegas and Chicago. He started his long association with *The New Yorker* in the early 1930s, becoming an editor of the magazine in 1935. He was promoted to managing editor early in World War II, and succeeded founding editor Harold Ross as chief editor when Ross retired in 1952. Ross had developed the light, witty, sometimes acerbic style that had made the magazine into one of the best-loved magazines of the 1920s, 30s, and 40s. Under Shawn, *The New Yorker* became far more serious, dealing directly with many of the issues of the day, while in its graphics and features maintaining some of the lightness that had previously distinguished it. For 35 years, Shawn was one of the most influential of American magazine editors, his rule at the magazine absolute. In 1985, *The New Yorker* was sold to the Newhouse publishing company, Advance Publications; in January 1987, the new owners forced Shawn's retirement, at the age of 80, a move hotly and unsuccessfully contested by many of the magazine's employees and contributors. Shawn attended the University of Michigan. He was survived by his wife, Cecille Lyon Shawn, a daughter, and two sons. (d. New York City; December 8, 1992)

FURTHER READING

Obituary. *New Yorker*, Dec. 21, 1992.
"A lover of the long shot." DAVID GATES. *Newsweek*, Dec. 21, 1992.
Obituary. *Variety*, Dec. 14, 1992.
Obituary. *The Times* (of London), Dec. 10, 1992
Obituary. *The New York Times*, Dec. 9, 1992.
The Last Days of the New Yorker. GIGI MAHON. McGraw-Hill, 1989.

Sheen, Martin (Ramon Estevez; 1940–)

Veteran stage and screen star Sheen ended his run as John Proctor in the National Actors Theater production of Arthur Miller's *The Crucible* in early 1992, and then returned to his film career, although he did star opposite Trish Van Devere in a one-week July Santa Barbara production of A.R. Gurney's *Love Letters*. On screen, Sheen starred in Amin Chaudhri's forthcoming film *Finnegan's Wake*, based on the James Joyce novel; Lara Flynn Boyle, F. Murray Abraham, and Martin Landau co-starred. He also hosted two television specials, one on *Columbus: The World's First Astronaut*, the other the National Geographic television film *Braving Alaska*, profiling several modern Alaskan pioneering families.

Sheen was as always also active on the political side of life, backing Barbara Boxer in the California senatorial campaign. He also co-sponsored a January 25th New York "Peace For Cuba" rally, that favored lifting U.S. economic sanctions and travel restrictions aimed at the Castro government, and drew some thousands of anti-Castro demonstrators.

Ohio-born Sheen played on stage with the Living Theatre from 1959, on Broadway in *The Subject Was Roses* (1964; and in the 1968 film version) and at the New York Shakespeare Festival in the late 1960s. On screen, he appeared in such films as *Catch-22* (1970), *Apocalypse Now* (1979), *Gandhi* (1982), *Wall Street* (1987), and *The Maid* (1991), and such telefilms as *The Execution of Private Slovik* (1974), *The Missiles of October* (1974; as Robert Kennedy), *Blind Ambition* (1979; as John Dean), *Kennedy* (1982; as John F. Kennedy), *Samaritan: The Mitch Snyder Story* (1986; as AIDS activist Snyder), and *Guilty Until Proven Innocent* (1991). He married Janet Sheen in 1961; they have four children, two them the actors Charlie Sheen and Emilio Estevez.

FURTHER READING

Martin Sheen: Actor and Activist. JIM HARGROVE. Childrens, 1991.

Sheets, Robert C. (1937–) As Hurricane Andrew stormed across south Florida, the Gulf of Mexico, and then Louisiana from August 24–26, 1992, Bob Sheets, director of the Hurricane Center, was seen and heard everywhere, as a voice of calm on virtually every television report, describing the expected course and passing on warnings to people in its path, in the process surely saving hundreds, perhaps thousands, of lives. He was there, of course, for the many other hurricanes of the year, as he has been for many years, but Andrew was one of the worst of the century, and certainly the costliest. Not only that, but the vicious storm headed straight for the Hurricane Center itself, just south of Miami proper. Sheets was personally involved, too; his own house and those of family members were damaged by Andrew's winds. How fast those winds were in Florida, Sheets and his staff could only estimate—they guessed sustained winds of 145 mph and gusts of 175 mph, based on barometric pressure, reconnaissance airplane data, and the last readings before meters were blown out of action, their wind-speed instruments out of operation, blown apart, damaged by flying debris, or taken out of harm's way before the storm hit directly.

After graduating from Ball State University in 1961, Indiana-born Sheets became an Air Weather Service Office officer in the U.S. Air Force (1961–64), and then obtained a Master's degree (1965) and later a Ph.D. (1972) in meteorology from the University of Oklahoma. He joined the National Hurricane Center in 1965, conducted and supervised field research until 1980, became a specialist in providing and improving forecasts and warnings (1980–85), was promoted to deputy director and, since 1987, has been director of the Center. Sheets lectures nationally and internationally on tropical cyclones, and has received numerous awards for his work. He and his wife, Mary Jane, have a son and two daughters.

FURTHER READING

"Eye on the storms." MARK LANG. *Connoisseur*, Mar. 1991.

Shevardnadze, Eduard Amvroslyevich (1928–) Former Soviet foreign minister Shevardnadze went home to Georgia in 1992, and in March was chosen to head the new country's State Council. In that position, he spent much of the year trying to unify a fragmented country, facing armed secession movements in South Ossetia and Abkhazia, and the armed forces of deposed Georgia President Zviad K. Gamsakhurdia in western Georgia. On June 24, he surived a coup attempt by Gamsakhurdia supporters in Tbilisi, the Georgian capital. On the same day, he and Russian President Boris Yeltsin arranged a ceasefire and placed a Russian-Georgian peacekeeping force on the South Ossetia-Georgia border.

On October 11, 1992, Shevardnadze was elected parliamentary Speaker, and as such effectively president of Georgia. He immediately moved to deal with the civil war in Abkhazia. He and Yeltsin had arranged a ceasefire in that war on September 3, followed by major Georgian force reductions in the area. Abkhazian rebel forces, helped by Russian "volunteers" and armed with Russian weapons and supplies, then quickly moved in to take much of Abkhazia, while Yeltsin ordered Russian forces in Abkhazia to protect Russians there.

Until December 20, 1990, Shevardnadze had spent his whole life in Communist Party and Soviet government work, beginning his career in the late 1940s, and rising through a series of Communist Party positions in his native Georgia through the early 1970s. His first major move came in 1972, when he led an anticorruption campaign in Georgia and replaced the Republic's party leader. He was first secretary of the Georgian Communist Party (1972–85), becoming a Soviet Central Committee member in 1976. Long associated with Mikhail Gorbachev, Shevardnadze replaced Andrei Gromyko as Soviet foreign minister in 1985 and remained in that position throughout most of the extraordinary Gorbachev era. He broke with Gorbachev and resigned as foreign minister on December 20, 1990, because of the too-slow pace of reform and Gorbachev's appointment of hardline conservative Communists to key positions; at the time, he warned against a restoration of rightwing Communist dictatorship, raising the prospect of a disastrous civil war should that happen. He then founded the Soviet Foreign Policy Association and the Democratic Reform Movement. In December 1991, he served briefly as the last Soviet foreign minister. Shevardnadze attended the Kutaisi Pedagogical Institute. He has published *The Future Belongs to Freedom: World Peace and Democracy in the U.S.S.R.* (1991).

FURTHER READING

" 'The dark forces. . . .' " *Time*, Oct. 5, 1992.
"Georgia preying. . . ." PETER PRINGLE. *Independent*, Sep. 24, 1992.
"Curious Georgia." SIMON SEBAG MONTEFIORE. *New Republic*, June 29, 1992.
" 'Mikhail Gorbachev has. . . .' " *U.S. News & World Report*, Sep. 2, 1991.
"A growing momentum. . . ." PIERRE BOCEV. *World Press Review*, Sep. 1991.
"Shevardnadze . . . ." *Time*, May 13, 1991.
"Shevardnadze. . . ." *Fortune*, May 20, 1991.
"The alternative is dictatorship." *Time*, Apr. 16, 1990.
"Falcon of the Kremlin." E. KAYE FULTON. *Maclean's*, Feb. 26, 1990.

Shuster, Joseph (1914–92) In 1933, Toronto-born Shuster and his friend Jerry Siegel were teenagers in Cleveland. There, writer Siegel conceived and artist Shuster drew the comic strip character Superman, who during the six decades that followed would become a worldwide hit and serve as an unending flow of riches for its owners—who were not to be Shuster and Siegel. As it turned out, it took five years for them to sell the idea, and when they did it was to a comic strip company that bought their idea for $130, and then put them to work creating the comic strip for next to nothing. Superman, in "Action Comics," became an extraordinary commercial success; but, when its creators asked for a share of the profits, they were refused, and, when they sued, they were fired. Meanwhile, billions of dollars of profits continued to flow from the property. Twenty-eight years of unsuccessful lawsuits against successive copyright owners followed. By 1975, Shuster was partially blind, broke, and desperate; that year, for the first time, he and Siegel publicly exposed what had been done to them. The then-owners of the copyright, Warner Communications, responded by paying them $20,000 yearly pensions, in 1981 raised to $30,000. Each also received a "bonus" of $15,000, when the first film in the Superman series grossed $275 million. It should be noted

that later copyright laws made it far more difficult for the creators of artistic or literary properties to be treated in this way. No information was available as to Shuster's survivors. (d. Los Angeles; June 30, 1992)

FURTHER READING

Obituary. *Independent*, Aug. 7, 1992.
Obituary. *Variety*, Aug. 4, 1992.
Obituary. *New York Times*, Aug. 3, 1992.

Sihanouk, Norodom (1922–)

During 1992, President of the Cambodian Supreme National Council, Prince Norodom Sihanouk, was engaged in carrying through the Cambodian peace process as provided in the October 23, 1991 Treaty of Paris, sponsored by the United States, the Soviet Union, and China, under United Nations auspices. The treaty, which ended—at least for a time—the long Cambodian Civil War, provided for an immediate ceasefire, the return home of an estimated 350,000 refugees, and the posting of thousands of UN trooops and civilian personnel to keep the peace, help set up a new government, and prepare for free elections to be held in 1993. The result of many years of negotiations among the three main Cambodian guerrilla factions, and between Cambodia and Vietnam as well, the treaty was a great triumph for Sihanouk, who since 1941, in and out of power, has been his country's leading politician on the world stage, and has repeatedly attempted to create an independent and democratic Cambodia.

Yet once again peace proved difficult to accomplish in Cambodia. As all had feared, the Khmer Rouge, strongest of the Cambodian military organizations, proved unwilling to abide by the terms of the peace treaty. In mid-March, Khmer Rouge forces attacked in central Cambodia, seeking territorial gains before UN forces arrived; a UN-brokered ceasefire went into effect two weeks later. In mid-June, Khmer Rouge forces attacked again in central Cambodia, and at the same time Khmer Rouge forces refused to give up their arms and go into demobilization camps as provided by the treaty. As the year progressed, the Khmer Rouge proved no more tractable, in November and December beginning to take groups of UN peacekeepers as hostages. Cambodia seemed on the brink of a return to full-scale civil war.

Eighteen-year-old Prince Sihanouk was named King of Cambodia by the French colonial occupiers of his country in 1941, and remained a nominal ruler under Vichy French collaborationist rule during much of the Japanese World War II occupation. Late in the war, the Japanese took control of Cambodia; Sihanouk then declared Cambodian independence, and led the national independence movement until Cambodian independence was won in 1953. He quit the throne in 1955, was prime minister of democratic Cambodia in the mid-1950s, and was the elected head of his country from 1960 to 1970. In 1970, his government was deposed by the Lon Nol military dictatorship, and Cambodia then endured the civil war that ended with the 1975 victory of the Khmer Rouge. Sihanouk, under Khmer Rouge house arrest, cooperated with the murderous new government and its Chinese allies, going into Chinese exile. He remained in exile through the balance of the Cambodian Holocaust and the 1979 Vietnamese invasion. In 1982, he became head of a new coalition government in exile, resigning after Khmer Rouge attacks on other Cambodian guerrilla groups. He returned to coalition leadership in 1988, and in 1989 started the long process of negotiation that led to the Vietnamese troop withdrawals that began in 1989, and the on-and-off negotiations during 1990 and 1991 that led to the 1991 peace treaty. In 1980 he published *War and Hope: The Case for Cambodia*. Sihanouk is married and has had fourteen children.

FURTHER READING

"Crazy in Cambodia." ROBERT SAM ANSON. *Esquire*, Aug. 1992.
"The man who would be king again." *Economist*, Sep. 29, 1990.
"The prince presses on." *Time*, Dec. 11, 1989.
"Sihanouk on the high wire. . . ." ADAM PLATT. *Newsweek*, May 15, 1989.
"An exiled leader. . . ." *Insight*, Jan. 20, 1989.
Prince Sihanouk. MADHARI KUCKREJA. Chelsea House, 1989.
"Bonnie Prince Norodom." *Economist*, Nov. 5, 1988.
"Now you see him. . . ." *Time*, July 25, 1988.
"Sihanouk's political circus. . . ." Ruth Marshall. *Newsweek*, Feb. 15, 1988.

Simon, Neil (Marvin Neil Simon; 1927–)

Once again, the celebrated playwright had a hit on Broadway in 1992. His play *Jake's Women*, a comedy about a warring couple and Jake's rec-

ollection of all the women in his life, opened on Broadway in March and ran into October. Alan Alda won a Tony nomination as Jake, in his first Broadway appearance in 20 years; Kate Burton and Tracy Pollan co-starred. It was a special kind of triumph for Simon, because in 1991 *Jake's Women* had been the first of his 24 plays to close on the road before reaching Broadway; he had then rewritten the play.

Simon also worked as a screenwriter in 1992, writing the script for Martha Coolidge's forthcoming film version of his Pulitzer and Tony-winning 1990 play *Lost In Yonkers*; Richard Dreyfuss and Mercedes Ruehl will star. His ABC television adaptation of his play *Broadway Bound* aired in late March. He was also working on the book of a musical adaptation of his film *The Goodbye Girl*, and on a new dramatic play.

New York City-born Simon worked as a radio and television comedy writer in the 1950s, most notably for Phil Silvers and Sid Caesar, and began his long career as a leading playwright with *Come Blow Your Horn* (1961). That work was followed by almost a score of other plays, including such hits as *Barefoot in the Park* (1963; and the 1967 film adaptation), *The Odd Couple* (1965; and the 1968 film), *The Star-Spangled Girl* (1966), *Plaza Suite* (1968; and the 1971 film), *Last of the Red Hot Lovers* (1969), *The Prisoner of Second Avenue* (1971; and the 1975 film), *The Sunshine Boys* (1972; and the 1975 film), and *California Suite* (1976; and the 1978 film). Much of Simon's work is to some extent autobiograph-

ical, and five plays are directly so: *Chapter Two* (1977; and the 1979 film), *I Ought to Be in Pictures* (1980; and the 1982 film), *Brighton Beach Memoirs* (1983; and the 1986 film), the Tony-winning *Biloxi Blues* (1985; and the 1988 film), and *Broadway Bound* (1986). He has also written the books for several musicals, including *Little Me* (1962), *Sweet Charity* (1966), and *Promises, Promises* (1968); and has written several film-scripts, most notably the *The Goodbye Girl* (1977), which starred his second wife, Marsha Mason. Simon attended New York University. He has been married three times, and has two children.

FURTHER READING

"All played out." Jay Rayner. *Guardian*, Nov. 13, 1992.
"King of comedy's serious work." Hap Epstein. *Insight*, Mar. 18, 1991.
"The last of the. . . ." David Richards. *New York Times Magazine*, Feb. 17, 1991.
"Simon, Marvin Neil." *Current Biography*, Mar. 1989.
Neil Simon. Robert K. Johnson. G.K. Hall, 1983.

Simon, Paul (1941–)

On January 11, 1992, Paul Simon became the first star foreign artist to appear in South Africa in eleven years, after the African National Congress and the United Nations had lifted their bans on such appearances. Climaxing a year-long tour, Simon took his "Born at the Right Time" 17-member concert band and ensemble to South Africa, where he appeared twice at Johannesburg, and at Port Elizabeth, Durban, and Cape Town. In South Africa, he was backed by three Black South Africans, guitarist Ray Phiri, saxophonist Barney Rachabane, and pianist Tony Cedras, as well as the a cappella group Ladysmith Black Mambazo, in such songs as "Bridge Over Troubled Water," "Cecilia," "The Boxer," "Mother and Child Reunion," "Graceland," and "Hearts and Bones." Although some radical Black South Africans opposed the tour, Nelson Mandela and other Black African leaders welcomed it, as did Black musicians, and masses of South Africans of all races. One South African musician was not there; Simon dedicated his concerts to his friend and *Graceland* colleague Headman Shabalala, of the Ladysmith Black Mambazo, who had been killed under highly suspicious circumstances on December 10, 1991.

On the personal side, Simon married songwriter and singer Edie Brickell in June; it was her first and his third marriage.

Newark-born Simon and Art Garfunkel were one of the leading folk-rock groups of the 1960s, beginning with their album *Wednesday Morning 3 A.M* (1965), with Simon's hit song "Sound of Silence," and ending with the extraordinarily popular Grammy-winning album *Bridge Over Troubled Water* (1970), its title song still a worldwide favorite. Their work together included the albums *Parsley, Sage, Rosemary, and Thyme* (1967), *Bookends* (1968), and the score of the film *The Graduate* (1968), with its Grammy-winning song "Mrs. Robinson." After 1971, Simon went on alone, creating such albums as *Paul Simon* (1972), *Still Crazy After All These Years* (1975), *Hearts and Bones* (1983), the Grammy-winning *Graceland* (1986), and *The Rhythm of the Saints* (1990). He also wrote, scored, and starred in the film *One Trick Pony* (1980). Simon attended Queens College. His second wife was actress-writer Carrie Fisher.

FURTHER READING

"Troubled waters." J.D. PODOLSKY and SUSAN HACK. *People*, Jan. 27, 1992.
"Profile. . . ." JESSE NASH and GEORGE FLOWERS. *Guitar Player*, Feb. 1991.
"In praise of midlife crisis. . . ." DAVID GATES. *Newsweek*, Jan. 14, 1991.
"Songs of a thinking man. . . ." JAY COCKS. *Time*, Nov. 12, 1990.
"Flying down to Rio. . . ." BRIAN D. JOHNSON. *Maclean's*, Nov. 12, 1990.
Paul Simon: Still Crazy after All These Years. PATRICK HUMPHRIES. Doubleday, 1989.
Written in My Soul: Rock's Great Songwriters . . . Talk about Creating Their Music. BILL FLANAGAN. Contemporary, 1986.

Sinatra, Frank (Francis Albert Sinatra; 1915–)

In his 77th year, the legendary performer was also a very live, very active performer, continuing to tour in concert, as in his soldout September Los Angeles Greek Theater concert with Shirley MacLaine, and their smash three-concert appearance at New York's Radio City Music Hall in October, which grossed more than $3 million. Forthcoming were more concert performances for Sinatra right into 1993.

At the same time, he was indeed a legend—so much so that that he was the subject of the CBS television two-part biographical film *Sinatra*, broadcast in November. His daughter, Tina Sinatra, was executive producer of the work, directed by James Sadwith and adapted for television by William Mastrosimone from his own story. Philip Casnoff played Sinatra in a cast that included Gina Gershon as Nancy Sinatra, his first wife; Marcia Gay Harden as Ava Gardner, his second wife; Nina Siemaszko as Mia Farrow, his third wife; and Olympia Dukakis as his mother.

Sinatra began his singing career in cabaret in 1935. He became a popular singer and recording artist in 1940, while appearing with Tommy Dorsey's band. In January 1943, at a four-week engagement at New York's Paramount Theater, he became the first of the modern teenage idols, whose fans "swooned" and rioted over him. He also became a radio and film star in "Your Hit Parade," and in such musicals as *Anchors Aweigh* (1945) and *On the Town* (1949), and won a special Oscar for his role in *The House I Live In* (1945), a plea for tolerance. But he ran into serious throat problems in 1952, and his career all but vanished. He then made an extraordinary comeback as a dramatic actor, winning a Best Supporting Actor Oscar as Maggio in *From Here to Eternity* (1953), and went on to such films as *Guys and Dolls* (1955), *The Joker Is Wild* (1957), *The Manchurian Candidate* (1962), and *The Detective* (1968). His vocal problems eased as well; he re-emerged as one of the leading song stylists of his time, continuing to tour in concert into his mid-70s. He celebrated his 75th birthday in performance on television in December 1990 before a nationwide audience, and began his year-long world tour in the same month. He has also written a book about his other vocation: *A Man and his Art* (1990), in 1991 retitled *Paintings: A Man and his Art*. Sinatra has been married four times, and has three children, including singers Nancy Sinatra and Frank Sinatra, Jr.

FURTHER READING

"Sinatra. . . ." SUSAN LITTWIN. *TV Guide*, Nov. 7, 1992.
"Really Frank? . . ." MARK HARRIS. *Entertainment*, Nov. 6, 1992.
"The man who was Sinatra." JOSEPH SOBRAN. *National Review*, Feb. 17, 1992.
Frank Sinatra. JESSICA HODGE. Outlet, 1992.

"Frank Sinatra. . . ." WALTER THOMAS. *Interview*, July 1991.

"Sinatra 101. " CHRISTIAN LOGAN WRIGHT. *Mademoiselle*, Apr. 1991.

Frank Sinatra: A Complete Recording History . . . 1939–1984. RICHARD W. ACKELSON. McFarland, 1991.

"Still good and saucy. . . ." CHARLES LEERHSEN. *Newsweek*, Dec. 17, 1990.

"Under my skin." WILLIAM KENNEDY. *New York Times Magazine*, Oct. 7, 1990.

His Way: The Unauthorized Biography of Frank Sinatra. KITTY KELLEY. Bantam, 1987.

Sinatra: The Man and the Myth (An Unauthorized Biography). B. ADLER. NAL-Dutton, 1987.

Frank Sinatra, My Father. NANCY SINATRA. Pocket Books, 1986.

Singleton, John (1969–)

The young African-American film director John Singleton was greatly honored by his peers in 1992. At the age of 23, he became the first African-American, and the youngest person, to win a Best Director Oscar nomination. He also won a Best Original Screenplay Oscar nomination. All were for his 1991 film *Boyz 'N the Hood*, about African-American life in south central Los Angeles; Larry Fishburne, Ice Cube, Cuba Gooding, Jr., Nia Long, and Angela Bassett starred. He had placed the script with Columbia just after graduating from the University of Southern California film writing program, successfully demanded that he be given the directing assignment, and against all the odds had made it all work. Forthcoming was the film *Poetic Justice*, written and directed by Singleton and starring Janet Jackson. It is another film about African-American life in California, this one set in south central Los Angeles and Oakland.

Singleton grew up in south central Los Angeles, the child of unmarried teenage parents Danny Singleton and Sheila Ward, who later both became rising professionals; his own father was his model for the caring father in *Boyz 'N the Hood*.

FURTHER READING

"Breakthroughs." WILEY MASON and DAMIEN BONA. *Entertainment*, Mar. 27, 1992.

"John Singleton. . . ." *People*, Dec. 30, 1991.

"John Singleton." BENILDE LITTLE. *Essence*, Sep. 1991.

"Not just one of the boyz." ALAN LIGHT. *Rolling Stone*, Sep. 5, 1991.

"Writer-director John Singleton." JAMES RYAN. *Premiere*, Aug. 1991.

"John Singleton. . . ." NANCY RANDLE. *Los Angeles*, Feb. 1991.

Sirica, John J. (1904–92)

Connecticut-born Sirica, a Republican, practiced law in Washington after his 1926 graduation from Georgetown University. He was a federal prosecutor (1930–34) and then in private practice until his appointment to the federal bench by President Dwight D. Eisenhower in 1957. In 1973, then chief judge for the U.S. District Court for the District of Columbia, he was the judge in the original 1973 Watergate "plumbers" trial. In the course of that trial and in all that followed from it, Sirica became a historic figure, as the judge who defied massive political pressures and ultimately brought down President Richard M. Nixon, though Sirica always regretted that Nixon himself had not been brought to trial. Sirica presided over the original trial and sentenced the "plumbers," ruled that Nixon must produce taped White House conversations, held hearings that disclosed that some of the crucial tapes were missing, and told the grand jury that its work would be protected. He then enforced subpoenas for tapes that revealed Nixon's participation in the conspiracy, as requested by the special prosecutor, setting the stage for Nixon's August 9, 1974 resignation, when facing three counts of impeachment. Sirica also presided over the trials of the other Watergate conspirators. He was survived by his wife, the former Lucile Camilier, two daughters, and a son. (d. Washington, D. C.; August 14, 1992)

FURTHER READING

Obituary. *The Times* (of London), Aug. 29, 1992.

Obituary. *Independent*, Aug. 20, 1992.

"John Sirica. . . ." LARRY MARTZ. *Newsweek*, Aug. 24, 1992.

Obituary. *New York Times*, Aug. 16, 1992.

Sisulu, Walter Max Ulyate (1912–) and Notsikelelo Albertina Sisulu (1919–)

One of the now-legendary leaders of the African National Congress (ANC), Walter Sisulu in his eightieth year continued to be a major and very active figure in the development of a united South African freedom movement, carrying through the work begun soon after his release from prison in 1989. He was elected Deputy President of the ANC in 1991, succeeding Nelson Mandela, who moved up to the presidency. A major contribution was his role in the October 27, 1991 establishment of a "patriotic united front" coalition of 90 freedom organizations, that for the first time featured an ANC—Pan-Africanist Congress alliance, although during 1992 elements of the Pan-Africanist Congress broke away from the alliance.

Sisulu became a leader of the then-nonviolent African National Congress soon after joining it in 1940. He defied the developing system of apartheid during the 1940s and 1950s, was tried for treason in 1956, and was acquitted in 1961. He was sentenced to six years imprisonment in 1963, jumped bail while his case was on appeal, was rearrested, and was then sentenced to life imprisonment. Walter Sisulu's 27-year imprisonment ended on October 15, 1989, as the new F.W. De Klerk government made its first substantial move toward peace and the end of apartheid in South Africa. He quickly moved back into the active leadership of the ANC, from February 1990 leading the ANC group planning the transition back to legal activity in South Africa.

Notsikelelo Albertina Sisulu became a leader of the South African freedom movement in her own right, and was restricted and in some periods under house arrest from the early 1960s through the mid-1980s. She was sentenced to four years in prison in 1984, but was freed on appeal. She has been Transvaal president of the United Democratic Front since 1983, was president of the Federation of South African Women in 1984, and is deputy president of the ANC Women's League.

Walter and Albertina Sisulu married in 1944; they had five children.

FURTHER READING

The Struggle: A History of the African National Congress. HEIDI HOLLAND. Braziller, 1990.
"Sisulu freed. . . ." FRANK DEXTER BROWN. *Black Enterprise,* Jan. 1990.
"Ex-ANC leader talks. . . ." *Jet,* Nov. 6, 1989.
"Sisulu. . . ." SCOTT MACLEOD. *Time,* Oct. 30, 1989.
"Freedom at last. . . ." MARY NEMETH. *Maclean's,* Oct. 23, 1989.
"Free at last. . . ." *Economist,* Oct. 21, 1989.

Skinner, Samuel Knox (1938–)

Former Secretary of Transportation Skinner succeeded John Sununu as White House Chief of Staff on December 5, 1991. With President George Bush's popularity sinking rapidly, a worsening economy, and an administration and White House in great disarray and plagued by political infighting, Skinner had an unenviable job ahead of him. By all accounts, and for whatever reasons, the job apparently did not get done. By early April, White House press secretary Marlin Fitzwater was threatening to quit because of frustrating White House "gridlock," and by late May many influential Republicans were calling for Skinner's replacement by then-Secretary of State James Baker. On August 13, Baker did finally replace Skinner, but far too late for the change to turn around George Bush's failing presidential campaign. On December 16, 1992 Illinois-based Commonwealth Edison, the third-largest American electric company, announced that Skinner would become its president, at an annual salary of $490,000.

Chicago-born Skinnner was an Illinois assistant U.S. attorney (1968–74). He has long been closely associated with former federal prosecutor and then Illinois governor James R. Thompson. He practiced law in Chicago (1977–84), and then moved into transportation, in 1984 becoming chairman of the regional transport authority. He became Secretary of Transportation in 1989. Skinner's 1930 B.S. was from the University of Illinois, and his 1966 J.D. from DePaul University. He is married and has three children.

FURTHER READING

"Skinner dipping." FRED BARNES. *New Republic,* Jan. 20, 1992.
"Samuel Knox. . . ." ANN GRIMES. *Chicago,* Oct. 1991.
"On the move. . . ." ANNA MARIA and TONYA ARIAS. *Hispanic,* Aug. 1991.
"Skinner, Samuel Knox." *Current Biography,* Aug. 1989.

Smiley, Jane Graves (1949–)

American novelist Jane Smiley emerged as a major literary figure in 1992, after her most recent novel, *A Thousand Acres,* published in November 1991, won a National Book Critics Circle award in January and a Pulitzer Prize in April. The book

quickly became a bestseller in hardcover and then in softcover; film rights were sold as well.

A Thousand Acres is a very modern retelling of the story of *King Lear*, now set in rural Iowa, in the present time, and on the underside of seemingly idyllic American farm life. In Smiley's work, Lear becomes an Iowa farmer who proposes to divide his thousand-acre farm among his three daughters, two of whom he has dominated all their lives and one who has managed to get away. Ultimately, the story becomes one of finally remembered rape and incest, as Ginny and Rose, the daughters who stayed, confront the real facts of their past and the real nature of their life with father.

Los Angeles-born Smiley became an assistant professor at Iowa State University in 1981, moving up to associate professor in 1984 and to full professor in 1989. At the same time, she began to produce the works for which she is by far best known, including *Barn Blind* (1980), *At Paradise Gate* (1981), *Duplicate Keys* (1984), *The Age of Grief* (1987), *The Greenlanders* (1988), and *Ordinary Love and Goodwill* (1989). Her 1971 B.A. was from Vassar College, and her 1976 M.F.A., 1978 M.A., and 1978 Ph.D. from the University of Iowa. She was a Fulbright Scholar (1976–77). Her third husband is Stephen Mark Mortensen; she has two children.

FURTHER READING

"Sharper than. . . ." Rupert Christiansen. *Observer*, Oct. 25, 1992.

"Of serpents' teeth. . . ." Michelle Green and Barbara Kleban Mills. *People*, Jan. 13, 1992.
"Smiley, Jane Graves." *Current Biography*, Apr. 1990.
"The problem is power." Laura Graeber. *New York Times Book Review*, Nov. 5, 1989.

Smith, Maggie (Margaret Natalie Smith; 1934–) Celebrated British actress Smith starred in 1992 opposite Whoopi Goldberg and Harvey Keitel in Emile Ardolino's comedy *Sister Act*; Smith plays the Mother Superior of the convent in which on-the-run singer Goldberg hides, masquerading as a nun. On a far more serious note, Smith also starred as Mrs. Mabel Pettigrew in Jack Clayton's television film adaptation of Muriel Spark's novel *Momento Mori* as the mysterious phone caller who tells a group of octogenarians one by one "Remember, you must die."

Forthcoming was a starring role as the housekeeper in Agnieszka Holland's film version of Frances Hodgson Burnett's children's story *The Secret Garden*, opposite ten-year-old British actress Kate Maberly; and anotehr in Lindsay Anderson's film adaptation of Anton Chekhov's *The Cherry Orchard*, opposite Alan Bates and Bob Hoskins, with a screenplay by Anderson and Frank Grimes.

Smith has been one of the leading actresses of the English-language theater since the mid-1960s. She played Desdemona to Laurence Olivier's Othello at the National Theatre in 1964, and went on to a long series of classic and modern roles, as in *Miss Julie* (1965), *Hedda Gabler* (1970), and *Private Lives* (1972). She won a 1990 Tony as best actress in a Broadway play, in Peter Shaffer's *Lettice & Lovage*, a role she had created on the London stage. She won a Best Actress Oscar in the title role of *The Prime of Miss Jean Brodie* (1969), a Best Supporting Actress Oscar for *California Suite* (1978), and starred in the telefilm *The Lonely Passion of Judith Hearne* (1987), as well as appearing in many key character roles on screen. She played Granny Wendy in Stephen Spielberg's 1991 *Hook*. She married playwright Beverley Cross in 1975. She has two children from her earlier relationship with actor Robert Stephens.

FURTHER READING

"The prime of Maggie Smith." Michael Coveney. *Observer*, Sep. 6, 1992.

"There's nothing. . . ." GEORGINA HOWELL. *Vogue*, Apr. 1990.

"English accents." MARK MATOUSEK. *Harper's Bazaar*, Apr. 1990.

"There is nothing. . . ." MATT WOLF. *New York Times Magazine*, Mar. 18, 1990.

Smoot, George F.

Smoot, George F. (1945–   ) On April 23, 1992, Dr. Smoot, a leading American astrophysicist, announced that his research team at the Lawrence Berkeley Laboratory of the University of California had found strong evidence that supported the "Big Bang" theory, which holds that the universe was created in a single moment approximately 15 billion years ago. Using data secured by instruments on the Cosmic Background Explorer (COBE) satellite, launched on November 18, 1989, his group reported that they had found minute variations in temperature between huge regions of the universe, which were described as "ripples" in the fabric of space-time that were made in the first trillionth of a second after the moment of the creation of the universe.

Smoot's announcement, accompanied by a meticulous description of the truly enormous research task involved, caused a sensation; the discovery was hailed as one of the most important scientific events of the 20th century. Overnight, Smoot became a major media celebrity, far beyond the world of science. His forthcoming book *Wrinkles In Time*, a popular explanation of the group's discovery, was scheduled for 1993 publication; before it was even written, publishers in many languages committed themselves to its publication.

Smoot's 1963 B.S. was from the Massachusetts Institute of Technology, as was his 1970 Ph.D. He began to search for validation of the Big Bang theory in the early 1970s, from 1974 focusing on the development of the set of measuring instruments designed to be carried by COBE; he saw his hopes begin to be realized 16 years later, a year after the satellite had been launched. He resisted any announcement as to what was being discovered for two more years, until far more validation had been secured.

FURTHER READING

"All this and. . . ." SARA WHEELER. *Independent*, May 13, 1992.

"The man who has the key." HILARY MACKENZIE. *Maclean's*, May 4, 1992

Solzhenitsyn, Alexander Isayevich

Solzhenitsyn, Alexander Isayevich (1918–   ) During 1992, dissident Soviet writer Solzhenitsyn prepared to return home to Russia. On September 17, 1991, chief Soviet—now Russian—prosecutor Nicolai Trubin dropped the treason charges that had been outstanding against Solzhenitsyn since 1974; the expatriate writer responded by declaring that he was ready to return home, but only after he finished his work in progress. In February, his wife Natalya Solzhenitsyn returned to Russia with two of their three sons, essentially to prepare for his arrival. In September, the author was reportedly ready to return home early in 1993, though retaining ownership of his family's Vermont home, should they choose to return to the United States.

Solzhenitsyn was one of the great Soviet dissenters, who survived imprisonment and exile to create a body of powerful work that strongly affected Soviet and world thinking, and helping to pave the way for the reforms of the Gorbachev era and the dissolution of the former Soviet Union. He was imprisoned in a labor camp (1948–53), and then internally exiled to Siberia (1953–57), but used these experiences to create his novel *One Day in the Life of Ivan Denisovich* (1962), a trailblazing exposé of the Soviet penal system. Denied publication in the Soviet Union, he published his major works abroad; these included the novels *The First Circle* (1968), *The Cancer Ward* (1968), *August 1914* (1971; republished in expanded form in 1989), and *The Gulag Archipelago* (1973–75). Some of his non-fictional reflections have been published in works such as *The Oak and the Calf: A Memoir* (1980) and *Solzhenitsyn at Harvard: The Address, Twelve Early Responses, and Six Later Reflections* (1980). His post-Cold War works include the essay "Rebuilding Russia" (1990), published in book form as *Rebuilding Russia: Toward Some Formulations* (1991). Solzhenitsyn won the 1970 Nobel Prize for literature. He attended Rostov University. He has been married twice, and has three children.

FURTHER READING

"The grand inquisitor. . . ." TATYANA TOLSTAYA and JAMEY GAMBRELL. *New Republic*, June 29, 1992.

The Great Reversal: Politics and Art in Solzhenitsyn. PAUL N. SIEGEL. Walnut, 1991.

"Writers. . . ." PETER HEBBLETHWAITE. *National Catholic Reporter*, Oct. 5, 1990.

Solzhenitsyn's Political Thought. JAMES F. PONTUSO. University Press of Virginia, 1990.

"Russia's prophet in exile. . . ." PAUL GRAY. *Time*, July 24, 1989.

"Solzhenitsyn, Aleksandr Isayevich." *Current Biography*, July 1988.

Solzhenitsyn: A Biography. MICHAEL SCAMMELL. Norton, 1986.

Solzhenitsyn in Exile: Critical Essays and Documentary Materials. JOHN B. DUNLOP et al; eds. Hoover Institute Press, 1985.

Sondheim, Stephen Joshua (1930–)

Some Stephen Sondheim show is being revived somewhere every year—or perhaps every week. *Anyone Can Whistle*, one of his most experimental shows, was revived off-Broadway in November 1992, garnering reviews more appreciative than those bestowed on its original 1964 Broadway production. Less well received was the 1992 London opening of his *Assassins*, which was as panned in London as it had been in New York the year before.

A new Sondheim show was in the making in 1992. *Putting It Together*, a revue starring Julie Andrews in a long-deferred return to the theater, was scheduled for a twelve-week Manhattan Theater Club off-Broadway run starting in

March 1993, to be directed by Julia McKenzie, with choreography by Bob Avian; the cast also included Christopher Durang, James Naughton, Michael Rupert, and Rachel York.

Sondheim also spoke out on a matter of principle in 1992, refusing to accept a National Medal of Arts in protest against the atmosphere of "censorship and repression" at the National Endowment for the Arts, which administers the award.

New York City-born Sondheim emerged as a leading American musical-theater lyricist in the late 1950s with the lyrics for *West Side Story* (1957) and *Gypsy* (1959), and then as a leading composer with both words and music for *A Funny Thing Happened on the Way to The Forum* (1962). As a composer and lyricist, he has won five Tonys, for *Company* (1970), *Follies* (1971), *A Little Night Music* (1973), *Sweeney Todd* (1979), and *Into the Woods* (1988), and a Pulitzer Prize for *Sunday in the Park with George* (1984). During 1990, he was Oxford University's first visiting professor of drama and musical theatre, resident at St. Catherine's College, a position funded by producer Cameron Mackintosh. Sondheim's 1950 B.A. was from Williams College.

FURTHER READING

Art Isn't Easy: The Theatre of Stephen Sondheim, rev. ed. JOANNE GORDON. Da Capo, 1992.

"Exploring along with Sondheim." HAP ERSTEIN. *Insight*, Aug. 28, 1989.

"Broadway's age. . . ." MIRIAM HORN. *U.S. News & World Report*, Feb. 1, 1988.

Sondheim & Co., 2nd ed. CRAIG ZADAN. Harper, 1988.

Sontag, Susan (1933–)

One of the leading literary essayists of her time, Sontag produced what was for her a remarkable change of pace in 1992, with *The Volcano Lover: A Romance*, a historical novel published by Farrar, Straus & Giroux in August 1992. Given her past history, the book attracted a great deal of critical attention, most of it favorable, and became a bestseller.

Sontag's book is another retelling of the love story involving Emma Hamilton, her husband Sir William Hamilton, and British national hero Admiral Horatio Nelson. It covers a period beginning about 1765 and ending in 1805, and is

"Sontag, Susan." *Current Biography*, Feb. 1992.
"Education of the heart." HARRIETT GILBERT. *New Statesman & Society*, Mar. 29, 1991.
Susan Sontag: The Elegiac Modernist. SOHNYA SAYRES. Routledge, 1990.
"Stand aside, Sisyphus." RICHARD LACAYO. *Time*, Oct. 24, 1988.

set largely in Naples. Although a romance, Sontag has also included a considerable body of political material, judging her main characters harshly for being on the side of Naples' rulers, who bloodily put down a democratic revolution. Alexander Korda's 1941 film version of the wholly romantic side of the story was titled *That Hamilton Woman*, and starred Vivien Leigh as Emma Hamilton and Laurence Olivier as Nelson.

Sontag attended the University of California at Berkeley, the University of Chicago, and Harvard University, where she received M.A.s in English literature and philosophy. Her first published work was *The Benefactor* (1963). With her 1964 *Partisan Review* essay "Notes On Camp," followed by her 1965 essay "On Style," and her 1966 essay collection *On Interpretation*, she emerged as one of the most notable literary essayists of her generation. Among her published works are *Death Kit* (1967), *Styles of Radical Will*(1969), *On Photography* (1977), *Illness as Metaphor* (1978), *Under the Sign of Saturn* (1980), and *AIDS and Its Metaphors* (1989). She has also written and directed the films *Duet for Cannibals* (1970) and *Brother Carl* (1971), and written the films *Promised Lands* (1974) and *Unguided Tour* (1983).

FURTHER READING

"Susan Sontag. . . ." LESLIE GARIS. *New York Times Magazine*, Aug. 2, 1992.

Souter, David Hackett (1939–) In his second Supreme Court term, Justice Souter identified himself as a "swing" figure within the Court, voting with the majority in 100 of the Court's 108 decisions, including 13 of the 14 decided by a 5–4 vote. He also emerged, with Justices O'Connor and Souter, as part of a new Court center with the joint O'Connor-Kennedy-Souter majority opinion in the landmark abortion rights case, *Planned Parenthood of Southeastern Pennsylvania v. Casey*, in which a 5–4 majority upheld the essence of *Roe v. Wade* (which in 1972 had established the right of a woman to choose to have an abortion), while at the same time upholding most of the restrictive 1989 Pennsylvania abortion law and giving the states broader powers to restrict abortion. He also joined all of his colleagues in a rare, unanimous landmark sexual harassment decision; in *Franklin v. Gwinnett County Public Schools*, the Court unanimously ruled that Title IX of the 1972 education act allowed a sexually harassed student to collect damages from a school district where a teacher-coach sexually harassed Christine Franklin and ultimately succeeded in pressing her to have sexual intercourse with him.

Some of the most important cases in which Souter voted with the majority during the 1991–92 Court term were *Georgia v. McCollum*, ruling that criminal case defendants could not bar prospective jurors solely because of their race; *Nordlinger v. Hahn*, upholding the right of California to enact Proposition 13, with its unequal property taxes on newcomers; *Lee v. Weisman*, barring nonsectarian or any other prayers at public high school graduations; *Hudson v. McMillian*, ruling that the excessive use of force by prison guards was an Eighth Amendment violation even if the prisoner was not seriously hurt; *Riggins v. Nevada*, ruling that the state could not force an insane criminal defendant to take medication during a trial; *U.S. v. Fordice*, ruling that Mississippi had not fulfilled its obligation to desegregate its public colleges and universities; *Jacobson v. U.S.*, ruling that the federal government had illegally entrapped a defendant into buying child pornography through the mail; *Lujan v. Defenders of Wildlife*, ruling that the plaintiff, an environmental organization, had no standing to bring suit because no determinable specific interest was at issue; *U.S. v. Alvarez Machain*, upholding the 1990 U.S. kidnapping of a Mexican doctor suspected of a role in the torture of a U.S. drug enforcement agent; *Lechmere Inc. v. National Labor Relations Board*, ruling that companies did not have to allow union organizers access to such company-owned lands as parking lots and shopping malls; *Keeney v. Tamayo-Reyes*, which sharply limited the federal habeas corpus appeals of state prisoners; *New York v. U.S.*, which invalidated a federal law forcing states to handle their own radioactive waste; and *Freeman v. Pitts*, ruling that schools being operated under court-supervised desegregation orders could be released from those orders step by step. Souter also ruled with the majority that the Coast Guard could continue to intercept at sea and return Haitian refugees to Haiti; and in the decision barring return of RU-486 pills to Leona Benten, a pregnant woman who tried to import them into the U.S. for her personal use, in a challenge to their ban. Two of his dissents were in *International Society for Krishna Consciousness v. Lee*, which ruled that airports could ban groups from soliciting money; and in *R.A.V. v. St. Paul*, which overturned a St. Paul, Minnesota ordinance making sexist, racist, or otherwise bigoted speech or behavior a crime.

Massachusetts-born Souter moved up in the New Hampshire attorney-general's office (1968–76), and was state attorney-general (1976–78). He was a state court judge (1978–83), and a state Supreme Court justice from 1983 until his 1989 appointment by George Bush to the U.S. Supreme Court. Souter's 1961 B.A. was from Harvard, as was his 1966 LL.B; he was also a Rhodes scholar.

FURTHER READING

David Souter. BOB ITALIA. Abdo & Daughters, 1992.
Turning Right: The Making of the Rehnquist Supreme Court. DAVID G. SAVAGE. Wiley, 1992.
"A new day in court." LAUREN TARSHIS and JAMES EARL HARDY. *Scholastic Update*, Nov. 1, 1991.
"Souter, David Hackett." *Current Biography*, Jan. 1991.
"Naturally right. . . ." JEFF ROSEN. *New Republic*, Sep. 24, 1990.
"A retiring Yankee judge. . . ." BILL HEWITT. *People*, Aug. 6, 1990.
"An 18th century man. . . ." MARGARET CARLSON. *Time*, Aug. 6, 1990.
"In search of Souter." DONALD BAER. *U.S. News & World Report*, Aug. 6, 1990.
"An old-fashioned judge." *Economist*, July 28, 1990.

Sissy Spacek (left) and Kevin Costner.

Spacek, Sissy (Mary Elizabeth Spacek; 1949–) Celebrated film star Spacek was highly visible throughout the world in 1992 as Liz Garrison, New Orleans District Attorney and Jim Garrison's wife, in Oliver Stone's highly controversial 1991 film *JFK*. She appeared in another controversial film in late June 1992, this one focusing on the issue of abortion, just before the U.S. Supreme Court was to rule on a landmark Pennsylvania abortion rights case. In Joan Micklin Silver's *A Private Matter*, an HBO television film, Spacek played Sherri Chessen Finkbine, mother of four children, who in 1962 decides to have an abortion after learning that her pregnancy has been damaged by taking Thalidomide pills, and who then decides to tell her story so that others may benefit from the knowledge. Chessen and her husband, Bob Finkbine, played by Aidan Quinn, find themselves attacked and vilified by anti-abortion advocates; she loses her job as the host of a televised children's show, he is pressed to resign his teaching job, and they and their children are harassed in the community, suffering deeply negative effects that last for many years.

On a much lighter note, Spacek starred opposite William Petersen in Martin Davidson's film comedy *Hard Promises*; the film was not well received. Forthcoming was a starring role in the Tia Brelis film *The Mommy Market*, based on the Nancy Brelis novel; co-starring are Anna Chlumsky and Maureen Stapleton.

Texas-born Spacek emerged as a star in the mid-1970s in such films as *Prime Cut* (1972), *Badlands* (1974), and in her breakthrough role in *Carrie* (1976), for which she won a best actress Oscar nomination. She went on to star in such films as *Three Women* (1977), *Coal Miner's Daughter* (1980), for which she won a best actress Oscar, *Raggedy Man* (1981), *Missing* (1982), *The River* (1984), *'Night Mother* (1986), *Crimes of the Heart* (1986), and *The Long Walk Home* (1989). Spacek attended the Lee Strasberg Theatrical Institute. She is married to art director Jack Fisk and has two children.

FURTHER READING

"Mettle of the belle." PAT DOWELL. *American Film*, Mar. 1991.
"Sissy Spacek's long walk home. . . ." JAN JARBOE. *Texas Monthly*, Feb. 1991.
" 'I've kinda found my rhythm.' " MICHAEL J. BANDLER. *McCall's*, Feb. 1991.
Country Girl: The Life of Sissy Spacek. MARK EMERSON and EUGENE E. PFAFF, JR. St. Martin's, 1988.

Spader, James (1960–)

After starring in the rather straightforward Washington-based corruption-in-high-places film *True Colors* in 1991, Spader starred in 1992 in an offbeat corruption-in-high-places film as Cray Fowler, heir to a rich, powerful New Orleans political dynasty, in Mark Frost's political crime melodrama *Storyville*. Jason Robards co-starred as corrupt New Orleans Congressman Clifford Fowler, along with Joanne Whalley-Kilmer and Piper Laurie. Forthcoming was a starring role opposite Theresa Russell in Nicolas Roeg's *Chicago Loop*, adapted for the screen from his own novel by Paul Theroux. Also reportedly forthcoming were starring roles in Nicholas Kazan's film *Dream Lover* and Philip Hase's film *The Music of Chance*.

Boston-born Spader made his film debut in *Endless Love* (1981), and went on to play in such popular films as *Tuff Turf* (1985), *The New Kids* (1985), *Pretty in Pink* (1986), *Mannequin* (1987), *Baby Boom* (1987), *Wall Street* (1987), *Less Than Zero* (1987), *sex, lies, and videotape* (1989), *Bad Influence* (1990), *White Palace* (1990), and *True Colors* (1991). Spader studied at the Michael Chekhov Studio. He and his wife, Victoria, have one son.

FURTHER READING

"James Spader. . . ." SUSAN SPILLMAN. *Cosmopolitan*, Aug. 1988.

Spielberg, Steven (1947–)

While his Christmas 1991 blockbuster *Hook* was during 1992 becoming another of his worldwide hits, Spielberg set to work on yet another big budget film. His sci-tech special effects blockbuster *Jurassic Park*, based on Michael Crichton's novel about modern genetically engineered theme park dinosaurs that become a menace, began shooting on Hawaii's Kauai Island on August 24. Spielberg directed a cast that included Sam Neill, Laura Dern, Jeff Goldblum, and Richard Attenborough. Cast and crew were trapped on the island briefly after a disastrous early-September hurricane. Release was scheduled for summer 1993.

Among Spielberg's many forthcoming projects were the television series "Sea Quest," about the underwater adventures of the crew of a research submarine, set early in the 21st century; and the Civil War period "Class of '61" television series. A "Mr. Magoo" feature film directed by Spielberg has also reportedly been planned.

Spielberg directed and in several instances produced many of the most successful action-adventure and science fiction spectacles of the 1970s and 1980s, including *Jaws* (1975), *Close Encounters of a Third Kind* (1977; and co-authored), *1941* (1979), *Raiders of the Lost Ark* (1981), *E.T.* (1982; and produced), *Indiana Jones and the Temple of Doom* (1984), *The Color Purple* (1985; and produced), *Indiana Jones and the Last Crusade* (1989; the third in the series), and *Always* (1989; a remake of *A Guy Named Joe*). He also wrote and produced *Poltergeist* (1982), and co-produced *Back to the Future* (1985). Spielberg attended California State College. Formerly married to actress Amy Irving, Spielberg married actress Kate Capshaw in 1991. He has five children, three of them with Capshaw.

FURTHER READING

"Steven Spielberg. . . ." SKIP PRESS. *Boys' Life*, July 1992.
"The panning of. . . ." HENRY SHEEHAN. *Film Comment*, May–June 1992.
Steven Spielberg: The Man, His Movies, and Their Meaning. PHILIP M. TAYLOR. Continuum, 1992.
"Peter pandemonium." FRED SCHRUERS. *Premiere*, Dec. 1991.
"Stephen Spielberg." MAURA J. MACKOWSKI. *Ad Astra*, July–Aug. 1991.
The Future of the Movies: Interviews with Martin Scorsese, George Lucas, and Steven Spielberg. ROGER EBERT and GENE SISKEL. Andrews & McMeel, 1991.
Icons: Intimate Portraits. DENISE WORRELL. Atlantic Monthly, 1989.
The Picture Life of Steven Spielberg. MICHAEL LEATHER. Watts, 1988.
Steven Spielberg: Amazing Filmmaker. JIM HARGROVE. Childrens, 1988.
The Fantastic Films of Steven Spielberg—Master Filmmaker. ROBERT G. MARRERO. RGM Publications, 1987.
Steven Spielberg. DONALD R. MOTT and CHERYL M. SAUNDERS. G.K. Hall, 1986.
Steven Spielberg. D.L. MABERY. Lerner, 1986.

Springsteen, Bruce (1949–) After a period of relative inactivity in the late 1980s, rock superstar Springsteen spent most of 1990 and 1991 creating two new albums. Both were released simultaneously in the spring of 1992, and both were worldwide hits, although more so abroad than in the United States. One was *Human Touch*, with its hit single "57 Channels (and Nothin' On)," and such songs as "With Every Wish," "Roll of the Dice," and "Real World." On this recording, Springsteen was backed by a band that included Wayne Isham, David Sancious, Roy Bittan, Randy Jackson, and Jeff Porcaro. The other album was *Lucky Town*, with its hit singles "Better Days" and "Leap of Faith," and such songs as "Book of Dreams, "Living Proof," and "If I Should Fall Behind." Springsteen toured in support of his albums in Europe in June and July, 1992, and then throughout the balance of the year and into 1993 in the United States. As part of the promotion, he made his first appearance before a live television audience in May on "Saturday Night Live," singing songs from his two new albums.

New Jersey-born Springsteen was discovered by legendary record producer John Hammond in 1972. Springsteen's first album, *Greetings from Asbury Park, New Jersey* (1973), was not very well received, although his second, *The Wild, The Innocent and the E-Street Shuffle* (1974), was promising. With his greatly successful third album, *Born to Run* (1975), Springsteen emerged as a rock superstar. He went on to record *Darkness on the Edge of Town* (1978), *The River* (1980), *Nebraska* (1982), the classic *Born in the U.S.A.* (1984), *Bruce Springsteen and the E Street Band Live/1975–1985* (1986), *Tunnel of Love* (1987), and *Chimes of Freedom* (1988), as well as such political and socially aware pieces as *No Nukes* (1979) and *We Are the World* (1985). Previously divorce, he married longtime companion, singer Patti Scialfa, in 1991; they have one child, born in 1990.

FURTHER READING

"Springsteen, Bruce." *Current Biography*, Aug. 1992.
"Springsteen. . . ." JAMES HENKE. *Rolling Stone*, Aug. 6, 1992.
"Boss tracks. . . ." DAVID BROWNE. "Who's the Boss?" GREG SANDOW. *Entertainment*, June 5, 1992.
Wild and Innocent: The Recordings of Bruce Springsteen, 1972–1985. BRAD ELLIOTT. Popular Culture, 1992.

Down Thunder Road: The Making of Bruce Springsteen. MARC ELIOT. Knightsbridge, 1991.

The Rolling Stone Interviews: The 1980s. St. Martin's, 1989.

"Romancing the boss." SUSAN SCHINDEHETTE. *People,* Oct. 10, 1988.

"The Catholic imagination of. . . ." ANDREW M. GREELEY. America, Feb. 6, 1988.

Bruce Springsteen Here and Now. CRAIG MACINNIS. Barron, 1988.

Dear Bruce Springsteen. KEVIN MAJOR. Delacorte, 1988.

Glory Days: The Bruce Springsteen Story Continues. DAVE MARSH. Pantheon, 1987.

Springsteen. ROBERT HILBURN. Scribner/Macmillan, 1986.

Bruce Springsteen: Blinded by the Light. PATRICK HUMPHRIES and CHRIS HUNT. Holt, 1986.

Picture Life of Bruce Springsteen. GERI BAIN and MICHAEL LEATHER. Watts, 1986.

Bruce Springsteen. KEITH E. GREENBERG. Lerner, 1986.

Stallone, Sylvester Enzio (1946–)

The star of the "Rambo" and "Rocky" films, which made him a worldwide celebrity, Stallone tried his hand at comedy once again in 1992, starring in Roger Spottiswoode's film comedy *Stop! Or My Mom Will Shoot* as a Los Angeles police sergeant whose mother, played by Estelle Getty, comes to visit him, with farcical consequences. JoBeth Williams also co-starred. The film was panned by most critics. Along far more familiar lines, Stallone also starred in the forthcoming Renny Harlin action-adventure film *Cliffhanger*, which filmed in Rome in the summer of 1992. In late July, he was injured on the set while doing a stunt, suffering a cut on his hand that required nine stitches to close.

In March, he was made an Officer of Arts and Letters by the French government, an award that brought considerable protest from many French critics of his films.

On the personal side, he won an apology and financial settlement in another libel suit against a British newspaper, this one the *Independent,* which had accused him of attempted draft evasion during the Vietnam War.

In 1976, New York City-born Stallone starred in *Rocky*; he also wrote the screenplay. The movie won a best film Oscar, was a worldwide hit, and Stallone was immediately an international star. He did four sequels: *Rocky II* (1979; he wrote the screenplay and directed); *Rocky III* (1982); *Rocky IV* (1985; he directed); and *Rocky V* (1990). He also starred as Rambo in *First Blood* (1982), *Rambo: First Blood Part II* (1985), and *Rambo III* (1988), and in such other action films as *F.I.S.T.* (1978), *Paradise Alley* (1978), *Nighthawks* (1981), *Rhinestone* (1984), *Cobra* (1986), *Over the Top* (1987), *Lock Up* (1989), *Tango and Cash* (1989), and *Oscar* (1991). Stallone attended the American College of Switzerland and Miami University. He has been married twice and has two children.

FURTHER READING

"Stallone on the range." GRAYDON CARTER. *Vogue,* Dec. 1991.

"The shaping of an icon. . . ." DAVID KLINGHOFFER. *Insight,* May 20, 1991.

"Rocky: the article. . . ." FRANZ LIDZ. *Sports Illustrated,* Nov. 12, 1990.

"Move over, Rambo. . . ." LAURA MORICE. *Mademoiselle,* Feb. 1990.

"Sly Stallone's rocky road. . . ." LEO JANOS. *Cosmopolitan,* Jan. 1990.

"Requiem for a heavyweight. . . ." CAMERON STAUTH. *American Film,* Jan. 1990.

Rocky and the Films of Sylvester Stallone. ED GROSS. Movie Publications Services, 1990.

Sylvester. A.C. CRISPIN. Tor, 1985.

Stallone! JEFF ROVIN. Pocket Books, 1985.

Starr, Ringo (Richard Starkey; 1940–)

As a former Beatle, Ringo Starr is a historic figure in popular music, but proved in 1992 that he is also a fine contemporary musician with the comeback album *Time Takes Time*, a ten-song recording that included the hit single "Weight of the World," and such songs as "Don't Go Where the Road Don't Go," "What Goes Around," "Don't Know a Thing About Love," and "I Don't Believe You." His album was applauded by most critics, also becoming a hit. Starr toured the United States and Europe during the spring and summer of 1992 with his All Starr Band that in 1992 included Burton Cummings, Todd Rundgren, Joe Walsh, Timothy B. Schmidt, Nils Lofgren, Tim Capella, and his son, Zak Starkey.

Liverpool-born Starr played with The Hurricanes (1959–62), and joined the Beatles in 1962. He became a worldwide celebrity in the 1960s, as he, Paul McCartney, John Lennon, and George Harrison created a revolution in popular music, in concert and with such records as

Please, Please Me (1963), *She Loves You* (1963), *I Want to Hold Your Hand* (1963), *Yesterday* (1965), *Revolver* (1966), and *Sergeant Pepper's Lonely Hearts Club Band* (1967), and in such films as *A Hard Day's Night* (1964), *Magical Mystery Tour* (1967), and *The Yellow Submarine* (1968). After the group broke up in 1970, Starr recorded several albums and appeared in such films as *200 Motels* (1969), *Stardust* (1975), *Son of Dracula* (1975), *Caveman* (1981), and *Give My Regards to Broad Street* (1984). His first solo tour came in 1989. He has been married twice, most recently to Barbara Bach, and has three children.

FURTHER READING

"Ringo." DAVID WILD. *Rolling Stone*, July 9, 1992.
"Ringo Starr. . . ." TOM PETTY. *Interview*, June 1992.
"In search of. . . ." GILES SMITH. *Independent*, Apr. 16, 1992.
Ringo Starr: Straight Man or Joker? ALAN CLAYSON. Paragon House, 1992.
Strange Days: The Music of John, Paul, George and Ringo Twenty Years On. WALTER PODRAZIK. Popular Culture, 1991.
"Ringo on the rebound." STEVE DOUGHERTY. *People*, Aug. 28, 1989.
"A Starr is reborn." DAVID WILD. *Rolling Stone*, Aug. 24, 1989.
It Was Twenty Years Ago Today. DEREK TAYLOR. Simon & Schuster, 1987.
The Beatles, 2nd ed. HUNTER DAVIES. McGraw-Hill, 1985.

Starzl, Thomas Earl (1926–) Liver-transplant pioneer Starzl, the surgeon who in 1967 led the team that performed the first successful liver transplant, pioneered once again in 1992. Although he had given up surgery in 1990, on June, 28, 1992 he led the University of Pittsburgh team that performed the first baboon liver transplant into a human, viewed by many medical researchers as a major step in the animal-to-human transplant area, though viewed with great alarm by animal-rights and endangered species advocates. Although the patient died on September 6, Starzl's team believed that the death was caused not by rejection of the baboon liver by its human recipient, but rather by other major medical problems. They planned a second baboon liver transplant in the near future. In a related development, on October 12th surgeons

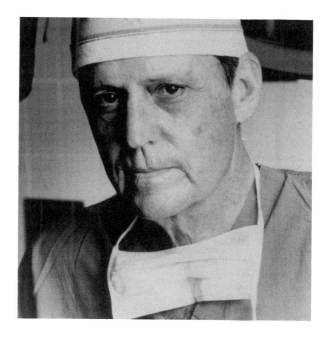

at Los Angeles' Cedars-Sinai Medical Center performed a transplant using a pig's liver, in an attempt to keep a dying patient alive for a few days until a human liver was available; but, although the patient stayed alive for more than 30 hours, her condition deteriorated so badly that the human transplant could not be performed. Starzl published his autobiography in August 1992: *The Puzzle People: Memoirs of a Transplant Surgeon.*

After completing his own medical education, Iowa-born Starzl briefly joined the faculty of the Northwestern University Medical School (1958–61) and then the University of Colorado Medical School at Denver in 1962, rising to become chairman of the surgery department (1972–80). While there he led the team that performed the first successful liver transplant in 1967 and helped develop a skilled team for kidney transplants. In 1981, he moved to the University of Pittsburgh, making its hospital-medical school complex one of the world's prime transplant centers, where most surgeons who perform organ transplants learned the techniques generally from Starzl himself, work for which he has received numerous awards and honors. In late 1990, he announced that he would no longer perform liver transplant surgery, but would focus on studying the drug FK-506, improvements in the system for locating organ donors and delivering the organs to needy patients, and liver transplants from other species into humans. Previously married to Barbara Brothers, Starzl was remarried in 1981 to Joy Conger. He has three children.

FURTHER READING

"Smart, social. . . ." STEVEN FINDLAY and DOUG PODOLSKY. U.S. News & World Report, July 13, 1992.
"Interview. . . ." Omni, Sep. 1990.

Steenburgen, Mary (1953–)

It was a highly political year for film star and political activist Steenburgen. She continued to be active in such organizations as the National Organization For Women (NOW), the Hollywood Women's Political Committee, and the anti-apartheid Artists for a Free South Africa; and she continued to speak out on a wide range of political issues, including the right to choose abortion and the need for increased AIDS research.

Little Rock native Steenburgen became a key Hollywood figure in the Clinton-for-President movement, endorsing Clinton on the basis of her long personal friendship with both Clintons. She toured with the Clinton campaign, ran fundraisers, and went to the Democratic National Convention as a highly visible Clinton delegate. She also campaigned for several other California Democratic candidates.

On the film side of her life, she starred opposite Tom Hanks, Denzel Washington, and Jason Robards, Jr. in Jonathan Demme's forthcoming film *Philadelphia*. She also starred opposite Johnny Depp and Juliette Lewis in Lasse Hallstrom's forthcoming film *Gilbert Grape*; filming began in November 1992. Also forthcoming was a starring role on Broadway in George Bernard Shaw's *Candida*, scheduled for March 1993.

Arkansan Steenburgen made her film debut in *Goin' South* (1978), and went on to such films as *Ragtime* (1981), *Time After Time* (1979), *Melvin and Howard* (1980; she won a Best Supporting Actress Oscar), *Cross Creek* (1983), *Dead of Winter* (1987), *End of the Line* (1987). *Parenthood* (1989), *Back to the Future Part III* (1990), and *The Butcher's Wife* (1991). She also produced and played a bit role in *The Whales of August* (1987). In addition, she appeared in such telefilms as *Tender Is the Night* (1985) and *The Attic: The Hiding of Anne Frank* (1988). Steen-

burgen attended Hendricks College and studied at New York's Neighborhood Playhouse. She has two children from her previous marriage to actor Malcolm McDowell.

FURTHER READING

"After years. . . ." MARY H.J. FARRELL. People, Aug. 28, 1989.
"Mary, Mary, quite contrary." TIM APPELO. Savvy Woman, May 1989.

Steinbrenner, George Michael, III (1930–)

What a difference a year makes! At the end of 1991, New York Yankees owner George Steinbrenner was still officially barred from day-to-day baseball activities, though baseball commissioner Fay Vincent was moving toward restoring Steinbrenner to regular ownership activities. But a year later, it was Vincent himself who was out of baseball, while the Yankees' "bad-boy" owner was moving right back into the catbird seat. In July 1992, Vincent announced that Steinbrenner would be allowed to return to head the New York Yankees beginning March 1, 1993, having settled two related law suits that had previously barred his return.

As a vice-president of the U.S. Olympic Committee, Steinbrenner spent considerable time during 1992 in France for the Albertville Winter Olympics and in Spain for the Barcelona Summer Olympics. He also branched out into other sports, becoming an owner of the Tampa Bay Lightning, a new franchise in the National Hockey League, and of New York's 1993 expansion team in the indoor Arena Football League. His autobiography was said to be forthcoming.

Ohio-born Steinbrenner is a leading ship-building company executive, who has since 1967 run the American Ship Building Company, co-founded by his grandfather. He bought a controlling interest in the New York Yankees in 1973, and quickly became a highly controversial figure, who hired and fired managers again and again, with 18 managerial changes from 1973 to 1992, and engaged in widely publicized feuds with key players. The Yankees won the World Series in 1977 and 1978, the last team to win back-to-back championships, and won the American League pennant in 1981, but the remainder of the 1980s were troubled years for the team. Steinbrenner was banned from day-to-day active participation in the management of the Yankees in 1990, because of his payments to a gambler as part of what were judged improper attempts to interfere with a trade of then-Yankee Dave Winfield. Steinbrenner's 1952 B.A. was from Williams College. He married Elizabeth Joan Zieg in 1956; they have four children.

FURTHER READING

"Welcome to hardball city." MIKE LUPICA. *Esquire*, June 1991.
"George Steinbrenner. . . ." JEFFREY KLUGER. *Playboy*, May 1991.
"The many woes. . . ." TOM CALLAHAN. *U.S. News & World Report*, Aug. 6, 1990.
Damned Yankees: A No-Holds-Barred Account of Life with "Boss" Steinbrenner. BILL MADDEN and MOSS KLEIN. Warner, 1990.

tial campaign, he was a deputy communications director for Michael Dukakis. He then returned again to Congress as an aide to Representative Richard Gephardt (1989–91).

Stephanopoulos began the 1992 presidential campaign as candidate Bill Clinton's assistant communications director, but soon became a key political advisor and main organizer of the day-to-day campaign, as well as Clinton's chief spokesperson throughout the entire electoral process. He continued on as communications director through the transition period.

FURTHER READING

"Clinton's boy wonder." MATTHEW COOPER. *U.S. News & World Report*, Dec. 7, 1992.
"Riding shotgun." JOE TREEN. *People*, Oct. 26, 1992.

Stephanopoulos, George Robert

(1961–) President Bill Clinton's Communications Director has spent almost all of his brief career in politics. He received his 1982 B.A. from Columbia University, and in that year worked for the Carnegie Endowment for International Peace. From 1983 to 1984, he was a Congressional aide to Representative Edward Feighan, then spent 1984–86 as a Rhodes Scholar at Oxford University, and returned to his work with Feighan (1986–88). During the 1988 presiden-

Stern, David Joel

(1942–) National Basketball Association (NBA) commissioner David Stern continued to preside over a highly successful league, the envy of other sports—so successful that, in December 1992, Stern's assistant, Gary Bettman, was tapped to be commissioner of the National Hockey League. The NBA's success continued to spawn rumors of further expansion, to cities such as Toronto, though Stern downplayed that possibility for the immediate future. Not surprisingly, Stern topped the

Sporting News January 1992 list of the most powerful people in sports.

Stern's most public actions centered around questions relating to star Earvin "Magic" Johnson and his infection with HIV, the virus that causes AIDS. Though Johnson had retired from basketball in November 1991, fans still voted him to the starting All-Star team. When Johnson indicated that he would play if allowed to do so, Stern responded by adding an additional 13th spot for him on the Western All-Star team for the February 9th game, so no other players would be penalized, with both Stern and Johnson regarding it as an opportunity to educate people about AIDS. As it turned out, Johnson put on a whale of a show and was named most valuable player of the game. Stern also gave his support when Johnson decided in September to return to active play, and then in November to retire again, this time for good. But some observers noted that Stern (as well as other sports commissioners) had failed to deal with the wider questions of AIDS and AIDS education in basketball, aside from the rule of stopping the game and treating any player with an open cut, with doctors and trainers wearing rubber gloves.

New York-born Stern was associated with Proskauer Rose Goetz & Mendelsohn (1966–78), the NBA's law firm, before being named NBA general counsel in 1978. He became executive vice president for business and legal affairs in 1980, and NBA commissioner in 1984. From 1983 he also served as adjunct professor of law at New York's Cardozo Law School. Stern received his B.A. from Rutgers University in 1963 and his LL.B. from Columbia University. He married Dianne Bock in 1963; they have two sons.

FURTHER READING

"Stern, David Joel." *Current Biography*, Apr. 1991.

Stern, Philip (1926–92) A philanthropist and leading critic of American political corruption, Philip Stern began his exposure to Washington politics as a Congressional aide in the late 1940s. In 1957, he founded a newspaper, the *North Virginia Sun*. He was appointed a deputy assistant secretary of state by President John F. Kennedy in 1961, but soon decided to spend his time outside government as a critic, and did so

for the following three decades. His best-known books include *The Great Treasury Raid* (1964), *The Rape of the Taxpayer* (1973), and *The Best Congress Money Can Buy* (1988), all of them and his other books and articles striking hard against what he saw as pervasive Washington corruption. In the latter book, he exposed the role of the Political Action Committee, a tool used by special interests to support Congressional candidates. He was survived by two daughters, three sons, and a brother. (d. June 1, 1992)

FURTHER READING

Obituary. *New York Times*, June 2, 1992.

Stevens, John Paul (1920–   ) With Justice Blackmun one of the two remaining Supreme Court liberals, Stevens still found himself able to vote with the majority in several landmark cases during the 1991–92 Court session, including *Planned Parenthood of Southeastern Pennsylvania v. Casey*, in which a slim 5–4 majority upheld the essence of *Roe v. Wade* (which in 1972 had established the right of a woman to choose to have an abortion), while at the same time upholding most of the restrictive 1989 Pennsylvania abortion law and giving the states broader powers to restrict abortion. Stevens also joined all of his colleagues in a rare, unanimous landmark sexual harassment decision; in *Franklin v. Gwinnett County Public Schools*, the Court unanimously ruled that Title IX of the 1972 education act allowed a sexually harassed student to collect damages from a school district where a teacher-coach sexually harassed Christine Franklin and ultimately succeeded in pressing her to have sexual intercourse with him.

Stevens also joined the majority in *Georgia v. McCollum*, ruling that criminal case defendants could not bar prospective jurors solely because of their race; *Freeman v. Pitts*, ruling that schools being operated under court-supervised desegregation orders could be released from those orders step by step; *Hudson v. McMillian*, ruling that the excessive use of force by prison guards was an Eighth Amendment violation even if the prisoner was not seriously hurt; *Lee v. Weisman*, barring nonsectarian or any other prayers at public high school graduations; *Riggins v. Nevada*, ruling that the state could not force an insane criminal defendant to take medication during a trial; *U.S. v. Fordice*, ruling that Mississippi had not fulfilled its obligation to desegregate its public colleges and universities; and *Jacobson v. U.S.*, ruling that the federal government had illegally entrapped a defendant into buying child pornography through the mail. He wrote a concurring opinion in the landmark *R.A.V. v. St. Paul*, overturning a St. Paul, Minnesota ordinance making sexist, racist, or otherwise bigoted speech or behavior a crime.

Stevens wrote a very strong dissenting opinion in *U.S. v. Alvarez Machain*, which upheld the 1990 U.S. kidnapping of a Mexican doctor suspected of a role in the torture of a U.S. drug enforcement agent. His 31 dissents included *Lechmere Inc. v. National Labor Relations Board*, which ruled that companies did not have to allow union organizers access to such company-owned lands as parking lots and shopping malls; *Keeney v. Tamayo-Reyes*, which sharply limited the federal habeas corpus appeals of state prisoners; *New York v. U.S.*, which invalidated a federal law forcing states to handle their own radioactive waste; *Nordlinger v. Hahn*, upholding the right of California to enact Proposition 13, with its unequal property taxes on newcomers; and *International Society for Krishna Consciousness v. Lee*, ruling that airports could ban groups from soliciting money. He also disagreed with the majority ruling that the Coast Guard could continue to intercept at sea and return Haitian refugees to Haiti; and in the decision barring return of RU-486 pills to Leona Benten, a pregnant woman who tried to import them into the U.S. for her personal use, in a challenge to their ban.

Chicago-born Stevens practiced law for two decades before being appointed to the Seventh Circuit U.S. Court of Appeals in 1970. President Gerald Ford appointed him to the Supreme Court in 1975. Stevens was thought to be a moderate conservative at the time of his appointment, as was Ford; the estimate was right, for Stevens often functioned as a middle force between the conservative and liberal wings of the court in the years that followed. But in later years, as the court turned sharply to the right, he was more often seen as a moderate liberal, in most instances agreeing with Justices Blackmun, Marshall, and Brennan, the latter two

since retired. Stevens' 1941 B.A. was from the University of Chicago, and his 1947 LL.B. from Northwestern. He has been married twice, last to Maryan Mulholland Simon in 1979, and has four children.

FURTHER READING

John Paul Stevens. BOB ITALIA and PAUL DEEGAN. Abdo & Daughters, 1992.
"A new day in court." LAUREN TARSHIS and JAMES EARL HARDY. *Scholastic Update*, Nov. 1, 1991.
"A voice of reason. . . ." *American Legion Magazine*, June 1990.
Eight Men and a Lady. HERMAN SCHWARTZ et al. National Press, 1990.
John Paul Stevens and the Constitution: The Search for Balance. ROBERT J. SICKELS. Pennsylvania State University Press, 1988.

Sting (Gordon Matthew Sumner; 1951–) Musician, songwriter, and actor Sting was honored by his musical peers in 1992, receiving a Best Rock Song Grammy for "Soul Cages," the title song of his hit 1991 album. He and Eric Clapton won a different kind of recognition as well from those who bought and made a hit of their single "It's Probably Me," from the soundtrack of *Lethal Weapon 3.* Forthcoming in 1993 was a new Sting album.

On the social service side, Sting continued to support a considerable range of social causes, perhaps most notably in March hosting the third annual Rainforest Foundation benefit at New York's Carnegie Hall, with Whoopi Goldberg, Natalie Cole, Elton John, and James Taylor, among others. On the personal side, Sting and his longtime companion, actress and television producer Trudie Styler, were married in August.

Sting, a former grade school schoolteacher, became a major rock star in the early 1980s, as lead singer of The Police, formed in 1977 with Andy Summers and Bill Copeland. Although the group continued, he largely went on his own in the late 1980s, recording such albums as *The Dream of the Blue Turtles* (1985) and *Nothing Like the Sun* (1987). He also developed a substantial film and stage career; his films include *Quadrophenia* (1978), *Brimstone and Treacle* (1982), *Dune* (1984), *Plenty* (1985), and *Rosencranz and Guildenstern Are Dead* (1989). In November 1989, he made his Broadway debut as

Mack the Knife in a revival of *The Threepenny Opera*. He and Trudie Styler have three children; he also has two children from a former marriage.

FURTHER READING

Sting: The Illustrated Lyrics. ROBERTO GILGROV. IRS Books, 1991.
"Twisting Mack the Knife. . . ." JOHN ISTEL. *Mother Jones*, Nov. 1989.
"Sting." RUDY MAXA. *Washingtonian*, Sep. 1989.
"Sting speaks." ART LANGE. *Down Beat*, Sep. 1989.
Written in My Soul: Rock's Great Songwriters. . . . Talk about Creating Their Music. BILL FLANAGAN. Contemporary, 1986.

Stirling, James Frazer (1926–1992)

Glasgow-born Stirling was a leading British architect. A 1950 graduate of the Liverpool University School of Architecture, he went into private practice in 1956. His early work was largely influenced by the stream in "modernism" that flowed from the rough-concrete work of Le Corbusier, as seen in his Ham Common apartment complex (1957) and the Leicester University engineering building (1959–63). Sharply criticized as "brutalist" by many, these two structures were also criticized—as was much of his other work—for not working very well as buildings in human comfort and environmental terms. Stirling later moved toward a more classic and at the same time more colorful style, called by many "post-modernist," although many of his structures still owed their basic forms to the industrial designs pioneered in Germany and Russia earlier in the century, that developed into the set of styles then called modernist. His Stuttgart museum, the Neue Staatsgalerie, is generally regarded as his most notable work. He was survived by his wife, the designer Mary Shand, two daughters, and a son. (d. London; June 25, 1992)

FURTHER READING

Obituary. *Independent*, June 27, 1992.
Obituary. *Variety*, June 22, 1992.
Obituary. *The Times* (of London), June 22, 1992.
Obituary. *New York Times*, June 19, 1992.
"Who's afraid of. . . . " DIANA KETCHAM. *ARTnews*, Feb. 1989.
*Norman Foster, Richard Rogers, James Stirling:

New Directions in British Architecture.* DEYAN SUDJIC. Thames Hudson, 1987.
James Stirling: A Select Bibliography. VALERIA J. NURCOMBE. Vance Biblios, 1985.
James Stirling: Buildings and Projects. PETER ARNELL and TED BICKFORD, eds. Rizzoli International, 1985.

Stone, Oliver (1946–)

For celebrated American film writer, director, and producer Stone, 1992 will always be remembered as the year of his classic, extraordinarily controversial film *JFK*, his view of the 1963 assassination of President John F. Kennedy as a conspiracy organized at the highest levels of American government. Stone wrote, directed, and co-produced the film with a multistar cast that included Kevin Costner, Sissy Spacek, Jay O. Sanders, Joe Pesci, Tommy Lee Jones, Gary Oldham, Michael Rooker, and Laurie Metcalf, with key smaller roles played by stars Jack Lemmon, Ed Asner, Walter Matthau, Donald Sutherland, and John Candy. The film, which opened on December 20, 1991, generated tremendous personal attacks on Stone; he and others defended his view, and the argument raged for much of the year, as the film went on to become a worldwide hit, grossing more than $150 million and generating worldwide controversy. Stone won a best director Golden Globe award for *JFK*, and a Best Director Oscar nomination; and with Zachary Sklar won a Best Screenplay Adaptation Oscar nomination. In the political arena, he and his film won the opening of many previously sealed government documents on the Kennedy assassination.

During 1992, Stone filmed yet another Vietnam story, titled *Heaven and Earth*, based on the books *Child of War* and *Women of Peace*, both autobiographical volumes of a Vietnamese woman, Le Ly Hayslip, as adapted by Stone for film, and covering a period stretching from the 1950s through the 1980s, from her days as a guerrilla soldier in Vietnam to her later life in America. The cast was to include an unknown in the lead, Tommy Lee Jones, and Debbie Reynolds as Jones' mother.

Stone was also involved in many other projects as a producer during 1992, among them the film *Eraserhead*; the forthcoming film *South Central*, about the 1992 Los Angeles riots; and a forthcoming six-episode television series based on the comic strip "Wild Palms."

New York-born Stone fought in Vietnam (1965–66), an experience that has deeply affected some of his most notable work. He has won three Oscars. His first was for his *Midnight Express* (1978) screenplay. His second was for his direction of *Platoon* (1986), a film that he also wrote and that won a Best Picture Oscar. His third was as best director for *Born on the Fourth of July* (1989), filmed from the Oscar-nominated screenplay by Stone and Ron Kovic based on Kovic's autobiography; Stone himself appeared in a small role in the film, which also won several other awards. Stone also co-wrote and directed such films as *Scarface* (1983), *Wall Street* (1987), *Talk Radio* (1988), and *The Doors* (1991). He attended Yale University; his 1971 B.F.A. was from the New York University Film School. He has been married twice, first to Najwa Sarkis, with whom he had a son, then in 1981 to former nurse Elizabeth Cox. Their son, Sean, at age six, played the young Jim Morrison in *The Doors*.

FURTHER READING

"Splinters to the brain." NATHAN GARDELS and LEILA CONNERS. *New Perspectives*, Spring 1992.
"Heart of stone." JEFF YARBROUGH. *Advocate*, Apr. 7, 1992.
"Ollie uber Alles. . . ." PETER COLLIER. *American Spectator*, Apr. 1992.
"No conspiracy!" *Independent*, Jan. 18, 1992.
"Camera obscura." STEVE DALY. *Entertainment*, Jan. 17, 1992.

"The man who shot 'JFK.' " JENNET CONANT. *GQ*, Jan. 1992.
"Plunging into the labyrinth." *Time*, Dec. 23, 1991.
"What does. . . ." DAVID ANSEN. *Newsweek*, Dec. 23, 1991.
"Can Hollywood solve. . . ." MARK SEAL. *Texas*, Dec. 1991.
"The shooting of JFK." ROBERT SAM ANSON. *Esquire*, Nov. 1991.
"Riders on the storm." ROBERT HORTON. *Film Comment*, May–June 1991.
"60s something. . . ." STEPHEN TALBOT. *Mother Jones*, Mar.–Apr. 1991.
"Oliver Stone. . . . " DAVID BRESKIN. *Rolling Stone*, Apr. 4, 1991.
"Unorthodox behaviour. . . ." *Economist*, Mar. 16, 1991.
"Stone unturned." MARK ROWLAND. *American Film*, Mar. 1991.
"Oliver Stone." JOHN CLARK. *Premiere*, Feb. 1990.
Icons: Intimate Portraits. DENISE WORRELL. Atlantic Monthly, 1989.

Streep, Meryl (Mary Louise Streep; 1949–) Celebrated film star Streep continued to move forward strongly in 1992, still finding substantial starring roles in a film trade that is notoriously empty of good leading roles for women over 40. Her major film in 1992 was Robert Zemeckis' dark comedy *Death Becomes Her*, the story of the lifelong—and post-death—rivalry of two Hollywood beauties, played by Streep and Goldie Hawn, and co-starring Bruce Willis. Forthcoming was a starring role in the film version of Isabel Allende's novel *House of the Spirits*. Set in Chile, the movie costars Jeremy Irons, Glenn Close, Winona Ryder, and Anthony Banderas.

New Jersey-born Streep was quickly recognized as a major dramatic star in the late 1970s; her work includes such films as *The Deer Hunter* (1978), *Manhattan* (1979), *Kramer vs. Kramer* (1980; she won a Best Supporting Actress Oscar), *Sophie's Choice* (1982; she won a Best Actress Oscar), *Silkwood* (1983), *Out of Africa* (1985), *Ironweed* (1987), *She-Devil* (1989), *Postcards from the Edge* (1990), and *Defending Your Life* (1991). Streep's B.A. was from Vassar in 1971; her M.F.A. from Yale in 1975. She married sculptor Donald J. Gummer in 1978; the couple have four children.

FURTHER READING

"Serious lady with a comic touch." RICHARD BROOKS. *Observer*, Oct. 18, 1992.

"Hope I die before I get old." TERESA CARPENTER. *Premiere*, Sep. 1992.

"Winning Streep." DAVID HANDELMAN. *Vogue*, Apr. 1992.

"Queen for a decade." MARC ELIOT. *California*, Sep. 1991.

"Getting the skinny. . . ." MICHAEL SEGELL. *Cosmopolitan*, May 1991.

"Meryl Streep. . . ." WENDY WASSERSTEIN. *Saturday Evening Post*, July–Aug. 1989.

"Ms. Streep goes. . . ." BONNIE JOHNSON. *People*, Mar. 20, 1989.

Meryl Streep: A Critical Biography. EUGENE E. PFAFF, JR., and MARK EMERSON. McFarland, 1987.

Streisand, Barbra

Streisand, Barbra (Barbara Joan Streisand; 1942–) At 50 still going strong, legendary singer and eight-time Grammy-winner Streisand won a 1992 Grammy Legend award for her whole body of work at the 34th annual Grammy Award ceremonies. She was honored for something new as well, winning a Directors Guild of America Best Feature Film nomination for *The Prince of Tides*, the third woman ever to be nominated. She was passed over at the Academy Awards ceremonies, though her film was not, winning a Best Picture nomination; her costar, Nick Nolte, won a Best Actor Oscar nomination, and Kate Nelligan won a Best Supporting Actress nomination, as did the film's cinematography, editing, original score, and screenplay adaptation. In 1992, Streisand issued the hit single "For All We Know," from the soundtrack of *The Prince of Tides*.

Streisand was active in political and social causes during 1992. Her foundation gave more than $100,000 to help rebuild riot-damaged Los Angeles areas, and she was personally active in the Clinton-Gore campaign, singing publicly for the first time since 1986 at a Democratic Party fundraiser on September 16 that Clinton attended. After the election, she called on entertainers to refuse to appear in Colorado to protest passage of the new state anti-gay referendum.

Brooklyn-born Streisand is one of the great popular music stars of the modern period, whose work also includes several very notable film, stage, and television credits. Her breakthrough roles came on stage in musical theater, in *I Can Get It for You Wholesale* (1962) and as Fanny Brice in *Funny Girl* (1964), a role for which she won a Best Actress Oscar in the 1968 film version. She became a worldwide recording star in the mid-1960s for such Grammy-winning songs as "People" (1964) and "Evergreen" (1977; also an Oscar winner), and such Grammy-winning albums as *The Barbra Streisand Album* (1963) and *My Name is Barbra* (1965). A six-time best vocalist Grammy-winner, she issued many old, but many new, songs in the four-CD *Just for the Record* (1991). She also starred in such films as *Hello Dolly* (1969), *On a Clear Day You Can See Forever* (1970), *The Owl and the Pussycat* (1971), *The Way We Were* (1973), *Funny Lady* (1975) and *Nuts* (1987). She produced and starred in *A Star is Born* (1976), and directed, produced, and starred in *Yentl* (1983). Her 1965 television special *My Name is Barbra* won five Emmys. She was formerly married to the actor Elliott Gould, and has one child.

FURTHER READING

"Streisand, Barbra." *Current Biography*, Sep. 1992.

"Barbra Streisand." JOHN CLARK. *Premiere*, Dec. 1991.

"The triumph of. . . ." JOE MORGENSTERN. *Cosmopolitan*, Oct. 1991.

"Queen of Tides." KEVIN SESSUMS. *Vanity Fair*, Sep. 1991.

Barbra—An Actress Who Sings, The Unauthorized Biography of Barbra Streisand. JAMES KIMBRELL. Branden, Vol I, 1989; Vol. II, 1992.

Barbra, the Second Decade: The Films and Career of Barbra Streisand. KAREN SWENSON. Carol, 1986.

Barbra Streisand: The Woman, the Myth, the Music. SHAUN CONSIDINE. Delacorte, 1985.

Sturges, John (1911–92) Illinois-born Sturges worked in film production and editing during the 1930s, and directed and edited armed forces training films during World War II. He began his Hollywood directing career with *The Man Who Dared* (1946), and emerged as a major director in the 1950s with such films as *Escape from Fort Bravo* (1953), *Bad Day at Black Rock* (1954; he won a Best Director Oscar nomination), *Gunfight at the O.K. Corral* (1957), *The Old Man and the Sea* (1958), and *Last Train from Gun Hill* (1959). He directed and produced *The Magnificent Seven* (1960), an adaptation of Akira Kurosawa's *The Seven Samurai*. His other major films included *By Love Possessed* (1961), *The Great Escape* (1963; he directed and produced), *Hour of the Gun* (1967), *Ice Station Zebra* (1968), *Joe Kidd* (1972), and *The Eagle Has Landed* (1974). He was survived by his second wife, Katherine, a daughter, and a son. (d. St. Luis Obispo, California; August 18, 1992)

FURTHER READING

Obituary. *Variety*, Aug. 24, 1992.
Obituary. *The Times* (of London), Aug. 24, 1992.
Obituary. *New York Times*, Aug. 22, 1992.

Sullivan, Louis Wade (1933–) On the positive side, Dr. Sullivan's last year in office as Health and Human Services Secretary was notable for his support of Dr. David Kessler, who as head of the Food and Drug Administration continued the series of major initiatives he had started in 1991. Sullivan was particularly supportive of the FDA's declaration of a 45-day moratorium on silicone gel breast implants, while a safety review was conducted, although that action cast doubt on the safety of the approximately 2 million silicone gel breast implants done since the early 1960s, and generated tremendous medical and drug industry pressures on Sullivan to derail Kessler's investigation. Sullivan also continued to support truthful food labeling, and to attack deceptive advertising. However, Sullivan continued to execute Bush administration policies on such matters as abortion counselling and AIDS, while leaving untouched such major national issues as the cost of medical care and the huge gaps in the national health insurance systems that left tens of millions uninsured. Sullivan unfortunately became

deeply involved in the partisan politics of the period. In September, deep into the campaign, he sharply blamed the Democrats for playing politics with medical care; Democratic Congressional leaders responded in kind, and deplored Sullivan's political involvement.

Atlanta-born Sullivan, a leading doctor and educator, went to Washington after a long and distinguished career that included teaching positions at Harvard Medical School, the New Jersey College of Medicine, and Boston University; he is an internist and hematologist. He was dean of the Morehouse College Medical School from 1975 until his cabinet appointment in 1989. Sullivan's B.S. was from Morehouse College, his M.D. from Boston University. He married Eve Williamson in 1955; they have two children.

FURTHER READING

"The CEO of health." Marjorie Whigham. *Black Enterprise*, Sep. 1991.
"How to keep America healthy." *American Legion Magazine*, July 1990.
"Louis Sullivan finds. . . ." Maria Wilhelm. *People*, Mar. 26, 1990.
"Sullivan, Louis Wade." *Current Biography*, July 1989.

Sununu, John H. (1939–) Out of power a year early, former White House Chief of Staff Sununu found another highly visible though far less powerful position in February 1992, replacing Pat Buchanan on CNN's "Crossfire," opposite liberal Michael Kinsley. He also became a lobbyist, in June registering to lobby Congress for W.R. Grace and Co., a diversified chemical manufacturer. He was not entirely out of Republican politics, though; in August, he made a non-prime-time brief televised speech to the Republican National Convention; and in October he helped rehearse President George Bush for the upcoming Presidential debates, playing Ross Perot.

Havana-born Sununu began his career an an engineer and educator, founding the Astro Dynamics company in 1960, and teaching mechanical engineering and then becoming associate engineering dean at Tufts University (1966–82). He moved into politics as a member of the New Hampshire legislature in 1973, ultimately becoming governer of his state (1983–89). He was a key member of the Bush presidential campaign staff in 1988, and after the election became the president-elect's chief of staff. Highly publicized expense account and other problems led to his resignation on December 3, 1991. Sununu's 1961 B.S. was from the Massachusetts Institute of Technology, as were his 1962 M.S. and his 1966 Ph.D. He married Nancy Hayes in 1958; they have four children.

FURTHER READING

"The political pleasures. . . ." HERB BRODY.
    Technology Review, Aug.–Sep. 1992.
"So long, Sununu." SIDNEY BLUMENTHAL. *Vanity Fair*,
    Feb. 1992.
"Sununu speaks. . . ." LEE WALCZAK and DOUGLAS
    HARBRECHT. *Business Week*, Dec. 2, 1991.
"The grounding of. . . ." BRIT HUME. *American
    Spectator*, Sep. 1991.
"The genius. . . ." SIDNEY BLUMENTHAL. *New Republic*.
    July 29, 1991.
"John Sununu's. . . ." KENNETH T. WALSH and STEPHEN
    J. HEDGES. *U.S. News & World Report*, May 13,
    1991.
"Profile. . . ." TIM BEARDSLEY. *Scientific American*,
    Apr. 1991.
"Beasts of the beltway. . . . " FRED BARNES. *New
    Republic*, Dec. 24, 1990.
"John Sununu. . . ." ROWLAND EVANS and ROBERT
    NOVAK. *Reader's Digest*, Nov. 1990.
"Big bad John Sununu. . . ." DAN GOODGAME. *Time*,
    May 21, 1990.
"Big bad John." MICHAEL KELLY. *Playboy*, Nov. 1990.
"John Sununu." CRAIG UNGER. *People*, Mar. 12, 1990.
"A talk with. . . ." LEE WALCZAK, et al. *Business
    Week*, Feb. 5, 1990.
"Sununu, John Henry." *Current Biography*, May
    1989.

Sutherland, Donald McNichol

(1934–   ) Canadian film star Sutherland was highly visible throughout the world in 1992–in one of his smallest roles, that of Colonel X, the highly placed covert operations U.S. intelligence officer who was James Garrison's key Washington informant in *JFK*. Also in 1992 Sutherland starred as an eccentric, maimed railroad enthusiast, opposite Julie Christie as the widow of an Irish Republican Army victim in Michael Whyte's romantic drama, *The Railway Station Man*, set in modern Ireland, which aired on TNT. He also starred opposite Kristy Swanson in Fran Rubel Kuzui's comedy *Buffy the Vampire Slayer*. Forthcoming were a starring role opposite Amy

Irving in Jonathan Heap's film *Benefit of the Doubt*; and another role in Werner Herzog's *Scream of Stone*, about a mountain-climbing team in Argentina.

Sutherland began his film career in the mid-1960s, and emerged as a star playing Korean War surgeon Benjamin Franklin "Hawkeye" Pierce in the original film *M*A*S*H* (1970). He went on to a wide variety of dramatic roles, many of them chosen primarily for their quality, in such films as *Klute* (1971), *The Day of the Locust* (1975), *1900* (1976), *Casanova* (1976), *Ordinary People* (1980), *Eye of the Needle* (1981), *Gaugin* (1986), *A Dry White Season* (1989), *Lock Up* (1989), *Eminent Domain* (1991), and *Backdraft*. On television, he starred in the Canadian miniseries "Bethune: The Making of a Hero." Sutherland attended the University of Toronto. He has been married three times, and has five children, including actor Kiefer Sutherland.

FURTHER READING

"Donald Sutherland and. . . ." GERMANO CELAND and
    BRIGITTE LACOMBE. *Interview*, Sep. 1990.

Swanberg, William Andrew (1907–92)

St. Paul-born Swanberg graduated from the University of Minnesota in 1930, with the United States in the grip of the Great Depression. After several difficult years, he went to work as an editor at Dell Publishing. He worked for the Office of War Information during World War II, and after the war became a freelance writer. His first published book was *Sickles the Incredible* (1956), a biography of Civil War General Daniel Sickles. It was followed by nine more books, including such notable biographies as *Jim Fisk* (1959); *Hearst: A Biography of William Randolph Hearst* (1961); *Dreiser* (1965), about author Theodore Dreiser; *Pulitzer* (1967), about editor and publisher Joseph Pulitzer; and his Pulitzer Prize-winning *Luce and His Empire* (1972). He was survived by his wife, the former Dorothy Green, a daughter, and a son. (d. Southbury, Connecticut; September 21, 1992)

FURTHER READING

Obituary. *Variety*, Sep. 21, 1992.
Obituary. *The Times* (of London), Sep. 14, 1992.
Obituary. *New York Times*, Sep. 14, 1992.

Swayze, Patrick (1954–) Film star

Swayze starred in what was for him a very different kind of film in 1992, playing Dr. Max Lowe in Roland Joffe's *City of Joy*. The City of Joy is scarcely that; it is a desperately poor neighborhood in Calcutta, as described in Dominique La Pierre's book, adapted for film by Mark Medoff. Lowe is a demoralized American surgeon; Pauline Collins is a British nurse who runs a clinic in the City of Joy; Art Malik and Shabana Azmi are an Indian couple in an otherwise all-Indian cast. In the course of the film, Lowe rediscovers himself and his calling as a healer. Unfortunately, the well-meaning, expensive film was rather poorly received by most critics, and did not do well at the box office. What was doing well for Swayze in 1992 was his 1991 bank robbery/car chase/sex-and-violence movie *Point Break*, which became a hit in home video.

Trained for ballet, Swayze began his career as a dancer, and danced and acted a lead in *Grease* for two years on Broadway before emerging as a leading film player late in the 1980s. His breakthrough role was as Johnny Castle in *Dirty Dancing* (1987). It was followed by a starring role opposite his wife, Lisa Niemi, in the fantasy-action film *Steel Dawn* (1987); and by starring roles in *Road House* (1989); *Next of Kin* (1989), *Ghost* (1990), and *Point Break* (1991). Swayze also appeared in the television miniseries

"North and South" (1990), and in several other television films.

FURTHER READING

"Patrick Swayze." *Playboy*, June 1992.
"Patrick Swayze. . . ." STEPHANIE MANSFIELD. *GQ—Gentleman's Quarterly*, Feb. 1992.
"Body and soul." JEANNIE PARK. *People*, Aug. 26, 1991.
"From here to maturity. . . ." *Seventeen*, July 1991.
"Patrick Swayze." *People*, Dec. 31, 1990
"Patrick Swayze. . . ." KATHRYN CASEY. *Ladies Home Journal*, Aug. 1990.
"A wild and Swayze guy." BILL ZEHME. *Cosmopolitan*, Aug. 1989.
"Going Swayze." LAURA MORICE. *Mademoiselle*, June 1989.
Patrick Swayze. MITCHELL KRUGEL. St. Martin's, 1988.
The New Breed: Actors Coming of Age. KAREN HARDY and KEVIN J. KOFFLER. Holt, 1988.

Sydow, Max von (Carl Adolf von Sydow;

1929–) The great Swedish actor Max von Sydow continued to appear in a wide range of substantial roles in 1992. Perhaps the most notable was his starring role as Anna Bergman's father opposite Pernilla August as Anna Bergman and Samuel Froler as Henrik Bergman in Bille August's *The Best Intentions*, the story of the courtship and very difficult early marriage of Ingmar Bergman's parents, with screenplay by Bergman. The film was shown first as a six-part television series in Scandinavia, and then premiered as a theatrical film at the 1992 Cannes International Film Festival, winning the Golden Palm award.

A second starring role was as the reborn old classical composer in Christof Zanussi's Polish film *The Silent Touch*, co-starring Lothaire Bluteau and Sarah Miles. In a third major art-film role, von Sydow appeared opposite Carol Drinkwater in John Power's *Father*, he as an ex-Nazi murderer hiding his past in Australia, she as the daughter who ultimately realizes that the charges against him are true. He also appeared in Sven Nykvist's *The Ox*, a story of hard times in the 1860s Swedish countryside that co-starred Liv Ullmann and Erland Josephson. He was also the narrator of Lars von Triers *Zentropa*, a surreal thriller set in devastated post-World War II Germany.

Forthcoming were a starring role in Fraser

Heston's film, *Needful Things*, adapted from the Stephen King novel and co-starring Ed Harris and Bonnie Bedelia; Dan Petrie's *A Dog In Flanders*; and John Irving's adaptation of his own novel, *Cider House Rules*.

The classic Ingmar Bergman films in which von Sydow made his greatest impact include *The Seventh Seal*, (1957), *The Magician* (1958), *The Virgin Spring* (1960), *Through a Glass Darkly* (1961), and *Winter Light* (1962). He also starred on television and in later theatrical release in two linked sagas of 19th-century Scandinavian-American immigration: *The Emigrants* (1969) and *The New Land* (1969). His later work included such films as *Three Days of the Condor* (1975), *Hannah and Her Sisters* (1985), *Pelle the Conqueror* (1986), and *Until the End of the World* (1991). He played a Catholic priest working in Hiroshima in the television film *Hiroshima: Out of the Ashes*, which premiered on August 6, 1990, the 45th anniversary of the atom bombing of city.

Von Sydow has long been recognized as one of Sweden's leading stage actors. He attended Stockholm's Royal Dramatic Theatre School, and has been associated with that theater since 1960. He married Christina Olin in 1951, and has two children.

FURTHER READING

"In step with: Max von Sydow." JAMES BRADY. *Parade*, Oct. 25, 1992.

"Scandinavia-hopping Von Sydow. . . ." LAWRENCE COHN. *Variety*, Dec. 21, 1988.

Syms, Sylvia (Sylvia Blagman; 1917–92)

New York City-born Syms, whose career as a jazz singer in cabaret spanned more than half a century, taught herself to sing as a teenager on New York's 52nd Street jazz strip. She was the young friend of many jazz musicians, and especially of her model, the singer Billie Holiday. Syms made her debut at New York's Kelly's Stable in 1941, and died on stage at the Oak Room of New York's Algonquin Hotel 51 years later, having become a highly respected figure in the jazz world. She made 15 records for Decca, and was well received, but had only one popular hit: "I Could Have Danced All Night (1956)," from *My Fair Lady*. Syms also had a second performing career as an actress in such plays as *Diamond Lil*, *Camino Real*, and *Hello, Dolly!*, and often played Bloody Mary in *South Pacific*. She was survived by a sister and a brother.

FURTHER READING

"Last set." WHITNEY BALLIETT. *New Yorker*, Oct. 19, 1992.
Obituary. *Variety*, May 18, 1992.
Obituary. *The Times* (of London), May 12, 1992.
Obituary. *New York Times*, May 11, 1992.

T

Tagliabue, Paul John (1940–   ) It was a turbulent year for National Football League (NFL) commissioner Paul Tagliabue. More than one commentator wondered aloud whether he might be booted out, as had his baseball counterpart Fay Vincent, especially early in the year, when the club owners voted against the instant replay that Tagliabue favored. But, as 1993 rolled around, Tagliabue's position seemed more secure, though professional football was going through massive changes.

His main task—and a formidable one—was to hammer out a new labor agreement between the players and owners after almost five years without one. The new contract would have to incorporate provisions that allowed free agency for veteran players to move to the teams of their choice, as provided for under a September 1992 court decision in a case brought by Jets' player Freeman McNeil and others, in which Tagliabue had argued strongly for maintaining the status quo so that the league could maintain competitive balance. At first constrained to take any proposed agreement back to the club owners for approval, Tagliabue in July was given complete authority to negotiate on behalf of the league. His work continued into January 1993, when he completed a seven-year labor agreement, running through 1999, allowing players with over five years' experience to seek the best deal for their services, once their present contracts have expired, though permitting each team to exempt one "franchise" player from free agency, if they meet or exceed the average of the salaries received by the top five players at his position.

Teams also had the right of first refusal for two other players, with payment of at least an average of the top ten players at that position. The settlement also provided for a salary cap (modeled on that successful in basketball), limitation on salaries for rookies, payments to settle oustanding litigation regarding free agency, and a reduction in the number of rounds in the college draft, allowing extra selections to teams that lose the most players to free agency. Some players who filed a companion suit to the McNeil case would have unrestricted free agency and could not be protected as "franchise" players.

Among the other problems Tagliabue was dealing with was the number of serious injuries to players; the possibility of foreign ownership of clubs, a question on which the NFL has had no policy; and, on the business side, extension of the NFL's television contract. While the labor questions remained unsettled, NFL owners tabled possible expansion of the league until after the 1993 season, and similarly suspended operations of the World League of American Football. Tagliabue's own contract is up for renewal at the end of the 1993 season.

After graduating from law school in 1965, Tagliabue worked at the defense department in Washington until 1969, and then for twenty years as a lawyer at Covington and Burling, becoming a partner in 1974. He became commissioner of the National Football League in 1989. Tagliabue's 1962 B.A. was from Georgetown University, where he played basketball; his 1965 J.D. is from New York University. He is married and has two children.

FURTHER READING

"The face of. . . ." RICK TELANDER. *Sports Illustrated*, Sep. 10, 1990.
"NFL commish's torch passed. . . ." *Sporting News*, Feb. 18, 1990.
"Tagliabue. . . ." PAUL ATTNER. *Sporting News*, Feb. 12, 1990.
"Tagliabue plans. . . ." STEVE HUBBARD. *Sporting News*, Dec. 4, 1989.
"A new quarterback. . . ." *U.S. News & World Report*, Nov. 6, 1989.
"In a blink. . . ." VITO STELLINO. *Sporting News*, Nov. 6, 1989.
"The NFL's new boss." PETER KING. *Sports Illustrated*, Nov. 6, 1989.

Tal, Mikhail (1936–92) Latvian chess grandmaster Tal, born in Riga, became Latvian chess champion while still in his teens, in 1953. He went on to win his first Soviet championship at Leningrad (now St. Petersburg) in 1957, and won a second Soviet championship at Riga in 1958. He won two major international matches in 1958 and 1959, both held in Yugoslavia, and in 1960 at Moscow defeated Mikhail Botvinnik, who had held the title for 12 years, for the world championship. Tal, then only 23, became the youngest 20th-century chess player until then to hold the world championship. But Tal, although an enormously talented and daring player, was also somewhat erratic, made even more so by lifelong physical problems. At a Moscow rematch with Botvinnik a year later, Tal was defeated by a large margin, and never again became a serious contender for the world championship, although he went forward to win further Soviet championships and major international matches. No information was available regarding his survivors. (d. Moscow; June 18, 1992)

FURTHER READING

Obituary. *The Times* (of London), June 30, 1992.
Obituary. *New York Times*, June 30, 1992.
Mikhail Tal: Master of Sacrifice. PETER CLARKE. Trafalgar, 1991.

Tandy, Jessica (1909–) Now in her mid-80s, more than half a century after she had been Ophelia to John Gielgud's *Hamlet*, and forty-five years after she created the Blanche Du Bois role

Jessica Tandy (right) and Hume Cronyn.

in Tennessee Williams' *A Streetcar Named Desire*, the great British actress Jessica Tandy was still going strong. In 1992, she followed up her 1990 Oscar for *Driving Miss Daisy* with a Best Supporting Actress Oscar nomination for *Fried Green Tomatoes*, also set in the smalltown South, but this one feminist-oriented. The film, which opened in December 1991, was successful commercially as well as artistically in early 1992, and enjoyed a second life in home video later in the year.

In 1992, Tandy starred as Shirley MacLaine's mother in Beeban Kidron's comedy-melodrama film *Used People*. Set in 1960s New York City, the film co-starred Marcello Mastroianni as MacLaine's long-adoring Italian-American suitor, Kathy Bates and Marcia Gay Harden as her daughters, and Sylvia Sidney as Tandy's best friend.

London-born Tandy appeared in London and New York during the 1930s, though mainly in London and in the classics, most notably as Ophelia to John Gielgud's *Hamlet* (1934). On the Broadway stage, she created the Blanche Du Bois role in Tennessee Williams's *A Streetcar Named Desire* (1947). After she and Hume Cronyn married in 1942, they created a lasting theater partnership, appearing together in such plays as *The Fourposter* (1951), *A Delicate Balance* (1966), and *Foxfire* (1982; and the 1987 television version). She has also appeared in strong character roles in several other films. Tandy and Cronyn were awarded the 1990 National Medal of the Arts. Cronyn wrote about their life and work together in his *A Terrible Liar: A Memoir* (1991). Tandy attended the Ben Greet Academy of Acting (1924–27). Her first husband was British actor Jack Hawkins, with whom she had a daughter. She and Cronyn have two children, one of them the actress Tandy Cronyn. (For additional photo, see Bates, Kathy.)

FURTHER READING

"Jessica Tandy." JOHN CLARK. *Premiere*, Feb. 1992.
"He drives Miss Daisy. . . ." EVE DROBOT. *Saturday Night*, Oct. 1991.
"Jessica Tandy. . . ." CINDY ADAMS. *Ladies Home Journal*, Apr. 1991.
Jessica Tandy: A Bio-Bibliography. MILLY S. BARRANGER. Greenwood, 1991.
"Two lives, one ambition. . . ." GERALD CLARKE. *Time*, Apr. 2, 1990.
"Happily ever after." JEANNE MARIE LASKAS. *Life*, Apr. 1990.
"She oughta be in pictures. . . ." NINA DARNTON. *Newsweek*, Jan. 1, 1990.
"Driving Miss Daisy. . . ." ROBERT SEIDENBERG. *American Film*, Jan. 1990.
"Two for the road." MARK MATOUSEK. *Harper's Bazaar*, Jan. 1990.
Actress to Actress. RITA GAM. Lyons & Burford, 1986.

Tanenbaum, Marc Herbert (1925–92)

Baltimore-born Rabbi Tanenbaum was a graduate of Yeshiva University and the Jewish Theological Seminary. He was ordained a Conservative rabbi in 1950. He served as a rabbi with two congregations (1951–54), was executive director of the Synagogue Council of America (1954–60), and was director of the department of interreligious affairs of the American Jewish Committee (1971–83), then becoming director of international affairs until his 1989 retirement. In both of the latter positions, he became a leading figure in the development of Jewish-Christian dialog, aimed at improving relations between the religions. He was an observer at the historic Second Vatican Council, and after the council spent much of his time in attempting to improve Jewish-Catholic relations, while continuing to work with those of other religious groups, as well. He was also active in international refugee and human rights work. Tanenbaum was a well-known radio broadcaster on religious matters, whose syndicated program began its long run on New York's WINS in 1965. Among his written works were

Religious Values in an Age of Violence (1976) and, as co-editor, *Speaking of God Today: Jews and Lutherans in Conversation* (1974), *Evangelicals and Jews in Conversation* (1978), *Evangelicals and Jews in an Age of Pluralism* (1984), *Twenty Years of Jewish-Christian Relations* (1986), and *Twenty Years of Jewish-Catholic Relations* (1986). He was survived by his wife, Georgette Bennett, two daughters, a son, and a sister. (d. New York City; July 3, 1992)

FURTHER READING

Obituary. *The Times* (of London), July 18, 1992.
Obituary. *New York Times*, July 4, 1992.

Elizabeth Taylor (left) and Johnny Carson.

Taylor, Elizabeth (1932–)

One of the world's leading figures in the fight against AIDS (acquired immune deficiency syndrome), Taylor in 1992 continued to develop fundraising and public awareness programs aimed at combatting the disease, which was spreading so rapidly that a late-1992 Harvard University study predicted that 50 million worldwide would be infected by the virus by the turn of the century. She continued to raise funds for the American Foundation for AIDS Research and for her own Elizabeth Taylor AIDS Foundation, in one mid-October benefit raising $600,000 for the latter organization. One individual donation from Taylor was for $250,000 to the AIDS Project Los Angeles. She also continued to combat fear and prejudice directly, as in her appearance as the voice of the mother of an HIV-positive teenager, played by the voice of Neil Patrick Harris, in the children's cartoon series "Captain Planet and the Planeteers."

On March 30, Taylor joined Paul Newman to present major awards at the 64th annual Academy Awards ceremonies. In late October, she was honored by her peers with a major award of her own, becoming the 21st recipient of the American Film Institute's Life Achievement Award, the ceremony to occur on March 11, 1993. She was also one of Johnny Carson's final guests on the "Tonight Show," her first-ever live talk-show appearance.

London-born Taylor began her film career as a young teenager with *Lassie Come Home* and *Jane Eyre*, both in 1943, and became a star at the age of 12 in *National Velvet* (1944). She went on to star in such films as *A Place in the Sun* (1951), *Giant* (1956), *Raintree Country* (1957), *Cat on a Hot Tin Roof* (1958), *Suddenly Last Summer* (1959), *Butterfield 8* (1960; she won a Best Actress Oscar), *Cleopatra* (1962), *Who's Afraid of Virginia Woolf?* (1966, and a second Best Actress Oscar), *Under Milk Wood* (1971), and *The Blue Bird* (1975). She has starred on Broadway in revivals of *The Little Foxes* (1979) and *Private Lives* (1983). Taylor has been married eight times, twice to actor Richard Burton, and has four children. She was married to Larry Fortensky in 1991. Her other husbands were socialite Nicky Hilton, actor Michael Wilding, producer Mike Todd, singer Eddie Fisher, and Senator John Warner.

FURTHER READING

"Liz's AIDS odyssey." NANCY COLLINS. *Vanity Fair*, Nov. 1992.

"Elizabeth at sixty." VERNON SCOTT. *Good Housekeeping*, Feb. 1992.

"Living with Liz." BRAD DARRACH and HARRY BENSON. *Life*, Feb. 1992.

"Elizabeth Taylor. . . ." SALLY OGLE DAVIS. *Ladies Home Journal*, Nov. 1991.

"He does, she does. . . ." JEANNIE PARK. *People*, Oct. 21, 1991.

"Liz: she's survived. . . ." GEORGINA HOWELL. *Vogue*, June 1991.

"Elizabeth." ALEXANDER WALKER. *Cosmopolitan*, Jan. 1991.

All About Elizabeth: Elizabeth Taylor, Public and Private. CAROLINE LATHAM and JEANNIE SAKOL. NAL-Dutton, 1991.

Elizabeth: The Life of Elizabeth Taylor. ALEXANDER WALKER. Grove-Weidenfeld, 1991.

Five for Hollywood: Their Friendship, Their Fame, Their Tragedies. JOHN PARKER. Carol, 1991.

Elizabeth Taylor: A Celebration. SHERIDAN MORLEY. Viking Penguin, 1990.

The Films of Elizabeth Taylor. JERRY VERMILYE and MARK RICCI. Carol, 1989.

The New Elizabeth. MARIANNE ROBIN-TANI. St. Martin's, 1988.

Terkel, Studs Louis (1912–) In his eightieth year and still going strong, Chicago author Terkel published his eighth book in 1992: *How Blacks and Whites Think and Feel About the American Obsession*. Like such other best-selling Terkel books as *Hard Times*, *Working*, and *The Good War*, it was an oral history, in this instance composed of nearly 100 interviews with Blacks and Whites, most of them in the Chicago area. As widely observed by the critics, however, the issues explored and attitudes exposed fully represented the whole modern American experience, and revealingly explored the depths of the prejudices that still drive many White and Black Americans apart. As with his other books, Terkel's work was very well received by both critics and public, sold well, and made a meaningful contribution to the dialog between American Blacks and Whites, so badly blocked and damaged in the 1980s.

New York City-born Terkel moved with his family to Chicago at the age of 8, and embarked on the long love affair with the city that has been a central feature of his life. After his 1932 graduation from the University of Chicago, he went on to a 1934 degree from the university's law school and a Washington job as a lawyer—and then quickly returned to Chicago, not to practice law, but to embark on a long and varied career as a radio and television show host, disc jockey, actor, and playwright. He had his own television show "Studs Place" (1950–53), and after being blacklisted for his political views during the McCarthy period turned to radio and four decades of his daily hour-long "Studs Terkel Show" on WFMT Chicago. He has also appeared in several plays, and wrote the play *Amazing Grace* (1959). Ultimately, Terkel began to publish the oral histories for which he is by far best known worldwide, including *Division Street America* (1966), *Hard Times: An Oral History of the Great Depression in America* (1970), *Working* (1974), and his Pulitzer Prize-winning *The Good War: An Oral History of World War II* (1985). His published works also include *Talking to Myself* (1977), *American Dreams: Lost and Found* (1980), and *The Great Divide: Second Thoughts on the American Dream* (1988).

FURTHER READING

"Studs Terkel." KURT JACOBSEN. *Progressive*, July 1992.
"Division street." GIOVANNA BREU. *People*, May 18, 1992.

Tharp, Twyla (1941–)

In 1992, celebrated choreographer Tharp came to New York City with a new company that included several dancers from the Paris Ballet, one of whom was Patrick Dupond, artistic director and leading male dancer of that company, who appeared only for Tharp's opening night. Tharp danced, as well, after a five-year pause, and was at 50 once again at the center of her company as dancer as well as choreographer. Several new Tharp pieces premiered, including *Grand Pas*, set to Paul Simon's "Rhythm of the Saints"; Simon flew in from Africa for the premiere. Tharp also premiered the highly acclamed *Men's Piece, Octet*, and later in her run *Sextet*. In late November, Tharp and Mikhail Baryshnikov set out on a 22-city North American tour, extending into 1993. They premiered Tharp's new ballet *Cutting Up* at Columbus, Ohio, on November 30, 1992. November saw publication of Tharp's autobiography *Push Comes to Shove*, accompanied by an author tour.

Indiana-born Tharp was a member of the Paul Taylor dance company (1963–65), and then developed her own company, also choreographing for other companies. Much of her work is developed around jazz and other contemporary themes, as in her *Tank Dive* (1965), *Re-Moves* (1966), *Forevermore* (1967), *The Bix Pieces* (1972), *As Time Goes By* (1974), *Eight Jelly Rolls* (1971), and *Push Comes to Shove* (1976). She also choreographed the films *Hair* (1979), *Amadeus* (1984), and *White Nights* (1985). Tharp attended Pomona College, Barnard College, and the American Ballet Theatre School, and studied with many leading dancers. She was formerly married, and has one child.

FURTHER READING

The Tail of the Dragon: New Dance, 1976–1982. MARCIA B. SIEGEL. Duke, 1991.
"Tharp's new shtick." JOAN ACOCELLA. *Connoisseur*, Feb. 1989.

Thatcher, Margaret (Margaret Hilda Roberts; 1925–)

Former British Prime Minister Thatcher continued to be a highly visible opponent of the controversial European Community Maastricht Treaty throughout 1992, remaining a focus for Conservative opposition to a treaty strongly supported by her successor, Prime Minister John Major. But, although she made it quite clear that she was highly critical of Major in several areas, she did support his winning candidacy in the April general election, and campaigned for him in a limited way, leaving for a United States visit late in the campaign. After the elections, she continued and widened her criticism of Major, most notably in an April *Newsweek* article and in her sharp attacks on his European Community commitment. Thatcher was named a life peer in June, to the title of baroness, taking her out of the House of Commons, and into the House of Lords. Forthcoming was her autobiography, to be published in two volumes, the first in 1993.

Thatcher was a chemist and then barrister before her 1959 election as a Conservative Member of Parliament. She became Conservative education spokesperson in 1969, and when her party came to power again was education and science minister (1970–74). In 1975, she succeeded Edward Heath as Conservative leader, becoming the first woman to lead any major British political party, and in 1979 became Britain's first woman prime minister; she was ultimately Britain's longest-serving prime minister of the 20th century, in office until 1990. Her era was marked by widescale privatization, the 1982 Falklands war, and the continuing civil war in Northern Ireland; she personally survived several IRA assassination attempts. She attended Somerville College, Oxford. She married Denis Thatcher in 1951; they have two children.

FURTHER READING

" 'It just won't do'. . . ." ROBERT LENZNER. *Forbes*, Oct. 26, 1992.

"Birth of a she-devil." SHIRLEY ROBIN LETWIN. *New Statesman & Society*, Oct. 2, 1992.

The Thatcher Era: And Its Legacy, 2nd ed. PETER RIDDELL. Blackwell, 1992.

Margaret Thatcher: In Victory and Downfall, 1987 and 1990. E. BRUCE GEELHOED. Praeger/Greenwood, 1992.

Margaret Thatcher: A Bibliography. FAYSAL H. MIKDADI. Meckler, 1992.

" 'That woman'. . . ." GEOFFREY WHEATCRAFT. *Atlantic*, Dec. 1991.

"Maggie's big problem." MAUREEN ORTH. *Vanity Fair*, June, 1991.

"A Woman for Four Seasons." OWEN HARRIES. *National Review*, Apr. 15, 1991.

Margaret Thatcher: The Woman Within. ANDREW THOMSON. Isis (NY), 1991.

Reagan and Thatcher. GEOFFREY SMITH. Norton, 1991.

Maggie: An Intimate Portrait of a Woman in Power. CHRIS OGDEN. L.J. Kaplan, 1990.

Margaret Thatcher: Britain's Prime Minister. DOROTHY HOLE. Enslow, 1990.

Margaret Thatcher: First Woman Prime Minister of Great Britain. LEILA M. FOSTER. Childrens, 1990.

Margaret, Daughter of Beatrice: A Politician's Psychobiography of Margaret Thatcher. LEO ABSE. Random, 1990.

Margaret Thatcher. MARIETTA D. MOSKIN. Messner, 1990.

Madame Prime Minister: A Biography of Margaret Thatcher. LIBBY HUGHES. Dillon, 1989.

The Iron Lady. HUGO YOUNG. Farrar, Straus & Giroux, 1989.

Thomas, Clarence (1948–) Still by far best known throughout the world for his 1991 confirmation hearing confrontation with Professor Anita Faye Hill on the issue of his alleged sexual harassment of Hill, Justice Thomas

maintained a low public profile during his first full year on the Supreme Court. On the Court, he became, with Chief Justice Rehnquist and Justice Scalia, part of the Court's most conservative wing. His presence, however, did not decisively shift the Court's balance; instead, a new centrist group emerged, consisting of Justices O'Connor, Souter, and Kennedy, which refused to erase *Roe v. Wade* and many of the other landmark liberal and moderate decisions of the Warren and Burger Courts.

Thomas wrote the majority opinion in *Lechmere Inc. v. National Labor Relations Board*, ruling that companies did not have to allow union organizers access to such company-owned lands as parking lots and shopping malls. He also voted with the majority in such key cases as *Lujan v. Defenders of Wildlife*, ruling that the plaintiff, an environmental organization, had no standing to bring suit because no determinable specific interest was at issue; *International Society for Krishna Consciousness v. Lee*, ruling that airports could ban groups from soliciting money; *U.S. v. Alvarez Machain*, upholding the 1990 U.S. kidnapping of a Mexican doctor suspected of a role in the torture of a U.S. drug enforcement agent; *Nordlinger v. Hahn*, upholding the right of California to enact Proposition 13, with its unequal property taxes on newcomers; *Keeney v. Tamayo-Reyes*, which sharply limited the federal habeas corpus appeals of state prisoners; *New York v. U.S.*, which invalidated a federal law forcing states to handle their own radioactive waste; *Freeman v. Pitts*, ruling that schools being operated under court-supervised desegregation orders could be released from those orders step by step; *Georgia v. McCollum*, ruling that criminal case defendants could not bar prospective jurors solely because of their race; *U.S. v. Fordice*, ruling that Mississippi had not fulfilled its obligation to desegregate its public colleges and universities; and *Jacobson v. U.S.*, ruling that the federal government had illegally entrapped a defendant into buying child pornography through the mail. He also joined all of his colleagues in a rare, unanimous landmark sexual harassment decision; in *Franklin v. Gwinnett County Public Schools*, the Court unanimously ruled that under Title IX of the 1972 education act a sexually harassed student could collect damages from a school district where a teacher-coach sexually harassed Christine Franklin and ultimately succeeded in pressing her to have sexual intercourse with him. He also ruled with the majority that the Coast Guard could continue to intercept at sea and return Haitian refugees to Haiti; and in the decision barring return of RU-486 pills to Leona Benten, a pregnant woman who tried to import them into the U.S. for her personal use, in a challenge to their ban.

Thomas dissented in such key cases as *Planned Parenthood of Southeastern Pennsylvania v. Casey*, in which a 5–4 majority upheld the essence of *Roe v. Wade* (which in 1972 had established the right of a woman to choose to have an abortion) while at the same time upholding most of the restrictive 1989 Pennsylvania abortion law and giving the states broader powers to restrict abortion; *Lee v. Weisman*, barring non-sectarian or any other prayers at public high school graduations; *Hudson v. McMillian*, ruling that the excessive use of force by prison guards was an Eighth Amendment violation even if the prisoner was not seriously hurt; *Riggins v. Nevada*, ruling that the state could not force an insane criminal defendant to take medication during a trial; and *R.A.V. v. St. Paul*, overturning a St. Paul, Minnesota ordinance making sexist, racist, or otherwise bigoted speech or behavior a crime.

Savannah-born Thomas was from early in his career a protégé of John Danforth, currently U.S. senator from Missouri. Thomas was Missouri assistant attorney general (1974–77), when Danforth was state attorney general.

Thomas was a corporate lawyer for the Monsanto Company (1977–79), a legislative assistant to Senator Danforth (1979–81), assistant secretary for civil rights in the federal Education Department (1981–82), and chairman of the U.S. Equal Opportunity Employment Commission (1982–89), before being named by President Ronald Reagan to the U.S. Court of Appeals for the District of Columbia in 1989. Thomas' 1971 B.A. was from Holy Cross, and his 1974 J.D. from Yale Law School. His second wife is the former Virginia Lamp, a lawyer at the U.S. Labor Department, and formerly at the U.S. Chamber of Commerce. Thomas has one son, from a former marriage.

FURTHER READING

"One year later. . . ." RONALD M. DWORKIN. *New York Times Book Review*, Oct. 25, 1992.

"Never mind. . . ." JEFF ROSEN. *New Republic*, Sep. 21, 1992.

Clarence Thomas. PAUL DEEGAN. Abdo & Daughters, 1992.

Clarence Thomas: Confronting the Future. L. GORDON CROVITZ, ed. Regnery Gateway, 1992.

Court of Appeal: The Black Community Speaks Out on the Racial and Sexual Politics of Thomas vs. Hill. ROBERT CHRISMAN and ROBERT ALLEN, eds. Ballantine, 1992.

Capitol Games: Clarence Thomas, Anita Hill, and the Behind-the-Scenes Story of a Supreme Court Nomination. TIMOTHY M. PHELPS and HELEN WINTERNITZ. Disney, 1992.

Turning Right: The Making of the Rehnquist Supreme Court. DAVID G. SAVAGE. Wiley, 1992.

Advice and Consent: The Senators and the Justices. PAUL SIMON. National Press, 1992.

"Breaking silence." VIRGINIA LAMP THOMAS. *People*, Nov. 11, 1991.

"The lesson of. . . ." STEVE ALLEN. *America*, Nov. 9, 1991.

"A question of character." RICHARD LACAYO. "An ugly circus." NANCY GIBBS. *Time*, Oct. 21, 1991.

"Thomas and Hill. . . ." ELOISE SALHOLZ. "Anatomy of a debacle." DAVID A. KAPLAN. "A moment of truth." *Newsweek*, Oct. 21, 1991.

"Judging Thomas." GLORIA BORGER. "Asking the questions. . . ." DONALD BAER. *U.S. News & World Report*, Oct. 21, 1991.

"Thomas and Benedict. . . ." GEORGE KANNAR. *New Republic*, Oct. 14, 1991.

"The pain of being black." JACK E. WHITE. *Time*, Sep. 16, 1991.

"Supreme mystery." DAVID A. KAPLAN. *Newsweek*, Sep. 16, 1991.

"The crowning Thomas affair." STEVEN V. ROBERTS. *U.S. News & World Report*, Sep. 16, 1991.

Thomas, Thurman Lee (1966–) Thurman Thomas may be football's best all-purpose running back—that's a growing opinion among fans and other observers of the game. In 1992, for an unprecedented fourth straight year, Thomas led the league in total yards from scrimmage (rushing and receiving: 1,913 yards in 1989, 1,829 in 1990, 2,038 in 1991, and 2,113 in 1992), breaking the three-time record of the legendary Jim Brown. In early 1992, on the completion of the 1991–92 season, Thomas was showered with honors, being named the league's most valuable player by numerous organizations, and offensve player of the year by others. He helped lead his team, the Buffalo Bills, into three straight Super Bowls; the first two were losses, but in early 1993 he was hoping to come away with his first Super Bowl win, against the Dallas Cowboys (the Bills lost).

Texas-born Thomas became one of the country's leading running backs while playing for Oklahoma State University, being named an All-American for performances ranging from his MVP-winning 155 yards in the Gator Bowl as a freshman to a record four touchdowns in the Sun Bowl as a senior. In his rookie year as a professional, he totaled an impressive 881 yards, despite missing time with an injury, before taking off on his dominating subsequent four years.

FURTHER READING

"Thurman Thomas. . . ." WILLIAM LADSON. *Sport*, Dec. 1992.

"The many faces of. . . ." PAUL ATTNER. *Sporting News*, Oct. 5, 1992.

Tomasek, Frantisek (1899–1992) Born in Moravia, Cardinal Tomasek was ordained in 1922, and spent the rest of the interwar period as a teacher and student. He gained his second doctorate in theology in 1945, and taught until 1949, when the theology schools were closed by the Communist government. He was named an auxiliary bishop by Pope Pius XII in 1949. With many other clerics, he was imprisoned in 1951; released in 1954, he became a parish priest in Moravia. He attended the Second Vatican Council. Tomasek moved to Prague in 1965, as apostolic administrator for Prague. He supported the 1968 reform movement, but Soviet intervention followed, and Tomasek then pursued a very cautious course, becoming a more open supporter of democracy only in the late 1970s. He was secretly appointed a cardinal in 1976, and openly named Archbishop of Prague and Primate of Czechoslovaka in 1978. He strongly supported democracy from the late 1970s, defending religious and political freedom as the end of the Communist government approached. He retired in 1991. No information was available as to survivors. (d. Prague; August 4, 1992)

FURTHER READING

Obituary. *The Times* (of London), Aug. 5, 1992.
Obituary. *New York Times*, Aug. 5, 1992.
Obituary. *Independent*, Aug. 5, 1992.
"Czech cardinal. . . ." DANA EMINGEROVA. *National Catholic Reporter*, July 19, 1991.
"Frantsi Tomasek. . . ." TIM McCARTHY. *National Catholic Reporter*, Feb. 22, 1991.

Torretta, Gino Louis (1970–) Miami Hurricanes' quarterback Gino Torretta was the runaway winner of the 1992 Heisman Trophy, given to the oustanding college football player of the year. The win was no surprise. In completing an undefeated, untied 1992 season, the all-time leading Miami quarterback had racked up a notable won-lost record of 26–1 (.963), and set regular-season school records in number of passes (991), completions (555), total passing yards (7690), and total offensive yards (7772).

Torretta has been noted for not only his strength but also his accuracy—during his senior year, he made 123 consecutive attempts without an interception—and his ability to scramble helped him in compiling a total of 47 touchdowns. Torretta also won numerous other "player of the year" awards, including the Johnny Unitas Golden Arm Award, offered annually to the nation's outstanding senior quarterback. The only fly in the ointment was that the team failed to capture the unofficial national college football title; in the New Year's Day Sugar Bowl, No. 1-ranked Miami was beaten (34–13) by No. 2-ranked University of Alabama, as Torretta and various of his teammates fell down badly.

Californian Torretta is the youngest child of a football-loving family. Two older brothers were also quarterbacks, one a backup for the Hurricanes, and the other a receiver. Gino Torretta worked briefly as a child actor, in commercials and in a bit role in Clint Eastwood's *The Enforcer*. After graduating from Pinole Valley High, where he was coached by brother Gary, Torretta was backup quarterback for two years, though he started four games, before moving into the starting position for the 1991 and 1992 seasons. He graduated a semester early and is working on a master's degree in business administration.

FURTHER READING

"Sacked out." AUSTIN MURPHY. *Sports Illustrated*, Sep. 23, 1991.

Trump, Donald John (1946–　) During

1992, the real estate tycoon and celebrity author Donald Trump looked more and more like a left-over from the high-flying 1980s. He did continue to avoid personal bankruptcy with the help of loan extensions from some of his many creditors, and he did continue to try to go forward with his long-stalled $3 billion Riverside South plan, on Manhattan's largest piece of undeveloped water-front land, the Upper West Side railroad yards, though meeting massive opposition from community leaders. He also sued his former wife, Ivana Trump, for $25 million, the approximate size of their divorce settlement, alleging that her novel *For Love Alone* revealed much about him that she had in the settlement agreed to keep secret from the public.

New York City-born Trump became a major real estate developer and highly visible billionaire celebrity during the 1980s. He also became a celebrity author with the bestselling *The Art of the Deal* (1987), written with Tony Schwartz. He also published *Trump: Surviving at the Top* (1990); the paperback edition of the book was renamed *The Art of Survival* (1991). Trump encountered severe financial problems in 1990, when his heavy bank and junk bond interest payments called for much more cash than his properties were generating, ultimately lost effective control of his properties to the bankers who had funded his expansion, and in 1991 sold many properties to reduce the size of his debt. Trump's 1968 B.A. was from the Wharton School. He and his former wife, Ivana, have three children.

FURTHER READING

"Fighting back. . . ." JULIE BAUMGOLD. *New York*, Nov. 9, 1992.
"Back atop his tower. . . ." LESLEY WHITE. *Sunday Times*, May 31, 1992.
"Trumped! . . ." SUSAN LEE. *New York Times Book Review*, July 14, 1991.
"Donald Trump gets small. . . ." HARRY HURT, III. *Esquire*, May 1991.
Trumped!: The Inside Story of the Real Donald Trump—His Cunning Rise and Spectacular Fall. JOHN R. O'DONNELL and JAMES RUTHERFORD. Simon & Schuster, 1991.
"Trouble with a big T. . . ." CHRISTINE GORMAN. *Time*, June 18, 1990.
"Manhattan's favorite. . . ." RICHARD L. STERN and JOHN CONNOLLY. *Forbes*, May 14, 1990.
"Playboy interview. . . ." GLENN PLASKIN. *Playboy*, Mar. 1990.

Tsongas, Paul Efthemios (1941–) In

the early days of the 1992 Democratic presidential primary race, former Massachusetts Senator Tsongas emerged—very surprisingly—as a strong contender for the nomination. With hardly any campaign organization and little money, but coming forward as an utterly clean, straightforward campaigner on the issues of fiscal responsibility and the need to rebuild the economy, he won the February New Hampshire primary, the Maine and Arizona caucuses, the Massachusetts and Rhode Island primaries, and the Delaware caucuses, while showing strongly in several other primaries. But it was not to be. Bill Clinton swept the southern states, went on to win in Illinois and Michigan, and was clearly positioned to win the nomination, and without money Tsongas had no staying power. On March 19th, he withdrew from the race. In early July, he endorsed Clinton, spoke at the Democratic National Convention in support of Clinton's candidacy, and then campaigned for his party's nominees. In November, he suffered a recurrence of the cancer that had earlier been thought cured.

After his 1962 graduation from Dartmouth College, Massachusetts-born Tsongas took the kind of socially conscious step that was to characterize much of his public career, joining the Peace Corps for two years (1962–64). He then completed his education, graduating from Yale Law School in1967, and went into practice—and also into politics. He was a Massachusetts deputy assistant attorney general (1969–71) and also a city councillor in his hometown of Lowell (1969–72), before becoming Middlesex Country commissioner (1973–74). Moving onto the national scene, he served two terms in the House of Representatives (1975–79), and then a term in the Senate (1979–85). In 1983, Tsongas was diagnosed as having cancer, and cut short his political career, not running for re-election and moving into lucrative private practice for the sake of his family. In 1988, a then very new bone marrow transplant operation was thought to be entirely successful, and Tsongas literally had a new lease on life. His published work includes the books *The Road from Here: Liberalism and Reality in the 1980's* (1981) and *Heading Home* (1984). He is married to the former Nicola Sauvage, and has three children.

FURTHER READING

"Debt-busting duo. . . ." DAVID ELLIS. *People*, Nov. 2, 1992.

" 'Now that we're. . . .' " MICHAEL KRAMER and JOHN F. STACKS. *Time*, Mar. 23, 1992.

"A clash of visions." LAURENCE I. BARRETT and STANLEY W. CLOUD. *Time*, Mar. 23, 1992.

"The Puritan. . . ." SIDNEY BLUMENTHAL. *New Republic*, Mar. 23, 1992.

" 'I believed I was dying' . . . ." HOWARD FINEMAN. *Newsweek*, Feb. 24, 1992.

"Democratic disasters." RICHARD BROOKHISER. *National Review*, Feb. 17, 1992.

"Eight for the prize." STEVEN MANNING. *Scholastic Update*, Feb. 7, 1992.

"Nipping at Clinton's heels." LAURENCE I. BARRETT. *Time*, Jan. 27, 1992.

"The no bull campaign." HOWARD FINEMAN. *Newsweek*, Oct. 14, 1991.

"T snooze. . . ." JON KELLER. *New Republic*, Aug. 12, 1991.

"It's Tsongas—with a T." ROBERT AJEMIAN. *Time*, June 24, 1991.

"Testing the waters. . . . ." POPE BROCK. *People*, May 27, 1991.

"Tsongas ready to make his run." BILL WHALEN. *Insight*, Apr. 8, 1991.

"Paul Tsongas is alive and well. . . ." *Boston*, Apr. 1988.

Turner, Kathleen (1954–) Film star Kathleen Turner's major 1992 film release was to have been Michael Lessac's *House of Cards*, the story of a mother's attempt to deal with her daughter's withdrawal from reality; Tommy Lee Jones, Park Overall and Esther Rolle co-starred. The film was scheduled for fall 1992 release but was then postponed. During the summer of 1992, Turner starred in a BBC radio dramatization of Sarah Paretsky's mystery novel *Killing Orders*, as Paretsky's detective hero V. I. Warshawski, reprising the role she had created in the 1991 film *V. I. Warshawski*. Forthcoming was a starring role in Daniel Algrant's film *Naked in New York*, co-starring Timothy Dalton, Whoopi Goldberg, Eric Stolz, and Mary Louise Parker; and reportedly another opposite Dennis Quaid in Herbert Ross's *Undercover Blues*.

Missouri-born Turner moved from the theater into films in the early 1980s, and quickly emerged as a leading movie star, in such films as *Body Heat* (1981), *Romancing the Stone* (1984), *Prizzi's Honor* (1985), *The Jewel of the Nile* (1985), *Peggy Sue Got Married* (1986), *Switching Channels* (1988), *The Accidental Tourist* (1988), *The War of the Roses* (1989), and *V.I. Warshawski* (1991). She also starred in a 1989 New York revival of Tennessee Williams' *Cat on a Hot Tin Roof*, and was the voice of the sexy cartoon figure, Jessica, in *Who Framed Roger Rabbit* (1988). Turner attended Southwest Missouri State University and received her M.F.A. from the University of Maryland. She married Jay Weiss in 1984; they have one child.

FURTHER READING

"Kathleen Turner. . . ." MALCOLM MACPHERSON. *Premiere*, Nov. 1989.
"A new role for. . . ." JENNY CULLEN. *Ladies Home Journal*, July 1988.
Kathleen Turner. REBECCA STEFOFF. St. Martin's, 1987.

Turner, Ted (Robert Edward Turner, III; 1938–) The president and chairman of Turner Broadcasting, the owner of the Atlanta Braves and Hawks, Turner in 1992 continued to be a world figure in the communications industry and simultaneouly a leading figure in American professional sports. On January 6, 1992, he was

Time magazine's Man of the Year. He also received the Governor's Award for lifetime contributions to television at the August 1992 Emmy ceremonies,

For the first time since the mid-1980s, Turner Broadcasting was able to announce a substantial profit in 1992, on 1991 operations, a profit that had been accompanied by a massive strengthening of its broadcasting activities. His company now recognized as the world's primary newscaster, Turner had developed great momentum, even though the worldwide depression somewhat slowed growth. One key new project in 1992 was the inauguration of the 24-hours-a-day cable Cartoon Network. Turner also announced plans to develop an independent Moscow-based Russian television channel.

Turner also continued to be active on social questions, using his Turner Foundation to help fund environmental organizations, and directly buying Western land to hold it for environmental preservation purposes. Perhaps stung by Native American criticism of his Atlanta Braves team name and tomahawk symbol, he announced plans for a major television history project on American Indians, to air in 1993.

Turner began building what ultimately became a set of major enterprises in the 1960s, and emerged as a leading American industrial and sports figure during the 1970s. After encountering serious financial problems in the mid-1980s, Turner in the late 1980s emerged as a world communications industry leader at the head of the Turner Broadcasting System (TBS), the Cable News Network (CNN), and Turner Network Television (TNT). TNT began broadcasting its combination of old movies, sports, original television movies, and a potpourri of other programming in October 1988, and quickly grew into a major asset. From 1989 to 1991 CNN grew into a worldwide broadcast news network, with hundreds of millions of viewers, through its 24-hour coverage of such massive events as the Tiananmen Square demonstrations and massacre, the San Francisco earthquake, the tearing down of the Berlin Wall, the continuing events in Eastern Europe and the Soviet Union, the Palestinian uprising, and the Persian Gulf War.

A leading yachtsman, Turner won the America's Cup in 1977. He sponsored the Goodwill Games at Moscow in 1986 and at Atlanta in 1990. Turner attended Brown University. Before marrying Jane Fonda in 1991, he had been married twice previously, and has five children.

FURTHER READING

"Prince of the global village." "The taming of Ted Turner." PRISCILLA PAINTON. "History as it happens." WILLIAM A. HENRY, III. "Inside the world of CNN." RICHARD ZOGLIN. *Time*, Jan. 6, 1992. All in "Man of the Year" issue.

Ted Turner: Television's Triumphant Tiger. REBECCA STEFOFF. Garrett, 1992.

"Ted Turner turns it on." BRUCE STUTZ. *Audubon*, Nov.–Dec. 1991.

"Jane and Ted's. . . ." JERRY ADLER. *Esquire*, Feb. 1991.

"Terrible Ted. . . ." IVOR DAVIS. *Los Angeles Magazine*, Aug. 1990.

"Captain planet. . . ." JOHN MOTAVALLI. *Interview*, June 1989.

"Ted Turner. . . ." GREG DAWSON. *American Film*, Jan.–Feb. 1989.

The Alexander Complex: Six Businessmen and the Empires They Built. MICHAEL MEYER. Random, 1989.

The Corporate Warriors. DOUGLAS K. RAMSEY. Houghton Mifflin, 1987.

Turturro, John (1957–)

Actor and director Turturro won yet another prestigious prize in 1992: the Cannes film festival Caméra d'Or award as best first-time director, for *Mac*. Turturro also co-wrote the screenplay with Brandon Cole, and starred in the title role as one of three New York City brothers who decide to go into the construction business after the death of their father; Turturro called the film largely a homage to his father, a builder. Co-starring were Katherine Borowitz (Turturro's real-life wife) as his wife, and Michael Badalucco and Carl Capotorto as his brothers. Turturro also starred as Roland Flakfizer, a Groucho Marx clone in modern dress, in Dennis Dugan's film comedy *Brain Donors*; Bob Nelson, Mel Smith, and Nancy Marchand co-starred in the slapstick comedy

New York City-born Turturro first came to public notice in John Patrick Shanley's off-Broadway play *Danny and the Deep Blue Sea* (1984), winning an Obie. His films include *To Live and Die in L.A.* (1985), *Five Corners* (1987), *The Sicilian* (1987), *Do the Right Thing* (1989), *Miller's Crossing* (1990), *Mo' Better Blues* (1990), *Jungle Fever* (1991), and *Barton Fink* (1991; he won a Best Actor Golden Palm for the role at the Cannes Film Festival). Turturro graduated from the State University of New York's College at New Paltz in 1978 and later attended Yale University's School of Drama. He and Katherine Borowitz have one son. His younger brother, Nicholas Turturro, is also an actor.

FURTHER READING

"Homebody." JOSEPH A. CINCOTTI. *GQ—Gentlemen's Quarterly*, Oct. 1991.

"Not just another. . . ." ZOE F. CARTER. *Premiere*, Sep. 1991.

"Honest John. . . ." PHOEBE HOBAN. *New York*, Aug. 12, 1991.

"John Turturro finks twice." GAVIN SMITH. *Interview*, Sep. 1990.

"Getting down. . . ." MARLAINE GLICKSMAN. *Film Comment*, Sep.–Oct. 1990.

"John Turturro's. . . ." KATHERINE DIECKMANN. *Rolling Stone*, May 17, 1990.

Tutu, Desmond Mpilo (1931–)

In 1992, Archbishop Desmond Tutu, leader of the Anglican Church in South Africa and holder of the Nobel Peace Prize, once again pursued his great work of peace and reconciliation in a South Africa torn by civil war and mass murder, yet on the verge of establishing a multiracial democracy. On January 27, 1991, he had called for peace when conducting burial services for the victims of the Sebokeng massacre, a major incident in the Inkatha-African National Congress (ANC) civil war. On June 29, 1992, he conducted funeral services at Sharpeville for the victims of the Boipatong massacre, another major incident in that war—yet this time perhaps a turning point, as his country moved toward resolution of its long agony. After Boipatong, the African National Congress broke off negotiations with the government, and went over to mass demonstrations, while Nelson Mandela appealed to the United Nations Security Council for help in ending the killings in the Black townships. Tutu himself called for the International Olympic Committee to withdraw South Africa's invitation to the summer Barcelona games, while continuing to call for an end to the killings. Ultimately, late in 1992, negotiations resumed—after a government promise to disarm the Zulu militants in Inkatha by prohibiting the public carrying of arms—and, at least for then, the end and a new beginning seemed in sight.

Tutu has since his ordination as an Anglican minister in 1961 become South Africa's leading apostle of nonviolence within the South African freedom movement, and is an immensely respected world figure, much as was Martin Luther King, Jr., in the 1950s and 1960s. Tutu was awarded the Nobel Peace Prize in 1984. He rose steadily within his church, and has been the archbishop at the head of the Anglican church in South Africa since 1986. He was secretary of the South African Council of Churches (1979–84), and since 1987 has been president of the All-Africa Council of Churches. Among his published works are *Hope and Suffering: Sermons and Speeches* (1984), *The Words of Desmond Tutu* (1989; edited by his daughter, Naomi Tutu), and *Crying in the Wilderness: The Struggle for Justice in South Africa* (1990). Tutu attended St. Peter's Theological College and the University of London. He married Leah Nomalizo Tutu in 1955; they have four children.

FURTHER READING

"A prisoner of hope." TIMOTHY JONES and THOMAS GILES. *Christianity Today*, Oct. 5, 1992.
Desmond Tutu: Religious Leader Devoted to Freedom. PATRICIA LANTER. *Gareth Stevens*, 1991.
" 'No one will stop us. . . .' " *UNESCO Courier*, June 1990.
"South Africa. . . ." TICHARD BAUTCH. *America*, May 13, 1989.
"A skeptical view." JOHN BIERMAN. *Maclean's*, Mar. 13, 1989.

Desmond Tutu: The Courageous and Eloquent Archbishop Struggling Against Apartheid in South Africa. DAVID WINNER. Gareth Stevens, 1989.
Desmond Tutu. DENNIS WEPMAN. Watts, 1989.
The Rolling Stone Interviews: The 1980s. St. Martin's, 1989.
Archbishop Tutu of South Africa. JUDITH BENTLEY. Enslow, 1988.
Tutu: Voice of the Voiceless. SHIRLEY DU BOULAY. Eerdmans, 1988.
Desmond Tutu: Bishop of Peace. CAROL GREENE. Childrens, 1986.

Laura D'Andrea Tyson (right) and Bill Clinton.

Tyson, Laura D'Andrea (1947–   ) President Bill Clinton's incoming Chairwoman of the Council of Economic Advisors seemed to many to bring a far different view on such matters as free trade and competitiveness into the economic councils of the federal administration. Tyson is an economist who has expressed considerable doubts about unrestricted free trade, and has urged American stimulation and protection of high technology industries. Her work expresses her concerns; most recently, she has written the book *Who's Bashing Whom? Trade Conflict in High Technology Industries* (1992). Her work also includes such books as *American Industry in International Competition: Government Policies and Corporate Strategies* (1983; edited with John Zysman) and *The Dynamics of Trade and Politics and Productivity: The Real Story of How Japan Works* (1989; edited with Chalmers

Johnson and John Zysman). Among her other works are *The Yugoslav Economic System and Its Performance in the 1970s* (1980), *The Impact of International Economic Disturbances on the Soviet Union and Eastern Europe* (1980; edited with Egon Neuberger), *Power, Purpose and Collective Choice: Economic Strategy in Socialist States* (1986; edited with Ellen Comisso), and *Can Gorbachev's Reforms Succeed?* (1990; with various co-editors).

At the time of her appointment, Tyson was a professor of economics and business administration at the University of California at Berkeley, where she also served as the director of the Institute of International Studies and research director of the Berkeley Roundtable on International Economy. She was an economic advisor to the Clinton/Gore campaign. New Jersey-born Tyson's B.A. was from Smith College, and her Ph.D. from the Massachusetts Institute of Technology. She is married to Eric Tarloff; they have one child.

FURTHER READING

"Whatever you call it, ..." PAUL MAGNUSSON. *Business Week*, Dec. 28, 1992.
"Tyson's trade treatment." VIVIAN BROWNSTEIN. *Fortune*, Dec. 28, 1992.
"No longer home alone." *Time*, Dec. 21, 1992.
"Teaching Washington. . . ." DAVID HAGE. *U.S. News & World Report*, Dec. 14, 1992.

Tyson, Mike G. (1966–) There was a new heavyweight champion of the world in 1992, and winner, loser, and contenders all continued to be compared to Mike Tyson, who had hoped for the chance to regain the championship in early 1992. But Tyson was not going to meet any challengers in the ring for some time to come, for he rested in an Indiana prison, the result of a sensational, heavily reported (though not televised) trial in January 1992. A former Miss Black America, who later revealed her name to be Desiree Washington, accused Tyson of raping her in his hotel room in Indianapolis in July 1991. Tyson argued that the two had had consensual sex, but the jury found him guilty and in late March Judge Patricia J. Gifford sentenced him to three concurrent six-year terms in prison (actually 10 years with four years suspended on each of three convictions), noting particularly that he did not seem to grasp the fact that he had done anything wrong. Tyson lost his bid for release while his case was being appealed by Harvard Law School professor Alan M. Dershowitz. Oddly, the Associated Press named the Tyson trial 1992's top sports story, presumably a measure of the public's interest in such trials.

The transition to life at the Indiana Youth Center in Plainfield was difficult. As Tyson later reported to Ed Bradley of CBS News, other inmates jeered him on his arrival in late March. While in prison, Tyson was found guilty of threatening a guard and disorderly conduct; as a result, he lost "good-behavior time," so that his earliest release date at that point was reported to be April 9, 1995. At year's end, Washington reached an out-of-court settlement for her $100 million suit against Tyson, but he also faced at least six other civil law suits, three of them brought by women charging sexual abuse.

A related trial was set to start in early 1993 involving perjury charges against the Reverend T. J. Jemison, head of the National Baptist Convention U.S.A.; he was accused of falsely denying that he offered Washington's family up to $1 million to halt the rape action against Tyson, who had reportedly promised $5 million for the Black Baptist denomination's new headquarters building in Nashville. Meanwhile, boxing promoter Don King was being investigated by the FBI over charges that he pillaged Tyson's championship winnings.

Brooklyn-born Tyson turned professional in 1985, and quickly became a leading heavyweight title contender. From 1986 to 1988, he successively defeated several boxers, the last of them Michael Spinks in June 1988, uniting the three boxing titles to become sole world heavyweight champion, the youngest ever. He held the title until his unexpected defeat, his first as a professional, by James "Buster" Douglas in February 1990. Tyson was formerly married, to actress Robin Givens. After a 1991 suit, he acknowledged paternity of a daughter.

FURTHER READING

"The lost boy." PETER BOYER. *Vanity Fair*, Mar. 1992.
"Judgment day." JOE TREEN. *People*, Feb. 24, 1992.
"Destined to fall." RICHARD HOFFER. *Sports Illustrated*, Feb. 17, 1992.
"Lawyers to their corners." TOM CALLAHAN. *U.S. News & World Report*, Feb. 3, 1992.
"Tyson." KEITH BOTSFORD. *Independent*, Jan. 11, 1992.
"Mike Tyson. . . ." PHIL BERGER. Jan. 1992.

Mike Tyson: Money Myth Betrayal. MONTEIL ILLINGWORTH. Carol 1991.

"Is he back?" DAVID MILLER. *Sport*, Oct. 1990.

"Mike Tyson. . . ." ROBERT E. JOHNSON. *Jet*, June 25, 1990.

"Mike Tyson. . . ." RICHARD REGEN and MICHEL CONTE. *Interview*, Oct. 1990.

Mike Tyson. JOHN HENNESSEY. Smithmark, 1990.

Bad Intentions: The Mike Tyson Story. PETER HELLER. NAL-Dutton, 1990.

"Fire and fear. . . ." JOSE TORRES. *Playboy*, Aug. 1989.

Blood Season: Tyson and the World of Boxing. PHIL BERGER. Morrow, 1989.

Fire and Fear: The Inside Story of Mike Tyson. JOSE TORRES. Warner, 1989.

"Tyson, Mike." *Current Biography*, Apr. 1988.

Updike, John Hoyer (1932–) Celebrated novelist Updike published his fifteenth novel in 1992: *Memories of the Ford Administration*. Always an event, the new Updike novel was generally well received by the critics, though it was not seen as a major work, in contrast to his 1990 *Rabbit at Rest*, the fourth and final work in the "Rabbit" cycle, which yielded a 1991 Pulitzer Prize and National Book Critics Circle award—and which as part of the quartet would be dramatized in a forthcoming NBC miniseries.

In *Memories of the Ford Administration*, Updike once again explores modern American up-

per middle-class life, focusing on the sexual side of life, with an emphasis on adulterous relationships and shaken families, as substitutes for lives that do not otherwise work very well in what for him seems to be a sadly small and meaningless time. The book's narrator reflects on what his life was—and was not—during the brief 1974–76 post-Watergate Ford administration, and compares the life of that time with American life during the 1850's Buchanan administration, for the author a larger, better time.

Pennsylvania-born Updike, a novelist and essayist, is best known for his "Rabbit" novels— *Rabbit Run* (1960), *Rabbit Redux* (1977), *Rabbit Is Rich* (1981), and the National Book Award-winning *Rabbit at Rest* (1990)—and for other novels such as the National Book Award-winning *The Centaur* (1963), *Couples* (1968), *Bech: a Book* (1970, and its 1972 sequel), and *The Witches of Eastwick* (1984). He has also written short stories, many of them published in *The New Yorker*, as well as essays, poetry, and a play. His recent work also includes the autobiography *Self-Consciousness: Memoirs* (1990) and the collection *Odd Jobs: Essays and Criticism* (1990). Updike's 1954 B.A. was from Harvard University. Formerly married to Mary Pennington, he married Martha Bernhard in 1977, and has four children.

FURTHER READING

"Personally speaking." *Vogue*, Sep. 1992.
Something and Nothingness: The Fiction of John

UPDIKE, JOHN HOYER

Updike and John Fowles. JOHN NEARY. Southern
Illinois University Press, 1991.

John Updike. JUDIE NEWMAN. St. Martin's,
1988.

John Updike. HAROLD BLOOM, ed. Chelsea House,
1987.

John Updike Bibliography. E.A. GEARHART. Bern
Porter, 1985.

the Wide World (1959), *A Time of Bees* (1964), *To See, To Take* (1970), *Bedtime Stories* (1972), *Merciful Disguises* (1973), *Letters from a Father and Other Poems* (1983), and *Near Changes* (1990). Her awards include the 1970 Bollingen Prize, a 1970 National Book Award, a 1989 Lilly Prize, and a 1991 Pulitzer Prize for Poetry. She has taught English at the University of Iowa (1943–46), at the University of Louisville (1946–50), and at the University College of Washington University (1950–67). Her 1942 B.A. was from the University of Northern Iowa, and her M.A. from the University of Iowa. She is married to Jarvis A. Thurston.

FURTHER READING

"Talking with. . . ." LUCY LATANE GORDAN. *Wilson Library Bulletin*, Oct. 1992.

Van Duyn, Mona (1921–) The distinguished poet Mona Van Duyn won two great honors in 1992. On April 9, she was awarded the Pulitzer Prize for poetry, for *Near Changes*, her seventh volume of poems. On June 14, she was named Poet Laureate of the United States, succeeding Joseph Brodsky. She is the first woman poet laureate. Forthcoming in January 1993 were two collections of her poetry: *Firefall* and *Collected Poems, 1959–1982*.

Iowa-born Van Duyn has published seven collections of poetry, and her many awards and other honors include several major American poetry prizes. Her collections include *Valentines to*

Van Fleet, James Alward (1892–1992) New Jersey-born Van Fleet was a 1915 graduate of the United States Military Academy at West Point, and a fullback on the 1918 Army football team. He saw action as a machine gun company commander during World War I, and served in the peacetime army during the interwar period. Van Fleet commanded units that landed on Omaha Beach on D-Day, and rose rapidly as American forces moved into Europe, becoming a divisional commander and then corps commander. During the immediate postwar period, his most notable task was to lead U.S. advisors during the Greek Civil War. In 1950, he became commander of the U.S. First Army, and in April 1951 became field commander of United Nations forces in Korea, defending against North Korean offensives and leading a major counteroffensive that was broken off when peace talks began. He later told a Congressional committee that he could have led U.S. forces to victory had he been allowed to continue his offensive, and voiced several other criticisms of the American effort in Korea. His only son, an air force pilot, was killed in action during the Korean War. He retired in 1953, later becoming a business executive. There were no survivors. (d. Polk City, Florida; September 23, 1992)

FURTHER READING

Obituary. *The Times* (of London), Sep. 25, 1992.
Obituary. *New York Times*, Sep. 24, 1992.

Vidal, Gore (1925–) Surprisingly, in 1992 celebrated writer Vidal also turned out to be notable film actor Vidal. Co-starring in Tim Robbins's acclaimed political satire *Bob Roberts*, Vidal played Senator Brickley Paiste, the aging, worthy U.S. Senator who becomes the cynical far-right Robbins' victim in a dirty-tricks, mudslinging senatorial campaign. Vidal was very well reviewed in the role.

As always, though, Vidal's main contribution in 1992 was as a writer. The year saw publication of his bitterly satirical bestselling novel *Live From Golgotha*, a savage attack on Christianity, Judaism, Israel, the modern media industry, and several other targets along the way. The book's story line, which is only a vehicle for Vidal's attacks, involves time travel and a computer virus attack on the New Testament. Vidal also published *Screening History*, a slim volume of essays on film subjects and his own creative processes and history, based on a group of Harvard University lectures. Other 1992 publications included the essay collection *The Decline and Fall of the American Empire* and *Who Owns the U.S.?*.

Born at West Point, New York, Vidal is one of the most prolific novelists, satirists, and social critics of the last four decades. His celebrated series of related novels on American historical themes includes *Burr* (1972), *Lincoln* (1984), *Empire* (1987), and *Hollywood: A Novel of America in the 1920s* (1989). He has also written several novels set in the Greco-Roman world, including *Julian* (1964), *Myron* (1974), and *Creation* (1981). His many other works include the novel *Myra Breckenridge* (1968), the plays *Visit to a Small Planet* (1957) and *The Best Man* (1960), several screenplays, occasional nonfiction works such as *Vidal in Venice* (1987), and a wide range of essays, reviews, and letters. Under the pseudonym Edgar Box, the young Vidal wrote several mysteries, some of which were in the 1990s reprinted in special editions, including *Death in the Fifth Position* (1952), *Death Before Bedtime* (1953), and *Death Likes It Hot* (1954). A liberal, he was twice an unsuccessful candidate for public office, and was in 1971–72 head of the short-lived New Party. He graduated from Philips Exeter Academy in 1943.

FURTHER READING

"Gospel according to Gore." DAVID HUTCHINGS. *People*, Nov. 2, 1992.
"Gore's lore." ARTHUR LUBOW. *Vanity Fair*, Sep. 1992.
"A gadfly . . . ." MARTHA DUFFY. *Time*, Sep. 28, 1992.
" 'J.F.K.' is not. . . ." MICHAEL ANDERSON. *New York Times Book Review*, Aug. 30, 1992.
Gore Vidal: Writer Against the Grain. JAY PARINI, ed. Columbia University Press, 1992.
"Mailer and Vidal. . . ." CAROLE MALLORY. *Esquire*, May 1991.
"Through the looking glass." HOWARD MEANS. *Washingtonian*, Feb. 1990.
"Tug of war." COLIN WRIGHT. *New Statesman & Society*, Nov. 3, 1989.
"Gore Vidal's. . . ." EDWARD ALEXANDER. *Society*, Mar.–Apr., 1988.

"The chore of being Gore." ANDREW KOPKIND. *Interview*, June, 1988.

Vincent, Fay (Francis Thomas Vincent, Jr.; 1938–) During 1992, conflict between baseball commissioner Vincent and the league's club owners accelerated so quickly and so far that, in September, Vincent resigned his post, as he put it: "in the best interests of baseball." The integrity of baseball—certainly the independence established after a 1919 game-fixing scandal to uphold that integrity—was seriously damaged by the circumstances of his departure, and it remained to be seen if it could be recovered. Vincent had seen his role as an independent executive overseeing baseball as a whole, while the owners wanted him directly responsible to them, not to the needs of fans, players, or umpires. Also, looking forward to the coming negotiations for the next collective-bargaining agreement, the owners apparently wanted to take a harder-nosed stance than they felt Vincent would take. Some were also concerned about how effectively Vincent would be able to negotiate the next television contract, with some also being upset by Vincent's attempts to reduce the negative impact on local markets of games televised on so-called "superstations." Many were still irked by 1991 battles over expansion, especially Vincent's insistence on realigning teams (which the Chicago Cubs filed a legal suit to block) and allocating expansion money. Some owners even went so far as to accuse Vincent of attending too many games and of acting arrogantly, sitting on the field before games in a golf cart (since a college accident injured his legs), and of talking too much to players, umpires, and reporters.

By September 3, the two sides had reached an impasse, when the owners passed an 18–9 no-confidence vote, with one abstention. Vincent initially said that he could not be fired, nor would he resign, but would complete his term, which was to have run through March 31, 1994. But by September 7th he had decided that a lengthy and bitter legal battle would benefit no one, certainly not baseball as a sport.

Earlier, in July, Vincent had announced that George Steinbrenner could return to active participation in the New York Yankees. He had also issued a lifetime ban on Yankees pitcher Steve Howe, who had pleaded guilty to attempting to buy cocaine; in relation to the Howe hearing, Vincent had summoned to his office three Yankee officials to give testimony on baseball's drug policy, an action that also irked some owners. At Vincent's departure, Pete Rose remained under the lifetime ban imposed by Vincent's predecessor, A. Bartlett Giametti. In addition, Vincent helped push through approval of the sale of the Seattle Mariners to a group of investors that included a Japanese company. Milwaukee Brewers owner Bud Selig became interim commissioner; at year's end a new commissioner had not been named. Some people have charged that, in spirit if not in letter, Vincent may have been the last commissioner of baseball.

Before joining major league baseball, Connecticut-born Vincent was a corporate lawyer and executive, a former president of Columbia Pictures and vice-president of Coca-Cola. His 1960 B.A. was from Williams College and his 1963 LL.D. from Yale. He became deputy commissioner of baseball in April 1989, and commissioner five months later, on Giamatti's death. Vincent married Valerie McMahon in 1965; they have three children.

FURTHER READING

"The emperor of China: baseball." *Economist*, Sep. 12, 1992.
"Stepping up to the plate." MARK HYMAN. *Sporting News*, Aug. 24, 1992.
"Take him out to a ball game." DAVID A. KAPLAN. *Newsweek*, July 20, 1992.
"Vincent, Fay." *Current Biography*, May 1991.
"Welcome to hardball city." MIKE LUPICA. *Esquire*, June 1991.
"Fay Vincent. . . ." RICHARD SANDOMIR. *Manhattan, inc.*, May 1990.
"Baseball's unlikely. . . ." TOM CALLAHAN. *U.S. News & World Report*, Oct. 15, 1990.
"Vincent. . . ." DAVE NIGHTINGALE. *Sporting News*, Feb. 12, 1990.

Walcott, Derek Alton (1930–) The celebrated West Indian poet and playwright Derek Walcott was awarded the 1992 Nobel Prize for Literature. The work of Saint Lucia-born Walcott reflects the several European and African influences that have shaped his personal history and the life of his region. Much of his early work was for the theater, and he was in the late 1950s a founder of the Trinidad Theatre Workshop, which produced his works and those of other West Indian playwrights. He has taught at several U.S. colleges and universities, including Harvard University, Columbia University, and Yale University, and was a visiting professor at Boston University when he was awarded the Nobel. His poetic works include *In A Green Night* (1962), *Selected Poems* (1964), *Castaway* (1965), *The Gulf* (1969), *Another Life* (1973), *Sea Grapes* (1976), *The Star-Apple Kingdom* (1979), *The Fortunate Traveler* (1982), *Midsummer* (1984), *Collected Poems 1948–84* (1986), *The Arkansas Testament* (1987), and *Omeros* (1989). His plays include *Henri Christophe* (1950), *Drums and Colors* (1958), *The Sea at Dauphin* (1960), *Six in the Rain* (1969), *In a Fine Castle* (1972), *Dream on Monkey Mountain* (1970), *Ti-Jean and His Brothers* (1971), *The Charlatan* (1974), *The Joker of Seville* (1978), *O Babylon* (1978), *Remembrance* (1980), *Pantomime* (1980), *The Isle Is Full of Noises* (1982), *The Last Carnival* (1986), and *The Odyssey* (1992). His 1953 B.A. was from the University of the West Indies, at Kingston, Jamaica. His third wife is Norlin Metiver; he has three children.

FURTHER READING

"Derek Walcott's. . . ." JERVIS ANDERSON. *New Yorker*, Dec. 21, 1992.
Critical Perspectives on Derek Walcott. ROBERT V. HAMNER, ed. Three Continents, 1992.
Art of Derek Walcott. STEWART BROWN. Dufour, 1992.
Derek Walcott's Poetry: American Mimicry. REI TERADA. New England University Press, 1992.
"The mango and the oak." *Economist*, Oct. 27, 1990.

Walesa, Lech (1943–) Polish President Walesa led a fragmented political system during 1992, his ability to lead greatly damaged by the need to shuffle and reshuffle premiers, as shifting parliamentary alliances made it very difficult to achieve stable government. Walesa had lost his election law fight in 1991, ultimately accepting proportional representation based on party lists of candidates, rather than direct majority election of individuals. As a result, the October 27, 1991 parliamentary elections resulted in a fragmented parliament in which no party had more than 13 percent of the votes, making it difficult to form any government at all, and even more difficult to hold one in power. Walesa had asked for a grant of emergency economic powers in 1991, as Polish economic problems multiplied, but was rebuffed by parliament; repeating his pleas again in early 1992, he was again rebuffed. However, his third premier of the year, Hanna Suchocka, was in August granted such powers, and proceeded to further implement austerity and investment programs, in the process moving against public sector strikers far more aggressively than Walesa might have done.

On the international side, Walesa continued to present Poland's face to the world in such areas as Poland's new association with the European Community, Poland's new and equal relationship with the countries of the former Soviet Union and Eastern Europe, and Poland's support for United Nations action to mediate the wars in what was formerly Yugoslavia.

Walesa became an electrician at the Lenin Shipyard in Gdansk in 1966; fired after leading the 1970 strike, he continued to organize Poland's developing labor movement. In 1980, he led the successful Lenin Shipyard strike, which sparked a nationwide series of largely successful strikes, and, in September 1980, he was a founder and first president of the Polish trade union confederation, Solidarity. He was imprisoned for a year after Solidarity was outlawed in 1981, but continued to serve as underground leader of the union and movement. As the Gorbachev era developed, he and Solidarity emerged openly once again, and Solidarity was legalized under his leadership in 1989. He led in the negotiations that resulted in the Polish turn toward democracy, and to the free elections of June 1989, won by Solidarity. Walesa refused the Polish presidency at that point, but in June 1990 decided to run, then defeating Tadeusz Mazowiecki and Stanislaw Tyminski in a three-way vote, and in the December runoff defeating Tyminski 3–1. Walesa was awarded the 1983 Nobel Peace Prize. In 1987 he published *A Way of Hope: An Autobiography*. He married Danuta Walesa in 1969; they have eight children.

FURTHER READING

"Walesa's poisoned chalice." NICHOLAS BETHELL. *Observer*, Aug. 16, 1992.

"L'état, c'est Lech: Poland." *Economist*, May 2, 1992.

Lech Walesa. ANN ANGEL. Gareth Stevens, 1992.

Lech Walesa: The Road to Democracy. REBECCA STEFOFF. Fawcett, 1992.

"Lech-luster. . . ." VICTORIA POPE. *New Republic*, Dec. 3, 1990.

"Walesa answers. . . ." MARTIN POLLACK. *World Press Review*, Aug. 1990.

"Walesa's war. . . ." ANNA HUSARSKA. *New Republic*, July 23, 1990.

"Walesa's drive. . . ." PETER HEBBLETHWAITE. *National Catholic Reporter*, June 1, 1990.

Lech Walesa: The Leader of Solidarity and Campaigner for Freedom and Human Rights in Poland. MARY CRAIG. Gareth Stevens, 1990.

"A symbol of hope." PHIL SUDA. *Scholastic Update*, Oct. 20, 1989.

"The struggle for solidarity. . . ." BARRY CAME. *Maclean's*, Apr. 17, 1989.

Lech Walesa. TONY KAYE. Chelsea House, 1989.

Crystal Spirit: Lech Walesa and His Poland. MARY CRAIG. ABC-CLIO, 1987.

Lech Walesa and His Poland. MARY CRAIG. Continuum, 1987.

Walken, Christopher (1943–) Stage and screen star Walken starred in another offbeat role in 1992 as villainous industrialist Max Schreck in the *Batman* sequel, Tim Burton's summer blockbuster *Batman Returns*, in a cast that included Michael Keaton, Michelle Pfeiffer, Danny DeVito, Michael Gough, Pat Hingle, Michael Murphy, and Marlon Wayans. Like the original *Batman*, the sequel became a worldwide hit. Walken also appeared in Barry Primus' comedy-drama *Mistress*, set on the fringes of the movie business in modern Hollywood. A third starring role was in Alexander Arcady's French film *Day of Atonement*, which opened in Paris in December 1992.

Forthcoming was a starring role opposite Glenn Close in *Skylark*, a sequel to the highly successful 1991 television film *Sarah, Plain and Tall*, in which he plays a Kansas man with two children who advertises for a mail order bride; Close plays the New England spinster who answers his advertisement. Also reportedly forthcoming was a starring role opposite Lorraine Bracco in the film *Scam*.

New York City-born Walken gained his early experience in a wide range of regional theater and New York stage roles, making his 1959 Broadway debut in *J.B.* His early work also included a notable appearance in *The Lion in Winter* (1966), and his later work a New York Shakespeare Festival appearance in *Coriolanus* (1988). He made his film debut in *The Anderson Tapes* (1972), played substantial roles in *Next Stop Greenwich Village* (1976), *Roseland* (1977), and *Annie Hall* (1977), and had a breakthrough role in *The Deer Hunter* (1978), winning a Best Supporting Actor Oscar. He went on to major roles in such films as *The Dogs of War* (1980), *Heaven's Gate* (1980), *Pennies from Heaven* (1981), *The Milagro Beanfield War* (1988), *Biloxi Blues* (1988), *Communion* (1989), *McBain* (1991), and *The Comfort of Strangers* (1991). Walken attended Hofstra University. He is married to casting director Georgianne Walken.

FURTHER READING

"Out there on a visit." GAVIN SMITH. *Film Comment*, July–Aug. 1992.
"Walken, Christopher." *Current Biography*, Oct. 1990.
"In the danger zone." CHUCK PFEIFER and MARK MATOUSEK. *Interview*, Mar. 1988.

Walker, Alice (1944–) In her fifth novel, *Possessing the Secret of Joy,* Walker continues to explore the experience of U.S. African-American women and the African cultural roots of that experience. In this novel, her central character is Tashi, who was a minor character in *The Color Purple*; Walker's subject is clitoridectomy, the widespread ritual genital mutilation of women in many African countries, an historical fact that is still a current practice affecting tens of millions of African women today. Tashi returns to Africa, to go through the ritual as part of her search for full identification with her roots, but nearly dies because of the mutilation, goes mad, and eventually finds her way to salvation; in the process, Walker writes an indictment of the practice and calls it one of the ultimate expressions of male domination of women. Walker's novel was received very respectfully, though some reviewers criticized it for its heavily political tone.

Georgia-born Walker is a leading African-American writer and feminist—or "womanist," as she calls it—whose work largely focuses on sexism and racism. Her novels include *The Third Life of Grange Copeland* (1970), *Meridian* (1976), *The Temple of My Familiar* (1989), and her bestselling and Pulitzer Prize-winning *The Color Purple* (1982), the story of an African-American Southern woman. It was adapted into Steven Spielberg's 1985 film, starring Whoopi Goldberg. Her work includes several volumes of poems, including *Once* (1968) and *Revolutionary Petunias* (1973), as well as a biography of Langston Hughes, and several volumes of essays, including *In Search of our Mother's Gardens* (1983) and *Living By the Word* (1991). Her 1966 B.A. was from Sarah Lawrence College. She was previously married, to lawyer Melvyn Leventhal, and has one child.

FURTHER READING

Alice Walker: Critical Perspectives Past and Present. HENRY L. GATES, JR., and K.A. APPIAH. Amistad, 1993.
"Alice Walker's appeal." PAULA GIDDINGS. *Essence*, July 1992.
"Alice Walker. . . ." CHARLES WHITAKER. *Ebony*, May 1992.
Alice Walker. TONY GENTRY. Chelsea House, 1992.
"The craft of survival." ALVIN P. SANOFF. *U.S. News & World Report*, June 3, 1991.
Alice Walker. HAROLD BLOOM, ed. Chelsea House, 1990.
"Alice Walker." ALEXIS DE VEAUX. *Essence*, Sep. 1989.
"Alice Walker. . . ." CLAUDIA DREIFUS. *Progressive*, Aug. 1989.
"I dream a world." BRIAN LANKER and MAYA ANGELOU. *National Geographic*, Aug. 1989.
"Living by the word. . . ." GREGORY JAYMES. *Life*, May 1989.
"Alice Walker." *U.S. News & World Report*, Feb. 13, 1989.
Alice Malsenior Walker: An Annotated Bibliography. L. H. PRATT and DARNELL D. PRATT. Greenwood; Series 1, 1987; Series 2, 1988.

Walker, Nancy (Anna Myrtle Swoyer; 1922–92) Philadelphia-born Walker, child of a show business family, made her Broadway debut in 1942 as a singer and comedian in *Best Foot Forward* (1941), and her film debut in the 1943 movie version of the musical. She appeared

frequently on Broadway in the 1940s and 1950s, starring in such plays as *On the Town* (1944) and *Barefoot Boy With Cheek* (1947). She also appeared in such films as *Forty Carats* (1973) and *Murder By Death* (1976). She was best known by far for her work in television, which included roles in the long-running "The Mary Tyler Moore Show," "Rhoda," and "McMillan and Wife." In 1978, she was briefly star of her own television show. Walker was perhaps equally well known for her extraordinarily popular television commercials. She was survived by her husband, David Craig, a daughter, and a sister. (d. Studio City, California; March 25, 1992)

FURTHER READING

"Good night, Mrs. Morgenstern." *People*, Apr. 13, 1992.
Obituary. *Variety*, Mar. 30, 1992.
Obituary. *The Times* (of London), Mar. 30, 1992.
Obituary. *New York Times*, Mar. 27, 1992.

Walton, Samuel Moore (1918–92)

Oklahoma-born Walton, creator of the Wal-Mart retail chain, began his retailing career in 1945, after World War II service. His first store was a Ben Franklin franchise in Newport, Arkansas. In 1962, he opened his own first Wal-Mart Discount City store in Rogers, Arkansas, and in the following three decades built a retail empire that in 1991 included more than 1,700 stores, grossed more than $45 billion, and had become the largest United States retailer. As his business grew, the Walton family share of the company grew in value to more than $23 billion, and he was in 1985 named by *Forbes* the wealthiest man in the United States. Walton built his chain of low-cost, low-overhead, non-union discount stores largely in rural areas, creating great competitive advantages as compared to other large retailers, and even greater advantages as compared to smalltown "Main Street" small businesses, many of whom went out of business because of their inability to compete with him. He retired from operational control in 1988, remaining chairman until his death. Walton was awarded a Presidential Medal of Freedom in 1992. He was survived by his wife, a daughter, and three sons. (d. Little Rock, Arkansas; April 5, 1992)

FURTHER READING

"Sam Walton in his own words." *Fortune*, June 29, 1992.
"The man who. . . ." LEWIS LORD. *U.S. News & World Report*, Apr. 20, 1992.
Obituary. *The Times* (of London), Apr. 8, 1992.
Obituary. *New York Times*, Apr. 6, 1992.
"Walton, Sam." *Current Biography*, Mar. 1992.
Sam Walton: The Giant of Wal-Mart. ANNE CANADEO. Garrett, 1992.
Sam Walton Story: The Retailing of Middle America. AUSTIN TEUTSCH. Golden Touch, 1991; Berkley, 1992.
"America's most successful merchant." JOHN HUEY. *Fortune*, Sep. 23, 1991.

Wang Hongwen (1934–92)

Wang Hongwen, until then a factory employee in Shanghai, emerged as a major figure during China's Cultural Revolution (1966–76), as a symbol of the supposed commitment of the young to the movement. From the late 1960s, Wang became very close to Jiang Qing, Mao's wife and after Mao the leading figure of the Cultural Revolution, and with Jiang encouraged the massive attacks on China's intellectuals and its cultural heritage mounted by the Red Guards in that period. Wang rose very quickly in those years, in 1973 becoming deputy chairman of the Communist Party. All this changed after the death of Mao in 1976; in October, Cultural Revolution leaders Jiang Qing, Zhang Chunqiao, Yao Wenhuan, and Wang were arrested and accused of a variety of crimes as the "Gang of Four," who were allegedly responsible for all the crimes committed in the name of the Cultural Revolution. Wang was sentenced to life imprisonment after the 1981 show trials of the Gang of Four. No information was available as to survivors. (d. Beijing; August 3, 1992)

FURTHER READING

Obituary. *The Times* (of London), Aug. 5, 1992.
Obituary. *New York Times*, Aug 5., 1992.

Washington, Denzel (1954–)

Stage and screen star Denzel Washington emerged as a worldwide film figure in 1992 in the title role of Spike Lee's epic, long-awaited, and heavily pub-

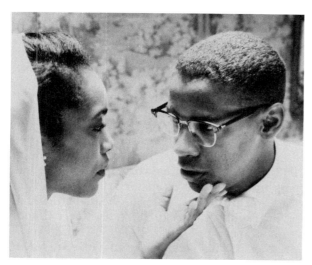

Denzel Washington (right) and Angela Bassett.

licized biographical film *Malcolm X*, based on the book *The Autobiography of Malcolm X*, as told to Alex Haley. Washington's portrayal of the African-American leader was very well received by critics and audiences, although the film itself received very respectful but mixed reviews, ranging from those who called it a film for the ages to those who called it dull, slow, and reverential.

Also in 1992, Washington and Louis Gossett, Jr., co-narrated the "American Experience" television series documentary *Liberators: Fighting on Two Fronts in World War II*, a story about African-American soldiers experiencing racism in their own segregated army, while at the same time liberating Dachau and other German death camps. On stage, Washington starred as murdered South African Black journalist Steve Biko in Priti Paintal's opera *Biko*, which premiered at Britain's Birmingham Repertory in June.

Forthcoming was a role as Don Pedro in Kenneth Branagh's film version of *Much Ado About Nothing*, in a cast that includes Branagh as Benedick, Emma Thompson as Beatrice, and Michael Keaton as Dogberry. Also forthcoming is a starring role opposite Tom Hanks and Mary Steenburgen in Jonathan Demme's *Philadelphia*. A third forthcoming lead was to be in the film *Invisible Man*.

Washington emerged as a strong stage player from the mid-1970s at the New York Shakespeare Festival and in several off-Broadway plays, one of them the Negro Ensemble Company's *A Soldier's Play*, a role he recreated in the 1984 film *A Soldier's Story*. He starred in the title role of *Richard III* (1990) at the New York Shakespeare Festival in Central Park. Washington became a television star in the 1980s as Dr. Otis Chandler in "St. Elsewhere" (1982–88). His films include *Cry Freedom* (1987) as South African Black leader Steve Biko, *For Queen and Country* (1989), *The Mighty Quinn* (1989), *Heart Condition* (1989), *Glory* (1989; he won the 1990 Best Supporting Actor Oscar), *Mo' Better Blues* (1990), *Ricochet* (1991), and *Mississippi Masala* (1991). Washington attended Fordham University, and studied at San Francisco's American Conservatory Theater. He is married to singer Paulette Pearson; they have two children.

FURTHER READING

"Denzel Washington." *People*, Dec. 28, 1992.
"Denzel Washington. . . ." LAURA B. RANDOLPH. *Ebony*, Dec. 1992.
"Denzel Washington." CLAUDE REED. *US*, Dec. 1992.
"Denzel Washington stars. . . ." *Jet*, Nov. 30, 1992.
"Denzel on Malcolm." JOE WOOD. *Rolling Stone*, Nov. 26, 1992.
"Denzel Washington." JOHN CLARK. *Premiere*, Nov. 1992.
"Playing with fire. . . ." LENA WILLIAMS. *New York Times Magazine*, Oct. 25, 1992.
"Washington, Denzel." *Current Biography*, July 1992.
"The glory days of. . . ." LAURA B. RANDOLPH. *Ebony*, Sep. 1990.
"The mo' better Denzel." ELVIS MITCHELL. *California*, Sep. 1990.
"Days of glory. . . ." PHOEBE HOBAN. *New York*, Aug. 13, 1990.
"Denzel delivers." SHARI ROMAN. *Video Magazine*, Aug. 1990.
"Denzel in the Swing." THULANI DAVIS. *American Film*, Aug. 1990
"Denzel Washington." VERONICA WEBB and HERB RITTS. *Interview*, July 1990.

Watkins, James David (1927–) Outgoing Secretary of Energy Watkins continued to grapple unsuccessfully with the enormous problems of nuclear industry control and effective nuclear waste disposal uncovered in previous years, as well as with sharply increased opposition within the Bush administration, staggered by the probable cost of a full-scale national atomic waste clean-up, estimated to run as high as $200 billion—if it could be accomplished at all, which was turning out to be increasingly questionable. During 1992, very serious safety questions again postponed the opening of the New Mexico national hazardous waste respository, the first to be built since the beginning of the nuclear age. Similarly, scheduled clean-ups at the Hanford, Washington and several other nuclear installations continued to be indefinitely stalled, due to massive technical and political problems. An example of the scope of the nuclear regulatory problems was the Savannah River nuclear plant, its scheduled January reopening once again delayed after a tritium leak into the river was found. On the wider question of developing a national energy policy, Watkins' goal since taking office in 1989, little progress was made, as a Republican President and Democratic Congress developed "gridlock" in a presidential campaign year.

Watkins was a career naval officer, who in 37 years moved up through a series of line and staff positions to become commander of the U.S. Sixth Fleet in 1978; vice chief of naval operations in 1979, the year he became an admiral; and commander-in-chief of the Pacific Fleet in 1981. From 1982 until his retirement in 1986, he served as chief of U.S. naval operations. In 1987, he began an entirely different kind of public career, when appointed head of the national AIDS advisory commission by President Ronald Reagan; he became a prime mover in the issuance of the landmark 1988 commission report that considerably helped to focus national attention on the fight against the disease, and especially on AIDS-connected discrimination. He was appointed Secretary of Energy by president-elect George Bush in January 1989. California-born Watkins received his 1949 B.S. from the U.S. Naval Academy at Annapolis and his 1958 M.S. from the Naval Postgraduate School. He married Sheila Jo McKinney in 1950; they have seven children.

FURTHER READING

"How to meet our energy needs." *Design News*, Mar. 11, 1991.
"Hands-on Energy leader." WILLIAM LANOUETTE. *Bulletin of the Atomic Scientists*, May 1990.
"The heat is on! . . ." THOMAS A. LEWIS. *National Wildlife*, Apr.–May 1990.
"James D. Watkins. . . ." WILLIAM LANOUETTE. *Bulletin of the Atomic Scientists*, Jan.–Feb. 1990.
"The new broom." *Economist*, Dec. 23, 1989.
"Admiral Watkins's. . . ." STEPHEN J. HEDGES. *U.S. News & World Report*, Aug. 14, 1989.
"Energy czar. . . ." VICKY CAHAN et al. *Business Week*, July 24, 1989.
"Watkins, James David." *Current Biography*, Mar. 1989.
"The metamorphosis of. . . ." LYNN ROSELLINI. *U.S. News & World Report*, July 4, 1988.

Weaver, Sigourney (Susan Weaver; 1949–)

Stage and screen star Weaver returned to what has been by far her best-known role in 1992. In 1979, her breakthrough film role had come in *Alien*, a blockbuster sci-tech film that was a worldwide hit. In 1986, she had starred in the hit sequel *Aliens*. In 1992, she starred once again as Warrant Officer Ripley in David Fincher's *Alien 3*. This version, set on a prison planet, reintroduces one of the aliens encountered in the previous films; Charles S. Dutton and Charles Dance co-starred.

Weaver starred in a second high-budget film as Queen Isabella in Ridley Scott's epic film *1492: Conquest of Paradise*, opposite Gérard Depardieu as Christopher Columbus and Armand Assante as Sanchez. The film received mixed reviews, and was a box-office disaster, possibly because of overwork of the Columbus theme, along with growing disillusion about Columbus and the European conquest of the Americas. Forthcoming was a starring role opposite Kevin Kline in Ivan Reitman's *Dave*, about a American Presidential lookalike called in to impersonate the President and fool all those around him, including his wife, played by Weaver.

New York City-born Weaver was on stage from the mid-1970s, most notably in *Hurlyburly* (1984), *The Merchant of Venice* (1987), and in the 1991 London stage run of Chekhov's *The Three Sisters*. She is best known by far for the "Aliens" films, and for such films as *Eyewitness* (1981), *Deal of the Century* (1983), *The Year of Living Dangerously* (1983), *Ghostbusters* (1984; and its 1989 sequel), *Gorillas in the Mist* (1988; in the Oscar-nominated role of Dian Fossey), and *Working Girl* (1988). Weaver attended Stanford University and the Yale Drama School. She married James Simpson in 1984; they have one child.

FURTHER READING

"Close encounter. . . ." STEVE GOLDMAN. *Sunday Times*, Aug. 23, 1992.
"Sigourney Weaver." ROBERT HOFLER. *US*, June 1992.
"Last in space." JAMES KAPLAN. *Entertainment*, May 29, 1992.

"Weaver, Sigourney." *Current Biography*, Mar. 1989.

Sigourney Weaver. T.D. MAGUFFEE. St. Martin's, 1989.

"Sigourney weaves. . . ." JESSE KORNBLUTH. *Cosmopolitan*, Dec. 1988.

"Dream Weaver. . . ." CHRISTOPHER DURANG and ROBERT MAPPLETHORPE. *Interview*, July 1988.

Webb, James Edwin (1906–92) North Carolina-born Webb, a lawyer, was a Marine flyer in the early 1930s, and served in the Marines again during World War II. A Democrat, he was President Harry S. Truman's Bureau of the Budget Director (1946–49) and an Undersecretary of State (1949–52). He left office with the election of Republican Dwight D. Eisenhower, working as an oil company executive (1952–61). In 1961, President John F. Kennedy appointed Webb administrator of the National Aeronautics and Space Administration (NASA), and for the following eight years he built the U.S. space program, which during his tenure took massive strides into space, including space probes of Mars and Venus, the development of the space satellite program, Alan Shepard's *Freedom 7* flight, John Glenn's *Friendship 7* first orbital flight, and Edward White's first space walk. Webb also prepared the historic *Apollo 11* moon flight, which occurred in 1969, after he had left office to make way for the Republican appointee. He was survived by his wife, Patsy, a daughter, and a son. (d. Washington, D. C.; March 27, 1992)

FURTHER READING

Obituary. *Aviation Week & Space Technology*. Apr. 6, 1992.

Obituary. *The Times* (of London), Mar. 30, 1992.

Obituary. *New York Times*, Mar. 29, 1992.

"James E. Webb." MAURA J. MACKOWSKI. *Ad Astra*, July–Aug. 1991.

Weiss, Ted (1927–92) Born in Hungary, Weiss emigrated to the United States with his family in 1930. A lawyer and lifelong liberal, he entered New York City politics as a Democratic reformer in the 1950s, and was elected to the New York City Council in 1961, serving for 14 years, until his 1976 election to the U.S. House of Representatives, succeeding Bella Abzug, who had resigned to make a Senate run. Weiss served in the House until his death, and was about to be nominated once again and elected to another term by his liberal Manhattan constituency, without significant opposition. During his three decades in elected office, Weiss was a consistently liberal voice, although very often in a distinct minority, as when he became an early proponent of research to combat AIDS long before it was fashionable to do so, became an early supporter of environmental initiatives, and resisted anti-pornography legislation as a violation of First Amendment rights. He was survived by his wife, Sonya, two sons, and a sister. (d. New York City; September 14, 1992)

FURTHER READING

Obituary. *The Times* (of London), Sep. 17, 1992.

Obituary. *New York Times*, Sep. 15, 1992.

Welk, Lawrence (1903–92) An accordionist and bandleader, Welk began his career with local band club dates in his native Strasburg, North Dakota. He organized his own Hotsy-Totsy Boys band in 1927, played throughout the Midwest and on radio until the late 1930s, and then moved to Los Angeles. Great commercial success came late, in television. In 1951, his band was broadcast on KTLA, Los Angeles, and his kind of dance band music began to find wide audiences. His many critics called his music terribly old-fashioned and all but featureless; his very large numbers of fans enjoyed it enormously. In 1955, the Welk band began a 16-year-long run on ABC television, and was syndicated on hundreds of stations. In 1971, after ABC finally dropped his show, he syndicated it with hundreds of independent stations, went on very successfully until 1982, and enjoyed widely carried reruns into the early 1990s. With Bernice McGeehan, he wrote *Ah-One, Ah-Two!: Life with My Musical Family* (1974), *My America, Your America* (1976), *Lawrence Welk's Joyous Family Album* (1977), *This I Believe* (1979), and *You're Never Too Young* (1981). He was survived by his wife, Fern Renner, two daughters, and a son. (d. Santa Monica, California; May 17, 1992)

FURTHER READING

"The death roll." *Maclean's*, Dec. 21, 1992.

"It was a wunnerful life." DAVID GATES. *Newsweek*, June 1, 1992.

Obituary. *Variety*, May 25, 1992.

Obituary. *The Times* (of London), May 20, 1992.

Obituary. *New York Times*, May 19, 1992.

Champagne Music: The Lawrence Welk Show. COYNE S. SANDERS and GINNY WEISSMAN. St. Martin's, 1985.

Wells, Mary (1942–92)

Detroit-born Wells began her singing career as a teenager, and was signed by Berry Gordy of Motown Records as a singer after she tried to sell him a song she had written, "Bye, Bye, Baby." Her 1960 recording of the song for Motown was her first hit. She went on to become one of Motown's earliest stars; in 1962, she had three major hits: "The One Who Loves You," "You Beat Me to the Punch," and "Two Lovers," all written and produced by Smokey Robinson. Robinson also wrote her greatest hit, "My Guy." But her career faltered with her switch from Motown to 20th Century Fox in 1964, and she had only a few minor hits during the balance of the 1960s. She made a modest comeback beginning in the late 1970s, in cabaret, on tour, and also making some recordings. Her career ended when she was afflicted with throat cancer in 1990. Short of money and without medical insurance, she lost her Los Angeles home, but was helped in her final years by several other artists. She was survived by two daughters, two sons, and a brother. (d. Los Angeles; July 26, 1992)

FURTHER READING

Obituary. ALAN LIGHT. *Rolling Stone*, Sep. 3, 1992.

"Singer Mary Wells. . . ." *Jet*, Aug. 10, 1992.

"Death of a soul survivor." GUY GARCIA. *People*, Aug. 10, 1992.

Obituary. *Variety*, Aug. 3, 1992.

Obituary. *The Times* (of London), July 28, 1992.

Obituary. *New York Times*, July 27, 1992.

Weltner, Charles Longstreet (1927–92)

Atlanta-born Weltner, child of a leading Southern family and an Atlanta lawyer, became a national figure during the civil rights struggles of the 1960s, sacrificing his political career to follow his conscience. In 1962, supported by a Black and White moderate coalition, he was elected to the U.S. House of Representatives. A year and a half later, he was one of only seven White Southerners to vote for the historic Civil Rights Act of 1964, stating before the House that he was voting his conscience. Even so, he won a second term in 1964, and in 1965 voted for a second Civil Rights Act. He won a third primary as well, but would not agree to sign a document supporting racist Lester Maddox for election as governor, and then withdrew from the Congressional race. Weltner then practiced law in Atlanta until appointed to the State Supreme Court in 1981. He was appointed Chief Justice of that court three months before his death. He was survived by his second wife, two daughters, two sons, two sisters, and a brother. (d. Atlanta, Georgia; August 31, 1992).

FURTHER READING

Obituary. *The Times* (of London), Sep. 8, 1992.

Obituary. *New York Times*, Sep. 2, 1992.

Wharton, Clifton R., Jr. (1926–)

President Bill Clinton's incoming deputy Secretary of State brings a considerable list of "firsts" to the job, beginning with his Ph.D., the first economics doctorate to be awarded to an African-American at the University of Chicago. He was also the first African-American to head a major U.S. foundation, to head a predominantly White university, and to head a Fortune 100 company.

Boston-born Wharton's B.A. was from Harvard University, his M.A. in international studies from Johns Hopkins University. He worked with the American International Association for Economic and Social Development (1948–53), was a research assistant at the University of Chicago (1953–57), and from 1958 to 1978 was with the Agricultural Development Council, spending 1958–64 in Southeast Asia. He was chancellor of the State University of New York (1978–87), and chairman and chief executive officer of the Teachers Insurance Fund and Annuity Association and the College Retirement Equities Fund (1987–92). He was chairman of the Board of Directors of the Rockefeller Foundation (1982–92). He is married to Dolores Duncan; they have two children.

FURTHER READING

Obituary. *Current Biography*, June 1990.
"$60 billion...." L.J. DAVIS. *New York Times Magazine*, Mar. 27, 1988.

White, Byron Raymond (1917–) Justice White continued to occupy a conservative-leaning, but far from ultraconservative position on the Supreme Court during the 1991–92 term. He wrote the majority opinions in several notable cases, including *U.S. v. Fordice*, ruling that Mississippi had not fulfilled its obligation to desegregate its public colleges and universities; *Keeney v. Tamayo-Reyes*, which sharply limited the federal habeas corpus appeals of state prisoners; and *Jacobson v. U.S.*, ruling that the federal government had illegally entrapped a defendant into buying child pornography through the mail. He also joined the majority in such key cases as *Lujan v. Defenders of Wildlife*, ruling that the plaintiff, an environmental organization, had no standing to bring suit because no determinable specific interest was at issue; *International Society for Krishna Consciousness v. Lee*, ruling that airports could ban groups from soliciting money; *U.S. v. Alvarez Machain*, upholding the 1990 U.S. kidnapping of a Mexican doctor suspected of a role in the torture of a U.S. drug enforcement agent; *Nordlinger v. Hahn*, upholding the right of California to enact Proposition 13, with its unequal property taxes on newcomers; *Freeman v. Pitts*, ruling that schools being operated under court-supervised desegre-

gation orders could be released from those orders step by step; *Georgia v. McCollum*, ruling that criminal case defendants could not bar prospective jurors solely because of their race; *Hudson v. McMillian*, ruling that the excessive use of force by prison guards was an Eighth Amendment violation even if the prisoner was not seriously hurt; *Riggins v. Nevada*, ruling that the state could not force an insane criminal defendant to take medication during a trial; and *R.A.V. v. St. Paul*, overturning a St. Paul, Minnesota ordinance making sexist, racist, or otherwise bigoted speech or behavior a crime. He also joined all of his colleagues in a rare, unanimous landmark sexual harassment decision; in *Franklin v. Gwinnett County Public Schools*, the Court unanimously ruled that under Title IX of the 1972 education act a sexually harassed student could collect damages from a school district where a teacher-coach sexually harassed Christine Franklin and ultimately succeeded in pressing her to have sexual intercourse with him. He also ruled with the majority that the Coast Guard could continue to intercept at sea and return Haitian refugees to Haiti; and in the decision barring return of RU-486 pills to Leona Benten, a pregnant woman who tried to import them into the U.S. for her personal use, in a challenge to their ban.

White wrote a dissenting opinion in *New York v. U.S.*, which invalidated a federal law forcing states to handle their own radioactive waste, also dissenting on such key cases as *Planned Parenthood of Southeastern Pennsylvania v. Casey*, in which a 5–4 majority upheld the essence of *Roe v. Wade* (which in 1972 had established the right of a woman to choose to have an abortion), while at the same time upholding most of the restrictive 1989 Pennsylvania abortion law and giving the states broader powers to restrict abortion; *Lee v. Weisman*, barring nonsectarian or any other prayers at public high school graduations; and *Lechmere Inc. v. National Labor Relations Board*, ruling that companies did not have to allow union organizers access to such company-owned lands as parking lots and shopping malls.

Colorado-born White was football star "Whizzer" White in the late 1930s. After World War II, he practiced law in Denver until 1960. He campaigned for John F. Kennedy in 1960; as president, Kennedy appointed him a deputy attorney general in 1961 and then a Supreme Court Justice in 1962. White's 1938 B.A. was from the University of Colorado, and his 1945 LL.B. from

Yale. He is married to Marion Stearns; they have two children.

FURTHER READING

Byron White. BOB ITALIA. Abdo & Daughters, 1992.
"A new day in court." LAUREN TARSHIS and JAMES EARL HARDY. *Scholastic Update,* Nov. 1, 1991.
"Byron White leads. . . ." DAVID A. KAPLAN. *Newsweek,* Apr. 30, 1990.
Eight Men and a Lady. HERMAN SCHWARTZ et al. National Press, 1990.

Wilder, L. Douglas (Lawrence Douglas Wilder; 1931–)

The first African-American Governor in the history of the United States was a candidate for the Democratic presidential nomination until withdrawing on January 8, 1992; he had not stirred much interest, and was having great difficulty raising enough money to even qualify for federal matching funds. He remained highly visible on the national and international scene, however, visiting South Africa in late June and meeting with Prime Minister De Klerk on July 2. Members of his staff had meetings with Ross Perot in mid-July on a possible Wilder vice-presidential nomination. In the end, he endorsed Clinton on July 14, and made one of the three nominating speeches for vice-presidential nominee Al Gore on July 16th. He then campaigned actively for the Clinton-Gore ticket.

Another political development was the continuation of the 1991 feud between Wilder and Democratic U.S. Senator Charles S. Robb, which had supposedly been patched up in June 1991. Robb had been accused of illegally taping a Wilder telephone call, and was the subject of a grand jury investigation.

Richmond-born Wilder became Governor after a long career in state government. He was a Democratic member of the Virginia Senate (1969–85), and was lieutenant governor of his state (1986–89). On November 7, 1989, he won the Virginia gubernatorial election by a razor-thin 50.1 percent to 49.9 percent margin, surviving a recount. Wilder's 1961 B.S. was from Virginia Union University, his 1969 J.D. from Howard University. He has three children.

FURTHER READING

"Wilder's flier." B. DRUMMOND AYRES, JR. *New York Times Magazine,* Jan. 12, 1992.
"Can Doug Wilder's. . . ." RUSSELL MILLER. *Rolling Stone,* Oct. 31, 1991.
"The no bull campaign." HOWARD FINEMAN. *Newsweek,* Oct. 14, 1991.
"Terminators 2. . . ." FRED BARNES. *New Republic,* July 8, 1991.
"Wilder and Wilder. . . ." JOHN HOOD. *Reason,* Mar. 1991.
"Va. governor Wilder talks. . . ." *Jet,* Feb. 25, 1991.
"L. Douglas Wilder. . . ." LYNN NORMENT. *Ebony,* Feb. 1991.
Racism As a Factor in the 1989 Gubernatorial Election of Doug Wilder. DAVID R. JONES. E. Mellen, 1991.
"Mild Wilder. . . ." FRED BARNES. *New Republic,* Aug. 13, 1990.
"Wilder, Lawrence Douglas." *Current Biography,* Apr. 1990.
"The first Black elected governor. . . ." LAURA B. RANDOLPH. *Ebony,* Feb. 1990.
Wilder: Hold Fast to Dreams: A Biography of L. Douglas Wilder. DONALD P. BAKER. Seven Locks, 1990.
Claiming the Dream: The Victorious Campaign of Douglas Wilder of Virginia. MARGARET EDDS. Algonquin, 1990.

Williams, Martin (1924–92)

Virginia-born Williams was a jazz scholar and critic, and an American cultural historian. He began his career with articles on musical matters for such publications as *The New York Times* and the *Saturday Review.* In 1958, he and Nat Hentoff founded the monthly magazine *The Jazz Review.* He also wrote several books on jazz, including *Where's the Melody* (1966), and his highly regarded *The Jazz Tradition* (1970). From 1971 to 1981, he was director of jazz and cultural programs at the Smithsonian Institution, responsible for lecture and concert series, collections, and recordings. In 1973, he issued the historic "Smithsonian Collection of Classic Jazz," also writing several books in cultural history. He became a special projects editor at the Smithsonian Press in 1983. He was survived by three sons. (d. Washington, D. C.; April 12, 1992)

FURTHER READING

Obituary. *The Times* (of London), Apr. 25, 1992.
Obituary. *New York Times,* Apr. 14, 1992.

Williams, Robin (1952–) Stage and screen star Robin Williams was honored by his peers in 1992, winning a Best Actor Oscar nomination and a Golden Globe as best actor for his role in *The Fisher King*.

While his role as Peter in Steven Spielberg's 1991 Christmas film *Hook* was being seen around the world, Williams was at work on another blockbuster Christmas film; he starred as the Genie in the animated film *Aladdin*, the major Disney entry in the Christmas 1992 film sweepstakes, in a cast that included Scott Weinger as Aladdin, Linda Larkin, the singers Brad Kane and Lea Salonga, and Jonathan Freeman. In the spring of 1992, he starred as the voice of Batty Koda in Bill Kroyer's animated film *Ferngully . . . the Last Rainforest*.

Williams also starred in Barry Levinson's comedy-fantasy film *Toys*, co-starring Michael Gambon, Joan Cusack, Robin Wright, and Donald O'Connor, about a toymaking factory gone mad in the hands of a mad general. He was also set to star in Bill Forsyth's forthcoming film *Being Human*, produced by David Puttnam. For a fifth year, Williams, Billy Crystal and Whoopi Goldberg joined their talents in a benefit for the homeless; their *Comic Relief V* raised more than $5 million in pledges. On the business side, Williams and his wife, Marsha, signed a two-year development and production agreement with TriStar Pictures.

Chicago-born Williams began his career as a comic in cabaret, playing many West Coast clubs, and then moved into television, in variety and then as a star in "Mork and Mindy" (1978–82). He became a leading film star of the 1980s, in such movies as *The World According to Garp* (1982), *Moscow on the Hudson* (1984), *Good Morning Vietnam* (1987), *The Adventures of Baron Munchausen* (1989), *Dead Poets Society* (1989; he won a Best Actor Oscar nomination), *Cadillac Man* (1989), *Awakenings* (1990), and *Dead Again* (1991). With Whoopi Goldberg and Billy Crystal, Williams has been a prime mover in the *Comic Relief* benefits for the homeless. In 1989, he published *To Be Somebody*. Williams attended Claremont College, Marin College, and the Juilliard School. Formerly married to Valerie Velardi, he married Marsha Garces in 1989; he has three children.

FURTHER READING

"Playboy interview. . . ." *Playboy*, Jan. 1992.
"A Peter Pan for yuppies." KURT ANDERSEN. *Time*, Dec. 16, 1991.
"Peter pandemonium." FRED SCHRUERS. *Premiere*, Dec. 1991.
"Robin Williams. . . ." JEFF GILES and MARK SELIGER. *Rolling Stone*, Feb. 21, 1991.
"Awake and sing." FRED SCHRUERS. *Premiere*, Jan. 1991.
"Talking with. . . ." CARSON JONES. *Redbook*, Jan. 1991.
"Robin Williams. . . ." JOE MORGENSTERN. *New York Times Magazine*, Nov. 11, 1990.
"Robin Williams has. . . ." LISA GRUNWALD. *Esquire*, June 1989.
"Actor. . . ." *Life*, Spring 1989.

Williams, Vanessa (1963–) Singer and actress Williams continued to develop both sides of her career in 1992. On the musical side, she made a major move forward with her single "Save the Best for Last," which became her first number one single on Billboard's Hot 100 chart and Hot Rhythm and Blues chart. She also issued the single "Work to Do," the fifth from her album *The Comfort Zone*. Williams was named Billboard's top female rhythm and blues artist of the year, and her "Save the Best for Last" was Billboard's number one adult contemporary hit.

Williams also starred in several telefilms broadcast in 1992. Perhaps most notable was *Stompin' at the Savoy*, directed by Debbie Allen; she played a young Harlem woman in the 1930s and during World War II, one of four friends whose interlinked stories are told in the film; Lynn Whitfield, Jasmine Guy, and Vanessa Bell Calloway co-starred. She also starred opposite Raymond Burr in the television film *Perry Mason: The Case of the Silenced Singer*. A third starring role came as Motown executive Suzanne de Passe in *The Jacksons—An American Dream*, about the singing Jackson family. She also starred in the Bernard Rose horror feature film *The Candyman.*

Williams began her career already a celebrity. In 1983, while attending Syracuse University, she became the first African-American Miss America, and then went the entire promotion route, complete with an audience with President and Mrs. Reagan in the White House. Then *Penthouse* magazine found and printed extraordinarily destructive nude photographs of her, and in July 1984 she was forced to resign as Miss America. Instead of folding up, she went on with her planned career, which included roles in such films as *Pickup Artist* (1986), *Harley Davidson and the Marlboro Man* (1991), and *Another You* (1991). She also began her recording career, making her breakthrough with the hit album *The Right Stuff* (1988), which won three Grammy nominations. Her second album was *The Comfort Zone* (1991).

Williams grew up in Millwood, New York, and attended Syracuse University. She married Ramon Hervey II, formerly her publicist and now her manager, in 1987; they have two children, and late in 1992 were expecting a third.

FURTHER READING

"Vanessa Williams." BETSY BORNS. *Harper's Bazaar*, June 1992.
"Vanessa on top." MARK HARRIS. *Entertainment*, Apr. 24, 1992.
"Too legit to quit." ROB TANNENBAUM. *US*, Apr. 1992.
"Vanessa Williams' . . . ." DEBORAH NORVILLE. *McCall's*, Apr. 1992.
"Vanessa Williams tells of intimate life. . . ." *Jet*, Feb. 3, 1992.
"Vanessa Williams." LANCE LOUD. *Interview*, Mar. 1991.
"Vanessa redressed." PAT JORDAN. *GQ*, June 1990.

Willis, Bruce (1955–) After his tremendous box-office success in the two *Die Hard* films, Willis seemed one of Hollywood's most "bankable" stars. But with his equally tremendous box-office failure in *Hudson Hawk*, followed by a series of films that were only moderately commercially successful, his career faded considerably. The cancellation of his projected *Die Hard III* in 1992 strongly indicated his falling star.

However, Willis did star in Robert Zemeckis's dark comedy *Death Becomes Her*, the story of the lifelong—and post-death—rivalry of two Hollywood beauties, played by Meryl Streep and Goldie Hawn. He also appeared as himself in *The Player*, Robert Altman's merciless, multistar lampoon of modern Hollywood. Forthcoming was a starring role in Rowdy Herrington's film *Three Rivers*. Willis was also highly visible in 1992 in support of the unsuccessful re-election campaign of President George Bush.

German-born Willis worked in the New York theater from the late 1970s, and appeared in several small film roles in the early 1980s. He emerged as a television star in the long-running series "Moonlighting" (1985–89), and with *Blind Date* (1987) moved into starring roles in films. He starred in *Sunset* (1988), *Die Hard* (1988; and its 1989 sequel), *In Country* (1989), *The Bonfire of the Vanities* (1990), *Hudson Hawk* (1991), *Mortal Thoughts* (1991), and *The Last Boy Scout* (1991). He was also the featured voice of baby Mikey in *Look Who's Talking* (1989) and *Look Who's Talking Too* (1990). Willis attended

Montclair State College. He and Demi Moore married in 1987; they have two daughters.

FURTHER READING

"Demi's big moment." NANCY COLLINS and ANNIE LEIBOVITZ. *Vanity Fair*, Aug. 1991.
"Bruce on the loose." ANTHONY HADEN-GUEST. *Vanity Fair*, Jan. 1991.
"Bruce Willis. . . ." FRED ROBBINS. *McCall's*, June 1989.
"Bruce Willis. . . ." *Video Review*, Feb. 1989.
"Playboy interview. . . ." LAWRENCE GROBEL. *Playboy*, Nov. 1988.
"Bruce Willis. . . ." DENNIS WATLINGTON. *Cosmopolitan*, Sep. 1988.
"Bruce Willis. . . ." AUDREY LAVIN. *Redbook*, Aug. 1988.

Wilson, August (1945–) In April 1992, August Wilson's new play *Two Trains Running* opened at Broadway's Walter Kerr Theater. Set in a Pittsburgh restaurant in 1969, it was the sixth in Wilson's series of plays on the African-American 20th-century experience. Lloyd Richards directed a cast that included Al White as restaurant proprietor Memphis Lee, Cynthia Martells as Risa, Roscoe Lee Browne as Holloway, Sullivan Walker as Hambone, Larry Fishburne as ex-con Sterling, Anthony Chisholm as bookie Wolf, and Chuck Patterson as undertaker West. The play, which had toured nationally in 1991, was a critical and box-office hit on Broadway. It won a Best Play Tony nomination, and was named best American play by the New York Drama Critics' Circle. Fishburne won a Tony as best featured actor in a play. A screen adaptation of Wilson's earlier *Fences* was reportedly forthcoming.

Playwright and poet Wilson emerged as a major figure in the American theater during the 1980s. His plays include *Jitney* (1982); *Ma Rainey's Black Bottom* (1984); *Fences* (1987), which won a Best Play Tony and a Pulitzer Prize, and for which James Earl Jones won a Best Actor Tony; and *The Piano Lesson*, for which he won a second Pulitzer Prize and which was named best play of the season by the New York Drama Critics Circle. Wilson dropped out of school in the ninth grade at age 15. He was formerly married.

FURTHER READING

"An elegant duet. . . ." RACHAEL MIGLER. *GQ—Gentlemen's Quarterly*, Apr. 1990.

"Fine-tuning. . . ." MEL GUSSOW. *New York Times Magazine*, Sep. 10, 1989.
"The light in August." CHIP BROWN. *Esquire*, Apr. 1989.
"On Broadway. . . ." CHARLAYNE HUNTER-GAULT. *Vogue*, Aug. 1988.
"Exorcising the demons. . . ." WILLIAM A. HENRY, III. *Time*, Apr. 11, 1988.

Winfield, Dave (David Mark Winfield; 1951–) How sweet it was! As a free agent, Winfield started a new season with a new team, the Toronto Blue Jays, and came away with the World Series ring that had previously eluded him. Not only that, but he played a crucial role in the win. During the season, he scored 26 home runs and batted in 108 runs, making him the first 40-year-old player to drive in more than 100 runs. Though his numbers were not always so good in the playoffs, his contributions were well timed. On October 7th, against the Oakland Athletics, he became the oldest player to hit a post-season home run, starting the comeback drive that took the Blue Jays into the American League Championship Series. Then in game six of the World Series itself, Winfield hit a game-winning two-out, two-run double in the 11th inning to clinch the 4–2 championship over the Atlanta Braves.

With that Winfield effectively wiped away the

sting of his 1-for-22 performance for the Yankees in the 1981 World Series—a slump Yankees' owners George Steinbrenner never let Winfield forget. But even Steinbrenner applauded Winfield's 1992 performance, and the Toronto fans went wild, redoubling the warm support they had shown for him all season. Winfield pronounced it quite simply "my biggest game, my best day in baseball." At season's end, Winfield's statistics stood this way: .285 career hitting average, 2,866 hits, 432 home runs, and 1,710 runs batted in. In December, it was reported that Winfield was heading back home, to join the Minnesota Twins.

Minnesota-born Winfield became a star outfielder in the major leagues immediately after graduating from the University of Minnesota. He played with the San Diego Padres (1973–1980) before going to the Yankees (1980–1990), and made 12 straight All-Star appearances (1977–88), before losing all of 1989 due to back surgery. He had numerous disagreements with owner George Steinbrenner, going to court to force Steinbrenner to make what Winfield alleged were agreed-upon payments to his charitable foundation. In 1990, Steinbrenner allegedly paid a bribe to a gambler for information thought to be derogatory to Winfield, intending to derail a proposed trade of Winfield to the California Angels; as a result, Steinbrenner was banned from day-to-day participation in baseball from mid-1990 until early 1993. In 1990, after being traded to the Angels, Winfield was named Comeback Player of the Year. With Tom Parker, Winfield wrote *Winfield: A Player's Life* (1988). Winfield married Tonya Turner in 1988, and has one child.

FURTHER READING

" 'I feel a whole lot better now.' " RICK REILLY. *Sports Illustrated*, June 29, 1992.
"Dave Winfield: 'My career is. . . .' " WILLIAM LADSON. *Sport*, Aug. 1991.
Dave Winfield. JUDY MONROE. Crestwood House, 1988.

Winfrey, Oprah (1954–) In 1992, Winfrey continued to be among the most successful people in the entertainment world. Indeed, she came in second to Bill Cosby on *Forbes*'s 1992 list of the highest-paid entertainers. Her afternoon talk show continued to be highly rated; she also hosted two prime-time interview specials in 1992. Starting in September, Winfrey became producer and host of ABC's award-winning "Afterschool Specials," shifting from drama to "reality-based programming," as a forum to teach and help young people. In an area of personal interest, Winfrey narrated a highly praised program called *Scared Silent*, focusing especially on child abuse within families, which—in an unprecedented move—was shown simultaneously by CBS, NBC, and PBS, and then two days later on ABC. In May, as part of her own series on racism in America, Winfrey took her show to Los Angeles in the wake of the riots over the Rodney King verdict. Winfrey was the voice of Elizabeth Keckley, as one of many narrators in the documentary *Lincoln*, which aired in late December. She was one of various African-American celebrities to provide funds to complete Spike Lee's over-budget *Malcolm X*.

On the personal side, Winfrey and her long-time companion, Stedman Graham, won a defamation lawsuit against the *News Extra* supermarket tabloid for falsely accusing Graham of having an affair with a male cousin. In November, Winfrey announced that she and Graham were engaged, though the wedding date had not been set. Previously divorced, Graham runs a Chicago public relations firm, and is cofounder of Athletes Against Drugs.

Mississippi-born Winfrey began her broadcasting career in 1972, as a reporter for WVOL radio while still in school and then for WTVF-TV (both in Nashville), then moved to Baltimore's WJZ-TV as co-anchor in 1976. Becoming co-host of the station's morning show, she entered a new career, scoring a major success as the host of "AM Chicago" for Chicago's WLS-TV, which was renamed "The Oprah Winfrey Show" in 1984, and became a nationally syndicated hit show. She also starred in the 1989 television miniseries *The Women of Brewster Place*, later developing the role in the short-lived television primetime series, "Brewster Place." Winfrey attended Tennessee State University. She has appeared in several films, including *The Color Purple* (1985) and *Native Son* (1986).

FURTHER READING

"The mystery of Oprah. . . ." KATHRYN CASEY. *Ladies Home Journal*, Nov. 1992.
"Her man Stedman." ELIZABETH SPORKIN. *People*, Nov. 23, 1992.

"The prime time of Ms. Oprah Winfrey." DAVID RENSIN. *TV Guide*, May 16, 1992.

Oprah Winfrey: Television Star. STEVE OTFINOSKI. Blackbirch, 1992.

"Oprah's crusade." MARY H.J. FARRELL et al. *People*, Dec. 2, 1991.

"The companies they keep." FRED GOODMAN. *Working Woman*, Dec. 1991.

"Oprah Winfrey. . . ." ALAN EBERT. *Good Housekeeping*, Sep. 1991.

"Next on Oprah." BILL BRASHLER. *Ladies Home Journal*, Aug. 1991.

"Walking in the light." PEARL CLEADGE. *Essence*, June 1991.

Oprah Winfrey. GERALDINE WOODS. Dillon, 1991.

"Oprah Winfrey tells. . . ." *Jet*, Sep. 17, 1990.

"A brain for. . . ." MATTHEW SCHIFRIN and PETER NEWCOMB. *Forbes*, Oct. 1, 1990.

Oprah Winfrey: TV Talk Show Host. MARGARET BEATON. Childrens, 1990.

Oprah Winfrey: Talk Show Host and Actress. LILLIE PATTERSON and CORNELIA H. WRIGHT. Enslow, 1990.

Oprah Winfrey: Media Success Story. ANNE SAIDMAN. Lerner, 1990.

Everybody Loves Oprah!: Her Remarkable Life Story. NORMAN KING. Morrow, 1988.

Oprah! ROBERT WALDRON. St. Martin, 1987.

Winger, Debra (1955–) Film star

Debra Winger starred opposite Steve Martin in Richard Pearce's film *Leap of Faith*, which opened during the 1992 Christmas season. Martin played fraudulent faith healer Jonas Nightengale, whose traveling road show finds itself stranded in little Rustwater, Kansas when its bus breaks down, and does a tent show there, with ultimately surprising results. Winger costarred as his highly efficient—and highly manipulative—manager, in a cast that included Lolita Davidovich, Liam Neeson, and Lukas Haas. Still forthcoming was a starring role opposite Dennis Quaid in the Glenn Gordon Caron film *Wilder Napalm*, which started production in November 1991.

Winger's name remained in the media early in 1992 because of her highly publicized friendship with Nebraska Senator Bob Kerrey, a candidate for the 1992 Democratic presidential nomination.

Cleveland-born Winger began her career in television, most notably in the series "Wonder Woman" (1976–77), and then moved into films. She emerged as a highly regarded dramatic actress in such films as *French Postcards* (1979),

Urban Cowboy (1980), *Cannery Row* (1982), *An Officer and a Gentleman* (1982), *Terms of Endearment* (1983), *Legal Eagles* (1986), *Black Widow* (1987), *Betrayed* (1988), *The Sheltering Sky* (1990), and *Everybody Wins* (1990). Winger attended California State University. She was formerly married to actor Timothy Hutton; she has one child.

FURTHER READING

"Debra Winger." STEVE POND. *Harper's Bazaar*, June 1992.

"Straight shooting star." LYNN HIRSCHBERG. *American Film*, July–Aug. 1988.

Woods, James (1947–) Film and televi-

sion star Woods starred in one of 1992's mostanticipated television films. In *Citizen Cohn*, he played New York lawyer Roy Cohn, from his days as a Red-hunting aide to Senator Joseph McCarthy to his death from AIDS after having led a life as a closet homosexual who professed to hate homosexuals. David Franzoni wrote the filmscript, based on Nicholas von Hoffman's biography of Cohn; Frank Pierson directed, and Joe Don Baker co-starred as McCarthy, in a cast that included Joseph Bologna, Ed Flanders, Frederic Forrest, Lee Grant, and Pat Hingle. Woods' portrayal of Cohn as a thoroughly evil man was well-received by critics and audiences.

Woods also starred as boxing manager Gabriel Caine opposite Louis Gossett, Jr., as boxer

Honey Roy Palmer in Michael Ritchie's film *Diggstown*, about a boxing scam that victimizes a villain. The versatile Woods also starred as a Chicago reporter opposite Dolly Parton as a singer who becomes a celebrity radio pop psychologist—with false credentials—in Barnett Kellman's film comedy *Straight Talk*.

Utah-born Woods appeared on the New York stage and in films in the early 1970s, and emerged as a star in such films as *The Onion Field* (1979), *Fast Walking* (1982), *Split Image* (1982), *Videodrome* (1983), *Once Upon a Time in America* (1984), *Against All Odds* (1984), *Joshua Then and Now* (1985), *Best Seller* (1987), *Cop* (1987), *True Believer* (1989), *Immediate Family* (1989), *The Hard Way* (1991), and *The Boys* (1991). He has also appeared in many telefilms, winning an Emmy for *Promise* (1986), and a second Emmy as Bill Wilson, a co-founder of Alcoholics Anonymous, in *My Name is Bill W* (1989). Woods attended the University of California and the Massachusetts Institute of Technology. He has been married twice.

FURTHER READING

"James Woods is. . . ." MICHAEL SZYMANSKI. *Advocate*, Sep. 8, 1992.

"James Woods. . . ." *American Film*, May 1990.

"Woods, James." *Current Biography*, Nov. 1989.

"Fighting his way. . . ." RICHARD B. WOODWARD. *New York Times Magazine*, Aug. 20, 1989.

"Arresting appeal. . . ." BETSY BORNS. *Harper's Bazaar*, Feb. 1989.

Woolsey, R. James, Jr. (1941–) President Bill Clinton's incoming Director of the Central Intelligence Agency is a Washington lawyer with considerable experience of government. Woolsey began his Washington career as a program analyst with the Defense Department (1968–70) and the National Security Council (1970). He was general counsel to the Senate Armed Services Committee (1970–73), and then became an associate with the law firm of Shea and Gardner (1973–77), leaving the firm to become a Carter Administration assistant Navy secretary (1977–79). He returned to Shea and Gardner as a partner (1979–89), leaving for another government post, as ambassador and U.S. representative to the Negotiation on Conventional Armed Forces in Europe (1989–91), returning to Shea and Gardner in 1991. Woolsey also served on several presidential commissions, and was an advisor in several sets of armed forces stabilization and reduction negotiations with the Soviet Union during the Cold War. Among his published works are *Keeping America Safe: Studies in Strategic Military Policy* (1982; with Paul Warnke), *Nuclear Arms: Ethics, Strategy, Politics* (1984; co-edited with Michael Quinlan), *Defending Peace & Freedom: Toward Strategic Stability in the Year 2000* (1988; co-edited with Brent Scowcroft and Thomas Etzold), and *The Atlantic Alliance Transformed* (1992; with David M. Abshire and Richard B. Burt).

Woolsey's 1963 B.A. was from Stanford University, his 1965 M.A. from Oxford University, and his 1968 LL.B. from Yale University. He is married to Suzanne Haley; they have three children.

FURTHER READING

"Some old, some new, some borrowed. . . ." *Time*, Jan. 4, 1993.

X-Y-Z

Yamaguchi, Kristi Tsuya (1971–) Women's figure skating honored a new queen in 1992: a 5-foot-tall, under-100-pound, 20-year-old American named Kristi Yamaguchi. The story had not been scripted that way. Even though Yamaguchi had been 1991 World Champion, her predecessor as champion, Japanese skater Midori Ito, was favored to take the gold medal at the Albertville Winter Olympics in February 1992. But Ito faltered, and Yamaguchi glided to the top, with a highly successful combination of athletic skill and artistry, most notable in her programs to the Spanish music of "Malaguena" and the Viennese waltz "The Blue Danube." She then reaffirmed her position as the world's premiere woman figure skater by taking a second world championship in March 1992, becoming the first American woman to do so since Peggy Fleming in 1968. After the championships, Yamaguchi went on a traditional post-Olympic tour of 45 cities and Europe with other Olympic champions. Under more liberal International Skating Union eligibility rules, she could be able to compete in the 1994 Winter Olympics in Lillehammer, Norway.

Yamaguchi is credited with having sparked something of a revival in figure skating among young girls. However, though she has some commercial endorsements, they do not near the number attained by the last American gold medalist, Dorothy Hamill, in 1976. Some suggest that U.S.-Japanese trade tensions are the reason for this, or more generally that Yamaguchi is "too ethnic" to have wide popular appeal. Kristi herself is a fourth-generation American; her American-born grandparents and parents were interned (and her mother born) in United States camps for American citizens of Japanese descent during World War II. Yamaguchi's own feeling on the matter was expressed in her traditional gold-medal exhibition dance, draped in red, white, and blue, and skating to "Yankee Doodle Dandy." Her other exhibition, with a nod to her French hosts, was to the music of Edith Piaf.

California-born Yamaguchi was born with club feet, but the condition was corrected and she learned to walk wearing special shoes with connecting bars, making her grace and delicacy all the more remarkable. She began skating at age 6. Yamaguchi has trained with Christy Kjarsgaard-Ness since 1989 and, after graduating from high school in 1990, followed her coach to Edmonton, Alberta.

FURTHER READING

"When dreams come true." MARTHA DUFFY. *Time*, Mar. 2, 1992.
"The gold rush. . . ." STEVEN LANG. *New Woman*, Feb. 1992.
"Spun gold." DAVID M. KOGER. *Science World*, Jan. 24, 1992.
"A skating sprite. . . ." *People*, Mar. 20, 1989.

Yeakel, Lynn Hardy (1942–) One of the first signs that 1992 was to be the "Year of the Woman" was the surprise victory of political unknown Yeakel in the Pennsylvania Democratic

U.S. senatorial primary. On April 28th, in a five-way contest, Yeakel won a landslide victory, gaining 44 percent of the vote to Lt. Governor Mark S. Singel's 33 percent Singel had been heavily favored to win the nomination. Like so many other women who decided to run for high office in 1992, Yeakel said that it was seeing the treatment of Anita Faye Hill by the all-male Senate Judiciary Committee during the Clarence Thomas Supreme Court nomination hearings that caused her to run—and especially to run against Pennsylvania Republican Senator Arlen Specter, who had been chief Republican "prosecutor" of Hill at the hearings, at one point even directly accusing her of perjury, a charge that was never pursued.

After her primary victory, Yeakel became a national figure, gained support from all over the country, and on July 13th addressed the Democratic National Convention. But back home in Pennsylvania, her campaign foundered. She was outspent 3–1 by Specter, and lost many traditionally Democratic labor and African-American voters to him. She also failed to handle Specter's many personal attacks well, and compounded her problems by using negative tactics of her own, losing some of the high moral standing that was the mainspring of her appeal. In the end, what had been a huge Yeakel lead over Specter slipped away; on November 3, he won by a narrow margin, 51 percent to 49 percent

Yeakel's 1963 B.A. was from Randolph-Macon Women's College. She is the director of the non-profit charitable organization Women's Way, and serves on the boards of several philanthropic organizations. She is married and has two children.

FURTHER READING

"The lady or the tiger?" CAROL SALINE and MAGGIE JONES. *Philadelphia*, Sep. 1992.

Yeltsin, Boris Nikolayevich (1931–   )

In his first full year in power, Russian President Yeltsin gambled much on crash market economy reforms, without much success. On January 1, 1992 he ended price controls on a wide range of goods and services, and within the next several months lifted most other price controls, doubled oil prices, and limited wage increases; he was blocked on his move to privatize landholding, and did not lift rent controls. But there was no effective move to rebuild the Russian manufacturing and distribution systems. As a result, produce rotted in the fields, factories ground to a stop without necessary components, and an already very badly damaged Russian economy proved itself unable to feed, clothe, house, and adequately care for its people.

The winter of 1991–92 was a disaster for the Russian people, especially in the cities but also in the countryside; and it was Yeltsin who bore the main burden of blame. The winter of 1992–93 started out no better. Using Russia's extraordinarily hard times as political ammunition, Yeltsin's conservative foes made a major comeback, and on December 14, 1992 were able in the Russian Congress to derail many of Yeltsin's economic reform programs, and to replace Premier Yegor T. Gaidar, chief architect of those programs, with conservative Viktor S. Chernomyrdin, who called himself an advocate of reform, but clearly spoke for those who wanted to slow and perhaps reverse Yeltsin's programs.

As Russian President, Yeltsin remained a major player on the world stage, particularly because Russia continued to hold major stockpiles of nuclear weapons and delivery systems. At the June 16–17 Russian-American Washington summit meeting, Presidents Yeltsin and Bush agreed to massive cuts in nuclear warheads, to be accomplished by the year 2003; a formal treaty was to follow. Yeltsin also addressed both houses of Congress, stressing friendship and appealing for U.S. aid. He received a $24 billion aid package pledge from the Group of Seven—the United States, Britain, France, Germany, Japan, Canada, and Italy—and concluded bilateral aid and trade pacts with several other countries. Presidents Yeltsin and Bush signed a major arms reduction treaty in Moscow on January 3, 1993.

Yeltsin in 1992 was also involved in negotiating a set of new relationships and disputes with the other nations of the former Soviet Union, including a major dispute with Ukraine over the ownership of the former Soviet Black Sea fleet; in August, he and Ukraine President Leonid M. Kravchuk agreed on a division of the fleet. During the year, Yeltsin sent Russian troops into several new countries, including Moldova and Georgia, and refused to move Russian troops out of the Baltic countries on schedule.

Yeltsin worked as an engineer (1955–68), then going into Communist Party work in his home city of Sverdlovsk. During the early 1980s, he strongly supported and was close to Mikhail Gorbachev; Yeltsin moved into far higher party positions in 1985, when Gorbachev came to power. He was mayor of Moscow (1985–87) and secretary of the Communist Party central committee (1985–86). He moved into opposition in 1987, becoming a leader of those who felt that reform was not proceeding quickly enough, and was for some years a "maverick" in Soviet politics, who was not taken very seriously, and whose relations with Gorbachev were often abrasive.

In 1989, Yeltsin won the Moscow elections to the Congress of People's Deputies by an overwhelming majority, and became an opposition leader in the Soviet parliament. In March 1990, he refocused, winning election as a delegate to the Russian Federation's Supreme Soviet. On May 29, 1990 he was elected president of the Russian Federation, and began a campaign to secure greater Russian autonomy from the central government. In July 1990 he also resigned from the Communist Party.

On August 19, 1991 Gorbachev was placed under house arrest while vacationing in the Crimea, and a rightwing Communist coup began. Yeltsin became the center of opposition to the coup, gathering huge unarmed crowds and then key capital military units around him at the White House, the Russian parliament building in Moscow. On August 21st, the aborted coup collapsed, Yeltsin was a national hero, and a

second, democratic Russian Revolution quickly swept away the remnants of Soviet communism and the Soviet state. Gorbachev on his return to Moscow was unable to hold the Soviet state together, or in the following period to resist the rise of Yeltsin to effective power in the Russian Republic.

Yeltsin has published an autobiography, *Against the Grain* (1990); forthcoming was his book on the August 1991 events. He attended the Urals Polytechnic Institute. Little is known of his personal life, except that he is married to Naina Yeltsin.

FURTHER READING

"What makes Boris tick?" Jonathan Steele. *Guardian*, Dec. 21, 1992.

"Holding Russia's fate in his hands." John Kohan. *Time*, Dec. 7, 1992.

"One nation under Boris." Stephen Sestanovich. *New Republic*, June 29, 1992.

" 'Yeltsin. . . . has made mistakes, ...' " Paul Klebnikov. *Forbes*, June 8, 1992.

Boris Yeltsin: A Political Biography. Vladimir Solovyov and Elena Klepikova. Putnam, 1992.

Gorbachev-Yeltsin: The Fall of Communism. Stuart A. Kallen. Abdo & Daughters, 1992.

Gorbachev, Yeltsin and the Last Days of the Soviet Empire. Neil Felshman. Thomas Dunne/St. Martin's, 1992.

Boris Yeltsin: Man of the People. Eleanor H. Ayer. Dillon/Macmillan, 1992.

"The end of the U.S.S.R." George J. Church. *Time*, Dec. 23, 1991.

"The man who saved the future." T.D. Allman. *Vanity Fair*, Oct. 1991.

"When putsch comes to shove. . . ." Tatyana Tolstaya. *New Republic*, Sep. 16, 1991.

"In excelsis Yeltsin." Helle Bering-Jensen. *Insight*, Sep. 9, 1991.

"A chastened character. . . ." John Kohan. *Time*, Sep. 9, 1991.

"Profiles of courage." Mary Nemeth. *Maclean's*, Sep. 2, 1991.

"The man who rules Russia." David Aikman. "Desperate moves." Bruce W. Nelan. *Time*, Sep. 2, 1991.

"Yeltsin's triumph." Rose Brady et al. *Business Week*, Sep. 2, 1991.

"Sober statesman. . . ." Bill Hewitt. *People*, July 8, 1991.

"Is Boris Yeltsin for real?" Rowland Evans and Robert Novak. *Reader's Digest*, July 1991.

"Mother Russia's freedom fighter." Paul Hofheinz. *Fortune*, Apr. 8, 1991.

"The conductor of discord." Strobe Talbott. "Portrait of a populist." David Aikman. "Boris vs.

Mikhail. . . ." BRUCE W. NELAN. *Time*, Mar. 25, 1991.
"Yeltsin. . . ." JOHN KOHAN. *Time*, Jan. 7, 1991.
Boris Yeltsin: Russia's First President. JOHN MORRISON. NAL-Dutton, 1991.

Yerby, Frank (1916–91) A very popular author of historical romances, born in Augusta, Georgia, Yerby began his career as a college teacher in the late 1930s, after receiving his M.A. from Fisk College. He also began writing short stories, and was regarded as a promising young African-American writer for such short stories as "The Thunder of God" (1939) and "Health Card" (1944). He worked in war plants during World War II, and began his long career as a novelist in 1946, with publication of his bestseller *The Foxes of Harrow*, a romance set in the pre-Civil War South, which in 1947 became the Rex Harrison-Maureen O'Hara film vehicle. Ultimately, he published more than 30 such works—he called them "costume novels"—several of them adapted into films. Yerby soon became an expatriate, living in France and from 1954 in Spain. In some of his later work, he focused upon his African heritage, perhaps most notably in *The Dahomean* (1971). He was survived by his second wife, Blanca Calle Perez, two daughters, two sons, and two brothers. (d. Madrid, Spain; November 29, 1991)

FURTHER READING

"Author Frank Yerby. . . ." *Jet*, Jan. 27, 1992.
Obituary. *Variety*, Jan. 13, 1992.
Obituary. *The Times* (of London), Jan. 11, 1992.
Obituary. *New York Times*, Jan. 8, 1992.

Young, Steve (Jon Steven Young; 1961–) Strange though it may seem, Steve Young has managed to be the highest-rated quarterback in the National Football League two seasons running (1991–92 and 1992–93), both times with over a 100 point rating, and was named the NFL's most valuable player for the 1992–93 season—but he still stands in the shadow of the man he replaced: the legendary Joe Montana. In those two seasons, Young compiled an enviable record, leading his team to the league's best record two years in a row and into the conference championships, though both times falling short of their ultimate goal—the Super Bowl. Coach George Seifert reportedly has stressed to Young, "It's your team now," noting that, when Montana was ready to return, it would be as a backup; and commentators pointed out that, with all the player turnover, perhaps half of the 49ers had never even played under Montana. Still, when Montana was healthy enough to return, San Francisco and, indeed, football fans across the country went wild to see him back at the helm—even if just for the last two quarters of a meaningless late-season game in mid-January 1993. The media were full of commentary about who should be the 49ers' quarterback for the 1993–4 season: the NFL's still-young top-rated quarterback or the aging legend, perhaps the greatest of all time, who led his team to four Super Bowl victories in the 1980s and is not ready to retire. It is greatly to the credit of both Young and Montana that they have, to all appearances, kept their balance in what is surely a touchy and difficult situation.

A great-great-great-grandson of the Mormon leader Brigham Young, Steve Young was born in Salt Lake City and attended high school in Greenwich, Connecticut. At Brigham Young University, he was a consensus All-American and runner-up for the Heisman Trophy, capped by an extraordinary senior year in which he completed 306 of 429 passes, for 3902 yards and 33 touchdowns, setting a then-record pass percentage of .713, and winning 11 of 12 games, passing for over 300 yards in all but two. In 1991, *Sports Illustrated* made a statistical analysis of college quarterback records—their personal statistics and team winning percentage—and found that Young led the list. After playing briefly for the L.A. Express of the U.S. Football League in 1984, when he became the first professional football player ever to rush for 100 yards and pass for 300 yards in the same game, Young moved to the Tampa Bay Buccaneers in 1985. Acquired by the San Francisco 49ers in 1987, he saw only sporadic playing time as backup to Montana until the 1991 season. Young completed law school at BYU in the off-season in 1992.

FURTHER READING

"There's no killing this quarterback. . . ." CHRIS MORTENSEN. *Sporting News*, Sep. 14, 1992.

"Quarterbacks quantified." DOUGLAS S. LOONEY. *Sports Illustrated*, Fall 1991.

"The Young 49ers." RICK REILLY. *Sports Illustrated*, Sep. 30, 1991.

"Young and rich." PETER KING. *Sports Illustrated*, Sep. 16, 1991.

"49ers reserve is. . . ." *Sporting News*, Feb. 5, 1990.

"Quarterback controversy. . . ." KEVIN DOYLE. *Sporting News*, Aug. 29, 1988.

"State of Montana. . . ." RALPH WILEY. *Sports Illustrated*. Aug. 15, 1988.

Zappa, Frank (Francis Vincent Zappa; 1940–   ) Performer and composer Zappa spent much of 1992 composing modern classical works for the Ensemble Modern, including "The Yellow Shark," a body of revised and new works, including new compositions such as "Welcome to America," "Chunnel Mr. Boogins," "None of the Above," and "Get Whitey." Appearing with the Ensemble Modern at the September 1992 Frankfurt Festival, he conducted two concerts before illness forced him to withdraw; the Ensemble completed Berlin and Vienna engagements without him. Zappa, who had been suffering from prostate cancer, said that he would continue composing, and that he had been negotiating to do an opera for the 1994 Vienna Festival.

Zappa continued in 1992 to issue more "bootleg" tapes of his own concert recordings in an attempt to frustrate real bootleggers, who had published more than 400 unauthorized recordings of his concerts. He also continued to issue

considerable quantities of old and new material, including three more double-CDs completing "You Can't Do That on Stage Anymore," a six-volume collection of his works. Forthcoming was a double-CD set of his "The Yellow Shark" concerts, as well as a symphonic work titled "Civilization: Phase III."

Zappa became a major rock music figure in the 1960s as founder of the group The Mothers of Invention (1964–77); the group's hit albums included *Freak Out!* (1966), *Absolutely Free* (1967), and *200 Motels* (1971; and the 1971 film). On his own, he made such records as *Hot Rats* (1969), *Apostrophe* (1974), and *Joe's Garage* (1979). His hit singles include "Don't Eat the Yellow Snow" (1974), "Dancin' Fool" (1979), and "Valley Girl" (1982), in which he teamed up with his daughter Moon Unit, then only 14. Zappa's most notable later work joins jazz and classical music, in such albums as *Boulez Conducts Zappa* (1982, 1987) and *The Perfect Stranger and Other Works* (1985). In 1989, Zappa published *A Mother of Necessity: The Real Frank Zappa Book*, written with Peter Occhiogrosso. In 1991, he published the double-CD sets *Make a Jazz Noise Here* and *The Greatest Band You Never Heard in Your Life*. Zappa married Gail Sloatman in 1967; they have four children. Moon Unit and Dweezil starred in the television situation comedy "Normal Life" (1990–91).

FURTHER READING

"Frank Zappa stricken. . . ." KIM NEELY. *Rolling Stone*, Jan. 9, 1992.

"Frank Zappa makes. . . ." MICHAEL DAVIS. *Down Beat*, July 1991.

"Frank Zappa—trading partner." DAVID CORN. *Nation*, Mar. 19, 1990.

"Zappa, Frank." *Current Biography*, Feb. 1990.

"Frank Zappa. . . ." TIM SCHNECKLOTH. *Down Beat*, Sep. 1989.

"Frank Zappa. . . ." STEVE DOUGHERTY. *People*, May 22, 1989.

PHOTO CREDITS

Abdul, Paula. Virgin Records (Photo: Alberto Tolot 0591)

Acuff, Roy. Opryland (Photo: Donnie Beauchamp)

Albright, Madeleine. Center for National Policy

Alda, Alan. Bill Evans Public Relations

Altman, Roger C. Presidential Transition Press Office

Andrew, Duke of York. British Information Services, Central Office of Information, London

Sarah, Duchess of York. British Information Services, Central Office of Information, London

Ashe, Arthur. Home Box Office, Inc. (Photo: Tony Triolo/HBO)

Aylwin, Patricio. Embassy of Chile

Baldwin, Alec. Copyright © 1992 Twentieth Century Fox (Photo: Herb Ritts)

Barkley, Charles. Phoenix Suns

Bates, Kathy. © 1992 Universal City Studios

Bentsen, Lloyd. U.S. Senate (Photo: Susan Noonan)

Bird, Larry. Boston Celtics (Photo: Steve Lipofsky, Copyright 1992)

Boutros Ghali, Boutros. United Nations Photo

Boxer, Barbara. Barbara Boxer for Senate

Bradley, Bill. U.S. Senate

Brando, Marlon. Copyright © 1992 Warner Bros.

Brandt, Willy. German Information Service

Braun, Carol Moseley. Carol Moseley Braun for U.S. Senate

Brooks, Garth. Gurley & Co., Capitol® Nashville (Photo: Beverly Parker 8/90 B)

Brown, Jerry. Brown for President (Photo: Michael R. Rodriguez)

Brown, Jesse. Presidential Transition Press Office

Gober, Hershel. Presidential Transition Press Office

Brown, Ron. Office of Ron Brown (Photo: Philip Bermingham Photography, McLean, VA)

Browner, Carol. Presidential Transition Press Office

Buchanan, Pat. Buchanan for President

Bush, George. Bush/Quayle '92

Caan, James. © 1992 Castle Rock Entertainment (Photo: Gemma La-Mana)

Cage, Nicolas. © 1992 Castle Rock Entertainment (Photo: Gemma La-Mana)

Caine, Michael. Turtle Bay Books (Photo: © Roman Salicki/Shooting Star)

Campbell, Ben Nighthorse. U.S. Senate

Capriati, Jennifer. International Management Group (Photo: John Russell)

Carson, Johnny. © National Broadcasting Company, Inc. 1992

Carter, Jimmy. Times Books (Photo: © Rick Diamond Photography, Inc.)

Cisneros, Henry. Presidential Transition Press Office

Clinton, Bill. Bill Clinton for President Committee

Clinton, Hillary. Bill Clinton for President Committee

Cole, Natalie. Elektra Entertainment, Dan Cleary Management (Photo: Nancy Ellison)

Costner, Kevin. © 1991 Warner Bros. Inc., Regency Enterprises V.O.F. and Le Studio Canal

Courier, Jim. International Management Group (Photo: Gus Bower Productions)

Cruise, Tom. © 1992 Castle Rock Entertainment (Photo: Andy Schwartz)

Crystal, Billy. © 1992 Castle Rock Entertainment ® (Photo: Bruce Mc-Broom)

Culkin, Macaulay. Copyright © Twentieth Century Fox

Cyrus, Billy Ray. Mercury Records (Photo: Peter Nash 9/91)

Danson, Ted. Wolf-Kasteler Public Relations

Davis, Geena. Copyright © 1992 Columbia Pictures

Davis, Ossie. Ossie Davis

Day-Lewis, Daniel. © Copyright 1992, Twentieth Century Fox (Photo: Frank Connor)

Dee, Ruby. Ruby Dee

De Niro, Robert. Copyright © 1992 Twentieth Century Fox (Photo: Louis Goldman)

Dern, Laura. Wolf-Kasteler

DeVito, Danny. © 1992 DC Comics, Inc.

Diana, Princess of Wales. British Information Services, London Pictures Service (Photo: Snowden)

Douglas, Kirk. Warner Books (Photo: Lori Hofferber)

Eastwood, Clint. Copyright © 1992 Warner Bros.

Eckersley, Dennis. Oakland Athletics

Edelman, Marian Wright. Beacon Press (Photo: Katherine Lambert)

Elders, Joycelyn. Presidential Transition Press Office

Elizabeth II. British Information Services, Central Office of Information, London (Photo: Karsh of Ottawa)

Espy, Mike. Presidential Transition Press Office

Ewing, Patrick. New York Knicks (Photo: George Kalinsky)

Feinstein, Dianne. Office of Dianne Feinstein (Photo: © Tom Gibbons)

Ford, Harrison. Paramount Pictures, Copyright © 1992 (Photo: Merrick Morton)

Freeman, Morgan. Copyright © 1992 Warner Bros.

Garrison, Jim. © 1991 Warner Bros. Inc., Regency Enterprises V.O.F. and Le Studio Canal

Gates, Daryl. Bantam Books (Photo: © Art Para)

Gates, Robert. Central Intelligence Agency

Gibson, Mel. Copyright © 1992, Warner Bros. Inc.

Glover, Danny, Copyright © 1992, Warner Bros. Inc.

Gorbachev, Mikhail. UN Photo 172547/Y. Nagata

Gore, Al. Clinton-Gore '92, National Campaign Headquarters

Gore, Tipper. Clinton-Gore '92, National Campaign Headquarters

Gossett, Louis, Jr. © 1992 Metro-Goldwyn-Mayer (Photo: Richard Foreman)

Grisham, John. Doubleday (Photo: Marion Silber)

Hackman, Gene. Copyright © 1992 Warner Bros.

Hanks, Tom. © 1992 Columbia Pictures

Harrison, George. © 1992 Warner Bros. Records (Photo: Carl Studna)

Havel, Václav. Knopf (Photo: Miloš Fikejz)

Hawking, Stephen. Bantam Books (Photo: Stephen Shames)

Hawn, Goldie. Copyright © 1992 University City Studios (Photo: Deana Newcomb)

Hines, Gregory. Richard Kornberg/ Carol Fineman (Photo: Martha Swope)

Hirsch, Judd. Jeffrey Richards Associates

Hoffman, Dustin. © 1992, Columbia Pictures Industries, Inc.

Holyfield, Evander. Caesar's Palace

Houston, Whitney. Arista/Nippy, Inc.

Ice-T. Universal City Studios, Inc., Copyright © 1992 (Photo: Sam Emerson)

Jackson, Janet. Virgin; Levine/Schneider Public Relations (Photo: Steve Granitz)

Jackson, Jesse. National Rainbow Coalition

Jackson, Michael. © 1991 Sony Music (Photo: Herb Ritts)

Jackson, Phil. Chicago Bulls

Johnson, Earvin "Magic." Times Books, © Andrew Eccles/Outline

Jones, James Earl. Paramount Pictures, Copyright © 1992 (Photo: Merrick Morton)

Jordan, Michael. Chicago Bulls

Keating, Paul. Embassy of Australia

Keaton, Michael. © 1992 DC Comics, Inc.

Kennedy, William. Viking (Photo: Mariana Cook)

Kesey, Ken. Viking (Photo © Roy Sebern)

Kidman, Nicole. © Universal City Studios, Inc.

King, Larry. © 1990 Cable News Network, Inc. (Photo: George Bennett)

Kite, Tom. Pros, Inc.

Kohl, Helmut. German Information Center

Koppel, Ted. ABC News/Nightline

Laettner, Christian. Duke University Sports Information Office

lang, k.d. © 1992 Sire Records Co., Warner Bros. Records (Photo Albert Sanchez)

Lange, Jessica. Copyright © 1992 Twentieth Century Fox (Photo: Louis Goldman)

Lee, Spike. Copyright © 1991 Universal City Studios, Inc. (Photo: David Lee)

Lehrer, Jim. MacNeil/Lehrer Productions (Photo: Christopher Little)

Leno, Jay. National Broadcasting Company

Lindros, Eric. Philadelphia Flyers

Lithgow, John. © 1992 University City Studios

McClintock, Barbara. Cold Spring Harbor Laboratory (Photo: Margot Bennett)

McEntire, Reba. Starstruck, MCA® Nashville (Photo: McGuire 0991C)

McInerney, Jay. Knopf (Photo: © Marion Ettlinger)

McKellen, Ian. Brooklyn Academy of Music, Boneau/Bryan-Brown (Photo: John Haynes)

McLarty, Thomas "Mack." Office of Mack McLarty

MacNeil, Robert. MacNeil/Lehrer Productions (Photo: Christopher Little)

Madonna. © 1992 Columbia Pictures Industries, Inc.

Major, John. British Information Services

Mamet, David. Turtle Bay Books (Photo: Rebecca Pidgeon)

Marsalis, Branford. Kathryn Schenker, Columbia Records (Photo: Timothy White)

Marshall, Penny. © 1992 Columbia Pictures

Michener, James. Random House (Photo: Steve Pumphrey, © 1991)

Mikulski, Barbara. U.S. Senate

Mitterand, François. Embassy of France

Miyazawa, Kiichi. Embassy of Japan

Moore, Demi. © 1992 Castle Rock Entertainment (Photo: Sidney Baldwin)

Morrison, Toni. Knopf (Photo © Brian Lanker)

Murdoch, Rupert. Howard Rubenstein Associates, Public Relations

Murphy, Eddie. Copyright © 1992 Paramount Pictures (Photo: Bruce W. Talamon)

Murray, Patty. People for Patty Murray U.S. Senate Campaign

Nicholson, Jack. © 1992 Castle Rock Entertainment (Photo: Sidney Baldwin)

O'Leary, Hazel. Presidential Transition Press Office

O'Neal, Shaquille. Orlando Magic

O'Rourke, P.J. Atlantic Monthly Press (Photo: Maxwell Mackenzie)

Pacino, Al. Universal City Studios, Copyright © 1992 (Photo: Myles Aronowitz)

Paglia, Camille. Vintage (Photo: © Larry Ford)

Panetta, Leon. Presidential Transition Press Office

Perot, H. Ross. Office of H. Ross Perot

Pesci, Joe. Copyright © 1992, Warner Bros. Inc.

Pfeiffer, Michelle. © 1992 DC Comics, Inc.

Powell, Colin. U.S. Department of Defense

Pryce, Jonathan. *Miss Saigon* Press Office (Photo: Michael LePoer Trench)

Rabin, Yitzhak. Embassy of Israel

Raitt, Bonnie. Capitol Records (Photo: Merlyn Rosenberg/1991)

Ramos, Fidel V. Embassy of the Philippines

Randall, Tony and Redgrave, Lynn. Spring Associates, Inc. (Photo: Joan Marcus)

Redford, Robert. © Copyright 1992, Columbia Pictures Industries, Inc.

Redgrave, Vanessa. Sony Pictures

Reich, Robert. Harvard University News Office

Reiner, Rob. © 1992 Castle Rock Entertainment (Photo: Sidney Baldwin)

Rice, Jerry. San Francisco 49ers

Riley, Pat. New York Knicks (Photo: George Kalinsky)

Riley, Richard. Presidential Transition Press Office

Rivlin, Alice. Presidential Transition Press Office

Robards, Jason. Shirley Herz Associations (Photo: Joan Marcus)

Rubin, Robert E. Presidential Transition Press Office

Rypien, Mark. Washington Redskins

Salk, Lee. Simon & Schuster

Sarandon, Susan. © 1992 New Line Cinema (Photo: Steve Sands)

Schmidt, Benno. Whittle Communications

Schrader, Paul. © 1992 New Line Cinema (Photo: Steve Sands)

Schroeder, Pat. Office of Pat Schroeder (Photo: Jim Richardson—*Denver Post*)

Scowcroft, Brent. The White House

Selleck, Tom. © Copyright 1992, Universal City Studios, Inc. (Photo: Emilio Lari)

Shalala, Donna. University of Wisconsin-Madison, University News and Information Service (Photo: Todd Rosenburg)

Sheets, Robert C. National Hurricane Center

Simon, Neil. Bill Evans Public Relations (Photo: Jay Thompson)

Smiley, Jane. Knopf (Photo: Stephen Mortensen)

Smoot, George F. University of California Lawrence Berkeley Laboratory Photo Services

Sontag, Susan. Farrar, Straus and Giroux (Photo: © Annie Leibovitz, 1992)

Spacek, Sissy. © 1991 Warner Bros. Inc., Regency Enterprises V.O.F. and Le Studio Canal

Springsteen, Bruce. © 1992 Sony Music (Photo: Pamela Springsteen)

Starzl, Thomas E. University of Pittsburgh Press

Steinbrenner, George. New York Yankees

Stephanopoulos, George. Clinton-Gore '92, National Campaign Headquarters

Stone, Oliver. © 1991 Warner Bros. Inc., Regency Enterprises V.O.F. and Le Studio Canal

Streep, Meryl. Copyright © 1992 Universal City Studios, Inc. (Photo: Deana Newcomb)

Sutherland, Donald. © 1991 Warner Bros. Inc., Regency Enterprises V.O.F. and Le Studio Canal

Tandy, Jessica. Office of Jessica Tandy and Hume Cronyn (Photo: Roddy McDowell)

Taylor, Elizabeth. © National Broadcasting Company, Inc. 1992

Terkel, Studs. WFMT, Chicago

Thomas, Clarence. U.S. Supreme Court, Public Information Office. © National Geographic Society

Thomas, Thurman. Buffalo Bills

Torretta, Gino. University of Miami

Tsongas, Paul. Foley, Hoag & Eliot

Turner, Ted. Turner Broadcasting System

Tyson, Laura D'Andrea. Presidential Transition Press Office

Updike, John. Knopf (Photo: Richard Kalvar)

Van Duyn, Mona. Library of Congress

Vidal, Gore. Random House (Photo: © Jane Bown)

Walcott, Derek. Boston University Photo Services

Washington, Denzel. Copyright © 1992 Warner Bros. Inc. (Photo: David Lee/ Warner Bros.)

Wharton, Clifton, Jr. Presidential Transition Press Office

Williams, Vanessa. Mercury Records (Photo: Peter Nash 9/91)

Willis, Bruce. Copyright © 1992 University City Studies (Photo: Deana Newcomb)

Winfield, Dave. Toronto Blue Jays

Woods, James. © 1992 Metro-Goldwyn-Mayer (Photo: Richard Foreman)

Yeakel, Lynn. Lynn Yeakel for U.S. Senate

Young, Steve. San Francisco 49ers

Zappa, Frank. Rykodisc USA (Photo: Lynn Goldsmith)

Cumulative Alphabetical Index

For ease of access, we have here provided a cumulative alphabetical index of all those who have appeared in any edition of **People in the News.** For each person, the index gives the year of any edition in which he or she appears, and (after the colon) the page number where the entry begins. So for Corazon Aquino, who appears in the first three editions, the index entry reads:

Aquino, Corazon   '93:13 / '92:11/ '91:11

Note that this 1993 edition of **People in the News** also includes a cumulative index by occupation beginning on page 443.

Cumulative Index by Occupation

For ease of access, we have here indexed those profiled in **People in the News** by occupation or other area of news interest. Under the appropriate headings, such as "Law and Court Cases" or "Stage and Screen," readers will find volume and page references for all who have appeared in any edition of **People in the News**.

For each person, the index gives the year of any editions in which he or she appears, and (after the colon) the page number where the entry begins. So for Corazon Aquino, who appears in the first three editions, the index entry is found under the heading "Politics" and reads:

Aquino, Corazon '93:13 / '92:11 / '91:11

Note that some people are listed under more than one heading, such as Willie Nelson, who appears under both "Music" and "Stage and Screen."

The main body of each edition of **People in the News** is, of course, self-indexed, with individuals listed alphabetically. However, the second and succeeding volumes also contain a cumulative alphabetical index, in the 1993 edition beginning on page 433.

Dance

Education

Journalism and Publishing

Law and Court Cases

Literature

Visual Arts